THE SHORTER CAMBRIDGE
MEDIEVAL HISTORY

BY THE LATE
C. W. PREVITÉ-ORTON

IN TWO VOLUMES

VOLUME II
THE TWELFTH CENTURY TO
THE RENAISSANCE

CAMBRIDGE UNIVERSITY PRESS

CAMBRIDGE
LONDON · NEW YORK · MELBOURNE

Published by
The Syndics of the Cambridge University Press

The Pitt Building, Trumpington Street, Cambridge CB2 1RP
Bentley House, 200 Euston Road, London NW1 2DB
32 East 57th Street, New York, NY 10022, USA
296 Beaconsfield Parade, Middle Park, Melbourne 3206, Australia

Library of Congress catalogue card number: 75-31398

ISBN 0 521 20963 3 hard covers
ISBN 0 521 09977 3 paperback
ISBN 0 521 05993 3 set of two volumes (hard covers)

First published in 1952
Reprinted with corrections 1953 1960 1962
Reprinted 1966 1971
First paperback edition 1975
Reprinted 1977 1978

First printed in Great Britain at the University Press, Cambridge
Reprinted at the Alden Press, Oxford

CONTENTS

BOOK VII

THE PAPACY AT ITS ZENITH AND THE SECULAR KINGDOMS

BOOK VIII

THE LEADERSHIP OF FRANCE

CONTENTS

BOOK IX

THE FOURTEENTH CENTURY

BOOK X

THE END OF THE MIDDLE AGES

CONTENTS

BOOK XI

THE TRANSITION TO MODERN TIMES

LIST OF ILLUSTRATIONS

Most of the illustrations have been greatly reduced

LIST OF ILLUSTRATIONS

LIST OF MAPS

LIST OF GENEALOGICAL TABLES

BOOK VII

THE PAPACY AT ITS ZENITH AND THE SECULAR KINGDOMS

༈

CHAPTER 21

POPE INNOCENT III

(I) INNOCENT III AND THE EMPIRE

Immediately after Henry VI's death, the revolt, long simmering in Italy broke out. His brother Philip of Swabia fled back to Germany from southern Tuscany; everywhere German officials and garrisons were driven out; the Tuscan cities, save Pisa, hastily formed a short-lived league at St Genesio under the Pope's patronage (November 1197); and the Empress Constance herself recalled the infant King Frederick from Foligno, on his way to Germany, to Palermo, where discord between Germans, Sicilians and Saracens flared up. At this juncture the nonagenarian Pope Celestine III died, and was immediately succeeded by the youngest cardinal, Lothar dei Conti, as Innocent III (8 January 1198).

The electors knew their time and the man. He was a legislator and a consummate lawyer, an organizing administrator of singular efficiency, but above all a statesman and diplomatist, resolute and versatile, with a width of view and a readiness in emergency unequalled in his generation. He was a profound believer in the highest curial doctrine of the papal plenitude of power to guide the Church and the world, but displayed a delicate skill in urging its secular exercise on lay rulers by less far-reaching arguments they found it harder to combat. Daring and sober prudence were strangely combined in him. Few have equalled him in the capacity to administer, judge, negotiate, and decide in affairs political and ecclesiastical involving all Europe.

With unfaltering promptitude Innocent exploited the vacancy of the Empire in Italy. Himself a Roman, he secured the appointment of a friendly and single senator, and, although he met with opposition later, did finally in 1205 obtain the continuance of this system, which resembled the northern institution of the podestà. He could be more aggressive in Central Italy, which he claimed for the Papacy. The communes of the duchy of Spoleto (Umbria), driving out their German duke, acknowledged

IRELAND

N. WALES

SCOTLAND

KINGDOM OF NORWAY

KINGDOM OF ENGLAND

London

KINGDOM OF DENMARK

•Cologne

HOLY

Mainz •

ROMAN

KINGDOM OF FRANCE

•Basle

EMPIRE

NAVARRE

Venice •

LEON

Milan •

PORTUGAL

CASTILE

ARAGON

•Lisbon

•Toledo

Rome •

KINGDOM OF SICILY

ALMOHADE KINGDOM

•Tunis

EUROPE AT THE
ACCESSION OF
INNOCENT III

Map 16

Map 16

papal suzerainty; so did some of the March of Ancona, whence Markward withdrew to Sicily. Communal independence, however, both checked further advance and rendered his annexations mainly titular. In the Regno his success was more effectual, if hardly won. The Empress Constance in her straits obtained his protection for her son by acknowledging vassalage and surrendering the legateship and its privileges. When she died (November 1198), she left him guardian of the boy, for whom he appointed a council of regency. Its leading spirit, Walter of Palear, Bishop of Troia, sought only his personal ends, while Markward arrived (October 1199) and raised the Moslems in revolt. Although he was defeated by papal troops (July 1200), he was joined by the bishop when Innocent gave King Tancred's son-in-law, the Frenchman Count Walter of Brienne, Tancred's Apulian lands. But Markward died (September 1202) and Brienne, after some victories, was killed (June 1205). Then the German leader on the mainland, Dietrich of Vohburg, went over to the Pope, and next year induced Markward's successor in Sicily, William Capparone, to surrender power and the custody of young Frederick. Two years more were spent in quelling disorder on the mainland, until the king was declared of age at fourteen (December 1208) and married to Constance of Aragon. He began his reign impoverished, in debt to the Papacy, and with mutiny rampant among the nobles, but Innocent had preserved his crown and seen to his education.

Fig. 133. Pope Innocent III

The time for the Pope's operations in Italy had been given by the civil war in Germany. Philip of Swabia returned to find his nephew's cause hopeless—although elected, he was an infant not yet crowned—but most princes were well disposed to the Hohenstaufen and to Philip himself. Yet anarchy was prevalent, and it was not till March 1198 that he was elected king by a large assembly in Thuringia. The opponents of his house were then already on the move. Their centre was in Lower Germany on the Rhine and in Westphalia, where the lead was taken by Adolf, Archbishop of Cologne, and what with the hankering of the princes for a purely elective kingship and their general desire to sell their support, defections from Philip were likely enough. The archbishop's difficulty was to find a candidate to undertake the dangerous and costly honour. The Dukes of Saxony and Zähringen declined. Then King Richard of England, freed from his vassalage by the dying Henry VI, supported his own nephew, the Welf Otto, second son of Henry the Lion, and Count of Poitou, who was thereupon elected by a small group and crowned at Aachen in July 1198. The civil war, which was to enfeeble the German monarchy, had begun.

Neither rival was well fitted for the contest. Philip was an amiable, popular knight, more disposed and able to buy adherents than to war down his foes. Otto IV was a blundering, stupid warrior, prodigal of promises he hoped to break. His best asset was the gold of King Richard, to whom he was a most useful ally against Philip of France. He had also the highly prized advantage of being crowned in the coronation city by the archbishop whose right it was to anoint the King of Germany, and he could appeal to the faithless particularism of the princes. Philip of Swabia on the other hand possessed the Hohenstaufen treasure and lands and a large majority of adherents, while he reknitted the alliance with Richard's deadly foe, his namesake of France. But his coronation in September 1198 at Mainz by the Archbishop of Tarantaise was so irregular as to damage his prestige. Medieval formalism told against it.

Desolation and ruin were spread over Germany by the sixteen years of brutal warfare which followed, ravaging the country, burning towns, and maltreating non-combatants. It was conducted by partisan raids, in which the worst offenders were the Bohemians on Philip's side. Each prince was ready for a bribe to change his party—Landgrave Herman of Thuringia, the cultured patron of poetry and art, did so six times to his great profit—but decisive campaigns did not occur, while royal rights and lands were recklessly alienated. By 1199 Otto was losing ground. The death of King Richard on 6 April deprived him of his mainstay, and the alliance of the Pope became more desirable than ever. Innocent had declared his neutrality. The mere interregnum was useful to him, but he could not be neglected by either party both for his influence over the German Church and for his prerogative of crowning the Emperor. Otto's electors had at once created a new precedent by requesting his confirmation of their choice, while Philip's had merely insisted on the imperial rights in their announcement. Partisanship, still officially veiled, became Innocent's policy. In a secret address to the cardinals he outlined his views, the *Deliberatio de facto Imperii* (1200). The Empire, he said, belonged to the Apostolic See, which had transferred it from the Greeks to the Germans in 800—the *Translatio*, a legend thus made official—and which invested the Emperor at his Roman coronation. Of the candidates, Frederick was too young to reign, Philip was excommunicate and a hereditary enemy, while Otto was

Fig. 134. Landgrave Herman of Thuringia and Landgravine Sophia

a hereditary friend and devoted to the Church. Therefore Otto was his choice. His open steps were more tortuous until in June 1201 Otto, in growing alarm, sealed a treaty with his legate at Neuss. He ceded to the Papacy Spoleto, Ancona, the Exarchate of Ravenna, and the Matildine lands on the strength of the Carolingian donations, and promised to follow the Pope's lead in Sicily and France and to repeat his engagements when crowned Emperor, for he, detected by Innocent, hoped to declare his merely royal engagement invalid. To Philip's supporters the Pope addressed (March 1202) a famous Bull, *Venerabilem*. He reaffirmed the *Translatio*, and pointed out that he could not sacre a madman, a heretic, or an infidel, if the princes should elect one; he must examine the fitness of their choice, and Philip was an excommunicate.

Meanwhile, fortune, after somewhat veering in Otto's favour, turned slowly again to Philip. The customary desertions were repeated. Even the Archbishop of Cologne changed sides (1204), although the citizens of Cologne, dependent on trade with England, remained firm for Otto. Excommunications of Philip's supporters had little effect on the laity. In fact Philip could be re-elected and duly crowned at Aachen (1205). Next year he defeated Otto near Cologne, which eventually surrendered. The struggle was really kept alive by Innocent. Yet the Pope had already (1201) treated with Philip, and the Hohenstaufen was eager to negotiate. For two years, while there was hope of English and Danish intervention, Innocent spun out the bargaining until in 1208 he suddenly capitulated. He would recognize Philip, crown him Emperor, withdraw from Spoleto and the March of Ancona. Perhaps it was the offer of the hand of Philip's daughter for his nephew along with these territories which convinced him, for the Pope was not free from nepotism, but he was on the verge of a dispute with John of England, Frederick was securely seated in Sicily, and a struggle with the Albigensian heretics was looming near. He might well wish to extricate himself on good ecclesiastical terms from the hopeless

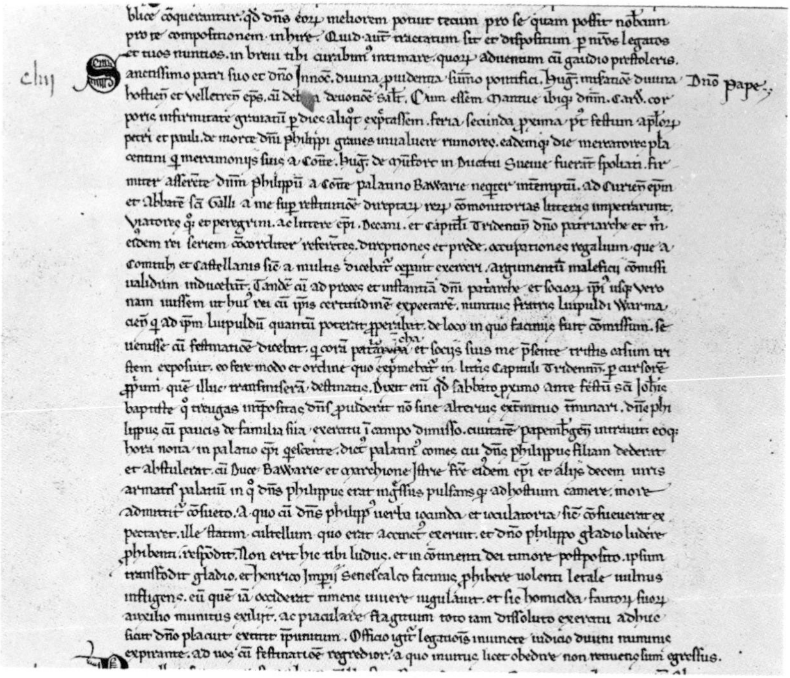

Fig. 135. Report by the Cardinal Bishop Ugolino of Ostia and Velletri to Pope Innocent III on the assassination of King Philip

contest in Germany. The treaty was all but completed when King Philip was unexpectedly murdered on 9 June 1208 by Count Otto of Wittelsbach for a private grudge, and the whole situation was changed. Otto IV was left alone in the field, vehemently upheld by Innocent; the natural Hohenstaufen candidate, King Frederick, had his hands full in Sicily. By submitting to a fresh election and betrothing himself to his dead rival's daughter Otto gained over the princes. Next year (March 1209) he made sure of the Pope by complete acceptance of the papal claims in his charter of Speier. Central Italy, the *spolia* and the *regalia* (occupation of vacant sees), interference in elections, were all given up and unrestricted appeals to the Papacy were conceded. In short, the monarchy's control of the German Church was to be at an end.

Otto, however, did not intend to be bound by his charter. When he entered Italy in force in 1209, he was resuming the Hohenstaufen aims for his own benefit. Scarcely was he crowned in October than he reclaimed the ceded lands and then began an invasion to conquer Sicily from Frederick. In this strait Innocent for once faltered, but mere ecclesiastical

651

Fig. 136. The Emperor Otto IV and the three Magi

penalties proved unavailing, and he resigned himself to accepting the King of France's advice of promoting rebellion in Germany and Italy in favour of the last Hohenstaufen (1211). Otto, who had won Apulia, was obliged to return to meet the danger. The Pope, however, in this dangerous expedient was resolved to keep Sicily and the Empire separate. He compelled Frederick, who was no less in peril, to crown his little son Henry and promise to abdicate in his favour when himself Emperor, besides yielding up border counties of the Terra di Lavoro to the Papacy.

With this arranged at a personal interview with Innocent, who had absolved Otto's vassals from their fealty, Frederick made the journey at extreme risk through Lombardy to Swabia. He left war raging in Italy among and within the communes and their factions, who sided with Otto or himself. It was now that in Tuscany his rival's partisans, temporary imperialists, began to be called Guelfs and his own, for the time papalists, Ghibellines, the Italian forms of Welf and Waiblingen.

In Germany the old tale of desertions and raids began again. Frederick was elected and crowned at Mainz by its archbishop in December 1212. As a whole South Germany was for him, North Germany for the Emperor. Each party was financed from abroad, Frederick by Philip Augustus and Otto by John of England, becoming thus the appendages of a foreign war. By that war of France and England, too, the contest was decided. In July 1214 Otto IV led the Netherlandish princes in the pay of John to the ruinous defeat of Bouvines by the French king. Epoch-making for France, the battle decided Otto's fate. One by one his supporters left him. His rival was crowned anew at Aachen. He was almost landless when he died unconquered in the Harzburg (19 May 1218).

Meanwhile Pope Innocent was making sure of his gains, somewhat embarrassed by the fact that his other opponent, John, became his vassal and ally (May 1213). The change may have helped to induce Frederick II to repeat Otto's concessions at Speier in the Golden Bull of Eger (July 1213), which was guaranteed by the princes and became irreversible law. To please the Pope and perhaps to gain the protected rights of a crusader, Frederick also took the cross (1215), thereby entailing a long train of troubles on himself. Finally, in his General Council of the Lateran in 1215 Innocent declared Otto deposed and Frederick confirmed, a precedent of fateful import. He had indeed emerged victorious, but by compromising his own policy of dividing the Empire from Sicily and by leading the Papacy into purely secular politics.

(2) INNOCENT III AND THE WESTERN KINGDOMS

In contrast with his action in the Empire, Innocent's dealings with the kingdoms of France and England arose from ecclesiastical causes, although even here his bent towards political measures and statecraft was manifest. A mixture of caution and courage was needed in his dispute with Philip Augustus of France if the vital friendship between France and the Papacy was not to be endangered, to which Innocent added a determination to prevent judicial perjury and some realization of the human problems involved. In 1193 Philip, seeking a Danish alliance against England and the Welfs, married Ingeborg of Denmark. Immediately on marriage he took an intense aversion to the bride, and obtained from his complaisant bishops a sentence of nullity on the false ground of her being within the prohibited degrees. She appealed to Pope Celestine III, who quashed the perjured verdict. Philip, however, who displayed a continuous and rancorous cruelty to his imprisoned wife, held on his way, finding at last (1196) a new consort in Agnes, daughter of the Bavarian Duke of Meran, who bore him a family. When persuasion proved useless, Innocent III boldly took his stand on principle and placed Philip's lands under interdict (1200), with the result that the king separated from Agnes and began fresh legal proceedings before papal legates. As he had no case, he interrupted the suit by suddenly taking back in name the unhappy Ingeborg. Agnes opportunely died, and the Pope legitimized her offspring. He had won a legal and moral victory of great moment, but Queen Ingeborg suffered no less than before, while the Pope corresponded with Philip more as an upright counsellor than as a moralist. He was clearly aware that there was a strong current of loyalty for the king. The sordid affair was not closed until 1213, for when he wished to become papal champion against King John, Philip suddenly put himself right by a reconciliation with the injured Ingeborg.

The Albigensian Crusade must be treated apart, but here too Innocent failed to lead King Philip as he wished. The king declined to be diverted from the English war, while firmly maintaining his legal rights as suzerain of Languedoc. He became all the more necessary an ally when Innocent broke with John and then with the Emperor Otto. The breach with John was due, likewise, to ecclesiastical causes, which were, however, bound to have political repercussions. When Hubert Walter, Archbishop of Canterbury, died, the king had his candidate ready, Bishop Grey of Norwich, but there was a contest between the monastic chapter and the provincial bishops as to the claim of the latter to share in the election. Both parties appealed to Rome, the monks secretly electing their sub-prior as well (1205). When John learnt of their action, he insisted on their electing Bishop Grey and asked for his pallium. But Innocent after inquiry decided that both elections, made pending appeal, were invalid, and that the bishops had no right to intervene. He summoned a delegation of the monks with full powers to elect. When they disagreed, he pressed on them the election of the eminent English cardinal and theologian, Stephen Langton, which they accepted. The fury of the king was unbounded. His control of the episcopate was challenged. Innocent had been scrupulously legal and had favoured a fit man of the highest character; now he was resolved to make his will prevail. He consecrated Langton without the king's assent (1207), and when John finally refused it, and ejected the monks of the cathedral monastery, he proclaimed an interdict over the whole kingdom (1208). John retaliated by seizing on the English endowments of the Church. For three years he ruled with an iron hand and much success—most of his bishops fled to exile—but in spite of his activity and his many alliances, he was unable to conjure the danger from abroad and the growing disaffection in England. Innocent at last (1213) enjoined his eager ally, John's mortal foe, Philip Augustus, to lead a crusade to deprive the excommunicated King of England of his crown. It was an exercise of the *plenitudo potestatis*, not quite equalled since the days of Gregory VII. But the formidable expedition was checked just when it was to start. John executed his sudden and humiliating surrender to the papal legate Pandulf, and became a tributary vassal of the Papacy. With his foe transmuted into his overlord and patron, he could wreck Philip's fleet by a swift blow, and proceed to patch up the damage of the interdict. It was, perhaps, the greatest of Innocent's triumphs. He had asserted his rule of the Church and had reduced a kingdom to vassalage. He had been the arbiter of Western politics. There was, however, much alloy in his success, won largely by secular diplomacy. His new vassal was still the ally of his enemy Otto IV and at war with the very independent Philip. When John's defeat and manifold oppression aroused revolt in England, Innocent, legal as ever, was found on the side of his vassal-tyrant. Yet he could not prevent the French invasion. Law, rather than right, was his criterion, a dubious precedent for his successors, and perhaps it was only his own death, followed by that of John (1216), which extricated the Papacy from more awkward entanglements, that would have tasked even his resourceful statesmanship.

France, England, and the Empire were by no means the only realms of the West in which Innocent was maintaining a restless vigilance and taking resolute action. Of Portugal and Aragon he was the acknowledged suzerain, which helped him to intervene in the government of the former, with effective persistence, when the kings attacked church privileges or were at variance with their kin. In León his action was of more doubtful benefit, for he denounced the marriage of King Alfonso IX with his cousin Berenguela of Castile as within the prohibited degrees. A seven years' interdict, detrimental to subjects more than kings, was needed to produce submission (1204), and then the Pope felt it wise to legitimize the children. More helpful to Spain was Innocent's share in co-ordinating the joint campaign of the peninsular rulers against the Moors which resulted in the decisive victory of Las Navas de Tolosa (1212).

Innocent used the same methods with less success in Norway. There the legate Nicholas Breakspear, the future Adrian IV, had in 1152 organized the Church in a province under Nidaros much as elsewhere, and in 1163 Archbishop Eystein, in return for his support in a civil war, extorted larger privileges, systematized the Canon Law, and secured for the bishops the chief voice in a doubtful succession to the crown. The clerical King Magnus, however, had fallen (1184) before the warrior Sverre, who championed ancient custom and the rule of the Church by the king. Excommunication was met by exile and by a skilful manifesto in defence of the older system. Innocent replied (1198) by interdict and by inciting the other Scandinavians to attack the rebel. No effect within or without Norway was attained, and when after Sverre's death (1202), his son Hakon IV induced Archbishop Eric and the bishops to compromise on the basis of 1152, the Pope's indignation could not alter the arrangement.

In all these dealings Innocent stood out as the masterful and adroit protagonist of the centralizing papal monarchy over the Church and the effective authority of the Canon Law. He was ready to use the extremest and most sweeping spiritual weapons in his armoury for that end, and he justified his action and the political manœuvres with which he supplemented it by his duty to intervene in cases of sin, *ratione peccati*, an argument hard to refute, but his proceedings merged insensibly into a claim to direct the secular rulers in politics, with the inevitable accompaniment of secular means and policy which infected the Papacy more and more. Indeed, he was profoundly convinced, although he did not flaunt the doctrine before kings, that his plenitude of power extended in the last resort over the whole sphere of temporal government. The Vicar of Christ was lord of lords in Christendom.

(3) THE FOURTH CRUSADE

No Pope, least of all the statesman Innocent, could neglect the Crusade. In 1199 he prepared to finance a fresh expedition by demanding a fortieth of clerical incomes. There was no Emperor or king now to snatch the lead, and from the first the new movement was an essentially feudal enterprise, in which the personal ambitions of the chiefs much outweighed the religious motive of a minority of their followers. The Crusade had become a business matter with most, a venture for power and wealth and fame, and the Pope, for all his skill, was to find himself little more able to direct it than his predecessors had been. In November 1199 a group of North French nobles began the enterprise, and were zealously assisted by papal preachers.

The lessons of the past were now thoroughly learned: transport by sea was required, and Venice was to be the naval power to provide it. In April 1201 the crusaders' envoys concluded negotiations. The Venetian Doge Dandolo's terms were business-like and shrewd. The sum of 85,000 silver marks, paid in advance, was to be the hire of ships and provisions, and the Venetians astutely joined in the Holy War themselves, the Doge himself, although old and blind, taking the cross. In reward they contracted for half the future conquests, besides gaining thereby an equal voice in the direction of the Crusade. This was all the more important as a divergence of views as to the immediate objective had already shown itself among the crusaders. The average knight wished to fight immediately in the Holy

Land itself, the politic great barons aimed at the conquest of Egypt, with its wealth, for which there was much to be said, since it was the heart of Moslem power and a first-rate and defensible base for the recovery of Palestine. Yet the Venetians possessed a lucrative trade by treaty with Egypt, and would in that case have to choose between their old and new obligations.

Meanwhile on the death of the original leader, Count Theobald III of Champagne, there was elected to succeed him Boniface, Marquess of Montferrat: he was warlike and ambitious, and closely connected with Eastern adventure, for one of his brothers (Conrad) had been King and another (William) regent of Jerusalem, and a third had been the Caesar Renier, who had married a Byzantine princess and aimed at the Byzantine throne. What private schemes Boniface may have cherished are not known, since his visit (1201) to King Philip of Germany, husband of another Byzantine princess, Irene Angela, would fit any of them. A year later, in the summer of 1202, a new factor was introduced by the appearance of the fugitive Alexius, son of the deposed Emperor Isaac Angelus,[1] in Italy, and his journey to Philip's court.

The crusaders by then were fully mustered at Venice in August 1202, but the easily foreseen difficulty of finding funds to pay Venice at once arose. The republic contrived to intern them on an island of the lagoon, and gave them their choice of paying or else reconquering the rebel city of Zara in Dalmatia, which had been seized by Hungary, in return for a respite. Innocent III and his legate denounced this scandalous perversion of a crusading army in attacking a Christian city under a king who, however insincerely—for he evaded his vow—had taken the cross, but Zara was stormed (November 1202), and the whole army, now excommunicate, sailed to Corfù. While the barons—but not the Venetians—sued for and obtained absolution, envoys of King Philip and the young Alexius had been busy with the crusaders. A new diversion of the Crusade was proposed to restore the imprisoned Isaac at Constantinople. The Venetians grasped at the opportunity of setting up a client Emperor of the East, and the chief barons, already mercenaries in the siege of Zara, were allured by the magnificent offers of Alexius. In May 1203 the definitive treaty was signed by him in Corfù: he would pay the crusaders' debt to Venice, provide them with money and supplies against Egypt and 10,000 troops as well, maintain 500 knights in the Holy Land, and effect the reunion of the Greek Church with Rome. Innocent had long known what was on foot and issued a formal prohibition of the attack on the Greeks, but he did no more—the reins had slipped from his hands. Only some plain-minded crusaders, among them Count Simon de Montfort, insisted on sailing for Syria, while the majority set out for Constantinople.

[1] See Genealogical Table 15b above, p. 537.

On 24 June 1203 the crusading fleet reached the Bosphorus. The chiefs found that the Greeks had rallied round the Emperor Alexius III, who, feeble as he was, represented their independence and their faith, but he proved unable to prevent the capture of Galata and the entrance to the harbour of the Golden Horn. An assault by sea and land stormed the walls on 17 July, the Emperor fled, and on 1 August the blind Isaac II and the young Alexius IV were enthroned by the Latins. Alexius IV now made an attempt to carry out the impossible terms to which he had subscribed at Corfù, while the crusaders passed the winter on the Asiatic shore. Their greed had been roused to exasperation by the sight of 'the sovereign city of the world' and its boundless wealth, and Doge Dandolo now set his heart on its real conquest and the enormous profit which would thereby accrue to his commercial republic. He exacerbated discord, by which the mutual hatred of Greeks and Latins was magnified and Alexius IV became a scapegoat to his subjects. In February 1204 Alexius and his father were overthrown by a revolution and replaced by a kinsman, Alexius V Ducas, nicknamed Mourtzouphlos. The crusaders had gone from bad to worse; inspired by Dandolo, they turned the Holy War into criminal brigandage. Now that the scheme of a client Emperor draining his treasury for their benefit had broken down, they resolved to seize the Empire for themselves by main force. In March 1204 they agreed on the division of the spoils to be won, 'to the honour of God, of the Pope, and of the Empire'. The schism was to be forcibly ended. The booty of the city was to be shared equally by Venice and the crusaders. Six Venetians and six crusaders were to elect a Latin Emperor, who was to receive a quarter of the Empire. The other three quarters were to be divided equally between Venice and the crusaders. Venice was to keep her commercial privileges, and the new Latin Patriarch of Constantinople was to be a Venetian if the Emperor (as was certain) was not. It was the most paying and unscrupulous bargain that Venice ever made.

After a first assault which failed, the crusaders on 12 April broke into the city by sea and land; Mourtzouphlos fled, and the terrible three days' sack began. Every atrocious outrage and cruelty was committed by the crusading plunderers, who unveiled themselves as worse than the infidels they were supposed to be combating. Irreparable loss was inflicted on civilization in the destruction of art and literature in this treasure-house of the ancient world. Irreparable, too, was the harm done to Christendom and Europe, for their bulwark against Islam and the Turks was shattered in the overthrow of the civilized European Empire which had so long held both at bay, for although, as will appear in the sequel, the Byzantine Empire survived and was renewed, it never recovered its old vitality and extent.

Organized extortion followed the restoration of order by the leaders, who proceeded to divide the spoil. To the new Latin Empire they elected

Baldwin, Count of Flanders (May 1204), who seemed less formidable to his compeers than Boniface of Montferrat. The lion's share went to the Venetians, who took three-eighths of Constantinople and most islands of the Aegean, besides valuable towns and coastlands round the Balkan peninsula and the Ecumenical Patriarchate. Boniface was allotted the kingdom of Salonika, reaching as far as Athens. Other barons received duchies and lordships in Asia Minor and Europe, a whole crop of feudal seigneuries. The Emperor Baldwin had to be content with both coasts of the Sea of Marmora. Most of these lands, however, were still to conquer. The brutal methods of conquest, the divergence of faith and civilization, and the confiscation of all Church property for the benefit of the Latins and their clergy had aroused the patriotism and the fighting spirit of the Greeks. Theodore Lascaris, son-in-law of Alexius III, rallied them at Nicaea in Asia Minor, and was crowned Emperor there by the new orthodox Patriarch (1206). Two Comneni founded a rival Empire at Trebizond in Pontus. An Angelus made himself Despot of Epirus, and other chiefs held out in Asia and Europe. At first the Latins seemed in a fair way of overthrowing resistance. King Boniface rapidly reached the Isthmus of Corinth, setting up a Burgundian friend, Othon de la Roche, as Sire of Athens. Two adventurers from Champagne, William de Champlitte and Geoffrey (the younger) de Villehardouin, under his aegis won the Morea (as the Peloponnese was now called) in a single battle, and founded (1205) the principality of Achaia. The Venetians secured two essential ports, Modon and Coron, on the littoral, but were chiefly occupied in obtaining the Aegean islands, including Crete, where they bought out the rights of Boniface. Meantime, the Emperor's brother Henry defeated Theodore Lascaris (1205), when the fruits of victory were lost by events in Europe.

Although Boniface and the Prince of Achaia endeavoured to conciliate their Greek subjects, the general treatment of the conquered was harsh enough, and the crusaders further made an enemy of the Bulgarian Tsar Johannitsa (Kaloyan), who had received a crown and legate from Innocent, and was then disposed to be friendly. They demanded the cession of his conquests from the Empire. He replied by invading Thrace at the appeal of the ill-used Greeks, overthrew the Emperor Baldwin, who was taken prisoner, at Adrianople (14 April 1205), and proceeded to ravage the land so cruelly as 'the Greek-slayer' that he produced a reaction in favour of the Latins. Since Baldwin was slaughtered by him and Dandolo died in Constantinople, the leadership of the ex-crusaders fell to Henry of Flanders, first as regent, then (August 1206) as Emperor. No better choice could have been made, for he was able and conciliatory. By defeating the Bulgarians and the Nicaean Greeks, and by humane government of his lands he was the real founder of the Latin Empire.

On the news of the atrocious sack, meanwhile, Innocent had written to

45-2

the crusaders with justified indignation, but the erection of a Latin Empire changed his attitude. He now looked on it as a miraculous event, a judgement of God to restore unity to Christendom. He was soon disillusioned in his hopes that the Crusade would be continued, but was active in his attempts to secure the submission of the Greeks to his supremacy and to obtain the restitution to the Latin clergy of the plundered Church lands. His legate, Cardinal Benedict of Santa Susanna, bargained with the Emperor Henry for the return of Church property with partial success, and endeavoured by negotiation and concession to win over the Greek clergy. His efforts, however, were mostly in vain, and were nullified by the persecuting methods of his successor, Cardinal Pelagius. The Emperor Henry found it necessary to intervene in favour of his injured subjects. Thus, although the Pope had extended the bounds of his jurisdiction, it was a barren conquest. The Crusade he had promoted had been perverted to brigandage and had even weakened fatally the defence of Christendom. He had vainly endeavoured to prevent the iniquity, and had ended by being an accomplice after the fact. It was of evil augury when a Pope so skilful and masterful had failed so signally to direct for the better the energies of Western Christendom.

(4) HERESIES AND THE ALBIGENSIAN CRUSADE

The great movement for Church reform with its ideals of asceticism and unworldliness was far from being limited to what may be called the official, hierarchical and rigidly orthodox organization led by the Papacy. Among no sections of the population did these ideals spread more widely than among the unprivileged and depressed classes, the struggling bourgeois and the peasant, who saw the reformed and the unreformed clergy as possessors of wealth and feudal power, and who looked on them as members of the ruling aristocracy, not as exemplars of the perfect Christian life. The Patarines of Lombardy, who had rioted against clerical marriage and simony in the eleventh century, were but in part satisfied with the official reform, and the same tendencies to alienation from the hierarchy were widespread in the West. Antisacerdotalism was a marked feature, as it was a predisposing cause, of these popular heresies. They were most prevalent where the clergy were most open to criticism. Not always doctrinal in origin, they tended to become so. The spontaneity of their beginnings led to variations in view not only of different groups, but within the same group, and besides the home-bred notions of religion which arose there was a steady infiltration of Eastern heretical ideas derived mainly, if not wholly, from the Bulgarian sect of the Bogomils.

A great impetus to this revolt from the official Church had been given by the famous ascetic preacher Arnold of Brescia, who taught that all the priesthood should live in strict asceticism, deprived of endowment and dominion and supported by the alms of the faithful. Less militant associations were formed *c.* 1150 by the groups of Humiliati in Lombardy, recruited chiefly among the poorest class, the employees of the traders in the ever growing cloth-manufacture. They founded little societies of their own, living in common a religious life and pursuing their vocation as weavers. Well before the close of the twelfth century, however, there were manifest fissures among them, some being orthodox and submissive, others near akin to the Waldensians, and others practically Catharans, with whom they became amalgamated.

The Poor Men of Lyons or Waldensians had a definite founder. About 1170 a rich, unlearned merchant of Lyons, Peter Waldo, resolved to devote himself to the furtherance of the law of Christ, the duty neglected by the clergy around him. He gave his wealth to the poor, and began to preach in the streets and private houses. At first his followers were approved by Pope Alexander III on condition that they received the sanction of the local clergy. When this limitation was disregarded and moreover the behaviour of the clergy was denounced by the Poor Men of Lyons, approval was converted into condemnation by the Council of Verona (1184). Thenceforward most Waldensians added to their early tenets, that poverty is the true Christian way of life and that Holy Scripture is the infallible guide in religion, the clearly heretical belief that every good man is competent to preach and expound Holy Writ, from which translations into the vulgar tongue were being made. They soon appointed elders (*barbani*) of their own, and offshoots, by no means unanimous in doctrine, appeared over Italy, Germany, and farther east in spite of persecution.

The austerity and simplicity which characterized the Waldensians as a body were not paralleled by the more formidable sect, or rather religion, of the Catharans (*Cathari*, the pure). The close connexion between them and the Bogomils of the Balkans is evident—indeed in the West they were often called Bulgari (*bougres*) among other names, such as Albigenses (which was derived from Albi in Languedoc, where they were numerous) or Patarines (which was due to their absorption of the extreme left wing of the old Church reform faction in Lombardy). Signs of the dualistic Manichaeanism of the Bogomils were already to be seen in North Italy and France in the eleventh century. The enlarged intercourse with the East following the First Crusade rapidly increased the number of Catharans, especially in Languedoc amid a prosperous and crudely intellectual population, disillusioned by the patent faults of the provincial hierarchy. So numerous and bold did they become, in spite of fulminations by the Church, that in 1167 they held a great council near Toulouse, attended by representatives from Bulgaria and Bosnia as well as from North Italy. They seem to have enjoyed full protection, if not more, from the secular authorities. In

Italy from Verona to Viterbo their adherents seem mostly to have been well-to-do bourgeois, but in Languedoc the lesser nobility and the poorer classes were also to a large degree gained over. In the north heresy was only sporadic and was detested by the populace.

Although there were differences in belief among the Catharans, they shared the same fundamental conception of the universe. The material world and matter were evil, the dominion of the evil spirit. Against him stood the good God of the New Testament, whose kingdom was of the spirit, not of this material world. Human souls were spirits imprisoned in the evil, material flesh, and to be freed by the Catharan belief and practices. The Catholic belief in bodily resurrection as well as the whole Church system of sacraments was untrue. Only the unregenerate passed into another material body. There followed from these extreme tenets an extreme of asceticism. All propagation of the evil flesh was the enlargement of the Devil's kingdom; marriage was thus one of the fleshly sins. All food that had been sexually begotten was unlawful—milk and eggs as well as meat— for it was the prison of a spirit. Fish were allowed owing to an ignorance of natural history, but otherwise the strictest vegetarianism was enjoined. In like manner, the Catharan creed in its crude simplicity forbade the taking of life and the swearing of oaths.

This creed, in which the reigning ideal of asceticism was driven to its utmost limits, seems indeed devised for the destruction of any organized human society and unlikely to attract a crowd of adherents, but it offered in fact a path to salvation less rigorous than that ordained for the orthodox laity. Only the fully initiate Catharan, the *perfectus* or *bonus homo*, was bound to obey these rigorous precepts, and the *perfecti* were few. They alone, and often near their deaths, went through the all-important initiation of the *consolamentum*. They were the chiefs of the faith. The mass of the Catharans were only *credentes* (believers) and their principal duty was to venerate the *perfecti*. Otherwise they could live ordinary lives and even lawfully deny their Catharism. It was a system which left a wide opening to misconduct among the mere *credentes* and a still wider to sweeping accusations of evil practices levelled against them by the orthodox.

Before these and other less notable heresies the attitude of the Church hierarchy increased in severity with their alarm. Burning alive appears to have begun in the West as a popular lay punishment of Manichaeanism, which was probably the allied creed of Catharism; it is noticeable that Alexius I Comnenus, with great reluctance, burnt a Bogomil heresiarch, who remained deaf to argument. The influence of the Civil Law helped to introduce the death-penalty for heresy. In 1184 Pope Lucius III and the Emperor Barbarossa agreed that the bishops should search out and ex-communicate these offenders against the Faith, and that the secular power should inflict on them exile and confiscation. In 1197 King Peter II of Aragon decreed death at the stake for heretics who did not obey the sentence of exile.

Innocent III was not without sympathy with the aspirations of the pious and low-born laity or knowledge of the clerical luxury and negligence which provoked unauthorized movements, but he insisted on obedience to Papacy and hierarchy. Submission was the test of orthodoxy. When groups of laity in the diocese of Metz read French translations from the Bible in defiance of priestly prohibition, he reproved them gently, and urged that preaching was the duty of the instructed clergy. Even the privilege of preaching was allowed to the large section of the Humiliati who submitted to the Roman see and were given an authorized Rule (1201). Such teaching, however, if by laymen, was to be moral, not doctrinal, in its aim. Heretical, antisacerdotal doctrine was another matter, and most formidable of all was the rival Church of the Catharans, which, besides its dubious tendencies, bid fair to undermine orthodox Christiantiy. That was to be rooted out. In 1200 Innocent was pressing King Emeric of Hungary to extirpate Catharism in Dalmatia and Bosnia, where the Ban Kulin was for some years a Catharan, and where the Bogomils, in spite of his re-conversion, remained strong. It needed a personal visit of the Pope (1207) to Viterbo to effect the banishment from the city, with confiscation of their property, of its leading Catharans. Elsewhere in North Italy little was done.

But the most dangerous centre was Languedoc, where Count Raymond VI of Toulouse himself was said to retain two *perfecti* ready to impart to him the *consolamentum,* and even some prelates were Catharans, while others were specimens of the ill-conducted clergy. Innocent's first measure was to send Cistercian monks as missioners to argue the heretics down, but they had little success and their wealth and the pomp of their abbots compared unfavourably with the genuine austerity of the *perfecti.* Nor did the efforts of the Spanish canon, St Dominic, who adopted a thorough asceticism (1205), fare very much better. In 1204 the Pope's legates, Peter de Castelnau and Arnold-Amalric, Abbot of Cîteaux, received a general commission to extirpate heresy and to call in the aid of the supreme suzerain, Philip Augustus of France. They were cautioned to use moderation, but the employment of armed force was envisaged. At the same time the reform of the peccant clergy was to be undertaken. As Philip Augustus, at war with England, declined to act and Raymond VI proved obdurate, the legates formed a league of the count's orthodox vassals to suppress the heresy, and on his refusal to join it, excommunicated him, laid his lands under interdict, and turned the league against him. So menaced, the count yielded, when the scene was changed by the murder of the hated de Castelnau (January 1208).

The deed, done by some underling of the Count's, finally turned the balance in favour of war. The Pope had already (1207) offered the spiritual benefits of a crusade to Philip and his vassals who should take up arms for the Church. Now he renewed Raymond's excommunication, absolving his vassals from their fealty, and had the crusade preached in North France. He hoped to avoid the uncontrollable behaviour of the Fourth Crusade and to conciliate all legal rights by inducing King Philip to take the lead. But a special legate failed to divert the king from his vital interests in the English war, and he had to be content with the permission given to the French barons to join. In result lords and prelates from the north assembled in great force in June 1209 at Lyons. It was soon seen that the crusaders were of the same metal as the conquerors of Constantinople: their greed and savagery were stimulated by their genuine fanaticism. Their leader was one of the best soldiers of the age, that Count Simon de Montfort who had honestly, but not for lack of ambition, insisted in 1202 on proceeding to Palestine. On 22 July they stormed the city of Béziers, perpetrating a frightful massacre of the inhabitants, Catharan and Catholic alike. Carcassonne capitulated after a brief siege; Narbonne and other places surrendered in terror on demand. The war was waged with relentless cruelty in Languedoc proper and the marquessate of Provence round Avignon. Differences of policy were soon apparent. De Montfort and his compeers aimed at dispossessing the southern nobility and seizing their lands. They drove the wretched Count of Toulouse, who had been forced to take the Cross, into opposition once more, and attacked his domain lands. Innocent's wish was to abolish heresy, but also to preserve an equitable legality, giving every opportunity to the Count of Toulouse to right himself, which the legate Arnold-Amalric and Simon de Montfort were zealous to prevent. Then there were the claims of Philip Augustus as king to be considered, and still more the protests of the indubitably orthodox King Peter II of Aragon, who claimed to be intermediate suzerain of Béziers and Foix and intervened to protect his injured vassals. Too late the Pope endeavoured to divert the crusaders against the Moors in Spain or the Saracens in the Holy Land.

King Peter had at first agreed to a compromise, by which Simon was acknowledged to be Viscount of Béziers and was put in charge of Peter's son James, the future husband of his daughter, but when Count Raymond was again condemned in a legatine council at Lavaur (1213) the king formed a league with the southern nobles and took up arms. He was overthrown and slain by De Montfort at Muret (12 September 1213), and the ferocious war went on. De Montfort was no less a diplomat than a soldier. He won over legate after legate and even Louis, the heir to France. He became Count of Toulouse and Duke of Narbonne. All the Pope could do was to grant an annuity to the dispossessed Raymond, rescue young King James I of Aragon from detention, and reserve the rights of Raymond's son to a remnant of his inheritance.

After Innocent III's death a new turn was given to the war by French intervention. The remorseless Simon de Montfort was killed in 1218 at the vain siege of revolted Toulouse, and his young son Amaury could not make head against the Catholic and popular son of Raymond VI, the young Raymond VII. The attempt of Louis of France to conquer England had just closed, and as it had been made in defiance of Pope Honorius III's prohibition, he was almost bound to go on the Crusade, but although he too perpetrated a ruthless massacre at Marmande, he could not retake Toulouse, and returned north. King Philip's policy was to wait until Church and crusaders would take him on his own terms. When he died (1223) the fruit was almost ripe, for Amaury de Montfort had resigned his nominal countship of Toulouse, and the true heir, Raymond VII, was no match for the King of France. The royal expedition, however, under King Louis VIII did not get under way for three years. Then the capture of Avignon in the marquessate of Provence (1226) was enough to cow Languedoc. King Louis declared that the lands of heretics belonged to the royal domain, but his death left Raymond VII still unsubdued, and able to join the rebel league against the regent, Queen Blanche. He shared in its defeat, the Toulousain was devastated, and he yielded to the Treaty of Paris (April 1229). The terms were harsh, yet he kept much of his domain lands. The Albigensian Crusade, set on foot by Innocent III, was at last over, and persecution of the heretics by the Inquisition, strengthened by Louis VIII's *ordonnance* which condemned them to the stake, could slowly continue the subjugation of Languedoc to North France and the Papacy. The Crusade with its horrors had already gone far to destroy the precocious culture of the land.

(5) INNOCENT III AND CHURCH ORGANIZATION

We have outrun the pontificate of Innocent III in order to follow to its close the terrible Albigensian Crusade for which, although he endeavoured to curb its evils, he was responsible. The effects of his ecclesiastical administration, too, cannot be confined to his own lifetime. He began a new era in the history of the Roman Curia. The chancery was systematically organized into departments and manned by men trained in law and office routine. With him begins the great series of papal registers which have been preserved. The documents were executed in different ways according to their purport. He drew up a set of rules for the detection of forgeries. The method of hearing appeals was elaborated, which resulted a little later in the formation of the rota of expert auditors to hear evidence and prepare cases for the papal sentence, which might be the remitting of the decision

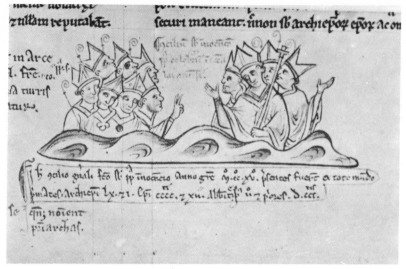

Fig. 137. The Lateran Council, 1215

to local delegates. Delay and venality were the vices of this elaborate machinery, but there was no denying the acute and logical legal justice dealt out by the Curia, unequalled by contemporaries.

Besides enforcing the law, Innocent created it, always in the sense of the papal plenitude of power, and he summed up his work in the Fourth Ecumenical Council of the Lateran, which he held in 1215 at the close of his life. Then he insisted on the duty of confession once a year at least, forbade the clergy to intervene in the barbaric survival of the ordeal, narrowed the limits of consanguinity as a bar to marriage, regulated the methods of election to bishoprics and the qualifications of the clergy, and endeavoured to check the decline and disorders of monastic life. The invention of new Rules for the religious life was forbidden, and a new principle was introduced into the old-fashioned Benedictine and Austinian houses. Their full autonomy under the inefficient supervision of bishop or Pope had proved a potent cause of decay. Relaxations and abuses became inveterate; a bad abbot's influence long outlived him; debts and disorders went hand in hand. The remedy adopted was the congregational system. Triennial chapters of both Benedictines and Austin canons were to be held in each province to issue fresh statutes and check abuses and to send round visitors for the same purpose. Autonomy and local customs were not interfered with as such, but an extra means of keeping up monastic standards was provided by mutual supervision in addition to episcopal investigations. To bring back earlier enthusiasm, generated in a half-anarchic state of Western society, was, however, a task too arduous for the monastic Orders, and the rigid statutes for the Benedictines, issued by Gregory IX, Innocent's second successor, were certainly not very sedulously regarded. Only the new ideals of the Mendicant Friars could reawaken the ancient fervour.

The tightening of control over the selection and activities of bishops remained a steady papal policy. They were to hold regular provincial and diocesan synods. The frequent employment of legates *a latere* had its effect. Innocent was prepared to annul an unfit or irregular election. In a disputed election he chose the claimant he approved. Translation from one see to another required his assent. He claimed the right of devolution, i.e. the power to appoint if a vacancy of a metropolis exceeded six months, and further the far-reaching right of provision to benefices. He used the latter with moderation. Literate and unbeneficed clerks of good reputation were collated by him to prebends along with some few members of the Curia. It was his successor, Honorius III, who first used this prerogative throughout Europe to pay his officials and escape the cost of his bureaucracy. Pope Innocent IV improved on the example by providing his relatives and friends or allies, a practice kept up by later Popes. If a whole series of checks was devised to test the provisors, they rarely seem to have been an obstacle to influential curialists. Ecclesiastical patrons of benefices, like the bishops, had little remedy, but lay patrons appear to have escaped. The good side of the practice was the endowment of neglected clerks and the teachers at universities.

As we have seen, in 1199, Innocent, first of the Popes, directly levied an income-tax on the beneficed clergy and the monasteries. That and a second higher levy in 1215 were to finance the Crusade in the East. Besides taxes for the genuine Crusades, Pope Gregory IX employed the same resource to raise money for his war with Frederick II, and this example was followed by his successors. The Lateran Council of 1215 confirmed the claim that clerical subsidies to the secular rulers required papal assent, a rule which led to frequent bitter controversies and to a startling dénouement under Pope Boniface VIII. Meantime, the exaction of income taxes had necessitated the assessment of the income of benefices, which in England ended in 1291 with the *Valuation* of Pope Nicholas IV. It was later used for the assessment of Annates, which became a prime source of the papal income.

On 16 July 1216 Innocent III died at Perugia, busied with the affairs of Europe and the preparations for the Fifth Crusade, and was at once succeeded in a natural reaction after the born autocrat by a tried financial official, the Chamberlain Cencio Savelli, who took the name of Honorius III (1216–27). He, too, was a Roman noble. Indeed, Innocent was, perhaps unconsciously, largely inspired by the tradition of the ancient Roman

Empire, with its centralized autocracy, its instinct for law and equity, its large and splendid solicitude for its subjects. He warred on turbulence, rebellion, and barbaric indiscipline. His political and legal temperament harmonized with his love of power, secular and ecclesiastical. With all his ability and merits, however, he was but half-successful in his endeavour to dominate the lay potentates, and he transmitted in a heightened form to his successors the secular methods and absorption in temporal aims which were to be the bane of the spiritual mission of the Papacy.

CHAPTER 22

THE FRIARS AND THE INQUISITION

It has been shown that the popular movements in religion had in many cases an orthodox wing, like the submissive, regularized Humiliati, or the Poor Catholics, who were a similar offshoot of the Waldensians. These communities had started by being indifferent or hostile to the priesthood and hierarchy, and when they accepted Church authority, the sap gradually ceased to flow in them. They sank into humdrum life, useful and admittedly upright, but also disliked, especially in North Italy, for they claimed, as religious, to be exempt under papal protection from the common burdens, military, financial, and official, of their unregenerate fellow-citizens. Something more, with a fresh inspiration, was needed if the imagination and devotion of the people, high and low, ignorant and learned, were to be recaptured for the Church. That inspiration was given by the arresting personality, at once original and in thorough harmony with contemporary ideals, of St Francis of Assisi.

(I) THE FRANCISCANS

St Francis (1181/2–1226) was the son of a cloth-merchant, Pietro Bernardone, to whose travels in North France he owed his name and perhaps his acquaintance with the ideals and the verse of chivalry. He had no taste for the trader's career. Open-handed, open-hearted, gay, and high-spirited, he became a leader of the young men of Assisi, and dreamed of becoming a knight of romance until perhaps illness turned the current of his thoughts. His definite 'conversion' may be dated from his sudden resolve to kiss a leper he met; hitherto he had shrunk with loathing from that horrible, then common, affliction. To tend lepers became for him a sacred duty. Devotion and self-renunciation were henceforth his ruling motives. His father disowned him when he gave the purchase money of some of his stock towards the repair of the ruined chapel of St Damian, and he lived as a wandering solitary until the day—24 February 1209—when his true vocation was revealed to him by the words of the Gospel (Matt. x) he heard read in the chapel of Sta Maria degli Angeli or Portiuncula. To preach that Gospel, following its precepts literally in utter poverty, became the end of his life, going barefoot and preaching repentance 'with words that were like fire, penetrating the heart'.

So far his aims were not unlike those of others of his century, but St Francis was no critic of the Church. He devoutly believed its doctrine and revered the priesthood. His originality lay in himself. His devotion and asceticism were interwoven with the romance of chivalry. To him Lady Poverty was the mistress of his heart; he was the minstrel of the Lord. He was not a gloomy precisian, but exhorted his friars to be glad and merry and becomingly courteous. He was so to all alike. 'More than a saint among saints, among sinners he was as one of themselves.' The same sympathy united him with all nature, animate and inanimate, and gave him power over beasts and birds. This sense of kinship received its highest expression at the close of his life in his *Praises of the Creatures*, which reveal the poet in him.

Fig. 138. *St Francis preaching to the birds*

At first hooted as a madman, his personal magnetism and the high romance of his ideal soon gained him followers, the rich Bernard of Quintavalle being the first and Giles, the ideal Franciscan friar, the third. For them he drew up a simple rule of poverty, asceticism, and preaching drawn from the Gospels, and proceeded to Rome (*c.* 1210) to obtain Innocent III's approval, which was only granted on the intercession of the Chancellor, Cardinal John of St Paul. The Order thus founded grew with great speed. The Friars Minor (as they were now named) wandered up and down Italy, winning universal veneration, living upon alms or casual work.

Once a year they met at their chosen rendezvous of Portiuncula where they erected wattle huts for the business of the Order. In 1212 they were joined by an heiress, Clara of Assisi, who was established with her imitators by Francis at St Damian's, where they were allowed to remain without possessions by Innocent III, who drew up the unprecedented privilege with his own hand. Missions outside Italy and among the infidels were among the chief aims of St Francis. At first they mostly failed, his own to the Saracens of Egypt as much as any, in spite of the kindly reception he met. Meantime (1219–20) the Order was deviating from the unsophisticated, formless idealism of its founder. Organizing, intellectual friars, patronized by his admirer, Cardinal Ugolino (the future Pope Gregory IX), were endeavouring to mould it into a formal society. They prescribed fasts, desired privileges and a constitution, and built a convent at Bologna, the university city, all things abhorrent to St Francis, who desired the spontaneous imitation of Christ and the Apostles without even corporate possessions. Francis in grief resigned his office of minister-general and asked Ugolino to be protector of the Order. The end was that the capable, despotic Elias became minister-general and a more elaborate Rule, although simple enough, was provided. Thenceforth St Francis lived as a model friar according to his first conception, which he formulated in his touching *Testament*. In August 1224 the stigmata of Christ's passion appeared on him at La Verna, and on 3 October 1226 he died at Portiuncula. In 1228 he was canonized.

Under Elias the Order went from success to success. Missions founded provinces over Europe. An elected General Chapter of ministers and others met every three years. The Rule was glossed by Gregory IX, who saw in the Friars Minor the very instrument to revive the Church. The spirit of its founder was still active in the Order, although formalism and rigidity were increasing, but learning and influence were now welcomed, while the 'spiritual' friars, who followed the exact footsteps of St Francis, took refuge in hermitages.

The despotism of Elias, however, who lived like a prince, aroused wide opposition and a revolt. In 1239 Gregory IX deposed him and authorized the subordination of the minister-general to the general chapter. The clerical members of the Order gained the upper hand, monopolizing office and imprisoning 'spirituals'. The rule of absolute poverty, softened by Gregory IX, was further relaxed by Innocent IV, who made (1245) the Papacy the owner of Franciscan belongings, unless the donors had retained the ownership. Against this relaxation the minister-general, John of Parma (1247–57), strove with some effect, but he and the stricter friars compromised themselves by their inclination towards the questionable doctrines of Abbot Joachim of Fiore.

Joachim (*ob*. 1202), the head of a group of strict Calabrian monasteries, had in several mystical works divided history into three eras, that of the Father or the Law, that of the Son or of the Crucifixion and the Sacraments, and that (which was to come) of the Holy Ghost, the Eternal Gospel of love and mystic contemplation. A spiritual universal Church was to arise, freed from the letter which killeth. His writings were dear to idealistic Franciscans, who believed that St Francis was the angel of the new era. One of them, Gerard of Borgo San Donnino, wrote (1254) an 'Introduction to the Eternal Gospel', in which by an amazing misconception he identified the new revelation with the works of Joachim himself. The rank heresy of his views earned him papal condemnation and his imprisonment by his Order, and caused the fall of John of Parma. John's successor, St Bonaventura (*ob*. 1274), orthodox philosopher and mystic, while endeavouring with little effect to check acknowledged abuses, was in sympathy with the opposite party. He believed in learning and privilege, in the Order's exemption from episcopal authority, in the Friars' right to preach and hear confessions without permission of the parish priests, to receive offerings, and to bury corpses of other than friars. Bitter hostility over fees

Fig. 139. Pope Boniface VIII receives
St Louis of Toulouse

and profits between the friars and the secular clergy was thus ensured to the discredit of both, all the more because the friars were better preachers and more expert confessors. The discord engendered continued even after a working compromise had been decreed in 1300 by Boniface VIII.

Bonaventura, however, could not heal the dissidence within the Order. In 1274 persecution of the spirituals by the majority again broke out. In vain Pope Nicholas III attempted in 1279 to close the breach by a stricter definition of poverty, and Celestine V's sensible division of the Order by forming the spirituals into a separate organization was promptly annulled by Boniface VIII. In 1312 Clement V defined once more the *usus pauper* of belongings without producing appeasement. The persecution was sharpened by Pope John XXII, who burned the spirituals of southern France as heretics. In Italy some grouped themselves independently under Angelo da Clareno, others in the south formed scattered communities of Fraticelli in the mountains and drifted into clear unorthodoxy. But John XXII was a hardheaded, matter-of-fact lawyer, who objected to mere technical poverty in which the laxer friars enjoyed the advantages without the name of property. In two decretals (1322–3) he withdrew the nominal ownership of Franciscan belongings by the Pope, and declared the Franciscan doctrine of the absolute poverty of Christ and the Apostles to be heretical. The general, Michael of Cesena, revolted with some of his followers, among whom was the famous William of Ockham, but the majority soon submitted. The decline in fervour and discipline was accelerated by the mortality among the friars in the Black Death and by the Great Schism. But at the same time there were symptoms of a regeneration. In 1334 certain friars, led by Giovanni Valle, were allowed to found a hermitage at Foligno for the strict observance of the Rule. Other foundations followed. The Friars of the Strict Observance, under the leadership of St Bernardino of Siena (1380–1444), became the most influential religious force in Italy. Their relations with the lax majority, now known as Conventuals, were strained until in 1517 Pope Leo X erected them into a separate Order. They made most headway in lands where the Conventuals were most careless of the Rule.

(2) THE DOMINICANS

The Friars Minor rose to their immense influence because, while practising the monastic virtues of poverty, chastity, and obedience, they had entered into active life among the people. A similar, though not identical, ideal led also to the success of the other great Order of Friars, the Dominicans or Friars Preachers. St Dominic (1170–1221) was a Castilian, who became a canon of Osma. Fervently orthodox, he adopted in 1205 voluntary poverty in his missionary journeys to convert the Albigensian heretics of Languedoc, gathering a band of like-minded men under him. In 1215 he attended the Lateran Council and petitioned for the establishment of an Order of Preachers, subject only to the Papacy. Since new Orders were forbidden by the Council, Innocent III gave him the choice of which existing Rule he would adopt, and he selected that of the Austin canons, under which he lived. It was so vague as to allow any kind of organization, and was immediately supplemented by a body of customs, largely borrowed from Prémontré, which really created a new Order of Friars. The Order was confirmed by Honorius III (1216). St Dominic sent friars to all parts, and in especial to the university cities of Paris and Bologna. In 1220 in the constitutions then drawn up he insisted on the absolute poverty of his Order. He drew up a Rule for Dominican nuns as an integral part of it, a position which in spite of a temporary abrogation (1252–67) they retained. He died at Bologna (6 August 1221) and was soon (1234) canonized. His courage and zeal were as unquestionable as was his capacity to rule and organize with a gentle sway. The originality of his conception of an Order of ascetic, learned defenders of the Faith is little affected by his imitation of the heretic *perfecti*.

Following his footsteps, the Dominicans excelled as organizers. They were the first religious Order to put intellectual work in the forefront, curtailing the hours in church for the purpose and giving the conventual superior powers of dispensation. They also gave elected representatives a large share in their government.The 'definitors' or effective part of the general chapter (annual till 1370) consisted for every two out of three years of elective representatives of the twelve provinces under the master-general and in the third year of the provincial priors. Every enactment had to be passed by three successive chapters. Besides legislation, the definitors could punish or depose officials. Both elected and official definitors met to elect the general. The yearly provincial chapters consisted in the main of the conventual priors and an elected representative from each convent. They elected the provincial prior, the visitors, and four definitors with the same powers in the province as the general chapter in the Order. Each convent elected its prior. It was a system of representative government. No other Order depended so much on election by a simple majority. The Franciscans appointed their 'guardians' of convents and 'custodians' of groups of convents from above, relying on frequent change of officers.

In the fourteenth and fifteenth centuries the Dominicans did not escape internal controversies and the general decay of discipline and the common life. Not only did most convents own property, but individual friars were allowed to have a private income. After the Black Death, apparently, there came in the practice of farming out at a fixed rent prescribed districts (*limites*) for preaching and confession. The 'limitor' had exclusive rights and made what he could out of them. During the Great Schism the Roman general established houses of Observant Friars to keep to the Constitutions, and the movement spread. But with the Dominicans, Observant or relaxed, absolute poverty was never an end in itself, but a means to influence the laity, and in 1475 the whole Order gladly accepted the papal bull which abolished the obsolete prescription.

Along with the Franciscans or Grey Friars and the Dominicans or Black Friars two other Mendicant Orders of less note obtained recognition at the General Council of Lyons in 1274, and must receive a bare mention. The Carmelites, who claimed Elijah as their founder, were originally a group of hermits in the Holy Land. Under their general prior, Simon Stock, they were transformed into friars by Pope Innocent IV and adopted a constitution and vocation modelled on the Dominicans. The Austin Friars sprang from several different groups of Italian hermits. They absorbed among others the Poor Catholics or orthodox Waldensians, and in 1256 were finally developed into a Mendicant Order by Alexander IV. They, too, submitted. to Dominican influence, but like the Carmelites played a minor part in the Church and universities.

(3) THE INFLUENCE OF THE FRIARS

After the first period of intense religious enthusiasm there followed about a century in which the Mendicant Friars supplied Europe with most of its leaders in thought and learning. From their beginning the Dominicans were a learned Order. The Jacobin convent at Paris was their intellectual centre, to which every province could send friars. Their original restriction to theology was soon superseded. They developed a system of *Studia* for Arts and natural philosophy and lastly theology. The chief *Studia* of theology were established in university towns, the eminent exception being that of Cologne. The Franciscans were not long in taking the same path in spite of St Francis's antipathy to learning. When in 1231 the distinguished professor, Alexander of Hales, entered the Order at Paris, and the still greater intellect, Robert Grosseteste, became lecturer to the friars at Oxford, their future was assured. Both Dominicans and Franciscans surpassed their secular rivals in the universities, and conflict with the strongly organized corporations of masters was inevitable. In 1250 Innocent IV definitely ordered the Chancellor of Paris to confer the licence to teach on such religious as were qualified. This ignored the right of the Doctors of Divinity to control admission into their faculty, and they resisted. In 1256 St Thomas Aquinas, the Dominican, and St Bonaventura, the Franciscan, were refused admission. At the papal court the secular masters found allies in the bishops and parish priests who were aggrieved at the friars' privileges. The peremptory bull, *Quasi lignum vitae* (1255), of Alexander IV in favour of the friars enforced submission only after prolonged recalcitrance. In Oxford a somewhat similar struggle left the Divinity Faculty in control of the grant of its degrees, but allowed the friars (who did not graduate first in Arts) to proceed by dispensation by a majority of votes in the fourteenth century. There was a difference in tendency between the two great Orders. The Dominicans, although they produced Albert the Great and St Thomas Aquinas, were distinguished by industry and learning rather than by originality. They compiled co-operative works, such as a revision of the Vulgate text, Biblical concordances, and the encyclopaedia edited by Vincent of Beauvais, the *Speculum maius*. In 1286 their general chapter decreed that they must defend the doctrine of Aquinas. This did not encourage intellectual freedom. On the other hand the Franciscans took the lead in the movement of ideas. Grosseteste (who was only their teacher) founded a school at Oxford, whose most eminent members were Adam Marsh and Roger Bacon. It championed independence of judgement and first-hand knowledge, the study of languages and physics, rather than dependence on authority, and its influence was still alive in the Order in the fourteenth century. Duns Scotus was the destroyer of systems, especially that of Aquinas, whose harmony of revelation and philosophy, arranged for foreordained conclusions, he showed to be largely illusory. Ockham went even further, and brought philosophy down from its speculative heights to common sense, direct observation, and induction.

As important as their intellectual achievements was the new vogue the friars gave to popular preaching. Their very churches were designed not so much for processions and the liturgy as for the audience of sermons. St Francis himself was unique. A learned hearer said: 'The words of the holy Francis alone escape me, and, if I commit any of them to memory, they do not seem to be the same that he had spoken.' Preaching in other friars was systematized. Instructions were compiled, and so were numerous collections of *exempla* or illustrative anecdotes. The learned Dominicans on the whole preferred stories of the great men of antiquity, the Franciscans the homely things of daily life. The sermons of two famous Franciscan preachers are preserved. Berthold of Regensburg (*ob.* 1272) needed no anecdotes. He was dramatic and inspired by a moral fervour which retains its vitality. St Bernardino of Siena (*ob.* 1444) was colloquial and practical. He was full of *exempla*, but careful to learn the everyday life and the local circumstances of his audiences. Merciless to witches, he was unusually tender to a shaken faith. He endeavoured to heal the inveterate canker of civil strife and was the promoter of the charitable institutions which are a characteristic of his country.

One effect of the early Franciscan preaching was the formation of fraternities of penitence among their hearers. In 1221 Cardinal Ugolino drew up a Rule for such communities, which in 1230 he referred to as the 'Third Order of St Francis'. They varied among themselves, and strongly resembled the Third Order of the Humiliati, who likewise were pledged to live an honest, peaceable, charitable, and devout life. Their relations with the Friars Minor varied, too, from place to place, and a party among the latter were averse to any responsibility for the 'Third Order', whose

Fig. 140. St Bernardino of Siena

freedom from heresy could not be guaranteed. At last in 1289 Pope Nicholas IV issued a stricter Rule for the Third Order and insisted on its supervision by the friars. Tertiaries of the Dominicans were also established at nearly the same time. Heresy, however, was by no means banished from the Franciscan Tertiaries, and they suffered much persecution from the Inquisition, in spite of the fact that eminent men and women joined them. They shared, too, in the dislike of the laity because of the exemption they claimed from civic duties.

Allied in spirit to the popular preaching, which combated ingrained paganism, were the missions to the infidel. St Francis had longed not to conquer but to convert the Moslems, a revival of the missionary spirit of older times. The Dominicans were the more methodical. About 1250 Raymond of Peñafort established schools to teach Hebrew and Arabic for their missionaries, an example which was imitated (1276) by Raymond Lull (martyred 1314) for the Franciscans. Meanwhile adventurous Franciscans, the Italian John de Plano Carpini sent by Innocent IV (1245) and the Fleming William of Rubruquis sent by Louis IX (1253), had penetrated to the Far East to the court of the Mongol Great Khan at Karakorum. The tolerance of the heathen Mongols allowed missionaries free scope, and they founded an archbishopric at Pekin. The Dominicans laboured less successfully in Persia. All these missions alike, however, were doomed to extinction in the fourteenth century, when the fall of the Mongol Yuan dynasty of China (1368) and the rise of the fervent Moslem Tamerlane in Transoxiana dealt them deadly blows and the Black Death diminished the supply of missionaries. None the less they had for a time opened the route to Central and Farther Asia to traders, including the famous Marco Polo.

(4) THE INQUISITION

The Church, however, relied on repression far more than on persuasion in its war with heresy, and made the friars its chief instruments. The bishops had originally been the judges of heretics and charged to search them out in their dioceses, and in 1184 the Council of Verona authorized them to act on common report (*diffamatio*) without an accuser. They were supplemented in the Albigensian proceedings by special papal delegates like de Castelnau. Pope Gregory IX thus appointed the ferocious Conrad of Marburg for Germany and the bloodthirsty convert, Robert le Bougre, in France, both of whom harried heretics and orthodox in their rabid zeal. But the Pope relied most on the two Mendicant Orders. In April 1233 two bulls virtually founded the Holy Office of the Inquisition. First established in southern France, where heresy was strongest, its powers and procedure were rapidly extended over Western Europe, although the British Isles, Scandinavia, Castile, and Portugal escaped, and Catharan Bosnia repelled it with slaughter. The Dominicans were called in first as inquisitors, but the Franciscans were soon also employed, and to prevent the quarrels which ensued separate districts were confided to them. The Dominicans were charged with France, Germany, and Lombardy, the Franciscans with the kingdom of Burgundy east of the Rhône, central Italy, and Bohemia.

As finally organized by Popes Innocent IV, Alexander IV, and Clement IV, the judges of the Inquisition were friars, who held local tribunals, independent of the bishops nominally associated with them and even of papal legates and their own superiors in the Orders, calling in the secular power when necessary, and inflicting penalties without appeal. They were attended by 'familiars' as a bodyguard, court police, and often spies. The inquisitors were picked men, fanatically devoted to orthodoxy. If monsters of wanton cruelty were the exception, their office was founded on unrelenting persecution, its procedure was bent to that end, and with its secrecy, ubiquity, and careful record acquired a sinister and dreadful reputation. The inquisitors' manuals abound in fine distinctions. In addition to the classification of heretics, there were the punishable categories of *suspicion*, *lightly suspect* for once speaking to a heretic, *vehemently suspect* for doing so twice or thrice, *violently suspect* for real frequency. Fautorship of heretics was a serious offence. Sorcery was soon labelled as heresy. *Diffamatio* in short was an easy pitfall.

The procedure was weighted against the accused. He was subjected to a prolonged interrogatory. He was not allowed to know who were the witnesses against him, and could only guess whom he could accuse of mortal enmity, the only valid defence against *diffamatio*. Any kind of evidence from persons however tainted was accepted against him. From 1254 he was not permitted to employ an advocate, in any case difficult to find for such a dangerous office. Torture was used to extort confessions. It was adopted from the Civil Law, and the secular power was at first called in to inflict it, but from 1255 the inquisitors were allowed to absolve one another for its use. The prohibition to torture twice was evaded by 'continuing' it on a subsequent day. Since a forced confession was invalid, the device was adopted of making the accused confirm it three days after as a 'voluntary' confession. It was the sick Pope Clement V who endeavoured to check these severities.

The 'penances'—not in name punishments—inflicted by the inquisitors varied. Pilgrimage more or less distant was a frequent one, public flogging in church was another, wearing a saffron cross was a third which perpetuated the disgrace. Fines, which led to extortion, were also much used. Confiscation of property for actual heresy was automatic, but the Church aggravated the Civil Law by disinheriting orthodox sons of the convicted. The division of the proceeds was diversely effected; latterly in France the Crown took all. Imprisonment varied from a more lenient detention to the terrible solitary confinement for life. Death at the stake was the most terrifying punishment inflicted on the obdurate and relapsed heretic, but it was a confession of failure to reconvert him, and in seventeen years the inquisitor Bernard Gui only sentenced to it 45 out of 613 culprits, something over seven per cent. The Church could not canonically decree death or the shedding of blood, but it *relaxed* the heretic to the secular power with a conventional prayer that those penalties should be avoided. It was known and expected, however, that they would be inflicted, and both the Emperor Frederick II and St Louis of France decreed them. Failure of the civil power to co-operate with the Church in extirpating heresy involved it in excommunication, and the penalty was popularly approved, although it did not become English law till the reign of Henry IV. So thoroughly did the Church believe in burning the obdurate heretic, as a traitor to Christendom, that, when his heresy was discovered after his death, it ordained that his bones should be exhumed and burnt.

In France in the thirteenth century, this terrible tribunal received the ardent support of St Louis. Count Raymond VII of Toulouse was no less zealous, and burnt heretics who had recanted and should have received a less penalty. His successor Count Alphonse was less barbarous but greedy of confiscations. His and the royal officials eagerly rounded off their masters' lands. As a result heresy was completely stamped out in Languedoc and northern France along with the remnants of the southern civilization. It left behind it a generation, orthodox in doctrine, but no lovers of the clergy. At the same time the methods of the Inquisition left a sinister influence on French criminal law.

In Italy the course of persecution was more chequered, for it was both assisted and impeded by city and party politics. Frederick II had decreed the severest penalties for heresy (1224, 1238), but the Popes were inclined to translate Ghibelline into heretic and both Guelf and Ghibelline city governments might favour or tolerate heretics. Verona, Brescia, and Mantua were their havens of refuge, and while the Dominican inquisitor, Peter Martyr, met with success in Florence, he was slaughtered (1252) at Milan, where the murderer went free. Towards the close of the century Catharism was being extinguished as well as wilder heresies which cropped up in Lombardy, like those of Segarelli (executed 1300) and of Fra Dolcino, whose followers were quelled by a Crusade (1305).

Waldensianism continued in the western Alps in spite of all, and forms of it spread half underground to Germany, Bohemia, and Hungary, where episcopal persecution could not suppress them. There they became an apt soil for the Hussite movement. In Germany there was a sudden savage outburst of persecution (1231), led by the frantically cruel Conrad of Marburg, a secular priest, with his Dominican coadjutors, backed by imperial and papal authority. No one accused could escape. Like Robert le Bougre in northern France (1233–9), he condemned his victims wholesale to the flames. When he attacked the upper classes, however, a reaction set in; almost all the bishops opposed him. The Count of Sayn, orthodox and blameless, was acquitted, and Conrad's murder (1233) sapped the rage for persecution. The Brethren of the Free Spirit and similar associations in the trading towns in Swabia, along the Rhine, and in the Netherlands, who were given to a mystical and sometimes antinomian pantheism, provided objects for the Inquisition for some two centuries.

CHAPTER 23

THE EMPIRE, FRANCE AND ENGLAND

(I) THE EMPEROR FREDERICK II

Frederick II, 'the wonder of the world' as some called him, began his reign in Germany under deplorable conditions. The imperial control over Church and prelates had been abandoned by Otto IV and himself; imperial demesnes, rights and dues had been squandered in grants to the greedy princes; and those princes and the great nobles had become used to rule their lands with little regard for the central authority. To restore the monarchy, if indeed it was feasible at all, would have required the long, patient, concentrated efforts of a resident sovereign, carefully avoiding the hostility of the Papacy and undazzled by the imperial tradition. But for such a role, improbable for any Emperor, Frederick of Hohenstaufen was most unfit. His heart was in the south. Born at Jesi (near Ancona) and brought up in Sicily, the heir of his Norman progenitors, he devoted his life to a new interpretation of Barbarossa's ambitions: the reduction of all Italy, the imperial *Regnum Italicum* along with the kingdom of Sicily, under his autocratic sway. The scheme was a chimera, opposed equally to the vital interests of the Papacy and to the passion of the northern communes for republican autonomy, and it led to the fall of his house and of the Empire itself.

The intricate web of German administration, with its involved, interlocking jurisdictions and piecemeal, fragmentary powers, with its intermingling of royal, tribal and feudal laws and courts, with the jealous restrictions imposed on royal action by the princes, and with papal legates steadily exercising control over the Church, can have had little attraction for the autocratic and orderly mind of Frederick II. Germany was becoming a conglomeration of semi-independent princedoms, confused and entangled as the process was. He looked on it rather as a source of influence, power and soldiers than as a state to be ruled. To secure the support and acquiescence of the princes, ecclesiastical and lay, was the mainspring of his policy. During the eight years of his sojourn north of the Alps with this and the restoration of some semblance of order in view, he granted away with a lavish hand regalian lands and rights. He bid for the loyalty of imperial towns by ample privileges, but the resistance of the lords prevented such action in seignorial towns. His attempt to effect an exchange for the benefit of the royal lands was equally rebuffed, but he obtained a share of the inheritance of the house of Zähringen on its extinction (1218). Bern, Zürich and two other towns became imperial, while his son, the child Henry, was invested with the duchy of Swabia and the rectorate of Burgundy.

The main object of Frederick, however, was to evade his pledges to the Pope to abdicate the kingdom of Sicily; his second was to defer the crusade, to which he was equally committed, to a somewhat nebulous future after he had performed the pressing tasks incumbent upon him of restoring order and stability to both Empire and Regno. The astute diplomacy by which he continued to make these disastrous engagements baffle one another gives the measure of his political adroitness and also of the falsity which confirmed the distrust and enmity of the Popes. He had sworn to abdicate Sicily when he received the imperial crown, the motive of Innocent's insistence on the renunciation being the dread of a permanent union of the two states. At the same time Pope Honorius III, like Innocent, was intensely anxious for the next Crusade to be led by the greatest monarch, the titular chief, of Europe, as well he might be, after the distortion and indiscipline of the Fourth and Albigensian Crusades. To play on this desire while rendering the abdication useless and a hindrance was Frederick's policy. He brought young Henry to Germany (1216) and prepared for his election by the princes as King of the Romans; thus the two crowns would still

Fig. 141. Frederick II with a falcon

be united. He bought the votes of the ecclesiastical princes when the election took place at Frankfurt in April 1220 by the far-reaching concessions of the famous *Confoederatio cum principibus ecclesiasticis*, by which he surrendered the right to erect castles and charter towns or to levy fresh tolls on Church lands, restricted the intervention of royal officials therein, and increased the prelates' control of their lay *Vögte*, while excommunication was to entail the ban of the Empire. Thus the royal executive was edged out of the prelates' fiefs. At the same time Frederick pretended to Pope Honorius that the election had been carried through without his knowledge in order to secure the peace of Germany during his crusade. He then departed to Italy to be crowned Emperor, leaving Engelbert, Archbishop of Cologne, the ablest of the prelates, as guardian of his son and the German kingdom.

Honorius III was a peace-loving Pope, seeking for a *modus vivendi* with his powerful ally and vassal, who had made such valuable concessions, had recently persuaded the insurgent Roman commune to recall him from Viterbo, and was prodigal of promises. In spite of suspicions and friction Frederick was crowned Emperor (22 November 1220) under promise of immediate help to the Fifth Crusade, then in difficulties in Egypt, and of joining it within nine months. The help he duly sent but in vain; his own sailing he postponed. In fact there was urgent need of him at home. In the *Regnum Italicum* he had sketched out a plan of control by appointing a General Legate with five provincial vicars. The measure had little effect, for the communes clung to their turbulent autonomy, and inter-city wars and internal faction strife blazed up fiercely everywhere. In the king-

Fig. 142. Castel del Monte near Andria

dom of Sicily he entered at once on the arduous task of reconstruction. The Norman monarchy was to be restored and developed. Two men served him well, the lawyer Roffredo of Benevento and the low-born Capuan, Piero della Vigna. He reunited usurped or extorted fiefs with the royal demesne. In December 1220 in a 'General Court' at Capua he enacted, as his 'will and pleasure', twenty reforming constitutions, dealing with fiefs, castles, invalid title to lands, and the judicial system; and he followed them up at Messina and subsequently with others whose object was the reform of abuses public and private. Meanwhile there was open rebellion to suppress. On the mainland the Count of Molise was exiled and his fiefs confiscated. In the island the Saracens under Morabit, who were supplied with munitions by the Genoese, wroth at the loss of their special privileges, were at length subdued by the Emperor, who transported large numbers to Lucera on the mainland. There they were made a prosperous agricultural colony, which provided invaluable and faithful soldiery to the Emperor, for they were indifferent to interdict and excommunication. By 1223 Frederick was master of his kingdom. All his subjects were under uniform laws; the administration was reorganized, the fleet rebuilt, agriculture, industry, and commerce were protected, talent and fidelity were the passports to office. First of medieval sovereigns, he founded (1224) and endowed a university, that of Naples, where his southern subjects were to learn the knowledge of the time.

The long wrangle with the Papacy had already begun. Honorius complained of the Emperor's tardiness as a crusader and of his infringements of clerical liberties in the Regno, besides a suspicious intervention of one of his vicars in the duchy of Spoleto. To lure the widower Frederick on, he arranged his marriage (1225) to Yolande (Isabella), heiress of the kingdom of Jerusalem, and consented to the dethronement of her father John of Brienne, while after repeated delays the Emperor's voyage was finally fixed for August 1227. Frederick used the respite to advance his schemes in North Italy by convoking a General Diet of the whole Empire for Easter 1226 at Cremona. The communes at once took alarm. The Second Lombard League of recalcitrant cities was formed, and the outlet of the Brenner Pass at Verona, the Chiuse (*clusae*), was seized to prevent the Germans attending. The Emperor's fulminations had no effect, the Diet was a fiasco, and not till a year had passed did papal mediation produce a compromise. By that date the pacific Honorius was already dead (18 March 1227), and Cardinal Ugolino dei Conti, the nephew of Innocent III, reigned as Gregory IX.

The choice of his name declared the new Pope's ideals. He was a fiery, imperious nature, prone to persecution, eager to take the sword, the admirer and yet the dominator of St Francis and his Order. He left his mark as a legislator with the aid of Raymond of Peñafort in his code of Decretals. His political insight showed him the danger of Frederick's schemes to the Papacy, which a unified Italy under an autocrat of genius would dominate. To wreck them he was impatiently ready to declare war. Meantime the crusaders gathered in Apulia and were being decimated by sickness. Frederick sailed indeed at the due date, but, himself ill, returned to Pozzuoli to recuperate. The Pope's wrath and suspicions burst out. He at once excommunicated the Emperor for breach of his vow, and when Frederick did sail next year, renewed the sentence. Frederick's reply was a manifesto, denouncing the secular ambitions of the political Papacy. Although driven from Rome, where he was not loved, Gregory sent an army into the Terra di Lavoro (Campania) and fomented the rebellion of towns which hoped to be communes. Against him Frederick's Vicar, Rainald, 'Duke of Spoleto', was sent into the March of Ancona. Much more formidable was the return of the Emperor himself (June 1229), now the regainer of Jerusalem. In vain was he excommunicated once more as a trafficker with Saracens in spite of his petition for peace. His personality was an overwhelming asset. He recovered lost and revolted territory almost without a blow, while the papal troops recoiled before him. Yet he was more desirous of a peace than the Pope, who was strengthened by the Romans recalling him under terror of a pestilence. The Treaty of San

Germano was not signed until 23 July 1230, when the Emperor bound himself to allow the fullest privileges to the clergy of the Regno. A fresh period of surly co-operation began, but the incurable discord of Papacy and Emperor had been unveiled by Gregory's premature aggression.

Frederick was now at liberty to stamp out the dying embers of revolt in the Regno. His main efforts, however, were directed to reform and

legislation. On 1 September 1231 he issued at Melfi the *Liber Augustalis* in both Latin and Greek (still a living language), the first code of law to be promulgated by a medieval secular monarch. Piero della Vigna and Giacomo, Archbishop of Capua, took part in the compilation of this imitation of Justinian, which was supplemented, like its prototype, by a series of *Novellae*. With all its absolutism and Draconian penalties it was far in advance of its century, replacing customary and feudal law. The administrative system was similarly precocious, developing that of Roger II. The king and his councillors ruled the State through efficient local officials. The feudal organization was subordinated to the royal bureaucracy, which was organized in departments and strictly supervised. Few great nobles belonged to it. The eleven provinces had each a justiciar and a

Fig. 143. St Elizabeth and her husband, Landgrave Lewis of Thuringia

master chamberlain for criminal and civil duties. The cities were equally kept in check, but the status of the bourgeoisie as a whole was raised, for their deputies were summoned to the periodic provincial courts which were instituted to redress abuses of power. In 1232 and 1240 two deputies from each town were even called to a general parliament for consultation along with the prelates and barons.

Economic prosperity was likewise Frederick's care. He built new cities and bridges. He stimulated agriculture and trade, largely by royal monopolies, but also by lower and fewer custom-duties and annual fairs. He reintroduced a gold coinage in Western Europe (outside the Spanish peninsula) by striking the augustale (1231). Under his vigorous and to some extent liberal administration, his kingdom surpassed in prosperity and civilization all its neighbours.

The fatal flaw in this structure was the costly ambition and the wars of Frederick. The wealth of the kingdom was drained to support them. After his crusade he added to his resources a hearth-tax, the *collecta*, which became annual and most oppressive. Even so he was obliged to have recourse to loans to pay his German and Saracen soldiery, which were the more burdensome because they were raised from foreign merchants. At the close of his reign he was barely solvent and his subjects were alienated by heavy taxation.

Meantime in Northern Italy the cities pursued their now normal course of discord and war, too multifarious to be narrated. Faction and class strife and the need of a unified executive were already producing a chief magistrate in the shape of the podestà and, in Lombardy, even foreshadowing the rise of the unfettered tyrant. The enmity of neighbouring cities in the race for independence, power, and trade was, if possible, more pronounced; Cremona and Pavia were the foes of Milan, Florence of Pisa and Siena, and so on, thus giving a foothold and excuse for Frederick's intervention. After first efforts in concert with the Pope, who was eager for his aid to extirpate the numerous heretics, the state of Germany gave Frederick a pressing occasion to deal with both sets of problems by summoning a General Diet of the Empire for November 1231 at Ravenna.

Fig. 144. Golden Augustale, coined by Frederick II in the Regno

A sudden concord fell upon the Lombards, who renewed their League and barred the Alpine passes, and to meet the German princes, Frederick was forced to sail to Aquileia.

The administration of Germany by Engelbert of Cologne had not been unsuccessful. There had not been any serious feuds. The greatest danger lay in the alarming conquests of King Waldemar II of Denmark, who annexed Holstein with Lübeck and Hamburg. When he was treacherously captured by the Count of Schwerin (1223), the Danes refused a treaty, and the war continued; Waldemar on the strength of a papal absolution broke the terms to which he had sworn for his release. It required his decisive defeat at Bornhövede by the Saxon princes (July 1227) to recover Holstein and give free field for German expansion eastwards on the Baltic coast. To this enterprise of the Teutonic Knights and the Knights of the Sword the Emperor contributed nothing but diplomas. The *Drang nach Osten* went on as a particularist adventure.

Archbishop Engelbert was much more concerned with enhancing the English trade of his prosperous city of Cologne. To this end he attempted to marry young King Henry to an English princess, but the Emperor remained fast to the French alliance. Meantime the resentment aroused by

Engelbert's firm repression of lawlessness bore fruit in his murder (1225) by his own cousin Frederick of Isenburg, in which two Saxon bishops were involved. Though the conspirators were punished, the regime of peace was shaken. The new regent, a secular prince this time, Duke Lewis of Bavaria, let the feuds go on unchecked, although little heed was paid to Pope Gregory's efforts (1229) to stir up rebellion even when Duke Lewis himself took to a short-lived revolt. Henry, now married to a daughter of the Duke of Austria, was henceforth his father's vicegerent.

It turned out an inharmonious partnership. Frederick leant on the princes. Henry naturally wished to check their autonomy and to revive the royal power by encouraging the towns, at whose wealth and aspirations for self-government the princes looked askance. His chosen advisers came from the lower nobility and the *ministeriales* of his royal and patrimonial lands, who desired the resurrection of the old kingship. Unfortunately, King Henry had neither the means nor the character to carry through his designs. He was injudicious, prodigal, spasmodic, and ineffectual. He enraged his father, whom he disobeyed, and was no match for the over-mighty princes. During their absence in Italy after the Crusade, he infringed the Bishop of Liége's rights by a charter to Liége recognizing a league of Netherlandish towns. When the absentees returned he found himself helpless against the wrathful princes. They wrung from him a general edict against town leagues and in May 1231 the famous *Constitutio in favorem principum*, which took its place along with Frederick's *Confoederatio* of 1220 as the fundamental law of the new Germany. It practically made the prince, the *dominus terrae* as he was styled, the absolute ruler of his domain to the exclusion of the rights of the Crown. He could even legislate with the consent of his subjects, a provision which furthered the growth of the local diets. When the Emperor met the princes at Aquileia, he was obliged to ratify these new concessions, which exaggerated his own policy. He had already at Ravenna fulminated against all internal liberties and associations in episcopal towns not granted by the bishop, an edict of no effect, for the German townsmen were too strong to be quelled. He only forgave his blundering son on condition of an oath of strict obedience and of co-operation with the princes. If the oath was broken their fealty sworn to Henry was to be null (April 1232).

The wayward young king had the folly to break his oath. He was a crowned king, he thought, not a mere viceroy. His occasional friend Lewis of Bavaria had been mysteriously murdered (1231), and he put his trust in his rash entourage. Although his behaviour during the heresy-hunt was creditable and pleased the bishops, he fell out with most of the lay princes, while the old feuds raged unchecked. At last (1234) he openly revolted against his father, going so far as to ally with the Lombard League in order to prevent Frederick from crossing the Alps.

This was the unpardonable sin. No accord had been reached between the Lombard League and the Emperor, although the Dominican John of Vicenza gained a transitory renown as a preacher of general peace, and there was a *rapprochement* between Frederick and Pope Gregory, once more exiled from Rome and once more acting, vainly and tepidly, as mediator in Lombardy. The Pope was at least in favour of the persecuting Emperor against his undutiful son. So Frederick, assured of his own strength, was able to enter Germany by way of Aquileia in May 1235 with his court, his treasure, his menagerie, and a mere handful of soldiers. The princes rallied round him, resistance was hopeless, and Henry surrendered. At a diet at Worms in July he was deposed and imprisoned, to die years later (1242) in Apulia. The Emperor now proceeded to strengthen himself in Germany. He took as his third wife Isabella, sister of Henry III of England, thereby pleasing the Rhenish trading cities. He closed the feud with the Welfs by converting their lands into a new duchy, that of Brunswick-Lüneburg. At the Diet of Mainz in August he made a vigorous effort to restore internal peace by a general edict. Private war was in law restricted and regulated. A justiciar was set up to enforce the peace among lesser nobles; the Emperor remained the judge of the princes. The measure

Fig. 145. Marriage of the Emperor Frederick II and Isabella

was the foundation of the imperial court of justice, which lasted, but its real effectiveness was destroyed by subsequent events. Even the towns received charters with their bishops' consent, for the prelates were now more awake to their best interests. To crown all, the Emperor's son by Yolande, the boy Conrad IV, the King of Jerusalem, was in 1237 elected, but not crowned, King of the Romans. Civil war, however, was not over The last Babenberg, Frederick, Duke of Austria, rose in revolt, and, although all but conquered, recovered his land as a rebel.

The real preoccupation of the Emperor, however, was in North Italy. He was at the height of his power and was resolved to use the soldiers of Germany to put an end to the exasperating independence of the communes and their all but open alliance with the Pope, who had defeated the Romans with his aid. He threw down the gauntlet in a circular summoning a general diet at Piacenza (1236). Italy was 'to re-enter the unity of the Empire', and the lands ceded to the Roman Church were to be reannexed from the ungrateful recipient. To this Gregory replied with a sweeping assertion of the highest papal doctrine. The world was under the sway of the Papacy. He cited the Donation of Constantine and the new-fangled doctrine of the Translation of the Empire by Pope Leo III from the Greeks to the Germans. In short, the two heads of Christendom staked their irreconcilable claims. Frederick's first campaign conquered the whole Trevisan (or Veronese) March, where he possessed a formidable ally in Ezzelino da Romano, faction-chief and tyrant of Verona, but he was called back to Germany to deal with the Duke of Austria's rebellion. There were still negotiations with the commmunes and their mediator, or rather patron, the Pope. They brought no solution, and in September 1237 the Emperor took the field again. This time he completely routed the League's army at Cortenuova (27 November). Almost all the communes were ready for surrender, when Frederick drove them to desperate resistance by insisting that it must be unconditional. From that moment, in spite of some progress in west Lombardy, fortune began to veer. After great preparations he besieged Brescia in vain for two months, and his enemies regained heart (1238). The Pope, now master of and resident in Rome, redoubled his complaints and was further exasperated when the Emperor married his bastard son Enzo to a Sardinian heiress and created him King of Sardinia, thus flouting the papal claim to suzerainty over the island. Gregory made a secret alliance with the uneasy naval cities of Genoa and Venice. He knew that Frederick was deep in debt and exhausting the overtaxed Regno. On 20 March 1239 he launched the expected excommunication of the Emperor.

Each side appealed to Christendom, Gregory with denunciation of the grievous misdoings of the faithless, heretic Frederick, the Emperor with protestations of his orthodoxy and counter-accusations of the Church's ingratitude. Pamphlets seconded his letters, but the princes of Europe held aloof. The Pope raised money from the Lombard League, from taxing the Church, and from usurious bankers' loans. Frederick expelled foreign friars from the Regno and mulcted its clergy. He won ground in the Papal State, but lost it in Lombardy, where he failed in a siege of Milan. Tuscany, however, was almost all in his obedience. At last, marching from Viterbo, he attacked Rome itself. There the Pope (22 February 1240) turned the divided citizens to his side by a procession, bearing the heads of the Apostles, and a fiery harangue. The Emperor saw it was useless to proceed, and there followed negotiations initiated by the German prelates and conducted by the Pope through Cardinal John Colonna. Then Gregory abruptly broke them off by summoning a General Council at Rome for 1241. Colonna was so wroth that he revolted to the Emperor, while Frederick refused safe-conduct to the prelates and issued commands for their capture. When a large party

*Fig. 146. Capture of the anti-imperial prelates by the Pisans,
May 1241*

of them sailed from Genoa, they were assailed and many seized near the island of Giglio by a Pisan and Sicilian fleet under King Enzo, now his father's general legate in North Italy (3 May). The intended Council was balked, but the Emperor was in dire straits for funds and longing for peace; he had even issued stamped leather as a compulsory substitute for his gold augustales. Gregory in his own critical situation—for the Milanese were defeated by their rival Pavia at the same time—gained a respite by offering him absolution on undefined terms. On negotiations being begun those terms were revealed as unconditional surrender, and hostilities inside and outside Rome were renewed. At this juncture the septuagenarian Pope expired (21 August 1241). The future was to justify his indomitable courage and his intuition of victory, but under him Papacy and Curia had taken long strides on the downward path of secular politics and aims. He had set Christendom ablaze with internal strife at the moment of greatest external danger, for at this very time (1238–41) the tide of the heathen Mongol invasion of Europe was reaching its highest mark. Russia was subdued, Poland and Hungary devastated, a German army defeated. It was only the fortuitous death of the Great Khan Ogdai with the civil war that followed that saved Europe from utter calamity.

Gregory IX's death allowed the Emperor to subdue most of the Papal State and to prepare to attack the sea-cities of Genoa and Venice, but his main preoccupation was to secure the election of a yielding Pope. The cardinals, who dispersed after the transitory pontificate of Celestine IV (November 1241), proved hard to compel, and the vacancy was not ended until the election at Anagni (June 1243) of the eminent Genoese jurist, Sinibaldo dei Fieschi, as Innocent IV. Their choice was clear evidence that Frederick was warring not with one headstrong Pope but with the traditional, relentless policy of the Roman Curia, for Innocent IV proved the most formidable of his adversaries. Diplomatic subtlety and audacious firmness and resource were his, and he speedily outmanœuvred the Emperor, still under the illusion that he was master of the game. Frederick hoped at first to carry out his ambition of unifying Italy by paying a tribute

Fig. 147. Taddeo da Suessa leaves the Council of Lyons;
Innocent IV excommunicates Frederick II

for the Papal States as a fief, but the renewed vigour of his enemies, coupled with the distress of famine and pestilence, so shook his resolution that he agreed (March 1244) to a peace which left him the Empire and Sicily under conditions wholly favourable to the Pope. The humiliation was too extreme to make his sincerity credible, and the Pope refused his absolution until the conditions were performed, while Frederick, recovering heart, began to make fresh counter-claims. As the Romans showed signs of turning against him, Innocent departed for Civita Castellana, where he arranged for an interview with the Emperor at Rieti, but instead, disguised as a soldier, he fled to Civitavecchia on the coast. He had in fact determined on a masterly stroke of policy, to retreat across the Alps and thence summon a General Council to rally the Church and Christendom against Frederick. Ships from his native Genoa convoyed him at his call to the Riviera (7 July). Thence he crossed the Mont Cenis Pass to Lyons, nominally within the Empire, but within reach of the aid of King Louis IX of France if he was attacked. He convoked the General Council for June 1245 and excommunicated the Emperor and his chief lieutenants anew.

In consternation Frederick sent suppliant messages and envoys. He declared he would appeal to a future Council and Pope and to all rulers. Meanwhile the Council met and (27 July 1245) declared him deposed as a perjured foe of the Church, guilty of sacrilege and suspected of heresy. The Pope proclaimed a crusade against him in Germany; legates and friars stirred up the war in Italy and rebellion in the Regno. In Germany, where Frederick of Austria had been reconciled to the Emperor (1239) and then had died (1246), leaving his vacant duchy to be occupied by an imperial officer, the Archbishops of Mainz, Cologne, and Trier had joined the papal side. At the Pope's command they and other bishops elected (May 1246) Henry Raspe, Landgrave of Thuringia, anti-king. The new legate, Philip, Bishop-elect of Ferrara, and his agents stopped at nothing.

Excommunication and interdict were the portion of the loyalists, complete control was taken of Church appointments, bribery and dispensations rewarded adherents, civil war was rampant. But most lay princes, headed by Duke Otto of Bavaria, King Conrad's father-in-law, held by the Hohenstaufen, as did the townsmen, now at last favoured by the Emperor. Henry Raspe, who made some progress, died in February 1247 without heirs, when his relative, the Margrave of Meissen, was granted the lapsed fief of Thuringia. His successor (October 1247) as anti-king, William, Count of Holland, was unable to secure more than the lower Rhineland. The main result was that the feeble central government of Germany was moribund.

Frederick's appeals and the natural sympathy of monarchs for secular independence at least obtained him the continued recognition of the kings of France and England. But in the Italian warfare his resources, drawn from the overtaxed Regno, were unequal to his needs. Wherever he came with his army obedience was enforced, but when he departed there was insurrection or conspiracy, and the hard core of the Lombard League remained intact. A combined attack on Milan by himself from the west and by Enzo and Ezzelino from the east had failed, when news came of a dangerous conspiracy of his own officials of the Regno itself (February 1246). His hasty return to Salerno from Tuscany, however, quelled the plot, whose participants were ferociously punished, and the remnant of Moslems in Sicily, who had rebelled, were transported to swell the colony at Lucera. He still hoped to put pressure on the Pope, especially when Henry Raspe died. Peaceful overtures proved fruitless again, and he prepared to advance in arms through Savoy. But he never crossed the Alps. The papalist exiles of Parma seized their native city by a sudden stroke (June 1247), and their Lombard friends streamed in to aid them. By its position on the crossroads Parma was an indispensable link in Frederick's communications. He hastened back to besiege it in force, vowing to sow the rebel city with salt. In his over-confidence he gave his fortified camp the name of Vittoria (Victory), while his vicar in Tuscany, his bastard son Frederick of Antioch, expelled the papalist Guelfs from Florence (January 1248). Then came disaster. During the siege the Emperor fell ill and in convalescence spent his mornings hawking. In his absence on 18 February 1248 the Parmese surprised his troops in Vittoria, slaying many (among them his trusted minister, Taddeo da Suessa), capturing 3000, and seizing his treasure. The blow was severe, and Frederick again resorted to petitions for a peace, begging the intercession of Louis of France, while the Pope's legates made progress not only in Central Italy but in the Regno. Worse still another plot broke out, in which Frederick believed (perhaps wrongly) his confidant Piero della Vigna to be involved (February 1249). The unhappy man was blinded and committed suicide. Frederick meanwhile curbed his

693

enemies in Tuscany and sailed to Naples, where he received news of another heavy blow. On 26 May King Enzo, his general legate in the north, was defeated and captured at La Fossalta by the Bolognese, who held him prisoner till his death (1272). He was the most attractive of his house, a warrior and a poet. Yet, though Modena was lost, a general improvement set in for Frederick. His terrible ally Ezzelino was enlarging his tyranny; ground was gained in Romagna and the March of Ancona; and Marquess

Fig. 148. Tomb of Frederick II, Palermo Cathedral

Oberto Pelavicini, half tyrant, half imperial vicar, recovered Piacenza and even Parma. At this turn of fortune the ailing Emperor was overtaken by death at Fiorentino in Apulia (13 December 1250).

Frederick's death closed both his unhappy attempt to unite Italy, henceforth abandoned to the turmoil of communes and tyrannies, and the Holy Roman Empire as it had been moulded by Otto the Great. In Germany the monarchy never recovered from the troubles of his reign and the interregnum which succeeded him. The Norman kingdom of Sicily, whose government he had perfected almost in a modern spirit, was enfeebled by his wars and soon to be the prey of foreign and degrading conquest. It was the impossible imperial dream of the Hohenstaufen, condemned to the implacable enmity of the Popes and the communes, which wrecked Frederick and his house, not lack of ability. In the width and variety of his insatiably curious intellect he was perhaps the most gifted of medieval rulers. He ranged at will over law, administration, war, diplomacy, philosophy, precocious science (as in his work on hawking), poetry (his court was the nursery of Italian literature), and art. His faults are obvious: the oriental way of life he inherited from his Norman progenitors, his faithlessness, and his abominable cruelty. But in spite of his failure in the ambitions to which he devoted himself, he was the herald of future times. Based on his Byzantine and Norman inheritance, he created 'the state as a work of art'. His championship of the rights of the lay rulers, in his life and manifestos, fostered the revolt of the laity against the political domination of the Papacy. His cultural influence spread over Italy.

(2) THE FALL OF THE HOHENSTAUFEN

The loss of Frederick's commanding personality not only dispirited the imperialists, Ghibellines we may call them from their Tuscan name, it disunited them. He left the Regno to King Conrad IV[1] absent in Germany, and appointed his bastard son Manfred *Balio* (or regent) of both the Regno and North Italy. Manfred was faced with the discontent of barons and towns in the overtaxed Regno and the disaffection of the chief officials, headed by Margrave Berthold of Hohenburg, commander of the German troopers, who not unjustly suspected him of scant loyalty to Conrad. Revolt broke out in the Terra di Lavoro, and the papal legate Capocci recovered the central Italian cities for the Papacy. Florence, under the new regime called the *Primo Popolo*, recalled the Guelf faction. Innocent IV gave way to triumphant hopes. He schemed to annex the Regno and rule it through a lax combination of nobles and communes. His protégé, William of Holland, should oust Conrad from Germany. In May 1251 the Pope arrived in Genoa to rally the papal partisans or, to use the Tuscan term, Guelfs. But, although he made some progress in Piedmont, he found Ezzelino and Pelavicini firmly entrenched in the east and the Guelf cities engrossed in their own interests. When he reached Perugia (November 1251), the strongly organized bureaucracy of the Regno had thwarted further revolt, and his own lack of troops and money inhibited invasion. Meanwhile King Conrad arrived in Lombardy, where he met his partisans, and thence sailed to Apulia (January 1252). He spent a year in subduing the rebels of the Terra di Lavoro, while the Lombard allies increased in power, partly perhaps through the favour of heretics even in Guelf cities. Innocent, too, was not master of Rome itself. Wearied of the turbulent nobility, the Romans in November 1252 elected an eminent Ghibelline as sole senator,

---

[1] See Genealogical Table 16*b* above, p. 557.

the Bolognese Brancaleone degli Andalò, who restored order and took a haughty tone towards the Pope. In Tuscany, the Guelf communes led by Florence were waging victorious war against their Ghibelline rivals, Pisa and Siena, without regard to papal mediation.

Throughout, however, Innocent IV held fast to his policy. He rebuffed Conrad, and since his own means did not suffice, he looked about for a foreign champion. Neither Richard, Earl of Cornwall, nor Louis IX's brother, Charles, Count of Anjou, would accept his terms, but the folly of Henry III of England led him to swallow the bait on behalf of his own younger son, Edmund Crouchback, especially as his nephew Henry, son of the Empress Isabella, opportunely died. An agreement was being made when King Conrad, excommunicated once more by the implacable Pope, died in his camp (21 May 1254) just as he was about to return to Germany for the war there. Unlike his father, he had stood for the old conception of centring the Empire in Germany and treating Italy and the Regno as a treasure-producing dependency. For that conception he had fought with a stout heart.

How much Conrad IV had alienated the Regnicoli by his German outlook and his exactions at once appeared. Distrusting Manfred, he in despair recommended his infant son, Conrad V (Conradin), who was far away in Germany, to the Pope's dubious protection. For *Balio* he nominated Margrave Berthold. There were now three factions in the Regno: Berthold with the army and the chiefs of the bureaucracy, Manfred, who possessed such loyalty as there was, and restive towns and nobles, weary of the war and hankering after the 'liberty' promised by Innocent. In this disunion the elated Pope was master of the game with all his hopes revived. He demanded possession of the Regno along with an adjudication on Conradin's rights when the child came of age. Manfred, who became *Balio* on the more yielding Berthold's resignation, refused at first, but, when Innocent raked together an army on Henry III's credit and began the invasion, he had no sufficient backing to enable him to avoid surrender (September 1254). The Pope seemed at his goal, when his own lack of good faith led to his disappointment. He had ignored the claims of Henry III, he knew that no Staufen could abandon his ambitions, and he was resolved to absorb the Regno in the Papal States. His legate, Cardinal William dei Fieschi, in command of his army began to disregard the reserved rights of Conradin; he himself diminished the provincial vicariate and appanage stipulated for Manfred. The wavering prince in a chance affray killed one of his supplanters and fled to Apulia, preceding the papal army of occupation. There he appealed to the Saracens of Lucera, who joined him. He now disposed of the royal treasure and became the paymaster of the German soldiery, while his cause and Conradin's were united by the Pope's breach of faith. A small victory over Berthold's brother Otto sufficed to send the cardinal and his wretched army in panic rout over the Apennines again. In a few days Manfred was master of Apulia, the barons were declaring for him, and even Peter Ruffo, the vicar of Sicily and Calabria, accepted him as *Balio*.

The news reached Innocent on his deathbed. In view of the revolt he had renewed his negotiations with Henry III. The cardinal's rout was the parting stroke, and he died (7 December 1254) at Naples, murmuring the verse of the Psalm, 'Lord, for his sin thou hast chastened man' (Vulgate, Ps. xxxviii). Innocent IV cannot be said to have introduced the foreigner into Italy, for the Hohenstaufen and their subsidiary tyrants had depended on German and Saracen levies, and it may be claimed that in his alliance with free communes he stood, in spite of their factious tendencies, for a juster and more humane government than that of the ferocious Ezzelino or of Pelavicini. But the mainspring of his policy was the fear of encirclement by a combined Empire and Regno and the desire to dominate Italy as a collection of petty states. He was essentially a priestly politician. He used his spiritual powers constantly and without scruple to raise money, buy friends and injure foes. His dispensations and provisions were a scandal; there would be four papal nominees waiting one after another for the same benefice. Bad appointments were a natural consequence, and, further, legates and cardinals chosen for war and diplomacy were more likely than not to be thoroughly worldly in character, like Octavian Ubaldini, Gregory of Montelongo, or the truculent Philip of Pistoia, the Archbishop-elect of Ravenna. Of the loss of spiritual influence Innocent was unconscious. His equanimity was seldom shaken by disaster or good fortune; in the same calculating spirit he wrecked the Empire, started the Papacy on its decline, and moulded the destinies of Italy.

The Cardinals elected without delay a Pope who was the opposite of his predecessor, Rinaldo Conti as Alexander IV (1254–61). This nephew of Gregory IX was a pious, learned prelate, protector of the Friars Minor, mild save when heresy was in question, easy-tempered and easily led. 'He did not care for the affairs of princes and kingdoms', but would rely on an adviser. In the matter of the Regno Cardinal Octavian became his oracle. Edmund Crouchback was now invested; Henry III was to pay expenses and send an army. Meantime Cardinal Octavian, counselled by Berthold, led a large force to subdue the Saracens of Lucera. But Berthold played false and Manfred blockaded him in Foggia. Early in September 1255 Octavian was starved into a treaty recognizing Conradin as king in return for the cession of the Terra di Lavoro. All the Pope could do was to disown the bargain, while his ally Henry III proved a broken reed.

Two years were spent by Manfred in establishing his rule over the entire Regno while ridding himself of Berthold and Ruffo. Then on an invented report of Conradin's death he had himself crowned King of Sicily (August

1258). Although his ambition was thus gratified, the usurper endangered his cause, for St Louis of France lost sympathy with him, and Conradin's guardian, Duke Lewis of Bavaria, was indignant. As his troops and subjects were now loyal, he might perhaps have eventually kept his throne had he not embarked on his father's policy of dominating North Italy, but the Papacy was irreconcilable and dangerous. Brancaleone had been expelled from Rome (November 1255), and the Guelfs of Tuscany, headed by Florence, the Pope's allies and creditors, were supreme in their province.

Manfred's diplomacy was shrewd enough. He gained a foothold in the March of Ancona, helped to restore Brancaleone, and made the rivals, Venice and Genoa, his friends. In Lombardy and Tuscany his intervention seemed called for. Both Pelavicini and Ezzelino were prototypes of a new form of government, the city tyrant, which was arising. Pelavicini was a warlike noble who ruled a group of cities by alliance with local faction chiefs, supported by his German soldiery; Ezzelino was himself the faction chief of Verona. During the thirteenth century and its wars a fresh turn had been given to city politics in North Italy. Subject to endless divergencies in detail, the middle class of traders in their gilds claimed and were obtaining a separate organization, called generally the *popolo* (people), alongside of the older governing association, the commune, in which the nobles were preponderant. This was seldom done without bloodshed, in which the *popolani* were usually abetted by a minority of nobles at faction strife with others of their order. Unfortunately in Lombardy the *popolo* as a rule proved incapable of securing internal order and governing their city or even of overcoming the main body of the nobles. For one thing the wealthier gilds had neither sufficient support from nor control of the pettier tradesmen and employees beneath them. But a worse complication was the war, in which the cities were protagonists, between Pope and Emperor. The noble factions took sides on this question of foreign policy as Guelfs or Ghibellines. Save their passion for autonomy, what most interested the *popolani* was the rivalry of city with city and the attitude of the nobles towards themselves. Thus a multitude of cross-currents prevented all stability. The strife was embittered by the practice of exiling the defeated noble faction, which was indeed rendered necessary by their irreconcilable feuds if any sort of internal peace was to be kept. Sometimes a well-knit *popolo*, like that of Bologna, could keep both factions in check for a term of years, but more frequently the *popolani* would entrust the government to a noble faction chief, the beginning of tyranny. He would at first hold a principal city office such as *podestà* of the commune or captain of the people (*popolo*). Successive enactments increased his power till at length he would be captain-general for life with absolute power, and then *signore* or lord, i.e. no longer an official, and finally hereditary. Such in gross was the evolution, however varied from city to city.

Ezzelino da Romano, tyrant of Verona, was a variation. He was chief of the Ghibelline faction there and allied with the *popolo*. Frederick II, whose natural daughter he married, provided him with German troopers. But he held no office, and the imperial vicar of the March of Verona was his humble deputy to rule Padua. After years of despotism he fell at last through the streak of insanity in him. Enmity to faction rivals became mad cruelty in him, thirst for blood a perverse hatred of his species, which gave him a reputation for heresy. Thus lashed with scorpions, his *popolani* grew disaffected, especially in the miserable city of Padua. Something may be credited to the kindliness as well as the orthodoxy of Alexander IV in stirring up action against the monster. He proclaimed a crusade under Philip of Ravenna, who led a riff-raff army, fortified by efficient Venetian auxiliaries. In June 1256 he suddenly freed Padua. This was the first intervention of Venice in her hinterland, but it was not followed up by the disunited Lombard Guelfs. On the contrary, Ezzelino, aided by Pelavicini, now Manfred's vicar, seized Brescia and defeated Philip (1258). But he recklessly cheated his ally, who formed a league of all his neighbours, Guelf and Ghibelline, against him. Ezzelino was captured in the battle of Cassano, and committed suicide (1 October 1259). Tyranny was, however, far from receiving a set-back. The Ghibelline Mastino della Scala founded a dynasty at Verona; the Guelf Martino della Torre was first tyrant of Milan; Pelavicini, the ally of both, hoped to establish a real vicariate.

Tyranny was not the only way out of these city broils. After twenty years of internal troubles in Genoa, where the nobles were the chief shipowners and identified with the city's prosperity, the heads of the two greatest Ghibelline families, a Doria and a Spinola, were set up as joint Captains of the people in 1270 and governed constitutionally. The 'Primo Popolo' of Florence, based on the militia companies, was even more successful. The Captain of the people with his two councils enjoyed coordinate authority with the *podestà* of the commune and his councils. Cumbrous as it was the constitution worked well, controlled by the rich merchants and bankers who were on the way to nobility. Their wars with their neighbours prospered, and so did their finances. In 1252, usurping an imperial right, they coined the gold florin, and they kept it undebased, so that it became the standard commercial coin of Europe. Bankers and creditors of the Papacy, whose revenues from England and elsewhere they collected and transmitted in the course of trade, they were aiming at the domination of Tuscany when Manfred intervened.

The way was opened by Siena, the steady foe of Florence. Accepting from him a body of German horse, her league of Tuscan Ghibellines became definitely superior in fighting qualities to the Florentine militia. On 4 September 1260 the Florentines were routed with fearful slaughter at

Montaperto. Submission was made at once, the Guelf nobles and some leading *popolani* went into exile, and Florence might have been razed to the ground had not her most eminent Ghibelline, Farinata degli Uberti, interposed a flat refusal. With the *Primo Popolo* abolished and Tuscany falling under his sway, while Pelavicini was the strongest power in Lombardy, with Moslem Tunis his tributary and the rulers of Epirus and Aragon allied to him by marriage, Manfred seemed to be aiming at the union of Italy like his father. The tragic procession of the Flagellants, recruited and passing from city to city in 1260, showed the despair of the war-torn age, but did not affect his predominance. It was the unyielding Papacy which he could not overcome.

When Alexander IV died (May 1261), the cardinals recurred (August) to a political Pope, Urban IV, son of a shoemaker at Troyes. Urban, a born despot, 'who did what he willed', at once gave the Curia—he created fourteen new cardinals—and its policy a pro-French direction. Vigorous measures and new men revived his cause and alleviated his debts. He insisted on the merchant-bankers of Florence and Siena being Guelfs; he could forbid their overjoyed debtors to pay their debts. Subterfuges, like a concealed partnership with Guelf firms, were of no avail. He was resolved that the new champion to be found for the Papacy should be French, but the righteous Louis IX must first be converted to allow aggression. For this purpose long negotiations were undertaken with Manfred, which ended in the desired breakdown, this time with St Louis's approval and the fresh excommunication of the King of Sicily (March 1263). Meantime Urban was in treaty with Charles of Anjou, once the alternative candidate of Innocent IV, Edmund Crouchback being deservedly cashiered. The haggling over conditions was long, for the Pope feared a too powerful ally and Charles meant to be no catspaw. Charles had been already elected senator of Rome, the Guelfs there having gained the upper hand since Brancaleone's death in 1259, and the bargain was all but concluded when in October 1264 Urban died. He had set on foot the expulsion of the Germans from Italy and the introduction of the French.

Another Frenchman, Gui Foulquoi, ex-chancellor of Louis IX, succeeded to the Papacy as Clement IV (1265–8). He ratified the treaty with Charles of Anjou which formulated papal policy. The Regno and the Empire were to remain separated, and Charles was to hold no dominion in the Papal States, Lombardy, or Tuscany, except a three years' tenure of the Roman senatorship unless he gained the Regno earlier. On conquest he was to pay 50,000 marks down and 8000 gold ounces yearly, besides furnishing 300 knights if called upon. The clergy were to be tax-free and amenable only to ecclesiastical tribunals. In desperate need of money Pope and count borrowed and taxed. The French clergy gave a tenth of their possessions for the 'crusade'. The Tuscan bankers provided loans with the prospect of the future exploitation of the Regno. Charles equipped a fleet in Provence, and French crusaders flocked to his standard.

Charles's master motive was a devouring ambition. Unweariedly active, he cared for no diversion, and with this dour energy went a love of despotic rule. Heresy vanished before his zeal for orthodoxy. Without being in any way a monster, he was a grim character, and the narrow range of his sympathies, confined to Frenchmen who were noble, made him a harsh governor. In 1246 he acquired the county of Provence in Burgundy (the Arelate) by his marriage to the youngest daughter of Raymond-Berengar IV, its last native count. There in spite of revolts he became absolute master, and by 1264 he had obtained a foothold in Italy by conquering the little communes in southern Piedmont, which had been subjects of Asti. Now as the defender of Holy Church he had no doubt of the righteousness of his cause. He was convinced that his own exaltation was the chief need of Christendom. His adversary was of softer metal. For all his courage and ability Manfred was a child of the harem. Indolent and undecided, the 'Sultan of Lucera' spent his days in his delicious country palaces in the Apennines, a poet and a patron, unable to brace himself up to the pleasureless activity necessary for his ambitions and his safety. It was of first importance to expel Charles's vicar from Rome, his base of operations, but two ineffective attacks, not pressed home, left the situation unchanged. Very different were the actions of the Pope and the vicar, who, penniless and surrounded, held out dauntlessly in Perugia and Rome.

The plan of Charles was bold and simple, to sail himself to Rome, while his army, unable to cross the sea which Manfred commanded, made a circuit through Lombardy and Romagna to join him. It was made feasible by the accession of a new Della Torre to the tyranny of Milan and the formation and enlargement of a new Guelf league to the detriment of Pelavicini, who was losing his cities. The crusaders, a formidable array of 5000 horse and 25,000 foot, reached Rome, where Charles himself had withstood Manfred's feeble attacks for eight months, in January 1266. Manfred showed too late the energy of despair. He gathered his German troopers and Saracens and the feudal levy of his kingdom, but treason was at work among the latter, and the glowing prophecies of the Pope were taking effect. When Charles advanced, he retreated to his inner line of defence in the Apennine pass to Apulia. There at Benevento on 26 February 1266 his feudal levy fled and his fighting men were overwhelmed by the French. He charged and fell in the *mêlée*. With him the glory of the Regno departed. With all his faults he had been a merciful, indulgent prince, the fosterer of its culture and prosperity. Now the Regnicoli fell under a greedy, relentless king and expiated their own fickle treason. All Italy was transformed. The Guelfs took the lead in Tuscany, and the Ghibellines went into exile, mostly in the mountains. In Lombardy Pelavicini retired

701

to his estates, while the Guelfs came into power in every city save tyrant-ruled Verona and republican Pavia.

The tragedy of the Hohenstaufen was, however, not over. Charles's government of the Regno speedily became odious. He ruled through oppressive foreigners; only the tax-gatherers were natives. The Tuscans absorbed the country's trade. The promised parliaments were not held. The heavy *collecta* was still levied, not only to pay Charles's debts but to provide for his vast scheme of conquest in the Balkans and the East, where the schismatic Greek, Michael Palaeologus, had recovered Constantinople (1261). 'What do you wish me to rejoice at?' he said after Benevento, 'To a valiant man the whole world would not suffice.' The burdens of Hohenstaufen rule remained without its merits. Clement IV saw the evils and angrily reproached his vassal king. He forced Charles to vacate the Roman senatorship, but this allowed the election of a wealthy adventurer, the Infant Don Henry of Castile, who joined the Ghibellines. In Tuscany the Ghibellines were still active, and the Pope in alarm felt obliged to call in Charles as *Paciarius* (pacifier) for three years (1267), a grant which enabled him to usurp the vicariate of the Empire there, while Florence elected him her *signore*, a position giving him direction of her executive. The task of the 'pacifier', which he at once undertook, was to war down the Ghibelline cities and exiles of Tuscany.

The motive for these operations was the imminent invasion of Conradin. The last heir of the Hohenstaufen was in 1267 a boy of fifteen, precocious, bold, and ambitious; he was the only hope of the oppressed Regnicoli and the Ghibellines. A plan was devised by which he should invade the Regno through Tuscany while an exile, Conrad Capece, attacked Sicily from Tunis. Capece raised a formidable revolt in the island in August 1267, and Conradin in October entered Verona with 3000 German troopers. In February 1268 the Saracens of Lucera took up arms. The Pope, who was Charles's paymaster, insisted on his return from Tuscany to combat these infidels. His march to Apulia allowed Conradin to slip across the Apennines over an unguarded western pass. In July he reached Rome, now Ghibelline, and in August crossed the frontier of the Regno, avoiding the hostile Terra di Lavoro to the south and aiming at Lucera. But Charles was ready for him on the selected route. He left two-thirds of the Regno to rebel behind him and the siege of Lucera unfinished. The two armies, Conradin's now of 7000 horse, Charles's much inferior, met in the valley by Albe, where Charles's generalship won a complete victory, later named from the neighbouring town of Tagliacozzo (23 August). He wrote to the Pope 'to arise and eat of his son's venison'. It was indeed a feast of vengeance. Executions, mutilations, burning alive were the order of the day. Don Henry of Castile was imprisoned for many years; Conradin was soon taken, tried, and beheaded at Naples with his boy-friend, Frederick of Austria

(29 October 1268), although European opinion was shocked by the execution of a royal rival in cold blood. The extinction of the Hohenstaufen, however, was a safeguard for Charles and the Pope, for danger from the Empire and Germany was for long years brought to an end.

Charles could now gather in the spoils. The Pope, to whom he had given victory, created him senator of Rome for ten years and 'imperial vicar' of Tuscany. The rebellion on the mainland of the Regno collapsed, and Lucera surrendered (August 1269). Lastly, Capece was captured and executed in Sicily (July 1270). After the first vengeance only ringleaders and obstinate rebels were put to death, but wholesale confiscations replaced the native baronage by immigrant Frenchmen. The capital was moved from Palermo to Naples, which had long been hostile to the Hohenstaufen. Meanwhile Charles' hands were freed by the death of Clement IV (November 1268). He knew that the Guelf cardinals by no means desired a new lay and French master, and it became his object to exploit their political, national, and personal divisions so as to prevent the election of a Pope, who would probably curb his predominance in Italy and, in the interests of a crusade to the Holy Land, attempt to hinder his ambition to conquer the Byzantine Empire. During the vacancy he was extorting taxes from the prostrate Regno and increasing his power in the north, where he was master of the Tuscan cities. His progress might have been even greater had it not been for his brother St Louis' determination to lead a second Crusade.

(3) PHILIP AUGUSTUS AND THE CREATION OF A STRONG MONARCHY IN FRANCE

While the Holy Roman Empire was speeding to its decline, the kingdom of France was rising to be first in power among European states. This was mainly the work of Philip II (1180–1223), the Conqueror as he was sometimes called, whose more lasting sobriquet of Augustus was due to the medieval mistranslation of the word as 'increaser' (*augere*) of his kingdom. Although his predecessors had left him master of the royal domain round Paris and Orleans with all the prestige and formal rights of king and feudal suzerain and the Carolingian tradition to back him—he was the Carolingian *par excellence*, if he shared a descent from Charlemagne with many contemporaries—the use of 'France' in common parlance to denote only the lands, roughly speaking, in the north and east, and excluding the vast Angevin inheritance and the south, indicates the limitations of his actual power at the beginning of his reign. It was Philip Augustus, who by steady insistence on his feudal rights and the most dexterous use of every political opportunity enormously enlarged the directly ruled domain and thereby his material resources, and converted his formal suzerainty over the great fiefs into a genuine and deepening control. That done, the supremacy of

703

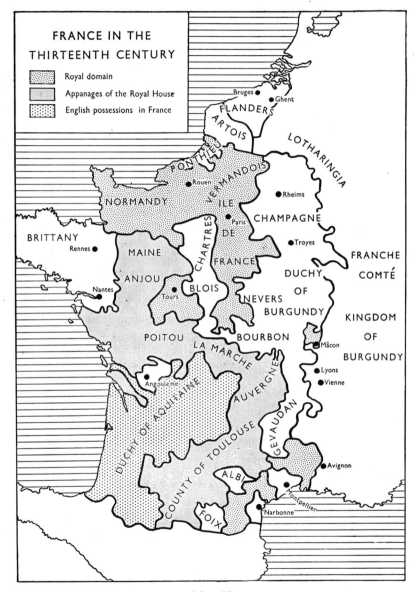

Map 17

the Crown, in spite of the continuing medley of local law and custom and variegated degrees of feudal autonomy, was assured.

No one has called Philip 'the Great'. He was an energetic, level-headed, practical Frenchman, conventionally pious, a stern and popular governor, far sighted and cautious for all the fits of passion which sometimes interfered with policy. When he wished he had a singular power of winning over men. The generosity of the regnant chivalry was wholly absent in him; he shunned danger and extravagance and took every advantage which occasion offered. The occasions were many and fruitful for this alert master of political intrigue.

His first marriage, when still only fourteen, proved his early independence and his keen eye for territorial gains. Against the wish of his maternal uncles of that house of Champagne and Blois whose possessions almost encircled the domain, he married Isabella, daughter of Count Baldwin of Hainault and niece of Philip of Alsace, Count of Flanders.[1] Her dowry, in prospect only, was to be the southern part of Flanders, called Artois. He soon fell out with his namesake and in five years of shifting hostilities and diplomacy out-played him. The death in 1182 of the childless Countess of Flanders, also an Isabella, added to the tangle, for she was Countess of Vermandois in her own right, and her sister Eleanor, the widower, and Philip Augustus himself on a distant relationship claimed her inheritance. At Boves in 1185, by a display of overwhelming force, Philip Augustus brought Philip of Alsace to terms, by which he added Amiens and its neighbourhood to the domain; Eleanor's share became his on her death (1213). By this treaty the royal domain reached the Channel, and, what was more remarkable, Flanders and imperial Hainault (united in 1191 under Baldwin V) and the whole house of Champagne were thenceforth firm allies of the king.

Even thus strengthened, however, Philip Augustus faced a far more formidable rival power in the house of Anjou. King Henry II of England, while wishing to keep and round off his continental fiefs, was far too feudally minded to aim at injuring his suzerain elsewhere. He felt unduly secure, too, in his own strength, and was deeply aware of the impossibility of keeping his heterogeneous fiefs permanently under one ruler, as his schemes of dividing them among his sons show. Their claims and the divergent characters of the provinces forbade it. Normandy and Anjou were strictly ruled monarchies; Brittany was intensely particularistic and Celtic; Aquitaine was a hot-bed of feudal disorder and privilege, filled with the explosive recklessness of the Midi. Henry II contemplated a family group like that of the house of Champagne. What ruined his plans was the heedless, grasping, treacherous ambitions of his quarrelsome sons. During the twenty years after the treaty of Boves, Philip Augustus seized every chance of fanning and exploiting their reckless discord.

[1] See Genealogical Table 13 above, p. 462.

The first chance came in 1183 when the three brothers, young King Henry, Duke Richard of Aquitaine, and Duke Geoffrey of Brittany, fell to war. Richard, aided by his father, showed his warlike genius at the head of the bands of routiers, professional mercenaries outside the pale of society and the Church, men who spared nothing in their atrocities. The sudden death of young Henry in June 1183 dissolved the rebel league, but the havoc and misery in Aquitaine did not cease so easily and produced a kind of peasant revolt, that of the *capuciati* (named from their white hoods), which lasted some two years. Richard, the Lion-heart (Cœur-de-lion), was now the heir of England, but he was resolved not to give up Aquitaine, which Henry II wished to be the portion of his youngest and favourite son John. In spite of reconciliations the cleft between father and son was never really closed. In 1187 Philip felt that the time was ripe for strong measures on plausible grounds. Henry II had retained the Norman Vexin on his eldest son's death without issue, and in return it was to be the dowry of Philip's sister Alice, whom Richard promised to marry. This promise was not performed. Then Geoffrey of Brittany died (1186), and Philip and Henry disputed for the wardship of his young son Duke Arthur. There were counter-claims, too, on the frontiers of Aquitaine, in which Raymond V of Toulouse was also involved. A first attack of Philip on contested lands in Berry ended in a truce, but, although the rivals took the cross for the Third Crusade, a fierce renewal of the war between Richard and Raymond led Philip to intervene (1188). Henry II and Richard joined forces until Philip, by playing on Richard's unceasing suspicions of being disinherited, effectually divided them. In a fateful meeting of the three at Bonmoulins in November 1188 the Duke of Aquitaine suddenly did homage to the King of France for all the Angevin fiefs and thenceforward was his intimate and his father's bitter enemy. Warlike genius was now on Philip's side against Henry, old and ill. A joint invasion of Maine drove him to surrender on all points at Colombières, and he died two days later at Chinon (6 July 1189), learning in his last moments that his favourite John had joined the league against him.

Wisely Philip did not drive a hard bargain with his partner. Richard was mulcted of no more than a little of Berry and the suzerainty of Auvergne, and he kept Quercy conquered from Toulouse. But the Angevin inheritance had begun to shrink, and the French royal domain to expand again. On the Crusade, as might be expected, the two temporary friends became mortal foes. Philip was outshone by his royal vassal, and was obliged to allow him to marry Berengaria of Navarre instead of Alice, while retaining the Norman Vexin. He returned in 1191, ailing and revengeful, to gather in the rest of Vermandois, allotted in 1185 to the dead Philip of Flanders. His opportunity came at the news of Richard's imprisonment by the Emperor Henry VI (1192). He seized the Norman Vexin, and allied with the ever-treacherous John of Anjou for the conquest of Normandy, while he tried to bribe the Emperor to hold on to his prisoner. But Richard was set free (1194), and the scene changed. He possessed the loyalty of the tried officials and the mass of his diverse subjects. He was himself a brilliant soldier. In a few weeks he was recovering lost towns and castles and driving Philip in flight at Fréteval, where the spoil included the French king's treasure and the records of his reign, among them the incriminating charters of John's partisans. There followed a chequer of brief truces and active war. If Philip nibbled off the south-eastern fringe of Normandy, Richard gained the alliance of Raymond VI of Toulouse by giving him his widowed sister, Queen Joan of Sicily, with the Agenais as her dowry (1196). The Counts of Flanders and Boulogne veered between the two kings. Richard's main preoccupation, however, was to fortify the Norman frontier with the key-point of his new castle of Château-Gaillard at Andeli on the Seine, built with all the engineering skill he had learnt in the crusading fortresses (1197–8). The omens of renewed war were in his favour when during a truce he was killed (6 April 1199) besieging a petty vassal's castle in Aquitaine in search of a non-existent treasure.

The loss of Richard's personality spelt ruin to the Angevin cause. His marriage was childless. For a time his dominions fell asunder, England and Normandy, with Aquitaine under his mother Queen Eleanor, were for his remaining brother John; Anjou, Touraine, and Maine sided with his boy-nephew Arthur of Brittany. But the worst Angevin stumbling-block was the character of John, Lackland as he was called from his lack of a portion in his early days. Able enough, almost a brilliant administrator, a dexterous weaver of combinations, he was false, blindly acquisitive, and cruel. There was no trusting him even in his own cause, and his energy alternated with a singular lethargy, which has made his sanity suspect. The personal dislike which clung to him wherever he went upset his adroitest plans and was a strain on the most loyal servants of his house. Loyalty and gratitude meant nothing to him. No sceptic, he was destitute of reverence for things sacred or secular. In short, he was a thoroughly bad, if gifted, man.

Philip could now play a waiting game. By the treaty of Le Goulet (1200) he retained his frontier gains and recognized John's heirship, while Arthur of Brittany was consigned to his own care. Within two years the decay of the cohesion of the Angevin lands, never great, had proceeded far enough for a new attack by law and by war. John set the disruption moving by an act violating the feudal bond. A great vassal of Aquitaine, Hugh IX of Lusignan, Count of La Marche, had been betrothed to the daughter and heiress Isabella of the neighbouring Count of Angoulême. John had freed himself from his first wife, and the charms of Isabella or rather of her valuable county led him suddenly (August 1200) to marry her himself, thus

707 48-2

breaking at least in legal form the suzerain's duty he owed to his vassal. The Lusignans' defiance—they had other grievances—was followed by the seizure of their lands by John and their appeal to the supreme suzerain, the King of France. John was summoned to answer their charges at Philip's court. When he naturally refused to appear, he was condemned in contumacy to forfeit all his fiefs, and Philip, well prepared, entered on the war to exact the forfeiture.

At the outset Philip's scheme was to annex Normandy and its Channel coastline, while investing Arthur with the rest of the Angevin fiefs. This would give France the richest and best organized part of John's continental lands and snap the link between them and England. But Arthur and the Lusignans were surprised and captured at Mirebeau in Touraine by John, and the report soon spread that Arthur was murdered by his uncle at Rouen in April 1203. This shameful crime was John's undoing. The Bretons rose against the murderer. Save the garrisoned castles, Anjou, Touraine and Maine accepted Philip as their immediate lord, while he had made substantial progress in disaffected Normandy. Although he had poured treasure and war material into the duchy, John lost his nerve and at the end of the year withdrew to England, leaving Normandy a willing conquest to Philip, who refused all papal mediation in this secular, feudal dispute. Château Gaillard was taken in March 1204 and Rouen surrendered on 24 June. When Chinon in Touraine fell (1205), only the Channel Islands remained to John of his possessions north of the Loire, which were united to the royal domain of France. Brittany was ruled by the second husband of its duchess and heiress Constance, mother of the dead Arthur.

Normandy and the central counties changed their allegiance with astonishing facility in spite of the discontents aroused by the fact that those barons who adhered to Philip lost their English estates, while those who, having larger lands in England, opted for John, lost their Norman fiefs. Normandy had in fact for years been a bureaucratic state which worked as well under one master as another. Provincial patriotism did not rally round the Angevins, least of all under their latest representative. The abolition of the war-torn frontier between Paris and the sea was soon seen as an economic advantage to townsman and peasant, even to the men of Rouen, who had profited most by the English connexion and its trade. Philip, too, was most wise in his procedure. Old rights and institutions, such as the Norman Exchequer, were sedulously preserved: the new French *baillis* took over the functions of the Norman officials. Little was changed save the size of the ex-ducal demesne-lands, which were greatly enlarged by the confiscation of the fiefs of John's Anglo-Norman partisans. The annexations settled down under the French king, whose preponderance in France was clear when the royal domain, directly ruled by him, and the demesne-lands of the Crown were more than doubled.

Aquitaine, however, was a different matter. Its turbulent barons might resist their duke and play off his suzerain against him, but they had no wish to exchange him for a stricter immediate lord, who belonged to the alien France of the north. In the critical year 1204 the Gascon lords accepted John's brother-in-law Alfonso VIII of Castile as their ruler. This revolt, however, was quickly put down in 1206, when John, once more energetic, sailed to the duchy, where, like Richard, he seems to have felt at home. He then turned north to recover the west of the frontier county of Poitou. But neither side felt equal to battle, and Philip had already abandoned (1205) the hazardous project of invading England, after which with true medieval insatiability he always hankered. So on 13 October 1206 a two years' truce was made at Thouars.

Thenceforward events were gradually shaping the formation of two hostile coalitions in what became a European conflict, in which the hostile kings lavished their diplomacy and their treasure. John's natural ally was the Emperor Otto IV, and when Otto became the Pope's enemy, Philip, whose interest it was to keep the Empire weak, promoted the bid of Frederick II of Hohenstaufen for the German throne. Both sides strove to gain the alliance of the Netherlandish princes, and in this John and Otto IV were the more successful. Renaud de Dammartin, Count of Boulogne, was indeed quickly dispossessed by his overlord, but Ferrand, the Portuguese Count of Flanders by marriage, was hostile to France, since Louis, Philip's elder son, had seized on all Artois as heir to his dead mother's dowry. Meanwhile, the long obduracy of John over the papal interdict (1209) led Innocent III to promote with characteristic policy the invasion of England by Philip as a holy war. Philip mustered a great fleet and army at Gravelines in Flanders (1213), and was proceeding with the conquest of the rebel count, when, on John's sudden submission to him, the Pope as suddenly forbade the invasion of England. Within a few days an English fleet under the Earl of Salisbury, John's bastard brother, destroyed the French armament in the Zwyn, the estuary leading to Bruges, and rescued Flanders thereby. John and Otto could execute an elaborate offensive. While John went to Aquitaine to attack the line of the river Loire, Otto with Ferrand, Renaud, Salisbury, and the princes of Saxony and the Rhineland assembled to meet Philip and his main forces in Flanders. The decisive victory of Bouvines (27 July 1214), won by the French knights arranged by Guérin, Bishop of Senlis, was one of the decisive battles of the world, and placed the French monarchy, more and more united, as a more efficient power than dissolving Germany. The future of the new France was secure. King John's own campaign in the south had been a less spectacular but as complete a failure. Although he gained over the Lusignans and invaded Anjou, he dared not join issue with the forces under the French heir-apparent Louis. After Bouvines a succession of truces under papal

709

mediation on the basis of *uti possidetis* suspended hostilities over Aquitaine until 1224. With his accustomed prudence Philip did not attempt to conquer that anarchic land of particularism. He was getting old and even his policy with regard to the Albigensian Crusade was dilatory. When John provoked civil war in England, he was no longer zealous for an invasion which had once tempted him. His son Louis was left to accept the barons' offer of the English throne and cross the Channel at his own risk. Until his death at Mantes (14 July 1223) Philip was preoccupied with the government of his enlarged domains.

Louis VIII was 'pious, determined, and shrewd', quite capable of continuing the work of expansion and royal supremacy. If his English adventure ended in failure (1217) and amends to the Papacy, those amends brought about his Albigensian Crusade and the subjection of Languedoc, which carried the royal domain to the Mediterranean. He rounded off his father's work by the conquest of Poitou and confined the French dominions of the minor Henry III to Bordeaux and the coastlands of Gascony (1224). His own will converted the custom of allotting appanages of younger sons, hitherto small, for the domain itself had been small, into a method of softening the transition from all but independent fiefs into half-royal lands. Artois, Anjou and Poitou were the portions of his younger sons.[1]

Philip Augustus had won his annexations and made himself effective King of France by the consistent exploitation of his rights as suzerain under the now well-developed feudal law. His task had been made easier by the errors of his Angevin adversaries, and also by the fact that some of the formidable great fiefs, like Champagne and Flanders, were crippled for years by being in the hands of regents. He was able to insist, too, on innovations, e.g. that the sharers in a divided inheritance should each hold directly from the Crown. Thus the Count of Blois was the vassal not of his kinsman the Count of Champagne but of Philip. The *Curia Regis* became a valid engine for the assertion of royal rights over the greatest, and they, now becoming distinguished as the 'peers of France', sat in it for the trial of their equals. But the members of the royal household (*familia*) formed the efficient part of the Curia for administration and justice. These clerks and knights of the king were a capable and growing bureaucracy. They furnished him with advisers and instruments. After the disaster of Fréteval, their records and archives, of which but few survive, were stored at Paris, which became a real capital. Elaborate record-keeping, initiated by the Papacy and the Normans, was a main implement in the growth of monarchic control, and for efficient finance. In the administration of the domain the system of *baillis*, nominated from Paris, resembling the English sheriffs, was already in being in 1190. The royal authority was thus stringently exercised from the centre. The introduction of parage by agreement, i.e.

[1] See Genealogical Table 13 above, p. 462.

710

joint-control by the Crown, especially in minor ecclesiastical fiefs, was a potent means of extending in practice the royal domain.

Philip was a wealthy and well-armed king. Even the original domain was not only fertile but rich from trade through its happy geographical situation at the centre and meeting-place of the main routes. The royal income was some £100,000, and was trebled later. The king's steady encouragement of communes, townsmen, and merchants was a political as well as a financial asset. In war and for garrisons he could call up some 2000 heavy armed knights, besides 'sergeants', but still more efficient were the professional mercenaries of the day, paid largely by the commutation-money levied in lieu of service from abbeys and towns. The fortification of towns and castles was Philip's especial care. In short, what with bureaucrats, soldiers, wealth, and territory, backed by a growing loyalty, Philip at the close of his reign had erected a monarchy supreme over its vassals and potent in Europe.

(4) THE REIGN OF ST LOUIS

Strange to say, the heir to this political being and to the practical, grasping Louis VIII was a secular saint, who formed his life on moral and religious principles, and whose aim was the salvation of souls. He is one of the best known kings of France, for he was happy in his biographer, his friend Joinville, not to mention plentiful other evidence. He was fortunate in his bringing up by his remarkable mother, Queen Blanche, the daughter of King Alfonso VIII, the Noble, of Castile, and grand-daughter of Henry II of England. She was regent during his minority (1226-34), and always his counsellor, and bred him austerely and piously. Though an ascetic, he was no sanctimonious devotee, but a strict ruler who lived up to the ideal of knighthood. Never was king more dearly and deservedly loved. His simple manners, his kingly majesty, his self-control in spite of ill health, his perfect good faith, his aversion to lying and hypocrisy, and his fervid piety roused the affectionate veneration of his subjects, for whose temporal and eternal weal he was so solicitous. He had no doubt of the authority he enforced. He was not only suzerain of France with feudal rights and duties; he was by his sacring the Lord's Anointed, charged to give justice and peace to his kingdom and to defend the Church and the true religion. If this conviction led him to be a relentless persecutor of heresy and a fanatical crusader, it added a mystic halo to the crown of France. He was really 'the most Christian king'.

Philip Augustus, first of his line, had been secure enough to dispense with the precaution of crowning his eldest son in his own life-time, a custom which was not renewed, so strong had hereditary right become. But a minority allowed every opportunity for a feudal reaction on the part of the great vassals chafing at their recent fetters. They declared against the regency of a Spanish woman and nicknamed her the she-wolf, 'Dame Hersent', from the satiric animal-fable, the *Roman de Renard*. Fortunately, the members of their coalition were of poor metal: Philip Hurepel, the king's uncle, Count of Boulogne, the unstable poet Theobald IV of Champagne, the restless Lusignans, the half-ruined Raymond VII of Toulouse, the inefficient Henry III of England. The most dangerous was Peter Mauclerc of Dreux, regent of Brittany in right of his wife and son. The struggle against the Crown was confused and useless, full of puerile intrigues and betrayals. The townsmen were firm for the queen-regent. Once the people of Paris came armed to rescue their young king from the barons' clutches (1227). But with the Church's aid Raymond VII was forced to peace (1229). Henry III's expedition was futile (1230), Peter Mauclerc after several revolts and submissions surrendered Brittany to his son (1237), and Theobald IV, rebel and ally by turns, left in humiliation for his new kingdom of Navarre (1236).

Louis IX, who attained his majority in 1234, had only one more serious outbreak to quell, partly due to the fierce persecution of the Inquisition he encouraged in Languedoc and the oppressive government of the royal domain there by his seneschals (the equivalent of the northern *baillis*), partly to the still contested lands of Aquitaine. The revolt of the wretched inhabitants of the seneschalship of Carcassonne, led by Raymond Trencavel, dispossessed heir of Béziers, was harshly crushed (1240), but Raymond VII, lured on by events in the west, then rose. In fulfilment of his father's will Louis IX conferred on his brother Robert the county of Artois, on Alphonse those of Poitou and Auvergne (1241), on Charles Anjou and Maine (1246). The appanage of Alphonse enraged the anarchic Poitevin nobles, headed by Hugh X of Lusignan, who was egged on by his wife Isabella, the widow of John of England. They called in their ancient suzerain, Henry III. He came with insufficient forces in 1242 to receive a contemptible rout near Saintes. There was nothing for Hugh and Isabella to do but make humble submission to Louis and Alphonse. Raymond VII was in like case. He bound himself to persecute the Catharan remnant, which he did till his death in 1249, when Alphonse of Poitiers, the husband of his daughter, succeeded him. As for Henry III, the efforts of St Louis for a reasonable settlement, which should establish a legal situation, bore fruit at last in 1258, when the pressure of the English barons induced Henry III to agree to the Peace of Paris (ratified 4 December 1259). By it Henry became the vassal of the King of France for the reduced duchy of Aquitaine and Gascony, and renounced his claims to Normandy, Maine, Anjou, and Poitou. Louis' counter-concessions were mostly in expectation, the retrocession of south Saintonge and of the Agenais when the childless Alphonse should die, and otherwise were illusory, for the French lawyers skilfully blocked in detail the unprecise cessions which were made in

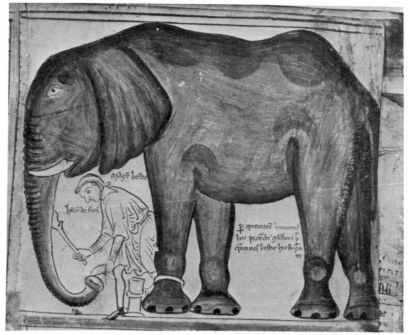

*Fig. 149. Elephant presented to Henry III of England
by Louis IX of France, 1255*

Périgord, Limousin and Quercy. In Louis's eyes the great gain was that his sovereignty was once more acknowledged, and indeed feudal law gave every opportunity for his successors to intervene in Aquitaine, but their piecemeal encroachments were to be a chief cause of the Hundred Years' War. Curiously enough, almost at the same time (11 May 1258) he concluded the contrasting Treaty of Corbeil with the King of Aragon, James I. Only the city of Montpellier was retained as a French fief by James, but Louis surrendered his nominal suzerainty of north Catalonia and Roussillon. Louis perhaps felt, rather than asserted, the naturalness of the frontier of the Pyrenees. Unnoticed by everyone, the linguistic territory of Languedoc was thus permanently divided into French and Catalan.

In the fatal contest between Frederick II and the Papacy St Louis was steadfastly neutral. He did not seek to fish in troubled waters, and, devout though he was, declined to recognize the papal sentence deposing a monarch like himself. If he insisted on the release of captured French prelates in 1241, and was prepared to defend Innocent IV from capture at Lyons, he permitted Frederick's propaganda in France, and it needed Manfred's usurpation to render him an active partisan of the invasion of his brother

713

Charles of Anjou. His known equity led to his selection as an arbitrator by his neighbours. His 'Mise of Amiens' (1264), based on his conviction of the inalienable rights of kings, was indeed a failure, but his 'Dit of Péronne' (1256), on the thorny question of the succession to Flanders and Hainault, was accepted by the disputants, and the like occurred in other cases. He was no self-seeking mediator, but the promoter of peace among Christians.

Very different was St Louis's attitude to the infidel. We have seen that he was ruthless in the suppression of heresy. The Crusade to the Holy Land was his chief aim in external affairs. The narrative of his first expedition (1248–54) must be left to the section on the Levant. Here, however, it should be said that the preparations were made with the greatest care—even the town and port of Aigues Mortes being constructed for the purpose—and at enormous cost, borne largely by the French Church and the towns. A total incapacity to learn from past experience marked the conduct of the campaign in Egypt, and the ransom of the Christian captives was a further drain on Louis' finances. He had shown heroic fortitude in his captivity, but his crusading obsession made him linger for years in Syria after his release, although the death of Queen Blanche, who acted as regent in France (November 1252), made his return an urgent matter. The fact was that his judgement was clouded when the Holy War was in question. Once back in France, his desire was to lead a second Crusade. The final victory of his brother Charles of Anjou made it possible, and France was again burdened for the armament. Almost at the last moment the Crusade was diverted (July 1270) to Tunis, for it might be a base whence to attack Egypt and St Louis cherished a chimerical hope of converting its emir, Mustansir. Charles of Anjou, who entertained vast schemes of his own, probably had a hand in the sudden change. But for St Louis it was only a change in the place of his death. He was unfit through weakness to travel when he started. The pestilence and dysentery, which decimated his army in Tunisia, ended his life on 25 August 1270. Miracles attended his relics almost at once, and in 1297 he was canonized. Few saints have earned the honour better.

Fig. 150. Aigues-Mortes, laid out by Louis IX, 1240

St Louis's chosen counsellors were mostly men from the old domain. Churchmen, like Eudes Rigaud, Archbishop of Rouen, Gui Foulquoi (the future Pope Clement IV), and Robert de Sorbon, the founder of the famous College of the Sorbonne in Paris University, played the leading part, but there were also petty nobles. We do not yet find in the *Curia Regis* those lawyers from the Midi, devoid of scruples, who exercised such a sinister influence under Philip the Fair. Louis IX's policy was conservative, to maintain existing rights and exact acknowledged duties. None the less, his local officials, the *baillis* in the north and seneschals in the south, possessed unlimited powers far from the king's eye. They were aggressive in extending the royal power and demesne, and oppression was the more rife the farther they were from Paris. The Curia was steadily growing more organized and specialized. Its legal functions were becoming a department, to which the once general name for an assembly, the Parlement, was slowly tending to be restricted. The 'Parlement's' seat was fixed at Paris, while its procedure and system of recording cases were strongly influenced by imitation of Normandy, as may be seen from the registers called *Olim*. Although, when magnates were concerned, some of the 'peers of France' and bishops for clerical trials sat in it, some twenty to thirty expert professional lawyers came to form its permanent staff. Yet they were still members of the undivided *Curia Regis*, and hence the Parlement of Paris in its future complete development would never renounce its political claims.

The progress of the financial department of the Curia, which in the early fourteenth century was named the *Chambre des Comptes*, is still more obscure owing to the lack of surviving documents. But sessions of experts of the Curia to receive the *baillis'* accounts were older than St Louis' reign and under him their methods were improved by imitation of the Norman Exchequer. The king's income remained on the old lines, receipts from the demesne, fines, commutations for service in the host, 'donations' from the towns, which proved ruinous to their finances, heavy tallages on the Italian bankers and the Jews from time to time, and for the Crusades large levies from the clergy authorized by the Popes. These sufficed for a policy which was pacific save for the Holy War, and few novelties were attempted. The supposed reform of the taxes of the city of Paris merely meant that the provost could no longer afford to farm them but became an agent only. His subordinates still farmed their offices, and in the rest of the royal demesne the farming-out system and its abuses remained in use, not superseded by direct collection. In finance, however, the king's uprightness permitted one valuable gain. The royal currency inspired such confidence that he could ordain that it should be accepted throughout the kingdom. That from established seignorial mints was only valid in the fief concerned. Fresh mints were not allowed. It was reserved for Philip the Fair to make coinage the plaything of politics and cause men to regret the good and honest coins of King Louis.

If the fervent piety of St Louis induced him to become a cruel persecutor, it also led him to practise and spread Christian conduct among his court and subjects. He was an encourager of sermons and builder of abbeys. The Sainte Chapelle at Paris enshrined the relics of the Passion in the most beautiful Gothic architecture. His charity to the poor and sick was a part of his religious duties. So was his action as a judge. He would try cases himself. He superintended trials by his counsellors in the open air in his garden, altering their sentences, if he thought right, and his justice was equal to all—no rank received special favour from him. He was horrified by the ancient customs of vengeance, private war, and the judicial duel. The last he forbade in trials before the royal judges. He decreed a truce of forty days for an arrangement in cases of blood-feud. Finally, in 1258 he prohibited private war altogether and the carrying of arms, a reform not easily enforced. The misdeeds of his officials were as hard to curb; indeed in their aggressions and misgovernment they profited by the halo which surrounded their master. St Louis knew that the monarchy and its agents had much to answer for, and before starting on his first Crusade he founded the system (1247) of sending round commissions of *enquêteurs*, mostly Franciscan friars, to receive evidence of abuses. After 1254 they were despatched annually. The scheme, lamentably perverted later, was during his life a real and popular remedy for grievances new and old, and the records that survive throw light on the time and his government.

The traditional wary and reverent policy of the kingship towards the Church was not modified by St Louis, save in that he was most scrupulous in his appointments to benefices. He aimed at suppressing abuses and safeguarding the rights of the monarchy, not hesitating to rebuke his prelates' failings or to protest (1247) against the Pope's bestowal of provisions on foreigners. With regard to the barons, great and small, St Louis rarely exceeded the ambit of feudal law, but he frequently punished misuse of power, and monarchical control steadily grew, while the multiplication of the privileged *bourgeois du roi* removed many from seigneurial jurisdiction. The kings's policy was to protect the 'good towns and communes'. They were now under oligarchic rule, which mismanaged their finances, crippled, too, by royal taxation. The result was that in 1262 he ordered that every November their accounts were to be brought for audit to Paris. This short-lived decree began the government's superintendence of town administration, which was not to slacken. The peasantry suffered from official oppression, as was shown by the Inquests, but protection and tranquillity were given as well. So popular was the king himself that at the news of his captivity the so-called Peasants' Crusade was led from *Francia* by a visionary to release him. They soon began to plunder the towns on their route, and had to be repressed, but the movement showed the king's hold on them.

After 1254, Louis and his brother Alphonse set themselves to heal the wounds of Languedoc. Seneschals and minor officials were kept in hand; so were the new barons who had succeeded the old aristocracy. The towns were encouraged and *villes neuves* charted. The brilliant seigneurial life of the twelfth century had disappeared, but bourgeois and peasant, now forcibly orthodox, regained security and prosperity under the Capetian rule.

The pacific age of St Louis indeed, for all its darker features, was one to gratify the optimist. Population was still increasing, waste and forest being reclaimed for cultivation. If the nobles were already becoming impoverished and dependent on the Crown, the peasants were prospering and personal serfdom decreasing. The townsmen were more solvent than the town finances. Travel was more secure. It was the time of perfection in Gothic architecture. Vernacular literature also flourished, in verse perhaps more tedious and allegoric than of old, save in the genre of shrewd, contemporary satire, but in narrative prose a living picture of the day. The racy tongue of Northern France seemed to other peoples the most delightful of vernaculars. The monarchy in St Louis' hands was a contributor to the renown and greatness of France.

(5) THE SONS OF HENRY II

In strong contrast to the progress of the monarchy in France was the evolution of English institutions. Centralization was in England of older growth, and the skilful combination of it with ancient local institutions by Henry II produced unforeseen checks on the overstrained despotism of the kings. Thus, although the period is full of dominating personalities and epoch-making events, its continuity is maintained by the development of the nation's organization and its institutions under their influence.

There was no doubt in 1189 that Richard I Cœur-de-Lion was his father's heir. His mother Queen Eleanor, set free from her long imprisonment, acted as regent with the assistance of Henry II's faithful ministers until his coronation on 3 September, a ceremony which served as a precedent for future sacrings. The peace was only marred by disgraceful outbreaks against the Jews in London and York, largely due to their defaulting debtors, who murdered the lenders and burnt their bonds, much to the loss of the royal revenue which by special exactions took its share. Richard was mainly concerned in raising money for his Crusade and in arranging for a secure government of the realm during his expedition. For the first purpose there was an unexampled sale of offices, central and local, supplemented by extortions from the displaced holders, among whom was the great justiciar, Ranulf de Glanville. William the Lion, the King of Scots, paid 10,000 marks for release from the stringent vassalage imposed on him in 1175. For the second end Richard endeavoured to quiet the insatiable cravings of his brother John by the earldom of Gloucester with its heiress and seven counties, besides baronies (or 'honours') with palatine jurisdiction like the great fiefs of Aquitaine. It was a state within the state, exempted from the central government, made the more dangerous by the permission given to John, on ill-advised second thoughts, to enter England.

The central government was left in charge of tried officials, among whom after various changes William Longchamp, Bishop of Ely, a low-born Norman, emerged the chief. He was chancellor, justiciar, and papal legate. Unfortunately he was overbearing, grasping, and imprudent, and soon set barons and clergy against him in his endeavours to enforce his authority. John speedily became the centre of intrigue and opposition. Open conflict between him and Longchamp was only partially stilled by a compromise, when in September 1191 a fresh handle was given against Longchamp by the sacrilegious arrest of the king's illegitimate brother, Geoffrey, Archbishop of York, who returned to England although under oath to remain abroad. The result was that Longchamp was hounded out of the country, while the Archbishop of Rouen as justiciar and the chief officials took control. Their rule might have been quiet had not King Richard fallen a captive to the Emperor. John now saw his chance to usurp the throne. He allied with Philip Augustus and revolted (1193). But the Archbishop of Rouen stood firm, Hubert Walter, Bishop of Salisbury, returned from the Crusade to support him, and Richard himself, ransomed in 1194, arrived in time to share in extinguishing the embers of the rebellion.

Richard celebrated his freedom by a fresh coronation. As before, he was in need of money, this time for his war with Philip, and sales of pardons to the rebels supplemented the proceeds of taxation. John recovered the earldom of Gloucester, but lost his other shires and palatine rights. Then the king left for the Continent, entrusting the government of England to Hubert Walter, promoted to be justiciar and Archbishop of Canterbury. It was his rule on behalf of an absentee monarch which further developed the powers of the Crown and the administrative system.

Hubert Walter was by no means a model ecclesiastic in life or learning, but he was a great administrator in Church and State, proud of his office and eager to do things well. He took the earliest opportunity of reducing Archbishop Geoffrey of York and the Bishop of Durham to impotence, for both were likely to be refractory. In 1194 he sent round commissions of justices to examine the state of the shires, in which the system of appointing local notables to keep the record of the pleas of the Crown was made general. Taught by recent experience he had compiled a government record of debts to the Jews. He attempted the revision of taxation and of the system of military service. For Richard's onerous ransom there had been levied an aid of 20s. per knight's fee, a fourth of all incomes, and a year's wool from the sheep-farming Cistercians, along with other exactions. Richard in 1194 had for the last time imposed a Danegeld, under the name of carucage, for the French war, and Hubert ordered a tallage of boroughs and royal demesne. In 1198 Hubert arranged a new assessment by ploughlands (carucates), estimated at 100 acres each, and demanded 3s. per ploughland, which would have produced a new Domesday, but he resigned the justiciarship to Geoffrey FitzPeter that year, and the survey was abandoned. Equally transitory was the attempt in 1198 to render the obligation of knight-service a basis for taxation to equip and pay a small long-service army for the war. Those who owed it were in a body to pay a tax sufficient to maintain 300 knights, but the opposition of St Hugh, Bishop of Lincoln, and the Bishop of Salisbury caused it to fail, and the old method of a mixture of personal service and scutage survived to provide a means of resistance to the baronage.

Although he ceased to be justiciar, Hubert did not cease to be a mainspring of the government and in 1199 he became King John's chancellor. But he served a different master. The frank, impetuous, generous Richard, the first soldier of the age, had won the loyalty of his subjects. His brother John, who was accepted to the exclusion of his nephew Arthur of Brittany (for the doctrine of the representation of an elder brother by his son was not yet an acknowledged rule), lacked the dead king's attractive qualities. As we have seen, he was able, he could be energetic and industrious, he was never a nonentity. But his peculiar temperament, which was unbalanced and erratic, put him at the mercy of fits of anger, cruelty, and lethargy. Loyalty to man, law, or God meant nothing to him. Active as he was, it is impossible to determine his share in the great administrative measures of his reign. The chancellor (Hubert Walter, *ob.* 1205), the justiciar (Geoffrey FitzPeter, Earl of Essex, *ob.* 1213), and the treasurer William of Ely were three of the most efficient men of the age. The lesser bureaucrats were trained and experienced. It was only during the demoralizing interdict that the loyalty of the baronage waned, while the influence of the court coterie congenial to his tyrannous nature waxed.

To Hubert Walter seems to belong the growth of systematic record, e.g. the series of Chancery and Exchequer documents. Both Exchequer and Chancery were becoming departments, yet they were still parts of the wider activities of the Curia Regis. The king's court, which moved about the kingdom with him, was the seat of government, and his household with its judicial, financial, and secretarial elements dealt with current business of all kinds, small and great, national and domestic. The household Chamber and its financial section, the Wardrobe, acted almost concurrently with the Exchequer as spending departments. A writ of the Privy Seal, kept in the household, would order the use of the Great Seal for state documents, if that were not with the king. Judicial cases came before the king and the justices at his court. Yet Exchequer and the Court of Common Pleas under the justiciar were stabilized at Westminster, the home of a professional civil service and official routine, not of arbitrary power. Apart from the king, the king's government always went on there.

The Exchequer was in touch with every section of the community, and its efficient yoke under the pressure of the king's needs grew more and more grievous. The profits from the shires, raised through the sheriffs, increased enormously. The revenue from the royal estates rose, sometimes to double. Alienated demesne was resumed. Constant tallages pressed hardly on the demesne, the boroughs, and the Jews, whose transactions, being registered in the Jewish Exchequer, left them open to royal exploitation (in 1210 they paid 66,000 marks). During the Interdict Church lands were similarly fleeced, and the landowners did not escape. Heavy scutages were levied annually, there was a plough-tax in 1200, a seventh on barons' movables in 1203, a thirteenth on chattels in 1207. In 1212–13 a great inquiry was carried through by the sheriffs on the services due from feudal tenures. A powerful fleet was commandeered from the ports. Efficiency and with it oppression reached their peak.

The large sums obtainable bear witness to the growing wealth of the land, in which trade bore its part. The townsmen were able to buy charters of self-administration; some 50 to 60 towns received them from John, enlarging their privileges and granting more. A real communal movement did not exist in the strictly governed land, although in the troubles of 1191 London exceptionally set up a short-lived commune, and retained an elective mayor, sheriffs and councillors. Otherwise, it was a question of allowing or commanding local notables to do the king's work. Taxes were assessed and inquests conducted by knights and burgesses at the king's orders. The practice of calling up knights from the shires to give authoritative testimony (*recordatio*) on judicial proceedings in the county courts led easily to the summons of them and of burgesses for conference, even in 1213 to 'discuss the affairs of the realm'. In fact the idea of representation of the local communities by some sort of election was becoming familiar as an administrative expedient. The effect, too, of the events and governmental institutions of the reigns of Henry II and his sons had been to give the baronage as a whole a new training and new conceptions, which went beyond old-fashioned feudalism. England, in spite of provincialism, had become an organized unity; John was King of England, not as formerly of the English. There was a common law and administration, which called for loyalty as well as the king. Beneath violence and impulsiveness, hatred and selfishness, personal and class interests, there existed a sense that there was a public duty in the functions of government. The temperamental tyranny of John divided this feeling between obedience to the head of the State and defence of the law and legal rights.

Hubert Walter died (1205) in the midst of the disasters of the French war, which perhaps show the limits of his effective influence over the unguidable king, who ruled in France as well as England. His death gave occasion to the dispute over the election to the see of Canterbury, which ended in John's refusal to receive the papal nominee Stephen Langton as archbishop and the papal interdict over the kingdom. The royal administration, more efficient than ever, had little difficulty in dealing with the actual facts. All but two of the bishops went into exile. The country as a whole was loyal and the lower clergy submissive to both king and Pope. All ecclesiastical property, spiritualities and temporalities alike, was seized into the king's hands, subsistence allowances being granted to the clergy, except those who defied the Interdict and were left untouched. Lay patrons seem to have controlled the churches on their estates. The losses of the clergy were exceedingly heavy, but as a whole the Interdict was observed, and the strain on men's minds from the cessation of religious observance, save private baptism and masses for the dying, was great. Yet John kept a bold front. Friendship with the King of Scots was cemented, the Anglo-Norman barons in Ireland were held in submission, and a formidable expedition against Llywelyn of North Wales was only prevented by the discovery of impending treachery (1212). John could depend on the mercenaries he had gathered round him, but the patience of the baronage was giving way in spite of his ruthless treatment of the hostages he exacted from them. It needed the near prospect of a French invasion to bring John suddenly to his knees and, as we have seen, to make submission and do homage to the Pope (May 1213). Langton and the bishops returned. Compensation was promised, if only partially carried out, to the churchmen.

For the moment John seemed more powerful than ever. In spite of his acknowledged delinquencies he was now the protected vassal and tributary of the Papacy. His alliances to strike a decisive blow at Philip Augustus were complete. But Bouvines and his own futile campaign in France (1214) sent him back foiled and discredited to meet an exasperated baronage.

The movement for administrative reform and the cessation of oppression had found a champion in Stephen Langton, the Archbishop of Canterbury, who in absolving John from excommunication in 1213 had exacted an oath of good government and of return to the good laws of his predecessors. Seemingly the justiciar Geoffrey FitzPeter before his death had inclined to Langton's side. A baronial party was forming, some of whom refused to do service in Poitou and on John's return to pay a scutage for non-performance. In November 1214 the opposition made a conspiracy at Bury St Edmunds, taking their stand on the charter of Henry I, which the archbishop had brought back to memory. While some of the leading malcontents were northerners, the real centre of the party lay in East Anglia and Essex, where Robert FitzWalter, Richard de Clare, Earl of Hertford, and the new Earl of Essex and Gloucester were great lords. Private wrongs and ambitions mixed in their motives with resentment at the general oppression. Allegiance had been strained till it snapped. John at first staved off revolt by promises, while he gathered forces and took the cross to obtain a crusader's immunities, but when the barons' demands were formulated, he flatly rejected them, with the words, 'Why not ask for my kingdom?' He appealed for papal arbitration, while the barons renounced their homage.

For the time the barons were the stronger. They gained over the Londoners (17 May 1215), and in a meeting at Runnymede on the Thames John submitted to seal the Great Charter—Magna Carta—on 15 June, to which he was urged by the archbishop and his more responsible advisers. In essence Magna Carta contained the principle that the king did not possess an arbitrary despotism. He was bound by feudal custom, and he was not to proceed against any of his free subjects save by legal process. Baronial rights were chiefly safeguarded, but the interests of other classes, even the serfs, were not wholly left out. The much-abused right of levying scutage was only to be exercised with the consent of the great council of tenants-in-chief, the amplest form of the Curia Regis. Many of the varied concessions were ratifications of old and reasonable custom, overstepped by the tyrannous, extortionate John. As such it became the symbol in the future of the fundamental law of the land, by and under which the king was to rule. It regulated the relations between the Crown and its vassals, and the administration of justice and finance. At the time, however, its sting lay in its appointment of twenty-five barons to see that the king carried out its clauses.

John fell back on the claim that the Pope's consent must be obtained to this charter of his 'crusading' vassal. Meantime, he relied on his bureaucrats and his able mercenary captains, as well as on an influential body of his moderate supporters, such as the celebrated William the Marshal, now Earl of Pembroke and lord of Leinster. The Twenty-five on their side, besides their merited distrust of John, were themselves infected with the desire to rule, and their actions paralysed the administration. Thus the party of loyalists rapidly grew as the lovers of order rallied to the king, who was preparing for civil war.

In this situation came Pope Innocent's annulment of the Charter and his suspension of Langton from his functions, followed by the excommunication of the leading rebels and an interdict on London, their headquarters. John and his professional soldiers far outmatched the feudal amateurs arrayed against them. By March 1216 he had hemmed in the barons in London. Their resource had been to offer the throne to Louis of France, whose wife was a grand-daughter of Henry II. In spite of the opposition

Fig. 151. Magna Carta

of Innocent and his new legate, Cardinal Guala, Louis, with his father King Philip's permission, accepted the offer and landed in Kent under favour of a storm which had scattered John's fleet. His mercenaries restored the balance of forces, resulting in a military deadlock, which was broken by the death of John. After an orgy of reckless ferocity round the Fens, he crossed the Wash before the tide went down, losing his treasure in the water, and died of dysentery at Newark on 19 October 1216.

(6) THE LIMITATION OF THE ENGLISH KINGSHIP

His death was the greatest benefit he could have conferred on the loyalists, who were now to be led by the capable and honest William the Marshal in concert with the well-chosen legate Guala, now acting for Pope

723

Honorius III. They crowned John's nine-year-old son Henry III at Gloucester on 28 October, and defections to their party soon began in earnest, while ecclesiastical penalties on Louis and his supporters produced other desertions, and the reissue of Magna Carta, with the scutage clause and the baronial committee omitted, remedied Pope Innocent's error. Papal support, which Henry III, the papal vassal, never forgot, was all-important at home and abroad, but two victories decided the war, one scored on land by the Marshal, now *rector regis et regni*, in the streets of Lincoln (20 May 1217), and the other at sea off Sandwich where Hubert de Burgh destroyed Louis's fleet and reinforcements (24 August). A wise treaty with Louis, besieged in London, which paid him an indemnity and pardoned his partisans, except the clerics, concluded the war at Kingston (12 September 1217).

The government during Henry III's minority was carried on by a regency of varying composition. Guala and William the Marshal (*ob.* 1219) were succeeded by the legate Pandulf, Peter des Roches, the Poitevin Bishop of Winchester (1205–35), who had been prominent as an administrator and man of war since John's days, and the justiciar Hubert de Burgh, who was similarly gifted. After Pandulf's departure (1221) and Henry's partial emancipation (1223) Hubert ousted his episcopal rival and in conjunction with the king, who became fully of age in 1227, managed affairs until his own fall. The recovery of the kingdom from disorder was a slow business, not achieved without dissension and mistakes, but it was done, and in 1224 Faukes de Bréauté, one of the ablest and most oppressive of John's mercenaries, was at last expelled. Magna Carta was reissued in its final redaction (1225). There were, however, serious shortcomings. Poitou was lost to Louis VIII largely through mismanagement, expeditions against Llywelyn of Wales failed dismally, Hubert's acquisitiveness—he had been made Earl of Kent—aroused enmities, and, to crown all, the justiciar was ousted from the king's confidence. In 1232 Henry resolved on a change of régime.

By this time Henry had begun to develop a personal policy. During his minority the staff of the Wardrobe, his household treasury, had steadily grown. In 1230 he revived the Privy Seal, kept in the Wardrobe, which thus became also a household chancery, the more so since 'the Great Chancery was ceasing to be merely a court office'. Henry's aim was to administer the country through his household staff dependent on himself, whereas the Chancery and Exchequer had independent traditions of their own. The first step was to get rid of the traditional justiciarship. Hubert de Burgh was dismissed, accused, and persecuted, his office lost its vice-regal character, and the Poitevin, Peter de Rivaux, an ally of the Bishop of Winchester and head of the Wardrobe, was made Treasurer as well with a variety of offices which included the sheriffdoms of most

Fig. 152. Map of England, Wales and Scotland, c. 1250

counties. Court official had triumphed over baronial minister: the Wardrobe was supreme.

A reaction soon set in against the Poitevins. Richard Marshal, Earl of Pembroke, carried on a civil war in conjunction with Llywelyn of North Wales and was treacherously brought to his death in Ireland. But Henry, pressed by Edmund Rich, the new Archbishop of Canterbury, and the baronage, gave way so far as to disgrace the Poitevins and to restore Hubert de Burgh to his lands (1234). To his system of personal government through the household he adhered. To his own misfortune he was a feckless statesman, who looked on the kingdom almost as a private estate and source of income. An artist and connoisseur to his finger-tips, he was incurably extravagant in his magnificent buildings, such as Westminster Abbey, and their adornment. He had some rare virtues; his family life was irreproachable, his piety and devotion were pronounced, and he was only too generous and affectionate to his foreign and greedy relatives. His marriage (1236) had been a skilful act of State. His queen was Eleanor, a daughter of Raymond Berengar V, Count of Provence, sister-in-law of St Louis, and niece of Amadeus IV, Count of Savoy. But she too well harmonized with Henry's propensities. Her active and adventurous Savoyard uncles were endowed in England. Boniface, the youngest, received the archbishopric of Canterbury (1245), Peter, later Count of Savoy, the earldom of Richmond (1241), Peter d'Aigueblanche, a hanger-on, Keeper of the Wardrobe, the see of Hereford. They were efficient men, although they took too ample a share of profitable favours, but Henry's Poitevin half-brothers, the Lusignans, who settled in England after 1246, earned general dislike by the excessive and undeserved gains they made: William (de Valence) became Earl of Pembroke, Aymer Bishop of Winchester.

Without foresight or judgement, taking things at their decorative value, Henry added to his unpopularity by the failures and ambitions of his foreign policy. We have seen his costly mismanagement in France. The expense of his brother Richard Earl of Cornwall's ill-advised election as King of the Romans (1257) luckily fell on that shrewd administrator's private fortune, but the folly of accepting the Pope's offer of the unwon crown of Sicily for his second son Edmund (1255) was Henry's own. Henry's lasting gratitude to his papal overlord had deprived the English clergy of all defence against the ever-increasing papal taxation and Innocent IV's unscrupulous profusion in provisions to benefices, all for his war with the Hohenstaufen. The expensive reforming visits of the legates Otto (1236) and Ottobono (1268) did not allay clerical resentment, which was kept alive by frequent papal collectors of the taxes. A kind of condominium of Pope and king over the English Church roused the ire of the clergy as the king's debts owing to the Sicilian war, and those with France and Wales, besides his needs for building, grew. The laity, whether baronage, lesser landowners, or townsmen, were being more and more irritated by a variety of discontents. The repeated demands for extraordinary aids (or subsidies) and scutages (for which the practice of consent of the payers had become customary), the anger at undeserving foreign favourites, the irresponsible centralization in the Wardrobe, the extortionate and abusive efficiency of the sheriffs and their underlings, and the screwing up by them of all means of profit to the Crown and themselves, all mingled together in this unrest, exacerbated by Henry's patent failure in his foreign dealings.

This age of grievances was in fact one of remarkable progress in organized administration and in the co-operative solidarity and practice in affairs of the suitors to the county courts and the bourgeois of the boroughs, which ran parallel with the decay of strictly feudal institutions. The purely feudal honour court was becoming a mere survival. The sheriff, surrounded by writs and documents, supervised the private franchises and held the county court. Hardworked knights in the county court served on juries under the multiplying writs of action and bore the record to Westminster. Mayor and aldermen in the boroughs, even in those freed from the sheriff, did the king's work. The king's bureaucracy was overstraining its powers, and was overreaching itself, for both in shire and franchise oppression was rife. In the end, force lay with the landowning barons and their followers, for the administration rested on their obedience more than on its own resources, and in the decay of personal military service since the reign of John the marcher lords of Wales, who necessarily were still well armed, acquired especial weight.

It had become customary for the king to ask for aids in a Parliament of barons, the version of the Great Council or largest form of the Curia Regis, sanctioned by the original Magna Carta, and it was in the Parliament of London (Easter 1258) that discontents came to a head. The barons would only make a grant to save Henry from bankruptcy on condition of the banishment of the Poitevins and the appointment of a commission of reform, the Twenty-four, half-royal and half-baronial nominees. The reforms were decreed in the Provisions of Oxford, by which the king was placed in tutelage of a Council of Fifteen, a responsible Justiciar, Treasurer, and Chancellor were appointed, and an inquest into the widespread abuses was undertaken, which was followed up by remedial provisions at Westminster (1259). The inquest indeed began to produce a fissure among the barons, for it showed the misdeeds of their own administration of their franchises. It brought to the fore a middle class, the lesser landowners, 'the community of the bachelry of England', who found a sympathetic leader in a great magnate. This was the king's brother-in-law, Simon de Montfort, Earl of Leicester through his mother. He was a son of the Albigensian crusader, and aggrieved by Henry, for whom he had governed

Gascony (1248–52). Private ambition and resentment were among his motives, but a sincere desire to bring about reforms and a sympathy with the English fabric of local self-administration and with the best political thought of the day, which emphasized royal duties and subjects' rights, took the first place in his mind. Other leading magnates, such as the Clares of Gloucester and Bigod of Norfolk, the Earl Marshal, were for restraining the king in oligarchical fashion and jealous of the domineering Simon. Henry, freed from the French war by the Peace of Paris (1259) and from his oath to the Provisions by the Papacy (1261), with the Provisions also annulled by the chosen arbitrator St Louis in the Mise of Amiens (1264), had freed himself from restraint, and challenged the reforming party. The outcome was Earl Simon's victory at Lewes (14 May 1264), and the captivity of Henry III, his heir Edward, Earl of Chester, and his brother King Richard 'of Almayne', Earl of Cornwall.

Earl Simon was now *de facto* master of the kingdom, and his policy and following were shown not only by the re-enactment of the Provisions enlarged (this time with a Council of Nine, not Fifteen), but by the composition of the Parliaments which the Council summoned. Not only the greater barons and prelates received their separate writs of summons, but two knights representing each shire (for which there was precedent) and two burgesses from a number of boroughs were called up (January 1265) through the sheriffs. It was a crucial step which helped to form the later constitution and the admitted advent of a middle class in State affairs. But Simon was masterful and grasping, his sons were deservedly disliked, and he alienated the marcher lords, like Gilbert, Earl of Gloucester, by forcing Edward to transfer to him the palatine earldom of Chester. Edward escaped, and joined by the marchers and Llywelyn of Gwynedd, who was recognized as Prince of Wales, was able to win the victory of Evesham (4 August 1265), where Simon met his death.

Civil war, however, was by no means over. King Henry was fast becoming a cipher, and his eldest son Edward had yet to learn moderation. Reckless confiscations and granting away of the lands of the defeated party provoked their bitter resistance. At Kenilworth, Axeholm, and Ely the 'Disinherited' held out, pillaging the countryside. Reconciliation was due to the action of two men. Cardinal Ottobono, the legate, helped to secure surrender by the *Dictum* of Kenilworth, by which 'repurchase', not confiscation, was laid down (1266). But the terms were hard, and it needed the rebellion of Gilbert of Gloucester, who restored his share of the confiscations to their owners, and seized on London, to bring the government to their senses. By the mediation of King Richard 'of Almayne' peace was made, and a special Eyre sent round to apply the *Dictum* mercifully (1267). At Shrewsbury a fresh treaty, making large concessions, was concluded with the Prince of Wales, who had been Gloucester's ally. Finally, the

Statute of Marlborough (1267) re-enacted the best part of the Provisions of Oxford or rather of their supplement at Westminster in 1259. The special restraints on the king disappeared, but not the administrative reforms which curbed both king and barons' officials. 'In many ways', says Maitland, it 'marks the end of feudalism.' So peaceful was the kingdom that Edward could start in 1270 on his crusade. King Henry was able to dedicate his abbey at Westminster before he closed his momentous reign (16 November 1272).

CHAPTER 24

THE SMALLER STATES OF EUROPE

(I) THE LATIN EMPIRE AND ITS RIVALS

The decay of the exotic Latin Empire is best told in the progress of its enemies. Of them the fragments of the Byzantine Empire were to prove the most formidable in the end, but for years their mutual rivalries and their inferiority to the 'Franks' in the field held them back. Only a passing mention can here be made of the Empire of impregnable and wealthy Trebizond on the Black Sea, founded by a fugitive Comnenus, Alexius (1204–22), grandson of Andronicus I. He and his brother David and his successors carried on a three-cornered warfare with Nicaea, the Franks, and the Seljūks of Rūm, the result of all which was a restricted dominion in vassalage to the Seljūks. Lascarids of Nicaea and the bastard Angeli of Epirus bore the brunt of the Frankish onset and began the reconquest. Although Theodore I Lascaris, who exchanged the title of Despot for that of Emperor (1206), suffered crushing defeats from the Latin Emperor Henry (1205, 1211) and had to fight desperately against the Seljūks of Rūm as well, the Bulgarians diverted the forces of the victors, and Theodore by his able government, which called out the patriotism of the Greeks, was able to refound the Byzantine Empire in western Asia Minor, where the Franks held little more than the shores of the Sea of Marmora when he died (1222). He had gathered up the battered remnants of Byzantine civilization at Nicaea.

The Despots of Epirus achieved more obvious reconquests. Michael I (1204–14) made himself master of Albania; his brother Theodore (1214–30) captured the new-elected Latin Emperor, Peter of Courtenay, brother-in-law of Henry, and later took Salonika, assuming the title of Emperor (1223). The feat was rendered easy by the weakness of King Demetrius, son of Boniface, slain years before (1207) in war with the Bulgarians. He thus entered into competition with the Nicaeans for the recovery of Constantinople, where Peter's son Robert (1221–8) and then the ex-King of Jerusalem, John of Brienne (1231–37), as colleague for the minor Baldwin II, another son of Peter, were ruling an imperilled state. The rivals of both Greeks and Latins for Balkan domination were the Slavs. Of these the Yugoslavs were divided between the two sons of Stephen Nemanya and Kulin, the Ban of Bosnia, and were preoccupied with their own discords and self-defence against Hungary. The Bulgarians, however, were intent on expansion. Tsar Kaloyan in the midst of his successes died in 1207, and his nephew and probable murderer, Tsar Boril, was worsted by the

Emperor Henry, but Kaloyan's son John Asên II (1218–41), restored by Russian aid, gave Bulgaria its second golden age. In 1230 he overthrew and captured Theodore Angelus at Klokotinitza, and placed his brother Manuel Angelus on the Salonikan throne. In 1235, in alliance with Vatatzes of Nicaea, he conquered Thrace from the Latins, although the siege of Constantinople itself proved vain. In 1240 he expelled Manuel, and re-

Map 18

placed him by Theodore's son John. He was a mild ruler, popular even with the Greeks. He revived, during his uncertain friendship with Nicaea, the Bulgarian patriarchate at his capital of Trnovo and fostered his country's trade. Yet these triumphs were due to his personality, as events after his death were to show.

More solid advance was the lot of the Empire of Nicaea. The chosen successor of Theodore I was his son-in-law John III Vatatzes (1222–54), a statesman and warrior, who justified his promotion. He began his reign by defeating the Franks and regaining territory. He retook Chios and

731

18. Emperors of Constantinople (and Nicaea), 1204–1453

(a) The Latin Emperors of Constantinople

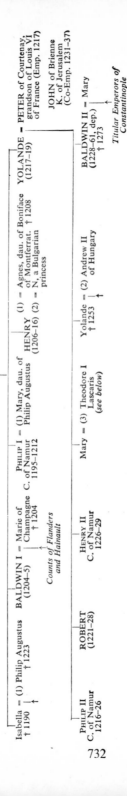

BALDWIN [V] of Hainault = Margaret, heiress of
and [VIII] of Flanders.   Flanders. † 1194
† 1195

BALDWIN I = Marie of
(1204–5)   Champagne
            † 1204

*Counts of Flanders
and Hainault*

PHILIP I = (1) Mary, dau. of
C. of Namur   Philip Augustus
1195–1212

HENRY (1) = Agnes, dau. of Boniface
(1206–16) (2)   of Montferrat. † 1208
         (2) = N, a Bulgarian
                princess

YOLANDE = PETER of Courtenay,
(1217–19)   grandson of Louis VI
             of France (Emp. 1217)

JOHN of Brienne
K. of Jerusalem
(Co-Emp. 1231–37)

HENRY II
C. of Namur
1226–29

ROBERT
(1221–28)

PHILIP II
C. of Namur
1216–26

Mary = (3) Theodore I
         Lascaris
         (*see below*)

Yolande = (2) Andrew II
† 1253   of Hungary

BALDWIN II = Mary
(1228–61, dep.)
† 1273

*Titular Emperors of
Constantinople*

Isabella = (1) Philip Augustus
† 1190

(b) The Emperors of Nicaea

Anna, dau. of Alexius III = (1) THEODORE I Lascaris (2) = Philippa of Armenia; div. 1219
Angelus. † 1212   (1206–22)   (3) = Mary of Courtenay (*see above*)

Irene = JOHN III Vatatzes
† 1241   (1222–54)

THEODORE II Lascaris = Helena, dau. of John
(1254–58)   Asén II of Bulgaria

JOHN IV
(1258–61, dep.)
† 1274

Irene = Constantine Asén
† 1270   of Bulgaria. † 1277

Mary = Nicephorus I, Despot
       of Epirus. † 1296

732

(c) The House of Palaeologus

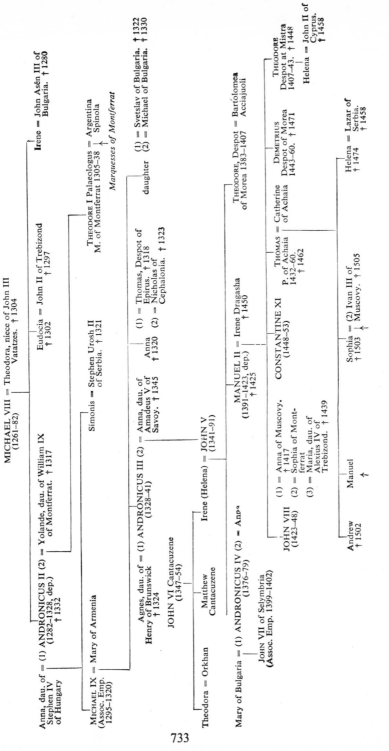

733

Samos in the Aegean Sea. His league with Bulgaria in 1235 gave back to the Greeks most of Thrace as far as river Maritza. When the alliance with John Asên II broke down owing to their incompatible ambitions, he held his own against a combination of Bulgarians, Franks, and savage Cumans from the Ukraine. With the death of the Bulgarian Tsar, who left a child, Kaliman I, as his heir, Vatatzes' chance came. John of Salonika was a feeble creature, whom he could compel (1242) to renounce the title of Emperor with all that it implied in exchange for that of Despot. The advance of the Mongols so weakened the Seljūks of Rūm that he was safe from their attacks. In 1246 Kaliman I's death and the succession of another child, Michael Asên, allowed him to snatch from Bulgaria her southern territory as far as Skoplie, and then to depose Demetrius, the last Despot of Salonika. Although Epirus was still left to the Angeli, the Nicaean Empire, now extended to Europe, surrounded the Latins of Constantinople, and unquestionably represented the Greek and orthodox cause.

A bare mention must suffice for Vatatzes' subsequent warfare to round off his dominions in Macedonia and vassal Rhodes, for his excellent administration of his Empire, and for his ineffective attempts to allay papal enmity by a compromise in religion. He died at Nymphaeum near Smyrna, his practical capital, leaving the throne to his able, but unbalanced son, Theodore II Lascaris (1254–8). The new Emperor's energy repelled an attempt of Michael Asên to reconquer his lost provinces, a failure which caused a civil war in Bulgaria and the extinction of the Asên dynasty, but his health gave way and he died, leaving his son John IV Lascaris a child of seven. The intrigue and turmoil that ensued ended in the elevation of the cleverest and most untrustworthy of the nobles, Michael Palaeologus, to the regency. This descendant of Alexius III was a popular and distinguished general, who had earned Theodore's suspicions and persecution. He quickly made himself Emperor (1259) with a prodigality of oaths of fidelity to his ward, whose coronation he evaded. His hands were strengthened by success. Michael II of Epirus was aiming at the conquest of Salonika and of Constantinople itself. He gained the alliance of William of Villehardouin, Prince of the powerful Frankish state of Achaia, by making him his son-in-law, and seized the opportunity of the Nicaean minority. But treachery within caused his own flight and the rout and captivity of William at Pelagonia (1259) at the hands of the Nicaeans. Epirus survived but out of the running. The Latin Empire was all but isolated, yet Baldwin II, supported by a Venetian fleet, had the optimism to challenge his inevitable foe. That fleet and the fiasco of a first attempt at surprise roused Palaeologus to a diplomatic triumph. By enormous trading concessions he induced Genoa to abandon the Latin cause for his in the Treaty of Nymphaeum (10 July 1261). The temptation of ousting Venice was too great. But the sacrifice of Byzantine interests proved needless, for, in a brief absence of the Venetian fleet, Constantinople fell on 25 July 1261 to the Nicaean general, Alexius Strategopoulos, by a lucky coup. Baldwin II and the Latins fled by sea, and Michael VIII reigned over the renewed Byzantine Empire. With characteristic perfidy he celebrated his triumph by blinding and deposing his child ward. Even Byzantine opinion was outraged, and he lived for years excommunicated.

If the Latin Empire had ceased to exist, however, its great vassals in Greece proper lived on, as did the colonies of the Italian towns, while ambitions to restore it continued in the West. The chief states in the south were the principality of Achaia and the duchy of Athens. The captivity of Prince William gave Palaeologus a diplomatic leverage over Achaia, and in 1262, in return for releasing his prisoners, he extorted the cession of a part of Morea (the medieval name of the Peloponnese) round Mistrà, thus gaining a foothold in the south. War was soon renewed, and became more threatening to the Byzantines when by the treaty of Viterbo (1267) the dethroned Baldwin II ceded the suzerainty of Achaia to Charles of Anjou, and when Charles himself became its prince (1278). The ruling ambition of the King of Sicily was to refound the Latin Empire by a 'crusade' against the schismatic Byzantines, and Michael VIII employed all his diplomacy for years to fend him off, gaining the protection of successive Popes by promises to effect the union of the Greek and Latin Churches. In 1274 he made complete submission to the Papacy in the Second Council of Lyons, but this fictitious reunion was resisted vehemently by clergy and people until in 1281 Pope Martin IV denounced it and Michael turned to other means of averting the coming invasion by Charles.

Partly because of these engrossing cares and partly because of his well justified fears of a treacherous usurper, Michael Palaeologus neglected the defence of Asia Minor against the multiplying Turkish tribes. In the Balkans, the Bulgarians were indignant at the Greeks obtaining the prize of Constantinople which they had marked out for themselves. Their Tsar was now Constantine Asên (1258–77). He was for a time kept in check by a Hungarian attempt to conquer his country. Later, Palaeologus' best resource was the internal turmoil of Bulgaria in the intervals of war and marriage alliance, which were complicated by the invasions of Nogai Khan, a Tartar chief of the Ukraine. For a while a Byzantine candidate, John Asên III, was placed by force on the perilous throne, but when Palaeologus died a fresh dynast, George Terteri I (1280–92), was struggling with Tartars and rebels. Bulgaria, although always an anxiety and injury to the Byzantine Empire, had fallen through dissension and invasion from its high estate.

Meantime the Yugoslavs, although linked to Byzantium by the orthodox religion of the majority, had been far more concerned with their western neighbours. In the early thirteenth century the dominant figure among them was St Sava (*ob*. 1236), youngest son of Stephen Nemanya and a great and patriotic ecclesiastical statesman. Besides their disunion among themselves they were endangered externally by the ambitions of the kings of Hungary, who already possessed Croatia, and internally by the Bogomil heretics, who were specially numerous in Bosnia. A ready means of defence from these perils and of attacking one another was to accept the Latin creed and papal supremacy, which carried with it papal protection. Kulin, the Ban of Bosnia (*ob*. 1204), after adopting Bogomilism, recanted in favour of Latin Christianity, and a subsequent Ban, Ninoslav (*ob*. 1250), went through a similar evolution with indifferent success. Bosnia fell under Hungarian suzerainty, but in spite of persecution the Bogomils remained a strong force there. St Sava's brother Stephen II had made a like submission to the Papacy to obtain a royal crown from Honorius III (1217). The saint, however, succeeded in cancelling this unpopular action and in obtaining from the Patriarch at Nicaea his own consecration as archbishop of an autonomous Serbian Orthodox Church (1219). He then recrowned his brother King of Serbia (1222). Neither step was retraced, and Serbia was still an orthodox kingdom under Stephen Urosh II at the death of Michael VIII. Although diminished in the north by Hungary, expansion at the cost of the Byzantine Empire and of Bulgaria had begun in the south. The way was being paved for Serbia to become the leading state in the Balkans.

Thus Michael VIII had after all restored a feeble Empire. The feudal Franks were entrenched in Greece proper; Serbia, Bulgaria, and Epirus were independent; and worst of all the Empire was losing ground in Asia Minor to the Turks. Degeneracy in arms and government had set in. Yet a real revival in culture, if in nothing else, was taking place. Literary studies were being renewed, and Byzantine art, becoming naturalistic and picturesque, akin to the Italian primitives, whom it influenced, was entering upon its last renaissance.

(2) THE KINGDOM OF HUNGARY, 955–1301

When once its conflicts with Germany were over, the ambitions of Hungary turned towards the south, and consequently, although its Latin faith kept it in a Western orbit, it is more convenient to summarize its history here from the time of its conversion to Western Christianity. After the disastrous slaughter of the Lechfeld (955) the Magyars or Hungarians began to settle down merely as troublesome neighbours of Germany in the Danubian plain. Christian missionaries, largely Czechs, were soon busy among them, and their work was crowned by the baptism and accession of the heir of the Arpáds, St Stephen I (997–1038). He enforced Christianity on his people, set up an ecclesiastical hierarchy, and in 1000 was crowned king, instead of duke, with insignia given by the Pope. The

EASTERN EUROPE
IN THE
THIRTEENTH CENTURY

Riga
KNIGHTS OF THE SWORD
COURLAND
Memel
LITHUANIA
Rügen
Konigsberg
Danzig
PRUSSIA
Stettin
Kulm
POMERANIA
KUJAWIA
BRANDENBURG
GREAT
POLAND
Poznan
MAZOVIA
LAUSITZ
Glogau
POLAND
Lublin
MEISSEN
Breslau
SILESIA
LESSER
Sandomierz
RUSSIA
POLAND
Prague
Cracow
Kuttenberg
BOHEMIA
MORAVIA
GALICIA
AUSTRIA
Gran
Buda-Pest
STYRIA
Veszprem
CARINTHIA
HUNGARY
TRANSYLVANIA
CROATIA
CUMANS
BOSNIA
SERBIA
BULGARIA

Map 19

Magyars had already contributed to the separation of the Czechs from the Eastern Church by driving a heathen wedge between them and Byzantium. Now they enlarged Latin Christendom by their own conversion. For years yet they were a thorn in the side of the Holy Roman Empire, which claimed suzerainty over them, but the frontier was finally established in 1043, and all idea of vassalage lapsed under St Ladislas (Laszló) (1077–95), a redoutable enemy of paganism. His nephew, Koloman I (1095–1114), like him looked southward for expansion. He achieved the permanent conquest of Yugoslav Croatia, which was formed into a separate kingdom Latin in faith, with its temporary province of Dalmatia on the Adriatic coast, also Yugoslav, but continually contested by Venice, to whom the suppression of its pirates and the supply of its timber were a matter of life and death. Thereby the division of Yugoslavia in creed and civilization was accomplished. Both the Crusades and the acquisition of Croatia brought closer contacts, often hostile, with the Byzantine Empire. The aim of the Comneni was, if possible, to promote a client Arpád prince to the Hungarian throne, and this end was gained by the Emperor Manuel when he established his protégé, Béla III (1173–96), as well as occupying for a time the much fought over Dalmatia. Béla III, however, was knitting relations with the West also, of which his marriage to the widowed Margaret, sister of Philip Augustus, was a symbol. Nor, as we have seen, were Hungarian ambitions in the Balkans, more especially in Yugoslavia, abandoned. But a crushing blow was dealt to Hungary and its monarchy by the Mongol invasion and the ruinous defeat of Béla IV (1235–70). The land was depopulated and disorganized, and the reception (1239) of 30,000 fugitive heathen Cumans from the Ukraine by King Béla added to the disintegration. King Ladislas IV 'the Cuman' (1272–90), whose mother was one of these ex-nomads, was hated for the favour he showed to them, and he was involved far more than his predecessors with his western neighbours. The extinction of the Babenbergs of Austria had led to a war with Přemysl Otakar II of Bohemia for their inheritance. Bohemia was the victor, but the hostility engendered made Ladislas an ally of the new King of the Romans, Rudolf of Habsburg, in his contest with Otakar and a sharer in the battle of the Marchfeld (1278), which established the Habsburgs in Austria. Ladislas' murder by the once-favoured Cumans produced a succession war. His cousin Andrew III (1290–1301), heir in the male line, was accepted in Hungary, but the next-of-kin in the female line, Charles Martel, grandson of Charles of Anjou, was accepted in Croatia until his death (1295). Finally, with the death of Andrew III, the male line of the Arpáds became extinct, and the disintegrating kingdom was left open to competition among his kindred.

From the outset Hungary, encircled by the Carpathian mountains, had contained a singular medley of peoples. The ruling tribes of Magyars

Fig. 153. King Andrew II and Queen Gertrude of Hungary

occupied chiefly the central steppes on the Danube. They kept their Ural-Altaic language, but through constant intermingling exchanged the physical type of their ancestors for that of the conquered nations. Around and beneath them were the earlier comers, Slovaks and Ruthenians in the Carpathian valleys, Vlachs, romance-speakers, in Transylvania, varieties of Yugoslavs in the south, and of course in Croatia and Dalmatia. Save in free Croatia, these submerged peoples were mainly peasant serfs. To them were added fresh ingredients by the policy of the twelfth-century kings, who wished to develop both trade and agriculture. Swarms of Germans and Flemings settled in towns and villages in this version of the *Drang nach Osten*—the block of 'Saxons' (in reality Rhinelanders) in Transylvania is one instance—and brought a higher civilization to the land.

The Christianization of the Magyars took long to complete, although St Stephen established Hungary as an ecclesiastical province, with an archbishop at Esztergom (Gran), dependent on the Pope, and founded monasteries. Ladislas I and Koloman brought it into line with the reform movement. The Hungarian Church became rich and powerful, but the pagan Cumans were not fully converted till the fourteenth century. The civil organization consisted of a royal council of considerable size and of counties, each under a nominated count (like the English sheriff), while colonists in town and country developed their own institutions. But barbarism in law and manners continued. The king's power was patriarchal, backed by enormous domains, and under him the old Magyar clans and chiefs subsisted. In the twelfth century, however, changes in economic and social structure were in process, which eventually undermined both patriarchal monarchy and clan. The immense royal estates were being contracted by grants of land to Church and nobles, while the spirit and institutions of Western feudalism entered the country, fostered by the policy of Géza II and Béla III, who linked the dynasty and kingdom to the West by

50-2

marriages, intercourse, and colonists. By the time of Andrew II (1205–35) the feudal age in Hungary had begun. Beneath the grades of prelates and magnates there appeared clearly the large class of turbulent lesser nobles, the Hungarian free gentry, while even Magyars outside these ranks were being degraded to a common serfdom with the subject peoples. Andrew, weak, ambitious, and prodigal, attempting with indifferent success to enlarge his kingdom, was by no means the man to curb his wild, clannish subjects. Rather, he weakened the kingship by his spendthrift grants. In 1222 the nobles extorted from him the Golden Bull, the fundamental charter of Hungarian liberties, which betrays not only the political consciousness acquired by the Magyars but Aragonese influence in its provisions. The mass Diet of all nobles, greater and lesser, was to meet at Székesfehérvár (Stuhlweissenburg) every year; nobles could only be tried and punished before the Count Palatine, one of themselves; their estates and those of the Church were to be tax-free; at the same time pure feudalism was checked by the removability and non-hereditary character of the 'counts', who ruled the counties with their local noble assemblies. Resistance to a breach of the Golden Bull was not to imply disloyalty. It was a primitive, but as it proved a durable consititution. Croatia, of course, retained its native autonomy. Transylvania, too, was in a special position, with regard both to its Magyar Szekels and to its privileged Saxon settlers.

The Golden Bull was a sign of the break-up of the old order. It was the Mongol devastation (1241) which finally ruined the patriarchal kingship. Complete anarchy marked the reign of Ladislas IV, and collapse that of Andrew III. The great clans, themselves decaying internally with the rise of the lesser nobles, defied central rule, and when the interregnum began, a number of overmighty magnates, tribal chiefs, ruled the fragments of Hungary.

(3) BOHEMIA, DUCHY AND KINGDOM, c. 900–1306

While Hungary remained a completely independent state on the outskirts of Latin Christendom, the Western Slav realm of the Czechs, or Bohemia, was a central European power, autonomous indeed, but bound by ties of vassalage to the Holy Roman Empire, of which it formed a part, and deeply influenced not only by German civilization and laws but by a wholesale immigration of German settlers.

The destruction of Great Moravia by the Magyars left the Slav tribes south of the Erzgebirge a mere congeries, nominally Christian and drifting towards the nearer Latin and German Church away from the influence of the now distant Eastern. Almost immediately the dukes of the Czech tribe round Prague (who traced their descent from the legendary Přemysl) began to outdistance the chiefs of other tribes. They nursed a zeal for Christianity, which linked Bohemia first to Bavaria and then to the Saxon dynasty, especially the Duchess St Ludmila (*ob.* 921) and her grandson St Wenceslas (Vaclav) (*ob.* 929). Both were murdered owing to domestic hatreds. Boleslav I (929–67), after an attempt at independence, was compelled by Otto the Great to submit to German suzerainty (950), and this vassalage was tightened in 973 by the foundation of the bishopric of Prague as a diocese in the province of Mainz. By this time the dukes ruled all Bohemia, and Boleslav II (967–99) was extending his dominion over Poles and Wends as well as over Moravia. After a revolt by Bratislav I (1034–55) German suzerainty was finally ensured (1041) and a long period of friendly dependence began. It was rewarded by the temporary conferment of the royal title (1085) on Duke Vratislav II (1061–92), and the acquisition of the dignity of Cup-bearer of the Empire, which gave the dukes a voice in German affairs. The feudal duty of supplying 300 knights for the *Romzug* of the Emperor was so well (and ferociously) performed that Frederick Barbarossa in 1158 once more gave the personal title of King to Duke Vladislav II (as King Vladislav I) (1140–73). Barbarossa, however, was shrewdly intent on increasing his control, when a disputed succession gave him the chance, an easy event through the mixture of seniority and election in the ducal house, which was the Czech custom. In 1182 he even nominated one claimant Duke of Bohemia and his rival Margrave of Moravia as an immediate vassal of the Empire. In practice the two lands were soon linked again, and the immediacy of Moravia in the end vanished too. The close of dynastic disputes (1197) and the German civil war gave Duke Přemysl Otakar I (1197–1230) the means of obtaining permanently the royal title (1198) and loosening the bonds of vassalage. After the usual changes of side in the war he received in 1212 a Golden Bull from Frederick II. The investiture of the kingdom was retained by the Emperor, but the right of election was recognized and the king was to invest the Bohemian bishops, while his own feudal duties were whittled down. Partly owing to lack of sons the rule of succession became in fact primogeniture.

The rule of the thirteenth-century Přemyslids was decisive for the future of their country. It was a time of increasing prosperity and independence, in which the kings aimed at creating an east-central European power. The disintegration of the Empire and Poland and the decline of Hungary gave the opportunity. Save for Moravia, the Czech realm by good fortune escaped the disasters of the Mongol invasion (1241). On the extinction of the Babenberg dukes of Austria (1246), followed by the death of the Emperor Frederick II (1250) in the midst of the duel between the Hohen-staufen and the Papacy, Přemysl Otakar II (1253–78), as yet only Margrave of Moravia, set up a claim for the vacant duchies of Austria and Styria. This led to wars with Béla IV of Hungary, closed at last by the victory of Bohemia (1260). When in 1269 Otakar II acquired by inheritance Carinthia and Carniola as well, he became the greatest prince in the Empire, anticipating in a way the later Austrian state. He was aspiring to be elected King of the Romans himself, for which his dignity as Cupbearer and the consequent claim to be one of the Electors, now restricted by custom to the seven imperial dignitaries, gave him a leverage. When Rudolf of Habsburg was elected instead without his participation, he refused his fealty. But his power was dreaded by every other prince, and they all followed King Rudolf to the field. There was rebellion in Bohemia. A first war deprived him of Austria and the other annexations (1276), a second, in which Hungary took part, produced his defeat and death on the Marchfeld (26 August 1278).

After an interlude of German rule, Otakar II's only son Wenceslas II (1278–1305), on coming of age, resumed the policy of expansion. His attempts to recover Austria were abortive, but, turning east, he aquired Silesia and much of divided Poland, where he was crowned king (1300). On the death of Andrew III of Hungary (1301) he entered the lists for the succession on behalf of his son Wenceslas. But he roused thereby the enmity of King Albert of Habsburg and the Papacy. When he himself died, his failure was clear, and Wenceslas III made peace. The young king's murder next year (4 August 1306) extinguished the Přemyslids, so that Bohemia, too, like its neighbours became the victim of a succession problem.

The internal development of Bohemia had been no less significant than these foreign ambitions. The earlier dukes had exercised a legally absolute sway, military, judicial, and financial, over their subjects. Their estates were very large, including all waste ground; they imposed tolls, taxes (especially an annual land-tax, the *tributum pacis*), forced labour, and *albergue*. They appointed the castellans of their castles, who were their local deputies for the subdivisions of the duchy, and were the chief factors in politics, for the primitive nobility had withered away. Gradually a new higher nobility was formed from court officials and castellans, and in the thirteenth century formed the barons with great estates due to royal grants. Beneath them appeared the class of knights, who held their lands by military service, a lesser nobility in short, of great importance. Below these ruling classes came two main groups, the slaves on the great estates and the much-burdened free peasants. Before 1200 the bulk of the latter had become dependent tenants (*hospites*) on the great estates, either by surrendering their holdings for protection or by settlement thereon for a livelihood. The Church had soon become extremely wealthy by donations, both the two sees of Prague and Olomouc (Olmütz), and the monasteries. The Benedictines introduced large-scale agriculture and literary education, but for long clergy and monks were under secular law and dominated by the lay rulers. Not till the mid-twelfth century did the Gregorian reforms effectually enter Bohemia, and the practice of grants of immunity from lay taxation and lay courts begin. Bishop Andrew of Prague in a contest with Otakar I secured full jurisdiction over the clergy in spiritual causes and the exemption of their lands from the state officials. Following the example of the clergy, the nobles, too, gained jurisdiction over their estates. As a consequence the old castle administration was replaced by feudalism.

The central government meanwhile was developing in a national direction. In the later twelfth century general assemblies were dealing with disputes between nobles, and in the later thirteenth century this function was taken over by a court of barons, which was also the royal council for state affairs. In the troubles after Otakar II's death, a kind of general diet appears for a time, in which clergy, nobles, and burghers took part.

The condition of the subject peasantry was being fundamentally changed by the German immigration, which began in the twelfth century and grew in volume in the thirteenth. These welcome colonists, who assarted waste land, did so under 'German Law', i.e. they were given hereditary tenure under fixed rents and conditions. The Czech peasants, with whom the former slaves were merged, for the most part gradually secured the same terms, while both races remained under feudal jurisdiction. But the German immigrants were also grouped as traders in privileged towns, thus creating a burgher class, which grew in importance. The result of immigration was to make Bohemia and Moravia a land of two races of different character and interests, a source of troubles and divisions up to the present day. But that and the close connexion with the Empire produced as well the Germanization of the Bohemian baronage, also with fateful results in external and internal relationships. In this evolution the Přemyslid kings led the way.

(4) POLAND AND THE TEUTONIC KNIGHTS, *c.* 950–1306

Whereas the Slavs of Bohemia were to some extent defended and confined by their mountains, and those between the Elbe and the Oder (the Wends) were exposed to the full German thrust eastward and thereby rendered more hostile to Christianity and less pervious to progress in civilization, save by sheer conquest, their kindred tribes in the borderless plain beyond the Oder and around the Vistula, the Poles, were forming a principality of considerable size under the dynasty of Piast. In the mid-tenth century their prince, or duke, Mieszko I, influenced by his Bohemian wife, was baptized (967) and accepted imperial overlordship, partly owing to his hostility to the more westerly Wends. His son Boleslav I the Mighty (992–1025) built up a powerful monarchy. With the help of the Emperor Otto III he obtained from Pope Sylvester the erection of Poland into a province with its archbishop at Gniezno (Gnesen) in 1000, by which a bound was set to the German archbishopric of Magdeburg. He speedily competed with Germany for the rule of the Western Slavs. He was unable to make a permanent conquest of Bohemia, but three wars with the Emperor Henry II left him in possession (1018) of Lusatia and more. Only his dread of his Russian neighbours to the east kept him partially in check. On Henry's death he took the style of king. His son, Mieszko II, hampered by Russian attacks and a rival brother, was shorn of these conquests by Conrad II, and his principality dissolved in anarchy. It was revived, with some assistance at first from the Empire, by his half-German son Casimir I the Restorer (1038–58). If the wide state of Boleslav the Mighty had vanished, Casimir united and developed the five central Polish tribes in a firm monarchy. On the model of Bohemia he set up an ecclesiastical and civil hierarchy superimposed on the clan system. The knights who were his armed force were maintained by land grants. The weakness of the State lay in the separation of the tribes and their mere veneer of Christianity. The civilized element was few in number and the clans opposed an obstinate resistance to the novel institutions. The error, tempting among the fluid kindred tribes of the time, of the capable and violent Boleslav II the Bold (1058–79) was to squander his energy in all-round aggression, which won him indeed a royal crown (1076) but lost the opportunity of annexing the Wends to the west, while transient successes against the Russians of Kiev, Hungary, and Bohemia and in the German civil war were offset by his quarrel with the Church and murder of St Stanislas, Bishop of Cracow. His incompetent brother Vladyslav I (1079–1102) left Poland weak and divided. His successor Boleslav III Wrymouth (1102–38) retrieved the situation, and in spite of prolonged civil war with his bastard brother Zbigniev, complicated with attacks by the Czechs and the Emperor Henry V, not to mention Russia, adopted a purposeful policy of expansion to the west and north. His wars there took on the character of a crusade, for the sea-coast Poles, or Pomeranians, were obstinate pagans. Years of war effected the conquest of Pomerania from the Vistula to Rügen, yet he was obliged to hold it of the Emperor Lothar III. No ruler did more for the Christianization and civilization of his country.

In his will, Boleslav Wrymouth endeavoured with poor results to alleviate dynastic disputes and tribal particularism by erecting a kind of family federation. He divided Poland into four hereditary principalities, Silesia, Mazovia, Greater Poland (round Gniezno), and Sandomierz, giving each to a son. Further, there was to be a suzerain principality of Cracow, which was to be held by seniority, falling to the eldest Piast for the time being. Poland was indeed too vast, too uncivilized, and too tribally disunited for one man, unless as gifted as Boleslav, to rule directly with the scanty means of a medieval monarch. A distinct nation had hardly been formed when Silesia was drawn towards Bohemia and Germany and Sandomierz towards Russia, while backward Mazovia was half heathen still. The rising magnates, too, dowered with estates, preferred a provincial prince. Although the constitution of Boleslav III was preserved and a succession of Great Princes strove to maintain their rights, their efforts failed in the civil wars which encouraged foreign intervention. Boleslav IV (1146–73) submitted (1157) for the last time to be the vassal of the Emperor Barbarossa. Worse still, the Wends and western Pomeranians became parts of the Empire, while the Piast Dukes of Silesia grew wholly Germanized. A flood of German colonists, townsmen and peasants, poured into these territories. Casimir II the Just (1177–94) won more by inheritance than by insisting on his suzerain rights. His son, Leszek I the White (1202–27), transformed the suzerain principality of Cracow (Lesser Poland) into his personal inheritance, but the change left the position of Great Prince still one to be fought for. More important, perhaps, was the entrance of effective Church reform into Poland in his reign. Gradually, clerical celibacy and ecclesiastical immunity were introduced in the several principalities. When in 1241 the Mongol invasion took place, the then regent, Henry II the Pious of Silesia, was defeated and slain in the battle of Liegnitz (9 April). Fortunately, the Mongols did not return, but the devastation they inflicted on Poland left weakness and depopulation behind.

During the twelfth century the Polish princes were not only distracted by rivalries with Germany and Bohemia to the west and with Hungary and Russia to the east; ambition and self-defence urged them to expand against the heathen towards the north and the Baltic coast. As we have seen, although they lost west Pomerania to Germany, they kept the suzerainty over the Christianized Poles of east Pomerania (Pomerellen) and its coastline by the mouth of the Vistula, but their attempts to conquer the southern Balts further east, who were stubborn heathen, were vain. All these barbaric tribes dwelt amid lakes, marshes, and dense primeval forest. Of the Balts, the Prussians held the seaboard from the Vistula to the Niemen; from the Niemen to the Dvina was roughly the land of the Lettish tribes; inland in the impenetrable woods round the Niemen were the Lithuanians; on the Narew, south of the Prussians, lived the restless Yatvags (Jadzwings). The northern neighbours of the Balts were Finnish tribes, the Ests, Livs, and others, who were exposed to Russians, Scandinavians, and eventually Germans but not to the Poles.

Apart from Danish conquest round Reval in Estonia, the first Western enterprise of conversion, which speedily became a crusade, in these parts was German. In 1201, after more peaceful beginnings, the Saxon Albert (*ob.* 1229), under the patronage of Innocent III, led a crusade from Lübeck to found Riga in Latvia, of which he became bishop. To maintain his conquests he obtained from the Pope (1204) the foundation of the Knights of the Sword, who, what with conversion and force applied equally against heathen and Russian rivals, founded a feudal crusading state ruled chiefly by a German aristocracy. Meanwhile, largely in self-defence against continual raids, the Polish Prince of Mazovia, Conrad, adopted the same programme of forcible conversion against the Prussians and Yatvags. His own crusades did little, and in 1228–30 he came to an agreement with Herman of Salza, the Grand Master of the Teutonic Order (1210–39). Herman had already diverted the energies of his wealthy and warlike knights from the Holy Land to a more hopeful crusading in Hungary. He eagerly seized the opportunity of conquering infidel territory in the north. Authorized to conquer by both Pope and Emperor, he received from Prince Conrad the grant of Chelmno (Kulm), and the Order began its new career. Admirably led and organized, supported by the Poles, the Knights completed the conquest of Prussia only after fifty years of hard fighting. They built great castles and fortified towns, they introduced large numbers of German settlers, both feudal nobles and peasants, and forcibly converted the stubborn natives. So high did their credit stand that in 1237 the Knights of the Sword were amalgamated with them at their own request. Now, however, their rapid expansion came to a halt. They schemed to enlarge their Livonian dominion by a crusade against the schismatics of northern orthodox Russia, and in 1242 on the ice of Lake Peipus endured a decisive rout from Alexander Nevsky, Prince of Novgorod. Against the Russians there was no more advance. A year earlier the prestige of the main Order suffered as severely when the Grand Master shared in the overthrow of the Poles in the battle of Liegnitz against the Mongols.

Meanwhile, a more organized foe than the Prussians had arisen in the Lithuanians, ensconced in their forests and marshes and united under an able prince Mendovg (Mindaugas) (1219–63), and westward the native Prince of Pomerellen, Sventopluk, not only attacked the Order himself but roused all the submissive Prussians, heathen at heart, to revolt against their harsh and German masters. Not till 1253 did Sventopluk come finally to terms, and it needed a supernumerary crusade, in which Otakar II of Bohemia—after whom Königsberg was named—and German princes took part (1254), to rescue the Order from the Prussians, who took years to subdue. Not till 1283 was the struggle, carried on by both sides with merciless atrocities, ended by the extermination or exile of the recalcitrants. At the same time the Order passed through a critical period in Livonia, where formidable revolt was fostered by Mendovg, himself threatened by the insatiable Knights, and by the Russians. At last the Order and the Danes each overcame their rebels, and the deaths in 1263 of Alexander Nevsky and of Mendovg, after which Novgorod was weakened and Lithuania fell into anarchy, relaxed the situation, while southern Prussia was left a desert. The extinction of the princely line and Polish feebleness enabled the Order to annex Pomerellen and Danzig (Gdansk) by unscrupulous proceedings and massacre, which showed its abandonment of the crusading ideal and earned the undying hatred of the Poles. In 1309 the Grand Master transferred his official residence from Venice to Marien-burg in Prussia, and the Order definitely set up as a territorial German power under the nominal suzerainty of Emperor and Pope.

Save for the lands governed independently by the bishops and chapters, the Teutonic Order now ruled the coastlands from Livonia to Pomerellen, to be increased in 1346 by the annexation of Danish Estonia on the Gulf of Finland. It was governed by a Grand Master, elected by the General Chapter of the professed Knights, and his Council of officials. Prussia and Livonia were under subordinate Landmeisters and were subdivided into *Komtureien* in charge of Houses of the Knights. From the first they were the chief German colony of the *Drang nach Osten.* Nobles and burghers were the principal emigrants to Livonia, where they exploited a native population of peasant serfs. Germans of every class swarmed to Prussia, where the surviving tribesmen were made serfs and Germanized. The nobles were given fiefs, and formed an important part of the army. The burghers of the towns received full autonomy and were allowed to join the Hansa League. The peasants, led by their locators, held their hereditary land by rent and services not too hard. For many years they were the most prosperous in Europe.

Similar migrations had long been in progress into Poland itself. Cistercian and Premonstratensian monks had led the way. The Piasts of Silesia from the start welcomed German settlers, and after the Mongol devastation all the Polish princes were anxious to repopulate their ruined lands. As in Prussia, the immigrants came in groups to found or reform both towns and villages. They only paid a rent and enjoyed autonomy under their own law, that of Magdeburg. Poland was permeated by these prosperous settlements, and Lower Silesia in particular, like its princes, became wholly Germanized—Wroclaw became Breslau. The influx of settlers brought a valuable element, which was a model for the native Poles. They learnt the use of the iron plough, the 'open-field' system, and the methods of assarting forest and reclaiming marshes. Imitation in tenure, too, came in. By concessions of the princes the Polish peasants obtained the Germans' privileges, and a period of prosperity began, in which the population increased and overflowed into the empty lands of the Yadvags and Prussians as well as eastward towards Brest-Litovsk and to the Carpathians.

All the same, the period after the Mongol invasion was one of political disaster and decline. The princes were at discord. Silesia became a fief of the Empire. After 1290 a foreign ruler, Wenceslas II of Bohemia, as we have seen, fought for the dominion of the country. Although Przemysl, Prince of Greater Poland, as leader of a nationalist movement, succeeded in being crowned king at Gniezno in 1295, he was murdered next year; so Wenceslas proceeded in his piecemeal conquest, and was crowned at Gniezno (1300).

But his death and that of his son left the fate of Poland still in the melting-pot.

As in Bohemia, these centuries in Poland saw a sweeping change in society. By 1100 the disruption of the ancient clans, although not of the wider tribal provinces, was accomplished. The rule of the prince and his castellans was supreme. But to secure the support of the Church and his own followers, he was obliged from 1100 to 1300 and beyond to make ample and continuous grants of lands and privileges, like the Frankish kings in the West. Bishops and monasteries earliest received exemption from taxation and secular officials. So in the sequel did magnates and knights. Townsmen and peasants were not slow to follow suit. But the evolution of the noble class was the most important, especially that of the knights. With hereditary land and jurisdiction over it, they retained enough of the clan spirit to adopt in the thirteenth century a common coat of arms for each clan and a common surname from the clan slogan. These helped to make them more linked together and more provincially minded than their like elsewhere. The class cohesion of magnates and knights limited the power of the provincial Piast princes; the castellans ceased to function as princely officials, and the prince's council, or *Wiec*, became composed of the provincial magnates. The conqueror Wenceslas did indeed introduce a new royal official, the *Starosta* (or sheriff), but of the solidarity of a Polish nation there was little trace.

(5) RUSSIA AND THE MONGOLS, 1015–1263

The dominating factors in Russian history after the death of St Vladimir I were the steady expansion of the Eastern or Russian Slavs, more especially towards the north-east, the perpetual subdivision of them among the multiplying scions of the house of Rurik, leading to endless civil war and rivalry for the Great or suzerain Princedom, and the Byzantine character of Russian civilization and Christianity, which was expressed and intensified by the fact that the Metropolitan of Kiev and Russia was all but invariably a Greek monk. Even when the wealth-giving trade-route between Novgorod and the Baltic and Constantinople was severed by the Cuman invasion of the Ukrainian steppes in 1068, the cultural and ecclesiastical connexion held fast. After a preliminary civil war, the Great Princedom of Kiev (1019) and then (1035) all Russia was attained by Vladimir's son Yaroslav, whose later reign was the golden age of Byzantine Kiev. It was a time of commerce, expansion and church-building in the beautiful Byzantine style. A last attack on Constantinople, which failed (1043–6), ended in the marriage of the Great Prince's son Vsévolod to a Byzantine princess, while his daughters married kings of France and Norway. When Yaroslav died (1054), discord among the princes again became the rule. In 1068 it was intensified when the Great Prince Izyaslav was overthrown and Russia cut short in the Ukraine by the Cumans (Pólovtsy), and was not comparatively appeased until Vsévolod (1078–93), beloved by clergy and people, succeeded. The civil wars on his death, in which the Cumans took part, produced at least a kind of family statute at Lyúbech (1096), if it did not much allay the strife.

The agreements of Lyúbech had a lasting effect on the territorial history of Russia, for they established the hereditary right of all princes to their father's appanage, and thus localized the branches of the family. The precedence of the original Russia of Kiev was maintained, and the eldest prince of the descendants of Vladimir I had a right to it and the Great Princedom, which more often than not he made effectual. But this did not mean administrative unity. The other princes ruled their shares uncontrolled after the death of Yaroslav (1054), and the incessant subdivision among co-heirs created a swarm of principalities, whose resources were developed by their owners. The two principal branches were those of Chernigov, the Ol'govichi, and of Pereyaslavl, the Monomakhovichi. The Ol'govichi's lands stretched far to the east to Ryazan and beyond; those of the Monomakhovichi included Smolensk, a great junction-town of Russia, and the north-east. Novgorod in the north was usually under a son of the Great Prince of Kiev, and did not acquire a dynast of its own, which had remarkable constitutional results. Polotsk and White Russia were something of a backwater, exposed to Lithuanian influences. Galicia (Halich) and Volhynia were bones of contention between Russia and Poland, although the people were Red Russians (Ruthenians).

Russian society was urban and aristocratic. The peasants (*smerdy*), whether free or slaves, grew in importance as a source of revenue to their lords, who organized them in manors as tillage increased. The aristocracy were the boyars, either members of the prince's *druzhina* (the German *comitatus*), who were the trained armed force, or wealthy townsmen who acquired rural estates. As landed boyars might well be members of the *druzhina*, the two classes might coalesce, but in Galicia the landed boyars formed an opposition to the prince and in commercial Novgorod they were quite independent of him. A third element was the people of the large towns, who formed a militia. In the twelfth century their assembly, the *vêche*, played a political role. The prince, who defended his subjects, was ruler and judge, drawing his revenue from his manors, fines, tolls, and dues. The Church was under Byzantine Canon Law, and with its dependants was immune from lay jurisdiction.

For a generation the dominating spirit in Russia was a son of Vsévolod, Vladimir Monomakh (so-called from his imperial, Byzantine grandfather), who devised the conference at Lyúbech, and another at Vitichev (1100) to quell the aggressions of David of Volhynia. He was at first Prince of

Pereyaslavl, Smolensk, and Rostov, and later succeeded to the Great Princedom of Kiev (1113–25). A brave warrior against the Cumans, a good Christian, a generous lord, a capable administrator, and an author, whose *Instructions* to his son are an attractive self-revelation, he established a peace which lasted till the death of his son, the Great Prince Mstislav (1125–32). Then the turmoil among the ambitious princes began again, punctuated by the able reign of Rostislav (of Smolensk and Novgorod) as

Fig. 154. Cathedral of St Demetrius, Vladimir

Great Prince (1159–68). Then Andrew (Andrey), Prince of north-eastern Suzdal', stormed Kiev with a pitiless massacre (1169), and transferred the Great Princedom to his own capital at Vladimir. The predominance of Kiev in Russian history was closed, although it was still the see of the metropolitan and retained its religious prestige. Its territory contracted as the Cumans seized the Ukrainian steppes.

In the ensuing period of disintegrations, Smolensk maintained best the unitary tradition, but Galicia and Volhynia cut a great figure. Roman (1198–1205) was a powerful prince. After thirty years of civil wars his son

Daniel (1235–65), who was crowned king by a papal legate, fostered the commerce and industry of his fertile land. Latin influences were strong in Galicia, although in the end Daniel broke with the Papacy, and helped to isolate it from its kindred principalities. On the other hand, a wholly Russian dominion was that of Suzdal', or Vladimir on the upper Volga. Its real founder was that Andrew Bogolubski (*ob.* 1174), a grandson of Monomakh, who wrecked Kiev. His brother the Great Prince Vsévolod 'Big-nest' (1176–1212) forced neighbouring princes into vassalage, laying the foundation of the future central state of Muscovy. Unlike the rest of Russia, the princedom of Vladimir looked eastward. It was in relations with the trading White Bulgars of the middle Volga. Its stone churches were built on Georgian and Armenian models. Vsévolod's numerous offspring, however, divided the principality.

The Cumans of the Ukraine had by no means been invariable foes of the southern princes. Now they were to become allies against a more terrible invasion of the nomad Ural-Altaic tribes, that of the Mongols, or Tartars, as they were called in Europe. For its origins we must turn to Far Eastern history. We have seen that the initial shock which produced the migrations in Europe was usually given, as by the Huns and Avars, by movements of the nomads on the Chinese frontier. Such a movement was that of the Mongols, the most formidable of all. Eastward of the Turkish tribes and north-west of China wandered the Mongols proper. One of their chieftains was the genius for war and domination, Temujin, the greatest conqueror in history, who was born about 1154 on the banks of river Onon. In continual warfare he united not only the Mongols but the neighbouring Turkish tribes, such as the Tatars (from whom the Western name of Tartars, due to a Latin pun with Tartarus, is derived) as far as the Altai mountains. In 1206 he assumed the title of Jenghiz Khan, 'the very mighty lord', in a Kuriltai or general assembly of his vassals, the majority of whom were Turkish tribes, now under Mongol supremacy. Illimitable conquest was the aim of Jenghiz Khan. He had the art of selecting generals of the greatest capacity, who knew how to use the nomads' method of fighting with forethought and organization. The submission of every fresh tribe, as well as the flight of the unsubmissive, added yearly to the barbaric flood which expanded on all sides. In 1213 Jenghiz Khan himself directed the first assault on the Empire of North China, then under the rule of the Manchu dynasty of the Kin, while South China formed the Empire of the native Sung. The desperate war with immense slaughter outlasted his life, but the final victory in 1234 was already certain. Meanwhile by 1218 the land now called Eastern Turkestan had fallen under his sway. Next year he led his armies farther west. The Turkish Shah of Khwarizm (Khiva), Ala-ad-Din Muhammad, had recently founded a wide empire, including Transoxiana and Persia. Appalling destruction and massacre marked the victories of

Jenghiz Khan, which reached the Zagros mountains. Eventually the last Khwarizm Shah, Jalal-ad-Din, with a horde of followers, broke westward (1231) to deal (1244) a fatal blow to the moribund kingdom of Jerusalem.

Jenghiz Khan died in 1227 in full career of his merciless conquests. No palliation of his atrocities is possible, but his genius as a ruler is undeniable. His Empire introduced safety for merchants and travellers throughout and linked for a hundred years Europe and Cathay in a spasmodic intercourse. He even showed favour to divines, physicians, and men of learning, the remnants of the civilization he destroyed. The Mongols, indeed, were tolerant of all religions, whether from indifference or all-embracing superstition.

Jenghiz Khan's choice of his third son, Ogdai, as his successor in the Great Khanate, was ratified by a Kuriltai (1229), as was also the allotment of tribes among his other descendants. Ogdai, who ruled in his capital of Karakorum, completed the conquest of North China, in concert with his brother Tule, and began the war with the Sung of South China. His brother Jagatai was chief Khan of Transoxiana and East Turkestan. To the sons of his dead eldest brother Juji were assigned the tribes west of the Oxus and the Sea of Aral and an advancing frontier. Already under Jenghiz Khan a Mongol army of conquest and reconnaissance had crossed the Volga and inflicted an overwhelming defeat on the Cumans and south Russian princes on the river Kalka (Kalmius) (1224). Now Bātu, a son of Juji, was sent under the guidance of the best Mongol general, Subatai, for more lasting conquest. In 1236 he conquered the White Bulgars. Next year he destroyed Ryazan and Vladimir, and only turned back from Novgorod (1238) because of the swamps in his way. The customary horrors of a Mongol invasion accompanied his march throughout. In 1240 he moved west. Kiev was burnt with a massacre. Then Bātu divided his forces. One division rode through Poland, met Duke Henry of Silesia and the Grand Master of the Teutonic Order at Liegnitz, inflicting on them a heavy defeat (1241), and turned south through Moravia to Hungary. The other division under Subatai himself crossed the Carpathian mountains into Hungary. There at Mohi on the river Theiss it completely routed the full force of Hungary under King Béla IV (11 April 1241). Hungary and Croatia were devastated and rendered helpless, while Pope and Emperor, at bitter odds, contented themselves with circulars. Dismay spread throughout the West, when salvation came from the news of the death of Ogdai and the vacancy of the Great Khanate. Bātu withdrew (1242) to intervene in the Kuriltai, and never renewed his invasion of Europe. Poland and Hungary were left to heal their wounds, but Russia and the Cumans remained under Bātu's domination. He fixed his residence at Saray on the lower Volga, where he and his successors ruled as Khans of the Golden Horde, or of Kipchak.

Besides the terrible destruction perpetrated, Bātu's campaigns fixed on the greater part of Russia the so-called 'Tartar Yoke', which lasted two centuries and profoundly influenced the land. Certain districts escaped its full weight. Novgorod, although tributary, was practically independent; Galicia, also a tributary, was little molested until the Golden Horde in 1282 wrecked it in a devastating passage towards Poland, after which it receded from daylight knowledge, to be annexed by Poland in the next century (1347). White Russia, on the other hand, was subdued by Mendovg of Lithuania and his successors. Meanwhile Great Russia and its many princes, as well as Kiev and its Little Russian territory, remained truly subject to the Golden Horde, whose overlordship was expressed by a poll-tax—the clergy being exempt—and occasional punitive raids. The Great Princes of Vladimir and their kindred princes received their authority by *yarlyks* (charters). To obtain and keep them involved frequent visits to Saray and even to Karakorum and liberal bribery and corruption. The most eminent Great Prince, St Alexander Nevsky (1246–63), the victor over Swedes and Teutonic Knights, spent most of his reign in these journeys in the endeavour to alleviate the lot of his subjects by unqualified sub mission. After his death a miserable rivalry for appointment to the pro fitable Great Princedom occupied the ever more numerous princes. The tribute meantime was collected by Tartar commissioners, who even insisted on censuses. The principal beneficiary in these subject years was at first the Orthodox Church, at last independent of the princes and receiving *yarlyks* direct from the Tartars, besides being tax-free and ruling its large estates.

An exceptional position and an exceptional history belonged to Novgorod, the northern metropolis. It derived its corn-supply from the region of the upper Volga, but its wealth and greatness were due to its immense northern hinterland reaching to the Arctic Ocean, from which came its exports, furs, fish, walrus, falcons, mica, and silver. These were distributed to Europe by the merchants of the German Hansa towns, who were friendly visitors. Swedes and Teutonic Knights both coveted the wealthy city. Fortunately the then Prince of Novgorod was Alexander, future Great Prince. In 1240 he won his surname of Nevsky by defeating the Swedes under Earl Birger on the river Neva; in 1242 he routed the Teutonic Knights on Lake Peipus. These victories kept Novgorod both Russian and orthodox. Its culture and art gave the lead to Great Russia, its architecture was both Byzantine and original, and its religious painting was the prelude to later schools. Its constitution and that of its dependent Pskov were really republican. With no hereditary line of princes, in the twelfth century they elected their *posadnik*, the prince's lieutenant, as well as their bishop. In the thirteenth century Novgorod elected its prince usually from the line of Vladimir with strictly limited powers as a chief magistrate. Ultimate authority was vested in the *vêche*, the general assembly, but it could only shout 'Aye' or 'No' to proposals, and fight the question out if the answer was not clear. The boyars were a plutocracy with enormous estates in the hinterland. Below them were the merchants organized in gilds, while the city was divided into an infinity of small local communities. The subject territory outside was composed of small districts and towns, governed by their own oligarchs.

Although the Mongol empire was loosely compounded of tribes and khanates, a certain amount of unity was maintained under the Great Khan

Fig. 155. Church of Spas Neredica near Novgorod

and the frontiers continued to advance. With the death of Ogdai's son Kuyuk (1246–8), Mangu (1251–9), a son of Tule, was elected Great Khan. Along with his brother Kublai he undertook the conquest of the Sung Empire of South China, during which he died. Civil war followed between Kublai (Kubla Khan) and his brother Arikbuka, which ended (1264) in the victory of Kublai. The Great Khan's ambitions were eastern. He finally subjugated southern China (1279), and reigned as a Chinese Emperor at his capital of Khan Balig (Cambalu, the modern Peking). The organization of Persia had been entrusted by Mangu to a third brother, Hūlāgū, founder of the dynasty of the Il-khans. Already the Mongol generals had invaded Asia

Minor, given a fatal blow to the Seljūks of Rūm in the battle of Kuza-Dagh (1243), and extended their suzerainty to the Mediterranean. Hūlāgū crushed the political power of the once formidable Assassins (1256). There remained the Abbasid Caliphate, which lingered on, a petty state, at Baghdad, upheld by the general reverence of orthodox Moslems. Its doom was now sealed. After a month's siege Baghdad surrendered (15 February 1258), and Hūlāgū perpetrated the worst of the Mongol butcheries. It is said that 800,000 captives, including Caliph Musta'sim and his family, were massacred. Another campaign reduced Syria in like manner as far as Damascus (1260), when Hūlāgū left his army to take part in the Kuriltai on Mangu's death. He thus escaped the defeat at Ain Jalut, the first check to Mongol conquest. Moslem civilization has never recovered from the destruction inflicted on the lands of Nearer Asia by the Mongols from the invasion of Transoxiana to that of Syria.

The reign of Kublai Khan (1259–94) marks an epoch in Mongol history.

Hitherto the sole achievement of the Mongols had been an invincible military organization. Their wars were wars of desolation. No victims survived their fury, and they learnt little or nothing from the civilizations they destroyed. Kublai, however, was of a new type. He became, as first of the Yuan dynasty, a genuine Chinese Emperor. He was not merciless and cared for the welfare of his subjects. He fostered learning and the arts. He undertook public works. He guarded communications, even the great route to the West. But the military spirit and hardihood of the Mongols

Fig. 156. Ulugh Begh medresseh, Samarkand

evaporated in a civilized, Chinese environment. Their rapid degeneracy resulted in their expulsion from China (1355–68) by the native Ming dynasty. The allegiance of the western khanates had grown nominal. Curiously enough, in the same period (1369) the Moslem Turk, Tīmūr Leng ('the Lame', Tamerlane), was founding a new empire in Transoxiana, whence he issued forth to conquer Persia and Nearer Asia. With him Islam renewed its military strength—the Il-khans of Persia had already adopted it for their religion—and incidentally the route between Europe and China was broken. Previously, however, the route, though long, was safe. The hope of converting the heathen but tolerant Mongols had first opened it. In 1245 Friar John of Plano Carpini had reached Karakorum as an envoy of Pope Innocent IV, and Friar William of Rubruck (Rubruquis) arrived in 1255 as the envoy of St Louis. Unsuccessful as missionaries, although others later gained some converts in China and Persia, their accounts informed Europe, and merchants followed in their wake. One of them, the famous Venetian, Marco Polo, spent eighteen years (1274–92) in China in the employment of Kublai, and returned (1295) to Venice by the sea-route from China to the Persian Gulf. His narrative of his travels, dictated or put together in a Genoese prison, was an account, wonderfully accurate for his time, of Asia and China itself under the Mongols. With the fall of the Yuan dynasty and the wars of Tamerlane, however, the Far East was once more shrouded by the veil which had been so marvellously lifted.

(6) THE KINGDOM OF JERUSALEM AND THE MAMLUKS

After the Third Crusade the kingdom of Jerusalem was confined to the coastal strip from Jaffa to Tyre; to the north Tripolis and Antioch maintained their autonomy. Elaborate fortifications protected all three, and the fact that the Latins possessed the Syrian ports, which were the exits of the caravan routes, was a source of strength. Besides, Venice and Genoa still commanded the sea. For a time the division of Saladin's dominions among his sons paralysed the Moslems, but when his brother Saphadin (Al-Adil) of Egypt (1199–1218) reunited most of them under his suzerainty the situation of the Latins deteriorated. After brief reigns of the Cypriote Lusignans, the King of Jerusalem, the adventurer John of Brienne, husband of Conrad of Montferrat's daughter Mary, was insistent on a new crusade to support him. Innocent III and Honorius III, as we have seen, organized and financed the Fifth Crusade for the recovery of the Holy Land. A great host from all the West assembled at Acre. With some strategic insight it was resolved on King John's advice to attack the Moslems in the heart of their power in Egypt. The port of Damietta, its eastern entrance, was besieged and at last captured (1218–19). Saphadin at its taking was already dead, and his son Sultan Kamil (1218–38) in despair at the danger offered to surrender Palestine if Damietta were restored to him. The soldier King John was ready to accept the terms, but the papal legate, Cardinal Pelagius, who had already mismanaged the Greek Church at Constantinople and considered himself now commander-in-chief, was too elated by the expectation of German reinforcements and even of the coming of Frederick II himself to assent with the glittering lure of the conquest of Egypt before his eyes. The crusaders' singular ignorance of the difficulties of advance among the rivers and canals of the Nile Delta strengthened his case, and after long delay the march on Cairo began (1221). The army was soon entangled in the inundation among the branches of the Nile at Mansurah, and starving and dying were glad to buy retreat at the cost of surrendering Damietta. The men were daft, said Philip Augustus, who for the sake of a town had refused a kingdom.

Very different was the policy of Frederick II in his long-delayed Sixth Crusade (1228). He well knew the straits of Kamil, perplexed by family dissensions and fears of new Turkish invasions from the East. By treaty Jerusalem and the Holy Places were ceded to him under promise of toleration. But Frederick, become king-consort of Jerusalem by his marriage with the heiress, King John's daughter, was at odds with Pope Gregory IX —he had to crown himself—and with the fanatical Military Orders. His reign was a failure, although his boy-son Conrad was acknowledged, while the Latins were rent with disputes. A straggling Crusade, in which Earl Richard of Cornwall took part (1239–41), recovered Ascalon. The Latins then allied with Damascus against Egypt with the consequence that Sultan Ayyub of Egypt called in the wandering Khwarazmian Turks, ousted, as we have seen, by the Mongols. The Khwarazmians sacked Jerusalem, and then with the Egyptian army under Baibars Bunduqdari routed the Latins in the fatal battle of Gaza (17 October 1244).

The disaster roused St Louis of France to his first Crusade. It was a remarkable replica of the Fifth, pursued with the same aims and the same ignorant unwisdom. He, too, took Damietta, easily this time (1249), advanced on Cairo, was defeated and blockaded at Mansurah, and compelled to surrender (1250). He bought his freedom with Damietta and a huge ransom. Meanwhile violent faction and suicidal rivalries vexed the moribund kingdom of Jerusalem. The death of Conradin (1268) opened a dispute over the succession, which was only nominally settled by the reigns of the Lusignans of Cyprus. Templars and Hospitallers were bitter enemies, while Venice and Genoa were at open or covert war.

On the other hand Egypt was becoming a military state of the first quality. More than his predecessors Sultan Ayyub had relied on his guard of Turkish and Circassian slaves, his Mamlūks, trained and tried soldiers. In 1250 they disposed of the throne, exalting one or other of their captains to be Sultan. It was an uncertain honour, for revolt might meet an unpopular conqueror, yet the Mamlūk Sultans did great things. On 3 October 1260 Sultan Qutuz inflicted on the Mongols their first defeat at Ain Jalut in Galilee. His general was the Emir Baibars Bunduqdari, who promptly murdered him and became Sultan. This was the death-knell of the Latin kingdom, for Baibars drove the Mongols beyond the Euphrates and showed himself a relentless foe of the Christians. In 1268 Jaffa and Antioch fell into his hands. St Louis's second Crusade, as we saw, miscarried at Tunis; Edward I of England, who came to Acre, did at least secure a long truce, but the disunited Latins drew little profit from the respite. Sultan Qala'un renewed the war. In 1289 he sacked Tripolis. Acre was now the only notable stronghold left to the Christians, and ill adapted to resist. It was 'the sink of Christendom', since the rascality of Europe gathered there. Owing to exemptions and trading colonies its government consisted of seventeen distinct communities. Help from the West was scant and feeble. After a six weeks' siege and stubborn fighting Sultan Khalil finally stormed the city on 18 May 1291, a few minor places were taken by July, and the Latin kingdom, save as an empty title, came to an end.

After their expulsion from Syria the Latins' Levantine territory consisted of the kingdom of Cyprus under the dynasty of Lusignan. It was thoroughly feudalized on the model of Jerusalem and was prosperous as a port of call for the eastern trade. On the coast of Asia and in the Taurus the kingdom of Little Armenia, under its fighting kings, kept at bay the Seljūks of Rūm and the Moslems of Syria, not to mention its Latin Christian neighbours of Antioch. The feudalism of the Latins was copied, but the Armenians, in spite of their politic kings, were firm in their Monophysitism. On the Mongol invasion they became vassals (1244) of the Great Khan, and this alliance stood them in good stead against the Mamlūks when Baibars and Qala'un attacked them, but it was at the cost of being involved in the defeats of the Il-khans of Persia. When the alliance was lost (1302), Little Armenia, torn by dynastic and religious dissension, was in the utmost danger. It, too, however, drew prosperity as an outlet of the oriental trade.

The great asset of the Latins in the Levant was their continued command of the sea, which was in the hands of the Italian sea-towns, Venice, Genoa, and Pisa. Unhappily, co-operation and mutual assistance were unknown to those fiercely rival powers. Open war between Venice and Genoa (1253–70, 1294–9) alternated with sullen, but hardly peaceful truce. Pisa collapsed before Genoa after her crushing overthrow at Meloria (1284). When Acre fell, Venice in a few years made a profitable commercial treaty with the Mamlūks (1299). The Papacy, in whose political schemes the Crusades had long taken a secondary place, was to be more concerned with the pressing defence of the Aegean Sea than with the visionary reconquest of the Holy Land. Crusading was still a fashion, but in other lands against other foes. The expansion of Christendom eastwards had in fact ceased, and was succeeded by an ebb. St Louis was the last to lead a Crusade with the old hopes and ideals.

(7) SCANDINAVIA, c. 1130–c. 1300

The Wars of Pretenders in Scandinavia, which began round about 1130, were primarily a conflict between dynastic claims and national unity, between the idea of the kingdom as a private property, in which all agnates of the royal house demanded a share, and the idea of an indivisible state with an existence of its own. Through the intermarriages of the dynasties civil war in each realm grew into a Scandinavian war.

Unity was attained earliest in Denmark. There by battle and murder Waldemar I the Great (1157–82), grandson of Eric the Evergood, a heavy-handed warrior, gained an undisputed crown. Luckily, he was counselled by a real statesman, Absalon, Archbishop of Lund (ob. 1201), the guiding spirit in Danish politics as long as he lived. In Sweden and Norway the strife lasted much longer and was influenced by Danish intervention. In all three clericalism and feudalism arose, making new demands in government, and from the wars a new society emerged. The Danish kings usually supported the clerical party, and acknowledged the Church as an independent body. Its leaders in each realm were naturally the three archbishops of Lund, Nidaros (Norway) and Upsala (Sweden), who championed the growing ecclesiastical claims. The contest had its vicissitudes. In Sweden, where two rival dynasties fought for the crown, one was anti-clerical. It provided the national saint, King Eric IX (1155–60); yet his grandson Eric X compromised matters by accepting coronation and unction from the Archbishop of Upsala (1210). In Norway, events fell out in a more fundamental and dramatic way, for the kingship was more developed and the Church was led by an aspiring archbishop, Eystein (or Augustine), a faithful papalist. Earl Erling Crooked-neck had set up for king his child son, Magnus V, who only derived Yngling blood from his mother, and remedied his defective title by a sacring at the hands of the archbishop (1163). In return for this alliance, the kingdom was to be held as a fief from St Olaf, the immunities of the Church were increased, and if a legitimate heir was lacking, the

Fig. 157. Gol Stave church, Hallingdal

bishops were to have a deciding voice in the election of a successor. Nowhere else had the Church won such a victory. The situation was reversed, however, by the appearance of a pretender of genius, Sverre, who may have been a Yngling or an impostor, but was a born ruler of men. He obtained the upper hand (1184–1202), and successfully defied the thunders of Innocent III himself. More clearly than the legal experts of Barbarossa he defined, in a pamphlet from his chancery, the supremacy of the kingship and the lay state. None the less his son King Haakon III made his peace with the Church.

In fact, in all Scandinavia the Church was gaining ground, economically, politically, and morally. The forces which made for feudalism made for it too. The kingship did not possess a revenue which could pay its local representatives: they could only be remunerated by their taking over the royal receipts of their districts. It is no accident that in Scandinavia as elsewhere the earliest charters of immunity were granted to the prelates, whose landed wealth equipped them for local rule.

All the same, the chief element in feudal devolution was the combining of military service with administrative power. Denmark was in the van. Already in 1134 a Danish pretender brought a troop of horse-soldiers to the field, doubtless imitating Germany. Expansion in the Baltic against Slavs, Balts, and Finns hastened the development under Waldemar I and his sons. But the new arm meant the decay of the old popular levy. The king needed an expert, immediately available force, with the complete equipment of knights, and must reward and endow this new nobility of king's men. Unlike the mere free farmers they were tax-free. They were charged with the king's local government. They received his local dues in kind as payment. Their offices became fiefs. In the general courts, the Dane-courts, they appeared as an estate of the realm. Dukes and counts and prelates took knights into their service in the same fashion. Meanwhile the old conscription of freemen for war, the *leidang*, was commuted into a money payment by the year 1200. The non-noble peasant became a tax-payer instead of a warrior.

Just as the Danish evolution of feudal tendencies was long behind that in more southerly lands, so was the Swedish half a century behind Denmark. The conquest of western Finland accelerated the movement (1249), and the second king of the Folkung dynasty, Magnus I Barn-lock (1275–90), besides grants of fiefs, decreed tax-freedom for the knight on horseback (1280). In Norway King Magnus V began the practice of appointing royal sheriffs alongside the ancient chiefs. Sverre in his wars so thinned the ranks of the old nobility that he was almost obliged to appoint his sheriffs for every district. The remnant of the nobles in 1208 agreed to accept sheriffdoms also. New and old sheriffs thereafter were fused in a single class of barons, whose élite formed the royal Council and gave assent to royal decrees. For the time being Norway, unlike Denmark and Sweden, was a strictly hereditary monarchy, but feudalism was nevertheless making way.

In foreign affairs during the period, Norway ceded Man and the Hebrides to Scotland in 1266, but expanded (1262) by the submission of the Icelandic chiefs, not to mention that of the tiny colony in Greenland. Sweden, on the other hand, after a century of wars, achieved the final conquest of Finland in 1249 under the great Earl Birger, the founder of the Folkung dynasty. The attempt to expand south of the Gulf of Finland, however, was frustrated by the victory of Novgorod captained by Alexander Nevsky (1240). Denmark, the most populous and wealthy kingdom of the three, was likewise the most ambitious. In alliance with Duke Henry the Lion of Saxony, Waldemar the Great conquered Rügen and part of the eastern coastline. His sons, Canute VI (1182–1202) and Waldemar II the Victorious (1202–41) utilized the fall of Henry the Lion and then the German civil war to extend their dominion over the coast of Mecklenburg and Pomerania. Waldemar II even laid hold of Holstein, Lübeck, and Hamburg, but he was stripped of his German and Wendish annexations when he was treacherously captured and later routed in the battle of Bornhövede (1227). His repeated conquest of Estonia round Reval was more lasting. Still, the Danish attempt to dominate the Baltic had failed.

The thirteenth century was a time of prosperity for all Scandinavia. The increasing population turned from Viking piracy to clearing forests for corn and cattle. Trade, although little of it was in native hands, was flourishing, its mainstay being the herring fisheries off Scania and the cod fisheries off Norway. Southern culture and art invaded the kingdoms, while the Icelandic sagas produced masterpieces in a purely native form. Political organization and unity were progressing. The king's functions were growing. In legislation and jurisdiction he was the mainspring. In Norway Magnus VI the Law-mender was able to create (1276) a common law for his kingdom. But the Church and the feudal nobility had begun to

Fig. 158. *King Magnus the Law-mender of Norway*

limit the king's power. The Church was the best organized and most aggressive element. In Denmark the strife lasted over fifty years from 1245. Archbishop Jacob Erlendson of Lund (1254–74) demanded that Church lands should be exempt from the *leidang*, and a violent struggle ensued, in which spiritual and temporal powers used all their weapons. Archbishop Jens Grand (1284–1302) renewed the strife till Pope Boniface VIII in 1303 accepted a compromise, by which the king retained the *leidang*, but confirmed other Church privileges. In Norway the Archbishop of Nidaros obtained (1277) from Magnus the Law-mender a charter confirming and extending Church privileges. The barons, however, objected to the extensions of economic favours to the clergy, and after a bitter contest secured their repeal (1290). About the same time the Swedish Church peacefully attained a similar position.

The feudal nobility also were paring away royal power. In 1282 the Danish nobles forced King Eric V Clipping (1259–86) to grant a charter, by which he was to summon a diet of nobles yearly and not to inflict punishment save by due process of law. The contest of king and nobles long outlasted his murder for recalcitrance. In Norway and Sweden feudal rights were defined, and by custom the kings could not act without the consent of their diets. The nobility in short was becoming predominant.

In Scandinavia, as in all the West, the Church had in fact taken the lead in political development. Although it was deeply concerned in gaining its special privileges, not to say, supremacy, it had created the idea of the State and had shown the way by example and precept to a civilized State organization. The thirteenth century saw the culmination of this clerical leadership, power, and organization centred in the ecumenic Papacy. Law emanated from it and grew under its influence. The indefinite, customary kingship was limited by charters. In the process, the crystallizing lay and feudal nobility took its share. In interstate relations, the Church had often taken the initiative and exerted a restraining hand. It had moralized political affairs, however imperfectly, however much its action was distorted by its own interests. In the Crusades, it had drawn Europe into a disjointed unity, deceptive indeed, yet a genuine, if passing, victory of the idea of Christendom. Its own European organization and activities under the Papacy had been fruitful of good and ill and had exercised a more durable influence in the trend away from barbarism which its saints inspired and its more mundane statesmen at their best had furthered. Mundane success, however, was accompanied by mundane sins. The Church was losing its spiritual ideals and its aureole of holiness by its own defects, its greed and secular ambitions, its patent lack of scruple, and the elaborate and subtle, but almost mechanical, soulless machinery of its administration and law. The heyday of the Papacy was imperceptibly fading before the developing secular State.

BOOK VIII

THE LEADERSHIP OF FRANCE

CHAPTER 25

ITALY, FRANCE AND GERMANY, 1270–1314

(I) THE PAPACY AND CHARLES OF ANJOU

The long vacancy of the Papacy (1268–71) after the death of Clement IV marks a stage in the decline of its predominance in European politics. Henceforth, whatever its majestic claims, it appears as one competitor among others for secular power. It was dragged down by its entanglement in Italian wars and ambitions, by the consequent secularization of the Roman Curia composed of worldly, if able, officials, statesmen, and even warriors, invaded by feuds and factions, who drove its legal and administrative machine with a shrewd efficiency little inspired by its still loudly professed ideals. Within the prevalent belief in its divine authority there lurked a justified distrust of its motives and methods, which emboldened covert and open resistance to its commands. The heavy taxation of ecclesiastical property, which was necessary to pay its bureaucracy and to finance its political schemes, made it unpopular everywhere, and provided continual occasions for dispute or unhandsome bargaining with lay governments. It was a time, too, when powerful rulers, themselves rival taxers for their wars and bureaucracies, could obtain support from their disillusioned subjects. There were plenty of lay-minded clerics and even educated laymen now to transact their business and maintain their independence with a skill in diplomacy and argument worthy of the Roman Curia itself. The fact that in the fighting world to which it had gradually descended the Papacy was essentially unarmed, and always required and feared a lay champion, reacted on its temporal politics and, although slowly, on its ecclesiastical control as well.

The symptoms of decay, however, were unobserved when the cardinals, resisting the pressure of Charles of Anjou, at last elected (1 September 1271) a Pope who believed in the old order of Papacy and Empire and longed to unite all Christendom for a crusade. Tedald Visconti of Vicenza, who became Gregory X, only reached Rome from Palestine next year with a policy already resolved on. A real Emperor, useful and not dangerous,

763

should terminate the German interregnum. The Greek Church should be reunited to the Latin, while Charles of Anjou should be curbed from his scheme of Byzantine conquests. For these ends Gregory summoned a General Council at Lyons. Meanwhile he turned a deaf ear to King Charles' wish that his nephew Philip III of France should be elected to the Empire, and readily accepted the German electors' choice (1273) of Rudolf of Habsburg to the vacant throne. The General Council of Lyons was a brilliant, but superficial success (1274). Michael Palaeologus purchased safety from Charles by submission to the Union under the Papacy and the papal creed. Papal diplomacy was then directed to North Italy, where the need was pressing. Genoa had become Ghibelline and had baffled (1273) King Charles's armaments to restore the Guelfs. King Alfonso X of Castile had long been a pretender to the Empire. He now could send troops by sea to the Lombard Ghibellines, led by Marquess William VII of Montferrat. A defeat from Marquess Thomas of Saluzzo at Roccavione (1275) shattered Charles's dominion in Piedmont. But Pope Gregory had already induced Alfonso to renounce a project unpopular in Castile, and in a meeting with Rudolf at Lausanne obtained German troopers to bolster up the Guelf tyrant of Milan. The Pope returned to Italy full of hope, when he died at Arezzo (12 January 1276). A friendly Emperor, a guided King of Sicily, a union of Christendom, and a crusade seemed on the point of achievement, but the appearance was hollow; the heavy feet of his contemporaries soon trod through his painted panorama.

After three ephemeral Popes, the cardinals, adhering to Gregory's policy, elected (25 November 1277) a Pope of a more secular mind, John Gaetan Orsini, as Nicholas III. The promotion of relatives was always a temptation to Popes surrounded by men of varying parties and independent power, but Nicholas's desire to exalt the Orsini went beyond older limits. He dreamed of giving them a kingdom in North Italy. Charles was to be confined to Sicily; Rudolf was to keep Germany as a hereditary Empire, while ceding the kingdom of Arles to Charles Martel, the eldest son of Charles of Anjou; the Papal State, enlarged as Gregory X had already demanded by the real government of Romagna, was to be safely cantoned between these balanced monarchies. The easiest point to secure was the formal surrender of Romagna by Rudolf, whose interests were wholly German. He made the surrender with every guarantee. Charles's power had waned further in the north. In January 1278 Archbishop Otto Visconti, the exiled chief of the Milanese Ghibellines, overthrew and captured at Desio the Guelf tyrant of Milan, Napoleon della Torre, and assumed the tyranny himself in alliance with William VII of Montferrat. Pope Nicholas, strong in his native Rome by his family influence and master of his cardinals by a large creation, could take a firm attitude. He removed

Charles from the senatorship and the vicariate of Tuscany (1278), while pressing forward an alliance between him and Rudolf. From the Roman commune he received the direct rule of the city, and exercised it through his brother. At the same time he was intervening in Romagna and Tuscany. Two nephews patched up a momentary peace in distracted Romagna, where the Guelfs of Bologna had driven out the Ghibellines. One of them, the worthy Cardinal Latino Mala-branca, then proceeded to Florence to assuage the troubles there. His new constitution (January 1280), although quickly modified, proved a landmark in Florentine history. He recalled the Ghibellines, and gave them an equal status with the Guelfs, which they lost in a trice. He set up once more the organization of the *popolo* and its captain. A new magistracy, the Four-teen, was to supervise administration and finance. In 1282 this feeble body was superseded by the Priors of the Arts, who, being based directly on the gilds (*Arti*), acquired and retained the rule of the city. In this way Florence passed definitely under the sway of the wealthy traders. She at any rate pro-duced a government of the *popolo* which would work, while in Lombardy city after city took refuge from dis-order under tyrannies.

Fig. 159. Pope Boniface VIII

By then, however, Nicholas III was dead (22 August 1280) and his schemes had vanished in smoke. Charles of Anjou at last succeeded in enforcing the election of a French Pope, Simon de Brie, as Martin IV (February 1281), an able, resolute man subservient to his interests, who gave the rein to his unquenched ambitions. The new Pope made his patron once more senator of Rome and master of the Papal States. He broke at once the sham Union with the Orthodox Church by excommunicating the recalcitrant Greeks, and thus freed Charles's hands for his war of conquest. The king was already overlord of Achaia; the titular Latin Emperor was his son-in-law and catspaw. The Regno was astir with preparations. It had been bitterly oppressed by foreign officials and troops and native tax-gatherers. Charles's remedies had been fruitless, for he kept adding to the

765

19. The Houses of Anjou and Aragon in Naples and Sicily

(a) The House of Anjou in Naples

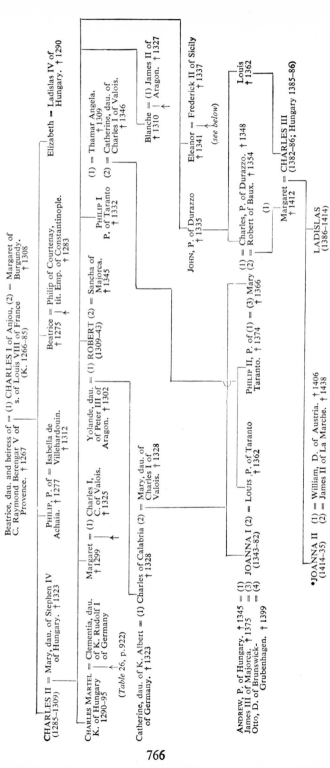

(b) The House of Aragon in Sicily

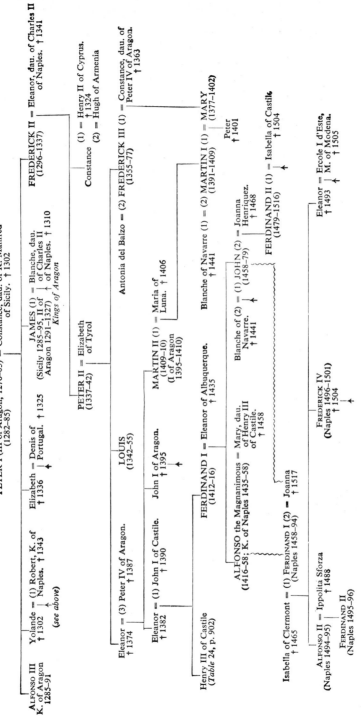

767

burden of taxation, and the yield of the yearly *collectae*, which he had sworn to abolish, was nearly doubled in spite of clerical exemption. The occasional parliaments were no longer assembled under this foreign and ultra-feudal regime.

The enemies of Charles abroad naturally joined hands. Peter III the Great of Aragon, the husband of Manfred's daughter Constance, had long schemed to recover her inheritance. His advisers were two Regnicoli, John of Procida and the Calabrian seaman, Roger Loria. It was John who kept up intelligence with the malcontents in the Regno, especially in Sicily, and who negotiated (1281) a treaty with Michael Palaeologus, now in the utmost danger, and ready to provide treasure for his impecunious new ally. Peter equipped his Catalan fleet, one of the best in the Mediterranean, and levied troops, including the formidable light infantry known as *almugaves*, proclaiming a crusade against Africa, where he landed. But already an explosion against the French, the Sicilian Vespers, had broken out at Palermo. On Easter Monday (30 March) 1282 a French soldier mishandled a young married woman on her way to the church of Santo Spirito. He was struck down, and on all sides the cry of 'Death to the French' was raised. It was the signal for a massacre of men, women, and children of the hated, insolent oppressors. The same atrocious vengeance spread over the island. The victims numbered some 3000 to 4000; and Charles's vicar withdrew from Messina. The impulse of the rebels was to set up communes in vassalage to the Papacy, but Martin IV sternly rejected their prayers, and Charles in wrath diverted his armaments for the East against them. In July he crossed the straits and besieged Messina. The city was nearly starved out when the Sicilians concurred in offering the crown to Peter III, who alone could save them. He landed at Trapani from Barbary on 30 August. Threatened by the Catalan fleet and army, Charles withdrew from the island.

The War of the Sicilian Vespers lasted twenty years. In it Sicily, upborne by a precocious national feeling, held out, with Aragonese aid, against the Angevins, the Papacy, and at times France. The Papacy's policy and prestige had become bound up to its lasting harm with this local and political war. Every resource, spiritual and temporal, was strained for the reconquest. At first both kings played for time with an insincere scheme to decide the issue by the ordeal of a knightly combat. More real was the Pope's decree of deposition against King Peter and of a crusade to make Charles, Count of Valois, younger son of Philip III, King of Aragon. The Catalan and Sicilian fleet under the victorious admiral Roger Loria was King Peter's best defence. When a new invasion of Sicily was imminent, Charles's heir, Charles the Lame, Prince of Salerno, was, in his father's absence, tempted out to a sea-fight in the Bay of Naples (5 June 1284) and captured by Loria. The baffled Charles himself died on 7 January 1285.

His career had ended in failure; he no longer guided Italy as a kind of inverted Hohenstaufen; he had been disappointed of his eastern ambitions; he had exhausted the mainland Regno, which may now be called the kingdom of Naples; and he had lost Sicily, bequeathing an unending, fruitless war to his descendants.

The two regents for the captive Charles II were fully supported by the Roman Curia under successive Popes, Honorius IV (1285–7) and Nicholas IV (1288–92), whose pontificates displayed the growing influence of the Roman factions of the Orsini and Colonna reflected in the cardinals. Some gain of Neapolitan loyalty was secured by reforms, but the French crusade against Aragon was a miserable failure, largely due to Loria's sea-victory by the coast. More hopes were roused by the death of King Peter (November 1285), for the interests of his eldest son, Alfonso III of Aragon, and his second, James of Sicily, drifted apart. The treaty of Canfranc (1288) took Aragon out of the war and released Charles II, leaving the Sicilians to shift for themselves. Alternations of truce and war, in which Sicily had the best by sea and land, were resultless until the sudden death of Alfonso III (1291) promoted James to the throne of Aragon and changed the centre of his interests. His rule of Sicily had been eventful. Under him the Sicilian Parliament had taken shape in imitation of the Aragonese, and become a permanent institution. The *Statuti di Giacomo* formed a basis for national liberties, which lasted till 1816 although unhappily sterilized.

Meanwhile, northern and central Italy had lapsed into a discordant congeries of petty states, to which the decadent Papacy and the feeble Charles the Lame could impart no common purpose. Signs of provincial consolidation, however, there were, although conflicting and unstable. In Tuscany, Florence and her friends put the Tuscan Guelf League on a permanent basis. It maintained a mercenary force of 500 non-Italian troopers. This was a notable step in the decline of the citizen militia and nobility, outclassed in war by these professional soldiers. In trade, goods to or from any ally passed toll-free within the League, much to the advantage of industrial Florence. Pope Martin IV, too, apportioned the collection of the papal tithes among the Tuscan firms, thus guaranteeing the staple of their banking and commercial operations. Ghibelline Pisa, on the other hand, was on the road to ruin. In her rivalry as a naval power with Genoa she was fatally hampered by her exposed *contado* and her enmities in Tuscany. A crushing blow was dealt her by Genoa in the sea-battle of Meloria (6 August 1284), which destroyed her navy and utterly depleted her man-power. She continued a gallant fight amid domestic tragedies, but lost her hold on Sardinia and ceased to be a Mediterranean sea power.

Tyranny and larger territorial units were visible among the Lombard cities, which wished for liberty and autonomy, but could neither keep nor give them. Pelavicini and Ezzelino and latterly the Della Torre of Milan had already ruled a coagulation of cities. Another war-lord, William VII Longsword of Montferrat, pieced together a wide dominion in the west, and led the armies of Milan and many cities in the centre. Yet he was essentially, like Pelavicini, an outside feudal lord with no roots in his towns. He could easily be turned out, and in 1290 was treacherously seized by the Alessandrians, while his waning dominion dissolved. The Visconti were proceeding more securely in Milan with rival dynasts all around them. Thus the last period of the Italian Middle Ages, independent development round sharply differentiated provincial centres, was well under way.

This turning-point of Italian history is rightly called the age of Dante. Although in the public life of his day he was doomed to failure and isolation, it is his genius which brings to life his contemporaries and his times. They are still classified under the categories in which he placed them in the *Divine Comedy*; they cannot escape his portraiture and his verdict. From his youth until his death we see them through his eyes in the colours, lurid, sombre, or sunlit in which he saw them.

(2) THE PAPACY AND THE ITALIAN STATES, 1292–1313

The harmful effects of the War of the Vespers on the Papacy were manifest when Nicholas IV died. The ten surviving Cardinals were divided into political factions embittered by family rivalry. One, headed by the Orsini, was pro-Angevin, determined to pursue the reconquest of Sicily; the other, grouped round the Colonna, was inclined towards a peace of compromise. After two years of deadlock the weary conclave with a sudden impulse to be non-political elected a celebrated hermit, Peter of Murrone, who had for years been secluded in a cave in the Abruzzi (5 July 1294). He took the name of Celestine V and was led to Naples by his monarch, Charles II. His reign was an absurdity; he never went to Rome; at the king's wish he created twelve pro-Angevin cardinals; and, quite unused to business, he reduced the Curia to chaos in a few months. Knowing his own incompetence, and spurred on (it was said) by a pseudo-angelic voice in his bedroom, he pronounced his own abdication, *il gran rifiuto* of Dante, in the hope of returning to his hermitage. The necessary two-thirds majority was then acquired by his reputed adviser, Cardinal Benedict Gaetani, who reigned as Boniface VIII (23 December 1294). The new Pope, a native of Anagni in the Campagna, stood head and shoulders above his colleagues in legal knowledge, diplomatic experience, and business talents, but his orthodoxy and morals were alike questionable, and his temperament was his greatest enemy. He was a law and an idol to himself. He treated men with a truculent scorn, exacerbated by his painful disease, the stone. He possessed a rough-handed dexterity in bribery and intimidation. Yet the hatred he inspired nullified it, just as his engrossing nepotism helped to lame his over-strained pretensions to rule and bend to his will Church and State in Western Christendom.

The new Pope undertook at once with a vigorous hand the government of the Western Church. He revoked the confusing acts of Celestine *en bloc*, with few exceptions, and all unacquired expectations by provision granted since 1285. He soon undertook to classify and add to the papal decretals since Gregory IX, which he published as the *Sext* (1298). His unlucky predecessor, the legality of whose abdication raised doubts, fled to the Abruzzi, but was captured and imprisoned until his death (1296). His memory turned out nearly as dangerous as his life. Nearest to Boniface's heart, however, were two purely secular aims: the subjugation of Sicily, which defied the Papacy, and the elevation of the hitherto undistinguished Gaetani to high rank and wide possessions. In June 1295 a great success was achieved. James II of Aragon, in danger of revolt, gave in, renounced the throne of Sicily, married Charles the Lame's daughter, and eventually brought over his invincible admiral, Roger Loria, as well as John of Procida, to the Angevin side. But the Sicilians, whom he deserted, proved as stubborn as ever. They elected his viceroy, his brother Frederick II, their king (January 1296), with conditions which gave the Parliament control of peace and war and legislation, and some degree of administrative supervision. Boniface, meantime, selected the ablest, but third, son of Charles II, Robert, as heir to Naples, while putting his main trust in bringing over King James and Loria with their Catalans to secure victory.

Domestic opponents of Boniface were the Colonna, led by their two cardinals. They were Ghibellines, desiring reconciliation with King Frederick; they doubted the validity of the Pope's election; and more than all their family greatness was threatened by his enormous purchases of land in the Campagna to endow the Gaetani as well as by a dubious acquisition by marriage of wide lands in the Tuscan patrimony north of the Tiber. In the true fashion of the wild Roman nobles their resentments led to a young lay Colonna, Stephen, later sung by Petrarch, raiding a great papal treasure as it was being brought to Rome (1297). Boniface in a towering rage deprived the Colonna cardinals. They restored the treasure, but declared Celestine's abdication invalid and appealed to a General Council. Interdict, confiscation, and a crusade, the last degradation of the Holy War, were the Pope's answer. By September 1298 he was victorious. Palestrina, the Colonna stronghold, surrendered under false expectations and was razed to the ground. The Colonna fled to exile (1299) to propagate scandal, true and untrue, against their enemy. It was the year after the publication of the *Sext*, and it was followed by the proclamation of 1300 as a Jubilee year. This was a brilliant device to make a pilgrimage to Rome equal in its benefits to a crusade, emphasizing the papal supremacy and enriching the papal coffers. Boniface's diplomacy, seconded by the self-interest of all parties in the crowds of pilgrims, secured a temporary peace in North Italy, and his ministers marvellously arranged plentiful food for them in the Eternal City. The popular impression has found voice in Dante's *Commedia* and Villani's *Chronicle*. By the irony of events the year was also signalized by war to conquer the Tuscan acquisition from its rightful possessors.

The War of the Vespers had not answered the Pope's designs. True that King James had been pricked on to attack his brother, and had won the command of the sea in the battle of Capo Orlando (4 July 1299). But then he had left to the Angevins the war by land. Robert, landing at Catania, attacked from the east, his brother Philip of Taranto from Trapani on the west. Fortune turned with King Frederick's victory over Philip at Falconaria (1 December 1299), where Philip was taken. Robert, no warrior, vainly blockaded Messina, while Boniface looked for a fighting champion in the ex-pretender to Aragon, Charles of Valois. He combined this expedient with his schemes in Tuscany.

There the strife of Florentine factions was reaching a crisis. Trade, manufacture, and banking, with the consequent wealth and population, were still expanding, but the *consorzerie*, whether of older nobles or of later-risen families who adopted their habits, rent the city with their feuds and insolence. They formed the class of magnates who dominated city politics. The middling and lesser gildsmen were more and more resentful, and in 1293, under a reforming noble, Giano della Bella, enacted the famous Ordinances of Justice, not unlike measures already taken at Bologna. By them, magnates, even if gildsmen, were excluded from the Priorate, and were placed under severe laws of exception with regard to their disorders. Giano himself quickly fell from power, but the Ordinances, although slightly modified (1296), were retained. It needed, however, much more than laws to prevent the greater magnates from controlling the legal magistrates and from feud and faction among themselves in doing so. There were besides wealthy *popolani* families, who had escaped being listed as magnates and yet lived as the magnates did. Two factions were speedily prominent, borrowing names from a feud in Pistoia, the Whites or moderate Guelfs to whom Dante belonged, headed by the Cerchi, whose nobility was recent, and the Blacks or extreme Guelfs, headed by Corso Donati, 'the baron,' of ancient Florentine stock. Sheer factious rivalry counted most, but Corso hankered after tyranny, and there were real differences in domestic and foreign policy. After all, the twelve Greater Gilds, who wielded official power, were themselves an oligarchy in the teeming city, where Lesser retail Gilds and the mass of subject workmen did not always accept their lead. The Blacks at first kept ahead, until in

1299 Corso's own misdeeds caused his banishment and put the Whites in power. A plot to overthrow them, almost contemporaneous with the outbreak of a blood-feud between Cerchi and Donati, involved the condemnation of a Spini, a favoured banker of the Papacy. Boniface, in his usual dictatorial manner, now intervened (1300). He nourished hopes of inducing the then King of the Romans, Albert I of Austria, to cede Tuscany to the Papacy, and of making Florence subservient to him. He sent first a mediator, Cardinal Acquasparta, to reconcile the factions. The exiled Blacks would agree to any terms for restoration, but the Whites in possession refused the award (Dante was then one of the Priors), and incurred an interdict. The Pope turned his thoughts to force. He made a compact with Charles of Valois, whose French army was to settle the affairs of Florence before taking up the reconquest of Sicily. The White government combined irresolute negotiations with provocative measures.

Charles of Valois, after a visit to the Pope, marched north towards Florence in October 1301 with the title of Peace-maker. The Whites, quite unprepared and no doubt fearful of the effect of papal hostility on their trade and banking, admitted him within the walls and gave him full powers (5 November). Under cover of his oath to pacify, he was ready to connive at forceful revolution. Corso Donati broke in and rallied his faction and the mob to plunder his opponents. They appointed new priors, but did not dare to touch the Ordinances of Justice. After a feigned reconciliation persecution began. A crowd of death sentences, mostly evaded, as in Dante's case, by flight into exile, were decreed, and a clique of Black Magnates pulled the strings. Charles, handsomely paid for 'jousting with the lance of Judas', departed to earn disgrace in Sicily.

Charles of Valois, who claimed the Latin Empire in right of his second wife, at length landed on the north coast of Sicily in May 1302. His campaign, feebly planned, was a mere fiasco, for his army struggled across the island to Sciacca in the south, taking no town. Isolated, his troops melting away from malaria, he made a peace at Caltabellotta (31 August 1302), which was soon ratified by the disillusioned Charles the Lame, and next year after an angry hesitation by Pope Boniface. Frederick, who married a daughter of his rival, was to be King of Trinacria for life as a vassal of the Papacy. Thus the long War of the Vespers came to an end, although hostilities between Naples and Sicily were renewed in a few years. The Papacy, which had made reconquest a cardinal aim for so long, was obliged to own its defeat in the face of the obstinate islanders. A secondary effect was the dispersal of the Catalan mercenaries. Some took service in Italy; the bulk crossed the sea to the Balkans, where they also made history.

Meanwhile Boniface was in the thick of his quarrel with Philip the Fair, which involved indeed the whole question of the relation of Papacy and Church to the secular governments, and had been growing in urgency in dealings with the Italian cities for over fifty years, but which must be told in the history of its decisive theatre, France. In November 1302, when French aid in the Sicilian war had been finally proved useless by the treaty of Caltabellotta, Boniface issued his bull *Unam Sanctam*, perhaps the high-water mark of papal claims, certainly their most incisive expression. But here the Pope's immoderate nepotism, his furious hectoring of kings, cardinals and cities, his enforced purchases of land from the petty nobles of the Campagna, and above all his family feud with the dispossessed Colonna, all came home to roost. Only with these assets of Colonna propaganda and simmering hatred could Philip have ventured to make his public charges against the Pope and to send his agent, Nogaret, to weave a plot to seize Boniface in his native city of Anagni (May 1303). Nothing is more singular than the Pope's ignorance of the scheme in train, while Nogaret, staying at Staggia, a castle of Philip's Tuscan financier, Musciatto Franzesi, prepared his forces. They included Sciarra Colonna, many Colonna ex-vassals, other nobles, bought out by Boniface and in his employ, and probably Cardinal Napoleon Orsini. The Pope was at Anagni, composing his final bull, *Super Petri solio*, releasing Philip's subjects from their allegiance, which was to be issued on 8 September. But Nogaret anticipated him. With 1600 horse and foot, hoisting the banners of the Papacy and of France, he entered Anagni by treason the day before (7 September 1303) and fought his way to the Gaetani palace. There he seized the Pope, but to carry him away was beyond his power. The supporters of Boniface rallied in the city and in the Campagna, the populace veered to the Pope's side with the cry of 'Death to the foreigners', Nogaret and his men were driven out, and the old Pope, broken and powerless, was released. On 12 September an escort of the Orsini led him to the Vatican, where after some sort of frenzy he died (12 October). Pride was his very being, and, his pride mortally wounded, he must die. A shock was given to the religious feeling of Western Christendom, but it is significant that no one stirred. A long course of greedy and grasping secular politics, often for petty, even nepotistic, ends, combined with flagrantly insolent, hectoring autocracy, had blunted the spiritual weapons, once so dread and so much misused. The magniloquent thunder of the papal bulls, which once could awe, could be truthfully described by Pierre Flote as verbiage compared with the steel sword of the King of France. As a battle-cry the Church was nearly as husky as the Empire.

How weak the unarmed, distrusted Papacy had become amid the chaotic factions of Italy and the organized secular monarchies, was shown by the difficulties of the speedily elected new Pope, unexceptionable in character, record and aims, the peace-maker Benedict XI. He absolved the Colonna ex-cardinals, and patched up an arrangement between them and the Gaetani, who nevertheless fought out their claims for thirty years in the

Campagna. It was impossible to defy Philip, yet inexcusable to condone the outrage of Anagni. So Philip was at once acquitted, while Nogaret and his compeers were threatened with trial. The compromise was rather politic than just.

Banking, trading Florence was the best ally of the Papacy with its European revenue, and Benedict strove for a general reconciliation of her factions. But though all classes below the highest longed for internal peace, the leading Blacks were not only hostile to the exiled Whites but bitter rivals to one another. They proceeded to tumult and outrage. The Pope's peace-making legate, Cardinal Nicholas of Prato, was deluded by false shows and fled, while an abominable use of Greek fire burnt out the heart of Florence (1304). Shortly after (July) the good Pope died. Owing to their own mismanagement the Whites were baffled in an armed attempt to re-enter the city, and the Black oligarchy remained in power. They could strike now with their allies of Lucca at the White stronghold of Pistoia, for Robert of Anjou as Captain of the Tuscan League brought a troop of mainly Catalan mercenaries under Diego de Rat to stiffen their forces in a relentless siege. Meantime, a deadlock existed in the conclave at Perugia. Ultimately Napoleon Orsini secured by unscrupulous intrigue the election of a Gascon, Bertrand de Got, Archbishop of Bordeaux, whom he knew to be in favour with Philip the Fair (5 June 1305). Unknowingly he had transferred the Papacy to France, for the new Pope, Clement V, had himself crowned at Lyons, ordered the Curia to join him, and not unnaturally delayed to enter the turmoil of Italy. The 'Babylonish Captivity' of the Pope at Avignon, where he fixed his residence in 1309, had begun, and was confirmed by a growing French majority of new cardinals.

Clement inherited the policy of Benedict XI as to Florence, but his agent, Cardinal Orsini, proved unequal to the Black leaders, who defied an interdict. Pistoia was starved out, Bologna drove out her moderates, and the Pope found it best to relent (1309). The ruling clique at Florence, however, rent by its own dissensions, was really weakening. Its members were bidding against one another for popularity. At length popular feeling asserted itself. The Ordinances of Justice were reinforced by the appointment of a new magistrate, the Executor of Justice, to maintain them with the aid of a revived militia. Corso Donati, outplayed by his rivals, made one last attempt at revolution, but was overcome and killed by the Catalan troopers (October 1307). The days of the fighting magnate were over. His cunning opponents, too, were dying off, and were replaced by new *popolani* families, who could serve as priors and broke with the tradition of street fighting. Their rivalries and factions and the discord between Greater and Lesser Arts were carried on with less violence and more circumspection. At any rate Florence had escaped tyranny. Astonishing is the contrast between the bloodshed, intrigue, truckling, and cruelty of the day and the

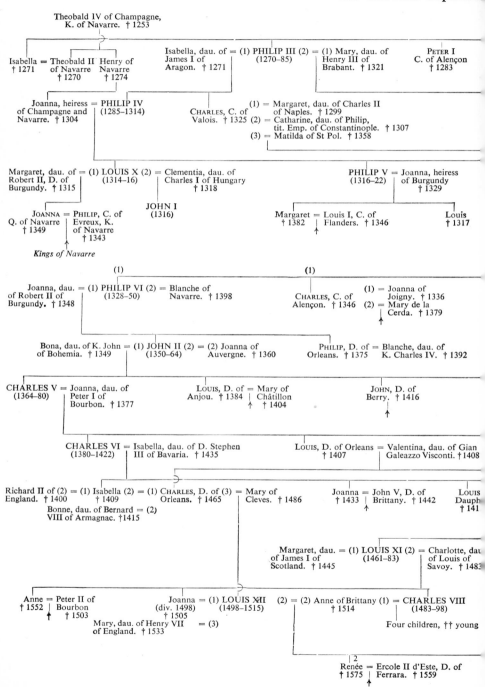

Theobald IV of Champagne,
K. of Navarre. † 1253

Isabella = Theobald II Henry of
† 1271   of Navarre Navarre
          † 1270   † 1274

Isabella, dau. of = (1) PHILIP III (2) = (1) Mary, dau. of   PETER I
James I of   (1270–85)   Henry III of   C. of Alençon
Aragon. † 1271   Brabant. † 1321   † 1283

Joanna, heiress = PHILIP IV
of Champagne and (1285–1314)
Navarre. † 1304

                  CHARLES, C. of
                  Valois. † 1325

(1) = Margaret, dau. of Charles II
      of Naples. † 1299
(2) = Catharine, dau. of Philip,
      tit. Emp. of Constantinople. † 1307
(3) = Matilda of St Pol. † 1358

Margaret, dau. of = (1) LOUIS X (2) = Clementia, dau. of
Robert II, D. of   (1314–16)   Charles I of Hungary
Burgundy. † 1315   † 1318

PHILIP V = Joanna, heiress
(1316–22) of Burgundy
           † 1329

JOANNA = PHILIP, C. of
Q. of Navarre Evreux, K.
† 1349   of Navarre
              † 1343

Kings of Navarre

JOHN I
(1316)

Margaret = Louis I, C. of
† 1382   Flanders. † 1346

Louis
† 1317

(1)

Joanna, dau. = (1) PHILIP VI (2) = Blanche of
of Robert II of   (1328–50)   Navarre. † 1398
Burgundy. † 1348

(1)

CHARLES, C. of
Alençon. † 1346

(1) = Joanna of
      Joigny. † 1336
(2) = Mary de la
      Cerda. † 1379

Bona, dau. of K. John = (1) JOHN II (2) = (2) Joanna of
of Bohemia. † 1349   (1350–64)   Auvergne. † 1360

PHILIP, D. of = Blanche, dau. of
Orleans. † 1375   K. Charles IV. † 1392

CHARLES V = Joanna, dau. of
(1364–80)   Peter I of
            Bourbon. † 1377

LOUIS, D. of = Mary of
Anjou. † 1384   Châtillon
                † 1404

JOHN, D. of
Berry. † 1416

CHARLES VI = Isabella, dau. of D. Stephen
(1380–1422)   III of Bavaria. † 1435

LOUIS, D. of Orleans = Valentina, dau. of Gian
† 1407   Galeazzo Visconti. †1408

Richard II of (2) = (1) Isabella (2) = (1) CHARLES, D. of (3) = Mary of
England. † 1400   † 1409   Orleans. † 1465   Cleves. † 1486
Bonne, dau. of Bernard = (2)
VIII of Armagnac. †1415

Joanna = John V, D. of
† 1433   Brittany. † 1442

LOUIS
Dauph
† 141

Margaret, dau. = (1) LOUIS XI (2) = Charlotte, dau
of James I of   (1461–83)   of Louis of
Scotland. † 1445   Savoy. † 148

Anne = Peter II of
† 1552 Bourbon
        † 1503

Joanna = (1) LOUIS XII (2) = (2) Anne of Brittany (1) = CHARLES VIII
(div. 1498) (1498–1515)   † 1514   (1483–98)
† 1505
Mary, dau. of Henry VII = (3)
of England. † 1533

Four children, †† young

2
Renée = Ercole II d'Este, D. of
† 1575   Ferrara. † 1559

and the House of Valois

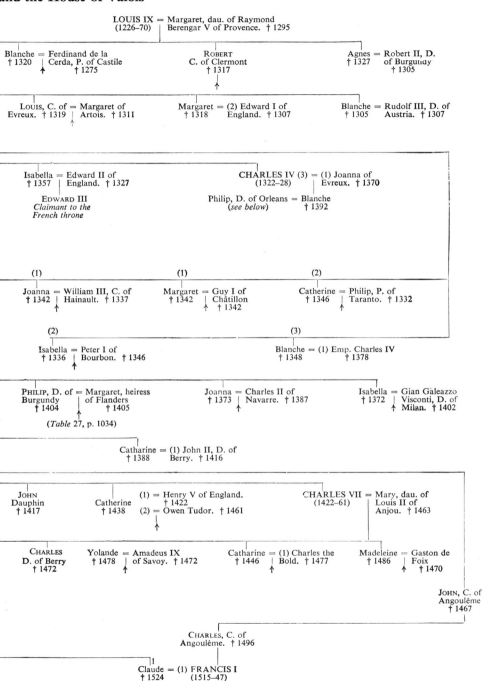

LOUIS IX = Margaret, dau. of Raymond
(1226–70) | Berengar V of Provence. † 1295

Blanche = Ferdinand de la
† 1320 | Cerda, P. of Castile
† 1275

ROBERT
C. of Clermont
† 1317

Agnes = Robert II, D.
† 1327 | of Burgundy
† 1305

LOUIS, C. of = Margaret of
Evreux. † 1319 | Artois. † 1311

Margaret = (2) Edward I of
† 1318 | England. † 1307

Blanche = Rudolf III, D. of
† 1305 | Austria. † 1307

Isabella = Edward II of
† 1357 | England. † 1327

EDWARD III
Claimant to the
French throne

CHARLES IV (3) = (1) Joanna of
(1322–28) | Evreux. † 1370

Philip, D. of Orleans = Blanche
(*see below*) | † 1392

(1)

Joanna = William III, C. of
† 1342 | Hainault. † 1337

(1)

Margaret = Guy I of
† 1342 | Châtillon
† 1342

(2)

Catherine = Philip, P. of
† 1346 | Taranto. † 1332

(2)

Isabella = Peter I of
† 1336 | Bourbon. † 1346

(3)

Blanche = (1) Emp. Charles IV
† 1348 | † 1378

PHILIP, D. of = Margaret, heiress
Burgundy | of Flanders
† 1404 | † 1405

(*Table* 27, p. 1034)

Joanna = Charles II of
† 1373 | Navarre. † 1387

Isabella = Gian Galeazzo
† 1372 | Visconti, D. of
| Milan. † 1402

Catharine = (1) John II, D. of
† 1388 | Berry. † 1416

JOHN
Dauphin
† 1417

Catherine
† 1438

(1) = Henry V of England.
† 1422
(2) = Owen Tudor. † 1461

CHARLES VII = Mary, dau. of
(1422–61) | Louis II of
| Anjou. † 1463

CHARLES
D. of Berry
† 1472

Yolande = Amadeus IX
† 1478 | of Savoy. † 1472

Catharine = (1) Charles the
† 1446 | Bold. † 1477

Madeleine = Gaston de
† 1486 | Foix
| † 1470

JOHN, C. of
Angoulême
† 1467

CHARLES, C. of
Angoulême. † 1496

Claude = (1) FRANCIS I
† 1524 | (1515–47)

idealism of Tuscan art and verse, but the same high level of intellect was conspicuous in the international finance, which gave Florence her power and dictated her manœuvres in European politics.

Other Italian cities, of which only Venice, and that at some distance, played a European role, must be dismissed more briefly. Matteo Visconti, great-nephew and successor of Archbishop Otto, overstrained his ambitions, and was forced to withdraw to exile in the Jubilee year by a coalition of Milanese malcontents and neighbouring tyrants. The Guelf leaders, the Della Torre, obtained control of Milan. Their chief, Guido, was finally

(a)   (b)

Fig. 160. The two earliest portraits of Dante, (a) by Giotto, c. 1336;
(b) by Nardo di Cione, c. 1355

(1307) elected Captain of the People for life with power to alter the city statutes. This was the tyranny in form, backed by a hired guard of 1000 men. He was also buttressed by a ring of allied Guelf tyrants in the Lombard cities, but his weakness lay in the discontent of his own kinsmen, including the archbishop, who resented his monopoly of power. Farther east, Padua was still a prosperous republic, but Verona was a popular tyranny under the plebeian Ghibelline house of Della Scala—the Scaligeri—who sternly repressed noble or feudal malcontents. The Scaligeri intermarried with ancient dynasts, and formed a court, of which Dante was at one time a member.

Venice in these years was passing through a crisis, which had a distant resemblance to the throes of Florence but a very different outcome, save that here too the republic was preserved. Oligarchical tendencies had long been visible in the city, testified by the institution of the Great Council (1172) and by the progressive limitation of the powers of the once unfettered Doge. It was a natural development when the merchant class, on whom the prosperity and guidance of Venice rested, were united by common interests identical with those of the people as a whole, however much in some immediate problem they might be at variance. What was growing was their jealousy of the more newly risen to wealth and the fear of individual pre-eminence and popular movements which might foster individual sway. The dangers of the time strengthened the party of oligarchy and its leader, the Doge Gradenigo, who, although unpopular, was elected in 1289. The fall of Acre and the loss of the Syrian ports, imperilling the Levantine trade, synchronized with the outbreak of a desperate war with rival Genoa for mastery of the sea, which ended in a disastrous defeat off Curzola in the Adriatic (1298) and a patched-up peace next year. It was during the stress of the conflict that a fundamental change in the constitution, aiming at internal stability, was carried out and gradually applied. The Venetian sense of governance and solidarity was brilliantly shown. The Great Council was the fundamental organ of legislation and election. Routine entrance to it was limited by the law of the *Serrata* (closing) in 1297 to families descended from members since its foundation. It became the practice to elect all who were thus qualified—the numbers rose from 210 in 1296 to 1017 in 1311—while elections of new men were difficult and rare. Thus was created the wide, legal oligarchy of Venice. Naturally the more select and much older Senate (the *Pregadi*) became steadily more charged with affairs and day-to-day debate. The stubborn constancy of the dominant party was soon proved, and indeed their skill in institution-making stimulated, by their unwisely ambitious foreign policy, which aimed at compensation for eastern failure by a monopoly of the outlets of Lombard trade by the river Po, while they renewed the all-important but much denounced trade with the Mamlūks at Alexandria. The opportunity on the river Po was furnished by dynastic disputes at Ferrara. Azzo VIII of Este, her tyrant, had in 1308 left his dominion to the child Folco, son of his bastard Fresco, to the wrath of his brothers. Pope Clement, in this matter resolute, claimed direct rule of his vassal town. So Fresco, the regent, in despair sold his son's rights to Venice, which occupied Ferrara. Clement's counterblow was an unprecedented bull (March 1309) outlawing the Venetians and decreeing a crusade against them. All the neighbouring cities joined in, the Ferrarese were for the legitimate heirs, and Venice suffered crushing defeats on the river Po, while in Dalmatia revolt was brewing. Venice bowed to surrender on the Pope's terms (November 1311), which were finally (1313) fulfilled, but meanwhile a combination of the peace party with the malcontents at the *Serrata* had produced a famous conspiracy and a new institution. The leaders, of whom Bajamonte Tiepolo, a showy young knight, was reckoned the most popular, were all men with a grievance and, it is noticeable, with estates on the mainland, whence they copied their methods. Their insurrection on 15 June 1310 was an ignominious failure, for Gradenigo had just time to be ready. Some were executed, others, like Tiepolo, submitted to banishment. The most important of the subsequent measures against disaffection was the institution of the Council of Ten, at first *ad hoc* and after constant renewals made permanent (1335). It was given overriding and secret powers to maintain the State. It consisted in fact of seventeen members, ten elected annually and not immediately re-eligible, and the Doge and his six Councillors. The quorum was twelve. Thus in the Middle Ages it was the concentrated essence of the Venetian patriciate as it developed after the *Serrata*. Swift, sudden, and secret in action, the Ten proved a sovereign remedy against tyranny and in emergencies of foreign war.

It was in this epoch of factious confusion and hatred—an absentee yet exacting Papacy, and inimical, ambitious, yet feeble kings of Naples and Sicily, amid the plots of embittered exiles, when men of good will, like Dante, were dreaming in their despair of an apocalyptic saviour to cure the incurable—that an idealistic King of the Romans, who believed in his divine mission as God's secular vicar of Christendom, Henry VII of Luxemburg, appeared on the scene to restore, as he thought, the Holy Roman Empire and give peace to the garden of the Empire. He possessed, too, the vacillating friendship of Pope Clement V, who had covertly favoured his election (1308) in order to avoid that of the eternal pretender, Charles of Valois, the candidate desired by the too formidable Philip the Fair. Henry, devout and chivalrous, would be a not unacceptable compromise, for he spoke French, not German, and had been brought up in Philip's court. A marriage alliance between Robert of Naples' heir and Henry's daughter was part of the Pope's policy, and he cherished hopes that Henry would still the turmoil of North Italy without impinging on papal claims and influence. He passed over the fact that Henry took the oath of obedience to and protection of the Papacy in the old non-feudal form, and not in the terms implying feudal subjection which Boniface VIII had extorted from Albert of Habsburg.

Henry, the idealist of the Empire in Italy, was a realist in Germany. There his object was to buy the loyalty of the princes and to gain the kingdom of Bohemia for his son John. He did both, and founded as successfully as the Habsburgs a new ruling house of the first rank, but his heart was in the Italian enterprise. Ghibelline exiles and Guelf spies thronged his court awaiting the event, while his ally, the Pope, anxious for the new conquest of Ferrara, reinsured himself by appointing Robert, now King of Naples (1309–43), his count (or governor) of Romagna, controlling the Emilian Way and the eastern route to Rome. Robert, a prey to timidity and suspicion, was as dubious in his attitude as the irresolute Pope. In contrast, the Blacks of Florence and the Tuscan League were openly and vigorously hostile to any renewal of the Empire, and they were the greatest financial power in Europe, their bills of credit easily surpassing the chests of gold which Henry brought over the Mont Cenis Pass. The adventure began well. Ghibelline exiles and Guelf tyrants gathered round him at Turin and Asti (November 1310), when he arrived with his Walloon soldiery. He declared he was neither Guelf nor Ghibelline, recalled all exiles as he proceeded, and replaced the tyrants by his vicars. He meant to be ruler and showed it. Milan was reached without opposition (23 December).

Guido della Torre, undermined and isolated, made but a faint gesture of recalcitrance. A forced and hollow reconciliation with the Visconti was followed by Henry's Italian coronation (6 January 1311) with an imitation of the iron crown, which was in pawn and unobtainable—too true an emblem of Henry's ideal. Trouble was already brewing, in which Matteo Visconti displayed his deft, treacherous 'wisdom'. Henry was needing money and men, and the levy provoked an outburst of the Guelfs, in which the Della Torre were driven out. After this Guelfic revolts were inevitable. Excessive harshness to Cremona stiffened the resistance of Brescia, where Henry lost time and men before the city surrendered. When he at length reached Genoa, he had become a Ghibelline, selling the imperial vicariates to native tyrants. In this way Matteo Visconti recovered the rule of Milan for his house. At Genoa King Henry, too, outstayed his welcome. He was occupied in negotiations with the shifty Robert of Naples for an alliance and with the alternative offers of Frederick of Sicily. Robert used the delay to send his brother John of Gravina with a Catalan troop to Rome, where the Orsini and Colonna as usual took opposite sides. At Pisa, to which he crossed by sea (March 1312), Henry at last heard Robert's impossible terms, which meant the evacuation of Italy in the form of an accord. He left defiant Florence on one side and entered Rome. Furious street fighting failed to capture the Vatican, and he was obliged to be content with his coronation by the papal legates, acting under severe pressure, at St John Lateran (29 June 1312).

Meanwhile Pope Clement's attitude had changed. Cowed by Philip the Fair, and fearing for Robert of Naples and for his own authority in Italy, he commanded Henry to leave the Papal State and to observe a truce with his unveiled enemy, Robert, for a year. The indignant Emperor, whose army was weakened by withdrawals of the northerners, declared as he retreated that intervention between the lord of the world and his vassal king was invalid. This time he vainly besieged Florence, for which he had no sufficient force, on his way to Ghibelline Pisa, where he was sure of devotion. He was resolved on war to the utmost. In vain did Clement threaten excommunication (13 June 1313). Henry put the King of Naples to the ban of the Empire, made an alliance with Frederick of Sicily, and called for large reinforcements from Germany and Bohemia. 'If God is for us,' he said, 'neither Pope nor Church can destroy us, and God we have not injured.' He was already suffering from Roman fever when he started southwards for the conquest of Naples. His victory over the unwarlike Robert seemed nearly certain, but he died of fever on 24 August 1313 at Buonconvento near Siena. His army dispersed, and the Italians were left to fight out their own destinies.

Whatever the prospects of immediate victory, failure was probably inevitable from the first. Henry, like his poet, Dante, was the victim of a mirage of the past, which neither his chivalry, nor his honesty, nor his benevolent intentions could make a reality. Italy had long outgrown the imperial system, which responded to no living need and merely brought invasion to exacerbate the bitter discords and the furious strife for power which reigned there. The future for centuries belonged to provincial particularism, and Dante's dream in his *Monarchia* of a worldwide Christian Empire, established by Divine Providence at Rome, the secular counterpart of the Church, awoke no echo save in barren controversy.

(3) PHILIP THE FAIR AND THE DEFEAT OF THE PAPACY

When we turn to France, we encounter hard facts, the growth of a national monarchy, ruthless and efficient, which aimed at being the chief of European states. It was moulded by feudal institutions which it dominated, it was draped in the colours of chivalry which it professed, but its essential power lay in the hold of the kingship over its subjects and in the ability of the bureaucrats in its employ. It was fitted to take up the challenge of the secularized Papacy with its claims of world dominion, and to insist on the independence of the lay governments.

Philip III the Bold (1270–85), St Louis' son, left by his father the most powerful king in Europe, was himself nearly a nonentity under the sway of his bureaucrats or his masterful uncle, Charles of Anjou. In 1271 he gathered in the great inheritance of another uncle, the childless Alphonse of Poitou and Toulouse, which united to the Crown the best of the Midi, less the Agenais, restored (1279) to Edward I of England, and the Comtat Venaissin, east of the river Rhône, given to the Papacy. A further acquisition was of the utmost value. In 1274 Henry II, Count of Champagne and King of Navarre, died, leaving an only daughter Joanna. The child queen was betrothed by her mother to Philip's son, Philip the Fair, who thus became King of Navarre and Count of Champagne. Navarre was of no vital importance, but rich Champagne in the heart of France was invaluable; it rounded off and solidified the royal domain on Philip the Fair's accession,

782

Fig. 161. King Philip IV of France, his son Louis, King of Navarre, with his Queen, Margaret of Burgundy, and three counsellors

and was never parted with thereafter. The king's own taste in the theatre for foreign war was for Spain. First, a move to interfere in the Castilian succession utterly miscarried. Next, Charles of Anjou influenced him to join in the War of the Vespers by accepting from the Pope the crown of Aragon for his younger son, Charles of Valois. The so-called crusade (1285) was an unredeemed failure, and Philip III was one of its victims.

His son Philip IV the Fair (1285–1314) has been thought a mystery. Silent and lethargic in the background, he consistently chose ministers whose aggressive daring and exaltation of the Crown left a deep mark on French and European history. The responsibility at any rate was his, and such as only a man of tough fibre and stark resolution could have endured during a thirty years' reign. His ministers, to whom he gave his unflinching support, were mainly lawyers from the Midi, whose abilities were hampered by no scruple save loyalty to their master. They depended entirely on his favour. Such were Pierre Flote, Guillaume de Plaisians, Guillaume de Nogaret, and Enguerrand de Marigny, all sordid makers of epoch-making history.

With some neglect of their constant interaction, the events of the reign may be grouped round certain main themes, the Papacy, the Templars, the great vassals and the eastern frontier, finance, and the growth of the States General. They all have one character in common, Philip's determination to be master in his kingdom, abandoning useless enterprises like Spanish affairs, but always intent on quelling rival powers, however formidable, within France, and ready for gains at the expense of the dislocated Empire.

Signs of uneasy relations with the Papacy on the frontiers of ecclesiastical and civil powers were already visible when there succeeded to the Papacy Boniface VIII, the worst man, with his arbitrary and explosive nature, to deal with delicate questions of competing and incompatible rights. The first friction occurred in 1296. Philip was embroiled with Edward I of England, his vassal for Gascony, and with his other vassal, the Count of Flanders. Both kings were in need of money for the war, their expenses far exceeding the traditional feudal payments incontestably due from their vassals, both lay and clerical. These emergencies had occurred before, but the necessary taxation of ecclesiastical wealth had been carried through by papal authority either in the name of a crusade or in return for royal assistance in raising the levies of tenths demanded by the Papacy from the Church. Certain Italian cities indeed had already insisted, to the wrath of the Popes, on taxing their clergy like their laity for objects of public utility. Now the two kings in similar manner required subventions from their clergy for the urgent needs of their war. Boniface took up the fundamental issue involving both the immunities of the Church and the control of Church property by the monarchical Papacy, which used its prerogative of taxation unsparingly. In the uncompromising bull, *Clericis laicos* (February 1296), he insisted that before such levies were exacted by kings or paid by clergy, papal consent must be obtained on pain of excommunication. The reaction of Edward I belongs to English history, that of Philip the Fair was a frontal attack on Boniface VIII. He forbade the exportation of bullion from France. This was not unprecedented as a war-time measure, but it was so worded as to endanger the solvency of the Italian bankers, who imported the papal revenues. After an interval of indignation Boniface slowly gave way. In February 1297 he admitted that Philip might accept voluntary grants from his clergy in case of pressing necessity, a current politico-religious doctrine; in July by the bull *Etsi de statu* he admitted the right of the king so to act even without consulting the Pope. Minor concessions were also made, culminating in the canonization of St Louis (August 1297). The king had won the first round. The Papacy needed him too much: it had overstretched its spiritual authority, with the result that its ban had not only been defied, as formerly, but rescinded in face of overmighty opponents.

The second quarrel, which ended so disastrously for the Papacy, began on the thorny question of the immunity of the clergy, and was extended by Boniface himself into the fundamental problem of the authority of the Papacy over lay rulers, which the Popes had claimed by spiritual and temporal means with alternate boldness and discretion since the *Dictatus Papae* of Gregory VII and more especially since the great days of Innocent III. Now, unseen by Boniface, the ebb-tide had begun, and its waves broke vainly on the rocks of national loyalty to a national king. Lay resentment had reached the sticking-point. The immediate cause was the resolve of Philip and his ministers to quell an unruly, rash, and unpopular bishop, who was a centre of trouble in Languedoc. Bernard Saisset, Bishop of Pamiers, a born *frondeur*, had fallen out with his neighbours and the government, and of him an example was to be made. The methods employed, of heaping up a mass of largely unproved accusations in a travesty of justice, were a terrible precedent for France and Europe. They ended in October 1301 in his condemnation by the king's court, and in an abrupt demand by Philip that the Pope should degrade the culprit from his orders so that condign punishment should be inflicted on him. Any Pope would have resented the invasion of ecclesiastical privilege; Boniface was up in arms, his pride inflated by the Jubilee. He demanded that Saisset should be sent to Rome for trial; by one bull, *Salvator mundi*, he revoked all privileges and concessions since *Clericis laicos*; in another, *Ausculta, fili* (6 December 1301), he recapitulated in the tone of a harsh pedagogue Philip's many offences in Church and State, proclaimed a Council at Rome for November 1302 to take measures for the reform of the kingdom, and warned the king that he was subordinate to the Papacy—only a fool would think otherwise. The terms of the bull, apart from their arrogant tone, might always be based on the doctrine, awkward to dispute, that the king, like others, was subject to the supreme pontiff *ratione peccati*, as a sinner, apart from the absolute claim of the Papacy to be possessed of the spiritual and temporal swords as Vicar of Christ; and acts of state might be sinful. Philip's advisers shrewdly put the absolute claim before their indignant public. They circulated a forged despotic abstract of *Ausculta, fili*, beginning *Deum time* and declaring that Philip was subject to the Pope in temporal and spiritual things. A forged and insulting reply asserted that the king was subject to none in temporalities. Saisset was forgotten in the greater contest.

Philip and his ministers were past masters in the ancient art of propaganda, which they developed with unconscionable cunning. In the independence of the French Crown they struck a vibrant chord, which was allied with nascent anti-clericalism. The bull was publicly burnt, and for the first time in his reign Philip summoned to Paris in April 1302 the three estates of clergy, nobles, and townsmen to hear his case and give their support. Each order addressed a letter to Rome unanimously asserting that the king held his kingdom from God alone, while the nobles rudely denounced Boniface's acts and implied a doubt of his being truly Pope. The crushing defeat of Philip's army by the Flemings at Courtrai in July weakened him, and in November nearly forty French prelates attended Boniface's Roman Council. There the Pope promulgated his bull *Unam Sanctam*, 'the most absolute proclamation of theocratic doctrine ever formulated in the Middle Ages', although it mainly reiterated well-worn similitudes and arguments. Negotiations still proceeded, while each side fortified its position. Boniface at last recognized Albert of Austria as King of the Romans, getting his own terms and stressing the universal Empire. Philip had made peace with Edward of England, and was won over to the plans of Nogaret, who succeeded to the dominant influence of Pierre Flote, slain at Courtrai. When the Pope insisted on complete submission with excommunication as the alternative, Philip in June 1303 held an assembly at the Louvre, where an indictment of him was read by Plaisians. Like Saisset, Boniface was charged with a precise and startling list of crimes, including heresy and base usurpation of the Papacy. The king had already appealed for a General Council to judge the Pope, and his agents broadcast the charges through France. The capture of Boniface at Anagni was to complete the scheme. As we have seen, the outrage at Anagni (September 1303) failed in its immediate purpose, but the shock to papal security was shown in the temporizing of Pope Benedict XI and the election under French influence of Clement V, who willingly or unwillingly transferred the Papacy to the banks of the river Rhône within range of Philip. He was, too, a good Frenchman, who in a few years made the College of Cardinals almost entirely French.

The overpowering influence over the Papacy that Philip's steady pressure could exert was shown in the destruction of the Order of the Temple. Like the Hospitallers, the Templars had amassed wide and scattered estates over the West, especially in France. For over a century they had won a profound unpopularity for their pride and avarice, and with the fall of Acre in 1291, the original purpose of the Order—the defence of the Holy Land against the infidel—disappeared. The Teutonic Knights had long diverted their energies to the Prussian crusade; the Hospitallers, with a base in Cyprus, made themselves into a naval police force to check the growing Turkish piracy, and obtained Pope Clement's support in conquering the island of Rhodes (1309), which became their headquarters. Both Orders were thus justified in public opinion, but the Templars remained inactive, and refused with blind obstinacy the suggestion of union with the zealous and useful Hospitallers. Rumour had long been busy with the heathen and immoral practices attributed to these wealthy celibate knights who lived at ease in France neglecting their mission under their secret rule. Their ill-repute, their wealth, and their dangerous power and ecclesiastical immunity—there were 2000 in France—attracted the cupidity and the pious indignation of the masterful needy king and his ruthless ministers. The knights' real preoccupation since Philip Augustus was with finance. They had been the

honest guardians of the royal treasure, and it may be presumed that
Philip, oppressed with debt, was glad to increase his resources with their
spoils and to believe that he was uprooting a pestilential society.

The methods used to accomplish this resolve were characteristic of the
reign and entangled in the aftermath of the conflict with Boniface with
Nogaret's usual skill. His master and he were determined to extort
condonation of their proceedings before and at Anagni from the embarrassed Pope, and the prosecution of Boniface's memory with the
accompanying scandal to the Papacy before Christendom was used both
to secure that end and to force his acquiescence in the ruin of the Templars.
The first move was to bring accusations of heresy and sordid vice against
the Order, which led in August 1307 to the Pope ordering an enquiry.
Then in October by a sudden act of power all the Templars in France were
arrested and their possessions seized by the king's officers. Royal commissioners examined the accused with such circumstances of terror or
torture as produced the required confessions of a degrading initiation,
blasphemy and idolatry, following certain general lines suggested to the
victims. Of those who were re-examined by the Inquisition hardly any
dared to incur the penalties of relapse by retractation. The Grand Master,
Jacques de Molai, and other elderly dignitaries led the way in terrified
self-accusation. No doubt the Order, like others, contained a number of
black sheep, but, e.g., the unanimity of the least credible charge, that of
adoring the idol Baphomet, combined with the contradictory descriptions
of it, would throw the gravest suspicion on such evidence in a more equitable
jurisprudence than that which prevailed under Philip the Fair. The impression on the vacillating Pope was strong enough to cause him to order
similar arrests and trials throughout the West (November 1307). With this
success Philip made the false step of handing over the captives to the papal
envoys. The immediate result was that many, led by the Grand Master,
retracted their confessions, and Clement suspended the process, reserving
it for his own investigation.

Now Nogaret turned to other weapons. Harangues and pamphlets
inflamed French opinion not only against the Templars but against
Clement himself as an unworthy Pope. The States General at Tours were
roused to follow the king's lead in their denunciations. King and Pope met
at Poitiers. Finally, Clement agreed to two trials, that of individual
Templars by the bishops and the king's emissaries and that of the Order by
papal commissioners, while he handed back the prisoners to the king. Thus
prisoners on trial for their lives in the usual cruel, unjust procedure were
witnesses against their Order in the papal process. The results were to be
reported to a General Council (1311) at Vienne. Burning alive was the fate
of the 'relapsed' who persisted, even under torture, in retracting their
earlier confessions. One poor wretch owned that he would have said that

he had killed God under these torments. The effect was reiterated confessions. Where torture and terrorism were sparingly or not employed the attack was less successful. Poor evidence was produced in the British Isles; in Spain and Germany the Templars were acquitted. In Italy and Cyprus, however, the affair went against them. Meantime the scandalous accusations against Boniface VIII were being pressed on the unwilling Pope. Clement moved in 1309 to Avignon out of French territory, but Philip was irresistible. The taking of evidence against Boniface began, and showed at least the indecorous, not to say dubious, sayings and doings of the late Pope. Clement at last gave way in a compromise which was a face-saving surrender (February 1311). Bulls were issued (April) annulling all bulls against Philip since 1300—they were even erased from the papal registers—praising the king's conduct, and absolving Nogaret and his accomplices on terms they did not carry out. The dangerous process was then allowed to drop, its last echo being the canonization of Peter Murrone (1313). The understanding on the Templars became visible at the Council of Vienne. In April 1312 the Pope decreed the abolition of their Order as a matter of expediency, not of conviction. Its belongings were given to the Hospitallers, save in Spain where they were given to the local Military Orders. The surviving dignitaries were left in prison, where the unhappy De Molai and another at last firmly declared their innocence and were burnt alive (1314). It took years and much money for the Hospitallers to recover their property. Philip had profited to some extent in cash, but his real triumph was that he had demonstrated the impotence of the Papacy in the hands of the King of France.

Philip's secular foreign policy had a domestic side. He and his bureaucrats were determined, firstly to exact from his great vassals full submission to his rights under the now completely developed system of feudal jurisprudence—a state of things very different from the practical autonomy they had enjoyed in the twelfth century;—secondly, to annex to the royal domain, as opportunity offered under feudal law, all or part of the lands of these too dangerous potentates. Two of them were especially aimed at, Guy of Dampierre, Count of Flanders, and Edward I of England, Duke of Aquitaine and Gascony. The wealth of Flanders and the discord between its count and the autonomous oligarchies of its trading towns opened the way to intervention. Philip became the patron of the *Leliaerts* (lily-men from the shield of France) as the oligarchs were called and the count sided with the lesser gilds and workmen. Guy's authority was all but annulled by the royal officials sent by the king. Meantime the friction between Philip and Edward had ripened into war. Since 1259 the appeals from the Gascon courts had multiplied, not to mention other exercise of French suzerain rights, while affrays between English and French seamen brought a new element into the perennial dispute. In 1294 Edward himself was

Fig. 162. Castle of the Counts of Flanders at Ghent

summoned to answer before the Parlement of Paris, and in a customary way his chief castles in Gascony were handed over to his suzerain for forty days during the investigation. But Philip meant war, and did not return them—the chance of laming a foreign king who held this desirable fief was too good. Edward could only protest and renounce his homage.

All the campaigning in the long war was done in its first four years. Edward, unlucky in Gascony, pinned his faith on a north-eastern frontier league like his grandfather John. Guy and King Adolf of the Romans became his allies. But Adolf proved a broken reed, Edward and Guy were unsuccessful, and Edward accepted (1297) a truce which abandoned his fellow-vassal. Guy was forced to submit to be a prisoner, while Jacques de Châtillon ruled Flanders for Philip (1300). The rule of Châtillon and his mercenaries, however, aroused the hatred of the Flemings, exacerbated by the economic oppression of the classes below them by the *Leliaert* oligarchs. The party of the *Clauwaerts* (claw-men, so named from the lion of the count's shield) was organized, led by the weaver Peter de Coningk, and on the night of 17–18 May 1302, the Matins of Bruges, a massacre of French and *Leliaerts*, similar to the Sicilian Vespers, began a general revolt. Then came one of the great events of the century. A magnificent army of French knights, led by the Count of Artois, was routed at Courtrai by the Flemish pikemen (11 July 1302). Bad and reckless generalship obscured the lesson that plebeian infantry if well-posted could match the reckless charges of armoured chivalry, but even so the hard fact remained that the Flemings had recovered their freedom. Although a victory in 1304 improved Philip's position and enabled him to insist on a harsh treaty with the new Count Robert at Athis-sur-Orge (June 1305), it was not carried out. A new treaty in 1312 ceded the Walloon towns of Lille and Douai to the king, but the friction involved caused a brief fresh war without changing the situation. Meantime, under the impression of Courtrai, Philip had come to a definite peace with Edward I (1303), who had already married (1299) his sister, and the duchy of Gascony was left as before the war.

The real failure of Philip's large ambitions with regard to Flanders and Aquitaine, not to mention the vain hopes of securing the Empire for his brother Charles of Valois, contrasts curiously with the less obtrusive success of his persistent nibbling all along the western border of the Empire, thus extending by small encroachments the eastern boundaries of France. Among these transfers of suzerainty the annexation after long intervention of once imperial Lyons in the Arelate (1307) was perhaps the most important owing to the commercial and strategic value of the city, but the significance of the whole was that Philip had begun the age-long expansion of the legal kingdom of France over the romance-speaking lands towards the Rhine and the Alps which had fallen to the Empire. The acquisition of the Free County of Burgundy (Franche Comté) by marriage for his son Philip was a step in the same direction, like the Angevin rule in Provence, but did not change the frontier.

The effect of the major conflicts, however, with the immense and mostly fruitless efforts they caused, was ruinous to Philip's finances. The customary and feudal revenue was insufficient from the start. It was supplemented either by old occasional levies, now made permanent, or by entirely fresh taxation. The clergy, for all Boniface VIII's resistance, frequently paid tenths. The nobles were taxed by heavy commutation-payments for their personal service. A new tax on sales, which became an exaction on necessaries, wheat, wine, and salt, was imposed in 1292 and continued. These burdens proved insufficient, and enormous loans were raised from Italian bankers and from native Frenchmen. Philip earned a bad name as 'the false coiner', by means of debasing the coinage, which gave a temporary profit to the Crown and a permanent loss to its subjects. Two sudden returns to a sounder basis (1306, 1313) were almost equally injurious by the dislocation they caused in all business. Nothing filled the king's empty purse, even when more desperate expedients were employed. In 1306 the Jews were driven out, in 1307 the property of the Templars was laid hands on, and in 1311 Philip's Italian bankers were likewise expelled. In each case the victims' possessions were seized, including debts due to them. This rapacity amid all its harm had one promising consequence: for his exactions Philip was obliged to woo consent in local or central consultations with notables, and in 1314 went so far as to summon to Paris the three Estates, later known as the States General, for the purpose.

In the thirteenth century assemblies of Estates were growing up under various names throughout Western Europe. They were not so much imitations of one another as developments from a common stock of institutions to be found in feudalized monarchies, where the efficiency of the central kingship and its control of its subjects were increasing. The royal Curia, besides throwing off specialized departments, was widening its range and the vassal's duty of counsel and aid. The greater solidarity of a territory was crystallizing into Estates the primary divisions of the population, fighting nobles, clergy, and townsmen, irrespective of their precise position in the graded feudal hierarchy. Thus the truly medieval society of groups received its latest and widest embodiment. The groups were based on the functions of their members; but they were still in separate layers, and the measure of their eventual unsuccess was the measure of the dissidence between the feudal and the non-feudal layers.

In France this development was, perhaps, retarded by the late union of its disparate provinces and by the prestige of the monarchy. As the thirteenth century wore on, besides assemblies in which prelates and barons took part, others of the bourgeois were occasionally summoned to obey the king's demands for aid. It was Philip the Fair who called all Estates to meet him at one assembly for the purpose of rallying public opinion round him. Some such meeting took place at Senlis (1301) over Bishop Saisset. The first well-known instance, which is reckoned as the beginning of the States General, was that at Paris (10 April 1302) in the thick of his conflict with Boniface VIII. Lay and spiritual tenants-in-chief were summoned as was customary for such a *grand conseil*, but beside them were representatives of the towns, whether directly subject to the king or belonging to some vassal (whose consent was demanded). The duties of direct vassalage were being extended to all subjects. From this beginning the States were summoned several times by Philip, full meetings being held to attack the Templars (1308) and to obtain supplies for the Flemish war (1314). Their organization was becoming clearer, nobles and clergy appearing in person or by proxy, the townsmen by their representatives. They all had little choice but to obey the king's will, but public feeling could be tested by them and they were an invaluable means of propaganda.

For real advice on his measures the king depended on his council. This would be large on important occasions, but a permanent *conseil secret*, whose members took a special oath, was in existence for the king to consult. In administration the Parlement of Paris, now well developed, acted as the supreme judicial court; the *Chambre des Comptes* dealt with public finance, the *Chambre aux Deniers* with the king's household moneys; the Chancery, of which Flote and Nogaret were chiefs, and subsequently

21. The House of Habsburg

The names of Kings of the Romans and Emperors are printed in heavy type.

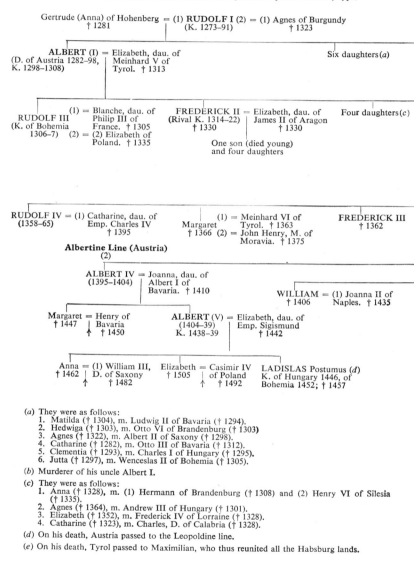

Gertrude (Anna) of Hohenberg = (1) **RUDOLF I** (2) = (1) Agnes of Burgundy
† 1281 (K. 1273–91) † 1323

ALBERT (I) = Elizabeth, dau. of   Six daughters (a)
(D. of Austria 1282–98, Meinhard V of
K. 1298–1308) Tyrol. † 1313

(1) = Blanche, dau. of   **FREDERICK II** = Elizabeth, dau. of   Four daughters (c)
RUDOLF III Philip III of (Rival K. 1314–22) James II of Aragon
(K. of Bohemia France. † 1305 † 1330 † 1330
1306–7) (2) = (2) Elizabeth of
Poland. † 1335   One son (died young)
and four daughters

RUDOLF IV = (1) Catharine, dau. of   (1) = Meinhard VI of   **FREDERICK III**
(1358–65) Emp. Charles IV Margaret Tyrol. † 1363 † 1362
† 1395 † 1366 (2) = John Henry, M. of
Moravia. † 1375

Albertine Line (Austria)
(2)

ALBERT IV = Joanna, dau. of
(1395–1404) Albert I of
Bavaria. † 1410 **WILLIAM** = (1) Joanna II of
† 1406 Naples. † 1435

Margaret = Henry of **ALBERT (V)** = Elizabeth, dau. of
† 1447 Bavaria (1404–39) Emp. Sigismund
↑ † 1450 K. 1438–39 † 1442

Anna = (1) William III, Elizabeth = Casimir IV **LADISLAS Postumus (d)**
† 1462 D. of Saxony † 1505 of Poland K. of Hungary 1446, of
↑ † 1482 ↑ † 1492 Bohemia 1452; † 1457

(a) They were as follows:
  1. Matilda († 1304), m. Ludwig II of Bavaria († 1294).
  2. Hedwiga († 1303), m. Otto VI of Brandenburg († 1303)
  3. Agnes († 1322), m. Albert II of Saxony († 1298).
  4. Catharine († 1282), m. Otto III of Bavaria († 1312).
  5. Clementia († 1293), m. Charles I of Hungary († 1295).
  6. Jutta († 1297), m. Wenceslas II of Bohemia († 1305).

(b) Murderer of his uncle Albert I.

(c) They were as follows:
  1. Anna († 1328), m. (1) Hermann of Brandenburg († 1308) and (2) Henry VI of Silesia
     († 1335).
  2. Agnes († 1364), m. Andrew III of Hungary († 1301).
  3. Elizabeth († 1352), m. Frederick IV of Lorraine († 1328).
  4. Catharine († 1323), m. Charles, D. of Calabria († 1328).

(d) On his death, Austria passed to the Leopoldine line.

(e) On his death, Tyrol passed to Maximilian, who thus reunited all the Habsburg lands.

NOTE. The succession of the Habsburg territories cannot be easily indicated by a table. They were held in common by the sons of Albert I and again by the sons of Albert II, but were divided after the death of Rudolf IV (1365) between the founders of the Albertine and Leopoldine lines and only reunited at the end of the fifteenth century.

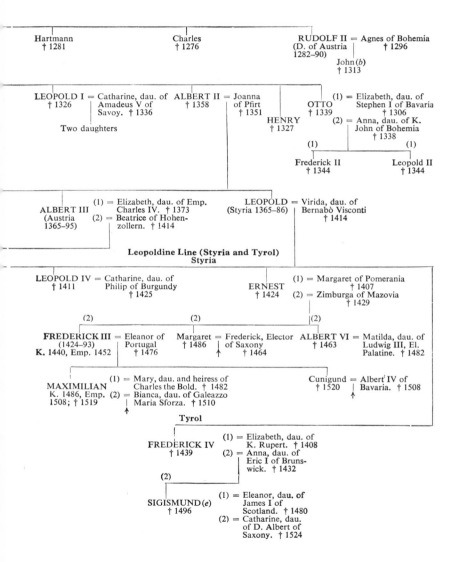

Hartmann
† 1281

Charles
† 1276

RUDOLF II = Agnes of Bohemia
(D. of Austria   † 1296
1282–90)
            John (b)
            † 1313

LEOPOLD I = Catharine, dau. of   ALBERT II = Joanna   (1) = Elizabeth, dau. of
   † 1326   Amadeus V of   † 1358   of Pfirt   OTTO   Stephen I of Bavaria
              Savoy. † 1336   † 1351   † 1339   † 1306
                                                HENRY   (2) = Anna, dau. of K.
   Two daughters   † 1327   John of Bohemia
                                                                       † 1338
                                          (1)   (1)

                                          Frederick II   Leopold II
                                          † 1344   † 1344

ALBERT III   (1) = Elizabeth, dau. of Emp.   LEOPOLD = Virida, dau. of
(Austria   Charles IV. † 1373   (Styria 1365–86) | Bernabò Visconti
1365–95)   (2) = Beatrice of Hohen-   † 1414
                  zollern. † 1414

Leopoldine Line (Styria and Tyrol)
Styria

LEOPOLD IV = Catharine, dau. of   (1) = Margaret of Pomerania
   † 1411   Philip of Burgundy   ERNEST   † 1407
               † 1425   † 1424   (2) = Zimburga of Mazovia
                                                            † 1429

      (2)   (2)   (2)

FREDERICK III = Eleanor of   Margaret = Frederick, Elector   ALBERT VI = Matilda, dau. of
(1424–93)   Portugal   † 1486 | of Saxony   † 1463   Ludwig III, El.
K. 1440, Emp. 1452 † 1476   ↑   † 1464   Palatine. † 1482

              (1) = Mary, dau. and heiress of   Cunigund = Albert IV of
MAXIMILIAN   Charles the Bold. † 1482   † 1520 | Bavaria. † 1508
K. 1486, Emp. (2) = Bianca, dau. of Galeazzo   ↑
1508; † 1519 | Maria Sforza. † 1510
              ↑
              Tyrol

                                   (1) = Elizabeth, dau. of
              FREDERICK IV   K. Rupert. † 1408
                 † 1439   (2) = Anna, dau. of
                                         Eric I of Bruns-
                                         wick. † 1432
              (2)

                                   (1) = Eleanor, dau. of
              SIGISMUND (e)   James I of
                 † 1496   Scotland. † 1480
                                   (2) = Catharine, dau.
                                         of D. Albert of
                                         Saxony. † 1524

Marigny Chancellor, issued the mass of more formal documents, while the *Chambre* under the Chamberlain acted as a domestic secretariat. Local government continued to be carried on by the *baillis* and *sénéschaux* and their subordinates. Oppression was rife, for the *enquêteurs* rather made mischief in these days than prevented it. So many were the grievances and discontents with fruitless wars and exactions that large districts in the north were in effervescence and leagues of the lesser nobles had been formed when in November 1314 Philip the Fair closed his epoch-making reign. He had proved what the kingship with an organized bureaucracy and national backing could do.

(4) GERMANY FROM 1250 TO 1313

The period named the Great Interregnum marks a decisive turning-point in the history of Germany and the Empire. Although rival Kings of the Romans existed throughout its twenty years, none of them acquired general recognition or was able to revive the central government, which since the death of Henry VI had been steadily decaying. In contrast to the unification of France, Germany had drifted into that aggregation of petty states loosely bound together which continued far into modern times. The crown was first fought for by Conrad IV of Hohenstaufen and the papal candidate, William, Count of Holland. When Conrad died in Italy (May 1254), King William seemed to be in a fair way to secure general acknowledgement and to re-erect the enfeebled kingship, but he, too, died fighting in a purely local Frisian warfare, and the throne was again vacant (28 January 1256).

By this time in a singularly obscure fashion a momentous change had come over the doctrine of the right to elect the King of the Romans. In the double election of 1198 all princes of the Empire, not a numerous body, were qualified to take part; in that of 1257 it was admitted that only seven of them were entitled to elect. Three of them were ecclesiastics, the Archbishops of Mainz, Cologne, and Trier; the four lay Electors were the holders of great offices in the imperial household, which were attached to their fiefs, but there were doubts with regard to these seculars. First, it was agreed that the Count Palatine of the Rhine, the Duke of Saxony, and the Margrave of Brandenburg were of the number, but the claims of the Duke of Bavaria (of the same family as the Count Palatine) and the King of Bohemia (a half-foreign prince) conflicted. Secondly, since the practice of dividing fiefs and dignities among the male co-heirs was coming in, doubts were arising which co-heir had the right to be the elector. Further, the majority rule, adopted in papal elections and in Italian city-councils, did not exist in Germany. Unanimity was the ideal; in the case of dissension each side could claim on various grounds to be the better part. Dissidence among the Electors, rendered likely by all these circumstances, was the more certain since all of them, like other princes, were indifferent to the interests of the Empire and Germany as a whole and engrossed in their personal and family independence, besides being strongly inclined to accept money bribes for their vote. They did not want to revive a powerful monarchy unless in their own persons; otherwise their instinct was to vote for a weak candidate, who would pay the best in privileges or cash.

The Electors and princes by no means exhausted the list of petty local potentates who now ruled Germany. Counts, abbots, and barons, often with wide possessions, who did not fulfil the technical qualifications of princely rank, were numerous. The *ministeriales* of imperial demesnes, released from strict dependence, and soon to be known as the Knights of the Empire, ruled their tiny fiefs as independently as other vassals, and losing their employ under the Hohenstaufen became a fruitful source of disorder owing to their brigandage and petty feuds. Against these robber knights and lesser barons like them the efforts of the towns were largely directed, for the *Landfrieden,* the only substitute for imperial control, were miserably ineffective. The fact was that Germany, where a slowly modified Carolingian monarchical control had so long subsisted, had arrived at the full feudal disintegration which France had experienced two centuries earlier.

Fig. 163. Tomb of Sigfrid von Eppstein, Archbishop of Mainz, crowning Kings Henry Raspe and William of Holland

The numerous self-governing towns, whether 'Free Cities' on imperial domain or on lands of a mesne lord, were the element in Germany which was making progress in civilized government. Their advance in trade, manufacture, and internal organization, mostly guided by oligarchic bodies, the 'patricians' to use a modern description, was marked during the abeyance of the kingship. Princes and lords, usually hostile, were unable to curb them within their walls, and they became the strongest antidote to the prevailing anarchy. Leagues of towns arose to secure peace and the abolition of arbitrary tolls and highway robbery. Not to mention earlier leagues, a great Rhine League stretching from Cologne to Basle was formed in 1254 for these objects. Unlike its predecessors it included the local nobles. It soon numbered seventy towns; it was recognized by William of Holland and its delegates took part in a Diet of the Empire held at Worms (1255). But the incompatibility of towns and feudal lords soon broke it down (1257). Smaller groups of towns were more lasting, among them (1259) that of the Baltic towns of Lübeck, Rostock and Wismar, which was the nucleus of the great Hanseatic League. Southern groups played a notable part in the contest for the crown.

On the death of William of Holland protracted negotiations were under-taken for the election of a successor. The Electors could not agree on a German prince, with the result that foreign powers took a hand in pursuance of their own interests. Alfonso X of Castile, who had Hohen-staufen blood in him, was backed by Ghibelline Pisa and France and at first by the Roman Curia, which feared the exaltation of Conradin. It was Italy that tempted his ambition. Henry III of England put forward his wealthy brother Richard, Earl of Cornwall. By dint of heavy bribes Richard secured the votes of the Archbishops of Cologne and Mainz and the Count Palatine (January 1257) and the adhesion of King Otakar of Bohemia. But the Archbishop of Trier and the Electors of Saxony and Brandenburg chose (April 1257) King Alfonso, also with the adhesion of Otakar. Alfonso took no further steps till much later and then in Italy. Richard came to Germany, scattering money and charters freely. He was crowned at Aachen (May 1257) and obtained recognition up the Rhine as far as Basle, but his rule was little more than a fiction. Twice he revisited Germany without much more effect, although he did his best to establish a *Landfriede* on the Rhine and finally won over Otakar by confirming his annexation of Austria and Styria (1262). For years until his death (2 April 1272) he was vainly attempting to gain the Pope's recognition and coronation at Rome.

Meantime the state of the country had been going from bad to worse. Feuds and private wars were waged unchecked all over Germany; there were struggles between bishops and their towns; disputes over succession seemed endless, like that over Thuringia on the death of Henry Raspe, which his kinsmen pursued. Even the narrow outlook of the lords began to be affected by the anarchy near them, and some local *Landfrieden* brought a little alleviation at last, while an inclination to re-establish the monarchy in some sort gathered a feeble momentum.

Yet in spite of all, individual vigour and fragmentary prosperity were not lacking. The outlet of German population, the refuge of the oppressed and enterprising, was towards the east. The thirteenth century is the culminating period of German colonization in the thinly peopled Slavonic lands, unaffected by the abeyance of the central monarchy, which had hardly heeded it. We have seen the fierce conquests of the Teutonic Order. But much migration was invited by native princes, the Kings of Bohemia and Hungary and the Polish dukes, more especially by those of Silesia and Pomerania, who were becoming German dynasties. Sheer aggression, on the other hand, was practised by the Margraves of Brandenburg, who extended their fief piecemeal to the river Oder and beyond. We have seen the growth of German towns and trade. Marked as it was along the trade-routes in Bavaria, Swabia and the Rhineland, it was still more promising in the north, where the new-born and rapidly increasing Hansa League was acquiring a monopoly of the fisheries and commerce of the Baltic and North Seas, backed by naval mastery of their waters. German expansion and German disunion went hand in hand.

Fig. 164. *Beatrix of Falkenburg, third wife of Richard, Earl of Cornwall and King of the Romans*

The death of King Richard opened the way for a new election, and now Pope Gregory X was eager to see the Interregnum end. The Electors were united in fearing the accession of a too powerful ruler, and as the Duke of Bavaria this time made good his claim to elect instead of Otakar of Bohemia, they could be unanimous in choosing, not the Czech king, the greatest of his line, a descendant of the Hohenstaufen, who had conquered the south-eastern duchies as far as the Adriatic, but an elderly Swabian count, Rudolf of Habsburg (1 October 1273). Although not a prince, he had large possessions in Alsace and in the modern Switzerland, and had earned general respect and liking for his solid character and uprightness. He was crowned at once and asked for the Pope's approbation. A meeting at Lausanne ratified the alliance between Papacy and Empire, for Rudolf

797

Fig. 165. Habsburg Castle, Aargau, Switzerland

was willing to accept the papal programme, and Gregory cleared the king's path by obtaining the renunciation of Alfonso of Castile. But Otakar was not so easily thrust aside. He insisted on his claim to be an Elector and refused his homage. Rudolf, however, was strong in the support of the German princes, all hostile to Otakar, and of the Church, which laid the rebellious Czech under excommunication. When he besieged Vienna, revolt broke out in Bohemia, and Otakar was obliged to submit (November 1276). He was shorn of his German conquests and did homage for his kingdom. As soon as he could, he renewed the war, but Rudolf, with the help of another jealous neighbour, King Ladislas of Hungary, overthrew him in the battle of the Marchfeld (26 August 1278), where the Czech king was killed. His young son Wenceslas II was married to Rudolf's daughter and only allowed to succeed to Bohemia, while Moravia was temporarily left in Rudolf's hands.

The overthrow of Otakar enabled Rudolf of Habsburg to embark on a policy which became characteristic of later German monarchs. Italy and the imperial coronation, although he was far from indifferent to them, were for him secondary considerations. He was content to obtain formal recognition and indeed gave armed aid to the Guelfs of Milan. He conciliated Pope Nicholas III by admitting the inferiority of the Empire to the Papacy and by complete abandonment of imperial claims on Bologna and Romagna. He allied with Charles I of Anjou, whose grandson, Charles Martel, married another of his daughters with an expectation (never realized) of the kingdom of Arles. Thus safe in the south, Rudolf concentrated on the exaltation of the Habsburgs in Germany. Law and custom, fortified by the jealous dread of the monarchy among the princes, forbade additions to the always too small royal domain, but the fresh enfeoffment of lapsed or confiscated fiefs, compelled by custom, roused less opposition, for the advantage went to a princely family, not to the elective monarchy. So Rudolf on 27 December 1282 conferred the spoils taken from Otakar— the duchies of Austria, Styria, Carniola, etc.—jointly on his two sons Albert and Rudolf, with the important provision, bred of the disintegration of a family power by the practice of co-heirship and division, that the actual rule should belong to Albert. In this way a great new princely house was founded in Germany, and kept its pre-eminence as long as the practice of single administration in it subsisted. The centre of that power, too, was inevitably transferred from Swabia to the south-eastern frontier lands of Austria, which were already acquiring a separatist provincial character of their own. By his action Rudolf prepared an evolution completely unforeseen.

King Rudolf's preoccupation with the endowment of the Habsburgs did not mean that he neglected the interests of the kingship. He hoped that it might remain in his house, fortified by its family possessions. He did make efforts, with partial success, to resume control of the depleted royal domain; he promoted *Landfrieden*, and even took armed measures to enforce them; he used force to insist on the homage of Franche Comté. But his revenue as king was insignificant and hard to levy, and in the desuetude of feudal service to the Crown, mercenary soldiers were an expense he could not always afford. He depended on his deserved popularity with princes and towns. To the former he was lavish of grants which confirmed what they had taken in return for help. He was content if his friends won in internecine wars, as when Duke John of Brabant defeated the Archbishop of Cologne and others at Worringen (July 1288). He won over Wenceslas II of Bohemia by recognizing his right to be an Elector (1290). As for the towns, he raised money by selling them trading privileges, and allowed the leagues they formed.

With these assets he cut a respectable figure in Germany and Europe. Impostors who pretended to be Frederick II or Conrad IV were put down. Yet his popularity ebbed. The towns were angry at the favours bestowed on the Electors and princes. The princes were alarmed at the growing Habsburg greatness, all the more when Rudolf endeavoured to obtain the kingdom of Hungary for his eldest son Albert and to renew the duchy of Swabia for his youngest son Rudolf. Still the prospect of securing the election of the latter, who was liked, as his successor in the Empire was good when the young prince died (May 1290). His father, now an old man, was employed in the uphill task of recommending Albert, who was dreaded, to the Electors, when he himself died on 15 July 1291. Shrewd and practical, he had not only founded a great princely house but also remade the German monarchy and its possession of the titular Roman Empire, although coronation at Rome had always eluded him in spite of his diplomacy.

It was perhaps due to his reign that the German kingdom and its association with the title and lands of the Holy Roman Empire continued to exist. Foreign princes aspired to the Empire, and the German princes had small mind to strengthen the kingship they had perforce re-created. Yet under his cautious rule it did survive and maintained at least the German section of the Empire—for this is the true rendering of the phrase 'Römisches Reich deutscher Nation'—as a political reality. The monarchy, however, was weak in resources and in power, without a revenue, an army, or an administrative machine. Real power was vested in its vassals, whether Electors, princes, lesser lords, or free towns, linked together in the lax union of the Empire.

How averse the Electors were to the restoration of a strong central control was shown in their choice of Rudolf's successors and their conduct towards them in the next twenty years. The power of Duke Albert of Austria, no less than his rough, tyrannical nature and his obvious ambitions, rendered him unacceptable, and the Electors, led by the archbishops, chose Adolf of Nassau, a valiant and capable count of small possessions, who submitted to give the usual bribes in money, lands, and promises. Thus buttressed, Adolf was crowned (June 1292), and Duke Albert found himself obliged to do homage. But King Adolf was soon in difficulties. Promises, not easy to keep, remained unfulfilled; he resumed the ambitions of a strong kingship and the endowment of his house. Controversy over the succession to the margraviate of Meissen and landgraviate of Thuringia furnished the opportunity for both. Two invasions (1295), conducted with ruthless pillage, which did not spare churches and their lands, conquered both Thuringia and Meissen, whose margrave, the heir of Thuringia, was driven out. Meantime Adolf was taking up the role of defender of the Empire's western frontier against the piecemeal encroachments of Philip the Fair of France. In return for subsidies he declared war as the ally of Edward I of England (August 1294). But Philip's position was stronger and his diplomacy better than Edward's or Adolf's, who never undertook the planned campaign. On the contrary, some great frontier vassals from Dauphiné to Luxemburg, as well as Albert of Austria, took Philip's side. At last, when it was clear that Edward could not help and that insurrection was brewing in the Empire, Adolf came to a truce. Church, Electors and princes had by this time taken umbrage at his ambitions and offences. Duke Albert saw the time was ripe, for the Electors were ready to revolt. In February 1298 he set out from Vienna with a motley army, largely non-German. A diet was called for May by the Archbishop of Mainz, and there the Electors declared the king deposed and elected Albert. On 2 July the valiant Adolf met his foe at Göllheim near Worms, and was defeated and slain. Albert I was promptly re-elected and crowned.

This powerful prince had been chosen because he alone had been able to overthrow Adolf, but he was feared more than loved, and the essence of his policy was the same, to exalt the Habsburgs and renew the kingly control of Germany; only his means and his success were greater than Adolf's while he lived. Of course, he had at first to make concessions to the princes. He began his reign with Philip of France as his friend and Pope Boniface VIII, who denounced him as a traitorous usurper, as his foe. The Rhenish Electors were soon (1300) in revolt. The rebels he subdued by force of arms, although the Netherland princes stood out. Boniface VIII, however, was still to be appeased, and his dispute with Philip the Fair offered the means. Albert was by no means easy over the French king's progress and overbearing power; Boniface was seeking for a counter-weight. An obstacle to the new alliance was the question of the subordination of the Empire to the Papacy, which was claimed by Boniface in the most pronounced form. Hitherto the Kings of the Romans, while taking the ancient oath of obedience to the head of the Church, and seeking papal approbation of their election and coronation (never achieved) at Rome, had evaded any precise acknowledgement of vassalage. Albert went further. He took an oath (not repeated by his successors) which approximated to, and was accepted by Boniface as, the oath of a vassal (1303). In return the Pope confirmed his election, and declared that the King and future Emperor of the Romans was the superior of all secular potentates.

The tragedy of Anagni soon put an end to this dear-bought alliance. Albert was far more deeply interested in the dangerous ambitions of his brother-in-law, Wenceslas II of Bohemia, who had secured the crown of Poland and intruded his son Wenceslas for a while on the throne of Hungary, a formidable but fragile combination. War broke out, but was ended by the Czech king's early death (June 1305). When the young Wenceslas III was murdered next year (August 1306), the male line of the Přemyslids became extinct and the Bohemian throne was vacant. Albert at once schemed to form such a collection of Habsburg states as came to pass long after his day. He obtained the election of his eldest son Rudolf as King of Bohemia. This meant another war with Wenceslas II's son-in-law, Henry, Duke of Carinthia, who on Rudolf's speedy death (1307) was chosen king. Albert did not give up the struggle, which was only ended by his own death.

Albert had indeed many foes to deal with. The long fought-over Meissen and Thuringia were being secured by the ancient line of Wettin margraves, and in his own lands in southern Swabia he was hampered by the birth of the Swiss confederation, which must be treated separately, but his most bitter foe was in his own family, created by his own injustice. Duke John, the son of his brother Rudolf, had been refused his share of the Habsburg lands. He now in revenge murdered his uncle (1 May 1308). With Albert's death the growth of Habsburg power over the Empire came to a temporary end. His eldest surviving son, Frederick the Handsome, made peace with King Henry of Bohemia. The Electors, although the murderers were banned, looked around for another, less formidable candidate for the Empire.

Their final decision was astute enough. No major prince should be elected; Philip's attempts to promote the eternal pretender, his brother Charles of Valois, were evaded despite all his bribery—there was too great a power behind him. But at the suggestion of Baldwin, Archbishop of Trier, and with the secret approval of Pope Clement V, they chose another minor count of ancient lineage, Henry of Luxemburg, who was duly crowned (January 1309). King Henry VII came from a German-speaking part of the Netherlands, but he had been brought up in the French court, and was therefore not unacceptable to Philip the Fair; his family inheritance was not large. Moreover, his character, upright, kindly, energetic, permeated with ideals of chivalry, was most attractive. The fact that he was a devotee of the Holy Roman Empire, setting his heart on its revival in Italy, seemed to be a guarantee that he would leave the German princes in practical autonomy. But, idealist as he was in Italy, in Germany Henry VII exhibited the natural policy of the revived kingship, that of using his acknowledged prerogative of filling vacant fiefs to establish the house of Luxemburg among the great princes of the Empire. He did so with amazing success. Approved by Pope Clement, he gained the friendship and homage of the Habsburg, Frederick the Handsome. Happily for him, the Bohemian crown was going begging. Henry of Carinthia was hated by the Czechs, who rallied round his sister-in-law, the younger daughter of Wenceslas II. They offered her hand to John, the only son of Henry VII. The marriage was celebrated, John invested with the kingdom of Bohemia, and Henry of Carinthia driven out (1310). Thus the Luxemburg dynasty became at a stroke a leading power, transferred from the west to the east. Henry VII could proceed on his romantic expedition to Italy, where, as we have seen, he was crowned Emperor, was embroiled with Naples, France, and the Pope, and died (24 August 1313).

By this time Germany had settled down in the form it kept for centuries. Power lay in the hands of the princes and free towns among the dislocated provinces, which were continually more subdivided owing to the practice of sharing among male heirs. Certain families, rarely added to, took the lead, the Luxemburgs in Bohemia, the Habsburgs in Austria, the Wittelsbachs in the Palatinate of the Rhine and Bavaria, the Wettins in Meissen and Thuringia, and the Ascanians in Brandenburg and the reduced duchy of Saxony, but division among co-heirs, who often were not harmonious, weakened their resources and influence. Feuds were always springing up

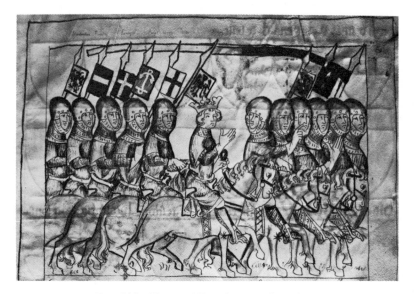

Fig. 166. Henry VII on his march to Rome

among them and other princes and counts, but feudal principles and
minute particularism maintained the many lesser potentates unless legal
claims to annex by inheritance were concerned. The crown was still an
object of ambition if only for the opportunities of family aggrandisement
it offered to its possessor. It, too, was rooted in tradition, and provided
a centre round which its disorderly bevy of satellites revolved in orbits
irregular and uncontrolled. That annex of the Empire, the kingdom of
Burgundy, now generally called Arles or the Arelate, and so often bandied
about in diplomatic negotiations, was ruled in nominal vassalage by its
great lords, such as the Count of Provence (who was King of Naples), the
Dauphin of Vienne, the Count of Savoy (who had extended his dominion
over Vaud in modern Switzerland), and the Count of Franche Comté (who
was now a son of Philip the Fair). Yet the dignity of the Holy Roman
Empire was not so tarnished as might appear. The Emperor (or King)
of the Romans was still acknowledged as the first of earthly rulers, and the
magic of the name helped to keep the crumbling Empire together. In spite
of feuds and dislocation, prosperity and population in the fragmentary
realm were increasing and expanding. Many fiefs were not ill ruled. The
towns were wealthy and self-governing; the peasants, free and unfree, had
gained in protective custom and by the competition induced by emigration,
and their depression in the later Middle Ages was still to come.

CHAPTER 26

THE BRITISH ISLES AND EDWARD I (1272–1307)

(I) THE ORGANIZATION OF ENGLAND

The years round about 1300 were the turning-point when the central Middle Ages with all their creative achievement and advance merged slowly and hazily into the later. The coming time develops from the past; it has its own creations in fact and thought; civilization grows as does the political and social machinery of life; new trends, which are to have a great future, make themselves felt; but along with their first florescence the symptoms of disintegration of the old feudal and scholastic world creep falteringly and unrecognized into view. The layman is more conscious of his power and better equipped to exercise it; Church and churchmen drift unknowingly from their leadership in thought and act into competitive politics displayed before the bar of a restive, almost formless public opinion.

In England these presages of change were as much to be found as in other western lands, but its insular history favoured, in spite of likeness, characteristic variations from the general evolution. Much, too, was due to the personality of Edward I, who, by an innovation, succeeded (20 November 1272) in his absence abroad to the kingship on his father's death, although he was not crowned till August 1274. Besides the gifts of leadership, industry, shrewd choice of ministers, and desire to rule his subjects well if autocratically, all characteristics of a great king, he had an instinct for order and system which made his reign a landmark in the formulation of law and organization. To be anti-feudal was no more in his thought than in that of his contemporaries; rather his aim was the strict royal supervision of the feudal fabric of society. Sovereign and suzerain rights were intertwined. He shared to the full in the legalistic outlook fostered by the methods of development in Church and State for three centuries. He exploited every legal claim he could advance, and pressed every legal evasion possible, however wire-drawn in either case. In his experiences in the civil wars he had learnt to know his people well, and his rule was congenial to them, but his grasping ambition imposed a disastrous strain on the country which bore evil fruit in the future.

Edward began his work of reorganization with the assistance of his friend and chancellor, Robert Burnell, Bishop of Bath and Wells (*ob.* 1292), soon after his return. Commissioners were sent round to obtain sworn information on the royal possessions, on infringements of them and usurpations, on administration and official misconduct, which was regis-

804

tered in the Hundred Rolls. It was the most efficient sequel of many such inquests. Armed with the returns, Edward enacted in his first Parliament (April 1275) the First Statute of Westminster, which largely dealt with administrative abuses. The Statute of Gloucester (1278) decreed the issue of writs *Quo Warranto*, demanding by what warrant the teeming feudal franchises were enjoyed. The object was not to destroy them but to define and register them. Prescription from 1190 was accepted as valid when no grant existed, and later usurpations were generally confirmed on payment of a fine, while the king retained his old right of entry on a franchise if his commands were not executed by its possessor. The feudal machinery, in short, was overhauled and exercised under royal control. An attempt was made (1285) by the Statute of Winchester to repress the constant local disorder, which in spite of all efforts and reforms vexed medieval England. The rights of feudal lords were safeguarded (1285) by a clause, *De Donis conditionalibus*, in the Second Statute of Westminster, which prevented donees alienating at will lands granted to them in entail, and by the Third Statute of Westminster (*Quia Emptores*) (1290), which laid down that the buyer of land in fee-simple became the direct vassal of the superior lord, not of the seller. Both king and great lords stood to gain by these statutes, but in the long run the king, the supreme suzerain, above all. The Statute of Mortmain (1279) controlled the transfer of land to the 'dead hand' of the Church by requiring a royal licence for the donation, by which adequate compensation could be secured for any loss in feudal obligations due to the Crown.

Definition was also applied to the revenues from customs at the ports. In the Parliament of 1275 the Ancient (or Great) Custom was fixed at 6*s*. 8*d*. per sack on the export of the main English commodity, wool, with a corresponding 'prise' on imported wine. Acknowledged royal rights were thus formulated. In the administration of the king's justice, three chief courts were by now at work competing with one another, each with its chief and staff: King's Bench, Common Pleas, and the Exchequer on its judicial side. In them custom enlarged by continual precedents reigned supreme. The 'Common Law' was an indigenous growth, less and less influenced by Roman Law. But above these courts there was still the jurisdiction of the king in his council, which was closely linked with the rise of Parliament. Two other functions of the king's Curia had become State departments, the Exchequer in its purely financial business under the Treasurer and the Chancery, or state secretariat, under the Chancellor, but the elastic Wardrobe under its Keeper remained in the king's household at his immediate orders, and dealt with all manner of business inside and outside routine, from kitchen supplies to the administration of war, which did not fall easily in with the traditional methods of Exchequer or Chancery. The king was the determined enemy of corruption and individual oppression among his swarming officials, central and local. A long absence in France (1286–9) produced a general breakdown of their honesty from top to bottom, which was chastised by him in exemplary fashion on his return. The weakness of his personal autocracy was that everything depended on the personal efficiency and conscientiousness of the king.

The name of Parliaments was being gradually confined to those solemn meetings of the reinforced Curia in which the king, in his search for co-operation, consulted his lieges. If this, too, was definition of a sort, it did not extend to the composition of these assemblies or much to their business. Their composition, even as regarded the magnates spiritual and lay who received a personal summons, varied with the matters for discussion. These were largely judicial, sometimes legislative, and in his earlier years Edward aimed at two such Parliaments a year, when only magnates as a rule would attend. But the practice of summoning knights representing the community of the shire and burgesses equally representative of the borough, which had begun under Henry III, was especially followed when the king desired a grant of money outside his feudal and pre-rogative revenue. The growth of these additions to Parliament, both in powers and functions, may be traced in the writs of summons. It was not until 1295 that a stable formula was invented, which lasted up to 1872. Knights and burgesses were then to come with full power to do and assent to what should be ordained by common counsel. Representatives of the lower clergy, as well as the dignitaries, were likewise summoned, thus completing the presence, personal or by representatives, of all men in the realm. The Parliament of 1295 was later known as the Model Parliament, a misnomer, for the clergy, save the prelates, gradually dropped out during the next century, preferring to make grants in their convocations, while the elected lay representatives, knights and burgesses, had not yet coalesced into a House of Commons—magnates, knights, burgesses, clergy all deliberated apart—nor were they yet an essential part of a Parliament. None the less the idea had become current that such a Parliament could be summoned which could bind all the nation by its acts. Parliament, the most characteristic English institution, which had developed from the Great Council of tenants-in-chief during the reign of Henry III, had become in wider or narrower form a durable and welcome organ of government.

(2) WALES, IRELAND AND SCOTLAND: WARS OF CONQUEST AND DEFENCE

The need of money, which had such a powerful influence on the expansion of Parliament and the tethering of the kingship, was mainly the effect of the wars which Edward undertook, whether moved by defence or aggression, and for which the normal revenue and its decaying feudal supplements were inadequate. The wars in Wales and Scotland, too, proved the inadequacy of the feudal array, that *servitium debitum* of the tenants-in-chief which had yielded fewer knights since the accession of Henry III, not to mention the time-limit of their service. The array had to be supplemented by paid troops and selected militia, while new weapons and tactics were evolved. As a military system feudalism was moribund in England.

Edward's first war was with the threatening power of the Prince of Wales, aiming at independence and the conquest of the Marches, whose Anglo-Norman lords with their palatine juris-diction and petty armies were a force in English politics. At this point it is necessary to turn back to the course of Welsh history since the death of the lord Rhys in South Wales (1197) left the field clear to the rulers of Gwynedd in the north as the champions of Welsh nationality. Llywelyn the Great (ap Iorwerth ap Owain), who ruled Gwynedd from 1194 to 1240, deserved his appellation. It was King John who removed from his path his chief rival Gwenwynwyn of Powys (1208) and gave him his own natural daughter Joan to wife, but it was also King John who all but ruined him by an invasion (1211). The Welsh rallied round Llywelyn, however; he took part in the barons' revolt, and in 1218 extorted from the English regency the Peace of Worcester, by

Fig. 167. Llywelyn ab Iorwerth on his death-bed, with his sons Gruffydd and David

which he secured his conquests in North and South Wales. Partly by deft alliances, partly by war, he retained his supremacy till his death. His son David (1240–6) was less fortunate. He was reduced to Gwynedd, and when he died internal divisions caused the loss of eastern Gwynedd to the English Crown, when it was granted to the future Edward I, then Earl of Chester. But Llywelyn ap Gruffydd, grandson of Llywelyn the Great, at last secured sole rule and resumed the task of expansion. The discord between Henry III and his barons gave the opportunity. In 1256 Llywelyn reconquered eastern Gwynedd, and very soon established his supremacy in the south, assuming the new title of Prince of Wales (1258). He became the ally of Simon de Montfort, and in spite of the earl's overthrow was able to make good terms with Henry III in the Peace of Montgomery (1267),

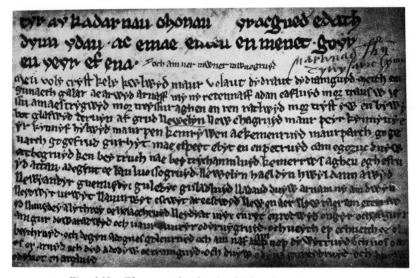

Fig. 168. Elegy on the death of Llywelyn ab Iorwerth

by which his title, his conquests, and suzerainty of most of the Marches were confirmed at the cost of renewed vassalage. No Welsh prince had stood higher since the Norman invasions.

But Llywelyn's head was turned by his success, and he misjudged the change in English leadership on Edward's accession. He refused homage to the new king, and brought on himself a carefully planned invasion. Well supported by the lords marcher, and adapting his strategy to the difficult mountain and forest lands, Edward turned the prince's defences by the use of a fleet to seize on corn-growing Anglesey. The wide principality fell like a house of cards, and Llywelyn, starved out in Snowdonia, was compelled to submit (1277). He was left as vassal Prince of Wales, with only western Gwynedd for his princedom. Untaught by experience of Edward's energy and generalship, and tempted by the exasperation of the Welsh at the alien and oppressive government of Edward's officials, which flouted Welsh customary law, he renewed the war (1282). This time Edward resolved to put an end to the Welsh danger. He mustered all his resources by land and sea, and once more blockaded Snowdonia. Llywelyn slipped out to lead a counter-movement in the south, but he was killed in a chance encounter there, and with him fell the fabric of Welsh independence. His untrustworthy brother David, who continued the resistance for months, was captured and executed as a traitor by the new, harsher law of treason come into use.

The political status of Wales was less altered than might be thought. By

Fig. 169. Ruins of Strata Florida Abbey, Cardiganshire

the Statute of Rhuddlan (1284) western Gwynedd was formed into three shires. Two similar shires (Cardigan and Carmarthen) were reorganized in the south. But these territories were kept, like the Marches, as palatinates. The new system of justice roughly combined English criminal and Welsh civil law. Strong castles of the latest concentric type held the country down—they proved invaluable in a dangerous rising of 1294—and round them boroughs of English immigrants were built. The king, too, gained a temporary victory, lost under his son, over the custom of private war among the lords marcher. The investiture of his son and heir Edward of Carnarvon, already Earl of Chester, as Prince of Wales in 1301 with suzerainty of the marcher lords was a concession to Welsh sentiment rather than a change of system. Wales remained a land of small, independent areas, a source of revenue and troops. No social revolution or change of culture was induced. The traditions of Wales, her language and literature, flourished, and old Welsh law was administered in the local courts. Thus the nationality lasted without a national centre.

Much had been learnt by Edward in the Welsh wars which was to print a new stamp on the English military system. Long campaigns had necessitated the payment of troopers fully or lightly armoured, at least after the term of feudal service expired. Payment for service abroad was soon to be the rule (1297). The archer, whether horsed for speed or on foot, had acquired a new importance. Hitherto, armed with the deadly but slow and cumbrous crossbow or with the weak short bow, drawn only to the breast, he had been a mere auxiliary. Now the longbow, drawn to the ear, was borrowed from the South Welsh to become the characteristic English weapon. It was light, it could rapidly shoot volley after volley, and yet in penetrating force it vied with the crossbow. It required long and early practice to use, and this was insisted on as the rustic exercise by Edward's revision of the old Assize of Arms in the Statute of Winchester (1285). A commission of array bringing archers from the shires produced an infantry force that Edward had the skill to combine with his armoured cavalry.

Although Edward I never set foot in Ireland, the Anglo-Norman half-conquest and organization reached their peak, from which they were shortly to descend, in his days, and there is a convenience in summarizing their history here. The tale is one of almost continuous fighting and a fitting prelude to the disaster which his Scottish ambitions brought about.

The opportunity for the Anglo-Norman invasion, which had long glimmered in the youthful dreams of Henry II, was given by the exile of Dermot MacMurrough of Okinselagh, King of Leinster, after his defeat by the High-king Rory of Connaught (1166). Next year Dermot obtained Henry's permission to engage the help of any of his subjects in a war for his restoration. Adventurous volunteers were soon found among the barons of the Welsh Marches. The highest in rank was Richard de Clare, surnamed Strongbow, Earl of Pembroke, who was promised Eva, Dermot's daughter, in marriage, but far more energetic were the Anglo-Welsh descendants of Nest, daughter of Rhys ap Teudwr of Deheubarth, a matriarch of conquerors, whose sons by her husband Gerald, castellan of Pembroke, and grandsons of varying descent were on fire to make their fortune like the Normans in Italy a century earlier. Dermot himself easily gained his restoration on terms with little help (1167), but he nursed both revenge and ambition for the high-kingship, and eagerly pressed for more. In 1169 a son of Nest, Robert FitzStephen, and others landed. All told, they were not more than 600 men, but they were inured to warfare, the horsemen armed in mail, the archers ('the flower of the youth of Wales') wielding a weapon unknown to and not to be parried by the Irish. The immediate result was the surrender of Scandinavian Wexford and widespread submission of Leinster clans. An attack by Rory was warded off by a feigned submission, which lasted only until fresh adventurers landed. This time Strongbow himself came, against Henry II's command, at the head of a large force (1170), and duly married Eva. The storm of Waterford and Dublin showed the prowess of the invaders, when King Dermot died (1171). The earl was now in an awkward position. Quite against Irish law he claimed to be Dermot's heir. The Leinster clans rose against him under Dermot's nephew, and the *Ard-rí* Rory besieged him in Dublin, while Henry II, suspicious of the enterprise, laid an embargo on supplies and recalled the adventurers. Only a reckless sortie, which put to flight Rory's army, saved him. It was the irresolute Rory's last attempt to expel the invaders.

Henry II was by this time determined to take over the conquest himself. Strongbow went to meet him in Wales, and made terms. Dublin and the seaports were to be royal domain; he was to hold the rest of Leinster of the

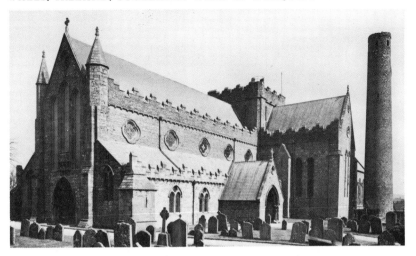

Fig. 170. St Canice's Cathedral, Kilkenny

king. During his absence the last Scandinavian attack on Ireland was made by Asgall, the expelled ruler of Dublin, with a host of Vikings, who besieged Dublin, but they were put to flight and Asgall beheaded by the governor, Miles de Cogan. Henry II landed near Waterford in October 1171 with 4000 men and marched to Dublin without having to unsheathe the sword. In fact, the Irish kings, even Rory O'Conor with reservation of his high-kingship, readily accepted him as overlord, and the churchmen were in his favour. The papal legate, who was the Irish Bishop of Lismore, held a fully attended synod at Cashel. It passed reforming decrees for the Irish Church, and acknowledged the new ruler. Dublin was given a charter on the lines of Bristol, and a rival to Strongbow was set up by the grant of Meath to Hugh de Lacy, who was made justiciar. In April 1172 the king could make his urgently needed return to England.

Henry II was by no means unmindful of the quasi-legality which a papal commission could afford his conquest. Early in his reign (1155) he had obtained some such grant from the English Pope Adrian IV, known in the dubious text of the bull *Laudabiliter*. Now, in the first flush of his reconciliation with Alexander III over the murder of Becket, and after the decrees of the synod of Cashel bringing the Irish Church into line with the Western Canon Law, the Pope confirmed his new sovereignty in bulls to him and to the Irish bishops and kings (September 1172). A further attempt at regularization was the Treaty of Windsor (1175) with King Rory of Connaught, but this proved unworkable from the first. Strongbow, who was a restraining influence, died next year, and neither Henry's representa-

811

tives nor the adventurers showed any inclination to refrain from fresh conquests. John de Courcy in a private campaign, begun in 1177, won for himself a lordship in Ulidia (Ulaid, Ulster) in the north-east. Hugh de Lacy in Meath and north Leinster was likewise building up a dominion fortified with castles of the old motte and bailey type, and by insisting on internal peace there was attracting the Irish peasants back to the soil until his murder by an Irishman (1186). Henry II himself broke the Treaty of Windsor by large grants in Munster to barons, which only took very partial effect, for the townsmen of Limerick burnt their city rather than surrender it.

A new experiment was made in 1185 when Henry II, who had already in 1177 created his son John Lackland Lord of Ireland, sent him with troops to undertake the government. It was a failure, for John angered both the Irish kinglets and the invading barons, and was soon recalled. Internecine wars among the Irish, the dispossession of native kinglets by the new barons, and speculative grants by the Lord of Ireland provide the events of these years. Rory of Connaught was expelled by his kindred and died a monk. Rapacity and plundering marked the progress of the Anglo-Normans, while the area under them gradually spread. Where they dominated there was peaceful consolidation of a feudal kind. William Marshal, the future regent, became lord of Leinster by marriage with Strongbow's daughter. The great stock of the Geraldines, under various surnames, possessed wide lands in the south; other immigrants were producing an Anglo-Irish baronage, like Theobald Walter, brother of the archbishop, who founded the Butlers of Ormonde, and William de Burgh who landed in Munster and endeavoured to conquer Connaught. The general trend was to come to terms with Irish kinglets who would accept vassalage and pay tribute for much reduced territories. The greatest of them was Cathal Redhand, who retained Connaught.

Changes among the great lordships were one feature of John's reign as king. John de Courcy was deprived of Ulster (1202), and it was given as an earldom to Hugh de Lacy the younger (1205). Then he and his brother Walter of Meath were deprived, but not permanently. John's second expedition to Ireland in 1210 had at least the wholesome effect of increasing the power of the Crown; much was done to improve the administration by forming counties and sheriff's courts and sending round itinerant justices outside the great liberties.

The fate of Connaught was sealed by a dynastic war on the death of Cathal Redhand (1224). His son Aedh foolishly used English aid to win and then revolted. The result was that Connaught was granted to Richard, son of William de Burgh, and years of fighting elapsed until the grant was made good and a kinglet found who would accept the fraction reserved for his dynasty. In 1254 the future Edward I was created Lord of Ireland by his father, but the success of his representatives was limited, although an

812

attempt of King Brian O'Neill of Cenel Eoghain (Tirowen, Tyrone) to revive the high-kingship was frustrated (1260) in spite of the importation of mailed soldiers from the Hebrides, the so-called galloglasses (*gall-óglaígh*). In Tirconnel (Donegal), Tyrone, part of Connaught, Thomond, and Desmond, the native kinglets could not be expelled. The galloglasses increased their military power. None the less, the area of English, or rather Anglo-Irish, domination had been extended, and the peace and prosperity of the east and south were maintained. Numerous small towns grew up under shelter of the castles, many of which received charters from their lords, formed gilds and became trading centres. Cathedrals, monasteries, and parish churches were built in the beautiful thirteenth-century style. Wars among and with the Irish kinglets, however, did not cease. One such was waged in Thomond between the rival factions of the O'Briens. Edward's remedy was to grant all Thomond to Thomas de Clare (hence the name of Co. Clare). It did not answer in the long run, for the O'Brien vendetta was inveterate, the De Clares were not equal to their task, and the De Burghs joined with their enemies. In Connaught and Ulster Earl Richard de Burgh expelled his rivals the FitzGeralds, and erected a great dominion from Carlingford to Galway, almost all Leth Cuinn.

The most successful of Edward's justiciars was John de Wogan, who summoned Parliaments on the English model. In 1295 knights of the shire or liberty were summoned, and in 1300 burgesses too. Unfortunately the experiment of summoning Irish kinglets was not tried. All Edward's great legislation for England was extended to Ireland, at least in the south. Growing prosperity was shown in the increase of the royal revenue from the customs and even in subsidies, in thriving towns and the acreage under the plough. It was rendered possible by the comparative order of the Anglo-Norman districts, which their business-like feudalism fostered. But there was another side. In large districts the Gaelic clans continued to live under their ancient customs, less influencing than influenced by the neighbouring barons. Norman feudalism and English direct supremacy were incompatible with their clannish way of life. They and their chieftains preferred their independence to a peace and order they did not value. The incomers regarded them as an inferior race, whereas they were only in an earlier stage of civilization, a stage which had already produced literary and artistic creations of high imaginative beauty. They hated the proud, rapacious aliens who had seized on their inheritance. Thus, whenever there was a sign of weakness, they pounced on the opportunity of retaliation, of plundering and destroying the wealth of their feudal neighbours. Edward I chose to devote himself to enlarging his dominion in Great Britain rather than to exploiting it in Ireland. With his death and the Scottish wars the chance of the clans and the ever more Hibernian baronage came, and they took it.

A very different fate than that of Ireland befell Scotland, where the introduction of feudal institutions came about by the infiltration of Anglo-Norman families, not by a marauding expedition, and where the Gaelic clans maintained themselves unbroken in a definite area north of what was called later the Highland line. Even so the kingdom of David I (1124–53) was disjointed enough with its triple division into Alban, Lothian, and Strathclyde and Galloway, and with its Norman barons absorbing a clannish spirit into their feudal jurisdictions, while the Highland chiefs were still patriarchal lords of their clans and Scandinavian kinglets and earls were ruling in the Orkneys and Hebrides. It needed the invasions of Edward I to weld these discrepant lands into a conscious Scottish nation. Much, however, had previously been done by the Kings of Scots.

It took up the reigns of four successive kings—Malcolm IV (1153–65), William I the Lion (1165–1214), Alexander II (1214–49), and Alexander III (1249–86)—to overcome completely the separatist spirit of the Gaelic clans and to effect the subjugation of the like-minded and often allied Norsemen of the Hebrides (Sodor) and Man. There was commonly a pretender among the kinsmen of the royal house for them to support. David's elder grandson, Malcolm IV, had to meet the attacks of Somerled, Lord or Kinglet of the Isles and Argyll, combined with a pretender, Donald Macbeth, which only ended with the overthrow and death of Somerled at Renfrew (1164). The rebel Lord of Galloway was not reduced until 1160. When William the Lion was captured by the English at Alnwick (1174), Galloway again rose in revolt until 1185, and on the extinction of the male line of its lords in 1234 Alexander II had to enforce by arms its subdivision among three co-heiresses by feudal law. The Gaels of Moray also had risen in favour of a new pretender, Donald MacWilliam, and had to be subdued (1187), and even then Alexander II in 1215 met and defeated another MacWilliam and another MacHeth, the last Gaelic pretenders.

The wars with the Norsemen were equally significant and long drawn out. Not to mention the hostilities and alliances of Viking times, King Magnus Bareleg of Norway had wrested from King Edgar (1097–1107) the admission of Norwegian sovranty over the western isles, and Somerled's activities later emphasized the danger to Scotland, where he was the ally of the Gaelic rebels. William the Lion took action against it (1197–8) when he reduced Harold, Norwegian Earl of Orkney but Scottish Earl of Caithness, to obedience. Alexander II subjugated Argyll in 1222, placing a royal sheriff there, and prepared to reconquer the Hebrides. His son Alexander III continued the project, defeated the fleet of Haakon IV of Norway off Largs in Ayrshire, and finally bought out the Norwegian suzerainty from Magnus VI by the Treaty of Perth (1266). Thus the Hebrides lastingly and Man for a time became subject to Scotland. Save for the Orkneys and Shetlands the kingdom was complete.

Very different were Scottish relations with England after the fixing in 1157 of the frontier. When William the Lion attempted to shift it southward, he was captured at Alnwick and compelled to admit the full vassalage of his kingdom to Henry II in return for his release (1174). This precise treaty, however, was abrogated by Richard I in 1189, and in 1192 the ties of the Scottish bishops to the English province of York were severed by Pope Celestine III, who declared the Scottish Church to be the especial daughter of and immediately subject to the Papacy. Yet an undefined claim to superiority remained, entangled with the Scottish king's possession of fiefs in England, and William the Lion submitted to have his children's marriages settled by King John. His son Alexander II, after a brief period of hostilities, married Henry III's sister Joan, and in 1237 exchanged his claim to the frontier counties for a fief within them. For a short while these cordial relations were interrupted by his second marriage to a Frenchwoman, but a show of force by Henry brought about their resumption and the marriage (1251) of Alexander III to Henry's daughter Margaret. Till an heir was born, claimants to the succession were disturbing the realm, but they agreed to the Council of Regency which Henry III set up (1258). Alexander III lived at peace with his father-in-law, and (1278) did his homage to Edward I under a mutual reservation of the independence or vassalage of Scotland. Then the problem of the succession arose again. Both Alexander's sons died young, and so did his daughter Margaret, wife of Eric II, later King of Norway. His second marriage was childless. When he died in March 1286, his only descendant was Margaret's infant daughter, Margaret, the 'Maid of Norway'. No woman had reigned in Scotland, but the Maid was proclaimed Queen and sent for. Her father King Eric was anxious to safeguard her, and Edward was eager to extend his power. After long negotiations, it was finally agreed by a Scottish assembly at Brigham in July 1290 that Queen Margaret should marry King Edward's heir, Edward of Carnarvon, under conditions which amply guaranteed Scotland's autonomy. Unhappily, the child queen died in September 1290 on the voyage to Scotland, and the peace of Scotland passed with her.

Competition for the vacant throne began among the nobility, allied legitimately or illegitimately, but seldom nearly, to the royal house. Norman in extraction or breeding and often possessors of English fiefs, they did not share the aversion to English paramountcy which was alive among the lower ranks of Scotsmen. They at once appealed to Edward, who in return pressed his claim to suzerainty; it would make his decision authoritative. He ordered an exhaustive search of documents; the resulting materials, some recording historical facts, some fantastic, but cogent to medieval eyes, were laid before the Scottish vassals at Norham in May 1291, and, although they elicited a protest from the lesser vassals, were accepted as valid evidence elsewhere. The competitors set their seals to a document binding them to accept Edward's award as lord paramount. The suit between thirteen claimants opened in August 1291 and lasted till November 1292. The three nearest to the dead queen in legitimate descent were John Balliol, Robert Bruce, and John Hastings, each representing a daughter of David, Earl of Huntingdon (*ob.* 1219), the brother of William the Lion. The case between Balliol and Bruce was a yet unresolved point of law, for Balliol, great-grandson of David, was descended from his eldest daughter, Bruce, his grandson, from his second, and it was doubtful whether the slightly closer kinship of Bruce outweighed the claim of seniority in line advanced by Balliol. Hastings, the great-grandson of the youngest daughter, could only argue that the kingdom should be divided among the co-heiresses' representatives, like an English fief: this the court (of whom 80 were named by the claimants, 25 by Edward) inevitably ruled out. In the end the decision gave the right to Balliol, as heir of the senior line, and Edward invested him as king and received his homage at Newcastle (26 December 1292).

Scotland had been saved from civil war, but John Balliol was unequal to his task as king, and the English suzerainty, unwelcome from the start to the Scots, was made exasperating by Edward's stringent legal interpretation of the obligations of vassalage. What he himself had to endure as Duke of Aquitaine, he demanded from the King of Scots—no other vassal king in Europe submitted to the like. The crisis came when Edward, at war with Philip the Fair, summoned King John to attend him abroad. Balliol refused to obey, and in 1295 made that defensive alliance with France which for three centuries profoundly influenced Scotland's cultural and political development. Directly the contemporary Welsh rebellion was quelled, Edward turned on him. Descending on Scotland in force, in July 1296 he compelled Balliol's surrender and abdication near Brechin. He treated Scotland as a forfeited fief, and annexed it to England, emphasizing the fact by carrying off from Scone the Stone of Destiny, on which Scottish kings were crowned, and placing it in Westminster Abbey.

He left behind him a triumvirate of Englishmen with garrisons to hold the country, but his ambition to create a single kingdom of Great Britain had overleapt itself. While he was in difficulties with his English subjects over his war-effort against Philip the Fair, in the spring of 1297, the angry Scottish commonalty rose under a brilliant guerrilla leader, William Wallace of Elderslie near Paisley, and before the autumn he was with his colleague, Andrew of Moray, master of the kingdom in the name of the captive King John. Their triumph was shortlived. Edward's hands were freed by his truce (1297) with Philip the Fair, and returning from his abortive expedition to Flanders, he bent all his energies to the subjugation of Scotland. In 1298 he led northward a large army, in which the majority of the archers were South Welsh longbowmen. At Falkirk he met the full force of the Scots under Wallace, who arrayed them in the customary manner of old-fashioned infantry, that is, in 'schiltrons' or close masses of pikemen. They beat back with ease the wild feudal charges of Edward's horse, but then Edward's archers riddled the schiltrons and broke their ranks until his cavalry could ride in and drive them in flight. The victory was a triumph for Edward's generalship in the combined use of cavalry and archers, but it was nearly fruitless in combating a national resistance. So long as Edward, tethered by internal and foreign difficulties, could only make a short summer campaign, the Scots held their own. Not till 1303 could the conquest be seriously undertaken by the king, who made it the object of his life. In 1305 the heroic Wallace was captured and executed as a traitor. Now, besides the instalment of English officials and garrisons, Scotland's ancient customary law was abolished and Anglo-Norman law substituted, though the ordinance to this effect was never operative.

Fig. 171. William the Lion captured at Alnwick: English caricature

Edward had been blind to the patriotism aroused by Wallace's wonderful career. The great Scottish nobles had throughout played an inglorious part in pursuit of their own interests. Two were pre-eminent. John (the Red) Comyn, lord of Badenoch and nephew of Balliol, had at one time leagued with Wallace as regent for his uncle, but submitted to Edward in 1304; Robert Bruce, Earl of Carrick and lord of Annandale, grandson of the claimant of 1290, had to this point exhibited remarkable duplicity and self-seeking. He too, had joined the patriots after Falkirk, but deserted them in 1302 and attended Edward's campaigns. In 1306 he was high in the king's confidence, while already he was in collusion with William Lamberton, Bishop of St Andrews, to raise a fresh revolt. In fact his father's death (1304) made him a pretender to the throne, and the murder of the Red Comyn at Dumfries before the altar both removed an adherent of the Balliol line and rendered revolt inevitable (January 1306). He rode to Glasgow, sought absolution, and, meagrely attended, was crowned at Scone. Three months later he was a hunted fugitive, but he returned to win the victory of Loudon Hill in Lanarkshire (May 1307). The death of King Edward (July) at Burg-on-Sands coming with an army to crush resistance made his fortunes secure, for the worthless Edward II abandoned the campaign. Bruce was free to subdue the Comyns—the vindictive harrying of Buchan became a proverb—and in 1310 obtained the adhesion of the Church. After a feeble invasion by Edward II, the blockade of the English garrisons was pressed. When Edinburgh and Roxburgh surrendered

(1314), only Stirling was left. At last Edward II and his barons were stirred to make the great expedition which ended disastrously at Bannockburn (21 June 1314). His father's generalship at Falkirk went for nothing. In the haste and disorder of the feudal charge in a mismanaged attack against a skilful defence the archers were deprived of their opportunity; those who were within range were ridden down by a Scottish squadron posted on their flank, and the unsupported English cavalry failed miserably for lack of their volleys. This crushing victory gave Bruce the heart of his people. He assumed the offensive by dispatching (1315) his brother Edward on that expedition to Ireland which broke up the fragile royal superiority there, and by fierce raids on the border English counties, in which Sir James Douglas won a grim renown. At length in 1323 Edward II accepted a truce. Under the regency of Mortimer this was converted into the Peace of Northampton (1328), which explicitly surrendered the English claim to suzerainty. The ambitious scheme of Edward I ended in planting a dangerous hereditary enemy on England's northern frontier and in exacerbating the savage, lawless turmoil of the Border. Robert I died next year, a man of rare force, sagacity, and decision. The greatness of his achievement cannot be exaggerated. If he did not create, he preserved the Scottish nation to develop its independence and national character.

(3) THE CONFIRMATION AND EXTENSION OF THE CHARTERS

The years 1290–2 form a dividing point in Edward's reign. He himself was ageing, more autocratic, and less adaptable. His intimate circle was contracted by the deaths of his much-loved queen, Eleanor of Castile (who brought him the French county of Ponthieu), his mother, and his friend, Bishop Burnell. Even the death of John Pecham, Archbishop of Canterbury (1278–92), was a loss. Pecham, who had been nominated by the Pope without consulting the king, had been a champion of ecclesiastical liberties, which brought him into open conflict with the king, but the dispute was quieted to a great degree in 1286 by Edward's writ of *Circumspecte agatis*, which allowed the most profitable rights of Canon Law jurisdiction to the Courts Christian. In one measure king and archbishop were in full accord. The Jews in England had for years been impoverished, and Edward, who shared the general aversion to them, relied for loans on the Italian merchant-bankers. He first forbade Jewish usury, while attempting to turn them to other occupations (1275). On the failure of this scheme he resorted to the ominous expedient of expelling them from England (1290), which he had already adopted in Aquitaine, setting an unhappy example to other monarchs.

The French war which began in 1294, followed by the Welsh revolt and the war with Scotland, put a disastrous strain on Edward's finances. The

'Model' Parliament, which he summoned to supply him with funds in November 1295, gave reluctant grants, and in Feburary 1296 appeared Boniface VIII's bull, *Clericis laicos*, which forbade subsidies from the clergy without papal consent. Under the leadership of Robert Winchelsey, the new Archbishop of Canterbury, the clergy in their convocation (January 1297) withdrew their consent to the grant. Indeed, what with crusading tenths to the king and his share of papal tenths, they had paid largely and were to pay more. Edward's answer was to outlaw them and to seize on their temporal fiefs. Even Winchelsey gradually gave way, and the retracting bull, *Etsi de statu* (July 1297), eased the situation. The fifth demanded by Edward was paid, and after a fierce raid by Wallace had demonstrated the danger of the realm, further grants were furnished in convocation. But, meantime, a still more serious controversy had arisen with the baronage. In February 1297, when Edward was ordering some to go with him to Flanders, and others to Gascony in the French war, the Earls of Hereford and Norfolk, respectively hereditary Constable and Marshal, refused to go to Gascony save with the king. The excuse was feudal and the two earls were disaffected owing to the king's recent attack on marcher privileges, but substantial grievances were also involved. Not only was the administration deteriorating and oppressive in the exaction of the king's prerogative rights (such as prise) and of a subsidy decreed in a narrow assembly, but arbitrary taxation on the wool-trade in the search for ready money was striking at the interests of all sheep-farmers (who were many, from earls to small-holders) in the kingdom. This was the heavy maletolt on exported wool in addition to authorized custom. In 1294 and 1297 Edward was levying this maletolt by agreement with the merchants, as well as seizing quantities of the wool as a loan in order to obtain the immediate price of the sales. The merchants did not lose for they passed on the duty, partly by enhancing the price abroad, partly—and here was the sting—by lowering the payment to the woolgrower at home. When Edward was about to quit England for his abortive campaign in Flanders, the two earls and their friends addressed to him a petition for the remedy of the burdens and arbitrary exactions of these years (July–August 1297). It was refused with excuses for his rigour, but when he had sailed, they persisted in their opposition, and the regency, hard beset with the Scottish war, felt bound to effect a compromise, for civil strife seemed imminent. On 10 October the council of regency, with the boy Edward of Carnarvon at its head, sealed not only the Confirmation of the Great and Forest Charters (which the king had already promised) but also undertook that the exactions complained of should not be repeated without common consent. The maletolt was withdrawn, not to be renewed without assent, and the earls received special pardons for their disobedience. The king retained his ancient prerogative of customs and prise; but from the Confirmation it was made clear that assent was needed for additions to the ancient rates. Both Edward and his subjects attached the highest importance to these concessions, as was shown by the king's attempts to minimize them, and the barons' to enforce them fully. In 1300 the king accepted twenty *Articuli super Cartas* for the relief of grievances; at Lincoln, in a full parliament in 1301, he assented to the disforestments already defined by a commission and for the last time solemnly confirmed the Charters. He was, in fact, driven to consent by his need of subsidies for the Scottish war. The same need caused him to tallage the royal demesne (an admitted right), and make an agreement with the foreign merchants for extra or petty customs (1303), but the English merchants assembled by him refused to follow suit and were left to the old rates. An absolution from Pope Clement V annulling his oaths to the Confirmation was hardly used. Some revenge he took, narrower entails of their earldoms on the marcher earls, and through the compliant Clement the exile of Winchelsey, who had played a leading part in the baronial resistance. But the net result remained. The Crown had been committed once more to the Charters and to the remedies for recent abuses appended to them. Common assent to new taxation, for which Parliament was the natural, though not the only, means, was made obligatory. The king had lost in a constitutional struggle due at root to his oppressive demands on his subjects for his exorbitant ambition.

Thus the reign closed with Scotland in full revolt, with internal disorder rampant, with a restive baronage, and with the royal authority checked and suspected. Yet Edward I had done great things. He developed national institutions and national law. He had made central control so much a thing of course that, while the feudal ethos remained, feudal government was growing obsolete and the aim of the baronage was rather to control the king's administration and policy than to break from it. The brewing crisis was to be seen when the crown passed to a weak and foolish king.

CHAPTER 27

SPAIN AND PORTUGAL: THE RECONQUEST

The dissolution of the Omayyad Caliphate of Cordova in 1031 and its replacement by a crowd of petty, mutually hostile Moslem principalities opened the way to the reconquest of Spain by the Christians of the north. That reconquest was a part of the general resurgence of the Christians in the Mediterranean which found expression in the Crusades to the East, but although connected in spirit and purpose, the Spanish Holy War for the most part ran its long course alone, and was essentially a local war of national revival and recovery. It was a Spanish enterprise, marked indelibly by the fundamental particularism of the variegated and semi-isolated Iberian peninsula.

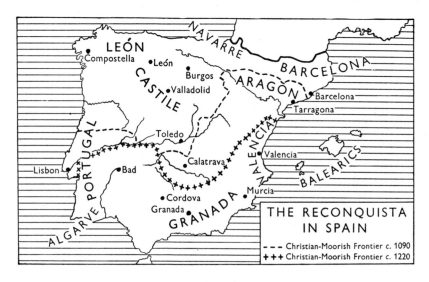

Map 20

While the Moslem kings of Seville, Granada, Málaga, and other cities were fighting for territory and predominance, Ferdinand I, King of Castile and León (1037–65), began his advance. He had already overthrown his brother Garcia of Navarre in 1054, but had preferred to leave Navarre unannexed, for his ambitions led southward. Before he died, he had conquered border-lands from Coimbra eastward, and had rendered the kings of Seville, Toledo, Badajoz, and Saragossa his tributaries. The situation of Almanzor's time was reversed. At the same time, the kings of little Aragon were nibbling at the Moorish kingdoms near them. Whether it was unwisdom or necessity, however, Ferdinand I in his will paralysed the Spanish advance by redividing his kingdoms among his three sons, with dower-towns for his daughters. Sancho II of Castile (1065–72) drove out his brothers from León and Galicia, but he was murdered while besieging his sister Urraca. He was succeeded by his brother Alfonso VI of León (1072–1109), who also took possession of Galicia, and recommenced the war of reconquest.

The Moslem kingdoms, although weakened, had not been unprosperous. The dynasty of Seville, especially under Mutamid (1069–91), had widely extended its dominion, and gave shelter to scientists and men of letters like the whilom Caliphate. Yet on the onslaughts of Alfonso, Mutamid only kept his throne by paying double tribute. King Qadir of Toledo fared worse. When he was expelled by his subjects, his ally Alfonso pretended to restore him, then besieged Toledo, and on 25 May 1085 took and annexed the city. It was a strategic gain of the highest value, for now Alfonso held the line of the river Tagus, and a base for further conquest. Qadir was thrust for a while on the throne of Valencia, and all the kings of the Taifas to the east and south became Castilian tributaries. About 1091, too, Raymond-Berengar II, Count of Barcelona, captured the city of Tarragona. If it was still small, his state possessed a historic importance, present and future. It was seafaring as well as fertile. Unlike the rest of Spain it was nominally a French fief, its language was Langue d'oc, its institutions and culture bore a south French imprint. It was a half-way house between true Spain and feudal France.

The resurgence of the Spanish Christians was largely due to their own increase in warlike skill, internal security, population, agriculture, and commerce, aided, it is true, in the eleventh century by not insignificant bands of adventurers from France, who were moved by the restless fighting spirit which found its chief outlets in Italy and the Crusades. But the Moslems contributed to it by an inferior military organization and above all by an incurable disunion even in self-defence, which made a combined attack on the uninviting north no object of their wishes. This was shown even in their desperate appeal for rescue from Africa. Betweeen 1056 and 1085 the Berber sect of Almorávides (Murābitīn), devotees of the Holy War against the infidel, had founded an empire over Barbary from Senegal to Algeria. Their leader Yūsuf ibn Tāshfīn was begged to repel the Christians by the kings of the Taifas. He came twice, routing Alfonso VI at Azagal (Zalaca) near Badajoz (1086) and checking the Christian progress. But Andalusia tempted him more than the Holy War. Instigated by his fanatic *faqihs*, he deposed (1091) the tolerant and wealthy kings of the

Taifas, while the border fighting was allowed to drag on. In fact, the Christians of Aragon made some advance.

During the first period of the Reconquest, however, the most famous and characteristic figure was not a king or ruler but a Castilian noble, Rodrigo (Ruy) Diaz de Vivar, 'the Cid', the national hero of Spain. He expressed the ideal of his people in his long career, which, after much unwarranted scepticism, is now clearly known. Born near Burgos, the capital, he distinguished himself under Ferdinand I and his son, so much so that Alfonso VI arranged his marriage with Jimena of Oviedo, a cousin of his own. But a raid on the King of Toledo, then Alfonso's ally, caused the Cid's exile from Castile (1081), and his career as a free-lance began. As stipendiary ally of the Moslem King of Saragossa, he fought the Aragonese and Catalans, capturing the Count of Barcelona himself (1082). A reconciliation with Alfonso did not last. In 1090 the suspicious king exiled him again and confiscated his lands, without allowing him the primitive judicial process of the day. Once again the Cid entered the service of Saragossa, and once again captured Berengar-Raymond II. The two became friends, and the Cid's daughter married the count's heir. The Cid was now dominant round the river Ebro, but failed to gain a lasting return to Castile, which he raided in revenge. Up to 1092 he had been the paid protector of Qadir of Valencia, and when the unpopular king was murdered, he assailed the city on his own account, took it (1094), and ruled it until his death (1099), more than repelling the vain attacks of Ibn Tāshfīn. His widow Jimena struggled on against the Almorávides for three years. Then at her call King Alfonso rescued her, and burned Valencia as he withdrew. The Cid was far more than a soldier of fortune in an anarchic time. He was a statesman and general, whose marvellous exploits fully earned the romantic glamour which surrounded his name for centuries.

In spite of some defeats—one at Uclés from Ibn Tāshfīn's successor, Ali (1108)—Alfonso VI maintained his hold on Toledo and his new-won frontier until he died (1109). A crisis supervened. His elder daughter and heiress, Queen Urraca (1109–26), had borne to her first husband, Raymond of Franche Comté, a boy Alfonso. Being a widow, her nobles forced her to marry a noted warrior, King Alfonso I of Aragon and Navarre (1104–34), who rapidly became unpopular and fell into bitter strife with the queen. To add to the confusion Diego Gelmirez, Bishop of Santiago, set up the boy Alfonso as King of Galicia, while the queen's younger sister Teresa, wife of Henry of Burgundy (*ob.* 1112), who had received the western county of Portugal (Oporto), endeavoured to enlarge the endowment of her husband and son. The result was complete anarchy, each party fighting for its own hand, and illustrating both the violent ingrained particularism of Spain and the reckless indiscipline of the warlike nobility. Castile, León, Galicia, Portugal, Aragon, and Navarre were all at odds. An improvement began

22. Castile and Aragon, 1033–c. 1300

(a) The House of Castile, 1033–1284

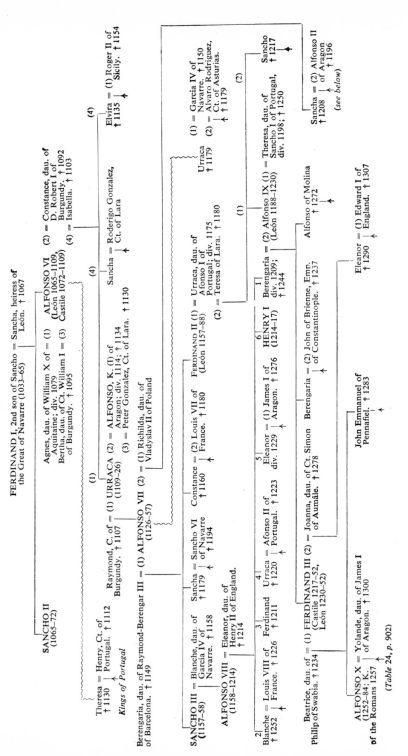

(Table 24, p. 902)

(b) The House of Aragon, 1033–1327

RAMIRO I, 4th son of Sancho = Gisberga of
the Great of Navarre (1035–63) | Bigorre

SANCHO RAMIREZ
(1063–94)

PETER I
(1094–1104)

ALFONSO I (2) = Urraca, Q. of Castile,
(1104–34) div. 1114. †1134

RAMIRO III
(1134–37, abd.)
†1147

PETRONILLA = Raymond-Berengar IV
(1137–62; †1172) of Barcelona. †1162

Dulcia = Sancho I of
†1198 | Portugal. †1211

SANCHO = Sancha Nuñez
C. of Provence of Lara
1181–85; †1223

Sancha = Raymond VII of
| Toulouse. †1249

ALFONSO II = Gersinda of
C. of Provence Sabran
1196–1209

Isabella = (1) Philip III of
†1271 | France. †1285

FREDERICK II = Eleanor, dau. of
(Sicily 1296–1337) | Charles II of Naples †1341

Kings of Sicily
(Table 19b, p. 767)

Matilda, dau. = (1) ALFONSO II (2) = Sancha, dau. of
of Afonso I (1162–96) Alfonso VII of
of Portugal Castile. †1208

RAYMOND BERENGAR III
C. of Provence 1167
†1181

Eleanor = (5) Raymond VI of
Toulouse. †1222

Yolande = Alfonso X of
†1300 Castile. †1284

Yolande = (1) Robert
†1302 | of Naples †1343

PETER II = Mary, heiress
(1196–1213) of Montpellier

Constance (1) = Emerich of Hungary. †1204
†1222 (2) = (1) Emp. Frederick II. †1250

Eleanor, dau. of Alfonso VIII = (1) JAMES I the Conqueror (2) = Yolande, dau. of Andrew II
of Castile, div. 1229 (1213–76) of Hungary. †1251

Alfonso
†1260

JAMES I = Sclarmonda
(Majorca 1278–1311) | of Foix

Kings of Majorca

Elizabeth = Dinis of
†1336 | Portugal †1325

PETER III (1276–85) = Constance, dau. of
(I of Sicily, 1282–85) K. Manfred of
Sicily. †1302

(1) = Blanche, dau. of Charles II
of Naples. †1310
(2) = Mary of Cyprus. †1321
(3) = Elisenda of Moncada

(Table 24b, p. 903)

JAMES II
(Sicily 1285–95;
Aragon 1291–1327)

ALFONSO III
(1285–91)

when Urraca died and her son Alfonso VII (1126–57) succeeded, but it took him some years to pacify his step-father and aunt and to quell his nobles. When Teresa was dead and her son Count Alfonso swore fealty for Portugal (1137), the Castilian king was secure.

Fortunately, the Almorávides, now centred in Spain, were thoroughly degenerate in pleasant Andalusia, and in 1125 lost all their African dominion to a new Berber sect, the Almohades (Muwahhid, Unitarians). In Spain, too, they were losing ground to rebel Moslems and Christians. In 1118 Alfonso I the Warrior of Aragon captured Saragossa from its petty king, and made it his capital. His victorious raids reached the sea near Granada. Meanwhile Count Raymond-Berengar III of Barcelona (1097–1130), was active in the same task of reconquest. He had wide lands in Languedoc, he acquired the county of Provence by marriage (1112), he consolidated his dominion in Catalonia. His best victory was maritime, when (1115) he joined with Pisa against the piratical Moors of the Balearic Isles. He left Catalonia a strong state and a Mediterranean sea-power.

The death of Alfonso the Warrior produced a war of succession. His brother, the monk Ramiro III (1134–7), reigned only long enough to beget a daughter, Queen Petronilla (1137–72), but Navarre went to another branch, and Alfonso VII attempted to conquer Aragon. Finally, Raymond-Berengar IV of Barcelona (1130–62), who had married the infant queen, was acknowledged as ruler (1140). The personal union of Aragon and Catalonia, one pure Spanish, the other half-French, was the first step in the formation of a singular tripartite state.

In the same time a new kingdom was being added to the jarring Christian states of the Peninsula. Emboldened by success against the Moors, Afonso I Henriques, Count of Portugal, assumed the title of king (1139). His new rank was confirmed by a brilliant victory over the Moslems at Ourique and by the conquest (1147) of the city and invaluable port of Lisbon at the mouth of the river Tagus, which was mainly due to a Crusading fleet from the Netherlands, induced to help him on their voyage to Palestine. Many remained as settlers, along with Spanish migrants, in the thinly peopled lands reconquered. Alfonso VII acknowledged the new title in 1143, when the new king became a tributary vassal of the Papacy. A shadow of superiority was retained by Alfonso VII in the style of Emperor, which he assumed (1135) following the example of Ferdinand I. It was, however, a title rather emphasizing the independence of the peninsula as against the Holy Roman Empire than giving effective suzerainty over its discordant kingdoms. The later history of Portugal, whose dialect became a literary language, only served to accentuate its separation and to create a nationality.

In face of Christian attacks, the Moorish kings who shared Andalusia with the decadent Almorávides made no headway. In 1146 one of them

*Fig. 172. King Alfonso VIII of Castile, Queen Eleanor and the
Master of the Order of Santiago*

called in the Almohades, who proceeded in years of warfare to reunite
Moslem Spain (by 1172). Meanwhile the Christians were at one another's
throats. Alfonso VII at his death gave Castile to one son, Sancho III, and
León to another, Ferdinand II (1157–88). Sancho was quickly succeeded
by his infant son, Alfonso VIII (1158–1214). Wars between the Christian
kings and civil war in Castile between the factions of Castro and Lara raged
for years. From 1166, however, the cause of Alfonso VIII gained ground.
The king drove back his assailants and subdued his vassals. He married
a daughter of Henry II of England. One of his own daughters he gave to
his cousin, Alfonso IX of León (1188–1230), another to Louis VIII of
France. He obtained the alliance of the Kings of Aragon. After repeated
conflicts he finally sheared the Basque provinces from Navarre (1200).
This age of strife naturally favoured the Moors, who regained Cordova,
lost to Alfonso VII, and repeatedly invaded Portugal, but internecine war
did not prevent the Christians attacking the infidel, as when Sancho I of
Portugal (1185–1211), again with the aid of voyaging crusaders, captured
Silves in Algarve (1189). At last the Almohade Yaqūb sent a strong force
from Africa and inflicted the crushing defeat of Alarcos on Alfonso VIII
(July 1196), who was compelled to beg for a truce. After 1200 it was evident
that the decisive contest between the two faiths was at hand. Alfonso VIII
appealed for aid all round. Pope Innocent III proclaimed a special
Crusade. In 1212 Alfonso marched from Toledo with an army from all

827

Iberian states save León, and inflicted a complete rout on Muhammad and the Almohade forces at Las Navas de Tolosa (16 July). The Almohades never recovered from this overthrow in Spain, where their dominion began to break into fractions.

Internal turbulence, external wars, and heedless personal ambition now intervened to halt the Christians' progress. Navarre, indeed, now confined to the Pyrenean slopes, was falling out of the main current of Spanish events. On the death of Sancho VII, the Navarrese elected his nephew, Theobald I (IV), Count of Champagne, who drew the kingdom into a French orbit (1234). In Castile the troublous, brief reign of Alfonso VIII's son, Henry I, a minor (1214–17), was followed by a singular war of succession. His sister, Berengaria, whose marriage to Alfonso IX of León had been annulled, resigned her rights to her son, Ferdinand III (1217–52), but he was opposed by his unnatural father, Alfonso IX. Supported by a majority of nobles, however, Ferdinand was able to ward off his father, and gradually to tame the Lara and other unruly lords. When Alfonso IX died in 1230, he made good his succession to the throne of León. Henceforward Castile and León were never divided, and slowly merged into a single kingdom of vastly greater power.

Portugal was torn by throes of a different nature. Sancho I, not too fortunate as a warrior, won a name as 'the Populator'. In the devastated lands north and even south of the Tagus, he rebuilt old towns and castles, founded new ones, and introduced settlers from the north. He especially endowed the Military Orders, Templars, Hospitallers, and the newer Spanish Knights of Alcántara (in Portugal Avis) and Santiago. These last had been founded and won renown in the Moorish wars under Alfonso VIII, and had already been encouraged by Afonso I. All alike possessed the discipline and system lacking in baronial and communal levies. In this advance of security and prosperity Sancho, like his predecessors, had been largely aided by the Church, and like them had rewarded bishops and monasteries with wide lands, which, since he was already a papal vassal, made them an over-mighty power in the land. With the Church he latterly fell out, for when the citizens of Oporto rose against their lord, the bishop, and imprisoned him, Sancho took their side. He fell out, too, with the Bishop of Coimbra, and exercised a strict hand over the Portuguese Church. Innocent III intervened, mildly for him, since the preparations for Las Navas de Tolosa were in progress, and the Archbishop of Braga was on the king's side. He received a startling reply, doubtless penned by the chancellor Julian, an old minister of the two kings, who suggested confiscation of the overgrown Church lands on the lines of Arnold of Brescia. None the less Sancho fell sick to death, and in alarm gave way on all points. He died shortly after, leaving his son Afonso II (1211–23) to carry out the terms imposed. In the Cortes of 1211 it was decreed that Canon

Law was part of the law of the realm, overriding any contrary secular law, and that the clergy were free from most taxes: only the right to buy fresh lands was withheld them.

This surrender was partly due to the imminence of civil war with his brothers and a Leónese invasion. Afonso II, with Innocent's eventual sanction and aided by Castile, came off victor and avoided dangerous alienations of the royal domain. But he later endeavoured to diminish the Church's immunities and its growing lands, and further (c. 1220) angered the nobles by an inquest into the titles to their domains. Insurrection and papal threats induced him, too, to surrender before he died. He left to his son Sancho II (1223–46) an unhappy legacy of a divided realm, in which both Church and barons were over-powerful.

Alfonso II of Aragon, who succeeded his parents in their realms, and expropriated the branch of his house in Provence in favour of his own line, was as much occupied in French and Mediterranean politics as in Spanish. He was the ally more often than the foe of Castile. For aid in the capture of Cuenca from the Moors he was released from the slender tie of vassalage for Aragon by Alfonso VIII (1177), and later (1179) made a treaty with him delimiting their spheres of the Reconquest, but his best achievement was the further consolidation of Catalonia. His son, Peter II (1196–1213), alarmed by the prospect of the Albigensian crusade on his heretic vassals in Languedoc, had attempted to insure himself by accepting the over-lordship of Innocent III (1204) to the indignation of his subjects, who denounced it. In the end he went to war, and fell in the defeat of Muret. It was the intervention of Innocent which rescued his minor son, James I the Conqueror (1213–76), from the clutches of Count Simon de Montfort. His early years were filled with the struggle to hold his own against kinsmen and nobles, but his strong and capable character in the end ensured his victory. By the close of 1227 he was ready to take his share in the Reconquest.

The rise to power of St Ferdinand III and James the Conqueror coincided with the collapse of the Almohades. On the death of Yūsuf II (1223) Moslem Spain once more broke into fragmentary kingdoms. Even in Africa the Almohades were losing territory, and in 1229 one of them, Mamūn, was aided by Ferdinand to regain a tottering throne. Alfonso IX of León was then conquering Badajoz. Ferdinand's progress in Andalusia was slow and steady. In 1236 he conquered Cordova, in 1248 Seville, and obtained the submission of Cadiz and the south-west coast. The Moorish Kings of Murcia and Granada became his vassals. Meanwhile James I was conquering (1229–35) Majorca and the Balearic Isles, which were made a new Catalan kingdom by colonization. While extirpating Moorish piracy, James was also pressing south by land; in 1238 he captured the great port of Valencia, and soon after occupied, in spite of revolts, the whole region allotted in 1179 to Alfonso II. When Alfonso X of Castile was faced with a Murcian revolt (1261), James came to his aid, and'took a small share of the conquest round Alicante in return (1266). Valencia was organized as one of his three confederate kingdoms alongside of Aragon proper and Catalonia. As has been said earlier, by treaty with St Louis of France Catalonia was freed in 1258 from French suzerainty, while James in return renounced his lost lordship in Languedoc, retaining only the seigneury of Montpellier. This and the kingdom of Majorca he bequeathed to his younger son, James (II), while his elder son, Peter III the Great (1276–85), the conqueror of Sicily, succeeded to Aragon.

In spite of internal disorder and Sancho II's inefficiency the advance of Portugal along the western coastlands kept pace with its neighbours'. Sancho himself reached the mouth of the river Guadiana and the coast of Algarve by 1240, and after much dispute with Castile the Algarve was finally in 1267 acknowledged to be Portuguese, thus practically completing the kingdom. The best of the Moorish fighting was done by the richly rewarded Military Orders.

Moors, free and serf, remained in plenty under Christian rule, but after the conquest of Murcia only one Moslem kingdom, and that tributary, was left in Spain, that of the Nasrids of Granada in southern Andalusia. It was founded in 1230 by Muhammad I al-Ahmar (*ob.* 1273), who in 1238 fixed his capital in the almost impregnable city of Granada. To him flowed a stream of refugees. He was obliged to accept vassalage and cede territory to Ferdinand III and even to Alfonso X, but the strength of his mountain stronghold and a skilful policy enabled him to become a considerable force in the faction-rid politics of Castile.

St Ferdinand's son, Alfonso X the Learned (1252–84), had many gifts, but not that of guiding a turbulent, much troubled state. He inherited from his grandfather, Philip of Swabia, Hohenstaufen blood, and wasted energy, treasure, and popularity in a vain attempt to secure the crown of the Holy Roman Empire, which he was forced to abandon in 1275 by Pope Gregory X. But he was an intellectual and learned monarch, and his influence on Spanish culture was considerable. He protected Moorish and Jewish culture, encouraged the production of lyrical poetry in the Galician dialect and the writing of Spanish history, and was a busy legislator. He was a student of Roman and Canon Law. In this sphere his greatest achievement was the composition with a band of jurisprudents of the *Siete Partidas*, an encyclopedia of law in the form of a code, which became a textbook for Spanish lawyers. In this he adopted the theory of royal absolutism, much resented by the undisciplined nobles, which, along with his own irresolution and extravagance, was a cause of the disorders of his reign. He was met by repeated rebellions, in which his kinsmen and the Moors of Granada took part and the new Moorish dynasty of Morocco, the Banu-Marin, intervened.

Fig. 173. King Alfonso X of León dictating his Book of Chess

The climax came when his eldest son, Ferdinand de la Cerda, died in 1275, leaving two young sons. In the *Siete Partidas* Alfonso had laid down the Roman principle of representation, soon to be adopted by his brother-in-law, Edward I, over the Scottish succession, by which his elder grandson became his heir, but his own second son Sancho and the nobles stood out for Sancho's heirship as nearest of kin. Alfonso gave way, and then tried to carve out a small kingdom in Andalusia for the disinherited grandson. The result was civil war once more between father and son, in the midst of which the king died (1284) and Sancho IV succeeded to a heritage of turmoil and invasion.

The lot of Portugal, worse at first than that of Castile, was improving at the close of the century. The expansion to the south in the reign of Sancho II was not accompanied with internal harmony. Noble contended with noble, Templar with Hospitaller, bishop with bishop, the prelates with the monasteries, clergy with laity; all were malcontent with the king; the kingdom was lapsing into anarchy. The greed and vast wealth of the Church was a perennial sore. At the instance of the prelates Pope Innocent IV intervened as suzerain, and appointed the king's brother and heir Afonso, Count of Boulogne, curator of the realm. Afonso III expelled his brother (1246), and succeeded him at his death (1248), but his very energy brought him into conflict with the Church. Allied with the townsmen, he surveyed the Crown estates and recalled illegal, extravagant, or fraudulent alienations. The dues were henceforth to be paid in money, not in kind, while the Military Orders, no longer at war with the infidel, were subjected to taxation. By an illuminating reform he renounced the right of debasing the coinage in return for a fixed tax to be paid once a reign. But the court was spendthrift and oppressive, and the clergy were up in arms at the continual invasion of their immunities. A long controversy with successive Popes ended in his excommunication (1277), when his son Dinis aided in the government. Afonso III yielded on his deathbed in 1279, but King Dinis carried on his policy until he obtained a reasonable compromise in 1289. Laws of 1286 and 1291 checked the further increase of Church lands. Although troubled by war with Castile and with his rebellious son Afonso, Dinis 'the Husbandman' gave his country good government. He drained marshes and planted woods and encouraged agriculture. He reorganized the navy, he had translated the Castilian *Siete Partidas*, he was a poet and patron, he founded the University of Coimbra. When he died in 1323, he left Portugal prosperous to a coming forty years of peace.

Social and constitutional conditions in the Christian states of Spain during the period of the Reconquest varied according to the state, but as a whole were more advanced, and, save in Catalonia, less feudalized in jurisdiction than was their neighbour France. Constant warfare and the repopulation of conquered territories, promoted by the monasteries, produced earlier freedom among peasants and townsmen, although they fostered the turbulent spirit and independence of all classes alike. Under and around the great lords (*ricos hombres*) the lesser nobles, the *infanzones* (later called *hidalgos*), became very numerous, including every freeman who possessed a horse for military service. Below them came the free peasants, although these were losing the right to choose their lord. The serfs in Castile, a large proportion of the peasantry, began to rise in the thirteenth century, often at the cost of severe struggles and bloodshed. A decree of Alfonso IX of León in 1215 for royal serfs marks a change which reached to freedom by 1300. The townsmen meanwhile with growing prosperity were gaining their charters or *fueros* and their customary local laws, which Alfonso X did much to unify by a typical *fuero* granted to certain cities. Nothing was more characteristic of Castile than the *Hermandades* (confraternities) of communes as a kind of police force to resist oppression and repress brigandage.

Moslem serfs suffered a hard lot, but those communities which surrendered under treaty enjoyed, like the numerous Jews, an ample degree of autonomy. So did the Christian Mozarabs who were freed from the Moorish yoke. All three exercised a marked influence on the culture and manners of Spain and Portugal.

In Portugal, as in Castile, personal serfdom disappeared by 1300, but in Aragon the peasantry were more hardly treated. Valencia was tilled by Moorish slaves and tenant-farmers under the immigrant nobility. In Aragon proper the lot of the serfs, Christian and Moslem alike, became even harsher in the thirteenth century. In feudal Catalonia they were crushed by dues and services, the 'evil usages', although above them there was a class of free dependants. But the townsmen of Aragon, and especially of sea-faring Catalonia, were freer and more important even than in Castile.

Fig. 174. Court of Lions, Granada

Connected with the prosperity of the towns was the early growth of the Cortes, assemblies like those of the English Parliaments and the French States General. Their development and powers outran their northern counterparts. The peninsula had long possessed assemblies of magnates, a form of the Curia Regis of France and England. The first undoubted appearance in them of delegates of the towns is recorded in 1188 in León. In the thirteenth century Cortes, so constituted, occur in every state except Navarre and with considerable powers. Under Alfonso X those of Castile and León met together. In Portugal, town deputies are first attested in 1254. The Cortes fell into the three divisions of magnates and knights, clergy, and townsmen, and in all states exercised, by their petitions, complaints, and grants, a strong influence on the government. In Aragon proper (where magnates and knights were separate 'arms' or *braços* of the Cortes) and in Catalonia they were a formidable check on the kings, and their consent became necessary to legislation, whereas in the rest of the peninsula the king was the sole law-maker, even when petitions and complaints induced his decrees. Two weaknesses had already begun: only the townsmen made grants, thus separating their interests from those of the nobles and clergy; and the free peasants were unrepresented, the knights being allied rather with the nobles than with the freemen of town or country. Their grants of money gave the townsmen bargaining power, but they were isolated from the other factors in the state. As yet, however, they had a great career before them.

BOOK IX

THE FOURTEENTH CENTURY

✿✣✿

CHAPTER 28

THE PAPACY, GERMANY AND ITALY

(I) THE PAPACY AT AVIGNON

The settlement of the Papacy at Avignon in Provence by Pope Clement V (1305–14), although prepared for by a long chain of events beginning at least with the election of the Frenchman Urban IV and the French and Angevin influence in the College of Cardinals, was due at the moment to almost casual contemporary circumstances. Rome was anything but a safe residence, the actions of Philip the Fair required close watching and personal contact, Henry VII was about to make his adventure in distracted Italy, a General Council was to be held at Vienne, and both Gascon Pope and French cardinals were loth to quit their native land. Avignon on the east bank of the Rhone was well fitted to be a temporary home. It was close to, yet outside, the French kingdom, the Count of Provence was the vassal king of Naples, and it was encircled by the Comtat Venaissin, a direct possession of the Papacy. In 1309 Clement moved there with the Curia as the safest place in Christendom, and in spite of tentatives for return to Italy there the Papacy remained fixed for two generations. Those tentatives and the continual intervention and ambitions of the Papacy in Italy are best treated in other sections. They were inspired by the conviction that Rome as the seat of the Roman Curia could only be safe if Italy were both removed from the effective action of the Holy Roman Emperors of Germany and under the strict control of the Popes. The more French and the more anchored in France the Popes were, the more they seemed anxious to assert their authority over Italy. It was a mainspring of their policy, which, besides the theoretical clash of the Two Swords, governed their attitude towards the Emperors.

The second persistent object of the Papacy was the furtherance of the Crusade, now directed against the dangerous advance of the Turks of Asia Minor, which threatened both Constantinople and, in piracy at sea, Christian trade in the Levant. Although never so much devoted to it as to their Italian domination, the Popes were the only potentates in Europe

Fig. 175. Avignon, the papal palace

who consistently perceived and endeavoured by diplomacy and subventions to fend off the common danger.

In some connexion with the Crusade stood the prolonged efforts of the Popes to bring about peace between France and England, which all shattered on the irremediable opposition of the two foes as well as on the suspicion in England of papal partiality. The Popes indeed were Frenchmen under the aegis of the French king. Though only the pontificate of the timorous Clement V could be reasonably described by Petrarch's phrase, 'the Babylonish Captivity', there were enough grounds to make them distrusted in England, disobeyed and flouted in Germany, and hated in Italy, which suffered from their wars and exorbitant claims without the profits of their residence.

Consistent as they were in their aims both in the secular affairs adumbrated above and in their organized over-centralization of Church government to be shortly described hereafter, the Popes of Avignon showed all the accustomed variety of men in their personal characters, aptitudes, and interests, which diversified their pontificates. Clement V was sickly, squeezable, nepotistic, accused of simony. John XXII (1316–34), elected after a dilatory, disgraceful conclave, was a rigid, harsh despot, an acute lawyer, a prudent financier, implacable and intolerant of opposition, not to be bent from his resolves. The Cistercian Benedict XII (1334–42) was an austere, conscientious reformer, disliked as such. He was succeeded by a great noble, Clement VI (1342–52), who scattered money far and wide, and lived in luxury and splendour in the fortress-palace he completed. His court was a centre of art and letters and learning, of feasting and display, which emptied the treasury. Innocent VI (1352–62), well meaning and impoverished, was unequal to his stormy times. Urban V (1362–70)

*Fig. 176. Pope Clement V consecrates Baldwin of Luxemburg
as Archbishop of Trier in Avignon*

showed himself an amiable, impulsive, popular ascetic, whom an experience of Rome soon sent back to Avignon. In Gregory XI (1370–8), for whom return to Rome was a firm determination at last carried out (1377), politics vied with the zealous persecution of heretics.

The period of the Papacy at Avignon saw the culmination of the centralizing process in the medieval Church. In papal autocracy, in administration, in finance it reached its utmost limits, and each Pope, whether saintly, political, reforming, splendid, or despotic, bent his efforts to that end. The work of the Curia fell into four main departments. The Camera Apostolica dealt with finance. Its head, the Chamberlain, was the Pope's right-hand man, and his office was charged with political relations as well as taxes and expenditure. The Chancery, elaborately organized, was charged with the papal letters of ecclesiastical administrative business. Its chief, the Vice-Chancellor, could only act on the Pope's mandate, unlike the Chamberlain. Owing to the enormous growth of judicial business, whether of appeal or first instance, a subdivision of courts and powers had become necessary. The Pope in Consistory was the highest, the most busy was the *Audientia Sacri Palatii*, known from 1336 as the *Rota*, which decided the numberless cases due to the processes of papal reservation and provision, while an allied court was concerned with the many pleas in bar of action. They were the happy hunting-grounds of the crowd of canon lawyers. Lastly, the Penitentiary's duties were to regulate the removal of ecclesiastical censures, to grant dispensations of all kinds, and absolutions in reserved cases. Taken altogether, the Curia at Avignon swarmed with officials of various grades, whose pay and rewards were derived from abundant fees and papal preferments.

The autocracy of the Popes, who reorganized and expanded their bureaucracy, was exemplified by Clement V in his treatment of the General Council of Vienne (1311–12) when he abolished the Order of the Temple. 'I will do it all the same whether you like it or no', he declared to the Council, and he acted on the assertion. In daily administration he and his successors multiplied their collations to benefices which were not elected and widened the net of their reservations. By the time of Urban V ecclesiastical patrons had almost everywhere lost their function of collation, although in England at least lay patrons fared better. At the same time a similar encroachment was practised in the provision to vacant sees, until at last Gregory XI reserved all sees for his own nomination. In point of fact in most countries a tacit concordat was reached between kings and Popes, the royal wishes being acceded to in the provisions in most cases. It was the electing chapters which suffered, and by their inability to agree on a candidate they prepared their own fate. In the Empire, however, where the Popes were at odds with the Emperors, and the chapters and abbeys were more independent, a prolonged struggle took place. In vain the Papacy quashed elections, made other nominations, and pronounced excommunication on elect and electors. The recalcitrants stood their ground. When Lewis the Bavarian was succeeded by Charles IV, things went no better. In law the Popes won a formal victory for their prerogative at the cost of a fiction. They quashed the election, and then provided the elect.

Provisions, great and small, apart from the special exacerbation in Germany, roused bitter and clamorous discontent over Europe. They produced absentees, foreigners, pluralists, neglect of the benefices, simony and hordes of benefice-hunters at Avignon, unfit provisors, heavy taxation and legal fees in interminable suits at the Rota. Cardinals and curialists battened on them. In England the indignation roused caused Statutes of Provisors and of Praemunire, enabling the king at least, who had a strong interest in rewarding his own ecclesiastical servants, to meet the Pope on more even terms in the competition for valuable preferments. In Germany the provisors were largely unsuccessful and might be repelled with crude violence. The fact that a provision, for the most part automatically given to a petitioner, was but the starting-point of a long, uncertain, and expensive legal process before it could take effect made the system the more unpopular among the smaller fry. Yet it had its merits. It checked the negligence, the narrowness, and the illegalities of the ordinary collators; it gave endowment to neglected men. The universities ended by sending up to the Papacy lists of meritorious scholars who deserved support by provisions.

It was not merely the desire to control Church appointments which moved the Papacy to this enormous extension of provisions. They furnished, especially if of bishoprics and abbeys, important financial resources in fees and dues. What with wars, lavish splendour, and an elaborate bureaucracy, the need of money was always in the forefront in Avignon. A vast fiscal system was developed to meet it, which tapped the wealth of the Church. Fees to the Pope, the Chancery, the cardinals, and the various officials, were a heavy burden on prelates at Avignon. Then there were the taxes levied locally by papal collectors, the annates or first fruits (i.e. a year's income of new incumbents), which were systematized by John XXII, the 'father of annates', the tenths (of ecclesiastical incomes) frequently demanded for crusades which might not be undertaken, the special subsidies, the property of dead prelates (*spolia*), and finally, the procurations due to bishops on their rounds of visitation and taken by the Popes, while legates and collectors were paid by local clergy. Add to this that debts were never forgiven by the insatiable Curia (itself in debt to its bankers), and their payment was enforced by the severest ecclesiastical penalties—a bishop might remain unburied until the Papacy was satisfied by his successor—and it will be seen how odious the luxurious court of Avignon became to Western Christendom. Its magnificence, greed, and vices were a byword.

In a somewhat spasmodic fashion the Popes were alive to the abuses in the Church. Clement V was fertile in wise rules on discipline. His better successors at times drove office-seekers from Avignon and enforced residence and particular reforms on the Orders. Of them the most systematic was Benedict XII. There was a general relaxation of their Rules among both monks and friars. In the monasteries, the manual labour, inculcated by St Benedict, was disused; the lay brothers, even of the Cistercians, ceased to function, and were succeeded by leaseholders, while the vigilant, direct administration of their lands by great abbeys made way for the same easier system, which encouraged inertia. Flesh-eating, personal property, careless finance, and lax claustration were typical failings. The numbers of vagabond monks, the *gyrovagi*, expelled or truant, was a prevalent evil, increased by the ravages of war. Discord in abbey and Order was recurrent. Benedict XII endeavoured to revive strictness and fervour by comprehensive reform in a series of constitutions (1330–9) for the Cistercians, Benedictines and Cluniacs, and Austin Canons. His regulations were moderate and far reaching had they been steadily obeyed, but obedience, not arising from unprompted zeal, was hard to gain even in reputable England, where the horrors of war and the pernicious habit of 'commending' an abbey to a high-placed personage, who sucked away its income, were not found. There at any rate the triennial provincial chapters, decreed in 1215, were held, and Benedict XII's canons ordering the maintenance of student monks at the universities were partially observed. In France, Italy, and Germany, however, disturbed by war, faction, or the strife between Papacy and Empire, and then by the Great Schism, the Benedictine constitutions were a dead letter, and monasteries ruled by a commendatory abbot were virtually secularized. Revival came from private enthusiasts, not from papal decrees.

More success attended the Popes in the persecution of heresy. John XXII fiercely attacked the Spiritual Franciscans in Provence, who denounced the worldliness of the hierarchy. He came into conflict with the majority of the Friars Minor over their tenet of the absolute poverty of Christ, which he declared heresy (1323). The revolt, which obtained the support of Lewis the Bavarian, was serious, but it faded away. The Friars submitted to own property in their own name. John XXII set the Inquisition on the rebels, in which the power of the bishops had been increased by the Council of Vienne. As a result heresy ebbed eastward. The Waldenses were too near Avignon not to suffer. Gregory XI sent expeditions against them in the Alps. His prisons were filled with those the sword and the stake had spared. Only the Great Schism allowed them to survive. The Inquisition, thus sharpened by the Popes, was, however, losing its general efficacy. The lay authorites viewed it with suspicion, and heretical opinions in spite of all were spreading above and below ground amid the simmering critical ill will towards the official Church. Oddly enough, the persecutor John XXII himself had propounded dubious opinions on the state of the departed before the Day of Judgement; they were exploited by his opponents, but he retracted them on his deathbed.

Not only, however, by persecution, crusade, and internal reforms did the early Popes of Avignon endeavour to fortify Christianity. They gave support and established hierarchies for the Franciscan and Dominican missions in China and Persia. For a time there were prospects of much success, but the overthrow of the Mongol dynasty in China (1368) and the erection of a new Turkish-Tartar empire in Transoxiana and Persia by the fervent Moslem Tamerlane (1369–1405), who proclaimed the Holy War, cut the life-lines to the West, and the missions faded away. More durable was the unofficial stir within the Church. The mystical impulse was abroad, and it is significant that it mainly found utterance in the vernacular tongues, not in learned Latin, and that its writers were not merely ecstatic visionaries and urgent preachers of the Christian virtues but fierce denouncers of the corruptions of the Church. Besides the pietists who fell clearly into heresy,

Fig. 177. Andrea da Firenze, 'Glorification of the Dominican Order'

there was a succession of the orthodox and their followers who kept within the pale. The English representative of the movement was the wandering hermit Richard Rolle (*c.* 1300–49). In Germany the Dominican Master Eckhart (*c.* 1260–1327) and his disciples Tauler (*c.* 1290–1361) and Suso (1295–1365) wielded a widely inspiring influence over pious laity along the Rhine. Ruysbroeck (1293–1381), a Flemish priest, was the exponent of a somewhat imperilled orthodoxy in the Netherlands, where heresy was rife. More sober and practical was the famous Gerard Groote (1340–84), the founder of the 'New Devotion' and the Brethren of the Common Life at Deventer. He initiated a renaissance of personal religion within the Church, which bore lasting fruit. There was less philosophy, but no less religious emotion in Italy. The fascinating romance of the mystical Franciscan ideal was given passionate expression in the *Lauds* of Jacopone da Todi (1228–1306) and in the *Fioretti del S. Francesco* of the fourteenth century. A Dominican tertiary, St Catherine of Siena (1347–80), came to grips with the evils of contemporary life, and left a deep impression on her generation. She even in a journey to Avignon strengthened the resolution of Gregory XI to return to Rome in spite of his reluctant Curia. These and many more show a new originality, however muffled in the frock and the gown. It was their obedient revolt from the stereotyped routine of passable salvation which had the greatest future significance. They wrote for the people in their own tongues and their seed sank deep in a fertile soil.

(2) THE IMPERIAL SUCCESSION, 1313–1349

A connecting thread for the history of Germany after the death of Henry VII is provided by the dreary final conflict of Papacy and Empire and by its inglorious extinction in mere phrases and claims that had lost real meaning. But more vital for the disintegrated land was the competition of leading dynasties for territory and power, the development of trading town-republics, and the remarkable growth of a new and unique state within the Empire, the half-peasant, half-urban Swiss Confederation. Save Switzerland, none of these rivalries and local evolutions, with their multifarious events, offer much of signal interest for a concise history, although their collective importance is great; and Switzerland, like the separation of the Netherlands from Germany proper under the Burgundian dukes, is most naturally treated apart from the main theme. That can at least be interwoven with the rivalry of Luxemburgs, Wittelsbachs, and Habsburgs.

Henry VII's death was followed by a disputed election, for which the doubts on certain electoral votes and the absence of a majority doctrine gave ample opportunity. King John of Bohemia fell out as too young. Duke Lewis of Bavaria, one of the several Wittelsbach princes who divided the possessions of their house, secured three undoubted and two disputed voters; Frederick the Handsome, the eldest Duke of Austria, two unchallenged and two doubtful voters, one being a claimant to vote as Duke of Saxony, and one Duke Henry of Carinthia, who still styled himself King of Bohemia (October 1314). The Electors seem to have unanimously given up the tendency to elect a petty prince, who was, experience showed, likely to intrude a new great house among them. The rival kings each had some excellent qualities, but each had a measure of instability and inconsequence, which perhaps furthered their election, since they seemed the less dangerous. They were already at war with one another and continued the uninspiring contest. North Germany took no part, the west and south were but languid, although princes and imperial cities were willingly bought by Lewis IV's concessions. Pitched battles were then a rarity: the fully armoured knight or trooper was too costly a soldier to be recklessly spent. Vain sieges and devastation were the rule. In 1317 Lewis IV prospered most, chiefly owing to the defeat of Duke Leopold, Frederick's energetic brother, by the Swiss at Morgarten. Then the troubles of King John, Lewis's best ally, in Bohemia gave the Habsburgs the advantage. But on 28 September 1322, repelling their invasion of Bavaria, Lewis and John caught Frederick without his brother's force at

Mühldorf, and inflicted on him a heavy defeat in which he and 1400 men were taken captive. Lewis IV was wisely clement, and most of Frederick's supporters changed sides.

Once secure, Lewis devoted himself, like his predecessors, to family aggrandisement. In pursuit of it, he most ungratefully crossed the ambitions of John of Bohemia. That prince, a model of contemporary chivalry, full of resources, always in a hurry, was incessantly active all over Europe in one scheme after another. The one country where he had no success was his kingdom of Bohemia, from which he was mostly an absentee. But he, too, was eager to increase his lands. The burning question of the moment was the future of the electoral mark of Brandenburg with its annex, the mark of Lusatia, where the ruling branch of the Ascanians became extinct in 1320. Lewis fobbed off King John with Upper Lusatia (Bautzen); but the lion's share, Brandenburg itself, was enfeoffed (1324) to Lewis of Wittelsbach, Lewis IV's eldest son. The gain, although disputed, was great, but the loss of John's amity greater, especially as Leopold of Austria was irreconcilable. Lewis IV's aims were at the same time directed south to Lombardy, which besides the unforgotten imperial rights was naturally attractive for commercial reasons to a Bavarian prince at the German side of the trade-routes. His intervention saved the Ghibellines, Can Grande, the tyrant of Verona, and the Visconti of Milan from overthrow by a papal 'crusade' (1323).

Fig.178. Peter of Aspelt, Archbishop of Mainz, crowning Henry VII, John of Bohemia and Lewis IV

This was to embroil him at once with the Papacy at Avignon, intent on Italian domination. Already Clement V before his death had formally declared the Empire to be a papal fief and in its vacancy to be under papal rule. John XXII utilized this far-reaching doctrine to justify his Italian campaigns. The double election of Lewis and Frederick, he said, left the Empire vacant until he should ratify the choice of one or other party. Till then he maintained an inflexible neutrality, addressing each claimant as

King-elect of the Romans, and proceeding as rightful ruler of imperial Italy. On the success of Lewis IV's intervention in Lombardy he was alarmed and furious, and hastened to extremities. On 8 October 1323 he fulminated a drastic bull; he accused Lewis of acting as ruler of the Empire without being legitimated by papal ratification and of lending aid to condemned heretics in the persons of the Visconti and their Ghibelline allies. Lewis, under pain of excommunication, was to lay down his power and annul his acts within three months, while his subjects were to renounce him under like penalty. When Lewis did not comply, another bull (23 March 1324) excommunicated him, summoned him to Avignon, deprived his obstinate clerical adherents, and again threatened his lay supporters. Thus the conflict of Papacy and Empire was renewed.

The Pope, however, had used too many threats at the start, and was disconcerted by the general indifference of the Germans and the annoyance of the Electors, although Leopold of Austria might intrigue with France for revenge. Lewis himself accepted the Pope's challenge by the Appeal of Sachsenhausen (23 May). John XXII was striving to usurp powers he did not possess. Lewis was lawfully elected and crowned and divinely sanctioned by victory. The Pope was himself a heretic, having denied the absolute poverty of Christ (here the Franciscan rebels had their say). The Catholic Lewis appealed to a General Council.

The dreary contest seemed for years to have no practical outcome. It was true that the Pope could do more harm to Lewis than Lewis to the Pope. If Lewis won the friendship of the Habsburgs by recognizing (1325) Frederick as joint-king (for that matter without validity), the greater part of the German episcopate went gradually at least in name to the Pope's side. Lewis's counterblow, in harmony with his Lombard interests, was in 1327 to make an expedition to Rome with the aid of his Italian friends. He was accompanied by the two political theorists who had fled to him, Marsilius of Padua and John of Jandun, and appears to have taken their counsel in his revolutionary proceedings. He was crowned at Milan and reached Rome in January 1328. There he was crowned Emperor by four syndics representing the Roman people. John XXII meanwhile was repeating his sentences of deposition, confiscation, interdict, and excommunication, winding up with declaring a crusade against the heretic. The new Emperor made a futile attempt to create a schism by setting up a puppet-Pope, Peter of Corvara, as Nicholas V by popular decree, but although he was joined by the leading revolted Franciscans, the ex-general Michael of Cesena and the philosopher William of Ockham, the attempt was abortive and Peter soon submitted to Avignon. With his great stroke a failure, Lewis returned to Germany (1330).

There he was still powerful, and still intent on family aggrandisement amid the bewildering and faithless manœuvres of the like-minded German princes. Frederick the Handsome's death in 1330 removed a possible rival, but no more. That of Pope John XXII in December 1334, after the collapse of a sort of compromise by which Lewis's cousin Duke Henry of Lower Bavaria was to replace him, aroused hopes of a more relenting Pope in Benedict XII, but the Roman Curia proved as implacable as ever. The Emperor, with dangerous enmities facing him in Germany, went step by step to great lengths to procure a peace. He would renounce his title of Emperor, annul his and Henry VII's imperial acts, never visit Rome save for one day to be duly crowned, go on crusade and perform penance. He shabbily threw the responsibility of the Sachsenhausen Appeal and similar documents on the Franciscans and other advisers. One thing only he refused, to admit that his election as King of the Romans required papal sanction to be effective, and on this fundamental question the negotiations broke down (1337).

Meanwhile the chief problem in German politics was the succession to Henry, Duke of Carinthia and Count of Tyrol, the ex-King of Bohemia.[1] Since he had no son, Lewis had promised him that a daughter or son-in-law should inherit his lands.

Fig. 179. Golden bull used by Lewis the Bavarian during his stay in Rome

One daughter, Margaret nicknamed Maultasch ('Bag-mouth'), married (1330) John Henry, second son of King John of Bohemia. Thereupon King John embarked on an expedition to Italy, where he erected a fleeting dominion, which cannot have been wholly pleasing to the Emperor with his Italian interests. In any case Lewis IV agreed with Duke Henry's Habsburg cousins to give them Carinthia, if the Wittelsbachs could take Tyrol. His aid was important for both candidates, and there was a long weaving of negotiations all round. In 1335 Duke Henry died, the Habsburgs annexed Carinthia, but in the war Margaret Maultasch kept Tyrol.

Defeated over Tyrol, at enmity with King John, rebuffed by the Papacy, Lewis now listened to the overtures of Edward III of England, who was planning an attack on France from Flanders with the assistance of German mercenary princes. Resistance to the persistent French nibbling at the frontier since Philip the Fair provoked in Germany a tepid fervour for resistance, and the King of France was the force behind the papal implacability to Lewis. The result was that in a meeting at Coblenz in September

---

[1] See Genealogical Table 25 below, p. 916.

1338 Lewis declared Edward III his vicar for the war with France: Edward was to give pay, Lewis to authorize and send troops. At the same time the Emperor was entrenching his constitutional position. The Pope's rejection of a compromise mission of German clergy had spurred the Electors, whose rights were threatened, into action. At Rense on the Rhine on 16 July 1338, they, with the exception of John of Bohemia, solemnly declared that whoever was elected, even if only by a majority of the Electors, needed no papal approbation to enter on his rights. The Pope's function was to crown him Emperor, which did not enlarge his powers over the Empire. The Diet at Frankfurt in August confirmed the Electors' decision, which was formulated in the law, *Licet iuris*, emphasizing that the Empire was held from God alone and pronouncing contraveners guilty of high treason.

This decisive legislation was never revoked, but the inconstant Lewis, who at first enforced submission, soon changed his policy. Edward's money was not forthcoming, nor were his campaigns successful. John of Bohemia was going blind, and Margaret Maultasch was on bad terms with her nominal husband, thus giving a new opening into Tyrol and Lombardy. In 1341 the Emperor changed sides and made a treaty with France. Next year he went to Tyrol, declared Margaret's marriage null, granted himself a dispensation of the bar of consanguinity, and then married his son Lewis of Brandenburg to the heiress of Tyrol and Carinthia. This grasping act made both Luxemburgs and Habsburgs his enemies once more, and gave Pope Clement VI a new handle against him. The Electors, too, were ceasing their support. In vain he repeated his largest offers to the Pope. Yet he still held his ground, although raising new grievances by taking quite legally the inheritance of his dead brother-in-law William, Count of Holland and Hainault, for his second wife and her sons to the detriment of other relatives (1345). At the same time he was scheming a new invasion of Italy. The Pope took the opportunity. A tremendous bull (1346) deprived Lewis and his descendants of their rights and called on the Electors to elect a King of the Romans.

A majority of the Electors, including a newly provided Archbishop of Mainz, obeyed, and chose at Rense (July 1346) a papal partisan, the Luxemburger Charles of Moravia, who ruled Bohemia in the name of his father John. This statesman had previously at Avignon subscribed to the papal demands. He was now crowned at Bonn, but Germany, princes and cities, as a whole held aloof, and Lewis IV was having the best of the little fighting when he died from an accident (October 1347). He had perhaps done little by Germany except to favour the free towns; his Italian ambitions had been futile; but he certainly achieved the great aim of a German prince in adding richly to the domains of his house. That their eminence did not last was due to the incompetence of the Wittelsbachs.

Charles IV had little difficulty in triumphing over the slack and belated opposition of the rival house, which after vainly enticing Edward III of England to be their candidate set up a phantom king in Count Günther of Schwarzburg (1349). Charles availed himself of a pretender to Brandenburg, who claimed to be Waldemar, the penultimate Ascanian margrave, emerging from concealment. When the Wittelsbachs, divided and endangered, submitted on terms which left them Brandenburg and Tyrol, the pretender was dropped and at last expelled.

Throughout the tedious conflict Germany was suffering in its turn under the terrible outbreak of bubonic plague named the Black Death, which, although it afflicted all Europe, may be outlined here. Its first progress was like the advance of a prairie fire, destroying and inescapable. Its way had been prepared by the unrecorded invasion of the black rat, the carrier of infected fleas, perhaps during the twelfth century, and the rat's distribution probably caused its patchy incidence—Bohemia escaped this first attack. In any case the Black Death came west from the great Crimean grain-port of Kaffa in 1346, and thence spread to Constantinople, Sicily, Genoa, and Provence in 1348. The same year it was in England, and by 1350 had traversed Germany and Scandinavia, reaching Poland from the west, a fact which showed how since the Mongol invasion intercourse between the Black Sea and the north had decayed. The plague followed the trade-routes, and the rat-infested ship and barge were more deadly than the march of an army. The immediate mortality was terrible; it may have carried off one-third of the population in the three years of this first visitation. But perhaps more important for the future was its recurrence almost every ten years. For three centuries the population of Western Europe had steadily increased. Now it was sharply diminished and remained almost stagnant until the close of the Middle Ages. The effect on both urban and peasant life was great, but by no means cataclysmic—it increased existing tendencies under new strains, and not least in Germany, where in the frantic panic there swept across most of the land the atrocious outburst of massacres of the hated Jews, accused of causing the plague. The major part of their settlements were exterminated, while the remnant fled eastward. Throughout Europe there was the debasement which follows great disasters: for a while men were more reckless, less dutiful, more callous.

(3) THE EMPEROR CHARLES IV

The new King of the Romans was a remarkable man, one of the new generation of statesmanlike, realistic rulers who replaced the warrior, high-flying knights that were their fathers. Charles IV was as acquisitive and ambitious as any, but he aimed at the practicable. He was businesslike, diplomatic, and shrewdly persevering, with little regard to honour or faith. Bred up in Paris, much travelled, and long regent of Bohemia, he was a linguist, proficient in French, German, Latin, Italian, and Czech. If he had a patriotism, it was for his kingdom of Bohemia, the solid basis of his power.[1] His imperial rights he used in Germany for his dynastic advantage with a secondary endeavour to sow some seeds of stability in the prevailing anarchic turmoil; in Italy to raise funds by sale of charters. His successor, the Emperor Maximilian, called him 'arch-father of Bohemia, arch-stepfather of the Empire', and there was truth in the epigram, although the mainsprings of his policy did not greatly differ from those of most later Emperors.

Charles regarded the Holy Roman Empire as an anachronism—the kingship in Germany was another matter—but he was none the less anxious to acquire the prestige and completeness of a valid coronation at Rome. For that end he toured Germany with gifts and concessions to secure a period of quiet, and then hastily departed for Italy with a small escort. He was crowned at Rome by the legate of a friendly Pope, coming and going on the same day (1355), and returning to Germany with the utmost celerity. He was accompanied by the ridicule of the Italians, but collected large sums from the sale of diplomas, which he found time to grant. The significance of this derided coronation was that it sealed the renunciation of any real imperial authority in Italy and removed the main motive of papal dread of the Empire.

Safely back, the Emperor, who had an orderly, formulating mind, endeavoured to give Germany a nucleus of organization by strengthening one institution at least. There was nothing in existence which could be called a constitution except traditions and miscellaneous laws. Germany was a collection of principalities and city-states. The monarchy was in a way to become a legal fiction, the convenient source of their privileges. The Crown lacked means to enforce its decisions or its laws, for its revenue was scant and uncertain and the domain now attached to it of little account, consisting mainly of free imperial towns, for it had been dissipated since the days of Frederick II. The imperial Diet was a formless assembly of princes, irregularly attended and a feeble instrument. There remained at any rate the Electors, few enough to act in concert and possessing some common interests. Their discord and the uncertainty of their composition had been hitherto a primary cause of civil war. Charles's attempt to define this body, and give it some solidarity and functions other than election, was the celebrated Golden Bull of 1356, which became a kind of fundamental law. He had prepared the way by settling rival claims to the electoral dignity. The Bavarian vote was excluded, the Saxon vote was assigned to the Duke of Saxe-Wittenberg. The Bull itself, along with many pompous, ceremonial futilities, arranged for the speedy election of a King of the Romans in a vacancy by a unanimous or majority vote of the seven

[1] His reign in Bohemia is dealt with below, pp. 917 ff.

Fig. 180. The Emperor and the seven Electors.
Bronze door-knocker, Lübeck, c. 1350

Electors (ecclesiastical: Mainz, Cologne, and Trier; secular: Bohemia, the
Palatinate of the Rhine, Saxony, and Brandenburg), each holding a
ceremonial arch-office. The secular Electorates, each with an indivisible
principality attached, were to descend by primogeniture, the first attempt
to prevent the continual subdivision among male heirs which splintered
Germany, while the semi-royal powers given to the Electors made them
more allies than subjects of the Emperor. Bohemia of course retained in
the clearest stipulations its ancient autonomy. In the vacancy of the
imperial throne, the Elector Palatine was to administer the Empire, but
where Saxon law prevailed the Elector of Saxony was to function, an
indirect denial of papal claims. More to the purpose was the attempt to
erect a sort of Concert of the Electors by prescribing their annual meeting.

Both this attempt and that to prevent leagues of the towns broke down. Yet the rule of primogeniture and the incidental sanction of the majority doctrine bore fruit, if slowly and at last.

Cheaply as he might hold the Empire, Charles IV was not the man to neglect any imposing ceremony or to abandon any formal rights which might at some time acquire a practical importance. He had assumed the iron crown of Italy on his way to Rome; in 1365 he had himself crowned King of Burgundy at Arles like Barbarossa. In 1356 at a brilliant Diet at Metz he obtained the homage of the heir to the French crown, Charles, for his recently acquired principality of Dauphiné. At the least there were privileges to be sold, even when Charles was made his Vicar for the realm, save Savoy where its Count was given the like office. In fact, the Empire was receding in all but name.

There was much more reality in Charles's astute dealings with the rival Wittelsbachs and the aspiring Rudolf IV of Habsburg, the senior Duke of Austria. With both there was friction, for Rudolf was claiming all the semi-regal privileges of the Electors, and his lands were becoming a separate province. The death of Lewis, the eldest Wittelsbach brother, followed by that of his son Meinhard, Count of Tyrol, caused Margaret Maultasch to cede Tyrol to Rudolf of Austria. Charles bought Rudolf's friendship by investing him with Tyrol and by the treaty of Brno (Brünn) in 1364, which provided that in case either Luxemburgs or Habsburgs became extinct, the surviving house should inherit their lands. Strangely enough, the treaty came into temporary effect within a century. Meantime Charles profited by the dissensions of the Wittelsbach brothers, Stephen of Bavaria and Lewis the Roman and Otto of Brandenburg. The two latter foolishly declared Charles their heir if they left no sons. The Emperor insisted on their bargain. When Otto the survivor repented, he isolated by skilful diplomacy the Wittelsbachs of Bavaria and finally bought them out (1373). Elector Otto, who ceased to rule his mark, died heirless, and the Emperor acquired Brandenburg and Lusatia for his house.

As time went on Charles became genuinely eager to see the 'Babylonish Captivity' ended and the Pope back in his see of Rome. The pro-French attitude as well as the exactions of the Curia at Avignon, particularly under Innocent VI, had made his relations with the Papacy uneasy. Rome and the Papal States, reduced to order by Cardinal Albornoz, appeared a safer residence than Avignon imperilled by the Free Companies, and Charles' consent that these freebooters should pass through Germany on a projected crusade had ended in his being obliged to repel them from Alsace by means of a no less villainous army (1365). With his views on the Empire he had no objection to a powerful Papacy dominant in Italy. It would be a counterpoise to the threatening conquest of Naples by Lewis of Hungary, a dangerous rival to the Luxemburgs of Bohemia. He proposed to assist

Fig. 181. King Charles V of France entertains the Emperor Charles IV and his son, King Wenceslas, January 1378

Pope Urban V's journey to Rome by an expedition of his own. But he came (1368) late after, not before, the Pope, and he reaped no profit in power or repute. In 1369 he came back to Germany and Urban, now a friend of Lewis, to Avignon. His next dealings with the Papacy were an instance of the slippery, false diplomacy, by which the papal claims of suzerainty over the Empire drifted into mere words and meaningless oaths. He saw his chance of avoiding the fate of the Wittelsbachs under a hostile King of the Romans by bribing the Electors to elect his son and heir Wenceslas in his lifetime. It was done and Pope Gregory XI taken by surprise (1376). Wenceslas was crowned without waiting for papal confirmation, and the matter was patched up by juggling with dates and a subsequent oath of Wenceslas confirming his father's undertakings of 1346. Thus both Electors and Pope were appeased in this double game.

Charles's need of money to finance his wars and bribe Electors and princes had always pressed hard on the Free Towns of the imperial domain, whom, unlike Lewis IV, he looked on rather as victims than supporters. The Golden Bull had forbidden their defensive leagues. In the north the Hanseatic League paid little regard to him, but the southern towns were endangered. The Emperor mulcted them repeatedly, and on Wenceslas's election proceeded to pledge many to princes as security for his bribes, which might often mean permanent subjection to a neighbouring prince. Thereupon fourteen Swabian free towns formed a league against fresh taxation or being pawned. Charles put them to the ban, but he and his princely allies were repulsed. After the league had won a victory (1377) over a Count of Württemberg, King Wenceslas on his father's behalf gave the required guarantees and recognized the league notwithstanding the Golden Bull. The league had won the first round. The ailing Emperor meanwhile was disposing of his territories. Long before he had created his younger brother Wenceslas Duke of Luxemburg. He now made one son, Sigismund, Elector of Brandenburg, and another, John, Duke of Görlitz in Lusatia. Bohemia and its dependencies were the share of King Wenceslas. Charles himself died in November 1378. His chief claim to fame lies in his work as King of Bohemia, but his reign left a deep mark on both German and Imperial history. His Golden Bull remained the constitution of the Empire until 1806.

(4) THE HANSEATIC LEAGUE AND THE SWISS CONFEDERATION

The Hanseatic League of northern towns went its way and achieved its greatest prosperity in the fourteenth century. Already in the twelfth and thirteenth centuries German traders had obtained privileged settlements or 'Kontors' in London, Bergen, Visby in Gotland, Novgorod, and Bruges. The leading cities were Cologne and Lübeck; Hamburg was important later. They exchanged the furs and other products of the north-east, and especially the herrings of the Danish Sound and the cod of Norway, for the cloth and manufactures of Flanders and the west. Their association in their Kontors led naturally to alliances among themselves. Such was the League of 'Wendish' towns under Lübeck, which shaped and directed the common policy of these Hansa towns. Their alliances were tested by the ambitions of Denmark. Eric VI Menved (1286–1319) compelled the Wendish towns to submit to his overlordship, from which they were rescued by a period of Danish anarchy. But in the same years the towns had forced Eric II the Priest-hater of Norway to agree to their terms in the Treaty of Tönsberg (1294) by means of a commercial blockade, with which Novgorod had

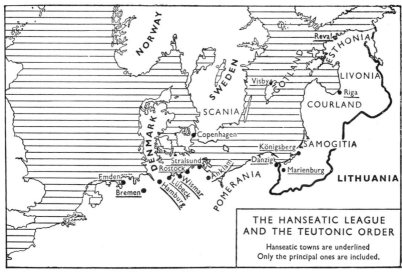

Map 21

already (1199) been and Bruges was soon (1307) to be coerced. In the Norwegian dispute Bremen was expelled from the growing league for not falling into line, a punishment (the *Verhansung*) which was used in future against recalcitrant towns. The full formation of the 'German Hanse', however, only came about c. 1356. The Baltic and Russian trade was largely controlled by Lübeck, Danzig, Rostock, Riga and Reval, the North Sea and English trade by Cologne, Dortmund, Hamburg and Emden, while many inland cities—Brunswick, Lüneburg, Magdeburg, Goslar, etc.—were also members and derived substantial advantages from the fact. The first success of the League was to compel Bruges to extend its privileges (1360). But it was immediately threatened by the expansion of Denmark, once more united under Waldemar IV. In 1360 he sacked

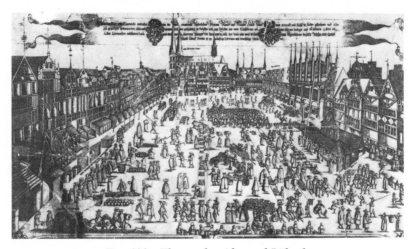

Fig. 182. The market-place of Lübeck

Visby, which never recovered from the blow. The Hansa replied by a great confederation, including Norway, Sweden, and the Teutonic Knights. The war went so badly that a first peace (1365) was unsatisfactory and did not restrain Waldemar from his hostility. In 1368 the Hansa renewed the war, and this time won a signal victory. By the peace of Stralsund (24 May 1370) complete freedom of trade and fishing off Scania was secured with territorial guarantees and the singular right of the League's assent being necessary for the accession of a King of Denmark. The last stipulation, however, was withdrawn in 1376 after Waldemar's death in agreements with Margaret, regent of Denmark, and her husband Haakon VI of Norway. The Hansa had soon enough to do in combating the piracy of the so-called Victualler Brethren, which grew up in the wars between the Scandinavian states and the claimants of their thrones. Not till 1404 was there comparative safety in the Baltic. For all that the Hansa dominated the Baltic commerce, the Sound fisheries, and the whole trade of Norway. They had a large share of English trade in spite of native rivalry, and maintained their position in Flanders. They, with the southern German towns, controlled the internal and foreign commerce of Germany.

Strange to say, the number of members of the Hansa League was always uncertain, even to the League itself. Round about seventy is perhaps the best average figure, but towns would slip out of or into the League according to circumstances. At the rare *Hansetage* or congresses of representatives the attendance of towns seldom exceeded thirty, yet the League was able to act as a powerful union. Only a few members, like Lübeck and Goslar, were practically sovereign states owing allegiance

854

direct to the Emperor; the rest were subject to the more effectual rule of territorial princes such as the Grand Master of the Teutonic Order, the Bishop of Münster, or the Duke of Mecklenburg. In internal government the Hansa towns in general were still ruled by close oligarchies, the so-called patricians, the descendants of the original merchants, who conducted their commerce and were the owners of their ground. In the fourteenth century,

Fig. 183. Session of the Hamburg Town Council, 1497

however, the discontent of the manufacturing gildsmen and employees was rising. Up to the death of Charles IV their revolts had been harshly suppressed, and in Nuremberg (outside the Hansa) Charles himself intervened (1349) to restore the patriciate. But more persistent and successful efforts were to come elsewhere.

Contemporaneously with the Hansa another league of far less pretensions was arising in southern Germany, the Swiss Confederation, which was to become a sovereign state of Europe. It was geographical conditions, the defensible, compact terrain and the common interests thereby developed, which gave permanence to a confederation of rural districts and towns as loosely constructed as any of the many similar leagues of the age. It began in the Alpine districts of the duchy of Swabia in resistance to the attempts of the house of Habsburg, native to the region, to extend and consolidate its territory and variegated feudal rights. The land indeed had once been feudally united under the Dukes of Zähringen, who by reason of their rectorate of Burgundy had ruled over the Burgundian lands within the

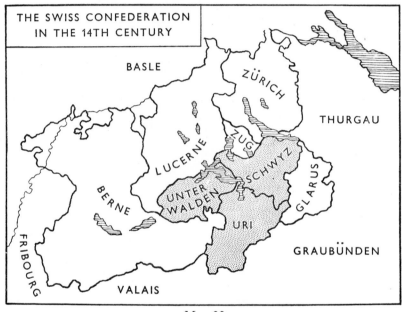

THE SWISS CONFEDERATION
IN THE 14TH CENTURY

BASLE

ZÜRICH

THURGAU

LUCERNE

ZUG

SCHWYZ

BERNE

UNTER WALDEN

GLARUS

URI

FRIBOURG

GRAUBÜNDEN

VALAIS

Map 22

Jura mountains as well as over Swabia south of the Rhine. When the Zähringen became extinct in 1218, a whole medley of intertangled feudal jurisdictions, ecclesiastical and lay, became direct vassals of the Emperor. At the same time the recent exploitation of the St Gothard Pass made the Swabian districts of great importance as a route into Italy for the Hohenstaufen and added to the wealth of their free towns, Zürich and Berne at their head. With a view to it, the Hohenstaufen chartered the districts or cantons of Uri and Schwyz as parts of the imperial domain. Both were lands of peasants, largely free in status, and with the neighbouring district of Unterwalden formed the Forest Cantons, which were to be the nucleus of the League. They commanded the approaches to the St Gothard. Their chief dread was subjection to the Counts of Habsburg, who ruled the lands to the north of them and by means of advocateships and vassalages were extending their sway and possessed rights within the Forest Cantons themselves. Some sort of league was made against Habsburg domination by the Three Cantons and the town of Lucerne, the immediate outlet from them. But the election (1273) of Rudolf of Habsburg (1239–91) to be King of the Romans endangered them once more. The charter to Schwyz was

Fig. 184. Silver dish with the imperial eagle,
the Lübeck coat-of-arms

annulled, and the imperial advocacy of Urseren between Uri and the St Gothard given to his sons. So threatening was the prospect of Habsburg rule and the loss of virtual autonomy in their small affairs that scarcely was King Rudolf dead when the Forest Cantons formed in August 1291 the pact of alliance, which, forbidding among other things officials not native to them, founded the Swiss Confederation. Duke Albert of Austria, however, had the best of the conflict outside the Cantons, and although his rival King Adolf of Nassau confirmed the charters to Uri and Schwyz, on becoming King of the Romans himself he compelled submission (1299) and levied heavy taxes. His own murder in 1308 produced a change, for King Henry VII renewed the privileges of Uri and Schwyz and gave the same right of being imperial domain to Unterwalden also.

The death of Henry VII again made war likely with the Habsburgs, who were by no means acquiescent, and the Forest League prepared for it by fortifying the approaches and attacking the Abbey of Einsiedeln on their frontier. They sided of course with Lewis IV against the Habsburg Frederick the Handsome, but Frederick's stirring brother, Duke Leopold I, determined to enforce the rights of his house by invasion in strength. His formidable array of knights and footmen, choosing an unblocked route, was utterly overthrown in the pass of Morgarten on 15 November 1315 by the mountaineers, skilfully led, and using their halberds and stones against the struggling mass of horsemen wedged between mountains and Lake Ägeri. The victory was decisive. Lewis IV renewed the three charters and named a native of Uri his bailiff over Urseren, while the Forest Cantons strengthened their confederation by the pact of Brunnen. Even Duke Leopold concluded a truce with them (July 1318). Morgarten in short guaranteed the future of their league.

The danger of a Habsburg reconquest, however, was not over, and the policy of the Forest Cantons was to ally with malcontent subjects and dependants of Austria. The first accession of such was the town of Lucerne, whose alliance in 1332, although formally abrogated, was in fact maintained. More important was the alliance with the Free Town of Zürich. There a revolution in 1336 had ousted the patriciate from control and given power to the craft gilds led by a burgomaster for life, Rudolf Brun. Imperilled by foes within and without, Zürich contracted a confederation with the three Cantons and Lucerne (1351). Next year the eastward district of Glarus and the little town of Zug severally joined in. A peace of compromise with Duke Albert of Austria soon after barely called a halt in operations to the east, but in 1353 a permanent and powerful member was added to the Swiss Confederation, as by the importance of the canton of Schwyz the Forest League began to be called. The Free Town of Berne had been increasing in power, wealth, and territory for a century. In 1339 she won an overwhelming victory at Laupen over a coalition of all the great and small lords round and her rival Fribourg. She now joined the League of the Three Forest Cantons on special terms. It meant that the Confederation had extended westwards. Meanwhile the intervention of the Emperor Charles IV against it produced a temporary setback in the peace of Regensburg (1355), but he soon was on bad terms with the Habsburgs, and the Swiss, by consequence in his favour, resumed hostilities. Zug was reconquered and readmitted as an ally. Zürich refused to be a subject of the Habsburgs. A new truce in 1368 suspended the war.

THE HANSEATIC LEAGUE AND THE SWISS CONFEDERATION

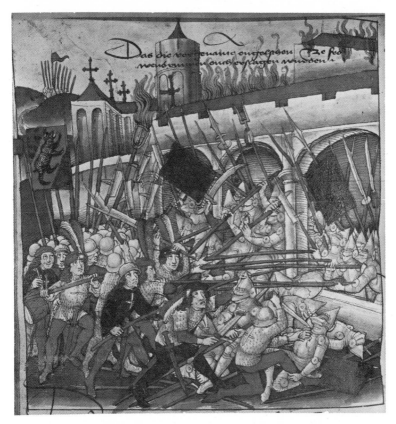

Fig. 185. The battle of the hooded men, 1375

The growing unity of the Confederation was shown in 1370 by a common regulation for keeping internal peace, named the *Pfaffenbrief* or Priests' Charter. It forbade highway robbery and private war, and imposed penalties on ecclesiastics who appealed to outside tribunals. The kernel of the League, now of six members, remained the Forest Cantons, who alone were allied with all their partners and pursued an undeviating anti-Habsburg policy. Berne, for instance, was temporarily allied with Duke Leopold III of Austria in repelling the incursion of English and Welsh Free Companies, called the Guglers, from France (1375).

Friction, however, due partly to the acquisitions of the Habsburg Duke Leopold III in Swabia and partly to the restiveness of the Swiss under the truce of 1368, caused war to break out anew in 1385. Its great events were the defeat and death of Leopold at Sempach in 1386, where his knights, dismounted in the new fashion, were outdone by the Swiss halberdiers,

859

and a like defeat of the Austrians at Näfels by the peasants of Glarus in 1388. During the truce that followed, the Swiss Cantons improved their military organization by the *Sempacherbrief*, while the Austrian dukes endeavoured to entice Zürich into a wide South German league. They failed, and in 1394 agreed to a twenty years' peace, abandoning their rights in Lucerne, Zug, and Glarus besides making small cessions. Thus the Swiss Confederation had established its freedom. It now consisted of eight cantons. Five—Uri, Schwyz, Unterwalden, Glarus, and Zug—were districts which enjoyed a popular government of freemen. Three—Berne, Zürich, and Lucerne—were city-states which ruled a subject countryside and within their walls were inclined to a kind of oligarchy. But for all that a common interest, common aims, and common foes held the complicated league together.

(5) ITALY AFTER THE DEATH OF HENRY VII

At the death of the Emperor Henry VII Italy had long been a heterogeneous collection of small, intensely particularist states, whether republics, tyrannies, surviving feudal lordships, or feudal kingdoms. They were the prey of incessant discord within and without. Even more than formerly their history dissolves into a series of entangled local dramas, in which sporadic attempts to control the whole land by the Papacy or Robert of Naples were rather elements of fresh confusion than means towards peace and unity. These potentates were merely the most ubiquitous competitors in the broil. Certain general characteristics and trends of the period were, however, apparent. First was the decadence of the city-commune as a republican government in North Italy. It was purely urban, for the countryman was just a subject, none too well treated. Within its walls the commune was dislocated by the inveterate conflict of classes and even cliques, nobles, merchants, retail traders and craftsmen, and simple employees, inextricably intermingled with family and personal rivalries, which, if they sometimes began in real differences of policy, were invariably carried on as unassuageable feuds. Again, these distracted republics were as of old in constant enmity with one another, and only in rare cases were able to mitigate their internal strife and pursue their external ambitions with steadfast efficiency. These troubles gave birth to the second characteristic, the predominance of the city tyrant, the Signore, who kept order with a firm, if not impartial, hand, and whose personal ambitions made for the larger state required for safety and for commerce without subjugating his cities to some hated rival republic but only to himself. But the tyranny, too, was showing its defects. It had no roots in ancient law or traditional right. It was the prize of the wiliest and strongest. All barriers of principle or kinship were overleapt in the race for power. Nor was there as a rule that continuous succession of hereditary ability which could create a sort

Fig. 186. The condottiere Guidoriccio da Fogliana

of loyalty. It is notable how much the more stable states depended on geographical advantages, the natural coherence or defensibility of their territories.

A third characteristic of the age was the continual scourge of the Free Companies. The old citizen militia had become unequal to the strain of long widespread warfare, and in battle was utterly inferior to the professional mercenary. The campaigns of Henry VII and Lewis IV, of the Popes and the Kings of Naples, introduced a swarm of fierce, marauding adventurers into Italy, who waged the wars of the century. They were not long in forming themselves into mercenary companies under noted captains, who were hired by the fighting states, and when unemployed wandered in predatory fashion over the country until hired once more or bribed to depart elsewhere. It is singular that in war and devastation the cities still carried on their commerce and increased in material civilization. They were still safe behind their walls, and the citizens lacked neither intellect, industry, nor perseverance.

The kingdom of Naples might seem from its size and its traditional monarchy, not to mention its alliance with the Papacy, fit to produce some kind of stability, but it was radically unequal to the task in itself and in the gifted mediocrity of its ruler. Naples was for the most part poor by nature, inert under a fossilizing, yet enhanced, feudalism, and growing poorer in the grip of extortionate taxation. It had no manufacturing or mercantile bourgeoisie; its exports and imports were in foreign, mainly Florentine, hands. There was a numerous baronage, often poor and always turbulent and fickle, and a multitude of plebeian townsmen and peasants tormented by poverty and the misgovernment of rapacious officials. The powerful Church was devoid of civilizing enterprise and at odds with barons and peasants. Native troops and fleets made a poor show, and the costly mercenaries were not to be trusted. The learned, timid, manœuvring King Robert (1309–43) was not the man to build on this quaking or indeed on a firmer foundation. Unhappily, too, he could never abandon his purpose of reconquering Sicily, from which he took his formal title. Time and again (1314, 1316, 1325–8, 1335, 1339–42), he endeavoured in vain to expel the hostile Aragonese dynasty, always to the exhaustion of his impoverished, debt-ridden kingdom and to the detriment of his ambitions in North Italy. Frederick II (1296–1337), on his side, broke the treaty of Caltabellotta and crowned (1321) his son Peter II, but had much ado to defend his kingdom against Pope and Naples and to deal with the unruly Sicilian barons, who lapsed more and more into factious anarchy.

Although King Robert headed the Guelfs in the Papal States and Tuscany as 'Imperial' and Papal Vicar and was Signore of faction-ridden Florence as well, he was not so powerful as he seemed. Pisa elected a Ghibelline soldier, Uguccione della Faggiuola, as her ruler. With his Netherlandish mercenaries to back him he obtained the submission of Lucca, and then routed the Tuscan Guelfs and Robert's troops at Montecatini (1315). He was himself expelled next year, but his brilliant supplanter in Lucca, Castruccio Castracani, continued the war intermittently, and after Robert's signory of Florence had expired (1322) inflicted another defeat on the Guelfs at Altopascio (1235). Meanwhile Robert had lost Ferrara to the native house of Este (1317) and had gained Genoa after a Guelf revolution, which he supported in an almost general war by an expedition in person, the one courageous act of his career (1318). But throughout the great Ghibelline tyrants of Lombardy, Matteo Visconti of Milan and Can Grande della Scala of Verona, one of Dante's patrons, held firm in spite of the denunciations and arms of the able papal legate Bertrand du Pouget. Matteo ruled with justice and conciliation a collection of central Lombard cities, including conquered Pavia, until his son Galeazzo took over the signory (1322). At the same time Cremona, after horrible vicissitudes, accepted Visconti domination. Can Grande (1308–29) of Verona extended his east Lombard state more slowly in spite of continual wars. The first result of his persistent attacks on Padua was to change that republic into a tyranny under Jacopo da Carrara (1318). Only when the power of the Austrian Habsburgs, sometimes his allies, sometimes his rivals, was diminished, did he become lord of Padua (1328).

During these years the distresses of Lombardy were exacerbated by foreign intervention. Cardinal du Pouget led a crusade against the Visconti from 1320; he was baffled by the action of Lewis of Bavaria, but in 1326–7 erected an evanescent dominion south of the Po. In 1327 Lewis IV himself descended into Italy on his way to his revolutionary coronation at Rome. His political schemes, however, like his schism, met with complete failure, his alliance with Sicily broke down, Castruccio, whom he created Duke of Lucca, died (1328), and he left with no profit gained (1330). The way was now open for a fresh competitor, the king-errant, John of Bohemia. Called in by Brescia against Mastino della Scala of Verona, and supported by Pope John XXII and Du Pouget, he acquired a sudden dominion north and south of the Po to the detriment of the Visconti. His triumph was ephemeral. Defeated by a wide league of Italian rulers (1333), John and his son Charles withdrew, followed soon by Du Pouget. This proved the opportunity of Mastino della Scala. For a few years he acquired a straggling chain of cities reaching from Vicenza to Lucca, but, met with general enmity, he was soon reduced to Verona and Vicenza (1341).

By this time the Visconti, reconciled for a while with the Papacy, were recovering ground. The popular Azzo, Galeazzo's son, who stabilized the government, overthrew at Parabiago (1337) a junior Visconti, Lodrisio, who was at the head of the fierce bands of mercenaries. His uncles, Luchino (1339–49) and Giovanni, Archbishop of Milan (1339–54), reformed and added to their central state. The archbishop was diplomatic and intensely ambitious. Called 'regulus super Lombardis,' Parma and Piacenza already his, he gained the signory of faction-ridden Genoa (1353), and aimed at Bologna and Tuscany. As to Bologna, Pope Clement VI's first anger at its seizure was mollified and Giovanni became its papal vicar. But Florence, backed by others, showed a stout front and war was deferred by the archbishop's death.

Pope Innocent VI was by now resolved to intervene in force in Italy. The States of the Church, divided in fact among petty despots and anarchic republics, was the first objective. Tyrants like the Malatesta of Rimini in the March of Ancona, and the Ordelaffi of Forlì and the Manfredi of Faenza in Romagna, pursued their schemes in defiance of the Papacy. Rome itself since the death of Henry VII had become a plague-spot of anarchy, which gave rise to a singular episode, the product of the legendary fame of the Eternal City, tinctured, if little more, with faint premonitions of the coming Renaissance. The barons, Colonna, Orsini, Gaetani and many others, waged incessant war, combined with brigandage, in the city and the Campagna, making the lot of the *popolani* intolerable. At last there arose a native would-be saviour. Cola di Rienzo, born in 1313 of very humble parentage, was an imaginative and fiery spirit, gifted with an intoxicating eloquence which imposed on himself as much as on others. He came suddenly to the front as a demagogue after 1344, equipped with a considerable knowledge of the Latin classics and longing to bring about a grandiose revolution. He would quell the nobles and revive the phantom of ancient Rome, subject the lingering Empire, and make Rome the capital of Italy and the Christian world. His mind, ill-balanced at best, was affected by the potent mirage of Roman greatness which blinded the Romans (and in some degree others) to reality. In 1347 his moment came. On 20 May the 'Roman people' on the Capitol gave him the signory with dictatorial and legislative powers. He took the title of Tribune, assumed royal pomp, held a congress of friendly cities, and began to defy the Pope, who at first had favoured him. None the less he started by ruling well, bringing in security and honest finance. His last victory was to rout the insurgent Colonna. Yet his own extravagance, the accusation of heresy and his excommunication by the legate, and the hatred of the barons undid him. On 15 December the mob changed sides, and Cola fled to the Abruzzi. For two years he lurked in a Franciscan convent. Then he went to Prague in the hope of inducing Charles IV of all men to be a real Roman Emperor to reform the world. Charles held him a prisoner for two years, and then sent him to Avignon. There he was tried and in danger of his life until Innocent VI sent him to Rome again as an instrument of Cardinal Gil Albornoz.

The cardinal was a Spaniard, promoted in the Church for his eminent services against the Moors. In 1353 he was despatched as legate to Italy to end the raging anarchy of Rome and bring the whole Papal States to obedience. A soldier and a statesman, Albornoz reduced the Patrimony to obedience, while he sent Rienzo to Rome as senator (1354). But the some-time reformer became both cruel and debauched in this latest phase. On 8 October the Romans revolted. He was caught by the mob and slaughtered at the foot of the Capitol. The streak of madness in him, however, should not wholly obscure the largeness of ideas and outlook in this half-genius. Albornoz was of a different stamp. Charles IV's journey to be crowned did not disturb him. In a few months the Malatesta surrendered and the March of Ancona was subjected (1355). In Romagna Ordelaffi put up a resistance, and behind him were the brothers Visconti, Galeazzo II (1354–78) and Bernabò (1354–85), whose cousin Giovanni Oleggio governed Bologna for them. While Albornoz was besieging Forlì, the astute Bernabò induced Pope Innocent to treat with him (1357), and send the Abbot of Cluny to take charge of negotiations. Albornoz indignantly resigned, but stayed long enough to enter the league against the Visconti. He also made his name as a legislator, promulgating at Fano the *Egidian Constitutions*, which became the code of the Papal States for centuries. The abbot, who succeeded him as legate, allowed by his utter incapacity the old mutinous disorder to revive within a year, and Albornoz returned in 1358 to his former post. In five years anarchy was tamed, Ordelaffi subdued, and Bologna subjected. Yet, in spite of his defeats, Bernabò's diplomacy at Avignon among the cardinals at length obtained from Pope Urban V his recall and the abbot's reappointment (1363). All the same the whole Papal State was now reduced to obedience.

To assess the perplexities of the papal Curia with regard to North and Central Italy it is necessary to hold in mind the contemporaneous events in the south and the deplorable condition of the vassal kingdom of Naples.

King Robert lost his son Charles of Calabria, sometime Signore of Florence, in 1328, and left his decaying realm (1343) to his elder granddaughter Joanna I, a mere girl. To accommodate the claims of the Angevins of Hungary, she was married to her cousin Andrew of Hungary, whom she at once learned to loathe, and to whom she was unfaithful. In 1345 he was murdered. Other members of the numerous royal family were involved in the crime, and the queen was loudly accused of complicity, while she herself was wishing to marry another cousin, Louis of Taranto. Her brother-in-law, King Lewis of Hungary, began a ruthless war of vengeance, conquering and hated, which lasted until

Fig. 187. Bernabò Visconti,
ruler of Milan

1350. Meanwhile Joanna fled to Avignon, where she obtained from Clement VI an acquittal and authorization of her second marriage. The Pope at last made her make peace with Hungary, but the dissensions of the princes of the blood continued. During these tragic years the kingdom was put to fire and sword by the Free Companies under the terrible adventurers, the Germans Conrad of Wolfort (Corrado Lupo, 'the Wolf') and Conrad of Landau (the Count of Lando), and Fra Moriale (Montréal), a recreant Hospitaller from Narbonne. For a decade, however, Queen Joanna maintained a comparative quiet with the aid of her latest paramour, the Florentine Niccolò Acciaiuoli, whom she made Grand Seneschal. He had extraordinary talents, without any scruples, and, taming the insolent barons, he defended the kingdom. He came nearest to victory over feud-torn Sicily of all the Neapolitan rulers (1354–62), but the death of King Louis of Taranto (1362) ended his progress. At last the Papacy itself was wearied of the endless war. Under the patronage of Gregory XI a treaty was made

(1373), which acknowledged the kingdom of 'Trinacria' as a vassal of Naples and the Pope. Joanna I had remarried, this time James III, titular King of Majorca, but her mainstay, Acciaiuoli, died (1366), and the gleam of prosperity was over. A fourth husband, Otto of Brunswick, did nothing to still the disputes over the succession and rearisen anarchy.

The two Visconti, shorn of Bologna and of Genoa, were yet the most powerful princes of Lombardy. They divided their signory, Galeazzo II ruling the west from Pavia, Bernabò the east from Milan. Bernabò, a cruel and restless tyrant, married his daughters to foreign princes. The milder Galeazzo II was fencing with a rival and kinsman, the Count of Savoy Amadeus VI, the 'Green Count' (1343–83). That Burgundian potentate, a crusader and schemer, pursued expansion on all sides, but especially in Italy, where he overthrew his cousin, the Prince of Achaia, and annexed Piedmont. He improved his status by gaining from Charles IV the dignity of imperial vicar over his territories (1365). His prestige was shown in his mediation between the two agelong enemies, Genoa and Venice.

(6) VENICE, GENOA AND FLORENCE

Venice showed her innate power of recuperation after the Ferrarese war. Under Doge Soranzo (1312–28), with the oligarchy established by the Serrata del Maggior Consiglio shaping itself and the Council of Ten watching over the State, commerce flourished and the population grew. Revolted Dalmatia was subdued and Genoa brought to terms. The city, secure in the lagoons, also possessed the inestimable advantage of the absence of the riotous blood-feuds and class-warfare which infested and deformed Lombard Italy and crippled Genoa. Apart from the maintenance of her dominion and trade in the Levant, her chief anxieties were the importation of her food-supply and the control of her land-outlets. These impelled her to the ambition of conquests in Italy, which were themselves an embarrassment. She headed the league against Mastino della Scala, and took Treviso as her share of the spoils (1338), making thereby enemies of the half-vassal da Carrara of Padua and the Austrian dukes, who pressed southward, as well as King Lewis of Hungary, who in any case was her foe over Dalmatia. Genoa, too, freed from Robert of Naples (1334), achieved some sort of stability by a popular revolution, which overthrew the ancient nobles and placed in power as doge Simone Boccanegra (1339). She took up anew the recovery of her dominion in the Levant and its complement, war with Venice. If her sea-defeat off La Loiera in Sardinia (1353) led her to accept the signory of Archbishop Giovanni Visconti, the conspiracy of the Venetian doge, Falier, against the oligarchy, although met by his prompt execution at the hands of the Ten (1355), checked Venice. Visconti made a peace, which was an ill-kept truce. On his death

Boccanegra was restored. Venice, meanwhile had the worse in conflict with da Carrara of Padua and King Lewis, to whom she was forced to cede Dalmatia (1358). It was a heavy blow to her sea-power, and she was in danger of losing Treviso and its cornfields, although her admirable government had made the city loyal.

In the Levant the two rivals were really in continuous war. They, of course, took opposite sides in the conflict between the Byzantine Emperor John Palaeologus and his rebel son Andronicus. The cession to each of the strategic island of Tenedos (1376) produced the most furious, now declared, conflict of the century. Aided by Hungary and da Carrara, the victorious Genoese fleet occupied Chioggia on the lagoon, and seemed on the point of conquering Venice herself. But under the heroic leadership of their admiral Vittor Pisani and the Doge Contarini the Venetians turned the tables, besieged the besiegers in midwinter (1379–80), and starved them to surrender. Venice was obliged to cede Treviso to Leopold III of Austria, but she won the war with Genoa. In 1381 Amadeus VI arranged the Peace of Turin. Both republics were half-ruined by their disasters in their blind rivalry, but Genoa, a prey to discord and revolutions, never really recovered and was soon glad to accept a French protectorate (1396), although still a naval power. Venice, on the other hand, united under her firm and sober government, was able in a few years to plan to regain her great losses and to make fresh acquisitions.

If the fortunes of Venice and Genoa were chequered, those of Florence, the great banking and manufacturing city of the West, were not less so. In spite of her ill-success in war, which led her to accept Charles of Calabria as Signore (1325–8), Florence was at the peak of her commercial wealth. By the revised statutes of 1328 the priors were appointed by lot, but this hardly diminished the control of the government by the wealthier *popolani grassi*. Yet both politics and finance were taking an ill turn. The competition for the possession of Lucca, in which Florence was engrossed, resulted in failure and debt. Further, the great banking-houses, some of them, like the Bardi, resentful of their magnate disabilities, had over-stretched their credit; their largest debtors, like Edward III of England, were defaulting, and they were on the verge of bankruptcy. They even attempted to save themselves by a *coup d'état* in 1340, which failed. The war with Pisa gave them another chance. Walter of Brienne, titular Duke of Athens, nephew of King Robert, a soldier of fortune, was appointed Captain of War and hired an army. With the aid of the magnates and acclaimed by the lesser folk, more especially the employees, he forced his way to the signory (September 1342). But he pursued without statesmanship his private ends. The magnates and the populace found themselves deluded of their hopes under his despotism; the *popolani grassi* prepared for a reaction. In July 1343 there broke out a furious insurrection, and in a few hours his power was gone. He was glad to escape under terms. Soon after, the populace rose against the magnate bankers with storm and pillage. In a new reform a larger share of the priorate was given to the lesser gilds, while many decayed magnates were made *popolani*.

Behind all these events there simmered a social and economic crisis, which the Duke of Athens had done nothing to resolve. The government was barely solvent; trade was declining; the teeming workmen of the Great Arts, with no organization or share in the State, and always ruthlessly exploited, were suffering from dearth and unemployment. The Free Companies made things worse. In 1342–3 Werner, Duke of Urslingen, and his men ravaged Romagna and Tuscany, leaving starvation behind them. In Florence incipient revolt was checked by the execution of an agitator, Ciuto Brandini (1345), but the discontent remained an unsolved problem. On these troubles came the European disaster of the Black Death, which may have halved the city's population. If wages went up, so did the price of food, and famine, whether due to bad seasons or to the Free Companies' incursions, increased the strain. The workmen had not been the only sufferers. The bankruptcy of the great houses, beginning in 1339, was consummated in 1346 by the ruin of the greatest, the Bardi and the Peruzzi. They dragged down in their fall a number of lesser houses and well-to-do Florentines, who were their creditors, among them Giovanni Villani, the chronicler. It was a testimony to the resilience of Florentine commerce and of Florentine expert banking skill that new firms, better aware of the limitations of credit, were able to rebuild their city's financial supremacy, just as the Bank of San Giorgio weathered all the political revolutions of Genoa.

In these circumstances two groups of Florentines formed in mutual opposition, the Parte Guelfa and the *popolo minuto* or workmen. The Parte Guelfa was the association of wealthy *popolani grassi* and magnates, who formed the half-concealed oligarchy dominating the commune. It retained its great wealth, being often a State-creditor, and watched over the interests of its members. Its preponderance reached its utmost with the laws of 1354–8, which enabled it to persecute any citizen on suspicion (often a fiction) of being a Ghibelline. The victims were 'warned' (*ammoniti*) and made political outcasts. So many were the malcontents even among the greater gilds that the law was modified (1366–7). What with dearths and the recurrent devastating passage of employed or unemployed Free Companies, among whom was the largely English White Company, a product of the Hundred Years' War, the hungry *popolo minuto* rioted and vainly struck in Florence, while in Siena it was repressed by slaughter. The Parte Guelfa succeeded in obtaining a veto on its own further restraint. On the other hand, the Lesser Arts obtained a share in the tribunal of the Mercanzia and a new court, the Ten of

Fig. 188. Palazzo Vecchio, Florence

Liberty, devised to remedy private oppression. The influence of the Lesser
Arts in foreign policy was less fortunate. The administration of the States
of the Church had degenerated after Albornoz's death (1368), nor did the
temporary return of Pope Urban V to Rome mend matters (1367–70). In

869

a dearth the legate of Romagna impeded the export of food to Florence, and he did not prevent the *condottiere* Sir John Hawkwood from invading Tuscany with his predatory bands. The incensed Florentines declared war on the Papacy (1375) and urged its restive subject cities to rebel. Pope Gregory XI, who was returning to Rome, replied with interdict and arms, in which the massacre perpetrated at revolted Cesena by the troops of another legate, Cardinal Robert of Geneva, added fuel to the flames. At Florence the popular war magistracy, nicknamed the 'Eight Saints' in defiance of papal censures, violated the interdict and pressed on the war. But the fighting was a stalemate, and the Parte Guelfa (representing the banker-magistrates, injured by Church enmity) proceeded to 'warn' their opponents. Peace was negotiated and after Gregory's death was ratified by Urban VI (1378).

The Parte Guelfa's action, however, had precipitated the brewing revolution. The *popolo grasso*, the Lesser Arts, and the workmen were momentarily united against it, more or less headed by Salvestro de' Medici, then Gonfalonier of Justice. Reforms began amid riots, which soon developed into an insurrection of the workmen, generally called the Ciompi from their most numerous section, the underlings of the Art of Wool. Led by a woolcarder, Michele di Lando, they stormed the Palazzo of the Commune and installed him as Gonfalonier of Justice in a new priorate. Three new employee gilds were created, the Dyers, Jerkin-makers, and Ciompi, with constitutional rights. But the revolution did not give employment or food: the shops remained shut in the tumultuous city. A mob of the poorest gathered and set up a committee, the 'Eight of Santa Maria Novella', to enforce violent change. They were met with unexpected vigour by Michele, who had developed a sense of responsibility. At the head of an armed force he scattered the insurgents (August 1378). The Art of the Ciompi was abolished, but the other two were allowed to stand. A coalition government,ᶠdemocratic in character, was now in power for three years, but it proved incapable of restoring the commerce on which Florence depended. The result was a counter-revolution (1382) which restored the domination of the *popolo grasso*, or more exactly of a narrow ring of wealthy oligarchs, which became narrower by the elimination of defeated competitors. Salvestro and Michele were both exiled, while the *popolo minuto* lost their two gilds. Whatever their defects and sins, however, the oligarchs knew how to deal with the essential problems of foreign affairs and foreign trade. Florence revived under them through critical times. She had fared better than her neighbours. Siena, with declining trade and industry, and more tormented by the Free Companies, passed through a bewildering series of sectional revolutions. Pisa fell under one tyrant after another, distracted, attacked by Florence, and impoverished.

The fourteenth century in Italy for all its woes was the golden age of the merchant and banker. If they did not invent, they at least brought into general commercial use the active or sleeping partnership, even at Genoa the joint-stock company, the bill of exchange, and the practice of insurance. Although the Church forbade the receiving of interest on loans as the mortal sin of usury, they either openly and safely flouted the prohibition (for churchmen were among the largest of borrowers) or evaded it by the employment of subterfuges allowed by the subtle canonists. Being both traders and bankers, they, imitating the Jews, developed the system of credit, if they had to learn by bitter experience its limitations. With pen, ink, and parchment, it was said, a Florentine could create a vast loan to a government. They performed miracles of ability and resource amid instability and danger and endless difficulties. By a mixture of freedom and gild-control they made their wares and products circulate over Europe and their finance conterminous with the Latin Church. But their political creation, the commune, although a triumph of varied ingenuity in construction, was, save in Venice, in full decay. Without, the incurable egoism and mutual enmity of the cities, their ingrained and exclusive particularism, exhausted them and prevented the growth of free states; within, the furious class and sectional strife prevented stable or equitable government and, along with external war, led sooner or later to the rule of tyrants who could impose internal peace and quasi-justice and govern impartially a collection of cities. The price was not only freedom but the tyrants' ambitious wars. It was not all the communes' fault that Pope and Emperor, King of Naples and Free Companies, added to the turmoil. But Pisa was ruined and Genoa cut short from mere inability to share peaceably an abundant commerce. In spite of all, however, these unbalanced cities produced not only an advance in political and commercial organization but new and exquisite growths in literature and art.

CHAPTER 29

THE STATES OF WESTERN EUROPE

(I) THE OPENING OF THE HUNDRED YEARS' WAR[1]

Louis X in his brief reign (1314–16) did little of importance save to appease the angry provincial leagues by a series of charters to them. The remedy of minor grievances was promised and partly performed. The significant fact was that the provinces acted separately and made no attempt to remove the overweening power of the royal administration, which soon resumed its unremitting sway. In fact there was union neither of France nor of classes, but a common allegiance to the Crown. Louis' death, however, leaving a child daughter, Joanna, and a pregnant queen, introduced the problem and prepared the solution of a fixed law of succession. Hitherto the Capetians had always left a son to succeed them. Now the throne was vacant until the expected birth. The first step was to recognize Louis' brother Philip as regent, not the foreign queen. When the infant John I was born only to die, Philip V the Tall took the crown himself to the exclusion of his niece. Thus the principle was established that a woman could not reign in France. It was confirmed when Philip himself died (1322), leaving only daughters. The next brother, Charles IV the Fair, succeeded unchallenged.

Of these two kings Philip V was an industrious organizing monarch, who gave completer form to the administrative departments and their procedure. While he was master, he was eager for advice. Besides other consultations, assemblies on the lines of the States General appeared at his summons. To give internal peace and order was the king's first aim; the Flemish controversy lingered on in alternate war and treaties. Charles IV was by contrast aggressive. In Flanders he found the new Count, Louis II of Nevers, a leader of the *leliaerts*; in Gascony the friction inherent in the English king's vassalage flamed up into war against Edward II, which ended in Edward III's cession of Agen and the mid-Garonne lands (1327).

Next year (1328) Charles IV died, leaving daughters and a widow with child, and the question of the regency and with it the right of succession at once arose. The male nearest of kin was Edward III of England, for his mother Isabella was sister to the dead king; but could she transmit a right which she could not possess? The nearest heir through male ancestry was a first cousin, Philip Count of Valois, son of Philip the Fair's brother. An assembly of barons gave its verdict for Philip, the native prince, and when the queen-dowager bore a daughter, he was crowned as Philip VI.

[1] See Genealogical Table 20 above, pp. 780–1.

Fig. 189. Philip VI and the French Estates, c. 1332

Edward III, after protesting, submitted to do homage for Gascony. It was agreed that Joanna, the daughter of Louis X, now Countess of Evreux, who as yet had borne no son, was Queen of Navarre, which was thus separated from France. The law of male succession to the crown, thus acted on in practice, was soon given a fabulous antiquity as 'the Salic Law'. It was indeed the most workable alternative in view of the possible future birth of grandsons of the three dead brother kings.

Philip VI, however, was neither by nature nor education well fitted for his new role. He was a knight of the fashionable, showy chivalry of the day with no strength of character or intellect. His court did not supply him

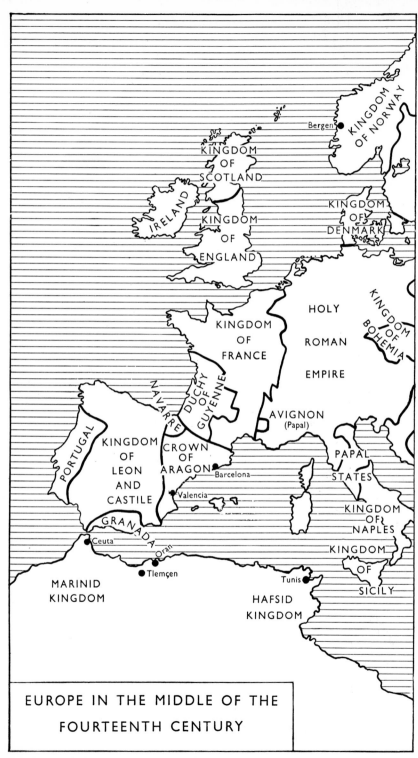

KINGDOM
OF NORWAY

Bergen

KINGDOM
OF
SCOTLAND

IRELAND

KINGDOM
OF
DENMARK

KINGDOM
OF
ENGLAND

HOLY

ROMAN

EMPIRE

KINGDOM
OF
BOHEMIA

KINGDOM
OF
FRANCE

NAVARRE

DUCHY
OF
GUYENNE

AVIGNON
(Papal)

PORTUGAL

KINGDOM
OF
LEON
AND
CASTILE

CROWN
OF
ARAGON

Barcelona

Valencia

PAPAL

STATES

KINGDOM
OF
NAPLES

GRANADA

Ceuta

Oran

KINGDOM

OF

SICILY

MARINID
KINGDOM

Tlemçen

Tunis

HAFSID
KINGDOM

EUROPE IN THE MIDDLE OF THE

FOURTEENTH CENTURY

Map 23

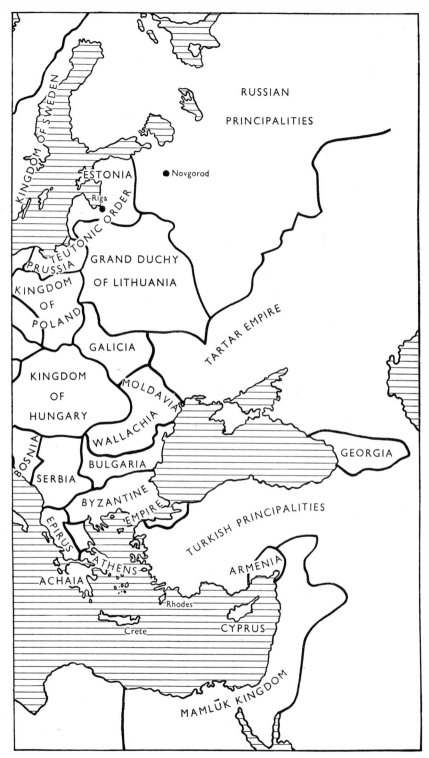

Map 23

with good counsel, the centralized bureaucracy remained superimposed on his subjects, and both were expensive—the normal revenue barely sufficed for peace-time. For war he relied on the feudal chivalry, coming largely for pay, the legal knight's and other services being commonly commuted for money, but although paid, neither mailed horsemen nor mercenary foot had advanced in military tactics since the last century. Their courage concealed their lack of skill and generalship. France was strong because she was rich and populous—there were some 12,000,000 inhabitants— since the merits of Capetian government, its peace and security, had far outweighed its defects. Trade and agriculture flourished, and the extent and the burdens of serfdom were much reduced.

With these advantages and with the benefit of a strict alliance with the Papacy at Avignon, Philip VI made a confident beginning. In Flanders Louis II appealed for help against a terrible insurrection of workmen and coastland peasants. King Philip overthrew the ill-led rebel footmen at Mount Cassel (1328), effacing the memory of Courtrai. With kinsmen ruling Naples and Hungary and allies in the Empire, he characteristically dreamed of leading a European crusade. But serious war was awaiting him with England. His ministers were steadily encroaching on Aquitaine by process of law, so that Edward III was being faced by the dilemma of war or expropriation. The duchy had been solicitously governed by the English kings, it was a loyal and valuable possession, and it was only Edward's strenuous attempt to reconquer Scotland, perhaps, which deferred his choice of war. It had in fact begun by Philip's assistance to King David Bruce. In 1336 the die was cast, and Edward renewed his claim to the French throne, although he would probably have been contented with the abolition of the intolerable vassalage of his duchy to France and territorial concessions.

The combatants seemed very unequal in strength, for England at most had a quarter of France's population, but Edward's personal superiority was great, his kingdom far more united and better organized, and its methods of warfare efficient to a degree unrealized in Europe. The military reforms of Edward I had been supplemented in the later Scottish wars by new battle tactics. An English army now consisted of paid 'retinues' of the king and barons—heavy mailed troopers, light horse, and archers—and paid levies called up from the yeomen of the shires by commissions of array, expert in the long-bow, whose practice had become a national exercise. Owing to the Scottish wars there was a plentiful supply of veterans. A campaign of these troops was in the main a devastating march, but their order of battle was skilled and professional. Their tactics were for the mailed troopers to dismount and act as pikemen on a selected terrain, while the archers were arrayed on the flanks or between their squadrons to break and enfilade the charging enemy, and a body of horsemen was kept in reserve. It was an infallible receipt for victory if the foe could be induced to attack the prepared position, for such as lasted through the volleys of arrows could make no impression on the lines of spearmen. The English, however, had achieved no advance in siege-operations beyond the slow and uncertain methods in vogue, and this was a fatal bar to success in the long run against a land of loyal, well-fortified towns and castles. They could not be captured within the time a costly campaign allowed—artillery was still in its infancy.

King Edward's first plan was to create a wide league on France's north-eastern frontier, herein following old precedents. He purchased allies among the border and German princes, not least of whom was the Emperor Lewis of Bavaria. In Flanders, by adroitly forbidding the export thither of the indispensable English wool, he provoked a revolution among the starving Flemings, who exiled the count and placed an influential clothier, James van Artevelde of Ghent, at the head of affairs (1337). To resolve their legal scruples Edward took in due form the title and arms of King of France (1340). But the campaigns of 1339 and 1340 were vain. Philip VI, although in force, declined to take the desired offensive, Tournai resisted a long siege, the German alliances broke down, and Edward returned baffled and in debt to England after making the truce of Espléchin. Yet he had scored (24 June 1340) the first of his victories. The English fleet, well furnished with bowmen and well handled, all but destroyed the great French fleet, incompetently manœuvred, at Sluys off the Flemish coast. For years Edward possessed the command of the sea and the choice of the theatre of war.

The value of Sluys was shown in the subsidiary war of the succession to the duchy of Brittany. On the death of Duke John III (1341), the dukedom was claimed by his half-brother John IV of Montfort and his niece of the full blood, Joanna, and her husband Charles of Blois. John was the choice of the Celtic-speaking Bretons and the townsmen; Charles of the French-speaking nobility. The Parlement of Paris decided for Charles, and John of Montfort gained over Edward III. Thus the two kings each championed the side opposite to their own claims to France. For years the Breton struggle, full of fighting, in which both kings took a transitory share, continued without a decision, a training ground for professional soldiers.

When the main war rekindled, Flanders was no longer a combatant and the eastern league had dissolved. Van Artevelde had been basely murdered by the factious Flemings. Edward turned his effort first to Gascony. His cousin Henry, Earl of Derby (and soon of Lancaster), brilliantly led a well-equipped army to Aquitaine in 1345, where he recovered in two years the lands lost by Edward II, baffling Philip's heir, John Duke of Normandy, in the warfare. Meantime Edward III had been attracted to Normandy by an injured Norman noble, Godfrey of Harcourt. In July 1346 he landed in the Côtentin with a strong force, took Caen, and made a devastating march eastwards towards Flanders. Philip gathered his host, but did not contrive to blockade and starve the English either at the Seine or the Somme. When he caught them up at Crécy, it was on ground chosen by Edward III, and he was lured on to attack (26 August). The English archers outshot his Genoese crossbowmen, the reckless charges of his cavalry ended in slaughter and rout, among the slain being the blind King John of Bohemia and Louis II of Flanders and among the fugitives Charles IV of Germany and Philip himself. After this resounding victory, Edward, with an unusual sense of strategy, resolved to secure an entry into northern France. He perseveringly besieged the port of Calais, and since Philip with a fresh army dared not take the offensive again, starved it to surrender after nearly a year. He could hardly be restrained from hanging six burgesses who volunteered to be scapegoats. Calais received a new English population and proved an invaluable acquisition, but the length of the siege made it clear how hard and long, not to say impossible, a task the conquest of France would be.

A long truce followed this exhausting campaign. Philip VI died in 1350 after both France and England had been scourged by the Black Death. He had not been all unfortunate in his foreign policy, for he had gained the succession to the wide land of Dauphiné between the Rhône and the Alps for his eldest grandson Charles from the last Dauphin of native stock. Henceforward the heir to France was a prince in the Empire. He issued, too, useful legislation, and his need of money made him an unwilling summoner both of States General and of provincial Estates. Heavy and new taxation was supplemented by debasement of the coinage. The clerical tenths which the Popes permitted, indeed, cast a doubt on papal neutrality and helped to frustrate the constant papal endeavour to bring about a peace. But the crucial point on which Edward naturally insisted was the absolute independence of his duchy of Aquitaine, for which alone he was prepared to barter his claim to the crown of France. On this the French were immovable.

(2) DISASTER AND RECOVERY IN FRANCE

The new king, John II, was still less fit for ruling than his father. Brave, passionate, and generous, he was stupid and obstinate, a prey to favourites, chosen ill. The times, too, were growing worse. His cousin Charles II the Bad, King of Navarre and Count of Evreux, the grandson of Louis X, born in 1332, was harbouring claims to the throne. He was a thorough-paced knave, treacherous and scheming, but eloquent and ingratiating, who could rely on his numerous vassals in northern France. He was to be the evil genius of the monarchy for years. He began his career of treason by stabbing the

878

Fig. 190. The Emperor Charles IV and King Charles V of France

king's favourite, Charles of Spain (de la Cerda), and by plotting with
Edward III he blackmailed King John, now his father-in-law, into fresh
grants of fiefs. Thus encouraged, King Edward renewed the war. In 1355
his son Edward, Prince of Wales (the Black Prince), began operations by
a devastating raid in Languedoc. King John was already in difficulties.
At that time the States General met in two assemblies, one for the north
and one for the south. In that of the north (Langue d'oïl) the lead was
taken by a clothier, Etienne Marcel, provost of the Merchants of Paris, and

879

the townsmen (Tiers État) showed themselves distrustful of the outlay of their subsidy. Next, an intrigue of Charles the Bad in Normandy led to his sudden arrest and the execution of Norman nobles, and then the king was obliged to repel a serious invasion by the Duke of Lancaster (1356). It was at the same time that the Black Prince with perhaps 7000 veteran soldiers

Fig. 191. *John II the Good*

was making a similar destructive raid in central France up to the Loire. King John turned to meet him and cut off his retreat. At Maupertuis close to Poitiers they joined battle. King John hoped to counter the English tactics by dismounting his main forces so that the disorder of the slain and wounded horses should not affect them. But the attack on a strong position, this time by wearied men in heavy armour, was retained. At the critical moment the Black Prince made a shattering counter-attack on the

880

main division of the arrow-riddled French, and won a complete victory, capturing the valiant King John himself (17 September 1356). Veteran skill had triumphed over clumsy courage and numbers. King John was carried to a chivalrous captivity in England.

This ruinous defeat, following pitiless ravage, intrigue, and discontent, placed the young Dauphin Charles, as his father's lieutenant, in a formidable quandary. The country was in a wretched state. Bands of English, Gascon and other mercenaries, in the process of turning into Free Companies, were desolating the land up to the gates of Paris. Bitter discontent at the helplessness of the monarchy and the nobles in defence was rampant. In the States General of Langue d'oïl, more especially in the Tiers État, it found voice. The leaders were the genuine and masterful reformer Marcel, who had all Paris behind him, and Robert Le Coq, Bishop of Laon, the agent of Charles the Bad. Dishonest officials and misgovernment were an easy target. To place the young dauphin under tutelage was the aim. In spite of shrewd temporizing, next year (1357) they extorted a reforming *ordonnance* in return for a subsidy. Yet they drew up no charter of liberties, while the captive John stultified their proceedings by his peremptory disapproval. The States General dwindled to certain town representatives of the Tiers État, allied to Charles the Bad, who had escaped from confinement. They were none the less exacting on the dauphin with his depleted treasury. When he thought the time was ripe to denounce the ministers they had thrust upon him, Marcel and the King of Navarre murdered two of his friends before his face, and, thinking him cowed, made the mistake of electing him regent with full powers. Within a month he found means of quitting Paris and thereby regaining his freedom. He assembled loyal Estates at Compiègne and levied soldiers. In reply Marcel in Paris prepared to fight.

Meanwhile the peasants were a prey to the wandering soldiery of all parties. In May 1358 their exasperation against the nobles who oppressed and did not defend them burst out in the Beauvaisis. The Jacquerie (so named from the *jacque*, the peasant's jerkin) spread from Picardy to the Seine, with a tale of burnt castles and hunted gentry. There was more pillage than bloodshed. The Jacques had a leader, Guillaume Cale; three towns, Beauvais, Senlis, and Clermont, joined them, besides stray craftsmen. Marcel imitated them and sent a troop of Parisians to capture the dauphiness and her court at Meaux. But the nobles and their men were rallying. A noted Gascon, the Captal de Buch, routed the assailants of Meaux, and the King of Navarre with his followers warred against the Jacques to the north, executing Cale with his wonted treachery. By midsummer the insurrection was drowned in blood.

By this time Marcel, the failure, and Charles the Bad, the egoist, had lost their popularity, while the dauphin with his troops was half-beleaguering

Paris. In desperation Marcel admitted an English band; the King of Navarre was intriguing all round. Before his plots were ripe, Marcel was murdered (31 July), and Paris opened her gates to the dauphin. He now earned his name of Charles the Wise by his lenient conduct. Marcel had but represented a section of the bourgeoisie in not too many towns, Charles the Bad only his own ambition, and a fraction of the Tiers État, posing as the States General, was unable either to reform or to control the royal government. The dauphin's aptitude to rule had restored its authority.

Charles the Wise had still to deal with the English and his namesake. Free Companies of both parties were overrunning the land from the Channel to the Garonne; towns near Paris were in their hands, and he was nearly moneyless. But he organized local defence against the raiders, and the general loyalty was shown when the States General rejected (May 1359) a peace agreed to by the captive king, which ceded all the lost dominions of Richard Cœur-de-lion. Charles the Bad found it best to make a hollow submission. Edward III, however, the official truce being expired, resolved on a vigorous effort to obtain his terms or the crown of France. In November 1359 he marched with a splendid army from Calais towards Rheims. But a new generalship had appeared among the French, typified by the famous Breton, Bertrand du Guesclin. No army came to attack the invaders and no fortress, least of all Rheims, where Edward hoped to be crowned, surrendered. Vainly ravaging, the English circled to Paris in the spring. By then they were suffering from shortage and loss of horses and men. The dauphin, too, was resigned to concessions. In May 1360 a preliminary peace was drawn up at Brétigny near Chartres. A much enlarged Aquitaine, including Poitou, Périgord, and Rouergue, was ceded to Edward in full sovranty, along with Calais and Ponthieu, while Edward abandoned his claim to the French throne. A ransom of 3,000,000 gold crowns was to be paid in instalments for King John. The treaty more or less embodied Edward III's primary aims. But here the dauphin's unpleasing astuteness and Edward's shortsightedness came into play. When the final treaty was sealed at Calais (24 October) and King John was freed, the mutual renunciations of suzerainty and claim were deferred until the transfers of largely reluctant territory were completed. They were never exchanged, and a legal loophole was preserved for the French government.

While the ceded lands were being slowly handed over, and instalments of the ransom still more slowly paid, the Free Companies—English, Gascons, Germans, and Spaniards—now out of employ, were overrunning the best of France. These mobile pillagers were organized and equipped like little armies. Their greed and cruelty were insatiable. Bertrand du Guesclin hunted them down in Normandy, but south of the Seine they endangered Avignon itself, and little relief was gained by some bands overflowing into Italy.

Fig. 192. Coronation of Charles V of France

King John exercised most influence in personal and dynastic politics. The old line of Capetian Dukes of Burgundy, which also possessed Franche Comté in the Empire and Artois in France, became extinct, and he conferred (1363) the duchy on his gallant youngest son Philip the Bold, for whom he also secured Franche Comté. Other claimants were appeased by lesser fiefs. Thus was founded the second Burgundian house, which became a European power. Another son, Louis Duke of Anjou, a hostage in England for the treaty, broke his parole and escaped. John's strict sense of honour made him return himself to captivity in London, where he died in April 1364.

His decease placed his heir on the throne, the first Valois fitted to reign. Charles V the Wise, unlike his ancestors, was of poor physique, probably from malnutrition in youth due to the change from the old hardy upbringing of royal courts, but his mental endowments were great. He possessed self-control, judgement of men and events, which degenerated into craft, and a love of order and magnificence, which fell in with his conception of himself as the Lord's Anointed, descended from St Louis. Devout, learned, and intellectual, he outwitted his blunter adversaries and burdened his subjects with taxes if he rescued them from anarchy. Like the Emperor Charles IV he belonged to the new type of rulers with a touch of the

Renaissance. His ministers were like himself, able and cultured, all save his brilliant constable, Bertrand du Guesclin. That Breton noble had been a born fighter from his youth up, but he also was one of the best new professional generals, upright and straightforward.

Du Guesclin forced Charles the Bad to a fresh, less advantageous peace, but he shared in the defeat of Auray at the hands of the English bands, in which Charles of Blois was killed (September 1364). In consequence the young John IV of Montfort was acknowledged as Duke of Brittany. The Free Companies remained to be got rid of. The first scheme to send them east as crusaders failed, as we have seen, in Alsace. The next opportunity was furnished by the revolt of the bastard, Don Henry of Trastamara, against his brother, King Peter the Cruel of Castile. Du Guesclin at the head of the Companies drove out King Peter in two months, and the bands streamed back to France. King Peter, however, persuaded the Black Prince, then ruling Aquitaine, to invade Castile through Navarre, when he won his last victory at Nájera (April 1367), and returned, fatally ill, and deluded by the restored king. Du Guesclin, who had been captured and ransomed, promptly led fresh bands to Spain, where Peter the Cruel was murdered and succeeded by Don Henry, henceforward a firm ally of France (1369).

One effect of these campaigns was to reduce the wild soldiery to a remnant who could be sternly dealt with. Charles the Wise could now proceed with his long-nursed plan of reconquest. Good government, justice, and peace in the royal domain were strengthening him. He obtained from the States General new taxes, especially the hearth-tax, which became permanent. The burden was somewhat alleviated by a stable reform of the currency. In spite of malversation and excessive expenditure Charles had acquired the sinews of war. The army was reorganized and paid—it largely consisted of nobles and was arrayed in trained companies. Fortresses were inspected, the artillery was at last becoming effective in sieges, and a fleet was created under the admiral, Jean de Vienne. Diplomacy was also at work. With the Pope's aid and by the retrocession of the long-lost south Flemish towns, Charles secured the hand of the heiress of Flanders, Margaret, for his brother Philip of Burgundy, thus preventing an English alliance.

Meanwhile the tension in Aquitaine was growing. The Black Prince's government was unpopular among the nobles and the ceded districts. When he, too, was obliged to levy a hearth-tax to pay for his Spanish expedition, the great malcontent Gascon houses of Armagnac and Albret appealed to the Parlement of Paris. The mutual renunciations had never been exchanged, and the Black Prince was cited to appear before the court (January 1369). On his refusal rebellion broke out in the ceded districts, and an ultimatum was despatched to Edward III, who then resumed the

Fig. 193. Charles V of France

title of King of France. Methodical reconquest by the French, and vain ravaging marches by the English armies, characterized the war. Du Guesclin refused battle save at advantage; his attacks were seconded by the population, to whom the sack and massacre at revolted Limoges (1370) by the Black Prince before he left for England were no deterrent. On the sea the effect of Sluys was reversed in 1372 by the defeat of the English by a Castilian fleet off La Rochelle. In three years Aquitaine north of the Garonne was recovered, and Duke John IV, who had held by Edward III, was driven out of Brittany. A great raiding march (1373) by John of Gaunt, Duke of Lancaster, from Calais to Bordeaux met no enemy in array. In 1375 the truce of Bruges preserved for the English only Calais and a coastal strip of Gascony.

Charles the Wise now turned on more domestic enemies. The treacherous Charles the Bad was evicted from all his lands, even Navarre, and reduced to destitution. The attempt to unite Brittany to the royal domain, however, proved a failure. The Bretons fought for autonomy, John IV was recalled, and even the loyal Du Guesclin showed no zeal (1379). The war with England, too, revived after Edward III's death with little profit to either side and abortive negotiations. Charles V had already recognized the Pope of Avignon in the Great Schism of the Church when he himself died on 16 September 1380, preceded by his constable Du Guesclin, who had spent his last days against the remnants of the brigand companies. He had been one of the greatest kings of France, but even so the kingdom was all but in ruins from the unending war and exhausted by taxation for his policy and magnificence.

(3) ENGLAND UNDER EDWARD II

The lassitude and discontent in England at Edward I's death were perhaps in tune with the speedy abandonment of his last expedition, but they were not allayed by the character of his heir, Edward II. The new king was incurably frivolous and careless of administration. He had robust health, but his diversions in the open air were peasant-like and mechanical, which alienated from him the fighting, hunting barons and lost him the respect of his subjects. What was worse, he was given to inordinate favouritism of the companion of his pastimes, who ruled him. The Gascon, Piers Gavaston, bred with him from boyhood, and banished by his father as an evil influence, was even more frivolous, insolent and vain. It was of ill omen when he was created Earl of Cornwall, married to an heiress, and flaunted as the king's chief counsellor. The offence taken was so great that Edward was forced to consent to Gavaston's banishment as lord lieutenant of Ireland (1308). Steady maladministration, however, enlarged the area of grievances and next year the king was obliged to consent to the reforming Articles of Stamford, in return for which he obtained Gavaston's recall. The concession aggravated the situation. When a baronial committee appointed in 1310, the Lords Ordainers, was drawing up ordinances to reform abuses in the government, they insisted once more on the exile of the hated favourite. Edward, who accepted in August 1311 the long series of ordinances they had devised for the reform and control of the government and officials, including those of the household and wardrobe, quickly recalled Gavaston and held aloof from the Ordainers in the north. The Ordainers replied by taking up arms: they chased Edward, captured his queen, Isabella of France, and forced Gavaston to surrender at Scarborough on terms of safe-conduct to a Parliament. On his way to Westminster, four of them, the Earls of Warwick, Lancaster, Hereford and Arundel, had him beheaded (June 1312). The outrage broke up their own party. The Earl of Pembroke especially felt that his safe-conduct had been dishonoured, but no one wished for civil war and a halting reconciliation was brought about. Little progress in reform was made by the Ordainers, hampered by an unwilling king and the stupid egoism of their overpowerful chief, his cousin Thomas of Lancaster, with his five earldoms. The disaster of Bannockburn (1314), the devastation of the northern shires by the Scots, the invasion of Ireland by Edward Bruce, brother of King Robert (1315), and a prolonged famine due to bad seasons added to the troubles.

At last Earl Thomas's incompetence weakened his hold on the magnates, and in 1317 he agreed to a treaty at Leake with them, which was followed by a full parliament at York (1318). The reins were now held by a middle party, led by the Earl of Pembroke and composed of moderate reformers and royalists. A standing council was set up, household and departmental reform really undertaken, a truce with Scotland secured for two years (1319), Edward Bruce overthrown and slain by the marcher baron, Roger Mortimer (1318), and an accommodation reached with France over Edward's fiefs of Aquitaine and Ponthieu (1319); even good harvests returned. The prospect, however, was soon overcast. Personal rivalries and ambitions, combined with Edward's ineradicable wilfulness and need of a favourite, divided the middle party. The new confidant was Hugh le Despenser the younger, an old intimate of the king and son of an elderly royalist baron of the same name. He used his household office of chamberlain to undermine all other influence and to lead Edward 'like a cat after a straw'. He had married one of the three co-heiresses of the last Clare, the Earl of Gloucester, who had been killed at Bannockburn, and his ambition was to enlarge the lordship of Glamorgan he had received with her into a still vaster marcher fief and to rise to an earldom. He was soon at private war with the other marcher lords and his brothers-in-law (1321). This gave the sullen Earl of Lancaster (himself a marcher lord) the opportunity to rally and reunite the opposition. A parliament, attended in arms, forced Edward to exile the two Despensers.

This proceeding roused the king to unwonted energy. An insult to the queen by the wife of Badlesmere, nominal steward of the household, gave him the means of a hasty siege of Badlesmere's castle of Leeds in Kent, which was taken. The Welsh marchers, who had again taken up arms, were overawed in a swift campaign, save the Earl of Hereford and others, who fled to the north, where they coalesced with Lancaster. With the same surprising vigour Edward, now counselled again by the Despensers, pursued them, and by the generalship of Harclay at the head of the Border levies utterly defeated his opponents at Boroughbridge (16 March 1322). For once in his life victorious, he took vengeance on them. Hereford had fallen at Boroughbridge, but Lancaster and his associates were executed, and a full Parliament at York annulled the Ordinances, which had limited the Crown, and, with reference doubtless to their baronial origin, declared that only a full Parliament including the commonalty could deal with the estate of the king and the realm. It was the victory of an unfettered kingship freed from baronial committees. But the rancorous feuds were not allayed by confiscations, and the king was more than ever involved in the success of his personal government.

Strangely enough, the latter reign of a weak and indolent monarch was marked by business-like reforms in the routine methods of administration. The greedy Despensers, the elder being created Earl of Winchester, were no patrons of muddle, and among the royal bureaucrats were men of high ability. Exchequer and Chancery were well organized; the Privy Seal became a state department, and the Wardrobe innocuous. But with the younger Despenser as Chamberlain, another department of the household,

23. England in the Later Middle Ages

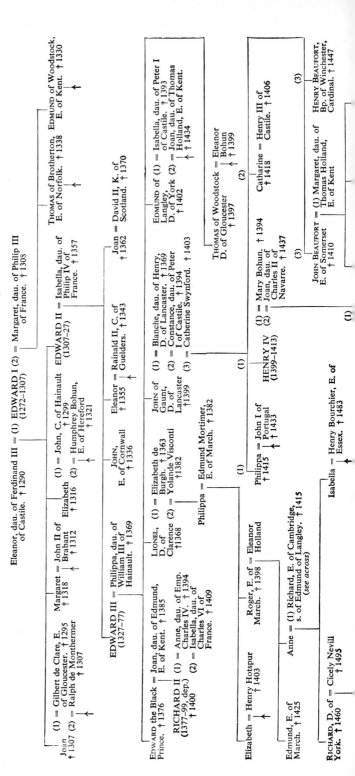

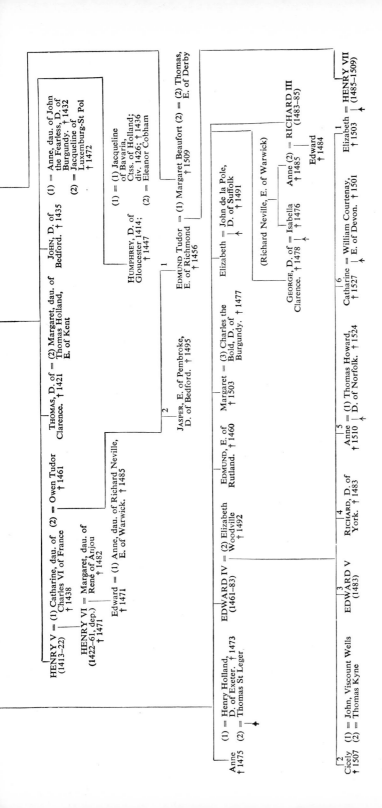

HENRY V = (1) Catharine, dau. of (2) = Owen Tudor
(1413–22) Charles VI of France † 1461
† 1438

THOMAS, D. of = (2) Margaret, dau. of JOHN, D. of (1) = Anne, dau. of John
Clarence. † 1421 Thomas Holland, Bedford. † 1435 the Fearless, D. of
E. of Kent Burgundy. † 1432
(2) = Jacqueline of
Luxemburg-St Pol
† 1472

HUMPHREY, D. of (1) = (1) Jacqueline
Gloucester 1414; of Bavaria,
† 1447 Ctss. of Holland;
div. 1426; † 1436
(2) = Eleanor Cobham

HENRY VI = Margaret, dau. of
(1422–61, dep.) René of Anjou
† 1471 † 1482

Edward = (1) Anne, dau. of Richard Neville,
† 1471 E. of Warwick. † 1485

EDMUND Tudor = (1) Margaret Beaufort (2) = (2) Thomas,
E. of Richmond † 1509 E. of Derby
† 1456

JASPER, E. of Pembroke,
D. of Bedford. † 1495

Margaret = (3) Charles the
† 1503 Bold, D. of
Burgundy. † 1477

EDMUND, E. of
Rutland. † 1460

RICHARD, D. of
York. † 1483

Elizabeth = John de la Pole,
D. of Suffolk
† 1491

(Richard Neville, E. of Warwick)

GEORGE, D. of = Isabella Anne (2) = RICHARD III
Clarence. † 1478 † 1476 † 1485 (1483–85)

Edward
† 1484

2 Catharine = William Courtenay,
† 1527 E. of Devon. † 1501

1 Elizabeth = HENRY VII
† 1503 (1485–1509)

EDWARD IV = (2) Elizabeth
(1461–83) Woodville
† 1492

3 EDWARD V
(1483)

Anne (1) = Henry Holland,
† 1475 D. of Exeter. † 1473
(2) = Thomas St Leger

Cicely (1) = John, Viscount Wells
† 1507 (2) = Thomas Kyne

Anne = (1) Thomas Howard,
† 1510 D. of Norfolk. † 1524

the Chamber, became the instrument of the king's personal action. Large revenues were paid into it apart from the Exchequer and Treasury. Good administration, however, in the central bureaucracy was no remedy for the general ills, and discontent, and unruliness. The northern shires were ravaged by the Scots, and the competent Harclay, now Earl of Carlisle, was executed as a traitor for treating with Bruce for the recognition of his kingship. Soon after (June 1323) the government itself secured a thirteen years' truce as a substitute. Next year the war with France began over Aquitaine with its misfortunes. As if to multiply his foes, Edward, under Despenser influence, seized his French queen's dower-lands, and then in excess of folly sent her, and later his heir, the boy Edward, to France to treat with her brother Charles IV. There she made a peace and also formed a friendship, ripening into adultery, with the Despensers' mortal enemy, the marcher Roger Mortimer, who had escaped from his imprisonment after Boroughbridge. Her fatuous husband thereupon denounced the treaty. He had few friends left amid these failures. Pembroke was dead, and his cousin Henry, Earl of Leicester, was aggrieved both at Earl Thomas's death and his own partial disinheritance. All but the Mortimer circle were estranged from him.

Isabella in France was well aware of the general feeling. Dismissed from Paris on account of the scandal of her amour, she took refuge in Hainault with Mortimer and her son, and obtained means for invading England by betrothing young Edward to its count's daughter. In September 1326 she and Mortimer landed in Suffolk. She met with almost universal adherence, so weary were men of their unprofitable king. The Londoners rioted in her favour, murdering one unpopular minister, the Treasurer, Bishop Stapledon. Edward II was chased to Wales and captured there. Both Despensers were also seized and immediately hanged. The king was held prisoner at Kenilworth by Henry of Lancaster and Leicester, while a parliament was summoned in his name to Westminster in January 1327. All, save some strong-minded bishops, were agreed like the London mob on his deposition, and he accepted his fate by abdicating. Thereupon the boy Edward III was proclaimed under a Council of Regency. A few months later his unhappy father was atrociously murdered at Berkeley Castle.

It was a sordid revolution, in which the fierce, adulterous queen and her brutal paramour played the chief part along with muddle-headed nobles and self-seeking prelates. Edward II paid the penalty for both his father's faults and his own folly. But the new government of Isabella and Mortimer, created Earl of the March of Wales, was no improvement either in methods or success. It, too, was the rule of a greedy faction. By necessity it made a losing peace with France, and by necessity after a feebly led campaign it acknowledged the independence of Scotland by the Treaty of Northampton

(May 1328). The union in deposing Edward II soon dissolved. Mortimer was chiefly intent on engrossing power and land. The royal earls, Lancaster, Kent, and Norfolk, attempted resistance, but Lancaster was blind, and the other two were irresolute. Lancaster was mulcted in estates, and Kent trapped into a plot and beheaded. Then Mortimer's own turn came. Edward III was growing up and had a son. With his intimates he contrived the sudden capture of the now hated Earl of March at Nottingham. A parliament condemned him to death, and Isabella was reduced to her dower-lands (November 1330). Edward III began to rule as well as reign.

(4) THE REIGN OF EDWARD III

In some ways Edward III was boyish all his life. His winning address never failed him with his subjects, and he was thoroughly in harmony in temperament and likings with his barons. Able, adroit, and strong-willed, he was not of the stuff of which tyrants are made. War, the hunt, and display in the current mode were his leading passions. He had little scruple in breaking his promises and recalling solemn concessions, but this very slipperiness made him short-sighted of the future if he gained his immediate end. The prestige that he acquired by his victories carried him easily over the chief domestic crisis of his reign, and it was almost in silence that the definite formation of a 'House' of Commons occurred and that the Crown was deprived of unparliamentary taxation, while feudal franchise faded out as a method of local government.

The king's earlier ambitions were directed towards Scotland, and the wiping out of the disgrace which he had endured under Mortimer. The Scottish neglect to restore English partisans to their lands, as following on the treaty of Northampton, supplied an incentive for conniving at the attempt of Edward Balliol, the son of King John, to recover his father's throne. In 1332 Balliol won a transient success by his victory at Dupplin Moor, a notable stage in the combined use of archers and dismounted men-at-arms in battle tactics. But the nationalists quickly drove him out, and he turned for aid to Edward III as his suzerain. A brilliant victory at Halidon Hill (1333), in which the new tactics, to be repeated at Crécy, were fully employed, caused the flight of young King David Bruce to France, and the nominal restoration of Balliol. In return he ceded the southern counties to the Forth to his protector. But he was a shadow king, whose support entailed a yearly English campaign. The Scots wisely refused battle, and although Edward III, especially in 1336, led very large armies to the field and reached the Moray Firth, he and his disheartened vassal never secured authority outside the districts held by their troops. After 1336 Edward III realized the failure and diverted his efforts against the French king, David's host and ally.

The domestic policy of the king during these early years was marked by slow increase of the influence of household officials in the administration: they were more amenable to the king's will. Not that Edward either excluded the magnates or was averse to frequent parliaments. Their main business was to grant money for the Scottish war, but their internal development possessed lasting importance. Knights of the shire and burgesses were now always summoned—frequently even in the occasional Great Councils which were called by writs of Privy Seal, whereas a true parliament was called under the Great Seal—and these elected representatives adopted the practice of consulting together, which produced 'the Commons', not yet named a 'House', but become a separate division of the assembly, while prelates and lay lords also deliberated together. Clerical proctors were also, if sporadically, sent, but since the clergy preferred to make their grants in the two Convocations of Canterbury and York, their interest in Parliament waned. Incidentally, the outbreak of the Hundred Years' War resulted in Parliament being invariably summoned to Westminster, the most convenient place for affairs.

The transfer of war to Europe brought on the major constitutional crisis of Edward's reign. It occasioned him to be long absent from England and to be in dire need of ready money for his costly alliances and armaments. Both facts put a severe strain on his harmony with his subjects. Edward's device for absence in the Walton Ordinances (1338) was to subordinate Treasury and Chancery, working at home, to the household officials, headed by Kilsby, his Privy Seal, who accompanied him abroad. This was a full return to the government by household of his father. It was speedily revoked, but still supplies of cash did not come in. Edward in 1340 made a personal bargain with Parliament. He obtained a grant in return for four statutes which abolished the occasional customary feudal aids and the right to tallage the demesne, and prescribed that future taxes on Englishmen should only be granted in Parliament. Still Edward found that money did not reach him, and came back again in wrath after a vain campaign, putting all the blame on the clerical chiefs of the Treasury and Chancery, including Archbishop Stratford of Canterbury, lately Chancellor and long his principal counsellor. A lay Treasurer and Chancellor were put in on the ground that they had no clerical immunity. A bitter controversy began between the king and archbishop, whose brother the Bishop of Chichester, just dismissed from the office of Chancellor after a brief tenure, was also involved. The archbishop, who modelled himself on Becket, adroitly combined a strong case with the magnates' dislike of government by mere household confidants. The king's personal popularity softened the compulsory reconciliation, but he was obliged to admit the right of magnates to be tried only by their peers in parliament, and also the audit of his accounts and the supervision of his appointments of ministers

(1341). The irksomeness of the latter restrictions was shown by his first annulling them, and then (1343) persuading Parliament to repeal them. None the less, henceforward he relied on baronial councillors and episcopal ministers. The policy championed by the Earls of Lancaster, the house to which the Stratford brothers had originally been attached, had achieved a certain measure of success.

The king's impecuniosity, which necessitated heavier and, if possible, anticipated taxation, produced in the long run, after many shifting expedients and broken promises—for his bad faith, like his empty purse, was incurable—a greater solidarity of the Commons and a greater control of revenue by the Parliament. Edward's earlier method was to impose a maletolt on exported wool (the most abundant source) by agreement with assemblies of merchants. They were to profit by monopoly prices and he by the anticipatory loans they made him, aided by his right of purveyance on credit from the wool-growers. The results were twofold. Group after group of rich and speculative merchant financiers, first Florentine, then English, were ruined by Edward's reckless breach of the agreements in his pressing need, and the lesser merchants and the multitudinous wool-growers, injured by monopoly and forced sales, tended to coalesce in their common meeting-ground of Parliament. It was only gradually that the conviction spread that the king must have the high tax on wool (1352), but then it was granted under conditions in Parliament. It was found in the end that the least objectionable way was to fix the Staple, or selling-place, of English wool at Calais, and its transport thither and sale there came into the hands of a fairly numerous body of merchants, the Company of the Staple. It was still a monopoly, but not so narrow as the former groups, and disconnected from the abuses of purveyance and forced sale. The king, too, unlike his rival of France, was more dependent than ever on his Parliament for the sinews of war and peace. His part in these transactions had no reference to economic policy but was that of an insolvent and insatiable spender, whose successive devices ended in uniting the interests on whom the burden fell.

War and its victories, in which that of Neville's Cross over the Scots (1346) and the capture of David II freed the king's hands for France, and its dubious finance were punctuated in England as elsewhere by the terrible Black Death (1348–50) and its recurrence in later years. The chief result was to reduce, and prevent the renewed increase of, the population and to embitter the relations between the landowners and the peasants, for the resistance of the former, who were masters in Parliament, to the rise in wages for scarcer labour added a new friction to an economic evolution already begun, as we shall see later. Here, however, mention should be made of the long drawn out change that was transforming the system of keeping public order and replacing in all but petty matters the feudal and semi-feudal organization. Ever since the latter days of Edward I the problem of suppressing crimes of violence, largely due to soldiers returned from the wars, had been acute, and caused the establishment of new officials for policing, the Keepers of the Peace, selected from the magnates and gentry of a county. The classes which had operated the older feudal methods were employed in the new. Characteristically, a long series of see-saw experiments were adopted in turn by Edward III. Was it magnates or gentry who were to be in charge, and were they to try culprits as well as arrest them? Eventually, by 1380, the erection of commissions of gentry as Justices of the Peace with power to try felonies in their county was the expedient which won the day. It was an innovation with a future in local government.

The reward of the king's officials, still mainly clerical, was achieved by ecclesiastical preferment, of which he disposed by law or influence. Here he came into conflict with the Papacy, which under John XXII had perfected its system of provisions. The conflict, which arose where ecclesiastical (not lay) patrons or electors were concerned, was fought out in detail in the respective courts of the contending parties, each working under their appropriate law, secular or canonical, with contradictory judgements. King and Pope might often agree on a candidate, but not infrequently they did not. The divergence became acute on the occasions when the Pope conferred profitable benefices not only on foreigners who hardly, if at all, came to England, but on Frenchmen when there was war with France. Edward III obtained statutes to strengthen his bargaining powers, the Statute of Provisors (1351) and the Statutes of Praemunire (1353, 1365). If a bull of provision was brought to England, the king was given the disposal of the benefice it concerned, and outlawry was threatened against those who had recourse to foreign (i.e. papal) courts in matters where the king's courts had cognisance. The king thus enjoyed a stronger position in his negotiations with the Papacy, which was a standing grievance of the Popes, but some form of collusion between them was the practice. The duties, if any, of the office and the rights of ecclesiastical patrons were not greatly regarded by either power. Both the statutes and the irritation that gave rise to them had their chief importance as signs that the over-strained centralization of Avignon had undermined obedience.

It was in harmony with this secular temper of Edward and his subjects that in 1365, when Pope Urban VI asked for the payment of the long arrears of the papal tribute, Parliament declared that King John had broken his coronation oath when he surrendered his kingdom to the Pope, and that his action was invalid. In 1374 Gregory XI reopened the question, which ended in 1377 with his being allowed to take a subsidy from the English clergy in return for moderation in the exercise of his ecclesiastical prerogative. The tribute was not obtained and dropped out of sight.

The renewal in 1369 and the failures of the French war, accompanied by the defects of a now ageing but still frivolous king, caused the reign to close in clouds and discontent. The ineffectiveness of the clerical ministers, among whom was William of Wykeham, Bishop of Winchester, the Chancellor, and their immunity from the lay courts, coupled with the pro-French tendencies of the Papacy, roused Parliament in 1371 to demand and Edward to appoint laymen in their place. But the new did no better than the old, and lawyers, the other literate class, were distrusted nearly as much as clerics. By 1376, what with the scandals of the household and the widowed king's subjection to a mistress, Alice Perrers, things were ripe for an explosion.

Fig. 194. The Black Prince praying to the Holy Trinity

By this time a considerable and, as it proved, a momentous change had evolved in the leadership of the baronage, whose chiefs were now sons or nearly allied to the king. Like his predecessors Edward III endowed his numerous sons with vacant fiefs and the hands of great heiresses, but his opportunities were greater than theirs. His heir was Prince of Wales, Duke of Cornwall, Earl of Chester, and husband of the Countess of Kent; a younger son, who predeceased him, was Lionel, Duke of Clarence and Earl of Ulster; younger again was John of Gaunt, the wealthiest peer in England, Duke of Lancaster and husband of its heiress; two others were earls and later dukes. Especially close to the throne was Edmund Mortimer, Earl of March, the husband of Philippa, daughter and heiress of Lionel of Clarence. The history of England for a century was to be shaped by the rivalries of these royal lines with their vast estates.

In 1376, with the Black Prince a dying man and the king senile, John of Gaunt, allied to the corrupt household ministers, was in charge and met the severe criticism of the 'Good Parliament'. The Lords, spiritual and lay, were led by Wykeham of Winchester and Courtenay of London; the Commons, who displayed a remarkable boldness and initiative, and acted with the Lords, chose as their 'Speaker' (the first, perhaps, who gave a permanent character to that function) Peter de la Mare, the steward of the Earl of March, an indication of the line of cleavage. Under their pressure the peccant officials were dismissed, Perrers banished the court, and nine lords, excluding Gaunt, were added to the Council. When the Black Prince died in June, his surviving son, Richard, was presented to Parliament at its demand, while the thorny question, who was next heir after him, John of Gaunt or Philippa of March and her son, was left unanswered. It is true that when the Good Parliament ended, Gaunt was supreme. He disgraced March, persecuted Wykeham, and imprisoned De la Mare. A new Parliament (1377) reversed many of its predecessor's acts. But the fact remained that the Commons had gained a new solidarity and importance and that Parliament as a whole had dictated to the Crown. On 21 June 1377 Edward III himself quitted the scene. Despite his masterful ability, his victories, and his splendour, the kingship had weakened under him. He left an exhausting and hopeless war, a group of over-mighty lords, jockeying for power, and a restive, over-taxed people to his grandson. The glamour of his personality no longer concealed the enfeeblement of the Crown.

Much else besides the crystallization of Parliament and central and local government was evolving, not unperceived but incidentally, in this reign of wars. In spite of the cosmopolitanism of regnant chivalry, the sentiment of English nationality became fully awake when France and Scotland were perennial foes and Gascony a small dependency. The upper classes, long and still bilingual in French and English, were finding English to be their native speech. In 1362 Parliament was opened by a speech in English. A new and cultured English literature was coming to birth for the educated reader, for the devout and the worldly alike. To name only the greatest, in Langland (*fl.* 1362–1400) and Chaucer (*ob.* 1400) we have the authentic voices of two chief sections of the English people, the plain, godly men of little town and countryside, awake to the crying sins of the time but at heart conservative and untouched by foreign influences, and the fashionable, go-ahead world of court and castle, secular, cosmopolitan, cynical, and kindly, its English woof dyed, like its composite language, with French and Italian colours, in touch with the long tradition of Latin and feudal civilization.

(5) SCOTLAND, 1329–1424

The history of Scotland in the century after Robert Bruce was warped by the long struggle against England, enhanced by the minority of David II and the weakness in character and resources of the first two Stewart kings. The natural consequence was to give excessive power to the fierce feudal lords who maintained Scottish independence by their hardiness in arms, but wrecked internal peace by their untamed unruliness, their incessant feuds and rivalries, their insatiable greed for land and power. These feudatories overshadowed the Crown both as valiant patriots and as selfish, turbulent vassals. The greatest of them was the house of Douglas, warden of the Marches, to whom Lord James, the companion of Robert Bruce, belonged.

The immediate provocation of the troubles of the reign of David II (1329-71) was the non-restitution of the disinherited partisans of England, who were mostly at blood-feud with Bruce since the murder of Comyn. It was with Edward III's connivance that under Edward Balliol they invaded Scotland and won the battle of Dupplin Moor (1332). Balliol's tottering throne was propped by Edward III, his suzerain, in some four years' campaigning, which, though victorious (as at Halidon Hill), failed completely to subjugate the Scots. King David, kept out of harm's way at the French court, was able to return in 1341. While Edward III was at the siege of Calais, he took the opportunity of a counter-invasion, but was defeated and captured at Neville's Cross near Durham (October 1346). Intermittent border warfare culminated in Edward III's devastation to the Forth, known as the 'Burnt Candlemas' (1356), and long negotiations ended in the Treaty of Berwick (1357), by which David was released on promise of an exorbitant ransom. Balliol had already transferred his hopeless claims to Edward, and certain fortresses including Berwick were left in English hands.

David's death in 1371 brought a new dynasty to the Scottish throne in the person of his sister's son, Robert II Stewart, the hereditary High Steward of Scotland. Sprung from Brittany and long settled under the name of FitzAlan in Shropshire, the family produced, besides the elder English line of the Earls of Arundel, a Scottish branch, the Stewarts, in Kyle. Unfortunately possessed of a private competence relatively trivial, they were hard put to it to hold their own against feudal arrogance, especially that of the Earls of Douglas and their kinsmen. Robert II (1371-90) himself took no personal part in the renewed border warfare with England, in which the second Earl of Douglas won the long-remembered victory of Otterburn over Hotspur at the cost of his own life (1388). His son Robert III (1390-1406) was still more a nonentity. Crippled and irresolute, he watched the increasing turbulence of the nobles, among whom the worst offenders were of his own house. The war with England continued in raid and counter-raid. His dissolute heir, David, Duke of Rothesay, died in prison, probably at the instigation of his uncle, the Duke of Albany (1402). This moved the king to a resolute act. He sent his remaining son, the boy James, to France for safety, only to hear that he had been captured by the English on the voyage. The broken-hearted king died, leaving Albany as regent, who ruled until his own death (1420). The most notable event of the time was a formidable invasion by the all but independent Lord of the Isles, Donald Macdonald, provoked by Albany's greed. But the Highland chief, a parallel to the Lowland Douglases, was overthrown at Harlaw near Aberdeen (1411). Murdoch, the second Duke of Albany, who succeeded as regent, had at least the wisdom to make a peace with England in 1423 which, unluckily for him, restored James I to liberty and the throne.

This half-anarchic period, however, was not devoid of constitutional growth or cultured activity. Robert Bruce in 1326 may have first called representatives of the burghs to his Parliament at Cambuskenneth, and they attended from time to time hereafter. They never reached the position

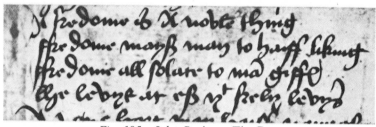

Fig. 195. John Barbour, The Brus

of meeting apart from the barons and prelates. By an innovation, not without a parallel where the kingship was weak, the majority in 1367 went home for the harvest, leaving a commission to keep a watch on affairs, and parliamentary authority passed gradually into the hands of the Committee of the Articles, set up in 1424 to consider business of the Crown. Yet Parliament for legislation and taxation was a further limitation on the exiguous monarchy. A definitely Scottish literature, in the north English dialect and without connexion with the Gaelic poetry common to the Highlands and Ireland, arose in Barbour's epic of *The Brus* and Wyntoun's *Chronicle* in verse, while the first Scottish university, that of St Andrews, was founded in 1413. Both poems and university were offsprings of the national spirit.

(6) IRELAND, 1315–1399

The victory of Robert Bruce at Bannockburn brought about the close of the flourishing period of Anglo-Norman domination in Ireland. He struck at his vanquished enemy there. In May 1315 his brother Edward Bruce landed with 6000 men in Co. Antrim. Ravaging the country, the Scots routed the Earl of Ulster near Connor. This was the signal for the rising of the Irish in Connaught and West Meath. Ulster was at Bruce's mercy, while he raided as far as Co. Kildare, returning to his base to be crowned King of Ireland (May 1316). Although the O'Connors of Connaught were crushed by the English under William de Burgh in August 1316 at Athenry,

Edward, joined by his brother King Robert, marched through Leinster and Munster as far as Limerick in 1317, doing incalculable damage to the open country. But, save in Ulster, they took no important stronghold, and the Irish themselves, though ready to attack their neighbours, were only half-hearted in supporting the invaders. Roger Mortimer, the future Earl of March, appeared as King's Lieutenant in 1317, and compelled some submission in the east, while King Robert left for Scotland. Not till October 1318 did Edward Bruce stir out of Ulster again, but he rashly gave battle to John de Bermingham and his more disciplined forces at Faughard near Dundalk, and met his death in his defeat (14 October). 'No better deed', says the Irish annalist, 'for the men of all Erin was performed since the beginning of the world than this deed, for theft and famine and destruction of men' had been rife during the invasion.

The Anglo-Norman dominion never recovered from the shock. General impoverishment, the decay of the Anglo-Normans, and turbulence by no means confined to the Gaelic septs were the consequence. Thomond (Co. Clare) was lost to the Irish in 1318, the first permanent retreat of English government, but the general insubordination, and the feuds among the barons and the Irish kinglets, were more fatal. The new earls, FitzThomas (a Geraldine) of Desmond, Butler of Ormond, FitzGerald of Kildare, the Berminghams, and the Le Poers carried on their private warfare involved with the hostilities of the Irish septs. The De Burghs of Ulster and Con-naught were not behindhand in turmoil, and fell out among themselves. In 1333 the Earl of Ulster was murdered by some of his vassals. He left a daughter and heiress, but his lands in Connaught were fought over by his kinsmen, the victors in the broil becoming known as the MacWilliams. The small authority of the Crown there disappeared. Meantime the heiress of Ulster was married (1352) to Edward III's son, Lionel of Clarence, but very soon the Clannaboy O'Neills expanded their possessions until the earldom was reduced to the littoral of Cos. Down and Antrim. In Leinster, too, the Irish septs encroached on the area of English rule, the most powerful kinglets, the MacMurrough, exacting what was really blackmail from the government.

The counter-action of the Crown, which found its revenue and authority steadily on the wane, was marred by vacillation and the evils of absenteeism, all Edward III's ambitions being engrossed elsewhere. They alternated between severity and leniency as the king's justiciars changed. The hostility of the Irish and the Hibernization of the Anglo-Irish had produced a new problem, of which the English government, becoming restricted to the ever narrower 'English Pale', was painfully aware. In 1341 a hasty remedy was adopted by decreeing the dismissal from office of all Anglo-Irish who had no English land and their replacement by such as had, as well as the re-sumption of all grants since 1307. The indignant colonists, led by the Earl of Desmond, held a meeting at Kilkenny, in which they drew up a petition of protest. Royal conciliation was then tried, followed by a successful campaign of a warlike justiciar, Ralph d'Ufford. In 1348–9 the Black Death added to the calamities of raids and feuds. The agricultural prosperity induced by the manorial system did not revive after the blow, and many Anglo-Irish drifted back to England in search of a securer life.

With the English Pale shrinking and disorder increasing, Edward III after the treaty of Brétigny resolved to send Lionel of Clarence with an army as his lieutenant to Ireland. The duke produced some approach to quiet, and in 1366 endeavoured to stabilize the situation by the Statute of Kilkenny. Its aims were twofold: (1) to prevent further Hibernization among the Anglo-Irish, so many of whom outside the Pale had, like the de Burghs and FitzGeralds, taken the position of Gaelic chiefs; (2) to obviate occasions of discord between the two races. For these purposes the statute forbade inter-marriage and fostering children of Irish and Anglo-Irish and the use of the Gaelic language and of the Irish Brehon law in the English districts. It was really a defensive attempt to preserve the dwindling English remnant, which was welcomed by the dwellers in the Pale and often re-enacted, and in no way a hopeless endeavour to extirpate the Irish tongue and law in the wider lands outside. But it was an acknowledgement of the failure of the Anglo-Norman conquest.

But even this defensive policy proved incapable of bringing peace. The English governors were rapidly changed and seldom liked. The Irish revenue was insufficient for defence and English assistance rare. Blackmail pensions to Irish chiefs, irregularly paid, tempted them to invade the settled districts, the Hibernization of the Anglo-Irish barons continued, and the English Pale shrank. Earl Edmund Mortimer of March, Earl of Ulster in right of his wife, Philippa of Clarence, took the offensive in 1380 with some success, but he died soon after, and, besides the internecine feuds, O'Brien of Thomond and O'Neill of Tyrone made war on their neighbours. It was at the petition of the Irish Parliament that Richard II, the first king since John to visit Ireland, landed at Waterford in 1394 with a large army. Characteristically, his policy had a statesmanlike side to it, but its execution was superficial, nor could he stay long enough to ensure its real effectiveness. With a little fighting and a great deal of parleying he obtained the submission of some fifty Irish chiefs, and knighted the four greater kings, O'Neill, O'Brien, MacMurrough, and O'Connor Roe, besides Hibernized barons. But the wars broke out again on his departure (1395). His Lieutenant Roger, Earl of March and Ulster, was defeated and slain in 1398, and his second expedition in 1399 was cut short by the news of Henry of Lancaster's invasion of England. With this the attempt to put the Irish question in the foreground of English policy and to insist on internal peace came to an end.

Fig. 196. Coronation ceremonies of the kings of Castile

(7) SPAIN AND PORTUGAL, 1276–1410

Castile and Aragon in the fourteenth century exhibited, like so many contemporary kingdoms, the struggle for supremacy between king and baronage, but in forms characteristically different from one another and from other states. In Castile, baronial turbulence and intense hatred of control combined with the reckless ambitions of the royal kinsmen to produce civil wars and anarchy. In the Aragonese complex, resistance to the kings was organized in the Cortes, and, not without rebellions, aimed at limiting the monarchy. But, although diverse, there was no isolation in these conflicts. Aragon, Castile, Portugal, and the Moors of Granada and Morocco took an active share in one another's broils. France and England intervened. Aragon and later Castile developed a foreign policy, which meant foreign rivals. In detail the entangled story is singularly picturesque, with heroism, atrocities, loyalty, faithlessness, policy, ambition, murder, and treason intermixed pell-mell. But the upshot of so many dramatic events was indecisive. After them, the kingdoms retained their boundaries, the kingships and the baronage held their own, but a solution was not yet in sight.

The triple state of Aragon, with its vassal, the kingdom of Majorca, came first into the main current of European events and thereby into constitutional change. The maritime power of Catalonia gave it Mediterranean ambitions of far-reaching portent. Peter III the Great (1276–85), had married Constance, daughter of Manfred of Sicily, thus showing the bent of his policy. He began his reign by throwing off the papal suzerainty

24. Castile and Aragon in the Later Middle Ages

(a) The House of Castile, 1252–1504

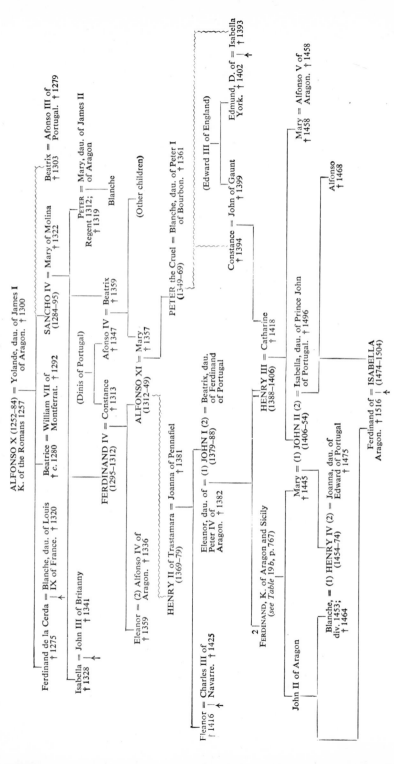

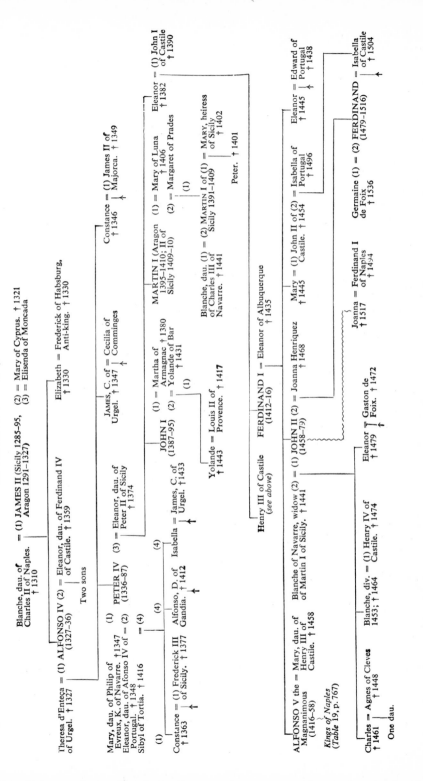

(b) The House of Aragon, 1285–1516

contracted by Peter II, and by establishing in a naval expedition a kind of protectorate over the weak Moslem kingdom of Tunis. Then he prepared to assert his claim to Sicily against its conqueror, Charles of Anjou. His wily diplomacy, his fictitious crusade to Barbary, the Sicilian Vespers, his conquest of island Sicily, the vicissitudes of the War of the Vespers, his naval victories, his deposition by the Pope, and the failure of the French invasion of Aragon, have already been briefly told. But there was a price to pay at home. In 1282 the League or 'Union' of the great nobles and towns of Aragon proper, less interested in the war, extorted from him the *Privilegio General*, recognizing their rights and privileges in a kind of aristocratic oligarchy. Next year, in Catalonia, he agreed to summon the Cortes, which henceforth included the town representatives, every year, and it was declared that their assent was necessary to legislation. His son Alfonso III (1285–91), although he conquered Majorca from his rebellious uncle James II, was obliged to go further. To the League in revolt in Aragon he granted in 1288 the still more irksome *Privilegio de la Unión*, which, among other clauses, gave the Cortes power to depose a king who transgressed their privileges.

Alfonso III drew his realm out of the War of the Vespers by abandoning his brother James of Sicily in the treaties of Canfranc (1288) and Tarascon (1291) as well as by renewing the papal tribute. James, on succeeding him as James II of Aragon (1291–1327), made a final peace with Pope Boniface VIII by much the same policy in the treaty of Anagni (1295), under which he even joined in the attack on his brother, Frederick II, his own successor in Sicily. But after the treaty of Caltabellotta (1302) he was able to follow his own wishes and give Frederick diplomatic support and good advice. He had restored his uncle and namesake to the vassal kingdom of Majorca. By the Pope's grant he took the style of King of Sardinia, but little progress had been made in its conquest before he died. Indeed, although he acquired a small strip of Murcia, and the adventurous Catalan mercenaries were making history in Italy and Greece, very little tangible seemed to result from his watchful and widespread diplomacy. In organizing the administration, however, he left a name, and he dealt skilfully with the three Cortes of his threefold realm, even with the Unión of Aragon proper.

In Castile there was far less constitutional liberty but far more mutinous self will. Sancho IV (1284–95) fought for his crown against his nephew, his brother Don John, and the Moors of Granada and Morocco. At first Aragon was his enemy, but later under James II his ally. At least, he denied the Banu-Marīn an entry into Spain by taking Tarifa on the bay of Gibraltar. The accession of his boy son, Ferdinand IV (1295–1312), made matters worse, for James II and Muhammad II of Granada supported Alfonso de la Cerda, and Dinis of Portugal Don John. Only the political

Fig. 197. Coronation of an Aragonese king

genius of the queen-mother Mary of Molina preserved the young king. She won over towns and nobles with privileges and concessions. She obtained grants from the Cortes and peace from Aragon and Portugal. But Ferdinand IV failed in war against the Moors, and dying early, left the throne to an infant, Alfonso XI (1312–49). This time the regency was fought for with the old anarchy and loss of territory to Granada until the king came of age (1325).

Under Alfonso XI the monarchy revived once more. He brought the nobles to reason, favoured the towns, and reformed the finances. The war with Granada and Morocco was renewed and at last victorious. He was besieging Gibraltar when the Black Death carried him off. He left behind him one legitimate son, Peter the Cruel (1349–69), and five bastards by a favourite mistress, Doña Leonor de Guzmán. This was enough to re-awaken the strife of factions and the old lawless oppression by nobles and prelates, against which the Crown struggled. Peter, cruel in a cruel age, fought ferociously for his authority against treason and revolt, which filled his violent reign. Perhaps it was only his mother and his favourite, the Portuguese Albuquerque, and not he, who had Doña Leonor murdered, but the deed roused a blood-feud with his bastard brothers. Fresh fuel was added to the flames by Peter's marriage to a French princess, Blanche of Bourbon (1353), and his immediate desertion of her for his mistress, Doña Maria de Padilla, while he imprisoned Queen Blanche. Albuquerque, the queen-mother, and the bastards thereupon joined hands in a rebellion, which was quelled. King Peter IV of Aragon, a shrewder parallel of Peter the Cruel, now joined in the turmoil in successive wars, bolstering up the eldest bastard, Don Henry of Trastamara. Peter the Cruel for long had the better, winning battles and executing or murdering his captives, men and women, among them two of his bastard brothers. He killed a defeated and suppliant King of Granada with his own hand. At last, with the aid of Aragon, Trastamara claimed the crown (1363). The King of France and the Pope at Avignon were eager to rid themselves of the Free Companies which infested France, and Bertrand du Guesclin was sent to lead them into Spain. They soon placed Henry of Trastamara on the throne of Castile (1366). As we have seen, the exiled Peter the Cruel gained the intervention of the Black Prince, who reinstated him after his victory at Nájera (1367), but Peter's immediate breach of faith and his slaughter of prisoners soon caused the departure of his protector, and he was left to face his enemies alone. His cruelties had increased their number. Before long he was defeated near Montiel and besieged in the castle. Tempted out by Du Guesclin, he was killed by his brother in a personal struggle in the Frenchman's tent (28 March 1369).

This atrocity ended neither the atrocious civil war, nor the conflict between the nobles and the Crown. Henry II of Trastamara (1369–79), as false and cruel as his brother, had to war down the partisans of Peter the Cruel's daughters by Maria de Padilla, and to meet the onslaughts of all his neighbours: Aragon, his quondam ally, now cheated of his concessions, Navarre, Granada, and Portugal. A Cortes had acknowledged the legitimacy of Peter's daughters on the ground of a precontract with their mother (1363), and in 1372 the elder, Constance, married John of Gaunt, Duke of Lancaster, who thereupon styled himself King of Castile. Henry II secured peace with Aragon by marrying his son and heir John to Peter IV's daughter, and he made a like alliance with Navarre. Portugal was met by a counter-offensive. Under Afonso IV (1325–57) and Peter I (1357–67) that country had enjoyed internal and foreign peace, seldom

Fig. 198. John I of Portugal entertains John of Gaunt, 1387

disturbed, and a good government which brought prosperity, but Ferdinand I (1367–83) now was advancing a claim to the Castilian throne, for which his military strength was unequal. After an invasion by Henry II he was forced to accept his enemy's terms (1373). The year before, the Castilian fleet as the ally of France had won its victory of La Rochelle over the English. Castile shared in the truce of Bruges (1375), and also made peace with Granada. Henry II used this unwonted tranquillity to buy support for his dynasty by lavishing grants of lands and lordships on friends and former foes, a proceeding which earned him the name of the 'Bounteous' (*El de las mercedes*).

John I (1379–88), however, had still to deal with dynastic disputes, partly of his own raising. After a brief, victorious war, which had been provoked by Ferdinand of Portugal, he took for his second wife Ferdinand's only child Beatrix, and on Ferdinand's death in 1383 assumed by treaty the style of King of Portugal. This arrangement, hated by the anti-Castilian Portuguese, was the more unpopular with them owing

Fig. 199. Battle of Aljubarotta, 1385

to the scandalous life of the queen-dowager, his mother-in-law, who actually ruled the land. There was a royal bastard, John, the Master of the Order of Aviz, son of Peter I, for them to turn to. He killed the queen-dowager's lover, and was proclaimed Defender of the Realm. John of Castile responded by a largely successful invasion and conquest. But the patriots held out in Lisbon and Oporto, and crowned the Master of Aviz as their king. Fortunately, he secured the alliance of England, where John of Gaunt was aiming at the crown of Castile, and with the alliance received 200 of the invaluable English archers. On 14 August 1385, by a variation of the tactics of Poitiers, the Portuguese won a crushing victory over a vastly superior Castilian army at Aljubarotta. It was this battle which sealed the independence of Portugal as a nation and its separation from the rest of the peninsula. The war was widened by the invasion of John of Gaunt, who landed in Galicia (1386). But John of Castile now met him with the strategy of refusing battle which had proved so effective in France. In 1387 the three Johns came to terms, a peace for Lancaster and a truce for Portugal. John of Gaunt's elder daughter by Constance—Catherine—was to marry John of Castile's son and heir Henry, thus uniting the rival claims. Gaunt's daughter by Blanche—Philippa—had already married John I of Portugal.

John of Gaunt's son-in-law, Henry III the Invalid (1388–1406), was still a minor when he succeeded to the throne, and under the regency the innate anarchy of Castile was renewed. The nobles fought among themselves, and the populace turned with terrible massacres on the Jews (1391), a catastrophe which wrecked their prosperity and produced a crowd of feigned conversions. Henry III, however, although sickly, possessed great force of character. He put down the nobles, recalled extravagant grants, repelled a Portuguese attack, destroyed the lair of Moroccan pirates, Tetuan, and was preparing to invade Granada when in 1406 he died. Thus the crucial questions of the enforcement of order and the subjection of the over-mighty subjects, as well as the completion of the Reconquest, were left over to a future generation.

The strength of Aragonese institutions by no means preserved the threefold state from internal troubles, but, combined with the capacity of the kings, it gave them a better outcome. Alfonso IV (1327–36) was engaged in a protracted effort to conquer Sardinia, which his son Peter IV the Ceremonious (1336–87) continued with but partial success, although he had Venice on his side against the rival competitor, Genoa. On the other hand, he conquered the kingdom of Majorca from his ill-used cousin James III. It was definitely united to the now fourfold Aragonese state (1354). Peter's nominal dominion was also extended, much to his pride, by the voluntary submission of the Catalan duchy of Athens in the Levant (1381). But more valuable than his foreign wars was his decisive victory over the unruly nobles of Aragon and Valencia. It was a stern struggle, but Peter IV had a hard, statesmanlike instinct, however marred by treachery and savage cruelty. The trouble began when Peter, being then without a son, declared his daughter Constance his heiress. The Unión of Aragon, which spread to Valencia, took sides in favour of his full brother, the Count of Urgel, and forced him in the Cortes of Saragossa to confirm the *Privilegio de la Unión* and to dismiss his councillors from Catalonia, the province on whose loyalty he could rely (1347). Soon after his partisans in Valencia were overcome, and he himself was detained there in humiliating subjection. The Black Death, however, enabled him to escape. Joining the loyalists, he this time overthrew the Unión in the decisive battle of Epila in Aragon (21 July 1348). The conquest of Valencia followed. Peter abolished the *Privilegio de la Unión*, and took ferocious vengeance on his opponents, but he shrewdly did not touch the older charters of liberty. The monarchy remained limited, but not in leading-strings.

Little need be said of the later reign of Peter IV. He intervened in the Castilian civil wars, as we have seen, and secured possession of his grand-daughter Mary, the little Queen of Sicily, though not of her kingdom. The last years of the grim king were embittered by his alienation of his last wife and his children. He died deserted. The reigns of his two sons, John I (1387–95) and Martin (1395–1410) were chiefly notable for the acquisition of island Sicily. Martin's son of the same name married (1391) his cousin Mary, under his father's regency, and succeeded her when she died childless (1402). He, too, died without issue (1409), so that his father became Martin II of Sicily. The personal union of the two crowns was thus established, giving along with Sardinia a valuable foothold to Aragon in the central Mediterranean.

In spite of the turmoil of the fourteenth century the Cortes in Castile did not lose their powers. They were frequently summoned for legislation and financial aid. In the Aragonese states, as we have seen, they limited the monarchy, although the Unión was dissolved by Peter IV. Two special institutions increased their control. One was the *Diputación General*, which was a permanent committee of the Cortes of each province. Between the sessions it watched over the royal administration and expenditure to prevent infringements of the law. The other was the *Justizia mayor* of Aragon, an officer whose powers were enlarged and made tenable for life by Peter IV in 1348. Besides acting as a judge, he had the duty of preventing the violation of chartered rights (the *fueros*) and of protecting an accused litigant until he was legally condemned. The fundamental defect of these constitutional liberties in Aragon as well as in Castile was the separation of classes. Clergy and nobles were subsidy-free, and the bourgeois who gave the grants represented the townsfolk, not the countryside. Thus the formation of a House of Commons, in which knights of the shire and townsmen coalesced, was out of the question. Yet the progress of the towns, although segregated, was great. The craftsmen were strictly organized in their gilds. The towns elected their own judges. In general, but not without strife, oligarchies of the well-to-do monopolized town government. Pre-eminent in power and wealth and also in internal conflict were the great commercial towns of Barcelona and Valencia, eager participants in the Mediterranean sea-trade. For them the kings created the Consulate of the Sea which adjudged mercantile disputes, and applied the now written maritime law.

CHAPTER 30

NORTHERN AND EASTERN EUROPE

(I) SCANDINAVIA, c. 1300–1412

There was visible in Scandinavia the struggle of the feudal nobility either to control the central government, or to secure their local independence, or both together, which was characteristic of the century. Against them was arrayed the kingship, sometimes fettered or submerged, yet indispensable. The three great powers of the period remained the nobles, the king and the Hansa, for the Church was no longer aggressive and it wavered between king and nobles. The strength of the nobles consisted in their predominance over small, none too populous agricultural communities. By intermarriage and common class interests they had become denationalized or at best Scandinavian. Except in Sweden, the old self-conscious literature, with its pride in a national past, was extinct. There was a natural tendency of nobles and kings towards a union of the three crowns, due rather to intertangled relationships and scattered estates than to a sense of Scandinavian unity. The growth of commerce with new sources of revenue only partially favoured the kings, for their creditors, the Hansa League, reaped the main profit.

The murder of Eric V Clipping of Denmark in 1286 and the succession of an infant, Eric VI Menved, began a series of wars, in which the nobles profited in all three kingdoms. Eric VI (1286–1319) fought with persistence against them, but his ambitions to quell his German neighbours, including the Wendish towns, overtaxed his strength. Denmark grew more feudal, and his brother and successor, Christopher II (1320–32), autonomous Duke of Slesvig, an ex-rebel, was obliged to subscribe to an election-capitulation, which placed the kingdom under the control of a parliament of nobles. In the same period King Birger of Sweden (1290–1319) was struggling against his nobles, led by his brilliant brother, Eric, Duke of Södermanland, the most unscrupulous of them all, who possessed lands in Sweden, Norway, and Denmark and had married the only daughter of Haakon V of Norway (1290–1319). True, Eric was at last imprisoned (1317) and died, but the nobles thereupon drove out Birger, and elected Eric's child-son, Magnus II (1319–43), already King of Norway.

Thus the nobles were triumphant. Save in Denmark, they did not possess the feudal jurisdictions of the south, but they formed an organized class with a monopoly of local government, the leading part in central government, and a control of the wealth and fighting force of Scandinavia. King Christopher II of Denmark in vain pledged the royal demesne. He passed

911

Fig. 200. Visby, Gotland, part of the north walls

some years in exile, while the German Count Gerard of Holstein, the leader of the nobles, ruled most of the land. An eight years' interregnum ended with the murder of Gerard, whose grievous burdens became odious, and the election of Christopher's son, Waldemar IV Atterdag (1340–75), a prince of indomitable perseverance—'Tomorrow is a new day', was his favourite saying—and soaring ambition. Bit by bit, assisted by the much vexed Church, he repieced his kingdom and recovered his revenues. He wisely sold Danish Estonia for more useful cash. By 1360 he had quelled noble revolts and attained a compromise, which safeguarded royal as well as noble rights.

Although he did carry through (1347) the introduction of a single code of law for all Sweden, King Magnus II was less fortunate, and his reputation was blackened by the vitriolic denigration of St Bridget, a violent noble partisan. The Black Death came (1349–50) to thin the population of both Sweden and Norway and to increase the power of the surviving nobles, mainly of Swedish extraction. The steady political decline of Norway began thereby. In 1355 one son of Magnus, Haakon VI (1355–80), took over Norway; egged on by a faction and aided by 'the fox of foxes', Duke Albert of Mecklenburg, the husband of his aunt, who already con-

912

trolled the herring-staples of Scania, for the moment a Swedish possession, the elder son, Eric XII, revolted and obtained a share of Sweden. In 1359 King Eric died.

This was the opportunity of Walde-mar Atterdag. He had already married his daughter Margaret to Haakon VI for a consideration. Now he recon-quered Scania for Denmark (1360), and proceeded to seize the island of Gotland and to ruin the great Hansa port of Visby (1361). Thereby he came into collision with Duke Albert, who retaliated by obtaining the deposition of Magnus II and the election to the Swedish throne of his own younger son Albert, a pawn of the nobility (1363).

Waldemar Atterdag had challenged too many rivals. With the support of Norway alone, he was now obliged to wage war against a coalition of all the Baltic powers led by the mighty Hansa League, the masters of Scan-dinavian commerce. As we have already seen, his earlier victories were followed by disasters, which induced the Danish Council to accept the un-equal peace of Stralsund. The Hansa obtained full protection for their com-merce, lower customs, territorial guarantees in Scania, and a dominating voice in the succession to Denmark. In Norway their privileges were restored, while Albert was recognized as King of Sweden.

Fig. 201. Epitaph in honour of the Gotlanders killed in battle by the Danes, 27 July 1361

Waldemar's death in 1375 intro-duced to Baltic and Scandinavian politics the most able woman of their history, his younger daughter Margaret, the Queen of Norway. She was as ambitious, flexible, and resolved as he, and more adroit and statesmanlike in her dealings with men and their conflicting interests. She had now at the age of 22 one son Olaf, for whom she was determined to gain the Danish throne, although her father had promised it to his other grandson,

Albert, son of Henry of Mecklenburg and nephew of Albert of Sweden. She knew that the Wendish towns of the Hansa did not wish to see the Mecklenburgs sole rulers of the Baltic lands. Hastening to Denmark, she won over the nobles for her son, while the Hansa League did not use their veto. The war with the Mecklenburgs was a languid affair. When her husband Haakon VI died (1380), she became virtual ruler of Norway also. She dominated the nobles there and in Denmark, although she was obliged to buy off the Counts of Holstein by granting them the duchy of Slesvig (1385). She was already coveting Sweden when in 1387 her son King Olaf died.

Characteristically, Margaret took control of the situation. Neither she nor her peoples would submit to the next heirs, the uncle and nephew, King Albert of Sweden and Duke Albert of Mecklenburg. Against all law and precedent, she was acknowledged as 'regent' both in Denmark and Norway. At that very time King Albert had fallen out with many Swedish nobles, with kindred in her realms. She went to war and captured him in her victory of Falköping (24 February 1389). Thus she became ruler of Sweden. There was an infant heir in whose name she could rule, her great-nephew, Eric of Pomerania, who was duly proclaimed king of all three kingdoms. She now worked for a durable union. In 1397, when Eric came of age, she held an assembly of Scandinavian lords at Calmar, where he was crowned. An act of union was drawn up, which prescribed a common law of succession and mutual alliance, but left each state to its own laws. Unfortunately the Norwegian prelates held aloof from the whole proceedings, and the union never became ratified. The coronation made no difference to Margaret's power, for King Eric was her docile pupil. Their aim was to make a permanent unity of Scandinavia. They filled the bishoprics with their friends, and intruded Danes into fiefs in Sweden and Norway. In fact, they unified the administration in Denmark, the richest and most populous of the three lands, while the other two were subordinate; but they also made use of German immigrants in their service. Margaret imitated her father in resuming royal demesne, and as far as possible appointed royal bailiffs for local administration, a system which resulted in more and oppressive burdens for the peasantry. Before she died in 1412 she even recovered the duchy of Slesvig during the minority of its heir. Yet all this imposing success, due to her personality, covered radical flaws. The Swedes, and to a less extent the Norwegians, grudged their subservience, and the nobles in Denmark also were unchanged at heart. The union was to break on the several grievances of nations, nobles, clergy, and peasants.

(2) BOHEMIA, 1306–1378

The fourteenth century was the period of the partial westernization and feudalization of the central East European kingdoms, and in this movement Bohemia, already feudalized and made bilingual by the German immigration and the policy of the Přemyslid kings, led the way. The death of Wenceslas III in 1306 without male heirs opened up a new problem of succession, in which the right of the Estates to elect, that of the suzerain, the King of the Romans, to appoint, and that of the relatives in the female line to inherit, were all involved. The suzerain, King Albert I of Habsburg, won the first round by obtaining the election of his son Rudolf, but when the young king died next year, the nearest relative, Duke Henry of

Fig. 202. The Emperor Charles IV and his son Wenceslas

Carinthia, husband of Wenceslas III's eldest sister, was chosen and maintained himself. His reign (1307–10), however, proved a time of disorder; the Bohemians deposed him and offered their crown, together with the hand of Elizabeth, Wenceslas's younger sister, to John, the son of the Emperor Henry VII of Luxemburg.

John's accession provided Bohemia with a new dynasty. He, too, was not a success in governing his kingdom. He quarrelled with Queen Elizabeth and alienated the Czech nobles, at first by favouring Germans. In 1318 he came to an agreement with his subjects to dismiss his German mercenaries and officials and to employ only the native born. Thenceforward he chiefly lived out of the country, following his singular career

25. Bohemia in the Later Middle Ages

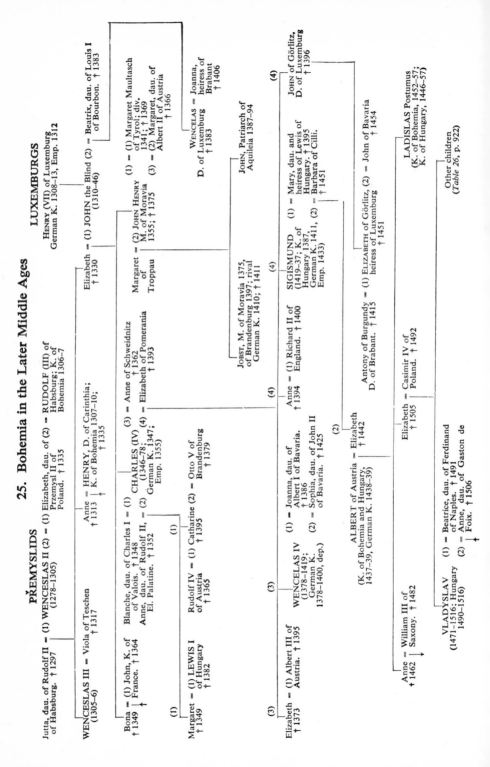

of adventurous king-errant and leaving the government to a few noble families, headed by his marshal, Henry of Lipa. He was an expensive king, but popular for the fame he brought and the accretion of territory won by his prowess and diplomacy. To the Bohemian crown he added Eger (Cheb), Upper Lusatia, and nearly all Silesia, which the Polish king at last admitted to be his (1335). Even his chivalrous death at Crécy (1346), when he had become blind, threw a glamour over him and his dynasty.

As in France, to the chivalrous king succeeded the statesman. John had brought up his son, Wenceslas, whom he renamed Charles, at Paris, and the French environment had a permanent effect on the boy without diminishing his predilection for Bohemia, the land of his birth. He was given an early experience of great affairs, by acting first as his father's lieutenant in Lombardy (1331) and then in Bohemia itself with the title of Margrave of Moravia (1333). He spent an interlude of two years (1336-8) in maintaining his youngest brother, John Henry, as Count of Tyrol. As travelled as his father, and a remarkable linguist, he knitted a close relationship with the Papacy at Avignon. The first fruits of this intimacy were the elevation of Prague to be an archbishopric with the Bohemian lands for its province (1344). Thus the old dependence on German Mainz was abolished and Bohemia made a self-contained ecclesiastical unit. His election as King of the Romans (1346) in his father's lifetime and his subsequent coronation as Emperor have been already told, and added little to his fame in spite of his importance in that role.

It was as 'Father of Bohemia,' of which he was the real ruler long before his official reign (1346-78), that Charles displayed his remarkable and varied talents and his high ideals as a ruler. Full of intellectual interests, he was also eminently practical; in both respects, as in his wiliness, he resembled his namesake of France. He took care both as Emperor and king (being his own suzerain) to formulate the unity and autonomy of the Bohemian state, and to regulate the succession of his dynasty. To him was due the treaty of 1346 with the Duke of Austria, by which, if either Habsburgs or the Luxemburgs became extinct, the surviving house should inherit the vacant territories. This gamble on the future ended in the Habsburgs acquiring Bohemia and shows that, like Otakar II, Charles conceived the formation of the later Austrian dominion. He had already annexed Lower Lusatia and the remaining fragments of Silesia to the Bohemian Crown, and by too ingenious manœuvres he acquired the electoral Mark of Brandenburg for his family. The election of his eldest son, Wenceslas IV, co-regent of Bohemia, as King of the Romans in 1376 completed the aggrandizement of the Luxemburgs, seated in their hereditary kingdom.

To improve the government, to nurture the material prosperity, and to raise the civilization of that kingdom was the purpose and the best

Fig. 203. Karlštejn Castle

achievement of Charles. He found it a prey to brigandage and oppression. He crushed violence and gave it a peace hitherto unknown. In the diet of 1356 a new law enabled the peasants to prosecute their lords in the royal courts. He would attend the sessions to see justice done. Had the diet agreed, he would have promulgated his new, revised code, the *Maiestas Carolina*, to reform the laws, but its emphasis on the Civil Law's doctrine of monarchical supremacy prevented its acceptance. In economic development he introduced vineyards, and encouraged the trading impulse among the Czechs. Whereas towns had previously been founded for Germans alone, and Czech immigrants had only later filtered in, Charles made his New Town of Prague open to all, and it was overwhelmingly Czech.

Nothing was more characteristic of the king than his foundation in 1348 of the University of Prague, to which he gave all the privileges of Paris and Bologna. It was the first university to be established east of the Rhine and north of the Alps, and in a few years was imitated in Germany and Poland. In his days it was, like its prototypes, international, and the majority of its students were Germans. Law and the other three faculties proved incompatible, so that in 1372 the lawyers seceded as a separate university, but henceforth Prague was an intellectual centre for Bohemia and for all central Europe, a breeding-place of ideas. Charles was a builder and patron of art, bringing in the French style and foreign artists. He founded the new

918

cathedral of St Vitus, the new royal palace, the royal castle of Karlštejn, along with other buildings, bringing in a golden age of art of all kinds, which acquired a national imprint.

Incidentally, but in true fourteenth-century fashion, Charles's large expenditure as king and Emperor led to constitutional advance. He needed

Fig. 204. The Emperor Charles IV in his private chapel at Karlštejn

frequent grants from his subjects. Besides separate diets of the provinces he called general diets of the Bohemian lands, whose consent was necessary for the validity of his decrees, and who displayed considerable independence. The Estates acquired a constantly increasing influence on affairs, and with the king represented the community of the realm. In short, the monarchy became limited, like England and Aragon. It was the general trend of the century.

This development was unavoidable, but the advance of the Bohemian Church was Charles's own policy. He completed the array of Church privileges in harmony with his congenial archbishop, the Czech noble, Ernest of Pardubice. The wealth of the Bohemian Church was enormous—one half of the land—and their opulence was not beneficial to the conduct and repute of the over-numerous monks and clergy. Pluralities and unfit appointments by papal provisions abounded. Charles and his archbishop made endeavours at reform—the most effective was a law of mortmain. Far more important than their authoritarian measures were the lives of two popular preachers who stirred men's minds, the Austrian Conrad Waldhauser (*ob.* 1369), who preached to the Germans, and Ján Milič (*ob.* 1374) of Kremsier in Moravia, who preached both to Czech and German. They re-awoke religious fervour in a land where furtive, fantastic heresy had for years been its chief expression. Both of them, too, fell foul of the friars, monks, and clergy, were denounced, and had to defend themselves at Avignon. Milič was a victim as well to his own apocalyptic views, which impelled him to point to the sober, crafty, yet well-meaning king as Anti-Christ. But they had begun a fervid religious movement, which was allied to the nationalism of the popular Czech audience to which Milič preached in its native tongue.

Charles, in fact, by his tastes and actions had fostered a Czech nationalism, with which he was in sympathy, but of which he did not foresee the outcome. The Czech nation, proud of its past, advancing in civilization in town and country, was finding its natural leaders in these churchmen and in the University of Prague, where and elsewhere they began to stand in opposition to the German element, once predominant. This evolution the cosmopolitan Emperor, at home in five languages, had not anticipated. Enthusiasm was strange to his nature.

(3) HUNGARY, 1301–1382

The death in 1301 of the last Arpád, Andrew III, left the Hungarian monarchy in a state of collapse. The greater part of the land was in the hands of certain overmighty magnates, who ruled whole provinces. In the moot question of the succession to the throne, their leagues favoured different candidates descended in the female line from the extinct dynasty. The next-of-kin was Charles Robert (Carobert) of Anjou, the son of the dead pretender, Charles Martel. He held Croatia, and was nominated by Pope Boniface VIII, but this very papal investiture set the majority against him, for it infringed Hungary's independence. Yet neither his widely supported rival, Wenceslas of Bohemia, nor his successor, Otto of Bavaria,[1] were able to hold the field, largely owing to the skilful diplomacy of the

[1] For the claims of these princes, see Genealogical Table 26 below, p. 922.

papal legates, who tacitly accepted the right of the diet to elect. In 1308 Charles I was chosen by acclamation.

He was the ablest of his house and began a new era. He did not try to revive the defunct patriarchal kingship, but in fifteen years of struggle he broke the power of the provincial dynasts, and then proceeded to create a new organization. The ancient clans had dissolved. Now there was a new aristocracy of prelates, magnates, and the wide class of lesser nobles, all feudalized. Next came the bourgeoisie, largely of foreign origin, and the remnant of free peasants, and last the multitude of serfs of various race and speech, the *jobbagy*, who comprised the rightless peasantry in general.

A new army was formed, consisting of the troops (*banderia*) of the king, prelates, magnates, and lesser nobles (the last serving in county battalions), while the king's authority was also maintained by the garrisons of his many castles and their castellans.

Charles also created a sound financial basis for the kingship. He reorganized the royal estates, encouraging immigration, so that he became the wealthiest landowner of Hungary. Still more did he encourage the townsmen, giving new privileges and founding new towns. They were a tax-paying population, and their economic prosperity was of great importance. Charles abolished the stifling internal custom-dues, and built up the frontier customs, while he fostered foreign trade by commercial treaties with his neighbours. At the same time, he restored the credit of the coinage and even minted an Hungarian gold florin of constant value. The precious metals—Hungary had gold mines—he made a royal monopoly. By levying a house-tax and taking a third of the Church tithes, he rendered the monarchy independent of the diet, which he ceased to summon save for form after 1324. For local administration he developed the county court of nobles. Thus in Hungary the fighting nobles and the tax-paying bourgeois were balanced against one another to the profit of the monarchy.

Charles I's foreign policy, when his hands were freed, was a system of alliances with Poland and the Papacy, linking up with the family friendships of the branches of the French house of Capet, France and Naples, and of the Luxemburgs. His adversaries were Venice, his rival for Dalmatia, and Stephen Dushan, king of Serbia, who coveted Yugoslav Croatia. The aims, however, of his son, Lewis I the Great (1342–82), were for a time deflected by a fierce family vendetta. His brother Andrew, king-consort of Naples, was murdered in a court intrigue, in which Queen Joanna of Naples was involved. Denouncing her as a murderess, Lewis, who had claims to Naples himself, invaded the kingdom and held it for three years (1347–50). This meant a breach with the Papacy, which upheld Joanna, and with France and the Luxemburgs as well. Although Lewis withdrew, the old family friendships were not restored. Henceforth his interests

26. Hungary and Poland in the Later Middle Ages

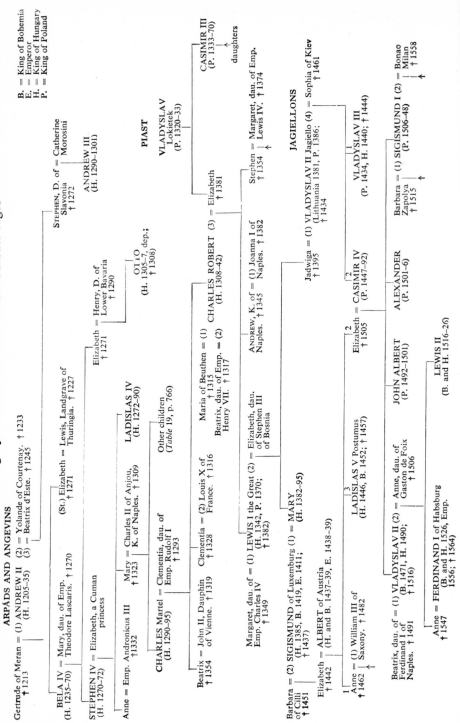

were eastern, and his commanding ability gained him pronounced success. In 1358 he wrested Dalmatia from Venice, a conquest confirmed by the treaty of Turin which closed the War of Chioggia (1381). The death of Stephen Dushan (1355) opened the way to hegemony in the Balkans.

Lewis annexed Belgrade and north Bulgaria; he became the suzerain of Bosnia and Wallachia. Nor was this all. After the death of his uncle, King Casimir III, Lewis was elected King of Poland (1370). The union of the two crowns was personal and temporary, but it enhanced Lewis's power as the head of an east-central European system of states. It was a fragile edifice, however, as the future was to prove.

The splendid and active Lewis was a monarch of the chivalric type, so much admired and dreaded that no insurrection occurred in his reign. In a land where rude club-law had been long predominant he introduced the manners and ideals of French chivalry

Fig. 205. Tsar Stephen Dushan of Serbia

in all their artificiality. Like the Emperor Charles IV he was a patron of art and building: the church architecture of Hungary became a version of French Gothic. In a similar emulation he founded the short-lived University of Pécs. In short, Hungary was being, at least superficially, westernized as a land of Latin civilization. His legislation showed his love of order and precise system. His Act of 1351 confirmed the Golden Bull of 1222 and fixed the rights of the nobility for centuries. The same law defined the heavy obligations of the now fully formed class of peasant-serfs.

(4) POLAND, LITHUANIA, AND THE TEUTONIC KNIGHTS, 1306–84

The resurrection of the dismembered kingdom of Poland was the work of Vladyslav the Short, a prince of that branch of the descendants of Piast who ruled in Kujavia, the province on the lower Vistula abutting on Kulm (Chelmno). On inheriting the lands of his elder brother in 1288 he laid claim to the dignity of Grand Prince, and on the extinction of the Bohemian Přemyslids in 1306 his claim was acknowledged in Lesser Poland on the upper Vistula and in Pomerellen. His chief opponents were the Germanized Piast princes of Silesia and the powerful German communities in Greater and Lesser Poland. In 1310–11 he crushed their revolts in Lesser and

Greater Poland (round Poznan), which he had just annexed. Most un-wisely he asked the aid of the Teutonic Order to subdue the rebellious prince of Pomerellen, with the result that the Order to his indignation took the seaboard province for itself. He had also to face the enmity of the Margraves of Brandenburg and the Luxemburg King John of Bohemia. To gain allies he married his daughter to the Angevin Charles I (Carobert) of Hungary and his son Casimir to the daughter of Gedymin, who was making Lithuania a formidable power. In 1320 Vladyslav I was strong enough to be crowned King of Poland at Cracow. His lengthy lawsuit at Avignon, however, against the faithless Teutonic Order over Pomerellen ended in a merely Pyrrhic victory, and his war with the Order brought more loss than gain. Even so, the indomitable king had renewed the Polish state and had called out a long-lacking Polish patriotism.

His only son, King Casimir III the Great (1333–70), was a statesman of wide outlook, prepared to sacrifice ideals to expediency. He abandoned the hopeless war with the Teutonic Order, and, finding papal support unavailing, consented by the treaty of Kalisz in 1343 to cede his claim to Pomerellen and Chelmno. Similarly, by the second treaty of Vyšehrad in 1339 with John of Bohemia he admitted the loss of Silesia in return for John's renunciation of his claim to the Polish crown and acceptance of the eventual succession to it of Casimir's nephew, Lewis of Hungary. His subsequent treaty of Buda with Lewis (1355) safeguarded the independence and liberties of Poland with the injunction added that Pomerellen should be recovered. On the other hand Casimir enforced the vassalage of his kindred princes of Mazovia, inherited Kujavia, and began the expansion of Poland to the south-east, as will be seen.

It was during this period that the most ferocious war of the Middle Ages was being waged between the aggressive Teutonic Order and the still heathen Lithuanians, a war which displayed the Order at the height of its fame and raised Lithuania into a great power. The Order was still colonizing Prussia with German immigrants, building town after town in the desolation— 'the Wilderness'—it had made, assimilating its Prussian serfs, and being frequently reinforced by crusaders, men who could bring substantial aid like John of Bohemia, Lewis of Hungary, Henry of Derby (later Henry IV), and other princes, delighted to prove their fashionable chivalry in smiting the infidel. Merciless guerrilla warfare and merciless systematic destruction and massacre, the uttermost cruelty, were the order of the day on both sides. Captured Teutonic Knights were burnt in their armour by the Lithuanians; extermination was the strategy of the Order. The vital aim of the Order was the conquest of Samogitia with the key-point of Kaunas, but it took a hundred years to achieve (1382). Nevertheless, this time of hideous strife marked the Order's apogee. In spite of an Estonian revolt (1343) and the Black Death it advanced, and the rule of the Grand Master,

Winrich von Kniprode (1352–82), ended in victory. The Order dominated the Baltic coastland from Estonia to Pomerellen.

But the other combatant, Lithuania, prospered also, not only in preserving its freedom but in expanding to south and east. The perpetual warfare turned the Lithuanians into a warrior nation. Secure in their forests and marshes from the Tartar inroads, they became the protectors of the White Russian princelings to the east. The founder of this greatness and of a dynasty was Gedymin (1315–41). By conquest and protection he became the suzerain of White and Little Russia as far as Vitebsk and Kiev. Over Red Russia to the south he came into collision with Poland. The native princes were extinguished in 1324 in battle with the Golden Horde. Their elected successor, Boleslav of Mazovia, proved a tyrant, and when he was murdered in 1340, one of Gedymin's sons, Lubart, who had married a princess of the ancient dynasty, occupied Volhynia, while Casimir III seized on Galicia. Lewis of Hungary, being Casimir's heir, postponed an old Hungarian claim, but war between Lithuania and Poland at once broke out. Meanwhile civil war in Lithuania ended with the accession of Olgierd, a son of Gedymin, as Great Prince (1345–77). In 1352 a peace divided Red Russia; Volhynia went to Lithuania, Galicia to Poland. Although it was rather a truce, it allowed the rivals to attack in concert the declining Golden Horde. Olgierd had best fortune, for he conquered the Black Sea coast nearly to the Crimea. He was in fact the head of a confederate Russo-Lithuanian state, the heir of ancient Kiev. The mobility of the armies of his brother Keystut of Troki (*ob.* 1382) and himself was remarkable. They moved rapidly from south to north and from east to west. Oddly enough, the ruling dynasty and people of this mainly Greek Orthodox state were still heathen.

Casimir III began the expansion of Poland to the south-east in his conquest of Ruthenian Galicia. He made room for Polish emigration, but it was among an Orthodox and alien people. It did not mean that he ceased to covet Polish Pomerellen and a coastline on the Baltic. This desire he bequeathed to his successors. In Poland itself, meanwhile, he was faced with the hard task of producing unity in a land divided into particularistic tribal provinces, of which Mazovia was under its own line of Piast princes, while Galicia was hardly Polish at all. Furthermore, there were the scattered alien populations, the German settlers and the Jews, who were increased by fugitives after the terrible massacres of them in 1348–9 in Germany. The real link of the kingdom was the person of the king with his seat in Lesser Poland at Cracow, where the provincial officials became a central administration. The large provinces had fortunately broken up owing to subdivisions in their extinct princely lines. Following the example of Wenceslas II of Bohemia, when he was king, and of his own father, Casimir III appointed a *Starosta*, like the French *bailli*, in each subdivision

925

to be his deputy and administer the government and royal estates. The older voivodes (*Wojewoda*) and castellans became the chiefs of the provincial nobility. To keep in touch with the nobles the custom grew up of calling frequent provincial assemblies (*Wiec*), eight or more in number, for consultation. These became the source of Polish parliamentary institutions.

Of more immediate importance was the reform of the law. The varying customary laws of the provinces, overlaid by sporadic edicts, were chaotic and inconsistent. Casimir III, assisted by councillors, promulgated a systematic code for all Poland based on the laws of Lesser Poland and imitative of the Canon Law (1347). A separate statute was issued for Greater Poland. The reign was one of internal prosperity. Casimir was known as 'the peasants' king' and the protector of townsmen and Jews. Of all classes, the knights or plain gentry profited most. Under numerous charters they became conscious of their rights. They assumed coats of arms on the Western model, but they denoted their clan, not their family. The peasants, too, benefited: they absorbed the foreign colonists, they could migrate at will and they had the right of appeal to the royal courts. The townsmen gained from the trade-routes from the Black Sea. The fact that so many of them were Germans, Jews, and even Armenians created a serious political problem, but Casimir protected their autonomy and was tolerant in religion, while he snapped the connexion with Germany by establishing a municipal court of appeal at Cracow to judge by 'Magdeburg law' and forbidding resort to German towns in their litigation. In Galicia, he fostered the Orthodox and Armenian bishoprics, although he also set up a Catholic hierarchy. But throughout he imitated the West, like his Angevin kinsmen, in chivalry, building, and learning. In 1364 he founded a Polish university at Cracow.

His desire to draw Poland from the petty, tribal politics of the past made Casimir III exclude his distant kindred of the Piast dynasty, and declare his successor to be his sister's son, King Lewis the Great of Hungary, an Angevin whose ideals agreed with his own. The misfortune of his choice lay in the facts that King Lewis's (1370–82) interests were Hungarian, that he had to buy the Polish nobles, and that he had only two daughters to succeed him. He schemed a plan of succession, giving a different combination. His elder daughter, Mary, was to marry the Luxemburg, Margrave Sigismund of Brandenburg, and inherit Poland; his younger, Hedwig (Jadwiga), was to marry Duke William of Austria and inherit Hungary. In the meantime he annexed Galicia to Hungary. He obtained the consent of the Poles in 1374 by the far-reaching concessions of the Pact of Koszice. (1) A daughter to be chosen should succeed in Poland; (2) the lands of the Polish crown should not be diminished; (3) the whole class of the nobles, by now named the *Szlachta*, were to be tax-free; and (4) officials should be natives of their province. Thus the Szlachta were recognized as a privileged class, and the resources of the Crown were impaired. The precedent, too, paved the way to an elective monarchy.

Lewis's absentee reign was disturbed enough. Two Piast princes claimed the throne, Lithuania fought for Galicia, and the Poles hated the Hungarians. When he died, there was war between Sigismund and the Prince of Mazovia. Lewis's widow selected her still unmarried daughter Jadwiga to succeed in Poland, but she came to be crowned only in 1384. The influence of the Polish magnates then induced her to agree to marry Jagiello (Yagaylo), the Grand Prince of Lithuania, who was to become a Christian and unite the two states. Common hatred of the Teutonic Knights was the motive of this brilliant stroke of diplomacy.

The general trend of the history of these lands of East Central Europe in the fourteenth century was that of their fuller reception into the common Latin civilization of the West. Bohemia was much the most affected. Its institutions and its culture became Westernized. Its most original feature was the religious revival which had such portentous consequences in the days of the Great Schism, and even that drew much of its doctrines from the teachings of English Wyclif and combined them with an ardent form of the nationalism which was coming clearly to the surface in Latin Europe. Poland and Hungary, so far as culture went, were copying Western models. While their kingships and nobilities, however, were reconstructed on the lines of the feudal monarchies, their native political tendencies were shown in the formation of the class of nobles, irrespective of wealth and jurisdiction, who in their assemblies showed themselves to be the basis of political power.

(5) THE BALKAN PENINSULA AND THE OTTOMAN TURKS, 1282–1389

During the long and disastrous reign (1282–1328) of Michael VIII's son, Andronicus II, the eventual fate of the Byzantine Empire was sealed. After the Sicilian Vespers and the death of Charles of Anjou he was safe from attack from the West. There was a violent reaction against the sham Union of the Churches, and its adherents were persecuted. The monks took control of the Eastern Church, preferring the Empire's ruin to reunion with Rome. The invertebrate Emperor allowed the state fabric of his father to go to pieces.

A new and at first inconsiderable foe had arisen on the Asiatic frontier. After the collapse of the Seljūks of Rūm, a stream of wandering Turkish tribes, set in motion by the Mongol invasions, had been pouring into Persia and Asia Minor. Among these nomads was a clan, by no means large, under a chief named Ertoghrul (*ob.* 1281), who established it on the borders

Map 24 a

of Bithynia round Dorylaeum (Eskishehir) and enlarged it by incorporating other similar Turkish bands. Other chiefs to the south were already curtailing the Empire, and reaching the Aegean Sea. Andronicus and his co-regent son, Michael IX (1295–1320), were unable to fend them off with mercenary forces of 'Alans' (possibly Tartars or Vlachs) from beyond the Danube. The Turks took to the sea and piracy as well and seized on the nearer islands, while Osman, the famous son of Ertoghrul, won a victory near Nicaea (1301). This conqueror, from whom his Turkish subjects took their historic name of Osmanlis or Ottomans, pursued throughout his reign a similar aim to that of his fellow emirs, i.e. to expand

Map 24b

northward and westward to the coast, in his case the Sea of Marmora
(the Propontis) and the Black Sea. The methods of these fighting nomads
were also much the same and hard to counter: to overrun the open country
and starve the fortified towns into submission. They were falling one by
one.

A new resource was opened to the hard-pressed Emperors by the end
of the War of the Sicilian Vespers in August 1302. A host of mercenaries,

Fig. 206. Church of Staro Nagoričino

mainly Catalans, were left out of employ. Under a well-known leader, a German, Roger de Flor, they were hired (1303) for the Turkish war. The Catalan Grand Company, as they were called, duly defeated Osman, but their ravages, partly due to the imperial treasury being unable to pay them, were worse than the raids of the Turks. They then crossed back to Europe to wreak havoc on Thrace and Macedonia, and called in as allies (1308) a band of mercenary Turks (Turcopuli), who had entered the Byzantine service, in their attack on their moneyless ex-employer. This was the first time that the Anatolian Turks entered Europe. In 1306 Roger de Flor had been murdered, but the internal quarrels of the Company did not diminish their devastation of the helpless Empire, although in 1309 the main body transferred themselves to Thessaly, after inflicting irremediable harm on the decaying state.

To complete the confusion came civil war. When Michael IX died, Andronicus II was compelled to recognize his son, Andronicus III (1321–41), as co-regent.[1] The new Emperor endeavoured to wrest the crown from his feeble grandfather. What with internal strife, Serbian and Bulgarian wars, and a Tartar invasion, the Empire was paralysed till Andronicus II was at last deposed from power in 1328. Meantime in Asia Minor the

---

[1] See Genealogical Table 18*b* above, p. 733.

losses continued. The only effective counter-move was not Byzantine; it was the occupation of Rhodes in 1309 by the Knights Hospitallers, who repelled attacks and warred against Turkish piracy thenceforward. In 1308 Ephesus had been lost to the Empire; in 1326, after years of resistance, the key town of Brusa (Prusa) surrendered to Osman's forces under his son Orkhan. It was the crowning victory of the old warrior, who had made a growing nation, and endangered the scattered remnants left to the Byzantines. Although Andronicus III fought valiantly and found allies in other Turkish emirs, he continued to lose ground, Nicaea (Iznik) in 1329, Nicomedia (Izmid) in 1337. Orkhan (1326–59), who styled himself Sultan, was an organizer as well as a conqueror. He was tolerant to the subject Christian *rayahs*, and they were safer and more lightly taxed by him than by their Emperors. So loyal did they become that he was able to recruit a Christian regiment of permanent troops, the Janissaries (*Yeni-cheri*, 'new troops'). With the help of his brother Ala-et-tin he traced the outline of a new organization of the army, the Timariots who held land for military service, the Sipahis who were enlisted and paid for a campaign, and the irregulars, light horse and foot, who depended on plunder.

The Catalan Grand Company was meantime causing a revolution among the Frankish states of Greece proper. While they were in Thessaly, they entered the service of Walter of Brienne, who had succeeded the Villehardouins in the duchy of Athens. They soon fell out with their new employer, and by sheer generalship and fighting quality annihilated him and the Frankish baronage in the battle of the Cephisus (1311). To marry the widows and take possession of the duchy was their next and final move. They accepted absentee dukes from the Aragonese Kings of Sicily, but the principality of Achaia, tossed about among nominees of the Angevin Kings of Naples, escaped them, as did the Byzantine province of Mistra, by a curious chance the happiest fragment of the Eastern Empire.

More important history was being made in the north. The main foreign objective of Stephen Urosh II (1281–1321) of Serbia was the conquest of territory from the Byzantine Empire. The best defence that Andronicus II could find was to marry a daughter to the barbaric, if very orthodox, king. The device was productive of tortuous intrigues for the succession to both thrones, and Urosh II played fast and loose with both Roman and orthodox Churches and all his neighbours. On his death his bastard Stephen Urosh III (1321–31) took the crown, and proceeded to vie with his neighbour and erstwhile brother-in-law, Tsar Michael, founder of a new dynasty in declining Bulgaria, in drawing profit from the civil war between the two Andronici of Byzantium. They alternately supported the rival Emperors, and Michael nearly seized Constantinople for himself in the process. Michael and Stephen Urosh III then fought out their quarrel directly. At Velbuzhd (Köstendil) the Serbian won a decisive victory on 28 June 1330, and set up his nephew as client tsar. Serbia became the greatest Balkan power, while Andronicus III, then Michael's ally, grasped the opportunity to reannex some territory.

The characteristic family disunion, in which Urosh III had taken his full share, now proved fatal to him. In September 1331 his unnatural son, Stephen Urosh IV, surnamed Dushan, overthrew him and at least connived at his murder. This sordid tragedy was the beginning of a great reign (1331–55), in which Serbia seemed to become an organized and semi-civilized state and the heir to Byzantium. Dushan not only maintained his suzerainty over Bulgaria, by allying himself with a new Tsar, John Alexander, whom a revolution had set up, but gained the friendship of a new-come power in the Balkans. The Vlach (or Wallachian) remnants of the plain beyond the Danube had in the thirteenth century been reinforced by emigrants from the mountains of Transylvania, who founded the principalities of Wallachia and Moldavia. Wallachia was taking a part now in Bulgarian and Balkan politics. In this unwonted harmony, Bulgaria recovered her lost districts and Dushan conquered western Macedonia from the Byzantines.

Fig. 207. Tsar John Alexander of Bulgaria, his Queen Theodora and their sons John Shishman and John Asên

Incurable discord in the Eastern Empire provided the Serbian king his next chance of expansion. John Cantacuzene had been the commander-in-chief and right-hand man of Andronicus III, but when he was expelled from the regency in the name of the dead Emperor's son, John V Palaeologus (1341–91), by a palace intrigue of the Empress Anna of Savoy, he sought safety in rebellion. Dushan at once overran Macedonia except Salonika, while both parties sued for his alliance. Anna bought Bulgarian support by ceding Philippopolis (Plovdiv), while John VI Cantacuzene (1347–54) bought that of Orkhan by giving a daughter to his harem. Turks were introduced into Europe in the employ of both antagonists. A lull in the strife was brought about by Cantacuzene's capture of Constantinople (1347) and his joint reign with his namesake and son-in-law, but in 1352 the two were at war again. It was Cantacuzene who then (1353) admitted

932

Orkhan's troops again into Europe, and this time their occupation of Gallipoli, the key of the Hellespont or Dardanelles, was permanent.

Dushan's progress meanwhile was continuous. In 1346 he assumed the title of Emperor of the Serbs and raised the Serbian archbishop to be Patriarch of Ipek. His court was an imitation of Byzantium. He conquered Epirus and Thessaly, and with Bulgaria took up the cause of John V. He recaptured Belgrade from Hungary, which had held the fortress for years, attacked the Ban of Bosnia, and toyed, as all these princes did, with the reunion of the Churches as a diplomatic means of gaining papal assistance. At this time Cantacuzene was involved in a war with Genoa, and, losing all popularity, was obliged to take the cowl and abdicate. John V succeeded to the dissevered fragments of the Empire. Dushan determined to bid for the possession of Constantinople himself, but on 20 December 1355 he died on the march, and his hopes died with him. Although a ferocious tyrant, he was no mere soldier, but a statesman and a legislator. He codified the Serbian laws in the *Zakonnik*. He encouraged trade, was the friend of the seaport of Ragusa and of Venice, and worked silver mines. He conciliated the Greek towns he conquered. The weakness of his Empire lay in the heterogeneous races—Yugoslavs, Greeks, Albanians, and Vlachs—and the rival religions—Orthodox Serbs, Orthodox Greeks, Roman Catholics, and Catharan Bogomils. Nor did it contain all Yugoslavs, for Bosnia under its Ban and Catholic Croatia under the King of Hungary lay outside it. Such unity as it possessed was due to its ruler. Dushan could not be a true autocrat. He had to keep the loyalty of the great Serbian nobles, then the dominant class, who ruled their estates and serfs at their pleasure. The lesser nobles, too, were privileged in law. The Orthodox churchmen also were favoured and powerful. Agriculture and pasturing were the main industry of Serbia, but the peasants, whether free or serf, were held in strict subjection, if protected by law. It needed more than one reign and one man to solidify and civilize this still primitive state.

Dushan's son, the Emperor Stephen Urosh V (1355–66), was a mere failure. Thessaly, Epirus, and Albania broke off at once under rebellious governors and native chiefs. Other fragments to north and south became practically independent. Feuds gave the opportunity of a Hungarian invasion, while Bulgaria, also torn by discord, suffered the like as well as Byzantine enmity. In 1366 the great noble, Vukashin, who ruled central Serbia, deposed Urosh V and took the title of king, while his brother Uglyesha governed in Macedonia. All these contending powers were oblivious of the Turkish danger.

Once in possession of Gallipoli, the Ottomans were spreading fast. Although crusading was fashionable and the Western kings rendered lip-service to it, only the Popes of Avignon made serious efforts to promote it, efforts which were always linked with delusive hopes, encouraged insincerely by the hapless Byzantine Emperors, of a new Union of the Churches. In 1344 a naval league, in which Venice and the Hospitallers took a leading part, actually recovered Smyrna for a while, but this was a blow to the local Turkish emir, not to the Ottomans, and the crusade, captained by Humbert II, last native Dauphin of Vienne, which was to supplement it, proved a miserable failure (1346). In 1363 the valiant King of Cyprus, Peter I, again with the aid of the Hospitallers, sacked Satalia in Asia Minor, but this exploit too did not affect the Ottomans. Their Sultan, Murat I (1359–89), Orkhan's second son, was in possession of Adrianople, which he made his European capital, and of most of Thrace, and was attacking Bulgaria and Serbian Macedonia. The Emperor John V, travelling to implore for help, was treacherously imprisoned by the Bulgarian Tsar, John Alexander (1365). In consequence, the brief crusade of Amadeus VI of Savoy ('the Green Count') was mainly spent in his rescue. The count's important reconquest of Gallipoli from the Ottomans, his other achievement, was nullified by its retrocession next year (1367). The decisive event fell on 26 September 1371. Vukashin of Serbia and Uglyesha fought Murat on the River Maritza in full force, and were routed and slain. All Macedonia, save Byzantine Salonika, submitted to the sultan. The Bulgarian Tsar and John V (1373) were compelled to become his vassals. The Ottoman Turks were now firmly cantoned in Europe, which was rapidly becoming the centre of their power.

John V in vain journeyed to Avignon and personally renounced the schism. In Yugoslavia Tvertko of Bosnia (1353–91) outshone the Serbian ruler Lazar I (1371–89). He formed a Balkan league against the Ottoman invader and scored one victory at Toplitsa (1387). But Murat was a single despot, more prompt and resolute than his bundle of enemies. He quickly reduced Bulgaria to submission, and then faced Lazar and his allies in the first battle of Kossovo (15 June 1389). He was killed by a Serb just before the action, but his army utterly defeated the confederates. Lazar, a prisoner, was slain by the new Sultan Beyazit's order. Lazar's son became a Turkish vassal. Tvertko devoted his energies to the conquest of Dalmatia until his death in 1391, which broke the power of Bosnia. The supremacy of the Ottomans was incontestable, largely through the ineradicable divisions of their foes.

The misfortunes and discord of the Palaeologi increased as their territory shrank. In 1373 John V associated his second son, Manuel II, on the throne, thereby offending his elder son, Andronicus. The latter, in concert with Sauji, a discontented son of Murat, revolted against both fathers. The sultan put down the rebellion with relentless cruelty, blinding Sauji, while John V made a like example, but less effectively, of his son. It was not long before (1376) Andronicus IV again revolted and imprisoned

934

his father and brother. An outbreak restored them to the throne, but as a last humiliation they were compelled to aid Murat to capture the sturdy town of Philadelphia, the last loyal Byzantine possession in Asia Minor. Even so Andronicus IV and his son John VII retained the scanty remnant of the Empire outside the walls of Constantinople. The conquest of isolated

Fig. 208. John VI Cantacuzene, as emperor and monk

Salonika (1386) gave the Sultan all the rest save distant Mistra. In this dishonoured state of civil war, vassalage, and imminent danger from his Turkish suzerain, Manuel II, worthy of a better time, succeeded his father (1391).

Murat I, eminent as a general and ruler, who moulded the destiny of the Ottoman Turks and of the Balkans, was the son of a Greek mother, and brought new traits of luxury and cruelty into his singularly gifted house. Perhaps his most characteristic innovation was the imposition, attested for his reign, of the ruthless tax of Christian boys to recruit the Janissaries. The likeliest of the conquered races were taken and brought up as fanatical Moslems, the best of them for war, as the standing army of the Sultan, others in the civil service. By this means the most virile elements of the Christians were absorbed into the Ottomans and used for further conquests. They acquired the discipline and unity their subject kinsmen never achieved. At the same time the flood of Turkish immigration into Thrace and Macedonia was augmented by settlement on the land. Adrianople became the real centre of the Ottoman state.

CHAPTER 31

SOCIAL AND POLITICAL CONCEPTIONS OF THE MIDDLE AGES

(I) CHIVALRY

In many of the preceding sections, the dominance of the chivalric view of life, now almost a formal code, among the ruling classes of society has been suggested, and some account has been incidentally given of its rise and development. As might be expected, its general prevalence as an institution, embodied in the 'Order of Knighthood', made it more and more ceremonial and superficial, nor, since it was, so to say, international, did it escape unceasing variations when it was introduced north and south. An elaborate initiation of the new knight had been devised under Church influence, which was exemplified in the induction of the English Knights of the Bath, first actually described in the fifteenth century, and the ideal of knighthood, typified in similar ceremonies, was already formulated in the thirteenth century in the poem, *L'Ordene de Chevalerie*. The asceticism of St Bernard's admonitions for the Knights Templar was one source of the development. On more ordinary occasions, as on the field of battle, the dubbing of the new knight was sufficiently performed by the accolade or by the girding of the sword-belt.

Unflinching courage, loyalty, courtesy, fair play, uprightness, fidelity to promise, generosity, the protection of the weak and injured, the defence of Holy Church and Christendom, and above all the passion for adventure and devotion to the lady of his choice were the chief qualities which made up a perfect knight 'without fear and without reproach'. They were embodied in but few real personages and perhaps best of all in the fabulous Don Quixote. The workaday reality was on a much lower plane. Yet the ideal produced a genuine effect, however limited, artificial, and superficial it might be. It can be seen in the high sense of honour and the strong 'sporting' instinct of the knights of Froissart's *Chronicles*, along with the narrow class feeling, the showy and formal display, and the hollow good breeding and reckless profusion that tarnished it. All the same, although the reigning fashion was indifferent to those not nobly born and knighted and coexisted with most unchivalrous behaviour, yet it had raised the public standard of the feudal class above the rank lawlessness of its precursors.

The grades by which knightly status was acquired by the page and the squire, with the appropriate training in horsemanship, martial exercises, and courtly behaviour, have already been mentioned. More and more they

Fig. 209. Charles the Bold of Burgundy presiding at the chapter of the Golden Fleece at Valenciennes, 1473

implied some degree of literary education, as well as physical and moral culture; Chaucer's squire and knight are instances of the ideal. Within the egalitarian pale of the Order of Knighthood itself there were distinctions. Some were due to feudal status and the feudal array in arms. The plain knight was a knight bachelor; but the knight commanding permanently other knights, whether his vassals or not, was a banneret, entitled to display his square banner, not a mere pointed pennon, in the field. The fourteenth century, too, saw the creation of secular Military

Orders by great potentates, who thus indulged the passion for show and pomp, and linked celebrated warriors to themselves by special ties. Such were Edward III's Order of the Garter, John of France's Order of the Star, and Amadeus VI of Savoy's Order of the Love Knots (afterwards the Annunziata). In the fifteenth century Philip the Good of Burgundy founded the Golden Fleece and Louis XI of France the Order of St Michael. The members of all these orders were few and select.

The growth of the 'science' of heraldry kept pace with these aristocratic developments. Nobles and knights had a right to a hereditary coat of arms, the device on shield and surcoat, which rendered them recognizable in armour. The experts in these matters were the heralds, who acquired an inviolable status in warfare. They adjudged the right to bear coat-armour in courts of chivalry, not a trivial question, since the arms were involved in disputes of inheritance, as when Edward III quartered the lilies of France.

The typical sport of chivalry from the eleventh century, if not earlier in some form, was the mimic warfare of the tournament. The two main varieties, usually seen on the same occasion, were the joust or single combat with lance and sword, and the *mêlée* when two opposed parties fought. They were frequent and popular in the twelfth century; a skilful knight could support himself on the ransoms of those he vanquished. But the loss of life and limb in these murderous conflicts led the Church to condemn them under pain of excommunication of the participants. The Lateran Council of 1179 denied Christian burial to the slain. The effect, however, of these canons was small enough, although a steady tendency was shown from the thirteenth century towards lessening the danger by the use of blunted weapons. They gradually became more ceremonial and artificial. In the fifteenth century the *mêlée* almost disappeared, and the joust was mostly a test of skill in unhorsing an adversary with all precautions against collisions of the chargers and the like. Even so, sharp weapons might be used and men be killed outright. In Germany it was necessary for the jousters in these noble sports to prove ancestry unblemished by recent mésalliance. In general the tournament by these restrictions became more and more divorced from actual warfare, but in fact in its cruder form it had already lost touch with the advance of military science. To counter the long-bow, indeed, the knight's armour had been much developed. Breast-plates and leg-armour of plate or leather had been added to chain mail, and the fifteenth-century complete suit of plate steel as well as the armoured horse were well in sight, but the result was cumbrous to a degree; the knight thrown to the ground was nearly helpless. Further, the nobles who rushed to their death at Crécy, Agincourt, and Aljubarotta had small conception of contemporary tactics and strategy, and, in spite of their courage and skill in arms, were hopelessly inferior as a military force to the seasoned and able mercenary companies. The professional captains were often knights and nobles, but their conduct was far removed from the ideals of chivalry, which were receding to courts and ceremonies, and not too real there. In fact, in England and France the ordinary squires tended to shirk the costly honour of knighthood with its burdensome public obligations. To do them justice, they might make more approach to the chivalric virtues than the dubbed knight, whose glittering career might be deeply stained. The romance of chivalry had, after all, created a new and higher standard of conduct.

(2) POLITICAL THOUGHT IN ITS CHRISTIAN SETTING

Whatever its sources in antiquity, which were multiplied as time went by, medieval political theorizing drew its first inspiration from the epoch-making work of St Augustine of Hippo, the *De Civitate Dei*. From that masterpiece it took its theological bias, and for good reason. Not for centuries was it really occupied with questions of the best forms of secular government. Those institutions which were in existence were matters of fact and tradition, changing slowly as facts and traditions changed. But St Augustine dealt with the then novel situation brought about by the rise of the Christian Church, and the Church was the most potent factor in medieval Christendom. Pledged to convert the world to a new allegiance, to control every human activity, to define the boundaries of right and wrong, the new society could not allow the final authority of any sovereign power outside itself. That part of the Civitas Dei which was living on earth was a pilgrim society journeying to the life to come; it was set amid the secular society, which gave indeed a kind of peace and an inferior justice, but whose law and institutions, with their merely terrestrial aims, could not possess the absolute justice and righteousness of the Divine City.

The difficulty arose when the Roman Empire was without dissent officially and irrevocably Christian, and when the earthly part of the City of God was already envisaged as the organized Church. What was now the relation of the Church, guided by its hierarchy, to the secular Empire, claiming the same ends under Christian rulers? The first and the most lasting answer was that of Pope Gelasius (*ob.* 496) to the Emperor Anastasius: 'there are two by which this world is ruled in chief, the sacred authority of the pontiffs and the regal power. In which so much heavier is the load of priests as they are to render account for kings themselves in the divine judgement of men.' It was the implications of this superiority of the spiritual, ecclesiastical hierarchy over the secular rulers within the Civitas Dei of Christendom that were to be worked out and contested in the Middle Ages. In the East in the palmy days of the Empire the solution, although attacked at times, may be roughly styled Caesaropapism: the

Emperor was 'equal to the Apostles', the governor of Church and State. In the Latin West, however, where the intellectual tradition was ecclesiastical and centred in the independent Papacy, and was only countered by the actual powers of the secular monarchy and the customs of its feudalized nobles, things went differently. It was not there, any more than in the orthodox East, a question of two separate communities—Church and State—living side by side, but one of the relative powers, functions, and pre-eminence of two sets of authorities, the priestly and the lay, ruling in a kind of partnership the same community, and of what borderline could be drawn between their activities.

The early Carolingian solution showed a distinct resemblance to Byzantine Caesaropapism. Merovingian tradition, fortified by remembrance of the Hebrew monarchy of the Old Testament and the accompanying unction of the king, making him a sacred, semi-ecclesiastical person, placed him in charge of the priesthood and the spiritual welfare of his subjects. This was exemplified by the authority wielded by Charlemagne. Yet, even so, the public lead taken by Pope Leo III in its embodiment in the new Empire of the West, no less than the previous forgery of the 'Donation of Constantine' and the later legend of the 'Translation of the Empire' from the Greeks to the Germans, was a witness to the higher claims of the spiritual hierarchy. The doctrine of ecclesiastical supremacy was emphatically maintained by Pope Nicholas I when he excommunicated King Lothar II of Lotharingia for bigamy, and, like other bishops, admonished the decadent Carolingians in a tone of unquestioned superiority.

Contemporary facts, indeed, the moral and temporal degradation of the Papacy and ecclesiastical hierarchy, and the restoration of order by devout Emperors, prolonged the life of what may be called the royal leadership of the Church in their dominions. A singular instance of the theory is to be seen in the so-called *York Anonymus* (c. 1100). But Church reform and the more than revival of papal authority, as we have seen, produced at the least the most unbalanced form of the Gelasian definition. The lay power might draw its authority from God, but only in subordination to the sacerdotal power embodied in its head, the Pope, the successor of St Peter. Henceforward, from the early twelfth century, the claim of secular monarchs was merely for independence in their own sphere: they were the defenders of the Church, not its masters. According to the reigning allegorical interpretation, the two swords of the Gospel (St Luke XXII, 38) betokened the two powers, spiritual and temporal, to which was allotted the rule of Christendom. The imperialists maintained that the Emperor held the temporal sword immediately from God. But the papalists contended, and their view was voiced by St Bernard in his *De Consideratione*, that both swords were entrusted to the Pope, the spiritual to be wielded by him directly, the temporal by the secular rulers under the guidance of

Fig. 210. The two-sword theory; the Emperor as marshal of the Pope

the priesthood, or at least at its sufferance. The weakness of the imperialists' case was that they admitted the higher function of the spiritual sword. It was a consequence of this superiority that the clergy were amenable in the main only to the jurisdiction of their own Courts Christian, which also dealt with the laity when faith and moral duties were in question.

The relation of the ecclesiastical and secular authorities, however, was but one aspect of the incipient political thought of the twelfth and thirteenth centuries. Their conception of law was also fundamental. For them it was essentially not man-made.

The Divine Law, revealed in Scripture, was binding on all men. The Code of Justinian was permeated by the belief that Justice was an eternal fact and that human law owed its moral validity to a Law of Nature binding on mankind, as rational beings. From this *Ius Naturale*, really a part of Divine Law, all species of human law, whether written or customary, were or should be derived; if human decrees or customs contravened its principles, they had no claim to obedience. Ideally, human positive laws were but expansions, explanations, and adaptations of those principles according to circumstances, local conditions, and the needs of the time. This limitation even applies, according to Gratian, to the Canon Law of the Church. It may err by contravening Natural Law, but the Church has the gift of authoritative interpretation, and the canonists' attitude practically implied that it overrides the less inspired secular legislation.

The belief that in the last resort the law was divinely imposed upon the human race made against any ideal of secular absolutism. Even the professors of the Roman Civil Law held that the law-giving power of the Emperor was due to a transference to him of the authority of the Roman people, who had originally framed their institutions by the light of Natural Law. The unusually cultured John of Salisbury (*ob.* 1180), whose *Policraticus* was long a source of ideas, is led to the distinction between the king, who respects the law and is not to be resisted, and the law-breaking tyrant, whom it is lawful to slay, a dim reflection perhaps of classic tradition mingled with feudal conceptions in real life. But John, the theologian, for long a member of the Roman Curia, also declares with St Bernard that the temporal sword is delegated to the prince by its possessor, the priest, of whose sacred hands its actual exercise is unworthy.

This ecclesiastical doctrine, as well as practical considerations, lay behind the persistent policy of the Popes in obtaining the feudal vassalage of secular rulers. It linked the papal theory to contemporary custom. The kings of Sicily and Jerusalem, the kings of Portugal, Aragon, and England, all at various times became papal vassals. Gregory VII had claimed in 1080 the fealty of the Emperor. Adrian IV, the one English Pope, had sent a ring to Henry II to invest him with Ireland. Even where there was admitted vassalage, however, the Popes were chary of intervening in matters of feudal law, and Innocent III declared that he exercised his possible jurisdiction outside the Papal States only in certain cases (*casualiter*). In any event, as pastor of souls, he could intervene in political actions *ratione peccati*. The most clear-cut definition of the Pope's possession of the two swords was given in Boniface VIII's famous bull *Unam Sanctam*, which stressed the unity of Christendom under its single head. A feudal turn was given to the argument by Aegidius Romanus (*c.* 1301–2) in his *De ecclesiastica potestate*, in which he maintained that secular rulers are vassals of God and can have no just dominion unless they are dutiful and obedient servants of the Church, whose powers are summed up in the Pope, the Vicar of God.

It was in defence of the independence of the temporal sword in the hands of the Holy Roman Emperor, who is rightful lord of Christendom and mankind, that Dante wrote his *De Monarchia*, the best known and most vivid, if not the most realistic, work of political thought in the Middle Ages. In the first book he gathers up all the scholastic arguments for unity and a single head for mankind, if it is to attain the felicity and peace designed for it by God. In the second, by an appeal to history and law, produced in arguments strange to modern eyes, he proves that the Roman Empire was providentially ordained to construct that temporal unity. In the third, while admitting that the spiritual sword and supremacy over that unity belongs to the Pope as guide to salvation, he insists strongly on the temporal headship of the Emperor, who is to maintain the peace and felicity of men in this life. The *Donation of Constantine* was *ultra vires*, and has no legal validity. The difficulty that the ideal of unity, so strongly pressed, is not very consistent with two independent heads of Christendom, is met by pointing out the mingled nature of man (soul and body) and the single headship of Christ, Who has conferred the two swords on his Vicars.

In this debate of the two swords, medieval political thought has barely emerged from a theological outline. But a new and truly political element had already been introduced into it by the acquisition of Moerbeke's Latin translation of Aristotle's *Politics*. The signs of this Aristotelian element are visible in St Thomas Aquinas's share (Bk. I and the early chapters of Bk. II) in the treatise *De Regimine Principum*. He does not examine the claims of the Empire, but discusses the merits and dangers of kingship over the 'perfect community' of city or province compared with the other forms of government set forth by Aristotle. He sums up in favour of a limited monarchy to secure unity, peace and good government. But since salvation is the end of human life, the *sacerdotium* is on a higher plane, and secular rulers and peoples should be subject to the Pope, the Vicar of Christ. Aquinas's continuator, Ptolemy of Lucca, is a genuine Aristotelian of the sacerdotal type. For him, apart from the Fall and Sin, men, being unequal, would need a government. He divided government (*dominium*) into *despoticum* and *politicum*. One or other is the more suitable according to the climate, character, and tradition of a people. The republican polity admired by Aristotle is suitable for cities (as in Italy), but provinces require a king. Rulers must be able to temper the rigidity of the law. Private property is not a consequence of the Fall but of men's natural inequality. He is most radical when he deals with the Empire, which is universal and elective. But the Empire is now really the fifth monarchy, the Church, under the elective Pope. The secular Emperors are merely delegates, selected in whatever manner has seemed expedient to the Popes. Thus we come back to the extreme doctrine of the two swords in the possession of the Papacy. Ptolemy is Aristotelian, we may say, only in the local governments within Christendom. The same exaltation of the Papacy, as we see it in Aegidius Romanus, is expressed with still greater exuberance, under John XXII, by Augustinus Triumphus in his treatise *On the Power of the Pope*. He is vicegerent of God with full powers, entitled to absolute obedience without appeal. Forms of government, whether the Empire or kingdoms, exist by his permission. He is the universal proprietor and legislator.

(3) THE SECULAR REACTION IN FOURTEENTH-CENTURY POLITICAL THOUGHT

When Triumphus wrote, the overstrained papal theory had already been challenged by a stronger foe than the unreal and moribund Empire. In the world of fact, Philip the Fair was repelling the attempts of Boniface VIII to interfere with his secular government, and he was backed by a loyal and already nationalistic kingdom. The contest gave occasion to political treatises, which began to break away from allegoric theology and to suggest dimly the movement towards modern political thought. They represent both the growing anger of the laity at the exorbitant priesthood and the self-assertion of a well-knit secular bureaucracy trained in Roman Law. The most naive and revealing of these works is the fanciful yet oddly realistic *De Recuperatione Terrae Sanctae* (*c.* 1300) of Pierre Dubois. He proposes to secure the peace of Christendom by its domination by the King of France, for which the French are qualified by their national wisdom. The Pope certainly has the legal temporal possession of the West by the Donation of Constantine, but he is too weak to exercise it. Let him transfer it in return for a pension to the king, who can compel submission by arms or treaty. The temporal claims of the Popes have been a source of mischief, wars, and injustice. More matter-of-fact and more influential was John of Paris in his tract on *Royal and Papal Power*. He declines, like Dubois, to accept allegorical interpretations of Scripture as arguments: we must adhere to the literal sense—a position of immense consequence. In actual fact, the temporal possessions of the Church have been due to lay grants like any others, not to a divine scheme. The *Respublica Christiana* embodied in the imperial idea is met by the pregnant assertion, already in use among the jurists, that every king is possessed of full powers, including legislation, in his realm. The growth of a civil polity is the product of human natural instinct implanted by God. The independent functions of Church and State are emphasized.

From these and similar precursors of the theory of the natural secular State it is a wide but not incongruous leap to the elaborate political structure reared by Marsilius of Padua. This restless Paduan physician was already distinguished enough in 1312 to be Rector of the University of Paris, and after obscure wanderings in the Lombard courts was settled again at Paris, where in June 1324 with the aid of his friend, an eminent Aristotelian and Averroist, John of Jandun, he completed his great work, the *Defensor Pacis*. The impending discovery of their authorship in 1326 sent both friends flying to the court of Lewis the Bavarian. Marsilius seems to have inspired the singular proceedings of Lewis IV in Rome. He was never given up to the Inquisition at Avignon by his vacillating patron, and died in 1343, after supplementing his thesis in the *Defensor Minor*.

The *Defensor Pacis* had been influenced both by the recent French controversialists and by the strict Franciscan party, who upheld the absolute poverty of Christ and the Apostles and were being condemned by Pope John XXII, but it went far beyond them. Marsilius was a thorough-going student of Aristotle's *Politics*. His understanding of the city-state was made more realistic by his knowledge of the institutions of the Lombard city-republics of his day, and he built an ideal scheme of the 'perfect' form of government, intended by Nature by gradual growth for human communities, and therefore obligatory on them, if a peaceful and full human life was to be realized. The community is composed of classes of men defined by their function in it, and of these classes the priesthood, whether heathen or Christian, was one. Another, and the most important part, was the *principans* which exercised the executive power. But the source and controller of power was the legislator, i.e. the whole body of the citizens in their general assembly. They alone decreed the laws of the community. The binding power of laws was derived from the legislator, for the salvo that, if they infringed the Divine Law explicitly and literally revealed in Scripture, they were wrong, was no more than an approval of individual passive resistance. The executive, whether one man or a board, is to carry them out and make them observed. Although Marsilius admits that the executive *pars principans* may be hereditary king, yet that must be due to a decree of the legislator at some time or other. In the legislator's assembly, a majority rule, which gave greater weight to the worthier citizens, was to be observed. But his crucial tenet was that the executive was a unity, supreme over all causes and persons in the community, including the priesthood. Religion in short was a function within and controlled by the secular polity.

If he was radical in his conception of the State and of law, Marsilius was still more so in his conception of the Church. He considered and attempted to prove by an elaborate chronological investigation of documents that the whole fabric of papal domination and Canon Law was a gradual perversion of the true principles of Christianity and a subversion of the rights of the 'legislator' and of the peace of Christendom. For him the Church is the whole body of believers. The priesthood, consisting essentially of priests and deacons (for bishops are merely priests, entrusted with duties of supervision), has the functions of celebrating the Eucharist, of hearing confessions and pronouncing possibly non-valid absolutions for sin, and of teaching and preaching the revealed Divine Law. Priests have no coercive powers, such as excommunication and interdict, nor can they own any property, for in his doctrine of apostolic poverty Marsilius is an extremist, who considers pious donations to be still owned and administered rightfully by the legislator or the donors. In appointments, emoluments, personnel, and functions the priesthood is completely subject to the 'legislator' and its deputy, the *principans*, like any other class of citizen. It is for the legislator to excommunicate, which is a civil punishment, and to make heresy a temporal crime, if that is really allowable at all.

Yet Christendom and the Church obviously transcend the boundaries of the states, great and small, which make it up. For the Universal Church, its doctrines and its rites, the proper authority is a General Council, consisting of both priests and laymen, elected for the purpose by their several legislators. Here only Marsilius has a real, if ambiguously worded, use for the Holy Roman Empire, which he suggests should take the first steps in summoning the General Council. Here also he allows a presiding and secretarial function to the Bishop of Rome, who is the most suitable ecclesiastic by tradition and prestige for the office, though there is no inherent right to it derived from a vicariate of Christ conferred on St Peter. That St Peter was Bishop of Rome even is dubious. The General Council, besides the interpretation of Scripture, where Scripture is really doubtful, has even the authority to excommunicate a *pars principans* and declare an interdict, but the execution of its sentences depends on the 'legislator', the sole possessor of coercive power in the State. Similarly, even the most beneficial prescriptions of Canon Law are only valid if endorsed by the legislator. As the Decretals of Popes and canons of purely ecclesiastical synods they should have no coercive authority in themselves.

The far-reaching character of Marsilius's revolutionary thesis is manifest. His conceptions foreshadow most modern political theory, the secular State, the sovereign people, the unitary government, besides being the negation of the papal domination of Christendom expressed by the 'plenitude of power' vested in the Pope. The natural state formed by man for temporal happiness makes a clear appearance, and the notion of historical development, linked with a rudimentary historical induction instead of allegoric deduction, has come to light.

In his own time the sweeping radicalism of Marsilius, which cut at the roots of the existing constitution of the Church and of traditional conceptions of law and government, could do little more than arouse the horror of the papalists and percolate slowly into the minds of subsequent thinkers. A speedier influence was exerted by the voluminous works of his fellow refugee, William of Ockham, whose renown as a scholastic reasoner made him the founder of a school. Ockham had been under suspicion of doctrinal heresy, when in 1328 he fled from Avignon to Lewis along with the revolted Franciscan General, Michael of Cesena. Himself a Franciscan, he came to the conclusion that Pope John XXII was a heretic in condemning the Franciscan doctrine of the absolute poverty of Christ. At Lewis's court he began to write on the political questions of the day. His method was to explore the whole field from every point of view, discussing every argument with subtle distinctions and counter-distinctions and almost refraining from acknowledging a final decision of his own. This was to provide an armoury for disputants in the scholastic fashion they thoroughly understood. Yet his sceptical hesitation tended to be more disintegrating than the positive thesis of Marsilius. He was against the full-blown papal claims. A General Council may be fallible. He suggests that to be universal women should take part in such an assembly. He is confident of the self-sufficiency of the temporal power. But human institutions and circumstances are liable to change, and the boundary between temporal and spiritual functions may be crossed from either side in case of necessity or expediency. Thus, in place of the rival, clear-cut scheme of things devised by Marsilius, he induces an inquiring relativity, just as fatal to the dogmatic papalist theory.

The practice of these medieval theorists was to write in terms of the abstract and ideal remote from immediacy, however urgent the practical situation might be which called them forth. Aristotle might be a contemporary, the Civil Law of Justinian in full efficacy, and feudalism hardly in existence. The Law of Nature is assumed to be literally in force. Yet notions of another cast are visible in the fourteenth-century civil lawyers, who endeavour to reconcile and deduce them from these sublime authorities. They endeavour to discover what precisely natural law is and its application to particular occasions. Bartolus and Baldus acknowledge the existence *de facto* of sovereign states, which enjoy a quasi-imperial position. Positive law, emanating from the ruler, is insisted upon, and the division between public and private law is made. The former overrides the latter, and in the French *Somnium Viridarii* the lay spokesman, the knight, advocates *raison d'État*, which places legislation at the royal mercy. Unity within the state takes the place of the unity of Christendom. Inferior groups or corporations owe their rights to the revocable concessions of the sovereign power. Confiscation is justifiable for the benefit of the State. We are well on the way to the irresponsible ruler and legislator of the sovereign State. Indeed, the Neapolitan Lucas de Penna, steeped in the Byzantine traditions of Roger the Great and Frederick II, foreshadows the sixteenth-century Bodin.

In contrast with this legal trend of the cautious jurists, yet in all its unreality more subversive of the existing fabric and theory of the Church, was the theological argument of John Wyclif (*ob.* 1382) in his works headed by *De Civili Dominio* and *De Dominio Divino*. Although a staunch follower of Aquinas, he was clearly influenced also by such different

948

strains as the feudal conception of society and the root-and-branch radicalism of Marsilius. Following the teaching of an elder schoolman, FitzRalph of Armagh (*ob*. 1360), Wyclif worked out a new doctrine of dominion, which reversed that of Aegidius Romanus with startling results. Dominion is possession justified by right, as feudal dominion was justified by the performance of faithful service in return. The test of valid, just dominion for Aegidius had been loyal obedience to Pope and Church, from whom all temporalities were held. For him the *iusticia* of St Augustine, without which all earthly rule or possession was imperfect, was thus feudally conceived as a strict legal obligation to the visible Church. Wyclif now pronounced that *iusticia* was ethical personal righteousness due from every man direct to God. It was this alone which really counted, membership of God's elect, not of the visible fabric of the Church. Since truly rightful possession of power and property in the eyes of God is only granted to the righteous (who by a theoretical communism possess all things), the *de facto* possession of them by evil men has no such sanction. Further, the hierarchy from top to bottom of the visible Church, which sets up to be the bride of Christ, is to be judged by the most rigid ideal standard, and that hierarchy, being sinful and perverted by temporal greed, has lost the right to its powers and endowments. In every degree, including the wealthy monks and the propertied, gainful friars, it should be reduced by the lay rulers to apostolic poverty. A severe adherence to the literal meaning of Scripture led him soon to the denunciation of the traditional accretions of the Church in ritual, the penitential system, and government. His philosophic realism, on the other hand, made him deny the doctrine of Transubstantiation. In another line of thought his belief that human affairs are guided by Divine Providence made him stress the duty of submission to secular rulers in the confessedly unideal world of just and unjust. In lay politics he was a conservative: the portion of the righteous was in the life to come. His uncompromising judgement on the hierarchy was due to its dedication to ideal spiritual things which it had belied.

In the exceedingly abstract scholasticism of Wyclif lay the germs of many ideas which could have and did have momentous practical applications. Individualism in the direct relation of each man with his Maker, the independence and *de facto* supremacy of the lay state, the diminution of the visible Church into a man-made creation, while the true Church was the communion of the righteous elect, the exaltation of the Bible as the infallible rule of human actions, which made him the father of the scheme to render it into the English tongue for all to study, all these doctrines and others were to bear fruit in the next century and later. In the long, conflicting gestation and transformation of ideas, theological, legal, and

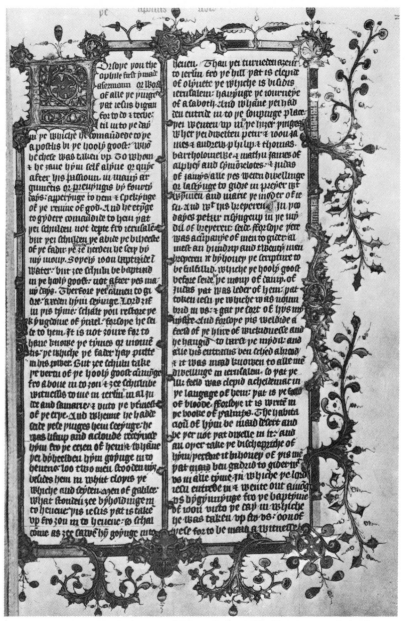

Fig. 211. Wyclif's Translation of the Bible (beginning of Acts)

social, which filled thinking minds in the fourteenth century, his part, curiously enough, was to present a body of formulated criticism and counter-doctrine, which could appeal to zealous, discontented, eager men of that age and through them reach the stirring elements in society, knight, bourgeois, and peasant, who were fumbling for remedies to present ills. The Great Schism, which broke the compelling organization of Papacy and Church, acted as a dissolvent of traditional submission and gave play in fluctuating degrees to the growing forces of kingship and nationality, criticism and reconstruction, individualism and consciously arbitrary law, the wrangling heirs round the sick-bed of the always disjointed Christian Commonwealth.

BOOK X
THE END OF THE MIDDLE AGES

❦❧

CHAPTER 32

THE GREAT SCHISM AND THE CONCILIAR MOVEMENT

(I) THE GREAT SCHISM

The historian of the Great Schism and the Conciliar Movement is confronted in an exaggerated form with the perennial difficulty of Church History in the Middle Ages. It is inextricably mingled with ecclesiastical and secular politics in the separate countries of the West. Thus series of events have to be segregated in each case from their natural surroundings and lose thereby much of their local and also European significance, while other series relegated to the story of particular countries suffer in the same way. Wars and diplomacy affected the whole course of ecclesiastical affairs, besides divergent views on the constitution of the Church and the desire for the reform of abuses and the general resentment at the intense and costly centralization established by the Popes of Avignon. The principle of the ecclesiastical unity of Christendom was on its defence against rival Popes and rival kingdoms.

The outbreak of the Schism was almost accidental, yet it had been long prepared for. The Papacy seemed less ecumenic in the provincial city of Avignon than in its traditional see of Rome. The pro-French leanings of Popes and cardinals, themselves French, had roused in England and Germany a deep suspicion of their impartiality. In Rome and Italy the anger occasioned by the loss of all the profits due to papal residence, and of the prestige and power thereto accruing, was exasperated by the continuous, aggressive intervention of the foreign Popes in Italian politics. It was because of this general ill feeling, which was rising to boiling point, that the Popes decided to take the unwilling Curia back to the dangers of tumultuous, unhealthy Rome.

The death of Pope Gregory XI (27 March 1387), when he was contemplating a return to Avignon, occurred with the cardinals still in Rome and subject to the violent pressure of the Roman mob, who demanded, if not a Roman, at least an Italian Pope. In fear they hastily proceeded (8 April) to an election, which they took pains to make appear wholly voluntary.

Their choice did no credit to their sagacity. Bartolomeo Prignano, Arch-bishop of Bari, who became Urban VI (1378–89), had been a reputable curialist and remained free from simony, but he revealed himself as a savagely cruel, wrathful, and repulsive autocrat, under whom it was unbearable to live. The cardinals slipped away from Rome, and thirteen of them met at Fondi in the kingdom of Naples, where they denounced the election as invalid. They then elected on 20 September 1379 their ablest man, Cardinal Robert of Geneva, as Pope Clement VII (1379–94). This was in effect a French election, but so much was Urban hated that the Italian cardinals assented, and Urban was obliged to create an entire College for his party. Clement was far from an ideal character—he was the author of the massacre at Cesena—but he was better than his rival. Thus began the Great Schism of the Western Church.

Each Pope at once resorted to spiritual and temporal arms, excom-municating the hostile party and hiring the Free Companies, who added desolation to the Roman Campagna. Urban VI won the first bout, for the Italian Company of Alberigo da Barbiano routed the Bretons, and Clement VII took ship for Avignon (1379). Of vital importance was the choice to be made by the rulers of the West between the two Popes. Charles V of France had already taken the lead by deciding after a solemn examination in favour of the Francophil claimant. With more or less hesitation he was imitated gradually by Scotland, by Castile and Aragon, and by those German princes who were amenable to French influence. On the other side, the Emperor Charles IV, Hungary, Scandinavia, and England held fast by Urban. The Italian states naturally were in favour of the Italian Pope. In fact, the Schism revealed itself as political. The French group was opposed by the rival or independent powers. This was shown by the reversion of Portugal, England's ally, to Urban after first accepting Clement, and still more by the wars in Naples. Queen Joanna took sides with Clement against the popular feeling, and against her Urban raised up her cousin Charles of Durazzo, who gained the throne (1381) and had her murdered. But she had adopted a French prince, Duke Louis I of Anjou, who occupied Provence and under Clement's patronage was invading Naples from the north. Meanwhile the fantastically violent character of Urban was alienating his own supporters. He quarrelled furiously with Charles of Durazzo. He tortured and executed recalcitrant cardinals, while roving deserted and unbending over southern Italy. The death of Louis (1384) gave the victory to Charles of Durazzo, but the victor was himself murdered just after acquiring the kingdom of Hungary (1386), and Naples was disputed between his widow and son and a new army sent by Clement to support Louis II of Anjou. The invaders were eventually overcome after the boy-king Ladislas was reconciled with the Roman Papacy, but only after years of warfare (1399).

The ferocious Urban VI was already dead (1389), and was succeeded by another Neapolitan, Boniface IX (1389–1404). Clement VII's death, too, made way for a new Pope at Avignon, the Aragonese Peter of Luna, who took the style of Benedict XIII (1394). Both Popes were able men endowed with much political craft, but Boniface's flagrant simony in his ceaseless search for funds and Benedict's patent absorption in the retention of personal power deprived them of the respect of one and all. Meantime the scandal of the Schism grew. The unity of the Church was divided into two obediences at strife with one another, each claiming the rightful Pope. The two rivals were wooing and cajoling the secular rulers, making empty appointments to sees and offices outside their own obedience, and making harder money demands on their own clergy to compensate for the decreased area they could tax. Abuses were magnified, and the grief of the pious was more outspoken and intense. The natural remedy was a General Council, but who was to convoke it, when each Pope regarded his rival as a mere rebel, and allowed no doubts on his own legitimacy? None the less it was soon advocated and old opinions on its authority were revived. The *Concilium Pacis* (1381) of Henry of Langenstein maintained that a General Council was superior to the Pope, that it was infallible, and that it could be summoned by the secular monarchs. Then there emerged another remedy, sponsored by the French king, Charles VI, and a council of his indignant clergy: the method of cession, i.e. the simultaneous abdication of both Popes (1395). This was welcomed by the cardinals of Avignon, but not by Benedict XIII. It was pressed on both rivals by the monarchs in 1397, only to meet with equal recalcitrance.

In the discussions over the ending of the Schism the University of Paris had taken a leading part. Its European prestige as the home of theology, sought from all nations, made it the chief representative of the *Studium*, which was vaunted to be a third power in Christendom alongside of the *Sacerdotium* and the *Regnum*. In spite of rebuffs and of the existence of an influential minority, it now induced the French king and an assembly of the French clergy to adopt a new measure of compulsion (1398), the withdrawal of obedience, and with it of the extortionate papal taxation and nomination to sees and benefices, from which Benedict XIII drew his resources. His refusal to abdicate, they said, was heresy in view of the Schism. The control of the Gallican Church and the interim exercise of papal functions passed to the bishops and the king. At the news fourteen out of nineteen of Benedict's cardinals deserted him, but the Pope held out. He was in vain blockaded in Avignon. In March 1403 he eluded the blockade and escaped to Provence. Then the opposition gave way. The cardinals and France returned to his obedience. Castile, which had joined in the withdrawal, had already done the same.

Besides the failure to compel Benedict, the French clergy had found the

Gallican system harder to bear than the Pope's. They paid as much or more to the king. The chapters did not in practice recover free election, and benefices were now given to nominees of the king, the princes, and the University of Paris instead of those of the Pope. The minority, too, of papalists among clergy and laity had always been numerous, and included the other universities of France. Yet Benedict felt obliged to conciliate opinion by fresh overtures to Boniface IX. The Roman Pope, however, took the same attitude as his competitor, unyielding insistence on his right. His successor, Innocent VII (1404–6), did likewise. Benedict showed his diplomatic talent by sailing to Genoa, a French dependency, and demanding a conference (1405). The lot of the Roman Pope had been more stormy and scandalous than that of the Pope of Avignon. At this time Innocent was labouring in the toils of King Ladislas of Naples, at once his enemy and supporter, while Rome and the Papal State were filled with war and anarchy. Amid corruption and abuses the European demand for reform, linked with the ending of the Schism, was growing louder. When Innocent VII died, his cardinals elected an aged Venetian, Gregory XII, under promise to close the Schism by his own abdication, if both Colleges met in conclave to elect a single Pope. Benedict gave an ambiguous consent, and the two rivals were to meet at Savona to carry out the way of 'cession'. Yet the meeting never occurred, although Benedict advanced first to Savona and then to Porto Venere (1407). Gregory never got nearer than Lucca; he would not venture into French-protected territory, and the two Popes haggled and manœuvred. Ladislas took the opportunity to conquer Rome.

But the patience of their obediences and their own cardinals was exhausted. In January 1408 the King of France declared for neutrality between the rivals. The two Colleges of Cardinals, in negotiating for their chiefs, came to an agreement to desert them and themselves to summon a General Council to meet at Pisa in 1409. At the news Benedict XIII took refuge at Perpignan, where he, too, proclaimed a Council. Gregory XII summoned another at Cividale in Friuli. The states of Europe took sides between the three. France, England, Poland and Portugal, most of Germany, and much of Italy adhered to the Council of Pisa; Castile, Aragon, and Scotland to Benedict; Naples, Hungary, parts of Germany, Scandinavia, and Venice to Gregory XII.

The Council of Pisa met on 25 March 1409, attended by 500 members. It promptly deposed both Popes, and under its aegis the combined cardinals elected Peter Philarges, Cardinal-Archbishop of Milan, as Pope Alexander V (June 1409). The immediate result was to add a third obedience to the existing Schism. Nor did the pressing demand for reform obtain satisfaction. Alexander V made the most limited and illusory concessions as to provisions and papal taxation. The main preoccupation of the Pope was the possession of Rome by the formidable King Ladislas of Naples, only to be expelled by war, and he was therefore dominated by the worst of the cardinals, Baldassare Cossa. This Neapolitan soldier, with nothing ecclesiastical about him, had done useful service to Boniface IX, and was ruling Bologna with a rod of iron. The pretender Louis II of Anjou was called in, and Ladislas had been turned out of the Papal State when the Pope died at Bologna in May 1410. Either from fear or fatuity the cardinals at once elected Cossa, who was rumoured to have poisoned him, as John XXIII. The choice of a scandalous pontiff might seem a cynical flout to all notions of reform, but John with Louis II won a brilliant victory over Ladislas. They did not know how to use it, however, while Bologna revolted from its hated tyrant (1411). In their straits both combatants came to dishonourable terms, deserting their allies. Pope John recognized King Ladislas, and Ladislas accepted John as Pope (1412). Gregory XII perforce fled to his only staunch protector, the *condottiere* and tyrant, Carlo Malatesta of Rimini. An all-but sham Council at Rome completed John XXIII's tactics. The fiction broke down before the European demand for a real General Council, voiced

Fig. 212. Tomb of Pope John XXIII by Donatello and Michelozzo

by the new King of the Romans, Sigismund of Luxemburg, King of Hungary. John XXIII promised it, and then found himself helpless in face of the renewed conquest of Rome by the no less faithless Ladislas.

(2) THE COUNCIL OF CONSTANCE

Sigismund was the first effective King of the Romans since his father Charles IV. His elder brother, the drunkard Wenceslas of Bohemia, had been deposed by the Electors for his neglect of the Empire. Rupert of the Palatinate, his successor, had died in 1410, and after disposing of rival claimants (both Luxemburgs) Sigismund had obtained (1411) an uncontested crown. The enemy of Ladislas over Hungary and of Venice over Dalmatia, he was an obvious ally for the Pope. But he was an active, indeed indefatigable, schemer with no small share of brains and resolution. Nothing could win him more renown than the healing of the Schism and its ills, which like others he sincerely desired, and which he felt was peculiarly his function as secular chief of Christendom. He adroitly pushed John XXIII into convoking a General Council to meet in November 1414 at the imperial city of Constance in Swabia. The death of Ladislas in August 1414 came too late for John to retract, his cardinals held him to his word, and full of foreboding he reached Constance by the time appointed.

By this time the year-long discussion on the calling of a General Council to end the Schism and to reform the manifold abuses in the Church, now at their height, had produced a certain amount of common ground, in spite of great diversity, among its exponents. They were essentially conservative in doctrine and organization, however radical might be their plans of reform. They held by the visible Church, its unity, and the institution of the Papacy. The revolutionary ideas of Wyclif, now adapted and extended by John Hus and his increasing followers in Bohemia, struck them with horror as a dangerous heresy, which it was one duty of the Council to crush. But in view of the baneful effects of papal autocratic centralization and the hopeless *impasse* created by the Schism in the Papacy and the rigid clutch of each of the three Popes on his power and the legitimacy he claimed, they were bound to find some other basis for the unity of Christendom in theory and in fact. The fitting home of the dispute was the University of Paris and the now numerous universities elsewhere, and among many controversialists some men, by no means unanimous in their opinions, stand out. There was Pierre d'Ailly, Bishop of Cambrai, a thorough-going reformer, who wished the Church to be governed by a succession of General Councils; his successor as Chancellor of Paris University, Jean Gerson, who, while eager for conciliar reform, by subtle distinctions made more room for papal rule although accountable and corrigible; Zabarella, the Bolognese doctor of laws, the champion of a practicable compromise; and, as influential as any, the German curialist, Dietrich of Niem, who stressed the supremacy of the universal Church, convinced by his long experience at Rome of the urgent necessity of conciliar reform of the abuses and corruption which were rife and bound up with papal autocracy.

The real centre of conciliar discussion before and during the Councils was the nature of sovereignty in the Church. There were Popes to be deposed and the evils of their centralized regime to be remedied. The Church itself, represented in its General Council, must therefore be the sovereign body superior to the Pope, with authority to depose him and to limit by its decrees his exorbitant powers. His office is a trust for the benefit of the Church and may be forfeited by misuse, while its overgrown functions should be curtailed. Here the influence of Marsilius and Ockham is evident. But precedent and the positive Canon Law of the Decretals were on the side of papal absolutism, and here the principle of the Law of Nature came into play. Positive law is only valid if it is consonant with the Law of Nature, which is the Divine command for the well-being of mankind. The Pope is essentially the minister, not the sovereign, of the Church. His powers, wrongfully used, may be pernicious to it. The Church in that case by the Law of Nature can unmake him and reform his office. Ultimate power therefore resides in the Christian community, against which prescription is of no avail. Government rests on the consent of the governed, a principle which could be, and was in later times, applied to secular governments as well.

In the actual proceedings of the Council of Constance the cardinals and the lay princes played an important rôle. Although under some parts of the cloud which enveloped John XXIII and his Curia, the cardinals were committed to reform since the Council of Pisa, and since then their attitude had been strengthened by the appointment of eminent reformers, the Frenchmen D'Ailly and Fillastre, and the Italian Zabarella. The lay princes were most important of all in the actual closing of the Schism. It was the unwearied diplomacy of Sigismund which brought about the adherence of those rulers who had maintained Benedict XIII. The French king, or rather the factions which ruled in his name, influenced his prelates. The English representatives were obedient to Henry V. Indeed, the progress of the Council was impeded and the insufficiency of its results partly explained by the enmity between France and England. The disunity of Christendom was only too manifest in the General Council which was to enforce unity.

When at its largest the Council of Constance, what with prelates and other doctors, numbered some six hundred, but it opened with a much smaller attendance. It began its work by proceeding against Hus as a heretic in spite of the safe-conduct he had received from Sigismund, a sign that it had no leanings towards revolutionary views. The next point was the crucial question of procedure and membership. The hopes of John XXIII, who had brought a large contingent of Italian prelates, were defeated both by the admission of theological graduates and by the division of the Council into 'nations', each of which was a voting unit. There were at first only four 'nations', the Italian, German, French, and English. The German included all eastern and northern Europe, the English all the British Isles, but they were less heterogeneous than they seemed, owing to the paucity of members from the included countries. Gregory XII had already offered to abdicate if his rivals did likewise. John XXIII, after wavering, decided to defy the Council. He had secured a temporal protector in the Habsburg Frederick of Tyrol and, fleeing in disguise to Laufenburg, denounced it. The Council took up the challenge with all-important decrees (April 1415). It held its power from Christ, and all, even the Pope, must obey it over the Faith, the Schism, and reform. The Pope was bound to abdicate if it so decided, and he was summoned to return. John's plans proved vain, for Sigismund forced his champion Frederick to complete submission. The Pope was captured at his last refuge in Freiburg-im-Breisgau, and imprisoned while he stood his trial. Such a catalogue of crimes was brought and largely proved against him

that he was easily deposed (29 May 1415) and himself ratified the act. Gregory XII gave way with more dignity. In July his envoys summoned the existing Council in his name, his cardinals were recognized, and his abdication was announced. He himself remained a cardinal until his death (1417). At the same time it was decreed that the Council should prescribe the method and time of electing a new Pope. Thus two of the three claimants had been removed. Benedict XIII, obstinate and safe in Aragon, was a more difficult problem. Heresy, it was thought, had received a deadly blow by the burning of John Hus, and it was hoped that the personal diplomacy of Sigismund would bring the Great Schism to an end.

Fig. 213. Burning at the stake of Jerome of Prague in Constance, 30 May 1416

Trust in Sigismund's powers of persuasion was not misplaced. In long negotiations at Perpignan he won over most of Benedict's supporters. A capitulation was sworn to at Narbonne on 13 December 1415, by which the lands of his obedience were to send representatives to join the Council of Constance. If Benedict should still prove obdurate, the Council then might depose him and proceed to the election of a new Pope. But Benedict had been craftily obdurate throughout the parleys and remained so at the Valencian castle of Peñiscola, whither he had withdrawn from Perpignan, still adhered to by some Aragonese and Scotland. However, late in 1416 Aragon and Navarre joined with Portugal to form a Spanish 'nation' at the Council, and Castile after long hesitation and haggling over the mode of the next papal election at last did the same in June 1417.

By the time, however, that Sigismund returned to Constance (January 1417) the brittle harmony of the Council had been much impaired. War had broken out between France and England and the French factions of Armagnacs and Burgundians were still at daggers drawn. Sigismund's own alliance with England during his absence made him suspect to the French. The Council meanwhile had only been unanimous in condemning Jerome of Prague, Hus's eloquent follower, to the flames (May 1416). The French delegates had fallen out bitterly over the Burgundian Petit's defence of 'tyrannicide', occasioned by the murder (1407) of the Duke of Orleans at the behest of John the Fearless, and they embarrassed the Council by thrusting their dispute upon it. Be-sides other ephemeral conflicts, the Council was endeavouring through a commission to discuss the burning question of reform. Papal taxation and provisions were the most vital problems, and most productive of variance. The Germans were most eager for change; the Italians were least; the English really felt secure behind their insular legislation; the French universities preferred papal provisions for their graduates to the caprice of patrons. Meantime the papalist party, rid of John XXIII and Gregory XII and all-but rid of Benedict XIII, was taking courage on the fundamental issue of conciliar or papal supremacy. The cardinals, who as such, in spite of their patronage of

Fig. 214. Coronation of Pope Martin V

reform, had been almost flouted in the earlier proceedings, were more and more given weight as a body, and were acting with the French 'nation'. Cardinal D'Ailly, who also became a proctor for Charles VI, was now more inspired by hostility to the small English 'nation' than by reform. It was difficult for the few English to maintain their separate status against his attacks, although they did. When the Castilians had joined the Spanish 'nation', and Benedict on 26 July 1417 was solemnly deposed as a heretic and incorrigible schismatic, a new commission on reform was discordant in its views, and cardinals and papalists were pressing for an early election of a new Pope before the reform measures were settled.

The deadlock between the 'nations'—French, Spanish, and Italian *versus* English and Germans with Sigismund—was suddenly ended by the death of the English leader, Bishop Hallam of Salisbury, and the receipt of instructions from King Henry V, which were reinforced by the arrival and mediation of Henry Beaufort, Bishop of Winchester. It was agreed to elect a Pope after passing those few decrees to which there was a general assent The most important was the decree *Frequens*, which laid down (9 October 1417) that General Councils should meet periodically, the first after five years, the second after another seven years, and subsequent assemblies at intervals of ten years. Soon after it was decreed that the new Pope should be elected by the cardinals jointly with representatives of the 'nations', and that before the Council dissolved he should agree with it on certain needed reforms. A two-thirds majority of cardinals and of each 'nation' was required. This was attained on 11 November 1417 by Cardinal Oddone Colonna, who had earned the reputation of a discreet and moderate, if undistinguished, curialist. He took the colourless name of Martin V, and soon showed a singular adroitness in diplomacy in dealing with the fatigued and discordant Council and a resolution to keep as much as he could to the old ways. Benedict XIII could be safely left to vegetate in his tiny schism, in which he died (1422), and which finally withered away (1429).

The diversity of opinions on reform was so great that Martin had little to fear from the Council's actions. It could only agree on a rigid bull against the Hussite heresy. Otherwise, it became content with separate concordats, mostly for five years only, with the five 'nations'. Such restrictions as they imposed on papal action were far below the early hope and were not effectively executed. Martin was at heart hostile to reform, and unwilling to lose revenue and power. On the question of the superiority of a General Council to the Pope he contrived to hedge. The Council was dissolved on 22 April 1418. Under great difficulties it had held together for years and had closed the Great Schism. In reform it had failed, not only because of dissension. Its successes and failures had been largely due to secular politics. The Fathers of the Council were drawn from different lands, unsympathetic and often hostile to one another. Their rulers were preoccupied with their temporal dominions, and the mastery over their particular Churches was their chief aim in matters ecclesiastical. They were weary of the confusion of the Schism, and they ended it. They were averse to the competing papal taxation, and they limited it. Their attitude to general reform was dubious and tepid, and it was left undone.

(3) BOHEMIA AND THE HUSSITES, 1378–1458

Its treatment of John Hus and his doctrines had been a fateful policy of the Council of Constance. Growing national consciousness had been a strong factor in the Council's proceedings, but it had been smothered by the belief in the unity of Christendom and the infallibility of the universal Church. In Bohemia, nationalism had become religious and doctrinal, for there two inharmonious nationalities lived side by side.

The reign of Wenceslas IV as King of the Romans was inglorious, ending in his deposition (1400); as King of Bohemia, it was a time of political upheaval and religious exaltation and revolution. The king was unfit to rule in calm weather and it was his lot to deal with the tempest. He was indolent, passionate, and a drunkard, without judgement or perseverance. He governed, for that matter, only Bohemia proper, for his cousin Jobst was Margrave of Moravia, as well as Elector of Brandenburg and Duke of Luxemburg. The king incurred the hatred of the nobles, headed by Jobst, partly owing to his favour to plain knights and burgesses. In the ups and downs of civil war Wenceslas was twice imprisoned, the second time by his mediating brother Sigismund of Hungary, and was compelled to submit to the control of a council of magnates. At last in 1403 he escaped to find himself restored to full power, for the experience of magnate rule had been a disillusion.

By this time the religious and racial atmosphere of Bohemia was in a ferment. The intervention of Wenceslas in ecclesiastical affairs had already been unfortunate. He had engaged in bitter quarrels with the ascetic and arbitrary Archbishop of Prague, John of Jenštejn, over the creation of a new bishopric and the immunity of the clergy, during which the archbishop's vicar-general, John of Pomuk (Nepomuk), much later exalted to be the national saint, was cruelly put to death (1393). The king's political alliance with Pope Boniface IX, however, gave him the upper hand. He obtained papal provisions for his favourites, and in return permitted papal taxation and dubious appointments. Clerical corruption and abuses were thus rampant in Bohemia at the very time when the religious and moral movement started under Charles IV was gaining ground. The layman, Thomas of Štitny, wrote devotional works in Czech, and Matthias of Janov (ob. 1394) attacked the corruption of the Church. In 1391 two laymen founded the Bethlehem Chapel at Prague for the dissemination of religious zeal. As time passed, the Czech element in the University of Prague was becoming more numerous, and was more open to the new movement than the diminishing German masters.

In this situation a leader of reforming opinion appeared, John Hus. He was born c. 1370 at Husinec (whence his abbreviated name), and became an influential figure in Prague University. It was as preacher in the Bethlehem Chapel from 1402 that he acquired a unique position among the Czech community. He roused a strong religious fervour in his hearers, in which the congregational hymnody he favoured had a share. At first he was in harmony with the court and the zealous Archbishop Zbynek, even while he attacked the prevalent corruption of the clergy, but gradually his views took a more radical cast. Owing to the contact established by the marriage of Wenceslas's sister Anne to Richard II of England, first the philosophical and then the doctrinal works of Wyclif percolated into Bohemia and won over numbers of the Czech masters in the university, among them Hus himself. It was in vain that the majority of the masters (largely German) twice (1403, 1408) condemned and forbade Wyclif's theological doctrines, and that their former champion, Stanislas of Znojmo, recanted under pressure. They gained ground among the Czechs, and Hus

Fig. 215. Hus's lecture on Wyclif's De veris universalibus, *1398*

from being tolerant of them slowly veered towards adopting them. The archbishop turned to persecution, confiscating Wyclif's works and forbidding attacks on the clergy. The debate was complicated by the progress of the Great Schism. Wenceslas IV wished to support the Council of Pisa; Zbynek continued his obedience to Gregory XII, and was upheld by the German masters, while the Czechs were for the Council. The archbishop excommunicated Hus. The king gave the Czech 'nation' a majority over foreigners in the university, with the result that most Germans deserted it to found a new university at Leipzig (1409). Interdict on Prague from the archbishop was countered by royal severities. But when Zbynek accepted Alexander V, he was freed to attack Hus and his followers. He forbade preaching, burnt the confiscated works of Wyclif, excommunicated Hus and his adherents, and renewed his interdict on Prague (1410). The king intervened forcibly to compel a truce. Hus meanwhile denied that he had

Fig. 216. Hus at the stake in Constance, 6 July 1415

taught Wyclif's more radical doctrines. Although Zbynek died (1411), Pope John XXIII, by his hostility and by the continuous scandals of his pontificate, gave an impetus to Hus's inclination toward Wyclifism. He denounced indulgences to finance the war with King Ladislas, and declared that disobedience to unrighteous papal commands was justified. He received popular support, although the university theologians turned against him, and John XXIII laid him under excommunication and interdict. The king, after shifting to the papal side, renewed his protection of Hus by persecuting his opponents.

By the time the Council of Constance opened, Hus had adopted Wyclif's doctrines with modifications of his own, and possessed the enthusiastic support of most Czechs. King Sigismund, the heir to his brother Wenceslas, and eager to clear Bohemia from the disgrace of heresy, invited him to attend the Council under his safe-conduct, and Hus rashly accepted the proposal. Soon after his arrival he was imprisoned as a heretic to be tried (November 1414), while Sigismund, anxious to conciliate the orthodox Council, withdrew his safe-conduct. A few months later Hus's disciple, Jerome of Prague, who came to Constance to defend him, was also imprisoned. The proceedings against Hus were lengthy and not unprejudiced, but it transpired from his defence that, although he did not go all the way with Wyclif (e.g. as to the denial of Transubstantiation), he accepted Wyclif's doctrine that the true Church consisted of those predestined to salvation, and that he was for the abolition of much of the existing Church order as abusive and not warranted by Scripture. He

*Fig. 217. Protest of 100 Bohemian and Moravian noblemen
against the burning of Hus, October 1415*

refused to recant what he admitted to have taught unless he could be convinced to do so by Scripture. Thus he opposed the authority and infallibility of the General Council, and his fate was sealed. After sentence as a heretic, he died bravely at the stake by Sigismund's order (6 July 1415). Jerome of Prague, who at first recanted, boldly withdrew his submission before the Council, and died with equal heroism (30 May 1416).

Hus was a martyr for the liberty of the individual conscience, and his death was as powerful as his life. His cause had become identified with that of the Czech nation which was inspired by him, and which incidentally owed to him the literary development of its vernacular tongue. The news of his execution and of Sigismund's breach of faith roused a storm of indignation among nobles and people. The nobles entered into a bond not to accept the Council's decrees, to obey Pope and bishops only in commands not contrary to Scripture, and only to allow the clergy to be convicted of heresy by Prague University (1416). The Council's ban on the university (now mainly Hussite) and its burning of Jerome produced exasperation and no more. However, the Hussites were much divided among themselves. They were unanimous indeed on one point. It had been since the thirteenth century the custom to give the Bread only to laymen in the Eucharist, reserving the chalice for the clergy. Shortly before Hus left for Constance, his followers began to maintain with his approval that laymen ought to partake in both kinds, and the moderate Hussites specially appropriated the name of Utraquists. But the more radical went far beyond this doctrine. In fact, besides the natural divergence on the degree of change, there had long existed subterraneously in Bohemia obscure and confused fragments of the older sects of Waldensians, Catharans, and the like, whom no persecution had rooted out, and who now provided a fertile soil for extreme and diverse doctrines. Yet by 1420 all were agreed at least on the Four Articles of Prague: free preaching, utraquism, the confiscation of the overgrown clerical and monastic possessions, and the punishment of simony and other deadly sins. Meanwhile Wenceslas IV had been spurred on by Sigismund to take the Council's side. One of his measures was to put in a new anti-Hussite town council of Prague. The Hussite mob broke into riot, and threw the councillors from the windows of the Town hall (30 July 1419). The king died of rage, and the Hussite revolution began.

The immediate question was whether the heir, Sigismund, should be recognized as king. He was accepted in the dependencies of Silesia, Lusatia and Moravia, where the Germans were numerous, but the Czechs would only admit him if he agreed to the Four Articles of Prague. Instead, he proclaimed a crusade to enforce obedience to the Church. In reply the Czechs formed an army, the best of which was organized round the new Hussite town of Tabor in south Bohemia. It was led by the one-eyed knight, Jan Žižka, sixty years old, who was an inventive general, a veteran of many private and foreign wars. For his ill-armed troops he devised new tactics, the fortification composed of wagons, supplemented by the hand-guns slowly coming into use. When the hostile armoured cavalry had dashed themselves in vain on the stationary wagons, the Czechs sallied out to rout them in their disorder. Two armies led by Sigismund successively received crushing defeats (1420), as did a further crusade, supported by the German princes (1421–2). Although Sigismund in 1420 had himself crowned at Prague, the Czechs held that the throne was vacant, and in search of allies elected the Polish prince Sigismund Korybut as regent and then king (1422). After attempts to effect a reconciliation with the Church he, too, was driven out (1427). Real power, however, all along was exercised by councils chosen by the Bohemian Diet, in which the towns, led by Prague and Tabor, enjoyed an important position along with the nobles.

Prague and Tabor became the centres of the two main parties among the Hussites. Prague the capital, with its university, knights, and burghers, was the home of the moderate Utraquists who did not wish to go beyond the Articles of Prague. Tabor the new town, with its sectaries, heretic exiles (among them the English Lollard, Peter Payne), farmers, and peasant serfs, was the focus of all radical views. There was the headquarters of the Chiliasts, who believed that the Second Coming of Christ was imminent and to be prepared for by a holy war against the godless and unreformed. There were the radicals, who rejected Transubstantiation, purgatory, saint-worship, and Church ritual. They destroyed altars, Church decorations, and monasteries. They elected their priests and a presiding bishop, and unlike the Utraquists broke definitely away from the visible, ecumenic Church. Besides, there was political radicalism, the abolition of serfdom and a passing attempt at communism. Somewhat less extreme was the party in East Bohemia, the Orphans, founded by Žižka before his death in 1424. Thus dissidence was prevalent in Hussitism from the start, and the parties fell to blows. But when repulse of invasion or attacks on their enemies in neighbouring Germany were in question, they were nationally united in the holy war.

In that war of defence and offence they possessed a first-rate chief in the Tabor priest, Prokop the Bald. They repeatedly invaded Silesia, Meissen (Saxony), Brandenburg, and Franconia, acquiring a secular passion for booty and forcing on their enemies humiliating truces. The crusades of the German princes against them were one after another miserable failures. The victory of Ústi (Aussig) in 1426 confirmed the belief in Hussite invincibility. In 1427 at Tachov and in 1431 at Domazlice (Taus) the crusading armies fled without fighting before the Czechs. This last collapse, at which the legate Cardinal Cesarini was present, determined the newly assembled Council of Basle to treat with the Hussites, whom it could not crush.

The divergencies among the Hussites favoured the new course. The Utraquists were disgusted with the internal anarchy, the radicalism, the iconoclasm of the Taborite regime, and began to draw nearer to the conservative catholic minority in Bohemia. There was even a section among them who would be content with the chalice for the laity and the removal of certain abuses. Yet all alike refused to make unqualified submission to the Council of Basle, and it was not until, after vain negotiations, the Council in October 1431 invited them to meet it on equal terms, that they met conciliar representatives at Cheb (Eger). There it was agreed that Scripture and the teaching of the early Church were to be the judge between them—the 'Cheb judge' the Hussites called it (May 1432). Meanwhile Hussite raids reached the Baltic. At Basle, however, the Czech envoys, led by Jan Rokycana, the vicar of the arch-see, found that only the chalice would be conceded, while they insisted on all the Articles of Prague. Thereat the Council sent a deputation to Prague, which skilfully induced (November 1433) the most moderate Utraquists to accept the Compacts of Prague. The Articles of Prague were therein whittled down with such adroit ambiguity that, save for the chalice clause, their original

968

meaning was almost lost. Utraquists and Council were long to dispute the meaning of the Compacts.

At the time, however, the irreconcilable Taborites and Orphans by continuing the civil war with the Catholics of Pilsen (Plzen) united their adversaries. Utraquists and Catholics, all the nobility, joined forces, and at Lipany on 30 May 1434 they overthrew the radicals, Prokop the Bald being among the slain. Agreement with Sigismund was now easy, if lengthy. The election of bishops was to be by a committeee of the diet, and Rokycana was to be Archbishop. The Compacts of Prague were ratified in July 1436. It seemed as if the contest of the Utraquists with the Catholics was over, although in reality it merely entered on another phase. Even so far, the struggle had produced radical changes in Bohemia. The Estates in their Diet greatly limited the king in government. Economically, the confiscation of the vast Church estates and their transference to the greater nobles and the gentry placed the wealth of the country in lay hands, and the burgesses of the towns shared in the spoils and in power. The German element in the population lost political importance. Against these changes was to be set the failure of the serfs and workmen of the towns to improve their condition. Further, Bohemia as a whole was impoverished by the long wars. The culture and art of the preceding time was destroyed, and a new start had to be made.

Accord between the Utraquists and the Council ceased almost at once. The Council refused to confirm Rokycana's election as archbishop, it declared that the partaking of the cup was not essential for the sacrament, and the zeal of its legates in restoring Catholic priests and rites was so vigorous that Rokycana left Prague for eastern Bohemia, where the sturdier Utraquists were predominant. At this juncture the Emperor Sigismund died (December 1437). His heir and son-in-law, Albert of Austria, who never attained an uncontested throne, died too (October 1439), leaving Bohemia divided and kingless, while Silesia and Lusatia went their own way. However, in east Bohemia proper the Utraquists formed a military union, led by Rokycana, Ptaček, and George Poděbrady, from whom it became known as the Poděbrady Unity, which succeeded in consolidating their whole party in the diet of 1444 against both Catholics and the conquered Taborites. They and the Compacts of Prague met the unbending opposition of the restored Papacy, but they occupied Prague, while the papal legate, Cardinal Carvajal, left the country. With the consent of the King of the Romans, Frederick III of Austria, the guardian of King Albert's posthumous son Ladislas, Poděbrady was elected governor for two years. He promptly quelled the Taborite remnant, but no consecration could be obtained for Rokycana, and the diminishing Hussite priesthood could only be recruited by surreptitious ordinations, for no bishop was on the Utraquist side. Ladislas Postumus, however, let go by Frederick III, was elected king (October 1452) under the guidance of Poděbrady. Peace and good government were restored, Silesia and Lusatia were acquiescent, and a possible reconciliation was under discussion with Pope Calixtus III when the young king died (1457).

With the extinction of the dynasty the problem of the succession was solved in March 1458 by the election of George Poděbrady as king. Thus a Czech and a Utraquist Hussite sat on the throne and a new set of internal and foreign complications arose.

(4) THE COUNCIL OF BASLE

After the close of the Council of Constance, Pope Martin V devoted himself to the recovery of the temporal power and spiritual authority of the Papacy. Partly by good fortune and partly by his ability he was able to return to his native Rome, and to restore to some obedience the States of the Church. But he was an enemy of Church reform and dreaded the doctrine of conciliar supremacy. The former would reduce papal revenue and power; the latter would limit papal autocracy. To burke the General Councils assembled under the decree *Frequens* was his aim. This he succeeded in doing with the ill-attended and spiritless Council of Pavia-Siena (1423–4), which lacked princely backing. Its only effective act was to fix Basle as the meeting-place of the next Council.

The pressure of the reanimated reform party, especially of some princes and the University of Paris, and the alarming successes of the Hussites, compelled Martin to observe this decree. He appointed the highly esteemed Cardinal Giulio Cesarini to be president of the coming Council of Basle just before his own death on 20 February 1431. His successor, a respectable, obstinate mediocrity, was the Venetian Eugenius IV, who was almost at once involved in troubles with the Romans. Meanwhile the Council gathered slowly at Basle. Cesarini was tepid until the shameful rout of the German crusaders, which he witnessed at Domazlice (Taus) (August 1431), convinced him that Hussitism could only be stemmed by the General Council. The clergy were pressed to attend, and it was declared that the extirpation of heresy, the peace of Christendom, and the reform of the Church were the objectives.

The main hold of the Council of Basle on the rulers and public opinion of Europe was due to the seriousness of the Hussite revolt and to the hopes that a way might therein be found of ending it, but the interest of its members, in majority reformers, lay in the long-needed reform of the Church and the dispute which at once arose with the Papacy. Its strength waxed as its deft handling of the negotiations with the Hussites led slowly with much vicissitude to the somewhat hollow Compacts of Prague and that partial and illusory reconciliation of Catholics and Utraquists; it

970

waned when the questions of reform and conciliar supremacy were left by themselves. The superiority and infallibility of a General Council with regard both to the Hussites and to the Pope was indeed the essential conviction of its members, which it upheld against both adversaries. The breach with Eugenius occurred almost at once. When the Council invited the Hussite leaders to conference under safe-conduct, Eugenius hastily declared the Council dissolved (December 1431), and the Council firmly refused to obey. It grew stronger in numbers and authority, for Sigismund, France, England, Burgundy, and Castile adhered to it. Papal absolutism was rejected by the Council, although the views of its members varied from considering the Pope the divinely appointed Head of the Church, if corrigible by a General Council, to holding the Papacy to be a human and alterable invention, and from thinking that the united episcopate was the essence of a General Council to maintaining that sovereignty in the Church belonged to the whole body of the clergy.

In spite of these internal divergencies the now numerous Council showed a steadfastness in action which contrasted with the vacillation and disingenuousness of the Pope. It called on Eugenius to revoke his bull of dissolution and to be represented. Cardinal Cesarini, who had at first resigned, resumed the presidency; a majority of the cardinals adhered; and in answer to a peremptory conciliar ultimatum with a threat of further action, Eugenius after a vain attempt at compromise, acknowledged in February 1433 that the General Council was in existence at Basle by a kind of re-summons. This concession was not sufficient for the Council. It threatened suspension and deposition unless he adhered unconditionally. In response the Pope, who had just crowned Sigismund Emperor and hoped for his support, became exceptionally tortuous in a series of bulls. By one bull he annulled its acts against the Papacy, by another, *Dudum sacrum* (August 1433)—prepared in two varying texts—he acknowledged the Council's continuous validity, withdrawing his bull (1431) of dissolution. A curious bull, *Deus novit*, whose authenticity he denied, obtained, genuine or not, wide circulation; it declared that to hold that a General Council was above the Pope was heresy. The effect of these utterances on the princes, however, was to make them protest, and at the same time he was losing the Papal States. In December 1433 he gave way in a new bull, also beginning *Dudum sacrum*, which promised co-operation and revoked his hostile bulls.

The Council was now at the height of its power and prestige. It was achieving the accommodation, however superficial, with the Utraquists, and the Taborites were overthrown at Lipany (1434). The question of reform remained. On this its lack of unanimity brought out all its weaknesses and the dubious nature of outside support. As we have seen, the members varied markedly in their views on the rightful position of the Pope, which meant that there would always be a dissatisfied minority. National animosities (for instance France and England were at war) rent the Council and influenced the voting. This was partially veiled by the official division into four 'deputations' allotted to heresy, peace, reform, and general business, but semi-official 'nations,' French, German, Italian, and Spanish (though the English did not secure recognition) existed too, and their roundabout influence on the 'deputations' was perhaps more hurtful to a well-considered course than the open division into 'nations' at Constance had been. Further, the qualification for membership was laxly interpreted, and, with a few striking exceptions, and those not always the most judicious minds, the members were not of high moral or intellectual calibre. They were carried away by success.

They began early to act as if the papal office was in suspension, setting up rival judicial courts, claiming the papal income, and meddling in administration at large. They decreed the abolition of papal reservations (1433), and if other decrees really reaffirmed existing prohibitions, a sweeping canon against abuses of June 1435, sponsored by Cesarini, did away with all curial fees as well as annates, while no provision to supply salaries instead was made. Eugenius, knowing that there was a weighty minority of moderate views, cautiously temporized. Although obliged to harbour in Florence from disorderly Rome, he was acquiring armed strength, and the urgent need of the unhappy Byzantines to buy Western help at the cost of Reunion placed a new diplomatic opportunity in his hands.

For the Pope, the Greek readiness for Reunion gave the occasion for acting as the effective head of the Church, and he possessed the inestimable advantages of all the fabric and means of an established central government in contact by long use with the secular rulers of the West, and of the natural desire of the Greeks for an accessible town in Italy as the place of negotiations, and for a responsible and permanent government with which to treat. For the Council's majority, the main object was still to curb the Pope's powers and to secure that the Reunion should, like the Utraquist reconciliation, take place under its own auspices at Basle or some place remote from papal influence. For both sides the prestige of closing the Schism was of vital importance. With pronounced ill judgement the conciliar majority linked its programme with a new offensive against the recalcitrant Pope. He was called upon (January 1436) to confirm all its decrees, he was denounced in a circular to Christian princes, further rules were laid down for him, and his overtures were rejected. Eugenius replied by a counter-attack and denunciation. The final breach came over the meeting-place with the Greeks. The Council's majority, led by the French Cardinal d'Aleman, insisted on Avignon, known to be unacceptable to them; the minority, mainly of prelates, and led by Cesarini, were for an Italian town.

972

At a riotous session on 7 May 1437 both parties simultaneously and indecorously passed their conflicting decrees.

Now that the Council was split, Eugenius could act decisively. The Greeks accepted his and the minority's invitation, and he transferred the Council to Ferrara to meet them. They rejected the majority's invitation. Cesarini and the minority left Basle for Ferrara, where and at Florence the lengthy and fundamentally insincere Council of Reunion was held (1438–9). At last their pressing need induced the Greeks, with one sturdy exception, Archbishop Mark of Ephesus, to acknowledge the Double Procession of the Holy Ghost and the Pope's supremacy. Eugenius in return sent troops to Constantinople, but in the Byzantine Empire the Reunion was a hated dead letter. The Pope's triumph was confined to the West.

Meanwhile the depleted Council of Basle kept up the fight. It declared the Pope guilty of contumacy, and then suspended him (January 1438). It still had the support of France and Germany. Charles VII and his prelates promulgated in 1438 the Pragmatic Sanction of Bourges, which applied the most notable of the reforms of Basle, and limited papal action in the Gallican Church. After Sigismund's death (1437), the German Electors made a declaration in much the same sense. Thus emboldened, the Council proceeded to depose Eugenius as a heretic, and after a while elected (November 1439) their chief lay adherent, Amadeus VIII, ex-duke of Savoy, as Pope Felix V. But he and the Council co-operated with difficulty, and their supporters were few outside Germany. The Electors and the Habsburg King Frederick III remained officially neutral in the Schism. A change in the situation, however, came about through the need in which Frederick III stood of papal assistance. The unscrupulous skill of his secretary, Aeneas Sylvius Piccolomini (a rat from the sinking Council), sold his adhesion to Eugenius for rights to nominate to certain bishoprics and for cash (1446). In a long process of bargaining the Electors and princes came in. They modified their demands for reform and accepted a still more diluted version from Eugenius. They were to share amply in the profits of the old system. The public good of Church and Empire was ignored. The final step to a concord was provided by the death of Eugenius IV (23 February 1447) and the election of the Tuscan humanist Parentucelli as Pope Nicholas V, who was free from the personal animosities felt for his predecessor. He was accepted, and a concordat was signed at Vienna (February 1448) by the King of the Romans and the astute Cardinal-legate Carvajal, which was acquiesced in by the princes.

The derelict Council of Basle was now helpless. By Frederick's orders it was expelled from Basle, and took refuge at Lausanne (1448). The mediation of both France and England brought it to a dignified close after amicable negotiations. Felix V abdicated, and became a cardinal. On

25 April 1449 the Council elected Nicholas V Pope, and decreed its own dissolution. It had, after all, made history. Under its influence the excessive centralization and taxation of the fourteenth-century Papacy had been diminished in favour of the secular monarchies, a fact of pregnant import. Of still more decisive significance was its failure: the failure of the medieval Church of the West to reform itself as a united body. Reform was left to come in the shape of, and as a consequence of, revolution.

CHAPTER 33

FRANCE, ENGLAND AND GERMANY,
*c.*1380–*c.* 1450

(I) CIVIL WAR AND DISASTER IN FRANCE[1]

The accession of Charles VI, a boy of twelve, who, when he grew up, was subject to recurrent insanity, unchained all the internal forces of evil in France. His uncles, the Dukes of Anjou, Berry, and Burgundy, were self-seeking to a degree. The people were in a state of turbulent unrest under the load of taxation. The new generation of nobles, debased by the long, hazardous havoc of the war, was reckless, extravagant, and febrile in its pleasures and politics.

It was a time of insurrection among peasants and workmen over Europe in England, in Tuscany, and in Flanders, where Ghent, at odds with the count, set up a despot, Philip van Artevelde. In France the crushing taxation caused the outbreaks. The government hastily suppressed the hated taxes, and then sought for aids from the local Estates to replace them. These led to riots in the towns. That in Paris (March 1382), where the people (hence named *maillotins*) armed themselves with leaden mallets, opened the prisons, and had some sympathy from the well-to-do and the university. The government replied by executions. The decisive event, however, occurred in Flanders. Philip of Burgundy was son-in-law and heir of the count. He induced the boy-king to bring an army to aid his vassal, and at Roosebeke on 27 November 1382 the well-led French chivalry trampled down the Flemish pikemen. This victory cowed the French insurgents. Unsparing executions, fines, and punishments were dealt out to rioters and moderates alike in north and south. The taxes were reimposed. Only in Flanders did the prudent Philip, alive to his own interest there, effect a reasonable reconciliation, after he inherited the county in 1384.

During these unhappy years of oppression Philip of Burgundy, entirely devoted to his own schemes, was the real head of the government, for Louis I of Anjou was engrossed in the war for Naples in which he died (1384). The war with England was Philip's affair. In 1383 he had to repulse an Urbanist pseudo-crusade in Flanders led by the Bishop of Norwich. In 1384 and 1386–7 he caused the king to prepare great forces for a descent on England from Flanders, but they never sailed. After 1388 long truces became the rule. In that year Charles VI, spurred on by his brother Louis, Duke of Touraine and soon of Orleans, took the government

[1] See Genealogical Table 20 above, pp. 780–1.

into his own hands. Old and trusty ministers of his father, the so-called 'Marmousets', took charge, and for a few years their wise rule gave France good administration and general reform. It was blasted in 1392 by the sudden madness of the king, whose neurotic brain had been fevered by a life of wild excesses, on an expedition against the lawless Duke of Brittany. Henceforward, even during his recurrent, but steadily shorter, lucid intervals, he was a puppet, for whose disposal his greedy uncles of Burgundy and Berry, his flighty queen Isabella of Bavaria, and his brother of Orleans, the best, if irresponsible, member of a harmful group, strove incessantly. The ladies ruled the court, in which the queen and Valentina Visconti, Duchess of Orleans, were bitter enemies. There was a vogue for extravagant fashions and showy exploits and ambitions. Orleans schemed for a kingdom of Adria in the Papal States in the service of Pope Clement VII; Louis II of Anjou was fighting for Naples; Philip of Burgundy, the ablest of the princes, was intent on building up a mid-European state composed of his French and imperial fiefs.

All these ambitions and rivalries in luxury, power, and display required money and lands at the expense of the Crown and the kingdom. The events of the Schism increased the unscrupulous competition. When the exasperation at the obstinacy of the rival Popes grew, the Duke of Burgundy, whose county of Flanders was for the Roman obedience, supported the University of Paris in the withdrawal of obedience from Benedict XIII (1398). After the vain siege of the Pope in Avignon, the Duke of Orleans championed him and secured the return of France to his obedience (May 1403). The Gallican Church suffered under both régimes. Abroad, also, the two princes ran counter to one another. There had been a prolonged truce with England, of which the seal was the marriage of Charles VI's daughter Isabella to Richard II (1396). When Henry IV of Lancaster usurped the English throne and Isabella was safe back in France, Orleans was wishful to break with the new king; Burgundy, more wisely, was for peace and arranged for Flanders to be untouched by a possible war. Louis cherished ambitions in the Empire, and obtained lands separating Philip's lands of Burgundy and Franche Comté from the Netherlands. Civil war seemed possible when Philip the Bold died (April 1404).

His son and successor, John the Fearless, was as ambitious as he, with an ability allied to cunning and devoid of the scruples of chivalry. He had been a leader in the crusade of Nicopolis and a prisoner of the Turkish Sultan. Louis of Orleans was then reconciled—too reconciled, men said—with his former enemy, the queen, and they were fleecing the kingdom for their pleasures. An all-but war was followed by a pretence of friendship, while John talked of the much needed reforms. War with England had begun, in which each cousin blamed the other for his unsuccess. Then on 23 November 1407 the Duke of Orleans was murdered in Paris by John's

976

cut-throats. Thus was created the irremediable blood-feud which delivered France into the hands of her enemies.

For the time being John the Fearless was too formidable to be brought to justice. He even found a theologian, Jean Petit, to justify the murder as a righteous act. The withdrawal of obedience from Benedict XIII was renewed. But a party formed during feigned reconciliations round the young Duke Charles of Orleans, which took its name from his father-in-law, the great Gascon lord, Count Bernard VII of Armagnac. To it belonged the princes and much of west and central France. With Duke John sided his brothers and dominions, together with the people of Paris and the university. The oppressive extravagance of the murdered Orleans enabled him to pose as a friend of the people, but his faction was essentially one of nobles, like the Armagnacs, and more open to foreign influences. Fighting became endemic, both factions called in the English, and Burgundy got them. In 1412 a kind of peace was patched up and the States General were summoned to fill the empty treasury.

The evils of the long misgovernment of the greedy rival princes and the vicious court now came home to roost. For years the Chambre des Comptes and the Parlement had been thoroughly corrupt. Honest finance and justice were not to be had. In Paris the gilds of the butchers, skinners and the like had since 1407 violently seized the lead among the thronging malcontents under the patronage of the Duke of Burgundy. Now the States General, at the instance of university and city, secured a commission of reform (1412), which worked to an accompaniment of violent rioting under the leadership of the skinner Caboche. To appease them the king, for the moment sane, promulgated in May 1413 the commission's reforms in the 'Ordonnance Cabochienne', so called from the name of the rioters and their chief. It was an elaborate and radical attempt to give permanent good government. The Council, the Parlement, and the Chambre des Comptes, and all officials, central and local, were to be elected. It was an honest, if then utopian, effort to put an end to corrupt appointments and corrupt administration. But the butchers were out of control, and anarchic violence continued, producing a reaction in Paris itself. The Armagnac faction were in arms, the Burgundian made peace with them. The Parisians veered to the side of order. When the Armagnacs entered the city, they restored the old officials, revoked the Ordonnance Cabochienne, and took vengeance on the rioters. It was in vain that the Duke of Burgundy tried to snatch power once more. He came to terms at Arras in February 1415.

By this time the danger from England had become imminent. Henry IV, ill and always preoccupied at home, had died in 1413, and his masterful, brilliant son Henry V, the first general of the time, was resolved to serve his ambition and his dynasty by the conquest of France. He obtained (1414) the half-alliance of John the Fearless. Insincere negotiations over his

Fig. 218. Holograph letter of Henry V

claim, a parody of Edward III's, to the French crown, and active, most businesslike preparations for invasion occupied 1414. On 13 August 1415 with a fully equipped army he besieged Harfleur on the Norman coast. The French did not impede his capture of Harfleur, but slowly gathered at Rouen, while John of Burgundy held aloof. Henry was determined to force a battle by recklessly marching across to Calais. He succeeded in inducing an attack from the French at Agincourt in Artois (24 October 1415). They greatly outnumbered his army, but almost wholly consisted of nobles, who had learnt nothing from Crécy and Poitiers. A mounted vanguard charged first, followed by the main body on foot. Both, in armour even heavier and more clogging than at Poitiers, were bogged in the mud from heavy rain and shot down by the English archers. So helpless was the mass of men that Henry was able to attack with his light-armed troops and slaughter them 'as though they were hammering on an anvil'. The death-roll of the vanquished was enormous, some 7000, that of the English 500. Among the prisoners was the young Duke of Orleans, destined to a long captivity. While Henry lived, no French army ventured to meet him in the field.

The kingdom's worst days now began. The deaths of two dauphins in succession and the youth of the third, Charles, the madness of the king, and the disgrace of the discredited queen left Paris and the government in the harsh hands of the constable, Bernard of Armagnac. The King of the Romans, Sigismund, travelling for the Council of Constance, was completely won over to the English alliance. John of Burgundy was in close understanding with Henry V. The English king in 1417–18 was systematically conquering Normandy. It became easy for John the Fearless to seize the government in the queen's name. Paris opened her gates to him in May 1418 and then burst into a cruel frenzy of anarchy which lasted till

October. After an heroic resistance Rouen at last capitulated to Henry in January 1419, driven thereto by starvation.

The Dauphin Charles however, had, escaped from Paris, and became the centre of resistance with the title of regent. All central France obeyed his government, which was organized at Bourges. John of Burgundy bargained with both sides till at a final and wrathful interview with the dauphin on the bridge of Montereau he was set on and killed by his enemy's followers (10 September 1419). The dauphin had retired and the murder was unpremeditated, but the effect was to exacerbate the deadly feud. John's son, Duke Philip the Good, and the whole Burgundian party were enraged. They had possession of the king, the queen, and their daughter Catherine, and on 21 May 1420 they concluded the Treaty of Troyes with Henry 'the Conqueror'. Henry V was recognized as heir to the French throne, and married Charles VI's daughter Catherine. Meantime he was to rule his conquests and share control of Charles with Philip of Burgundy. States General, university, and Paris all submitted.

The dauphin, however, was unconquered. Languedoc and the Duke of Brittany went over to him, and his troops defeated and killed Henry's brother, the Duke of Clarence, at Beaugé (May 1421). Then Henry returned to pursue his methodical

Fig. 219. Charles VII of France

conquest. He was as irresistible as ever, till he died of camp fever on 31 August 1422, leaving an infant son, Henry VI. The regency of France was assumed by his very able brother, the Duke of Bedford, who, when the unhappy Charles VI died on 21 October 1422, proclaimed his nephew king. The dauphin meanwhile reigned as Charles VII at Bourges. North of the Loire the country was under the strict, wise, and hated rule of Bedford; south of it, except for English Aquitaine, France was under the negligent, but popular government of Charles. In each case the inhabitants were miserable. Armed bands fought and plundered everywhere, earning their name of *écorcheurs* and turning the open country almost into desert, while the walled towns were a prey to overcrowding, famine, and disease.

(2) THE REVIVAL OF THE FRENCH MONARCHY AND THE END
OF THE HUNDRED YEARS' WAR

It was only slowly, and almost imperceptibly, that the tide began to turn in the French favour. Bedford's generalship, which disposed of a veteran army, and his diplomacy, which kept up the alliance with the Duke of Burgundy, and won over Brittany and the Pyrenean Count of Foix, gave him superiority at first. On 17 August 1424 he won the battle of Verneuil, the last of the great English victories. Charles VII was a drag on his own cause. With no taste for soldiering, slow to come to maturity, and morally paralysed by doubts of his own legitimacy, he remained inert, surrounded by low adventurers, and in dire straits for money. In 1425 there was a gleam of hope. Philip of Burgundy withdrew into neutrality, offended by the foolish attempt of Bedford's brother, the Duke of Gloucester, to obtain the county of Hainault in the Netherlands by marriage with its countess. Brittany and Foix changed sides again, and, what was more, the Duke of Brittany's martial brother, the Count of Richemont, took charge as Constable of Charles and his warfare for a while. The revival did not last, for Charles fell under the influence of the unworthy La Trémoïlle, while Bedford patched up the alliance with Burgundy, and in 1427 gathered force for a new offensive.

The campaign in 1428 was directed to the capture of Orleans, the key of the line of the Loire. But, though strategically sound, the action offended the chivalric code of the day, which forbade an attack on a prisoner's (as was the Duke of Orleans) lands, and it roused the French to a wrathful activity, in which an instinctive sense of the city's importance bore a part. The besieged citizens, captained by Dunois, bastard brother of the duke, held out with heroic tenacity, while the besiegers, making vain assaults, suffered in their turn from short rations. The convoy bringing them supplies, however, defeated a French attack in 'the battle of the herrings' (February 1429), and it seemed as if Orleans would be starved out, when a deliverer appeared on the scene.

St Joan of Arc (Jeanne d'Arc) was a peasant's daughter of Domrémy on the utmost verge of France towards Lorraine. After a blameless, pious childhood, her grief at the woes of France became linked with heavenly visions, in which the Archangel Michael, St Margaret, and St Catherine spoke to her and commanded her to rescue Orleans. It was with great difficulty that she obtained from the local dauphinois captain an escort to Chinon to impress her mission on Charles VII. There in a private interview she declared to him that he was the son of Charles VI and true heir to France, freeing him from his paralysing doubts. She even won over an ecclesiastical commission, which examined her. Her intuitions, indeed, were allied with an honest shrewdness and good sense, and all together

their dubious charters. Meanwhile the revolts in East Anglia were more violent and murderous still under Litster, 'the king of the commons'. The local gentry seemed helpless, but Despenser, Bishop of Norwich, who had a small force, showed fight, and quelled the rebels in a pitched battle. Magnates and veteran captains were now rallying, and the government had recovered its nerve, though sporadic disturbances continued. There followed severe, but legal, suppression of the rebels, without the brutality of the French Jacquerie. Few results came of the outbreak. The status of the peasants was not altered by the annulled charters. It does not even seem that the decease of the manorial system was hastened. There was a slow, long, and halting change towards money-rents and the disappearance of serfdom in progress at the time, which over half-a-century later was making villeinage a mere survival, and its successor, copyholding, a free tenure. The revolt may have caused a set-back for some years from the anger of the landowners.

For the next few years feeble divided government continued. Rival magnates, rival London factions combined with inefficient but obstinate warfare to produce discontent. But a new court party was growing up around the king, whose happy marriage to Anne of Bohemia (1382) made the leading-strings of the minority less effective. Richard II's personality and opinions became of importance. His worst handicap was his own neurotic temperament. At times he was less capable of self-control even than the tempestuous men of his day, with whom by an added misfortune he was fundamentally out of touch. Cultured, refined, with a keen feeling for art and literature, though a hunter he was no warrior and was wanting in the rough, fighting 'chivalry' of the time. He could inspire strong affection in a few intimates but not the respect and admiration of his people. Although not devoid of foolish, showy ambitions, there was an unpopular wisdom in his wider views of policy: he was for peace with France, he saw the importance of the neglected Irish problem and even of a balanced budget, he was no persecutor in religion, he saw, like others who were not magnates, the evils in government and justice of Livery and Maintenance. But he was not an industrious ruler. His remedy for the weakness of the Crown was a doctrinaire assertion of his indefeasible 'regality', doctrines of absolute monarchy derived from Roman Law and much in vogue in the circles of Charles V of France but alien in England. He attempted to cow or disregard an unresponsive public opinion, not to lead it. Tenacious in his general policy, he was subject to incalculable moods. Perhaps the anxieties of ruling affected the balance of his mind, for he was at his best after his seclusion from state affairs.

In contrast to Richard II stood two of his uncles, John of Gaunt, Duke of Lancaster, and Thomas, in 1385 created Duke of Gloucester. Both were typical magnates of their time, active, warlike, and ambitious.

989

Gaunt, although of average ability, showed good sense and moderation, and his vast estates rendered him the most powerful subject in the land. Conventionally orthodox, he was sympathetic towards Wyclif's teaching until the denial of Transubstantiation alienated him. In spite of a violent quarrel with the young king and his intimates, he was a steadying influence until he left England in 1386 on his private expedition to conquer Castile, which he claimed in right of his second wife, the heiress of Peter the Cruel. Thomas of Gloucester, on the other hand, was a stormy petrel, who placed himself at the head of the magnates averse to Richard and his ways and determined to keep him in tutelage.

Richard's new court party was a combination of tried and competent officials, like Michael de la Pole, Earl of Suffolk, his Chancellor, and personal intimates, like De Vere, Earl of Oxford, a young man of little capacity, whom he created Duke of Ireland. Their hold on the country was small, and when the storm burst in Parliament in October 1386, Richard found himself helpless. He was compelled to dismiss his ministers and to accept a Commission to control the government and his household for a year. He spent the time in endeavouring to enroll troops and in obtaining an opinion from five judges in favour of his prerogative and against the late proceedings. But Gloucester, and the Earls of Arundel and Warwick, Henry Earl of Derby, Gaunt's son and heir, and Mowbray, Earl of Nottingham, were before him with their 'retinues'. They forced him to summon the 'Merciless Parliament' to adjudge their 'appeal of treason' against Vere, Suffolk and others of his friends. Suffolk fled, and Vere's armed attempt at rescue was out-generalled and shattered at Radcot Bridge (December 1387). Richard himself barely escaped deposition, while Parliament, or rather the peers, condemned the exiled Vere and Suffolk to death and actually executed those leading royalists they could lay hands on. The five appellants secured a grant for their services. Yet they gained small credit by their tenure of power. Derby and Nottingham cooled towards Gloucester and the other two earls. It was known that Gaunt had made a treaty as to Castile and was likely to return. So by a sudden stroke Richard in May 1389 resumed the government with no opposition. He appointed veteran officials as his ministers, and started on a new career in harmony with his Parliaments and not at open feud with magnates.

The fact that the king's ministers were generally acceptable, and the influence of John of Gaunt, now firm friends with his nephew and at no time inclined to diminish the royal authority as such, together produced a period of quiet and not unwise government. The cessation of the war with France, achieved by a succession of truces, won acquiescence in view of its manifest advantages. Gloucester and Arundel, if thorns in Richard's side, were kept in check by Gaunt, while Derby sought adventure abroad and Nottingham was active in the royal service. Acts of Provisors (1390)

Fig. 224. Richard II

991

and Praemunire (1393) strengthened the royal hands in the customary bargaining with the Pope. More obnoxious to the churchmen was the growth of the dead Wyclif's followers, the Lollards, who formed a kind of sect, and found (1395) champions in the Commons. The government showed no zeal in their suppression. Richard was more interested in legislating against the pernicious Livery and Maintenance, and in asserting his prerogative, but he was putting his trust in granting his own livery to his tenants and his Cheshire archers, while he was forming a new court party among young magnates, like his half-brothers, the Hollands. The Londoners, against whom both he and Gaunt had grievances, were sharply punished for a riot.

Richard, however, for all his judicious moderation remained the same man, liable to unbalanced emotions and schemes and quite unable to rouse a genuine popularity among his subjects. The death of Queen Anne of Bohemia (1394) gave him a shock, from which perhaps he never fully recovered, and his wish for absolute monarchy was mingled with resentment against and fear of those magnates who had threatened him and executed his friends in 1388. The superficial success of his first Irish expedition did not impress English opinion, and his wise policy of a French alliance under colour of a perennial truce (to avoid unpopular surrender of English claims) did so still less. In 1396 he married the seven-year-old Isabella, daughter of the French king, and stipulated for French aid in case there were rebellion in England. The impossibility of the birth of a son for years may have been in harmony with his apprehensions, for there would be a dispute over the succession if his deposition were mooted again—the lines of Lancaster, March, and Gloucester might not agree. But Gloucester, Arundel, and Warwick were dangerously voicing the stubborn war-policy, with the unpopular redemption by the French of the Breton seaport of Brest to criticize, and Richard, unduly (as usual) elate at his own diplomacy and Gaunt's loyal support, and with his old rancours not unnaturally reviving, determined in an evil hour to get rid of them at the peak of his fortunes.

Parliament in 1397 was unusually submissive. The Commons apologized for criticizing the expense of his household, although a hare-brained scheme (yet it might remove unquiet magnates) for a Franco-English expedition to Italy was rejected. In July the decisive stroke was made. Gloucester, Arundel, and Warwick were arrested, and eight peers, among them Nottingham, 'appealed' them of treason. Arundel was beheaded, Warwick banished, and Gloucester—there is small doubt—murdered under Nottingham's charge. Arundel's brother, Archbishop of Canterbury and but lately Chancellor, was exiled, while Nottingham and Derby were made Dukes of Norfolk and Hereford for complicity and acquiescence. To cow opposition in Parliament the king had brought his archers to Westminster.

In January 1398 Richard continued to weave up his folly in the Parliament at Shrewsbury. The acts of the Merciless Parliament were repealed. It was declared treason to attempt to revoke the Shrewsbury Parliament's acts. In fact absolutism was needlessly unveiled. A new dissension was referred to a parliamentary committee. This was due to the two remaining Lords Appellant of 1388, Norfolk and Hereford, falling out owing to their mutual fears of the king's vengeance. The trial by combat was stopped by Richard, who condemned both to exile, Hereford for 10 years, Norfolk for life, and Norfolk to confiscation. Both obeyed, and Richard felt himself secure, if only the Lancastrian line did not turn against him. With singular blindness the now erratic king irritated the gentry, clergy, and merchants by small loans under pressure and arbitrary acts, even by extorting blank charters, which alarmed them for the future. He took no heed of the weakening of his position when in July 1398 the only possible rival to the Lancastrians for the succession to the throne became the new Earl of March, a child of six, and when in February 1399 his loyal uncle, John of Gaunt, died, he committed the crowning folly of confiscating the vast Lancaster estates, which were Hereford's admitted inheritance. No doubt he hoped to destroy the power of his popular cousin, but he gave the widespread discontents a capable and congenial leader, and alarmed every landowner in England at the same time. Oblivious of the risks he ran, he sailed to Ireland in May, leaving his uncle, the Duke of York, almost a nonentity, in charge at home.

Hereford took his opportunity. In July he landed in Yorkshire, declaring he came for his inheritance, and received a warm welcome. With his native generalship, he cut off York at Bristol, which he captured, beheading among others Bushy, Richard's expert in managing the Commons. Richard reached Wales on his return to find his forces dissolving. No soldier, he was induced by lying promises to surrender to his cousin at Conway. He was taken as a prisoner to the Tower, forced to call a Parliament and to abdicate (29–30 September 1399). A long indictment was drawn up against him, and Henry of Lancaster then claimed the throne by a mixture of fictitious genealogy, conquest, and election. He called a new Parliament which was merely the old resummoned.

Richard II had fallen by his own growing incapacity. Henry IV was in many ways well fitted to carry on the struggle to maintain the power of the Crown against the overmighty barons, who had raised him to the throne. He was no theorizing doctrinaire, but a popular fighting man, tenacious, unflagging in business, practical, and forceful. He was strengthened by the great Lancaster estates, but his disregard of his promises of better government, his extravagance, and his resolve to be a free king soon disillusioned his early supporters. Yet he fought down dangerous rebellions one by one, and resisted from the beginning attempts to impose on him a baronial council. The first revolt occurred in the days of his early popularity. Richard's friends, the Appellants of 1397, rose in January 1400 and were easily quelled and slaughtered. They sealed their patron's fate, for Richard was at once done to death in his prison at Pontefract.

There was war abroad as well as disaffection at home. France was temporarily appeased by the surrender of Richard's widow, Isabella (1401). The Scots, after a vain English invasion, were defeated by Henry's allies, the Percies of Northumberland, at Homildon Hill (1402), and were later kept in check by the capture of the boy James, the heir to their throne (1406). As variegated, but more lasting, was the insurrection in Wales, which began in 1400. Its leader was a distinguished and aggrieved landowner, of princely descent, Owain Glyn Dŵr (Glendower). Expeditions by the king and nobles, an alternation of successes and reverses, went on for years amid the mountains. Glyn Dŵr roused a nationalistic spirit of resistance. He took prisoner Edmund Mortimer, the uncle of the captive young Earl of March, and formed an alliance with him. In 1404 he assumed the title of Prince of Wales and set up a real government. The contemporary revolts in England favoured him, French help came, and he seemed within an ace of success. But Henry IV was mastering English rebels, and the French proved a broken reed. When in 1408 the king's heir, Prince Henry, took charge of the war, Glyn Dŵr's fortresses fell, and he was reduced to a hunted guerrilla chief. In 1416 he died, still at large. He had relit a national flame that lasted.

The Welsh rebellion had been fostered, and discontents multiplied, by Henry IV's irresponsible encouragement of piracy—he never quite outgrew the attitude of a turbulent magnate—which brought on a kind of anarchy in the Channel and French ravage of the English coast. Not until 1407–8 were treaties arranged with Flanders, Brittany, and the Hanseatic League. They did, indeed, secure the recognition of his kingship abroad, his main object in the strife.

Meantime the unruliness of the overmighty nobles, which Henry's usurpation had encouraged, was bearing its unwelcome fruits. The border house of the Percies of Northumberland were discontented at their little share in the government—perhaps they had not meant to exalt Henry so high—and began to think of playing the king-makers again for the Earl of March. Luckily for Henry they were at bitter feud with their neighbour borderers and king-makers, the Nevilles of Westmorland. This was Henry's salvation in his troubles, combined with his own prompt fighting spirit. In 1403 the Earl of Northumberland, his brother Thomas, Earl of Worcester, and his warrior son Henry Hotspur broke into revolt in the dead Richard's name. Hotspur and Worcester raised the men of Cheshire and the Welsh Marches, but were met and routed by the king and Prince Henry at Shrewsbury (21 July). Hotspur was killed and Worcester executed.

Northumberland, held in check by the Nevilles, surrendered and was acquitted of treason by the significantly friendly peers. He did not therefore give over his designs. In February 1405 he made an extraordinary agreement with Glyn Dŵr and Edmund Mortimer to divide the kingdom with them. The Earl of Nottingham and the saintly Archbishop Scrope of York were drawn in, the latter perhaps really indignant at the faults of Henry's government. What with promptitude and treachery (by the useful Westmorland) the king made quick work of the revolt. Nottingham and the archbishop were taken and beheaded in haste, Northumberland driven to Scotland, whence he emerged in 1408 to be killed in his defeat by the sheriff of Yorkshire. With him was crushed for a while the spirit of revolt. Henry IV's dogged energy had secured his dynasty at any rate, and is the more remarkable because the war with Wales had continually hampered him. Even the sacrilege of Archbishop Scrope's death did not loosen his hold on his subjects.

The abandonment of armed rebellion, however, strengthened the hands of his critics in Parliament. From the start, his prodigal expenditure and indifference to justice had aroused discontent, but it had been left to the Commons to endeavour to find remedies. In spite of contrary custom and their own diffidence of responsibility they were driven to invade the royal prerogative. Their weapon was the command over supply, for Henry, involved in necessary and unnecessary expense, could not 'live of his own'. They endeavoured to fix responsibility on the King's Council. In 1404 they appointed four special treasurers of their grant to prevent squandering. Although the king exercised pressure on elections, which retarded developments, the 'long' Parliament of 1406 engaged in a stubborn contest with him, while a party in his Council, led by his loyal but independent, legitimized half-brothers, were opposed to his methods. Although Henry at last got the grant of money, he submitted to parliamentary audit and to the provision that expenditure should be approved by the Council, which was to take an oath to observe directive articles.

It was a humiliating pact which Henry had no intention of observing. The clouds were lightening and he secured a potent ally. Thomas Arundel, the Archbishop of Canterbury, shared the somewhat sordid ambitions of his time. A partisan of the Appellants of 1386, he was later Richard's Chancellor and then Archbishop until the execution of his brother and his own exile in 1397 changed his views. Restored in 1399, he took part in Richard's deposition, and obtained what he and the prelates most desired, the Act of 1401, *De haeretico comburendo*, which engaged the civil power to burn condemned heretics. It was aimed at the Lollards who preached Church disendowment, but he feared as well those orthodox laymen who also wished to solve the financial problem by stripping the Church of its possessions. He was for some years in sympathy with magnate control until

Fig. 225. Thomas Occleve dedicating his De Regimine Principum
to the Prince of Wales, 1411–12

in January 1407 he became Chancellor once more. Immediately afterwards the legitimation of the Beauforts, granted by Richard in 1397 as a sop to their father John of Gaunt, was declared not to give them a place in the succession to the crown. For a time the king had his way with Parliament, but his health, which began to fail in 1405, now often incapacitated him, and his undutiful heir, Prince Henry, fresh from the conquest of Wales and eager to mount the throne, put himself at the head of the opposition in 1409. Arundel was forced to resign the Great Seal, and a council, in which the prince's friends predominated, took charge of the government. Prince Henry, however, found no general support in his demand for his father's abdication, while the archbishop quelled the Wyclifite party in Oxford University. At the Parliament of November 1411 the Council was dismissed and he was restored to power. The next year was disturbed by the attempts of the prince to put armed pressure on the king, one bone of contention being the conduct of war with France. They ended in reconciliation just before Henry IV's death on 20 March 1413. The archbishop was dismissed next day.

Henry IV had kept his crown and baffled his frequent and unavoidable Parliaments by his fighting qualities. Henry V was resolved to do the same, this time by leading the magnates to foreign conquest. The victim was to be France, to whose throne, like his father, he advanced a casuistical claim. He possessed immense strength of will, besides a genius for war and government. His subjects were amazed by the sudden change from a lawless, disreputable youth to a self-righteous bigot and disciplinarian, and they long remembered his breach with his old associates. Ambition, attained by war, became his sole passion, with the final aim of reconquering the Holy Land. To this all the energies of a powerful brain were devoted. He was aware of the inner vigour of his people, prospering in trade for all the disorders and acutely self-conscious, and he directed this nationalism to a long-drawn war of conquest which became hopeless when he died. Like his father, too, he was reckless in finance. He vastly enlarged the debt he inherited, while pressing for parliamentary grants and extorting loans. To the evils of Livery and Maintenance he seems to have been indifferent, for they gave him his armies. The glamour of his autocratic personality and of his victories secured obedience, although the Commons and even the soldiers at the close of his reign grew restive at the endless war.

The beginning of the reign quelled discontents. Active persecution produced a Lollard attempt at revolt in 1414, but it was quickly put down, and the heretics were mercilessly hunted until the revolutionary sect survived at most in obscure corners. One more magnate plot in favour of the nerveless Earl of March, in which Richard, Earl of Cambridge, his brother-in-law, and Lord Scrope of Masham, ex-Treasurer, were principals, was ended by their execution (1415). Agincourt acted as a prophylactic against further rebellion. Insubordination, as in his uncle Bishop Henry Beaufort, was severely checked.

Henry's administrative preparation for his war was beyond precedent thorough. Not less was his diplomacy to keep the Duke of Burgundy a friendly neutral. With this was linked his determination to command the Channel. For this end he repressed the piracy of the English shipmen, and wooed the favour of the Hansa and the Flemings. The Statute of Truces (1414) was designed to keep the peace of the seas for traders. The defeat of a Genoese squadron (1416) removed the only French naval ally, leaving the Channel uncontested. We have seen how he gained over Sigismund and worked through his bishops at Constance.

In the midst of his triumphs Henry V died on 31 August 1422. The evils he caused lived long after him, for his country and his infant son by Queen Catherine of Valois, Henry VI, to reap. In England the barons joyfully asserted their independence. Humphrey, Duke of Gloucester, the youngest son of Henry IV, who wished to continue to exercise the authority he had enjoyed as his brother's lieutenant, was obliged in spite of his resistance to be content with the title of Protector under the control of a Council elected in Parliament. In truth, the 'good Duke Humphrey' of legend, although a genuine and meritorious patron of the new revival of classic learning, was a rash and incompetent politician. The opposition to him was led by his far more able and equally selfish uncle, Cardinal Henry Beaufort, Bishop of Winchester. Something of a real statesman, Beaufort, the richest man in England, was greedy of wealth and power, a large creditor, often against his will, and a defrauder of the impoverished Crown. His weakness in home politics, however, was his desire to play a great part in papal and European affairs. He wished to serve two masters and fell between two stools. More weighty than either rival was John, Duke of Bedford, the loyal regent for Henry VI in France, who intervened with effect to keep the peace. The result of Livery and Maintenance was seen in the harmony between the peers and the knights of the shire: the Londoners, with whom Gloucester was popular, were more independent. The coronation of Henry VI (November 1429) closed the protectorate, but also the elected Council, and gave the duke more real power, all the more because Beaufort had lost Pope Martin's favour, and was looked at askance for his connexion with the Curia. So Gloucester was able to change the king's ministers (1432) and attack his rival under cover of *Praemunire*. It needed the return of Bedford, in great straits for money and men, to compose matters in 1433 and to reinstate the former Treasurer. But the government was almost bankrupt, and when he died in France on 14 September 1435, and Burgundy changed sides, the English government was faced with the choice of a peace or war policy.

The people were obstinately resolved on war, while grudging the sacrifices involved. Hence the more far-sighted councillors in their tentatives for peace were liable to their resentment. Yet the war was causing not only the insolvency and hand-to-mouth finance of the government but the decline of national prosperity. Meanwhile the Beaufort group of magnates re-captured control from the Duke of Gloucester, and they had the ear of the king. Henry VI grew up a nervous invalid with the seeds of insanity in him. The Valois in his heredity had cancelled the traits of the hard, war-loving Lancastrian stock. He was a pious, disinterested, sweet-natured weakling, remote in manners and morals from the rampant, remorseless egotism of his age. With the aid of Moleyns, who became Privy Seal and Bishop of Chichester, at the king's side and of the household officials under the Steward, the Earl of Suffolk, and supported by a group of peers, Beaufort did away with the control of the Council, reducing it to merely advisory functions. When in 1443 the old cardinal retired from public life, Suffolk stepped into his shoes, keeping the king secluded from all advisers not of his faction. The short-sighted Commons were preoccupied with their hatred of rival, foreign traders and their sympathy with English piracy. In 1435 they secured the suspension of the Statute of Truces and in 1440 its practical repeal, while taxes and disabilities were imposed on the alien merchants. The result was anarchy in the Channel and the loss of foreign markets, while the government gained no popular credit for its extorted submission to clamorous unwisdom.

Ill success in the war, both under the lay chief of the Beauforts, the Duke of Somerset, in 1443 and under the more capable Duke of York, had convinced Suffolk that peace must be sought. He obtained in 1444 a truce for two years and the hand of Margaret of Anjou for the king, but the effect of it was soon overclouded by Henry VI's cession of Maine to his father-in-law. Suffolk was indeed unpopular on his own account because of the greed and local tyrannies of himself and his adherents. The Duke of Gloucester, now heir-presumptive, and the Duke of York, who stood next in the succession if the Beauforts were excluded, were both enemies of him and the court circle. He dealt with Gloucester by impeaching him in February 1447 at a Parliament at Bury St Edmunds, and when the duke died under arrest, the suspicion of murder, even if unfounded, shortly won belief, involving Cardinal Beaufort, who was then dying at his see of Winchester. The Duke of York was appointed King's Lieutenant of Ireland, but delayed two years to go into that exile. These measures did not strengthen a feeble government. Private war among the magnates was spreading. Uncorrupt justice was not to be had in the face of Livery and Maintenance. The king's debts, large in 1433, had nearly trebled. By 1449 the country was ripe for civil war. In that year Normandy was lost, and the chief ministers ratted from the sinking ship, which did not save Moleyns from murder by mutinous seamen. Next year Suffolk was impeached by the Commons,

999

banished by the king's favour, and murdered on the high seas by English shipmen. He suffered for others' sins as well as his own.

This was the signal for outbreaks of disorders. The new Treasurer, Lord Say, had deserved an evil name in Kent, and there in June 1450 a certain Jack Cade, who called himself a Mortimer, led a large and disciplined force on London. Their manifesto summarized reasonably enough the evils of the long misgovernment, and demanded the repeal of the Statute of Labourers to which the gentry clung. They were no mere rabble, but drawn from all classes below the knights. The government showed its usual indecision, London was entered, Lord Say handed over and beheaded, and terms were made by the archbishops. The rebels mostly dispersed, but Cade renewed disorder in Kent, and then was hunted down. There seemed to be a lull in the general turbulence when the Duke of York returned uninvited from Ireland. Thus the stage was set for the Wars of the Roses, the nemesis of the Hundred Years' War, with its accompaniment of armed and over-mighty magnates, reckless finance, and government both weak, factious, and tyrannous, which has been miscalled 'the Lancastrian experiment'.

(4) GERMANY AND THE EMPIRE, *c*. 1378–1439

The dominating factor in strictly German history after the death of Charles IV in 1378 was an almost parochial particularism. There was a King or Emperor of the Romans, the council of the Electors, and frequent Diets, which were slowly assuming a more settled form. There were foreign alliances and wars, Church and international affairs and enterprises in which they took part, and schemes of internal reform, succeeding one another, seldom adopted and always nullified in action. But except the last all these chains of events seem more concerned with other countries than with Germany as a whole, even although German princes were conspicuous actors in them. The contest of German and Slav in the East belongs most suitably to Bohemian and Polish history. In the West, without a formal change, the Netherlands and Switzerland were slipping away from the Empire.

Within these receding frontiers Germany was in a state of chaos, the battle-ground of ambitious feudal lords, great and small, lay and ecclesiastical, of trading, self-governing towns and their leagues, all of them pursuing their individual and local aims, to which their horizon was limited, although the evils they caused and suffered were national. On all sides the laws were not observed and might was right. The nobles and the towns were mutually hostile. All alike cherished and exercised the pernicious right of private war. Not only the Electors since the Golden Bull were virtually autonomous; many lords, towns, and churches had in practice the same independence. The anarchy was imperfectly tempered in parts by the characteristic and revealing institution of the Veme. The local courts of the Veme were survivals of the old 'folkmoots' and now consisted of a 'free count' and his assessors, who might be princes or plain freemen. To have assessors in the Veme was the desire of every community and class, but the free knights, who held their tiny fiefs direct of the Emperor, were the most numerous. The proceedings of these courts were secret and dreaded. Spreading from its native Westphalia, the Veme became a power, but in the fifteenth century it deteriorated, for the knights were venal and inclined to wreak their private feuds, while there was no consistency in the decisions of its numberless courts. It outlived its usefulness.

The German king had small means of remedying anarchy, even when he was not engrossed in his dynastic and provincial schemes. He was elected and liable to deposition. Rights and revenues had been bartered away. His income, if collected, was 13,000 gold florins. The Empire was impossibly wide for administration, and the Papacy, even if his ally, locked its wheels. There was no capital, or compact domain, or bureaucracy. Only the local powers could at long last enforce their will. The imperial dignity had indeed its advantages and prestige: lapsed fiefs could be granted

Fig. 226. Session of the Westphalian Veme court

if not annexed; its service was a magnet to the ambitious; the Emperor could and did act as the head of Christendom; he could benefit his family, if not the Empire. The Reichstag or Diet was a poor instrument of union and order. Though all tenants-in-chief were nominally members, attendance save from the south was lacking. The Imperial Towns, which were really city-states, were mainly there to resist over-taxation, which fell on them, and to defend their liberty. The Electors, who dominated proceedings, were seldom in harmony. In short, the future lay with the stronger princes, who could survive the struggle for existence and consolidate their territorial power.

The defects of King Wenceslas, Charles IV's son, which did him so much damage in his Bohemian kingdom, were even more deleterious to him in Germany, where he seldom appeared in person. The general disorder, indeed, and the effects of the Great Schism might well have baffled a more efficient ruler. Wenceslas and the majority acknowledged the Roman Pope, but they could not carry many of the trans-Rhenane nobles nor the Austrian

Duke Leopold III with them. Meantime the discord between the princes and rural nobility and the towns was growing. Leagues were formed on each side. The Swabian town league entered into alliance with the Swiss against Leopold, now estranged from the king. The duke fell at Sempach (1386) against the Swiss, but a general war between nobles and towns lasted from 1386 to 1389, in which the towns had the worse and obtained an unsatisfactory peace at Eger by means of Wenceslas. The southern towns were hampered by their position as islets in feudal territory, and their oligarchies, which were not composed of indispensable great capitalists like those of the Hansa, were threatened by the petty craftsmen beneath them.

The dissensions in Bohemia and among the Luxemburgs themselves paralysed Wenceslas's further efforts to act as king. His meeting in 1398 with Charles VI of France for the ending of the Schism had no effect, and in 1400 the four Rhenish Electors deposed him for his inefficiency, and chose Rupert of the Palatinate as King of the Romans. This made a secular schism in the Empire, since Wenceslas and his supporters did not accept the decision. Rupert, although an honourable and active prince, did no better than his rival. His attempt to intervene in Italy was an utter failure. He became embroiled with his neighbours, while most of Germany was indifferent, and did not imitate his determined loyalty to the Roman Pope against the Council of Pisa. His death in 1410 produced a tangle of elections over the three Luxemburg candidates, Wenceslas, Jobst of Moravia, and Sigismund of Hungary. Wenceslas gave way to Jobst, who obtained five votes from the conciliar party, including his own for Brandenburg, Sigismund received three from the Gregorian Electors, including his own vote also for Brandenburg. The absurd situation, in which Wenceslas still claimed to be king, was ended by the death of Jobst in January 1411. Sigismund, who adopted a conciliar policy, and recovered Brandenburg without question, was unanimously elected in July. Wenceslas kept his title and a pension.

Sigismund had already had an eventful career, making good his claim to Hungary, intervening in Bohemia, and fighting in the Balkan wars. He was a vivid and versatile character, a stalwart knight, a cultured patron of letters, a linguist and diplomat, dignified, vain, and restlessly active. But his hands were always too full and his purse always too empty. His successes were remarkable and his failures glaring. Since Frederick II no Emperor had been such a leader of Europe.

Sigismund was as much of an absentee as Wenceslas had been. For years he had no territory in the Empire, for he alienated (1411) Brandenburg to his supporter Frederick of Hohenzollern, Burgrave of Nuremberg, who thus acquired an electorate (1417) and began the transference of his house from Franconia to the north-east. Yet the king did not so much neglect German interests as his brother had done. In 1411 his action and mediation obtained for the Teutonic Knights the lenient peace of Thorn (Torun) after

*Fig. 227. Investiture of the Hohenzollern Burgrave of Nuremberg
with the Electorate of Brandenburg*

their ruinous overthrow by the Poles and Lithuanians at Tannenberg (Grunwald). He failed, however, in his attempt to keep Friuli for the Empire and Dalmatia for Hungary in his war with Venice (1409–13). He was at his best in dealing with the Great Schism. Such success as the Council of Constance attained was largely due to him. The Holy Roman Empire and its head appeared once more as the effective centre of Christendom. Incidentally, his subjugation (1415) of the recalcitrant Habsburg, Frederick IV of Austria-Tyrol, manifested the union of the German princes under their king. Yet it was the Swiss who gained permanent profit for their loyal participation in the war at the imperial summons. When Frederick was forgiven (1418), they insisted on retaining Aargau. Since in a former war with Frederick IV (1403) they had extended their alliances eastward to the upper Rhine, the house of Habsburg was now practically expelled from Switzerland.

Sigismund was again able to mobilize many princes and the Diet in his support in the Hussite crusades. There was a national hatred between Germans and Slav Czechs, as yet the Germans were orthodox, and Austria, Bavaria, Franconia, and Meissen were Bohemia's neighbours and involved. Frederick of Brandenburg, although estranged from the king owing to his own Polish ambitions, soon joined in. Sigismund himself, whose absenteeism nearly caused his deposition from the Empire, possessed a strong party in Bohemia and Moravia and ruled the annexes of Silesia and Lusatia. But the Hussite crusades, though repeated again and again, were, as we have seen, disgraceful fiascos, which brought about the Hussites' invasions of their enemies' lands all round. It was Sigismund's diplomacy, the conciliation of the Council of Basle, and above all the victory of the Bohemian Catholics and moderate Hussites over the Taborites at Lipany (1434), not the efforts of the German Diets and princes, which closed the horrors of the war and gave Sigismund the uncontested crown of Bohemia.

Meantime Electors and Diets were engaged in projects of reforming the Empire, which all parties declared for and balked by their own behaviour. Sigismund discussed reform as much as any, and perhaps more wisely, but his preoccupations in his kingdom of Hungary and the East, which were a main cause of his absenteeism, and his regard for his imperial prerogatives, made him one more hindrance to agreement. In 1423, to fortify himself against the ambitions of Frederick of Brandenburg, he conferred the vacant electorate of Saxe-Wittenberg on Frederick the Quarrelsome, Margrave of Meissen, thus by chance causing the transference of the name of Saxony to Meissen, the most considerable part of the new Elector's dominions. It did not help him much, although a kind of regency established by the Electors (1424) broke up, and talk of his deposition as an absentee died away. After his coronation as Emperor at Rome in 1433 he mooted again a scheme of reform which he had vainly proposed in 1415–17. South and central Germany should be divided into four circles, each under an imperial governor (*Hauptmann*), with a view to enforcing the public peace. Its terms and how to give peace, justice, a sound currency, and defence were discussed without result at two Diets. The schism between the Papacy and the Council of Basle complicated matters as well. On 9 December 1437 the Emperor died in Moravia, and he was buried in Hungary. There on the eastern frontier of Europe, where his real power lay, was his spiritual home. He was the last male Luxemburg.

On Sigismund's death the Electors realized that the thankless task of leading the dissolving Empire could only be entrusted to a prince of wide territories and able to defend the eastern frontier. The centre of gravity had shifted by force of territorial concentration and what may be called the Eastern Question to the south-east. Fortunately, Sigismund's son-in-law and heir of Bohemia and Hungary, Albert V, the senior Habsburg duke and ruler of Austria proper, was ready to their choice as Albert II of the Empire (1438). Henceforward for centuries the senior Habsburg was always to be elected. Albert II was personally well fitted for the dignity, being honest, sturdy, and blameless, and a thorough German, knowing no other tongue. He repelled Polish invasions of Bohemia and Silesia, but no more than Sigismund induced his German Diets to agree on a scheme of reforms. Nor was any real progress made in ecclesiastical policy. In October 1439 he died of dysentery incurred in the Turkish war, and with him died the best hope of united action. His threefold dominion, Austria, Bohemia, and Hungary, broke up.

While Electors, princes, nobles of all degrees, and towns were engaged in strife for their local interests and ambitions, and the Hansa League was struggling for its sea-supremacy with Scandinavia, the Netherlands, English and Baltic pirates, and even Spain, and the southern towns were further undergoing an internal evolution towards a wider oligarchy in which the craft-gilds shared power with the patriciate, there was also in process a steady deterioration of the condition of the German peasantry, which began in the fourteenth century. Many causes contributed to this evolution. The subdivision of peasant holdings and the emergence of a landless rural proletariat were two. The decay over Europe of the old dual manorial economy of the lord's demesne and peasant holdings, which provided servile labour, was being replaced by paid labour and rented peasant holdings, an advantage for the capable well-to-do villager, but not necessarily for the less prosperous and landless. The Black Death and its sequels strained this situation. The bitter struggle over wages, which in France and England hastened the disappearance of serfdom, produced in feudal, decentralized Germany, where the knightly class was supreme, a manorial reaction and a recrudescence of serfdom. Feudal jurisdiction there did not fade but increased by the continual devolution of public and royal functions to the lords, whether as *Vögte* or otherwise. Add to this the evolution, principally east of the Elbe, of a new kind of great estate, organized for the outer market and worked by landless serfs. Even in central Germany jurisdictional rights were growing into landownership to the enlargement of the lord's original property. In Brandenburg, Pomerania, Prussia, Silesia, and Poland, the combination of jurisdiction and direct ownership, fostered by conquest of the natives, was pressing even the German settlers, once the freest peasants in Europe, into helpless, personal, landless serfdom. In these lands of corn-exporting great estates the degradation of the peasantry was the most general and ominous, but the same tendency was pronounced enough elsewhere with its revival and increase of servile burdens and its doctrine that settlement on a lord's land led to personal serfdom. As in other countries there were peasant revolts, so the slow-gathering resentment of the German villagers at their growing bondage showed itself in risings in the fifteenth century, the prelude to others after the Middle Ages. Their success in Germany was small indeed. But as in England earlier they had an effect on thought and literature. Democratic equality was mingled with criticism of the wealthy, landowning, and grasping hierarchy of the Church. The labouring peasant, in England Piers Plowman, became for a while the type of Christian holiness, not the priest.

CHAPTER 34

EASTERN AND NORTHERN EUROPE IN THE FIFTEENTH CENTURY

(I) THE TRIUMPH OF THE OTTOMAN EMPIRE

Beyazit I Yilderim ('the lightning'), a brilliant soldier but despicable for his debauchery, cruelty, and arrogance, reaped in his early reign the harvest of his father Murat's statesmanship. It was he who in two campaigns (1390, 1392–3) first united all the rival states of Asia Minor under the Osmanlis by subduing the lesser Turkish dynasties. In Europe he annexed Bulgaria with his usual ferocity, suppressing the Bulgarian patriarchate (1393), and invaded Wallachia, defeating its Vlach prince, Mircea (1394). Sigismund of Hungary now stood forth as the Christian champion. He restored Mircea, and assembled a crusading army from the West, in which French and Burgundian knights under John the Fearless, the heir of Burgundy, were prominent. They plundered the Serbian vassals of the sultan on their way to Nicopolis on the Danube. There, on 25 September 1396, they suffered an annihilating defeat from Beyazit, for which the headlong rashness of the French knights, the desertion of Mircea, and the skilful tactics of the sultan, who ambushed from the flanks their victorious charge, were responsible. The vassal prince of Serbia, Stephen Lazarevich, dealt the decisive blow. Sigismund escaped with much peril, John with the greatest barons was held captive to ransom, and most of the crusaders were massacred.

The end of the Byzantine Empire, reduced to Constantinople, seemed now impending. The French knight Boucicaut, with a fleet and troops from the West, took charge of a sturdy defence, and the Emperor Manuel II went off to Europe (1399–1402) to beg for assistance, after admitting his rival and nephew John VII as co-Emperor. The aid he was given was insufficient. Meantime Beyazit besieged Constantinople, threatening extermination if the city was not surrendered (1402). But the Empire was saved by another Asiatic conqueror.

Tamerlane (Timur Leng, 'the lame') was a Mongol or Turk of Transoxiana, the khanate of Jagatai, which was rapidly disintegrating. From vizier of the Jagatai Khan he forced himself to supremacy over the Turkish tribes (1369) and renewed the spirit of conquest. Unlike the Mongol Khans he was a fervent Moslem, and his rule meant the breaking of the commercial route from Europe to China and the extirpation of the missionary Christian Church in his widening dominions. He was above all a conqueror in the destructive Mongol-Turkish fashion, and his empire was loosely held together by his victories and the terror his incessant wars inspired. From 1380 to 1400 he was mainly occupied in the conquest of Nearer Asia, taking Baghdad in 1401 and Damascus from the Mamlūks in the same year. But he found time to subjugate his revolted protégé, Tuqtamish, whom he had placed over the Golden Horde of Kipchak, defeating, as we shall see, Vitovt of Lithuania in the war, and he had made his terrible and famous raid into India (1398). His first aggression against Beyazit was marked by the capture of Sivas. In 1402 this was followed by invasion in full force. Beyazit mustered all his powers, but was outgeneralled and outnumbered in the battle of Ankara (20 July 1402). The Osmanli Sultan was defeated and died in captivity, and Tamerlane's army reached the Aegean Sea. The conquered Turkish princes of Asia Minor were restored to their thrones, while Beyazit's sons fought over the remains, mostly European, of their empire. They had the opportunity to do so, for Tamerlane, a superb general, was devoid of constructive statesmanship, and died while preparing a Chinese campaign in 1405. The dominions he had devastated rather than ruled broke to pieces.

The fratricidal contest of Beyazit's three sons lasted for years. At first Suleyman dominated the European lands. He was ousted in 1409 by his brother Musa from Asia Minor. Musa renewed the attack on Manuel II, who had been Suleyman's ally and had received cessions from him. The third brother, Mahomet I, now joined in the fray from Asia Minor and overthrew Musa (1413). He spent his reign in consolidating his possessions, earning the title of 'the Gentleman' as the best and the most peaceful of the Ottoman sultans. For a few years Manuel II, his ally in turn, enjoyed a respite. The case of the Serbs and Wallachians was less creditable. The Despot Stephen, his rivals (his brother Vuk and his nephew George Brancovich) and Mircea of Wallachia helped and betrayed equally the Turkish combatants. Union against the Moslem was not in their calculations. Bosnia, too, was rent by rival chieftains with the addition of Sigismund of Hungary, whose ambitions were at least warranted by a kind of Christian patriotism. The general result was Turkish invasions and revival, while, as we have seen, Dalmatia accepted the safer rule of Venice.

By the time Mahomet I died (1421) the favourable moment had passed. His son Murat II (1421–51) resumed the policy of expansion. Owing to the migrations from the East during Tamerlane's expeditions the numbers of the Turks in Asia Minor and especially in Europe had greatly increased and made him more formidable. At the same time the Janissaries, recruited from the tribute of Christian boys, drained the Christians of their best blood and formed a standing army of the first quality: they were archers of terrible efficiency. By 1428 all but two of the independent Turkish emirates of Asia Minor had been reannexed. Only two strong powers fought Murat II. Venice, victorious at sea (1416–19) against his

Fig. 228. John VIII Palaeologus

father, could not counter him on land, and, preoccupied in Italy, came to a trader's peace. Salonika, which the republic had held since 1423, was taken by Murat and ceded in the treaty of 1430. The other power was Hungary, which acquired Belgrade from George Brancovich, now Despot of Danubian Serbia. The latter, however, lost almost all his territory to the Turks by 1439, but Belgrade was besieged in vain. Meanwhile, another crusade was brewing after Manuel II's son, the Emperor John VIII (1423–48), had perforce accepted the Union of the Churches at the Council of Florence. King Vladyslav of Hungary and Poland was naturally the protagonist, but he was supported by Brancovich and Vlad the Devil, Prince of Wallachia, and received a subvention and a legate, Cardinal Cesarini, from the Pope. At first, the war went well. The Turks were beaten by the warrior John Hunyadi, Brancovich was restored, and the Albanian ex-Janissary, the famous Skanderbeg, raised revolt in his native land. At the same time war with the Turkish Emir of Karamania in Asia Minor distracted the Sultan (1443). Murat bent to sign in July 1444 the treaty of Szegedin, which bound both parties not to cross the Danube. He then withdrew from affairs, while the western crusaders went home. But Cardinal Cesarini was eager to free the Balkans, and unhappily persuaded Vladyslav to break his oath and march forward once more. Murat II returned and encountered the Christians at Varna, where Vladyslav himself and Cesarini fell in their defeat (10 November 1444).

This disaster did not quench the hopes of Hunyadi, now the real ruler of Hungary. He put in a new prince in Wallachia to replace his enemy Vlad, and at the head of the Hungarians and Vlachs tried the fortune of invasion again. Brancovich remained an unfriendly neutral, as he had after the treaty of Szegedin. For three days Hunyadi fought with Murat the second battle of Kossovo (17–19 October 1448). On the third the Vlachs deserted and the Hungarians broke. The wily Brancovich, from whom Hunyadi, become his captive, escaped with difficulty and bad faith, ruled as an endangered Turkish tributary until his death in 1456. In that year, Murat's successor, Mahomet II, fresh from the capture of Constantinople, after shearing off part of Danubian Serbia, had been roundly defeated in his siege of Belgrade by the heroic Hunyadi, whose peasant troops were inspired by the Franciscan preacher, St Giovanni Capistrano. But the fate of Serbia was not long delayed. Dynastic disputes of the usual demoralized character made the annexation of the country easy for Mahomet II (1459). The medieval history of Serbia was closed. Native rulers continued to survive in discord in Bosnia for some years. Besides their conflicting ambitions and local divergencies, the mutual hatred of Bogomils, Catholics, and orthodox wrecked any co-operation. Mahomet II conquered the centre in 1463, while Matthias Corvinus of Hungary annexed the north. The remnants of Herzegovina (the ancient land of Hum) waited till 1483 for the Ottoman conquest. Even then a fragment of the Zeta maintained a harassed independence as Montenegro. Curiously enough, the obstinate Bosnian Bogomils were easily converted to Islam after the Turkish conquest, and thus in contrast to Serbia, where the nobles were extinguished and the Christian peasants remained, Bosnia was left under a native aristocratic caste of Moslems. To sum up, the Yugoslavs, still irremediably at discord among themselves, were at the close of the Middle Ages divided between the Turks, Hungary, which held Croatia, and Venice, which kept Dalmatia as a wisely governed and loyal province.

A parallel history was to be seen in the Vlach (or Rumanian) principalities beyond the Danube. Wallachia suffered most. An attempt at independence under the savage Vlad the Impaler ended in 1462 in the installation of a puppet Turkish vassal. Stephen the Great of Moldavia, who had assisted in Vlad's fall, threw off the Turkish yoke in a glorious victory in 1475, but he only postponed the day of vassalage (1513). These barbarous principalities, which were lamed by internal discord, still, however, kept a measure of autonomy under their vassal princes. In fact, the Yugoslavs, Bulgarians, and Vlachs, who could have repelled the Turks in union, were incapable of co-operating even with their own kinsfolk. They never fully emerged from barbarism for all their valour and natural gifts.

A relapse into barbarism had been the fate of the Albanians (the ancient Illyrians) since the utter decay of the Byzantine Empire. The people, at least after Stephen Dushan's death, were split up into wild rival clans. In the fifteenth century the coast-towns submitted to Venice, while the Turks occupied the interior. George Castriota became a Turkish janissary under the name of Skanderbeg, but in 1443 he took the lead in a revolt of his countrymen, seizing the impregnable fortress of Kroja and reverting to Christianity. The clans rallied to the guerrilla chief. Venice, the Pope, and the King of Naples sent aid. Murat II failed in a siege of Kroja. The more formidable Mahomet II had little better luck and agreed in 1461 to a ten years' truce. When Skanderbeg broke it, he too vainly besieged Kroja. The conquest of Albania was only achieved after Skanderbeg's death in 1468. Venice was driven out ten years later.

Long before, the greatest tragedy of the century, the fall of the Roman Empire, which had preserved ancient civilization, however tarnished, throughout the Middle Ages, had taken place. The conqueror was Mahomet II (1451–81), who, after a premature earlier reign due to his father's weariness of governing, finally ascended the throne at his death. He was the ablest of the Turkish sultans, as grim and merciless as any of them, devoured by ambition and indifferent to pleasure, a lover of learning (a rare trait in his dynasty), and a patron of art, going so far as to have his portrait painted by the Venetian Gentile Bellini. Constantinople was less ready for resistance than ever. The attempt of the hapless John VIII to enforce the Union of the Churches had encountered a bitter resistance. When he died in 1448, his gallant brother Constantine XI, who had ruled successfully as Despot of the Morea, could with difficulty, under papal pressure, proclaim the Union publicly in the face of furious opposition from the people and orthodox clergy (1452). In the Turkish dominions the orthodox bishops represented their flocks to the government, and they preferred the Sultan to the Pope. In return Constantine only received a few Venetian ships and some 900 fighting men commanded by the capable Genoese soldier, Giustiniani. He foolishly hastened the war by demanding a double subsidy for the detention of Orkhan, the only Ottoman prince whom the murderous custom of the house of Osman had left alive. Mahomet had laid his plans with thoroughness and skill, making truces with Hunyadi and the Balkan princelets. He amassed munitions and seized the west shore of the Bosphorus. On 5 April 1453 his army faced the landward wall of Constantinople from the harbour of the Golden Horn to the Sea of Marmora, while his fleet occupied the sea. To defend the wall of Theodosius against Mahomet's 150,000 men, Constantine disposed of only 8000, of whom 3000 were Venetians and Genoese. A chain was drawn across the entrance of the Golden Horn. The real danger was on the landward wall, which was battered by the heaviest cannon yet made. The walls crumbled and were replaced indefatigably by the garrison.

Three Genoese ships fought their way with supplies into the Golden Horn, but this was all the fresh help which the Emperor received, and it was more than nullified by Mahomet's device of bringing his ships on rollers by land and launching them in the harbour. This was to strain the weak garrison still more. They had early repulsed one general assault by land. After midnight on 29 May the second and last began. The protracted resistance of the Christians baffled two attacks until the wound and retreat of the veteran Giustiniani disheartened them just as the Janissaries made the third advance.

Fig. 229. Sultan Mahomet II

The Turks burst in victoriously, and Constantine, worthy to be the last Roman Emperor, died in the fighting.

Massacre and pillage were succeeded by the conversion of Constantinople, now known as Istanbul, into the capital of the Turkish Empire. St Sophia became a mosque with half the churches, while Gennadios, the new Patriarch, a fervid enemy of the Union, was made the civil head of the tribute-paying Christian subjects (*rayahs*) of the Sultan. Most of the subjugation of the Balkans has been already told. The conquest of the squabbling rulers of Greece proper had commenced when in 1423 an invasion had rendered them tributary. Constantine XI, when he was Despot of the Morea, had alone showed a militant patriotism. In 1458–60 Mahomet II dethroned the last miserable rivals. Venice still retained most of her ports on the coast and islands, such as her old possession Crete, and the newly (1489) acquired Cyprus. For years (1462–79) she fought the Ottomans single handed, save for the fiasco of the crusade of Pope Pius II. She lost Negropont (Euboea) in 1470, but kept her trading rights in the peace. Meanwhile, in 1461 Mahomet annexed the cowering vassal Empire of Trebizond, the last fragment of Greek autonomy. By the conquest of

1011

Karamania, the surviving Turkish emirate, he finally unified Asia Minor under the Ottoman sway (1471). Thus in all the lands from the Taurus to the Adriatic, an essentially barbaric state had taken the place of the long-lived East Roman Empire.

(2) HUNGARY, 1382–1490

The death of Lewis the Great in 1382 opened in Hungary a period of dissension from which the monarchy did not recover. His daughter Mary (1382–95) succeeded him with her husband Sigismund of Luxemburg, but her rights were contested by the King of Naples, her cousin Charles of Durazzo.[1] In 1385 he obtained the crown, only to be murdered next year. His son Ladislas of Naples was the next but vain claimant, while Tvertko of Bosnia seized part of Dalmatia. King Sigismund meantime had met with disaster. The advance of the Osmanli Turks to the Danube had become the greatest danger, and he led the last general European Crusade against them, but at Nicopolis suffered, as we have seen, a complete defeat (1396). He returned with difficulty to a shaken throne. The kingdom lost territory in these storms, for the Balkan vassals of Lewis the Great fell under Turkey, and Venice set about reconquering Dalmatia, buying out the claims of Ladislas (1409). Sigismund's wars to prevent her annexation of Friuli from the Patriarch of Aquileia and to check her in Dalmatia were closed in frustration (1409–13, 1418–20). Neither as King of the Romans nor as King of Hungary were his means sufficient, and as King of Bohemia he was engrossed in the Hussite wars.

In fact, the wars of succession had renewed the evils of a century before. New great magnate houses were as anarchic and grasping as the old. The Crown was once more poor and defied: Sigismund was once imprisoned by the rebels, and he sought the alliance of the great house of Cilli in his second marriage to gain the support of his overmighty vassals. Wisely enough, he counter-balanced them by developing the county courts of the lesser nobles and their power in the parliaments. Unfortunately he was not only poor but extravagant, and his wars and ambitious foreign policy involved crushing taxation on the towns, the Jews, and the peasantry. Not less burdensome was his new militia, the *portalis* (1435), necessary for defence against the Turks, which pressed upon nobles and peasants. The rightless peasants, indeed, oppressed without relief by the exactions of king and nobles, were driven into revolt in his last year, but gained no ameliora-tion of their lot.

The victories of Tamerlane had for a while suspended the Turkish conquests in the Balkans, but by the accession of Murat II (1421) the Osmanli empire had been reconstructed. Sigismund met with defeat in

[1] See Genealogical Table 19 above, p. 766.

1428, but he obtained an admirable frontier fortress by the cession of Belgrade on the Danube by the Serbian despot, George Brancovich. His son-in-law and successor, Albert of Austria (1437–39), died in the war, and then the Hungarian parliament, seeking for a strong ally against the overpowering Turk, elected Vladyslav I, the King of Poland, as their monarch.[1] But young Vladyslav and his Vlach-Hungarian general, John Hunyadi, beginning with victories, led their army to ruin in the battle of Varna (1444) on the Black Sea coast, where the king himself fell. Ladislas V, Albert's posthumous son, was then chosen king in the hope of renewing the alliance with Bohemia and Austria (1446). Real power, however, was exercised by Hunyadi while he lived; he had the full support of the lesser nobility, and was the hero of the day. Although he received disastrous defeats at Varna and at the second battle of Kossovo (1448), he repelled the most formidable attack of the Turks under Sultan Mahomet II the Conqueror by his splendid victory at Belgrade (1456). Unluckily he died of plague after his triumph.

Hunyadi represented a political party and programme. Himself half a Vlach, he led the lesser nobles, the gentry, against the overmighty magnates. The sovereignty of Hungary belonged to the Holy Crown of St Stephen, which meant the king and his parliament of nobles, of whom prelates and magnates were but a part. Since the death of Lewis I and his daughter Mary the kingship had become elective in spite of hereditary claims, and was weakened thereby.

On Hunyadi's death Ladislas V broke with his party. In the strife one of Hunyadi's sons was executed, and the other, Matthias, sent prisoner to Prague. Then Ladislas himself died (1457), and after a fervid competition between ambitious magnates and various foreign candidates the election of Matthias, surnamed Corvinus, was carried by the lesser nobles (1458). Although under age, the new king, released from Prague, speedily took over the government. He made short work of the revolt of recalcitrant magnates and of the attack of their candidate, the Emperor Frederick III, who was obliged to surrender the crown of St Stephen (1463). Matthias had many great gifts: he was a warrior, a ruler of inflexible justice who protected the oppressed, the petty nobles and the serfs, a legal reformer who abolished trial by combat and the barbaric custom of atoning for crime by money payments, an administrator who founded a professional bureaucracy and a standing army and remodelled taxation, and a book-lover, who patronized the new learning of the Renaissance. His memory was cherished for centuries.

In his Turkish wars, he kept Belgrade and rendered north Bosnia a Hungarian vassal, besides keeping some sort of superiority over Moldavia if not Wallachia. But these really defensive campaigns were secondary

[1] See Genealogical Table 26 above, p. 922.

with him. He appears to have understood that the Balkan Christians, hopelessly divided by personal ambitions, by religion, by racial and provincial feuds, could not be rescued from the Turk by the weakly based and none too large Hungarian kingdom. He spent his chief energies in the endeavour to conquer his western neighbours and to reconstruct a composite dominion, like that of Sigismund, a prelude to the future realm of the Habsburgs. He took the role of the Catholic champion against the Hussite Poděbrady of Bohemia. In 1468 he conquered Moravia and was crowned King of Bohemia next year. Poděbrady retorted by selecting the Pole Vladyslav as his heir, which brought Poland into the war. Not until 1478 was a peace concluded at Olomouc, by which Matthias kept Moravia, Silesia, and Lusatia and the title of King of Bohemia, while Vladyslav II only reigned in Bohemia proper. At this time Matthias was already at war again with the Habsburg Emperor, Frederick III. In three campaigns (1477–85) he conquered Lower Austria (with Vienna) and Styria, and held them till his death. But election as King of the Romans, for which he had hoped since 1471, eluded him finally when in 1486 Frederick's vigorous son Maximilian obtained the coveted dignity.

Matthias Corvinus, great as he was, had overstrained his kingdom and the loyalty of his subjects. He died in April 1490 without a legitimate heir, and the Hungarian Parliament elected his old rival, Vladyslav II of Bohemia, as king. In a way the policy of a composite realm was thus realized, although Austria was lost to Maximilian. But Vladyslav was weak; without excessive taxation the Hungarian monarchy was poor; magnates and nobles were glad to lack the restraint of the central power in their own feuds and devices; and the ill-used peasants were ripening for rebellion. In the collapse of the kingship the way was prepared for the Turkish conquest.

(3) POLAND AND THE TEUTONIC ORDER, 1384–1492

The personal union of Poland and Lithuania by the marriage of Jadwiga (*ob.* 1398) and Jagiello, who became as a Christian Vladyslav II (1386–1434) of Poland, was a bold as well as a brilliant move. That it lasted and became organic was largely due to the singular statesmanship of the long-lived king. Externally for years he faced the determined hostility of his brother-in-law, the Luxemburg Sigismund, who obtained Hungary and who feared the rise of a great Slav power endangering him both in Hungary and Bohemia. Internally he was met by difficulties, both racial, religious, and dynastic. The Lithuanians proper accepted the Catholicism he decreed, but the wilder Samogitians remained heathen, and the Russians, who inhabited the bulk of the principality, were firmly Orthodox. They found a leader in his cousin, the warrior Vitold (Vitautas, Vitovt), who seized the government of Lithuania and aimed at conquering an eastern realm, in which Russia and the Tartars should be subject to him. Ceding much-contested Samogitia to the Teutonic Order, he made much progress in his ambition of conquering Russia, reaching the boundaries of Muscovy. But in 1399 he was disillusioned when in support of the exiled Khan of the Golden Horde, Tuqtamish, he and his great host were overthrown on the river Vorskla by Tamerlane's general Edegey. He saw his failure and turned to co-operate with the patient Jagiello. At Vilna in 1401 it was agreed that Vitold as Grand Prince for life should be the vassal of Poland, and that the Poles should not elect a new king without Lithuanian consent.

The first-fruits of the agreement were seen in the recovery of Samogitia (1404). Meanwhile, the Teutonic Order, although widening its lands in 1402 by the purchase of a province of Brandenburg, was already afflicted by decline. The conversion of the Lithuanians had deprived it of its crusading spirit and of recruits. It had become merely a German outpost, ruled by an oligarchy of knights, none too strict in life and none too popular with their lay vassals. Spurred on by the Luxemburgs, Wenceslas and Sigismund, the Grand Master went to war in 1409. With foresight and speed Jagiello and Vitold gathered all their strength from their motley dominions, with a body of Czech mercenaries as well. The encounter of the two great armies took place on 15 July 1410 at Tannenberg (Grunwald) in Prussia, and ended in the disastrous rout of the Knights. The Grand Master Ulrich von Jungingen was among the slain. It was only King Sigismund's action which extorted an easy peace in 1411, and this was supplemented next year by the treaty of Buda, by which Sigismund renounced Ruthenia, and ceded a Hungarian district besides. A renewal of a ravaging war by the Order from 1414 to 1422 made no considerable change.

The victors, meanwhile, drew nearer together. The Samogitians were really converted to Catholicism. In 1413 the Union of Horodlo produced some uniformity. Lithuania was organized on the Polish model, and the Catholic nobles of the Principality received the privileges of the Polish *Szlachta*; only the more numerous Orthodox were left in the cold.

The Hussite revolution, however, caused a new divergence between Jagiello and Vitold. Both were inclined to tolerance when Hussite doctrines spread into Poland, and both were eager to reconcile their Orthodox subjects to the Western Church. But the Polish hierarchy, led by Olesnicki, later Bishop of Cracow, were violently opposed to the Hussites, and Jagiello was keenly alive to the dangers of estranging the Papacy and the West by aiding the Czechs. Vitold secured the despatch of a cousin, Zygmunt Korybut, to aid the Hussites, but he proved incompetent, and Jagiello concluded peace with King Sigismund (1423) and began to persecute the Polish heretics. Thereupon Vitold turned his thoughts again towards independence. In 1429 he held a glittering congress at Lutsk, which Sigismund attended, nominally for a Turkish crusade, but really to obtain the title of king. Olesnicki contrived to frustrate the attempt, and Vitold's death in 1430 ended it. Jagiello now had to deal with revolt in Lithuania and a fresh war with the Teutonic Order (1431–5). He won in both conflicts. Vitold's brother Zygmunt was made Grand Prince, while the Act of Grodno (1432) gave the orthodox Russian boyars the same rights as Catholics. The same policy was followed in Polish Galicia.

Before peace with the Order was signed Jagiello died, at the age of eighty-six (1434), leaving two young sons, Vladyslav III, who was elected king, and Casimir. The government was in the hands of the Polish oligarchy of magnates, whose chief was Olesnicki. They revived Casimir III's policy in accepting the crown of Hungary for Vladyslav, while refusing to intervene in Bohemia, when the Emperor Sigismund and Albert of Austria were dead (1439); the young Casimir, who had been offered the Bohemian throne, became Grand Prince of Lithuania. The ends of Olesnicki seemed largely achieved when Hussitism was suppressed in Poland under the aegis of the Council of Basle and when Isidore, the Metropolitan of Kiev (Moscow), and numbers of the Orthodox in Lithuania and Galicia accepted Union under the papacy at the Council of Florence (1439). But the Turkish war, in conjunction with Hungary, led to disaster. In the defeat of Varna (1444) King Vladyslav III vanished, and Hungary returned to the Bohemian alliance. For three years the Polish oligarchy, believing in their king's survival, delayed to elect his heir, Casimir IV (1447–92).

The new king, who continued to rule Lithuania directly, followed a new policy: to overthrow the oligarchy by concessions to the lesser gentry of *Szlachta*, to abandon the Turkish war, and to resume the national war with the Teutonic Order. He triumphed over Olesnicki in the nomination to bishoprics. The *Szlachta* were gained by statutes which required their consent to new laws and to the military levy. Thus fortified, Casimir undertook the decisive struggle with the Order. The opportunity was given by the Order's own subjects, who, both vassals and towns, were by this time thoroughly disgusted with the rule of the decadent Knights. In 1440 the Prussian League to resist oppression was formed among them, and in 1454 it appealed to Casimir for the annexation of Prussia and Pomerellen to Poland. The consequent thirteen years' war was fought by ferocious mercenaries on both sides with customary devastation, but after the battle of Puck in 1462 the Knights' fortresses were taken in succession. By the peace of Thorn (Torun) of 1466 the Order as a Polish vassal was reduced to East Prussia with Königsberg; Poland regained a seaboard with Pomerellen, Danzig, and west Prussia. Thenceforward until the Reformation the Order was a minor power. The Slav reaction had triumphed. Casimir even recovered some scraps of Silesia. He pursued dynastic aggrandisement. While his eldest son Vladyslav was elected King of Bohemia (1471) and Hungary (1490), two other sons succeeded him in

Poland and Lithuania. Yet he lost access to the Black Sea to the Crimean Tartars.

Although held together by a common supreme monarch and by some common institutions, Poland-Lithuania was not a unitary state. Lithuania was largely ruled by Lithuanian or Russian dynasts. Poland itself was made up of provinces (of which Mazovia had its own princely lines), and these were subdivided into voivodeships, under a royal *starosta*, each of which came to possess an assembly of its *Szlachta* known as its *Sejmik* (*Little Sejm*). The king since Lewis the Great's death had by force of events become elective, although invested with great powers. From time to time he held a general assembly of officials and magnates, called the *Sejm* (later the Senate). As the importance of the provincial *Szlachta* in politics and for taxation increased, a second house of this parliament grew up. At first all the *Sejmiks* were summoned to confer and grant, but soon each *Sejmik* sent a deputy. Thus was formed the House of Deputies, alongside the Senate. Since the separate *Sejmiks* abandoned none of their powers, they gave precise instructions to their deputies, and for a valid act of the whole parliament the consent of each deputy (that is, of his *Sejmik*) was necessary. In this way, owing to the separate action of each *Sejmik*, the pernicious rule of unanimity obtained in the House of Deputies. Each deputy could exercise a veto. The *Sejm*, like the *Sejmiks*, thus consisted of the *Szlachta*, the land-owning gentry, great and small, too numerous to be called an oligarchy. Of the towns only Cracow regularly sent a deputy. Meantime, with the disuse of the military levy, the *Szlachta* had settled down to agriculture, eager to develop the production and export of corn. As in Germany east of the Elbe, the peasant's freedom diminished and his burdens increased. The towns, too, with small exception lost in wealth and importance. Thus, although Poland was a great power, tolerant and free, and learning began to flourish, the seeds of decay were being thickly sown in a markedly ill-compacted society and State.

(4) RUSSIA, 1263–1484

The Tartar Yoke pressed with great severity on north-eastern (or Great) Russia, as we have seen, but it was accompanied by two developments of vast importance. The first was the migration of the Metropolitan of the Church to the northward. In 1300 Vladimir became his official see, and St Peter (1308–26), a Russian by birth, took up his residence in the town of Moscow, where his successors remained. Still more big with consequence was the fervent religious revival of the time, which led to the foundation of great new monasteries, no longer in towns, but in the forest wilderness of the north and east. They became social and economic centres, bringing about by well-organized colonization an immense extension of Great

Russia. The second development was that of centralized monarchy. It grew paradoxically out of the continuous subdivision of principalities among the male agnates of the house of Rurik. The numerous lesser princes were obliged to enter into contracts of 'younger brotherhood' or even of service with their wealthier kinsmen, becoming hardly distinguishable from the non-princely boyars, who possessed wide immunities and could change their suzerain. The free but tax-paying peasant was ranged beneath these landowners, while the upper section of the unfree, corresponding to the earlier German *ministeriales*, were better off than he was and produced a secondary gentry. Under these conditions the greater princes extended their territory and power.

The aim of each wealthier prince was to obtain from the Great Khan the *yarlyk* making him Prince of Vladimir and tribute-gatherer for the Tartars. Success in this ignoble competition was won by the Prince of Moscow. The town had been the share of Daniel (*ob.* 1304), the youngest son of St Alexander Nevsky, who began the increase of his appanage. His son Yuri (George) engaged in a contest of intrigue at the Tartar court with the rival Prince of Tver, and the prize of Vladimir was securely gained in 1328 by Yuri's brother Ivan (John) I, nicknamed Kalitá (i.e. the Purse), whose bribes were heaviest. Henceforward the Princes of Moscow were Great Princes of Vladimir, with but one interval. The foundations of their power were laid. Alliance with the Church, thrifty finances, and complete subservience to the Golden Horde were the keynotes of their policy. They bought up lands and subjected neighbours. The Khan's armies could be used against resisters. The Church, which alone preserved the ideal of Russian unity, sided with Moscow, where the Metropolitan dwelt and which the Great Prince ruled.

The predominance of the Church in the growth of Muscovy was manifest when Ivan I in 1341 left his dominions to his three sons. The eldest, Simeon (1341–53), and the younger, the feeble Ivan II (1353–59), easily obtained the Tartar *yarlyk* as Great Prince of Vladimir and suzerain of the other princes, and so too, after a brief interlude when the Prince of Suzdal bought the coveted dignity, did the infant son of Ivan II, Dimitri (Demetrius). The real ruler of Russia was the Metropolitan, St Alexis (1354–78), in concert with the Muscovite boyars, to whose class he belonged by birth. At this time the Russian princes were not autocrats: the council of boyars preserved a continuity of policy under the guidance of St Alexis. He worked for unity and obedience to the Great Prince at Moscow. The Golden Horde was obeyed, but was verging towards dissolution under the decadent dynasty of Batu. At length an able vizier, Mamay, usurped the Khanate and resolved to check Russian colonization on the steppe. Dimitri, encouraged by the Church, decided on resistance (1378). All but one of the northern princes followed him; he had become a national leader. On

8 September 1380 he conquered Mamay in the hard-fought battle of Kulikovo on the upper Don, which gave him the surname of Donskoy (of the Don). This victory of legendary fame did not, however, bring freedom to Russia. In 1382 Tuqtamish, set over the Golden Horde by Tamerlane, captured Moscow and renewed the Tartar Yoke. Dimitri's son Vasili I (Basil) (1389–1425) journeyed to the Horde on the Volga for his *yarlyk*. Tamerlane's campaign of 1395 against the rebel Tuqtamish, followed as it was by the internal conflicts of the Horde, did indeed, embolden Vasili to withhold the tribute, but the vigorous Khan-maker Edegey in 1408 besieged Moscow, though vainly, and reimposed the Yoke. It was the further disintegration of the Horde, not Russian revolt, which enabled Vasili's son Vasili II (1425–62) and grandson Ivan III (1462–1505) to be more and more independent until in 1480 tribute and nominal vassalage were thrown off together.

Apart from the slow release from Tartar servitude, the fortunes of Muscovy were chequered, but ended in steady growth, chiefly owing to the unfaltering help of the Church, dominated by the ideals of the venerated St Alexis and St Sergius of Radonezh, which surrounded it with a spiritual halo, and also to the memory of the victory of the Don. Moscow became the centre and symbol of national unity. Stone architecture, literature, and religious painting revived, with Moscow, no longer Novgorod, as their capital. Otherwise, the history is drab enough. In 1391, by means of a Tartar *yarlyk* and the treachery of the local boyars, Vasili I annexed the principality of Nizhni Novgorod, deporting its prince. He failed, however, in a similar attempt (1396–8) to seize on Novgorod the Great itself. Meantime, his hold on the principalities of Tver and Ryazan was weakened after the last Tartar invasions, and Lithuania, under Vitold (1388–1430), set up over western Russia a rival suzerainty which cut short the expansion of the Great Principality.

Internally, the change of the numerous minor princes from 'younger brotherhood' to 'servants', by which they became a higher rank of boyars, added both power and prestige to the Muscovite. The weakness of Vasili II lay in himself and his nearest kinsmen. He was a man of no talents and no virtues. His strength lay in the unfaltering support of the Church and boyars given to the legitimate ruler and in the patronage of the Golden Horde. When his cousin, Dimitri Shemyaka, seized and blinded him (1446), St Jonas, the Metropolitan, obtained his release and a counter-revolution. Shemyaka was poisoned at Novgorod, his place of refuge, and a victorious campaign of the Muscovites forced the Novgorod republic into a genuine vassalage to the Great Prince (1453).

At that very time the Russian Church was acquiring ecclesiastical independence from the patriarchate of Constantinople. In 1439 the then Metropolitan of Moscow, the Greek Isidore, had accepted at the Council of Florence papal supremacy and the Reunion. On his return to Moscow he was deposed by a Russian synod. The result was a declaration of complete autonomy and the election of a Russian Metropolitan, St Jonas (1448–61). Oddly enough, the Russian Church, become more national than ever, and growing still more in wealth and moral influence, was brought thereby into a new dependence on the secular State. The fall of Constantinople in 1453 was of primary importance for Muscovy. Moscow was now the head of the Orthodox world. It was not long before the monk Philotheos of Pskov voiced the theory of 'Moscow—the Third Rome'.

Ivan III, the first to style himself 'Great Prince and Autocrat (*Samoder-zhats*) of all Russia', had an easy task before him. He married a Palaeologus princess (1471) and took up the legacy of Byzantium. He threw off the Tartar yoke (1480). He conquered with little effort Tver (1484) and even Novgorod the Great (1478). At last Lithuania was forced back by the annexation of Smolensk and Chernigov (1500). A new, great and stable power had arisen in the far east of Europe, to be formally expressed when the title of Tsar (Caesar) was assumed by the Great Prince (1547) and that of Patriarch by the Metropolitan of Moscow (1589).

(5) SCANDINAVIA, 1412–1500

The unwieldy Union of Calmar even under the masterful rule of Margaret had been fruitful of discontents in each of her three kingdoms. These were exacerbated after her death by the very energy of her heir, King Eric, who continued her unifying policy. His determination to retain Slesvig, however natural, proved a cardinal mistake. The Count of Holstein, heir to the duchy, went to war after he came of age (1410). For over twenty years, with intervals of negotiations and lawsuits, in which the King of the Romans, Sigismund, was appealed to, the conflict went on. What was worse, it involved war with the reviving Hansa League, whose commerce was imperilled by his debased coinage and the continuous piracy practised by him and by that old pest, the Victualler Brethren. The sea-going trade of the Hansa suffered enormously by these depredations, worst of all when it came to war. In 1427 they endured several naval defeats, the entire Bay-salt fleet being once captured by the Danes. A five-years' truce in 1432 with Eric amended matters, but left the Victuallers' piracy unchecked. Not till 1435 did the king's own difficulties induce him to a real peace, which restored the Hansa's old privileged position in Scandinavia. Even so, there was a dearth of the commodities which they handled in the north, and they had to pay duties for the transit of the Sound.

Eric's own subjects were laden with heavier taxes for his war-policy, which was in the end unsuccessful, for in 1432 he was obliged to abandon his efforts to annex Slesvig. From 1420 there were peasant rebellions. In

Sweden the native nobility were also malcontent at Danish intruders, while a new force, the native merchant and industrialist, now entered the arena. A leader appeared in the iron-mining province of Dalecarlia. This was Engelbrecht, a mine-owner, who was free from the egoism of his contemporaries, and whose far-sighted views produced a constitutional revolution. At the head of the insurgents he expelled the foreign bailiffs and forced the Council to call for 1435 a general parliament at Arboga. Unlike its predecessors, this parliament contained, besides the two orders of spiritual and secular lords, two more, of the burghers and yeomen, an arrangement which persisted for centuries. It elected Engelbrecht regent of Sweden, although the aristocratic Council gave him a colleague in Karl (Charles) Knutsson, one of the greater nobles. A year later Engelbrecht was murdered, further yeoman risings were suppressed, and a purely nationalistic policy was adopted by the Council. But his ideas lived after him, and his example infected the other kingdoms. In 1436 a rising of the yeomen in southern Norway, led by a noble, Osmund Sigurdsson, resulted in prudent concessions from the Norwegian Council, which forbade fiefs being conferred on foreigners and filled up the vacant State offices. When the Danish peasants likewise rose against oppression, the Danish Council, too,

Fig. 230. King Charles VIII of Sweden by Bernt Notke

refused to obey King Eric. The whole movement had by now passed into the hands of the nobles, whose particularism was combined with a strict devotion to the interests of their class. In 1438 Eric fled from Denmark and established himself in the Swedish island of Gotland, whence he infested the Baltic with piracy.

The Danish Council elected (1440) as their new king Eric's nephew, Christopher, the Count Palatine; Norway followed suit in the same year, and Sweden in 1442. In all three kingdoms the nobility took undisputed control, while the Church exchanged the king's dominion for that of the

1021

secular lords. The burghers were sacrificed to the Hansa, for Christopher, powerless and poor, raised an income by confirming all the Hansa's privileges and giving up the transit dues of the Sound. In 1448 the personal union of the three kingdoms was broken by the death of the king without heirs. In Denmark the Council offered the crown to the Duke of Slesvig, who recommended instead of himself his nephew, Count Christian of Oldenburg. So Christian I was elected king under a capitulation which gave all power to the Council of the Realm. Both in Sweden and Norway the nobles were divided. In Sweden, a party elected and crowned the ex-regent Knutsson as Charles VIII. In Norway, one party elected Charles and the other Christian, each under a capitulation like the Danish (1449). The latter carried the day, and proceeded to agree to an act of union (August 1450), by which Denmark and Norway should always have the same king. Sweden fell into civil war coupled with invasion, but in 1457 Charles VIII was driven out and Christian crowned. For a time Christian I appeared to have restored the Union of Calmar and more. In 1460 he inherited under terms Slesvig and Holstein, with the fateful proviso that the two should never be separated. The long-dethroned Eric died in 1459. But actually the royal power reached its nadir in Christian's days. A lover of splendour, he was always in straits for money. As pledge for his daughter's dowry, he ceded his lands and rights in Orkney and Shetland to the King of the Scots (1468). He paid dearly for his acquisitions with borrowed funds. The Hansa and the nobles of Holstein were his creditors and masters.

The characteristic of the time was the rise of Sweden and the eclipse of Norway. For years Sweden had been the theatre of the ignoble, rival ambitions of the great nobles, for whom Christian I and Charles VIII were pretexts. Christian was turned out in 1464; Charles, three times enthroned, but always powerless, died in 1470. But the new burgher class was growing and animating with new ideas both lower nobility and yeomanry. In spite of the Council, Charles's nephew Sten Sture, who revived the programme of Engelbrecht, was elected regent and ruled for thirty years. He won the battle of Brunkeberg against King Christian (1471). The burghers were rewarded by the abolition of the law that half of each town council should be German. It was a sign of Sweden's economic independence of the Hansa. Sweden, too, was expanding to north and east, bringing the whole of Finland under her rule, just as Muscovy was absorbing Novgorod. Norway on the other hand, was sinking into dependence. The greater nobles were of foreign extraction. Native commerce was crippled by the monopoly of the Hansa, which engrossed the export of cod and timber. The yeomen and fishermen, who colonized the north, felt no interest in politics. The far-off colony in Greenland was starved out by neglect. When Christian I died in 1481, his son John (Hans) of Denmark was accepted after some vacillation

Fig. 231. St George and the Dragon by Bernt Notke

in Norway also. He issued a common capitulation for both kingdoms which reaffirmed the supremacy of their Councils.

John (1481–1513), however, had his triumphs. He was obliged to share Slesvig-Holstein with his brother Frederick, and he was fettered by the Councils. But he was popular with the Danish burghers, he curbed the declining Hansa, and in 1497 he was able in an invasion to assert his rights in Sweden, being helped by a simultaneous attack on Finland by Ivan III of Russia. The renewed Union of Calmar was not lasting, for in 1501 the Swedes deposed John and were ruled again by Sture. National feeling proved superior to the common aristocratic interests. In fact, both in Sweden and Denmark the power of the nobles was on the decline, for the burghers were gaining strength and supporting a national monarchy. Only Norway was lagging behind in the new development.

BOOK XI
THE TRANSITION TO MODERN TIMES

CHAPTER 35

FRANCE, BURGUNDY AND THE EMPIRE

The failure of the Councils of Constance and Basle to reform and reconstruct the Western Church had left the government of the Church in the hands of the Papacy, restricted far more than of old by the secular powers. Those powers were in the later fifteenth century gaining unprecedented strength. For a hundred years or more monarchy had developed its centralizing bureaucracy, but the assemblies of its subjects, the nobles, the clergy, and the bourgeois, which it had gathered round it, and the dominance of acknowledged law and custom, limited and controlled it. It was only by their grants in aid that it could meet the cost of government and war. Most of all it was crippled by the overmighty magnates, with their vast possessions and military force. Round about 1400 these magnates seemed to be triumphant, if not irresistible. But they had not the talent or the training or the union to use their power. They gave neither lasting victory nor peace and justice to their countries. No more could they appeal to the strong national feeling, which was now fully self-conscious. They were local, narrow, petty, capricious, and based after all on inadequate foundations. In the stresses of the fifteenth century their failure and anarchy were manifest, and the growth of untrammelled monarchy met a public need. It gave order, defence, and security. It stood above the strife of classes and personal ambitions. Supported by public opinion, welcomed by bourgeoisie and peasantry and even by the minor nobles, it rallied round it its ablest subjects. It could afford to levy disciplined armies. Forethought, co-ordination, system, and routine, which the Middle Ages had slowly brought forth, were at its service; they could never be the allies of spendthrift, turbulent lords with their narrow outlook. The progress of absolute monarchy was to be seen almost everywhere. Its variations and the speed of its growth were infinitely varied, but the need for it was proved by the fact that those lands, which like Poland did not achieve it, fell behind their neighbours in power and prosperity.

(I) FRANCE UNDER LOUIS XI

The harvest which had been sown by Charles '*le bien servi*' and his ministers was left to his son Louis XI first to imperil and then to reap. Few characters have been less attractive than that of the new king, even when the melodramatic legends with which it has been laden have been discarded. He was neurotic, diseased, suspicious, cruel, treacherous and false, without a moral sense. His religion was a strict and superstitious formalism, in which he believed he could bribe the celestial hierarchy as he did men in his dealings. He took a base delight in lying, tyranny, and revenge. Yet he was endowed with great gifts, which stamped his personality on the government and development of France. He was restlessly industrious, always on the move, and kept his hand on all the acts of government. No king knew his subjects better. He was, with all his loquacity and contempt of his species, a true master of men. He was shrewd, alert, energetic, and persevering. His aims were grandly conceived, original, and usually well judged. At the root of his policy lay a conviction of his duties as king, to whom absolute rule was given by right divine, and he claimed at the end of his life that he had fulfilled his task with all diligence to the benefit of France.

When Louis XI gleefully received the news of his father's death, and was escorted by his incautious patron, Philip the Good of Burgundy, to Paris, the kingship, although reconstructed, was not out of danger. Externally, there was always the risk of a new English invasion, the Papacy was still unreconciled to the Pragmatic Sanction of Bourges, and the Italian states were on their guard against renewed French interference. Internally, France was still suffering from the effects of the Hundred Years' War. She was depopulated and exhausted. The condition of the peasantry was miserable in the extreme. Worse still, the peril from the overmighty magnates had been scotched but far from killed. The great Gascon lords, Armagnac, Albret, and Foix, were dangerous and turbulent. The Duke of Brittany, of Capetian descent, claimed all but independence in his strongly particularist land. Most formidable of all were the princes of the blood royal of Valois, the Dukes of Orleans, Anjou, Burgundy, and Alençon, who had vast fiefs and prestige. The Duke of Burgundy, Philip the Good, was an independent prince. To his French fiefs (Burgundy, Flanders, Artois, etc.) he added wide lands in the Empire, mainly in the Netherlands, which he was forming into a kind of conglomerate of states by annexation and inheritance. A middle kingdom, resuscitating the ancient Lotharingia, was arising between France and Germany, and for Louis it was his chief enemy.

By his rancours and hasty aggressions Louis soon succeeded in creating distrust in every quarter. He disgraced the loyal, capable officials of his father and put in dubious favourites. He 'reduced to slavery' the clergy,

Fig. 232. King Charles VII, Louis XI as Dauphin and the Scots guard

Fig. 233. Paris, mid-fifteenth century

both when he abolished the Pragmatic Sanction (1461) and when he restored it. He offended the nobles by his economical disregard of show and his bourgeois tastes, while he encroached on their jurisdictions and arbitrarily abused his rights of wardship. He began a series of quarrels with the great vassals. Philip of Burgundy was old and lethargic, and at variance with his heir. So, naturally enough, Louis took the opportunity with the help of bribing his advisers to redeem the strategic Somme towns, and further raised troubles in the bishopric of Liége against the Burgundian protectorate and countered the Burgundian designs on the duchy of Lorraine, which divided the Netherlands from Franche Comté and Burgundy. When the heir, Charles the Bold, took control from his father (1465), a collision was certain. Meanwhile, Francis II of Brittany (1453–88) was in conflict with the king over his English alliance and the nomination to Breton bishoprics, and Louis needlessly flouted his old cousins, Charles of Orleans the poet

1028

and René of Anjou the art-loving claimant of Naples, besides seriously opposing their troublesome ambitions in Italy, which he wisely considered the wrong road for French expansion. To these enmities he added the alienation of the Duke of Bourbon and the hatred of the Catalans, from whom he wrested Roussillon on pledge. In the hope of winning Calais he compromised himself with the English Yorkists by a small loan to Queen Margaret of Anjou.

This was a heavy tale of errors, but Louis was fortunate in the internal difficulties of foreign powers, which prevented their coalition against him. Only his own ally, Sforza of Milan, sent serviceable troops. All the same, the 'League of the Public Weal', which was formed in 1465 by the malcontents, was a serious ordeal and began a long struggle between the Crown and the great nobles. Both sides wooed public opinion by their manifestos. Particularism, feudalism and clericalism were all arrayed against the king. The Count of Dunois, bastard of Orleans and hero of the English war, voiced the programme of the League and the grievances against Louis' tyranny. The princes were to have complete control of government, finance, and army, and of the king himself. They had many sympathizers in Church and bureaucracy, but their overt friends in both were few. They possessed no real leader and little unity of action. Save their own vassals, the petty nobility were for the king. The bourgeois were at most divided, and the artisans had no wish for several selfish rulers. Yet the armed strength of the League was great. After an initial success against Bourbon, Louis was reduced to parleys—his best weapon—by the drawn battle (15 July 1465) of Montlhéry close to Paris. In the peace of Conflans (October) he bought off the strongest of the egoistic rebels. His feeble brother Charles, once proposed as regent, was given the duchy of Normandy. Charles the Bold recovered the Somme towns with additions. The rest went empty away. No trace remained of the vain programme of the League.

Yet Louis had been beaten, and his next years were spent, with his native perfidy, in repairing his errors and losses. The very disorder and pillage which survived the civil war worked in his favour with his disillusioned subjects. He almost immediately reoccupied Normandy, and in 1468 he even convoked the States General at Tours to annul the grant of the duchy to his brother. He resumed the contest with Charles the Bold, invoking his suzerain rights, stirring up the city of Liége to revolt. Meantime, Duke Charles won the Yorkist alliance, and the Duke of Brittany was equally hostile. In 1468 Louis swiftly forced the latter to a peace. Charles the Bold he trusted to outwit by a personal negotiation. Thus he ventured on the famous interview at Péronne on the duke's land and under his safe-conduct (October). There came the news of the outbreak of Liége at Louis's instigation. The king only escaped imprisonment by heavy bribes and a humiliating surrender: he witnessed the burning of Liége, renounced the appeals from Flemish courts, and promised Champagne to his brother Charles.

Louis of course violated his promises, and his struggle with his foes, foreign and domestic, was resumed in intrigue and war. He could not trust his ministers, men of tainted character. Cardinal Balue and the shifty Duke of Alençon were imprisoned, the latter under sentence of death (1474). But Louis gained new counsellors; one was the historian Commynes, a deserter from Charles the Bold (1472). In 1469 he persuaded his brother to take Guienne (Aquitaine) in lieu of the vital Champagne. In 1470 his diplomacy succeeded in the brief expulsion of Edward IV and the restoration

Fig. 234. Exhibition of the Burgundian spoils in Lucerne, 1477

of Henry VI. But Aragon and Burgundy allied against him, with Brittany and the Gascon vassals and Charles of Guienne. The king was saved, not only by his own ingenious diplomacy but by the death of his brother (1472) and the stupidity of Charles the Bold. A Burgundian invasion failed at Beauvais, the Duke of Brittany was reduced to a new submission, the Count of Armagnac was killed, the Count of Foix died.

Charles the Bold now made a renewed coalition with the restored Edward IV, but, obstinately engrossed in a German war, he left Edward's invasion without support, and Louis scored his greatest success in the treaty of Picquigny (29 August 1475), in which he bribed the English king with an annual pension to cease hostilities. The English danger was averted, and truce with Burgundy followed. Next year King René of Anjou was brought to heel, while the Dukes of Brittany and Bourbon were cowed into loyalty.

All the time, 'the spider' Louis was spinning wide his web for Charles the Bold. With the invaluable aid of his enemy's folly he raised up wars against him. His master-stroke was to reconcile the Swiss, whose fighting quality he knew by experience, with their ancient adversary, Sigismund of Austria-Tyrol (1474), and to further their alliance with Duke René II of Lorraine, whose duchy was seized by Charles the Bold (1475). Thus began the war which ended in the defeat and death of Charles on 5 January 1477 at Nancy. He left only a young daughter, Mary, behind him, and Louis could proceed to open war.

The Burgundian state was exhausted, and Louis gave free rein to his violence and greed in his determination to oust the helpless heiress. Not only the duchy of Burgundy and Flanders but Hainault and Franche Comté should be annexed to the royal domain. But his remorseless attack aroused opposition. Mary in desperation gave her hand to the warlike Maximilian of Austria (18 August 1477), thus making the Habsburgs the rivals of France. The battle of Guinegate (7 August 1479) proved a severe check to Louis' arms, and in the treaty of Arras (December 1482) Louis accepted Maximilian as regent of Flanders for his little son Philip, father of the future Emperor Charles V. Only the duchy of Burgundy and the Somme towns were permanently and Artois and Franche Comté for a few years absorbed into the royal domain.

Fig. 235. King Charles VIII of France

The domain was further enlarged on the extinction of the house of Anjou in 1481. Anjou and Maine escheated to the Crown, and Louis seized the imperial county of Provence and the duchy of Bar from his whilom protégé, René II of Lorraine. The princes of the blood trembled before him: the Duke of Bourbon lost his special jurisdiction; the young Louis of Orleans (later Louis XII) was forced to marry a barren daughter of the king; the new Duke of Alençon was in dire captivity. Throughout Europe Louis XI's prestige stood high. His influence was great in Italy. He muzzled Edward IV with the pension, which was not paid to Richard III. His privateers had the best of a pirate war with overtasked Venice in the Mediterranean (1468–78). Only in Spain his tortuous ambitions met with defeat. John II of Aragon was a shrewd antagonist, and his son Ferdinand, married to Isabella of Castile, was a match in any perfidy and machination. A united Spain faced France over the Pyrenees.

1031

At the treaty of Arras Louis' own race was nearly run. He had ceased to perambulate his kingdom and kept to his trap-circled castles in Touraine, where on 30 August 1483 he died 'constantly saying something of sense'. His daughter Anne, aided by her husband, the Bourbon Sire de Beaujeu, exercised the government for her young brother Charles VIII, quelling the revolts of the Duke of Orleans and his complotters, and forcing Brittany into real vassalage and eventual union with the Crown. Charles VIII himself, in order to secure his Italian expedition from impediment, re-troceded (1493) Franche Comté and Artois to Maximilian and Roussillon to Ferdinand the Catholic. With these exceptions and the evacuation of Bar the great acquisitions of Louis XI were retained, while the absolute authority he had gained for the Crown was defended and made inveterate.

The oppressive despotism established by Louis XI did not mean indifference to public opinion. He sent round skilful manifestos and tendentious information on events. He often called assemblies of notables, although only once the States General. They were, however, kept in leading-strings, and the remaining provincial Estates merely voted money on demand. The characteristic of his rule was the intensification and enlargement of bureaucracy and of the arbitrary action of the king. He worked his councils hard in administration and advice. He increased the number of provincial Parlements for justice, but he would dictate the judgements of the courts when he willed. To be one of the swarming bureaucrats, exempt from taxation with opportunities for profit, was a common ambition, and purchase of office as well as heredity in it was a growing custom, although Louis loved to show his power by making and unmaking men. The network of royal post-services, which he instituted, kept him well informed; yet abuses remained rife. He was alive to the advantages of the long-standing alliance between the bourgeoisie and the Crown, but municipal liberties fared ill at his hands. The towns were reduced to complete subservience by his arbitrary rule of them. In short, their officials became, to continue for centuries, mere organs of royal authority. As for the feudal lords, their ancient rights and jurisdiction were so undermined by the vigilant royal officials that their freedom was gone.

A prime evil of the reign was excessive taxation. Louis' wars, his diplomacy, his standing army, his bribes to men and saints, purchases, and pensions, were all expensive. He was not a saving king. In consequence, the revenue from impoverished France, the main source being the *taille*, nearly quadrupled in his reign, besides the forced loans he exacted. And the long-lasting abuse of inequality and exemptions exacerbated burdens on those who bore them. This over-taxation inevitably retarded the recovery of the countryside from the devastation of the Hundred Years' War, especially as the king's troops were irregularly paid and prone to pillage. Although real progress was being made in resettlement and recultivation

Fig. 236. Louis XI presiding at a chapter of the Order of
St Michael

on easier terms for the farmer, it was as yet but partial, if not sporadic.
There was sickness, famine, and riots in Louis' gloomy closing years.

With Charles V he was the ablest and most successful of the Valois
kings. There was a resemblance, physical and mental, between the two.
But the comparison shows the decline in moral standards typical of the
fifteenth-century ruling class. Charles V was neither cruel nor devoid of
scruple, nor arbitrary and despotic. Louis XI was a tyrant of a kind also
to be seen in Italy, and not only there. It was his part in history to
accomplish in France the establishment of absolute monarchy, characteristic
of the age, which involved the crushing of feudal particularism and government by co-operation and consent, both of them decadent and, one might
say, diseased. The new State triumphed over great evils, but with great
benefits it combined other evils, old and new.

1033

27. The Unification of the Netherlands

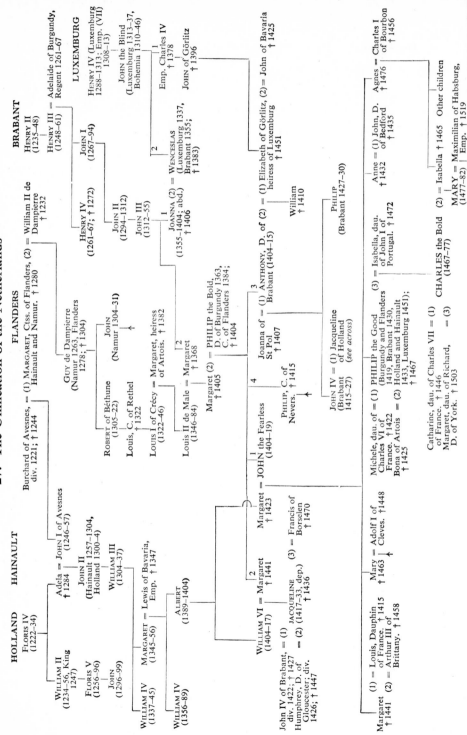

(2) THE HOUSE OF BURGUNDY AND THE NETHERLANDS

The lasting achievement of the Valois Dukes of Burgundy, and also their conscious aim, was the unification of the Netherlands, a development long foreshadowed by their slow alienation in language and spirit from Germany and France, between which their allegiance was divided. If the extended middle kingdom of Lothar II of Lotharingia was not revived, its northern provinces—the present Holland, Belgium, and Luxemburg—became a distinct political entity in Europe.

The Netherlands were composed of a number of great fiefs. To France belonged the counties of Flanders and Artois, to the Empire the three prince-bishoprics of Liége, Utrecht and Cambrai, the counties of Holland-Zeeland, Friesland, Hainault, Guelders (later a duchy), Luxemburg (later a duchy), the county of Namur, and the duchies of Brabant and Limburg. The linguistic frontier between Low German (Dutch) and Romance (Walloon) dialects did not correspond with any political division. Walloon (the most northerly variant of Langue d'oïl) was spoken from south of Dunkirk to south of Maestricht, thus including south Flanders, Hainault, south Brabant and Liége, and the Ardennes; Dutch-Flemish was the tongue to the north of this line, and east Luxemburg spoke High German. But if divided in language, the Netherlands were united in geographical situation on the cross-routes of Europe by sea and land. Taken as a whole, they were a land of industrial and commercial towns, importing their raw material, and exporting their manufactures. The cloth-trade was the staple product of Flanders and Brabant, that in copperwork of Dinant and Huy in the prince-bishopric of Liége. The European vogue of their handiwork brought about an immense influx of wealth and population, which redounded to the independence and power of the towns, more especially Bruges (which had then access to the sea), Ghent, and Ypres in Flanders, and Liége and Dinant. They enjoyed practical autonomy under their feudal overlord, and more than counterbalanced the rural nobility in his government.

But within the towns the character of their trade produced developments of the first importance, analogous to those in contemporary Tuscany. In the thirteenth century, these towns were ruled by merchant oligarchies (the so-called 'patricians'), which dealt in the export and import vital to their existence, and which alone possessed the expert knowledge and foreign connexions necessary for its exploitation. The weavers and fullers were in reality their mere employees, and were hardly pressed by them and despised as 'blue-nails'. Unlike the typical medieval system of the craft-gilds of 'small masters', which subsisted for that matter in these lands for crafts, like the butchers and bakers etc., the cloth and metal industries were under an early regime of capitalism, and they occupied, for instance, in Ghent 60 per cent of a population of some 50,000. The situation was by necessity

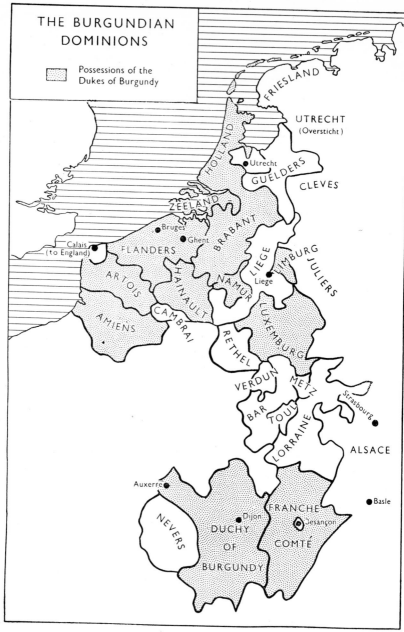

THE BURGUNDIAN DOMINIONS

Possessions of the
Dukes of Burgundy

FRIESLAND

UTRECHT
(Oversticht)

HOLLAND

Utrecht

GUELDERS

CLEVES

ZEELAND

Bruges

Ghent

BRABANT

Calais
(to England)

FLANDERS

LIEGE

LIMBURG

JULIERS

ARTOIS

HAINAULT

NAMUR

Liege

LUXEMBURG

AMIENS

CAMBRAI

RETHEL

VERDUN

METZ

Strasbourg

BAR

TOUL

LORRAINE

ALSACE

Auxerre

Basle

NEVERS

Dijon

FRANCHE

Besançon

DUCHY

OF

COMTÉ

BURGUNDY

Map 25

a strained one, especially when wars or other impediments restricted import and export and caused a stoppage. To make matters worse, the patricians in control were always concerned to keep wages low, and became more narrow and less efficient as the century wore on, which aroused the wrath

Fig. 237. Bruges. Traders' Hall

of the small craft-gilds not engaged in the dominant commerce. By 1280 there was a general movement of insurrection of the 'lesser folk' against the patricians.

The attitude of the princes varied. In Liége the bishop and chapter were concerned to maintain their own privileges. The Duke of Brabant sided with the patricians to keep the clothworkers in check. In Flanders and Hainault the counts endeavoured to protect the cloth workers against the very real abuses under which they suffered and to diminish the autonomy of the ruling class. The effect in Flanders was to turn the patricians into *leliarts* who, as we have seen, implored the intervention of the suzerain, Philip the Fair, against the count, Guy de Dampierre (1278–1305). It has been told how Philip conquered Flanders, roused a general revolt in favour of the count, and was defeated by an army of townsmen and peasants at Courtrai (1302). The war did not end then. Not till 1320 was there a definite peace between king and count, by which Walloon Flanders (Lille and Douai) was ceded to the royal domain.

The social and economic problem was not solved thereby. The patricians and the 'lesser folk' were at daggers drawn, whether the patricians had lost authority or, as in Ghent, had regained it. Affairs reached a crisis in 1323, when a revolt broke out in Bruges against a new count, Louis of Nevers, suspected of being a tool of the King of France. For five years a terrible civil war was waged, in which, besides the craftsmen of Bruges and Ypres, the coastland peasants took part with ferocious brutality against the count and the nobles in defence of their liberties. It was ended by Louis I invoking the aid of his suzerain, King Philip VI, who crushed the ill-led Flemings in the battle of Mount Cassel (23 August 1328). Thenceforward Louis of Nevers was the most devoted vassal of the house of Valois.

For a time he was able to wreak his anger on the rebels and was master of Flanders, but the war looming between Edward III and Philip VI destroyed his power. He firmly refused to join the alliances which Edward III was buying in the Netherlands, and the consequent English prohibition of the export of wool struck a blow at the heart of the cloth-industry. All parties, patricians and workmen, threatened with ruin and starvation, united against the obstinate count. In Ghent the townsmen organized a committee of the Public Weal under the patrician James van Artevelde, who rapidly acquired the power of a dictator. In 1337 he obtained the re-entry of the essential wool, and he induced the towns (1340) to acknowledge Edward as King of France. But the failure of the English king's campaigns based on Flanders and the cessation of the dearth of wool allowed all the inner dissensions of the townsmen to burst into flame. Ypres and Bruges envied the supremacy of Ghent. In Ghent, the weavers upset the equilibrium established in 1338 between the various groups. In May 1345 they slaughtered their rival workmen, the fullers. In July Artevelde, left unsupported by Edward III, was killed in a riot.

The craft of weavers now made itself supreme in Flanders, but its tyranny aroused opposition everywhere. In every town the fullers rose, massacring the weavers in Bruges and Ypres. The death of Louis I at Crécy in 1346 allowed a new coalition of parties, for his shrewd son, Count Louis II de Male, was free from the odium attached to him. In January

Fig. 238. Ypres. Clothiers' Hall, Town Hall and St Martin's Church

1349, by the capture of the weavers' stronghold of Ghent, he confirmed his authority, and by an adroit policy of balance he kept Flanders out of the Hundred Years' War. His tergiversations were mingled with marriage-projects for his daughter and heiress, Margaret. In the end (1361) Charles V of France won the prize for his brother Philip the Bold, Duke of Burgundy, by the retrocession of Walloon Flanders to the count, who was himself the heir of Artois and Franche Comté, held by his mother.

The spirit of social revolution, however, was by no means dead in Flanders. The weavers quickly recovered from their disasters, and the rise in prices after the Black Death added fuel to the flame. Against them were ranked all those who had something to lose, nobles, merchants, craftsmen —'the Good'—under the count. After risings, repressed without pity, the wage-earners—'the Bad' in contemporary parlance—set up a reign of terror in 1379, first in Ghent, then in Bruges and Ypres and all Flanders. The natural reaction was captained by Louis de Male with much effect, but the weavers, reduced to Ghent, found a new demagogic leader in Philip, son of James van Artevelde. In May 1382 he recaptured Bruges. The count's resource was to appeal to his suzerain, Charles VI, and his powerful son-in-law, Philip of Burgundy. On 27 November 1382 the French army won the decisive victory of Roosebeke, Artevelde, no general, being among the slain. Ghent still held out, assisted vainly by the sham English crusade under the Bishop of Norwich. But Philip the Bold, who succeeded Louis on 30 January 1384, had the best in arms and diplomacy. With a wise leniency he accepted Ghent's capitulation on generous terms (December 1385) and inaugurated the rule of his house in Flanders.

The disturbances in Flanders were not isolated. In Brabant, the duke and patricians easily crushed revolt so that not till 1378 did the craft-gilds of Louvain share in its government. The duke's personal power, however, had long been limited. A council of nobles and towns had been instituted in 1312 by the impecunious John II with large powers of control, and in 1356 Duke Wenceslas from Luxemburg swore to the charter, named the *Joyeuse Entrée*, on his accession. It forbade the duke to declare war, coin money, or conclude alliances without the consent of the delegates of clergy, nobles, and towns, which later were known as the Estates. In the prince-bishopric of Liége, the power of the bishop was still less, and he was the ally of the nobles. In a furious outburst of 1312 in Liége the 'lesser folk' burned a number of the 'great folk' in the church whither they had fled. The struggle raged unceasingly until 1384, when the 32 craft-gilds obtained exclusive possession of the city government, over which they quarrelled, for there was no predominant craft in Liége. In Dinant, however, from 1348 onwards, patricians, coppersmiths, and lesser craft-gilds each secured a third of the town council, similar to the arrangements which were the outcome in Brabant and Flanders. The Bishop of Liége was indeed tethered in his whole principality. From the peace of Fexhe in 1316 he was compelled to admit the control of the canons, the nobles, and the towns in legislation. Although successive bishops strove for independence, a peace was ordained in 1373 which placed all his officials under the supervision of a committee of twenty-two, four canons, four knights, and fourteen burgesses. He was rendered a mere figurehead. The Counts of Holland and Hainault were more fortunate. There, as in Brabant, clergy, nobles, and towns formed three Estates, which voted subsidies. In Flanders the strongest power was the three great towns—the Three Members—but they were discordant, and the count could rally the rest of the country against them.

Hitherto the Netherlands had been mainly a geographical expression, but there were signs of political amalgamation. Since 1288 the Dukes of Brabant were also Dukes of Limburg. In 1299 the Counts of Hainault succeeded to Holland-Zeeland, with which went half-conquered Friesland, and in 1345 these counties passed by marriage to a branch of the Wittels-bachs. In 1355 Duke Wenceslas of Luxemburg married the heiress of Brabant. None of these princes had real resources outside the Netherlands, however. It was Philip the Bold who could back his ambitions with Burgundy, Franche Comté, and Artois, and on occasion with the power of France. By timely aid and skilful diplomacy he induced the widowed and childless Duchess of Brabant to make him her heir, and to install (1404) his second son Anthony as duke. By a double marriage he allied his house to the Wittelsbachs of Hainault and Holland. When he died in 1404, the house of Burgundy was already dominant in the Netherlands.

Philip's eldest son, John the Fearless (1404–19), was, as we have seen, a sinister figure in French history. The clearest clue to his ambitions is his determination to solidify and enlarge his dominions in the Netherlands. It was rivalry for the duchy of Luxemburg, bandied about between the princes of its house, which was a main motive for his murder of his own cousin, the Duke of Orleans (1407), thus beginning the deadly feud of Burgundians and Armagnacs in France. In 1411 his brother, Anthony of Brabant, was married to Elizabeth, the heiress with the best claim, perhaps, to the duchy, but Anthony was among the slain at Agincourt. King Sigismund was bent on asserting his family claims to both Brabant and Luxemburg, and John the Fearless was the more inclined to his dubious negotiations with Henry V in consequence. On the death of William VI of Holland and Hainault (1417) he secured the hand of the heiress Jacqueline for his nephew John IV of Brabant, while Sigismund replied by investing her uncle John with these counties. John renounced his bishopric of Liége, and married Elizabeth of Luxemburg, Anthony's widow. During the complicated dispute John the Fearless himself was murdered, leaving his own dominions to his son Philip the Good (1419–67).

Philip the Good, magnificent, ambitious, and industrious, was the very man to complete the fabric of the unification of the Netherlands. In revenge and to fortify himself he made a firm alliance with England by the Treaty of Troyes in 1420, which left him free to pursue his aim. In 1421 he bought the county of Namur. The succession to Hainault and Holland was more difficult, for Jacqueline discarded her feeble husband John IV, and without a divorce married the English prince, Humphrey of Gloucester. Philip took energetic action, while the Duke of Bedford, to keep his alliance, dissociated himself from his foolish brother's cause. Gloucester was defeated and Jacqueline imprisoned. The ex-bishop John died in 1425, and in two years' war in Holland Philip with the aid of the townsmen gained the victory. By the treaty of Delft (3 July 1428) he was acknowledged as governor and heir of Holland and Hainault. Jacqueline, who had escaped, promised never to remarry, for John IV was dead (1427) and had been succeeded in Brabant by his brother Philip. The latter died childless in 1430, and Philip the Good was declared to be their duke by the Estates of Brabant. The irresponsible Jacqueline did remarry, but only saved her last husband's life by renouncing her counties to Philip, who already ruled them (1436). A year earlier he both purchased the succession to Luxemburg from the Duchess Elizabeth and renounced the English alliance, in return for the Somme towns and freedom from French suzerainty for his lifetime. The Emperor Sigismund, whose imperial and dynastic rights had been flouted throughout, declaimed in vain. His hopes from England's anger were frustrated when in 1439 Henry VI renewed, however ineffectually, the commercial truce with Philip. He was himself far too deeply engaged in the Turkish war and his German troubles to do more than send against his foe a small force, which was easily repelled by the Limburg peasants, who like the Brabantines were devotedly attached to their popular duke (1437). Philip took possession of Luxemburg, whose duchess he succeeded in 1451. The two next Kings of the Romans, Albert II and Frederick III,

were helpless when, one after another, Philip assumed the protectorate of the prince-bishoprics of Cambrai, Liége and Utrecht, to which he appointed his relatives (1439–57).

Thus, thanks to Philip's sagacity and address, the house of Burgundy had become a great power. In 1454, with all the pomp he loved, he vowed to lead a new crusade against the Turks, unfulfilled of course, and no more than the conventional phantom ideal with which medieval monarchs proposed to crown their triumphs. But wealthy and strong as he was, there were serious flaws in his greatness. The Emperor Frederick III steadily evaded even investing him with his imperial fiefs, and still more converting them into the kingdom which he desired. Defect in legality

Fig. 239. Philip the Good of Burgundy

was a genuine weakness within and without. Charles VII of France was an obvious enemy of the middle state, which was wrenching away valuable French fiefs from their vassalage and barring French expansion. Philip himself, worn out with business and pleasure, allowed the covenanted redemption of the Somme towns in 1461 by Louis XI. He had indeed never overcome the worst defect of all, the fatal gap of alien territory between the core of his wealth and power, the Netherlands, and Burgundy and Franche Comté, two blocks of territory only allied by the person of their common prince. In fact, the Netherlands themselves were still a collection of provinces straddled over France and the Empire.

The reign of his son, Charles the Bold (a mis-translation of *le Téméraire*, 'the Rash'), really began in 1465 owing to Philip's incapacity. He deserved the bitter characterization of Louis XI, 'arrogant and wrathful, only a brute'; he was the victim of a stupid obstinacy, but was not without some solid qualities and a consistent policy, that of connecting his severed dominions and creating them into a kingdom. His wars in France were almost inevitable. It was the blind aggression and self-confidence with which he stirred up enemies all round, fomented by the cunning diplomacy of Louis XI, which ruined him. His first encounter with Louis was in the League of the Public Weal, when he fought the battle of Montlhéry with skill (1465). If the Treaty of Conflans did not benefit the Public Weal, it did Charles, who regained the Somme towns. Louis, however, had long tampered with the townsmen of Liége, who with other townsmen drove out the Bishop, Louis of Bourbon, nephew and tool of Philip the Good. Charles enforced their submission, but a new revolt immediately broke out. Charles savagely sacked and burnt Dinant (1466), and next year (1467) defeated the Liégeois. Their liberties were abolished and the whole principality brought under his sway. This neither conciliated the Liégeois, nor caused Louis XI to cease to instigate them to a fresh revolt. It came just when Louis was in Charles's power at Péronne (1468), and the French king only escaped by surrendering the hearing of appeals from Flanders, and by personally attending the burning of Liége by the enraged duke.

Hitherto, Charles had had the best of the conflict with France. He had become a Yorkist ally by marrying the sister of Edward IV, whom he aided to recover the English crown in 1471. Charles, too, was adding to his dominions. He conquered Guelders in 1473, and the purchase of Upper Alsace from Sigismund of Austria-Tyrol (1469) did something to fill the gap between Franche Comté and Luxemburg. He thought the time had come for a kingly title, but the Emperor Frederick III slipped away by night from Trier where they met, and left Charles the laughing-stock of Europe (1473).

Pride and passion now took possession of Charles the Bold. He wrecked his own alliance with Edward IV in their combination against France by his obstinate persistence in the futile and vain siege of Neuss on the Rhine in order to spite his deluder, Frederick III, who was on its side (1474–5). Meantime, Louis XI by secret diplomacy, backed by bribes and pensions, was contriving the toils into which the duke was to rush headlong. The discontent aroused by the harsh governor of Upper Alsace produced a local league, while the neighbouring Swiss were both alarmed and eager to expand, and Sigismund was lured by cash and the desire to regain his lost territory. In 1474 the Perpetual Peace and alliance was concluded between Sigismund and the Swiss, who could now turn westward. René II of Lorraine was involved. Charles's own alliances proved his undoing, for in 1474–5 the Swiss, besides invading Franche Comté, conquered the district of Vaud from the duchy of Savoy. The reply of Charles was to seize Lorraine and recapture Grandson in Vaud. The campaign formed an epoch in military history. By this time the use of the trooper in plate-armour as a real cavalryman to charge on horseback had again come into vogue, and

Charles with his ally of Savoy was well supplied with such. But the Swiss foot now fought in deep columns of pikemen, invulnerable to a cavalry charge, whose weight as they advanced could bear down horses and men. At Grandson (2 March 1476) they inflicted an utter defeat on Charles's horse and artillery. With fresh forces he was again hopelessly routed at Morat (22 June). Now René II reoccupied Lorraine, and Charles, marching towards the Netherlands and besieging Nancy, was overthrown and slain by a superior army, of which the best component was Swiss, on 5 January 1477.

The Burgundian state seemed irretrievably ruined. Louis XI invaded Burgundy, Franche Comté, and Artois; the Netherlands were in turmoil; and Liége revolted. But the heiress, Duchess Mary, was rescued by the husband to whom Charles had betrothed her, Maximilian of Austria. As we have seen, he halted the advance of the French king, and, although the ensuing peace confirmed Louis' conquests, Artois and Franche Comté were restored in 1493 by Charles VIII to him and his son, the Archduke Philip. Thus, the middle state, created by the Burgundian dukes, still subsisted, linked by the persons of its rulers to the Austrian dominions and the Empire.

Although the Netherlands, apart from the quite separate duchy of Burgundy and Franche Comté, had been slowly pieced together by the dukes, principally Philip the Good, a more than personal union had been established under the dynasty, in which economic and semi-national factors were influential. For the most part, the rule of the dukes had been due to the consent of the populations, though Liége and Guelders were annexed by conquest. It is true that Bruges (1436) and Ghent (1450–3) rose against Philip, but this was merely the attempt of those towns to preserve outworn and now unprofitable privileges, which won no support from the rest of Flanders. The prosperity of the country, which found its centre and outlet in the free port of Antwerp untrammelled by meddling local greed and its narrow spirit of monopoly, fed the loyalty to the ducal house. The united Netherlands were able to defy the commercial blockade of the Hansa in 1448–58. If Bruges lost, Antwerp gained. In 1433 Philip the Good inaugurated a coinage current throughout his dominions, and the cloth-industry was migrating from the gild-bound towns to the unhampered conditions of the countryside. There was a steady progress in Dutch fishing and shipping under the duke's protection. The social peace resulting from prosperity and free enterprise rendered the bourgeoisie and nobility firm supporters of their monarch. The great nobles were bound to the sovran by his new Order of the Golden Fleece (1430). They all looked on him as their 'natural prince', and Commynes could call the wealthy Netherlands a 'promised land'.

The dukes created a set of central institutions, which amounted to federation. The Great Council, in which all the provinces were represented, little by little imposed its authority over all matters outside the local constitutions. Its judicial section became in 1473 the Parlement of Malines, the supreme court of appeal. In 1471 a standing army was created in the *Compagnies d'Ordonnance*. Most important was the summons (1463) by Philip the Good of the Estates General, consisting of representatives of the provincial Estates. Taxes could only be levied by consent of the local assemblies, and the Estates General were in fact a congress of them. The new federal monarchy remained limited in spite of the absolutist tendencies of its dukes, the common feature of the century. In short, with freedom of individual enterprise, with the organization of internal peace and justice and finance within a wide territory of a national character, the Netherlands were going through the slow and chequered evolution from late medieval to modern times.

(3) GERMANY AND THE EMPIRE

The death of King Albert II revealed more patently than ever the irremediable disunion and confusion of German politics. The Hansa League and the northern princes merely went their own way, without regard to national concerns. In the centre and south, these were discussed interminably in frequent Diets, whose action was paralysed by the divergent interests of Emperor, princes, and towns. The aim of all members of the Empire was autonomy, dynastic in the princes and lesser tenants-in-chief of the Empire and parochial in the Imperial Towns. Germany was a mass of warring authorities, from which was to emerge a collection of great and petty autocrats, from Electors to Knights of the Empire, fortified by the formal reception of the Roman Civil Law (1495), ruling and fighting over their intertangled fiefs, and of scattered town republics, wealthy and cultured and able to preserve their independence but not to influence the national destiny. Yet, although monarchical power was shattered in Germany as a whole, it was gaining in its fragments. The close of the fifteenth century saw the territorial lords masters in their own lands, whether lay or ecclesiastical. Their nobles and diets (where these existed) and their towns (even when they belonged to the Hansa League) were being reduced to submission, and their little bureaucracies had begun to grow.

In 1440 the choice of the Electors was dictated by their own preference for a weak overlord and by the dearth of candidates likely to defend the Empire. They elected the eldest Habsburg, Frederick of Austria-Styria, the natural guardian of Albert II's posthumous son, Ladislas.[1] Frederick III (1440–93) shared with his troublesome brother Albert VI the poor and mountainous duchies of Styria, Carinthia and Carniola; he was regent of Tyrol and the western Habsburg lands for his cousin Sigismund (1439–96), and of Austria proper for Ladislas. The Electors may have guessed that this

---

[1] See Genealogical Table 21 above, pp. 796–7.

Fig. 240. Vienna, 1483

poor, cultured, and lethargic prince, perplexed by his relatives, his local diets, and his nobles, and by the disputed successions to Bohemia and Hungary, was not likely to revive the power of the German Crown. Yet through a reign of disasters Frederick, even when helpless, was tenacious and diplomatic to a degree. In the game of passive and often adroit resistance he was never quite outplayed. He surrendered no right or claim. He had the firmest, indeed a superstitious, belief in the destiny of the house of Habsburg, which was bolstered by his confidence in astrology, the dominant pseudo-science of the day, and was shown in his monogram A.E.I.O.U. (*Austriae est imperare orbi universo*), and, strange to say, the close of his long reign witnessed the rise of his son to a genuine leadership of Germany.

Frederick's troubles began, or rather continued, on his accession. He was obliged to see native rulers in Bohemia (George Poděbrady) and in Hungary (John Hunyadi) in spite of his efforts, and when he at last surrendered his ward, King Ladislas (1453), the chief change was his own loss of Austria proper. Sigismund, too, obtained his heritage of Tyrol, while Albert VI received the western lands, such as Upper Alsace (1446). In the interval, his attempt to assert his family and imperial rights in Switzerland by allying with Zürich and calling in the French army of *écorcheurs* had ended in failure and the ravaging of Alsace by them (1443–5). Beyond his coronation at Aachen (1442) and a vain Diet he had achieved nothing but ignominy. In 1444 he withdrew to his own lands for twenty-seven years. The elevation of Austria proper into an archduchy (1453), and his imperial coronation at Rome (1452) were poor titular consolations. In the purely diplomatic question of the Schism he was more fortunate from a dynastic point of view. Advised by Aeneas Sylvius Piccolomini and his Chancellor Schlick, he gradually edged from official neutrality and made a final Concordat with Pope Nicholas V in 1448. One after another all Estates of the Empire acceded to it. Separate bargains, profitable to the greater princes, were made on the example of Frederick, who had acquired valuable rights over the Church in his own territories.

Meantime, the wars and anarchy within Germany went on unchecked. Princely houses fought to obtain prince-bishoprics for their members and to wreak their family feuds. In south Germany the most important war was that between the princes and the towns. Brigandage and tolls were the grievances of the townsmen, the reception of countryside citizens (*Pfahlbürger*) that of the lords. The princely protagonist was the Margrave Albert Achilles of Brandenburg, who ruled the Hohenzollern lands of Ansbach and Baireuth, a typical feudal warrior, fierce and ambitious. The leader of the towns was his neighbour, the rich Imperial City of Nuremberg. A Swabian league of towns was faced by a league of nobles in a savage war from 1449 to 1453. In spite of a victory at Pillenreut the townsmen could not parry the wasting of the open country, just as the feudal armies could not take the towns, and in the peace of Lauf, Albert Achilles secured a money indemnity. This peace formed an epoch. Henceforward the free towns, content with their own defence, would not help one another. They looked on when in 1462 Mainz was subdued by its overlord, the Elector-Archbishop. The future of Germany lay not with them but with the greater princes.

Frederick's fortunes were then at a low ebb. The death of Ladislas in 1457, which was followed by the elections of George Poděbrady as King of Bohemia and of Matthias Corvinus as King of Hungary, diminished the Habsburg inheritance, while Austria proper was disputed between the Emperor and his brother Archduke Albert VI. Although personally rescued by Poděbrady, Frederick was expelled from the archduchy in 1462, only to recover it in 1463 by Albert's sudden death without a son. Sigismund of Tyrol was being worsted by the Swiss, and lost the remaining original Habsburg lands in the war. But the Emperor had enough to deal with in his own duchies and in his relations with his neighbours of Bohemia and Hungary.

King Matthias had extorted (1463) the surrender of the crown of St Stephen, which the Emperor had kept, with the addendum (long afterwards made real) of the Habsburg succession to Hungary if the Hunyadi became extinct. King George was in a difficult but strong position. He owed his crown to his headship of the Utraquist party and to Czech national feeling, but his Hussitism involved the enmity of the irreconcilable Papacy and the disloyalty of the Catholics and the German element in his dominions. His investiture by the Emperor was repaid by support, which was contaminated by his desire for election as King of the Romans. Hence he intervened in the long and tangled disputes of the German princes, who debated the provision of a colleague for their absentee Emperor. The Wittelsbachs led the opposition to Frederick in a considerable war, while Albert Achilles was the imperial champion, and Archduke Albert VI, as we have seen, attacked his brother. In 1461 King George almost secured election at a conference at Eger. It fell through, but he did arrange a peace at Prague in August 1463.

Rival schemes of reform and mutually hostile leagues of princes filled the next few years. But George Poděbrady lost his pre-eminence. His endeavours to appease the Papacy were wrecked by the determined intransigence of Pius II, the erstwhile Aeneas Sylvius and now the upholder of the highest curial claims. Nor did Pius's death in 1464 help the Bohemian king. Pope Paul II deposed him as a heretic in 1466, and the Catholic Czech nobles, after leaguing together at Zelená Hora (Grünberg) rose in revolt. King George was gaining the upper hand when the insurgents were joined by his ex-son-in-law King Matthias of Hungary (1468), who coveted Bohemia for himself. With some reverses and some sacrifice of his personal honour, Matthias gained a footing in Moravia and Silesia as well as a coronation as king. King George abandoned his wish for the succession of his own son and bought the alliance of Poland by the election of King Casimir IV's son Vladyslav as his heir (1469). In the midst of this three-cornered war and of peace-negotiations George died (1471). He had become a great figure in Czech national history, and with all drawbacks his reign had been a period of revival in Bohemia itself. But he had not solved the religious and national problems before him, exacerbated as they were by foreign intervention. Not only were the subordinate provinces, Moravia, Silesia, and Lusatia, restive to his doubtful sway, but the Germans in Bohemia itself were recalcitrant. The disaffected found a common bond in their papalist, conservative belief. Nor were the ardent, nationalistic Utraquists able to obtain with his and their utmost efforts their minimum terms from the Papacy, the confirmation of the Compacts and the Chalice for the laity. At the same time they held firmly to episcopal ordination and the apostolic succession for the clergy. Hence, since Rokycana (*ob.* 1471) could never gain consecration as archbishop, the Utraquist clergy were unable to receive holy orders save by subterfuge in foreign parts and were diminishing in numbers. Their papalist opponents were as active in controversy as themselves, and the Hussite extremists, freed from Taborite extravagance, were forming a new, radical association of their own (1467), to which King George and the Utraquists dealt out bitter persecution. Add to this, that while nobles and townsmen prospered, the peasants were finding their burdens increasing and their liberty being curtailed. Only the stubborn spirit of the Czechs and the rivalries which prevailed around them preserved their harassed independence.

Vladyslav II (1471–1516) was immediately elected King by the Bohemians, while Matthias, supported by the Papacy, maintained his position. The war, interspersed with truces, lasted until the Peace of Olomouc (Olmütz) in 1478, which divided the country between the two combatants, Matthias taking Moravia, Silesia, and Lusatia, Vladyslav II Bohemia proper. Should Vladyslav die heirless before Matthias, the latter should succeed him. The contrary, however, happened. On Matthias's death in 1490, Vladyslav was elected to the throne of Hungary and took back the ceded provinces. Meantime the Utraquist schism continued. Since the king himself was a papalist, the Catholics at first gained ground, but the violent resistance of Prague produced the treaty of Kutná Hora (1485), which restored the *status quo* of King George's time. More striking was the growth of the Hussite dissidents, the Unity of the Brotherhood founded by the quietist Chelčicsky, which broke with the ideas of the Universal Church and the apostolic succession. Abandoning its absolute abstention from secular activities, the Unity spread rapidly, and influenced the Reformation movement. Turbulent elements had wandered off to the wars around. Otherwise the reign of a weak king was marked by depression of the peasantry, now tied to the soil, and the issue at long last of a Bohemian national code of law. The triumph of monarchy, suspended by the religious wars, was to come later under the Habsburg dynasty.

To return to German affairs, Frederick III, tormented in the Habsburg lands by the insubordinate nobles, was eluding the pressure of his powerful neighbours by his characteristically slippery diplomacy. For a while he warded off Matthias by a pretence of supporting his election as King of the Romans. The Wittelsbachs of the Palatinate and Bavaria had long been his constant enemies, and the Emperor's deposition was only prevented by the divisions among the Electors. Frederick's own contribution to reform, an imperial court of justice (1471), died away in a few years. This project was due to the danger looming from the Turks, whose raids reached Carniola. More adapted to Frederick's ambitions was the possibility of the Burgundian inheritance which was offered by the hand of Charles the Bold's daughter and heiress, Mary. Frederick put forward his own only son Maximilian, but Charles demanded either the kingship of the Romans or the erection of a new kingdom from his hereditary lands. Oddly enough, the Emperor's miserable evasion of the demand by his stealthy flight from Trier produced unusual help from the Electors to repel the angry Charles from his revengeful siege of Neuss (1475), and Charles's overthrow by the Swiss and Louis XI's invasion of the Netherlands caused Mary's marriage to the warlike Maximilian (August 1477). The balance of power was suddenly changed, for the possession of the wealthy Netherlands rendered the house of Habsburg incontestably the strongest German dynasty and the champion of the Empire to west and east.

Frederick's own embarrassments, however, were worse than ever. As we have seen, King Matthias drove him out of his hereditary lands. His dissipated cousin, Sigismund of Tyrol, was unbearable to his own subjects

and hostile to him, while the Wittelsbachs of Bavaria were insolently aggressive. The Emperor's prospects at last began to brighten when he allowed the election of his vigorous son as King of the Romans (1486). An effective League of Swabian lords and towns was then formed and provided an army, which fortified Maximilian in the Netherlands as regent for his son Archduke Philip, and checked the Bavarian dukes. In 1490 Sigismund surrendered Tyrol, Upper Alsace, etc., in return for a pension. In the same year Matthias died, and Maximilian entered on Austria, although he failed to oust Vladyslav from Hungary. The Habsburg inheritance was reunited in his popular hands when in 1493 the Emperor closed an invertebrate reign.

One cause of the turmoil of Germany and the survival of the Empire had been the continual subdivision of the fiefs among all the male heirs. That primogeniture was the cure for the multiplication of princelings was

Fig. 241. Tomb of the Emperor Frederick III

shown by the history of the Hohenzollerns. For long their electoral mark of Brandenburg attracted them less than their old possessions in Franconia. The Elector Frederick II (1440–70), however, established a firm rule in Brandenburg, and his brother Albert Achilles (1470–86), although mostly occupied in the south, defeated (1478) a league of all his northern neighbours, including Matthias of Hungary. He was the last of his house to rule in both Brandenburg and Franconia, and the *Dispositio Achillea* (1473) recognized the predominance of Brandenburg in establishing it as the share of his oldest son and his descendants. Thus a solid state was insured in the north, the future rival of the Habsburgs.

At the time northern Germany was more deeply concerned in the fortunes of the Hansa League. Some of the history of the League in the fifteenth century has transpired in that of its chief neighbours, Scandinavia, the Netherlands, France, and England, which disputed its monopoly of the Baltic, the fishing and the salt trades. There was little harmony among the chief Hansa towns. Riga and Danzig were inclined to pursue their own policy regardless of Lübeck. Russian Novgorod was an awkward customer and salesman. Only a commercial blockade (1388–92) restored the Hansa's treaty-rights. With England there was a standing controversy due to English attempts at competition in the Baltic and the piracy in the Channel. The contests with Scandinavia in the Baltic and the piracy there have been briefly indicated. A first conflict with the Flemish towns, complicated by dissensions within the Hansa League itself, was ended by a commercial blockade (1388–92) and the transfer of the Kontor from Bruges to Dordrecht in Holland, which induced Duke Philip the Bold to renew the Hansa's privileges.

The League was being weakened by the discontent of the craft-gilds in the towns with the merchant-oligarchs, the 'patricians'. The tendency was to admit the craft-gilds to the town council and to repress the mere employees. Lübeck was paralysed from 1408 to 1418 by these internal dissensions. But the real danger to the commercial monopoly and hegemony of the League, along with the varying independence of its scattered towns, was the growth of larger states, which could defy its commercial blockade in the face of the closer confederation, led by Lübeck, which was adopted in 1418. In spite of war and Baltic piracy, the League, as we have seen, could hold its own against Scandinavia until 1497, but the acquisition of Holland by Philip the Good in 1433 altered the situation in the Netherlands. Although the Hansa could break the resistance of Bruges (1436–8), which besides was losing its status as a port, it was to the advantage of Antwerp. The Hollanders became serious rivals in the North Sea fisheries, and the duke of Burgundy was a redoubtable enemy. The agreement of 1458 with him was a compromise, and the steady decentralization of trade and manufacture in the now united Netherlands made Hansa dominance at Bruges of less importance, and a renewed commercial blockade of Flanders (1448–58) of less effect. The Hansa could not afford to ban the whole Netherlands. Owing, perhaps, to the weak Lancastrian government and to the Wars of the Roses, the dealings of the Hansa with England were more fortunate at last. After long ups and downs and piratical wars and truces, complicated by the secession of Cologne and the Westphalian towns from the League for a decade and a destructive riot of the Londoners against the German settlement of the Steelyard, the stubborn Hansa won a complete victory in the treaties of Utrecht (1474). The English merchants failed entirely to obtain equal treatment. As arrangements were made with the Netherlands at the same time, and Louis XI was friendly, commercial peace reigned for a while in the West. In the East the situation in the later fifteenth century was not so happy for the Hansa. The decline of the Teutonic Order after 1410 deprived the League of a valuable ally, and after Poland's victory and the Peace of Thorn (Torun) in 1466 Danzig was really the only Hansa town left in Prussia. Riga, the chief Hansa town in Livonia, since c.1418 the equal of Lübeck in the Russian trade, and since 1459 enjoying a monopoly at Novgorod, lost its privileges in 1478 when Ivan III of Muscovy annexed that emporium. The Hansa here, too, was faced with a wide national state, and in 1494 the German settlement at Novgorod died out.

With the loss of its trade monopolies, the Hansa League was slowly ceasing to be a great power, and many of its members were slipping away. Yet Lübeck and the great ports were still the main trading communities of the north from Spain to Livonia and Norway, if the south-German towns, Nuremberg, Frankfurt-on-Main, and others were on the way to outstrip them on the continental routes, and Dutch and English fishers were at least rivalling them in the herring supply.

The Hansa League never ceased to be a part of Germany. On the other hand, like the Netherlands, Switzerland at the close of the Middle Ages was *de facto*, though not *de iure*, an independent state. Switzerland alone had found the way to form a durable federation of free communities subject to no dynastic house. Geography, common interest, and fighting qualities, together with sterling good sense, had produced this unique result. Not all the Swiss were equal or even self-governing. Within a canton like Berne the peasants might be subordinate to the town oligarchy. The alliances of the cantons among themselves and with subordinate allies were most complicated, and conquered districts were mere subjects. After the war with Duke Frederick IV of Austria-Tyrol the Aargau in 1415 became such. Lesser acquisitions may be passed over. In 1442 the Austrian King Frederick III endeavoured to split the Confederation by alliance with Zürich. The war which followed proved the prowess of the Swiss against the veteran *écorcheurs*, and confirmed their union. New districts, St Gall, Appenzell, and Glarus joined the Swiss complex. In further conflicts Duke Sigismund lost almost all the remnants of the old Habsburg lands south of the Rhine. At last, as we have seen, with the help of Louis XI's diplomacy, the Perpetual Peace of Constance was arranged with Duke Sigismund in 1474. The war with Charles the Bold (1476–7), then planned, meant war also with the duchy of Savoy, in which Vaud was for a time conquered, to be later annexed by Berne.

Subsequent events belong more to modern than medieval history. Here it must suffice to say that the divergence between the town cantons and the more aggressive country cantons went to the verge of civil war, which was happily averted by a compromise, the Covenant of Stanz (22 December 1481). A last attempt by King Maximilian to enforce his own and the imperial diet's authority ended in 1499 in war and Swiss victory. The Peace of Basle exempted Switzerland from even the claim of imperial jurisdiction, which meant in practice the acknowledgement of its independence. Through long-drawn various stages and preliminary alliances the number of full cantons rose to thirteen by the admission of Basle (1501), Schaffhausen, Fribourg, and Solothurn (1502), and Appenzell (1513). The Grisons, St Gall, Neufchâtel, and the Valais were free allies.

The victorious campaigns of the Swiss and the part they played in Europe were largely due to the efficiency of their military system. Training and service were compulsory from the age of sixteen, and the Confederation could, if it never did, muster 50,000 men. Arrayed in deep columns, armed with long pikes, which projected far beyond the leading ranks in a series of steel points, these footmen were invulnerable to frontal attack and could thrust down horse and man. They could suffer from artillery and hand-firearms, but these arms were yet to reach an overwhelming power, and the hardihood of the Swiss could endure heavy loss. But a population trained to war within a narrow and poor country found its outlet in mercenary service abroad. Louis XI had perceived the profit of hiring Swiss soldiers by means of an alliance with the Confederation, but plenty of Swiss soldiers were to be had by contending rulers without the sanction of a treaty. Fighting became the most paying trade of the Switzer. The same venality affected the statesmen of the Confederation. For bribes and pensions they sold their influence and votes in the diets of League and cantons in dealings with foreign powers. It was Switzerland's share in the lowered public morale of the fifteenth century.

Thus the Empire, with contracting frontiers and disintegrated into little states, appeared to be little more than a name in 1500. But its tradition was still strong and the Emperor-elect of the Romans, in virtue of the Habsburg dominions, was a potent prince. There were still common interests and institutions in Germany, which the Reformation and international politics were to display and strain to breaking-point.

CHAPTER 36

THE BRITISH ISLES

(I) ENGLAND: THE WARS OF THE ROSES, 1450–1485[1]

In England the progress of monarchy was delayed and disguised and eventually brought about by the dynastic conflict of York and Lancaster, to which the weakness and insanity of Henry VI gave an opening. King Henry at this time was childless, although married to Margaret of Anjou since 1445, and the question of the succession was undecided. His nearest kinsman in the male line was Edmund Beaufort, Duke of Somerset, grandson of John of Gaunt, but the Beauforts had been barred from succession to the crown when Henry IV confirmed their legitimation. The next nearest in the male line was Richard, Duke of York, grandson of Edmund of York, Edward III's fifth son, but in the female line Richard could propound a superior hereditary claim to Henry VI's own, for his father, the Richard of Cambridge executed in 1415, had married the heiress of Mortimer, and hence of Edward III's third son, Lionel of Clarence. Rivalry between York and Somerset and their respective allies for the control of the king was almost inevitable, and became expressed in popular story by the White and Red Roses they were said, fabulously perhaps, to have adopted as their emblems. The struggle was an amalgamation of the .many local feuds between the magnates rather than a choice between good and bad government. Each man among them chose as private ambition and connexion dictated. Duke Richard was, apart from the king, lord of more acres than any of his compeers. Mowbray of Norfolk and the Nevilles, father and son, of Salisbury and Warwick, his kinsmen and partisans, were only less endowed than he. Their enemies were the allies of Somerset and the house of Lancaster. The king was a saintly puppet. The middle and lower classes were, save on rare occasions, neutral between the baronial combatants, from whom they could hope for small profit. The smaller gentry had no choice but to follow the magnates, on whom they depended, but the townsfolk could manifest their indifference.

York, headstrong and after all, in spite of his professions, a rebel, was a poor tactician in politics. His preliminary advantage of surprise and force in 1450 was lost in face of the honest placability of the king and the adroitness of the reigning faction of Somerset and the court. For a time they won over the Commons and baffled York, until in August 1453 Henry VI fell into a state of imbecility. In November York took control, while Somerset was sent to the Tower. Meantime a new factor had been

[1] See Genealogical Table 23 above, pp. 892–3.

Fig. 242. Richard Beauchamp, Earl of Warwick

introduced into the struggle by the birth in October of Edward, Prince of Wales. Queen Margaret became a fierce and implacable defender of her son and his rights. For a year, however, York was content to be Protector, until about Christmas 1454 the king returned to his senses, and reinstated Somerset. York took to arms and fought the first battle of the Wars of the Roses at St Albans (22 May 1455). He won it, and captured the king and the government. The deaths of Somerset and other Lancastrian magnates in the fight added ferocious blood-feuds to the conflict, for the beaten faction was anything but overcome, and although, when a second access of insanity seized on Henry, York was made Protector, the king's speedy recovery deposed him again, and the rancorous queen prevented any compromise. Both sides prepared for a second civil war. When it came in 1459, York to begin with had the worse. He withdrew to Ireland, the Nevilles and his eldest son, Edward, Earl of March, to Warwick's government of Calais. Most unwisely the angry Lancastrians not only attainted their foes but also embarked on oppressive and extortionate government, which aroused general disfavour. When in June 1460 the Nevilles and March landed again in Kent, they were welcomed there and in London. They routed the Lancastrians and captured King Henry at Northampton (10 July). Duke Richard then appeared in a fresh Parliament, and abruptly claimed the crown in virtue of his descent from Lionel of Clarence (October). The peers were far from compliant, but a compromise declared

1055

him heir to Henry VI and Protector to the exclusion of the Prince of Wales. Time had been given to Queen Margaret to mass an army in Yorkshire, where near Wakefield on 30 December 1460 York was defeated and killed. A son of his and the Earl of Salisbury were slaughtered after the fight, while Richard's head with a paper crown was displayed at York. The queen, at the head of her bands of fierce borderers, English, Scots, and Welsh, next proceeded south, looting town and country on the way and defeating Warwick at the second battle of St Albans (17 February 1461). King Henry escaped to join her, but they hesitated to enter London with their unruly troops. March, however, had meanwhile defeated the Lancastrians in the west at Mortimer's Cross. He now re-entered London and was 'elected' King Edward IV by acclamation (26 February). He overtook the retreating Lancastrians at Towton in Yorkshire, where he crushed them with great slaughter (29 March). Henry, Margaret and their son fled to Scotland, and the victor was crowned. The 'judgement of God' by battle had more weight on opinion than the wire-drawn arguments on legitimacy through the female line—a debated theme—of the Yorkist claimant *versus* parliamentary sanction and long possession of the Lancastrian line.

The new king was a handsome, stalwart, popular youth, an excellent general and soldier, but in times of peace so given to indolence and his pleasures as to mask his strength of character and genuine ability. Far more active in the public eye was 'the King-maker', Richard Neville, Earl of Warwick and Salisbury, who was now the wealthiest subject in England. Distinguished as soldier, sailor and statesman for many years, at the head of an army of retainers, he held the reins of government. It was he who now with vindictive ruthlessness fought down the Lancastrian risings in the north. Slaughter or execution of captured magnates was now the order of the day, while attainders enriched the royal demesne.

The government, like all those founded on faction since 1450, with its Parliaments always submissive to the party in power, paid small heed to the rampant evils nurtured by Livery and Maintenance, but foreign policy was perforce its care. Louis XI of France, the hereditary enemy, gave for a while support to Queen Margaret in the north, but as the Yorkists grew more firmly seated, he changed his drift. Warwick, perhaps convinced that peace with France was desirable, was urging his king in 1464 to marry Louis' sister-in-law, Bona of Savoy, when Edward announced that he was already married to a Lancastrian lady, Elizabeth, widow of Lord Ferrers of Groby and daughter of Anthony Woodville, Lord Rivers. Favours were soon conferred on her numerous kinsfolk, who began to link a definite, if not over-powerful, group among the peers. Warwick and his connexions, still in high place and influence, found that the king had escaped from their leading-strings.

The divergence in policy and interest which the growing rift indicated, was shown in 1468 when Edward married his sister Margaret to Charles the Bold and concluded alliances with Burgundy and Brittany. There were good reasons for the move, for it benefited English merchants in the Flanders trade and enabled Edward to take a strong line in the recurrent disputes with the Hansa League. But it meant—and Edward seemed eager for—that war with France which Warwick was energetically working to preclude. The breach between king and earl, widened by dismissals of Warwick's friends and by competition for the profitable marriages of heiresses, was made manifest when in 1469 Warwick gave his elder daughter and co-heiress as wife to the king's brother, George, the 'false, fleeting' Duke of Clarence, at Calais, which he still governed. Clarence was only one of many malcontents. There were plots and risings, and 'Robin of Redesdale' (whoever he was) led a formidable gathering in Yorkshire. Starting from Calais, Warwick and Clarence invaded England and trapped Edward in the Midlands, while his dilatory army was defeated at Edgecote. Death was as usual meted out to the king's friends, and Edward himself, after a brief captivity, was led to London, where Henry VI, who had fallen into his hands in 1465, was still a prisoner in the Tower. Warwick seemed to be supreme, but other Yorkist nobles did not love the Neville group, and Edward was a master of the intrigue and dissimulation of the day. Warwick did not scheme to depose him, and in March 1470 the king mustered friendly magnates to repress a rising in Lincolnshire, and then drove the unwary earl from the country. Edward's triumph, too, was short lived. Warwick found a helper in Louis XI, who, with the view of keeping alive the internal riot of England, achieved the difficult task of reconciling him and Clarence with the exiled Queen Margaret. Once more a diversion was provided in a northern insurrection, while Warwick landed in the south-west. With Lancastrian aid he occupied London, and Edward, deserted by pretended supporters, had only time to take ship for Holland (October 1470). Henry VI, more numb and puppet-like than aforetime, was reinvested with the crown under the charge of Warwick.

The earl's hold on England, however, was far from secure. Norfolk and other Yorkists were against Neville domination and a Lancastrian king. Clarence, disappointed of his own hopes of the crown, had been long intriguing with King Edward. Queen Margaret, still in France with her son, justifiably suspected her new ally, although his other daughter Anne was now Princess of Wales. Warwick's pro-French policy set the reaction going. His treaty with Louis XI engaged him to attack Charles the Bold, who replied by aiding Edward IV to make another bid for the throne in Hansa ships. He landed in Yorkshire, outgeneralled Warwick, was joined by the turncoat Clarence, and entered London. Sallying thence, he won on 13 April 1471 the hard-fought battle of Barnet, in which Warwick himself

1057

was slain. With the King-maker fell the Neville greatness, for which he had contended. Queen Margaret landed in Dorset on the same day, and was joined by the south-western Lancastrians and the Duke of Somerset, fleeing from Barnet. Her army headed for the Severn to meet her Welsh partisans, but was caught up by King Edward at Tewkesbury. There (4 May) it was cut to pieces. Prince Edward of Wales was killed in the rout without mercy; Somerset, the last of the male Beauforts, and other leaders were beheaded by the victor; Margaret was kept a prisoner, while the unhappy Henry VI was murdered in the Tower (21 May). The house of Lancaster appeared to be extinguished.

Although there was some more sporadic fighting, Edward was now secure in uncontrolled power, but his character was rather worse than better for his vicissitudes. Cruel, faithless, and treacherous on occasion, an indolent, yet masterful voluptuary, his pleasant address made him personally popular. At any rate, what with confiscations, benevolences (i.e. forced loans), fines, and judicious trading, he was a solvent king, who rarely needed to summon his subservient Parliaments. After all, the benevolences exacted from the well-to-do were an arbitrary method of taxing wealth which escaped the fossilized tenths and fifteenths. Edward did not possess the activity or the creativeness of a vexatious despot, although embryos of some later Tudor institutions, such as the bureaucratic councils and the importance of the king's secretary, appear in his reign. Measures designed to protect and encourage English traders and industry show the bent of the government and the middle class. Edward ceased to check Livery and Maintenance. It sufficed him that so many of the greater magnate houses had been broken or rendered harmless in the slaughter and proscriptions of the wars. When his anger and suspicions were aroused, his native hardness knew no restraints. Clarence continued to be a factious, ambitious, and quite untrustworthy brother. Edward now had children and heirs, and perhaps was the more ruthless. In 1478 he called a Parliament for the purpose of attainting and condemning him to death, the execution or murder being carried out in dead secrecy, in itself a commentary on the men and the time.

A contributory cause of the fall of Clarence was his meddling in foreign affairs. In 1474 Edward, when giving way to the Hansa League at Utrecht, had arranged with Charles the Bold for a joint attack on France. Well supplied by benevolences and his obedient Parliament, the king led one of the finest English armies from Calais in 1475, but Charles lingered too long at Neuss, as we have seen, and Edward stooped to a money transaction with Louis XI at Picquigny in August. For a large sum down and an annual pension he withdrew and surrendered his prisoner Margaret of Anjou, while a match was arranged between the dauphin and his eldest daughter Elizabeth. It was a return to Warwick's policy and the winning side, however

Fig. 243. Jean de Wavrin dedicating his Chronicle to Edward IV

unpalatable to his deluded subjects. The situation changed again when
Charles was overthrown by the Swiss. Clarence, just then a widower,
schemed to marry Mary, the heiress of Burgundy; Edward, more wisely,
favoured her marriage to Archduke Maximilian, a far better antagonist to
French expansion. Maximilian secured the prize, but Edward was cheated
to his wrath in 1482, when the dauphin was promised to Maximilian's
daughter, and Louis had already stirred up trouble with the Scots. Since
1461, when Henry VI ceded Berwick to Scotland in return for armed
assistance, Edward had made use of Scottish malcontents and exiles, but in
1463 a long truce was arranged between the kingdoms. At Louis'

instigation the Scots renewed the border raids in 1480, and in concert with James III's exiled brother, the Duke of Albany, Edward's youngest brother, the Duke of Gloucester, was sent to invade Scotland (June 1482). Berwick was recaptured, but Albany, who had agreed to be vassal King of Scots, made his own terms—to be his brother's vice-regent—and the retrocession of Berwick was perhaps all that Edward earnestly desired, although he soon renewed his treaty with the then falling Albany.

Fig. 244. Richard III

The man who recovered Berwick permanently for England, Richard of Gloucester, had, unlike Clarence, hitherto borne a fair reputation according to the unexacting standards of the day. He had been faithful to Edward IV, and won loyalty in Yorkshire, where he owned the Neville lands by his marriage to Prince Edward's widow. His soldiership was unquestioned. Men knew that he would not hesitate at ruthless acts more than his compeers; that he would stop at nothing in pursuit of his personal ambition, they had yet to learn. When they did, it produced the Tudor tradition that he was a monster from birth. He was brought to the test by the death of Edward IV, who had worn out his strength, on 9 April 1483. The new king, Edward V, was a boy of twelve, and it was evident that there would be a contest for the regency between Gloucester and the Woodville clan, who were old enemies. By craft and energy Gloucester won. He gained possession of the king, and dispersed or imprisoned the unpopular Woodville group. Thereafter, with the aid of the Duke of Buckingham, he worked for the crown. On 13 June he suddenly beheaded Lord Hastings, who was likely to oppose him, and then induced Queen Elizabeth to hand over to him her second son, Richard, Duke of York. It was then publicly preached and spread abroad that Edward IV's children were illegitimate owing to a pre-contract with another lady, while the children of Clarence were under attainder. Forces had been assembled, and on 26 June an assembly of Estates (not a Parliament) declared Gloucester to be King Richard III as rightful heir. Such of the Woodville group as were captive were promptly executed. But, although Richard's accession was accepted and he strove for popularity, these disgraceful proceedings told against

1060

him, and to complete his work he ordered the murder of his young nephews in the Tower (August). It was a miscalculation. The murder of young boys went beyond the customary latitude, and thenceforward he had few friends. Further, he had thereby made his marriageable eldest niece the heiress of Edward IV, and, although he made overtures for marrying her himself, when his wife and his only son died, he only increased the general repulsion. It became possible for most Yorkist lords to scheme for a union of factions by plotting her marriage to a new pretender, Henry Tudor, the exiled Earl of Richmond. Richmond's mother, Lady Margaret Beaufort, was the daughter of John, Duke of Somerset (*ob.* 1444), and heiress of such claims as those illegitimate Lancastrians could put forward. His father, Edmund, was the son of a Welsh gentleman, Owen Tudor, by the French widow of Henry V. The French court entered into the scheme. A first rebellion, led by the repentant Duke of Buckingham, was put down with ease, but when Richmond landed in 1485 at Milford Haven, among the Welsh compatriots of his father and his uncle Jasper Tudor, Earl of Pembroke, the king found that he could not depend on many of his seeming supporters. One, Lord Stanley, the second husband of the Lady Margaret, hung back and joined Richmond during the decisive battle of Bosworth; another, Percy of Northumberland, made no attempt to resist the enemy. Richard III died fighting. He closed the ancient line of Plantagenet, while the victor, Henry VII, began a new dynasty and a new regime (22 August 1485).

The Yorkist dynasty had largely risen through the growing desire for peace and order. It fell because, bred in feud and faction, it had not supplied them. Edward IV was too indolent and inconstant, and Richard III not intelligent enough and too neurotic in his ambition to accomplish a slow pacification. Besides, the overmighty magnates, of whom they were in essence specimens, although much weakened and depleted, were not yet wholly quelled, and neither was quite the man to kindle a devotion to the Crown amid the lesser gentry, merchants, and officials who were longing for stable, monarchical government. They were not hampered by their none too frequent Parliaments, which registered their decisions. The acts were drafted from above rather than from below. It is noticeable that borough-members were now often lesser gentry, lawyers, or officials as well as trading townsmen. The distinction between classes was not so marked as in France or Germany. The large landowner was a trader in his wool. His younger son might well be a merchant in London or other great town, and, if prosperous, would seek to buy an estate. Thus there was a strong and variegated middle class, impatient of the wrangling baronage who misruled the land, and looking, as yet in vain, for the strong, consistent king, who would master factious disorder and local tyranny. These capable gentry and merchants, as may be seen from their letters, were a hard and

Fig. 245. Tomb of a galloglass at Glinsk, Co. Galway

money-seeking generation, little inclined to chivalry or scruples. Their ambition was to advance their families in wealth and place, which was the easier because their resources were not drained, like those of the nobles, by a host of retainers. The show they made was to rebuild their parish churches and their own houses. Thus under the troublous aftermath of the foreign war, whose nemesis was the Wars of the Roses, there was arising a new society ready for an autocratic king, who would answer its desires.

(2) IRELAND IN THE FIFTEENTH CENTURY

During the reigns of the three Lancastrian kings the condition of Ireland went in general from bad to worse. All three were preoccupied elsewhere, and gave but little aid to their most active viceroys. The raids and blackmail of the border Irish chiefs afflicted the narrowing English Pale. When the warrior Sir John Talbot (later Earl of Shrewsbury and Waterford) brought them (1414–20) into temporary submission, his exactions to support his troops gave the English loyalists the alternative of being plundered by their enemies or despoiled by their friends. From 1414 to 1449 the chief power in the government for the most part oscillated between the Talbots (Sir John and his brother Richard, Archbishop of Dublin), who came from England, and the Anglo-Irish Butlers of Ormonde, who were far from friends. In spite of their warlike activity, however, the Pale round Dublin only measured 30 miles by 20 in 1435. The long failure of the impoverished government to give order and equal justice wrecked any chance of gaining

Fig. 246. Holy Cross Abbey, Co. Tipperary

the confidence of the Irish septs. The small minority of loyalists became fewer and poorer. Many emigrated; others, especially the great Anglo-Norman barons, became hibernicized, a blend of feudalists and Irish chiefs. Methods of fighting had become identical. All the great chieftains maintained their galloglasses, professional and in some sort disciplined. What preserved the remnant of the settlers was the utter discord of the Irish septs. The old clans, always at enmity, were fissiparous as well, and could not unite. Each chief and fraction preferred to plunder the English for their own hand.

When in 1449 Richard, Duke of York and Earl of Ulster, the heir of the Mortimers and himself a royal prince, was exiled as King's Lieutenant of Ireland, he was well received by all parties, and his conciliation of them rendered the country predominantly Yorkist. He and the Anglo-Irish deputies he appointed, the fourth Earl of Ormonde, FitzEustace, and the seventh Earl of Kildare, held Parliaments and did their best to rule. The duke drew force from Ireland in the English civil war until he fell at Wakefield (30 December 1460). But since the FitzGeralds of Kildare and Desmond were Yorkists, their foes, the Butlers, became Lancastrians and waged the endemic clan warfare under the Red Rose.

The victory of King Edward IV furthered a development, already practised by his father York, of entrusting of such royal authority as existed to a group of Anglo-Irish baronial chiefs. The Yorkist Parliament of Drogheda in 1460 had already asserted the legal and legislative independence of

1063

Ireland in set terms. Now the FitzGerald, Thomas, seventh Earl of Desmond, was appointed Deputy under the absent Duke of Clarence. He had the characteristics of an Irish chieftain, and although beloved by the Irish and barons like himself, he was distrusted by the less hibernicized lords and unable to make head against greater chiefs like O'Conor of Offaly and O'Brien of Thomond. In 1467 he was superseded by the English Tiptoft, Earl of Worcester, who had earned the evil name of 'the butcher' for his vindictiveness in the civil war. Next year Desmond and his ally Kildare were attainted for leaguing with the Irish, and he was executed, but Kildare made his peace and, when Tiptoft was himself beheaded in the brief Lancastrian restoration in 1470, was appointed Justiciar. Whoever was King's Lieutenant, he and his successors, the eighth and ninth Earls of Kildare, became indispensable and the real governors of Ireland, with brief exceptions, for the next sixty-four years. Under this troubled, tribal, and baronial state of things, with the native Irish language, literature, and customs always in the ascendant, the revival of monarchy was impossible in Ireland without a new English conquest.

(3) SCOTLAND, 1424–1488

The return of James I (1406–37) to his kingdom in 1424 marks an epoch in Scottish history and in the hitherto ineffective house of Stewart. Unlike his father, he enjoyed full vigour of mind and body. He bent himself to one absorbing task, the revival of the power of the monarchy and the quelling of the anarchic nobles. 'There shall not be a spot in my kingdom', he said, 'where the key doth not keep the castle and the bracken the cow.' He set about his task with swift energy and at first with little resistance. In 1425 he strengthened the Crown and took his private vengeance by executing his cousin, the Duke of Albany, with his two sons and the Earl of Lennox. Besides confiscating their fiefs, he seized on the earldoms of Strathearn, March, and Mar. In 1427–9 Alexander, the Lord of the Isles, was brought to heel. First imprisoned, then revolted, he was forced to beg for mercy. Other chiefs had been executed. Of Highlands and Lowlands James was master. He was rapacious and burdened the Scots with taxation to remedy the poverty of the Crown, but he also endeavoured to remedy the poverty of the land by his legislation as well as to check the private feuds. Aeneas Sylvius, a visitor, terms Scotland 'a barren wilderness,' and Froissart tells a similar story. But in James I's day things began to mend, and by 1500 the Lowlands had attained to considerable prosperity. James's laws insist on the improvement of cultivation as well as armed musters and the maintenance of internal peace. In 1428 he empowered the lesser tenants-in-chief to elect county representatives to attend Parliaments, an imitation of England which was long in bearing full fruit. With England he was at peace for years. He married Joan Beaufort, his love-affair with whom is commemorated in his poems named the *Kingis Quair*. After the truce of 1423 expired, hostilities began again, and James in 1436 vainly besieged Roxburgh, since 1334 in English hands.

James I showed few scruples in his war with anarchy, and the rancour excited helped to bring about his death. Sir Robert Graham, embittered by family and personal wrongs, lent himself to the ambitions of the king's half-uncle, Walter, Earl of Atholl, who being born in wedlock, whereas Robert III had only been legitimated, nourished a hope to exalt his own grandson, Sir Robert Stewart, to the throne. Sir Robert, being the royal chamberlain, was able to admit Graham and his men into the Black Friars at Perth, where they murdered King James unawares. They were tortured to death by the loyalists.

James I with all his faults had begun the struggle to make the monarchy effective and to hold down the fierce magnates, but his aim, hard to reach in any case, was continually baffled by the fact that each of his successors, even if capable, began his reign as a minor, of which the baronage took full advantage. His son, James II (1437–60), was in youth under the tutelage of Sir William Crichton and Sir Alexander Livingstone, old servants of his father. These two carried out by treachery the execution (1440) of the young Earl of Douglas, with his brother, chiefs of the border house, which by its vast possessions and its warlike prestige was the rival of the Crown. Their great-uncle, the seventh earl (*ob.* 1443), did not take up the deadly feud thus begun, but his son William, the eighth earl, in alliance with Livingstone, procured the outlawry of Crichton and his own appointment as Lieutenant-general of the realm. His victory over an English force at Sark on the Border added to his fame (1448). But James II became of age in 1450, and found an able and loyal adviser in his Chancellor, James Kennedy, Bishop of St Andrews, who was intent on maintaining the power of the Crown against the overmighty barons. In 1444 Douglas had made a dangerous league with two northern compeers, the Earl of Crawford and John, Lord of the Isles and Earl of Ross. While Douglas was sent on a mission to Rome, James II showed his authority in his fiefs, and after the earl's return summoned him to Stirling. Douglas came, but when he refused to abandon his bond with Crawford and Ross, he was murdered by the king's own hand (1452). A trial of strength between the Douglas and the monarchy was bound to follow. Lavish grants brought the king adherents, and both the ninth earl, James, and the Earl of Crawford were forced into submission. James II may have been merely biding his time and the earl may have planned treason during a mission to England. At any rate, the king took the field again in 1455, and drove Douglas and his brothers into exile in England. Although the banished earl gave trouble almost until his death (1488), the ruin of the Douglases was consummated. The best of

1065

Fig. 247. Hermitage Castle, Roxburghshire

their domains were forfeited to the Crown, which thereby emerged from its comparative poverty. James II excelled his father in his appropriations.

James II, whose relations with England had been a chequer of border warfare and truce, was inclined to favour the weak Lancastrians in the Wars of the Roses. When the Yorkists were predominant, he besieged Roxburgh, and there met his death on 3 August 1460 by the explosion of one of his cannon, which he was watching. His premature end at the age of 29 deprived Scotland of a king who might have made the cause of monarchy triumphant. As it was, although the rival Douglases had fallen, there were many formidable barons left, to whom the errors and misfortunes of his son, James III (1460–88), were to give their opportunity. While Bishop Kennedy (*ob.* 1465) lived and ruled, in spite of the opposition of the queen-mother, Mary of Guelders, the government had some success. Roxburgh was taken, the Lancastrians were aided gainst the Yorkists and their friends, the exiled Douglases, and Berwick itself was ceded (1461) by Henry VI in return for assistance. But Edward IV was too dangerous, the Douglases were raiding, and John of the Isles was in formidable rebellion. So Kennedy changed his side, and in 1463 made a truce, lasting fifteen years, with England.

The place left vacant by Bishop Kennedy's death was speedily filled in 1466 by the family plot of the Boyds, of whom Sir Alexander was governor of Edinburgh Castle. They kidnapped the youthful king, and induced a Parliament to name Lord Boyd governor of the realm. Their main object was to exalt themselves—in 1467 the king's sister was married to Lord Boyd's eldest son, created Earl of Arran—but incidentally they completed the territorial extent of Scotland. Christian I of Denmark and Norway was pressing for the long arrears of the tribute for the Hebrides. The dispute was made up by James III's marriage to Christian's daughter, Margaret (1469). The tribute was abolished, and the Orkney and Shetlands were pledged for her dowry, which the impecunious Christian could not pay. In 1472 they were annexed to Scotland. Before that the Boyds had fallen before a combination of jealous nobles (1469).

So far the reign had not been unfortunate. In 1472 the kingdom, hitherto directly under the Papacy, was given a metropolitan in the archbishop of St Andrews. The always dubious relations with England were ameliorated in 1474 by a treaty with Edward IV. This enabled the government to take stern measures against the ever-mutinous John of the Isles. He was compelled to surrender the earldom of Ross to the Crown (1476). But James III's own character was telling against him in face of the turbulent barons. He had no kingly or knightly tastes, and chose for his counsellors plebeian, if clever, favourites. His brothers, the Duke of Albany and the Earl of Mar, were men of the ordinary mould and his enemies. Mar died in prison, Albany fled to incite an English invasion. When in 1482 it came, the gathered Scottish barons at Lauder Bridge, headed by Archibald Douglas 'Bell-the-cat', Earl of Angus, seized

Fig. 248. Tombstone of Donald son of Patrick son of Earl Celestine of Lochalsh, cadet of the Lords of the Isles

and hanged the king's favourites. Albany was installed as Lieutenant of the realm, and Berwick was finally lost to England. Albany, however, was justifiably suspect of treason, nor was James powerless. In 1483 he attainted his brother, who escaped to throw a last stake in vain with the Earl of Douglas next year.

But James III was still addicted to counsellors of low birth and was personally unpopular, while the nobles were factious and divided. In 1488 the storm broke. After a hollow reconciliation with the malcontents, it came to war. James was defeated in June at Sauchie Burn, and then killed in cold blood. His unfilial eldest son became James IV.

It was clear that the monarchy had not yet succeeded in taming its truculent baronage. Yet much had been done since the accession of James I. The king was now comparatively wealthy and, if apt for his task, could by hard fighting enforce his will. The Scottish Parliament functioned. There was the apparatus of an ordered state in being. There had been a notable progress in the prosperity of the nation. The alliance with France established contacts with European politics and culture. Two universities had been founded for learning, and there was a hardy vernacular literature, which in verse was the best inheritor of Chaucer. Under all drawbacks these were national achievements.

CHAPTER 37

THE STATES OF SOUTHERN EUROPE

(I) SPAIN AND PORTUGAL[1]

Even before the death of Henry III of Castile in 1406, and the conclusion in 1411 of a definite peace with Portugal after some thirty years of alternate truces and wars, Aragon had taken the lead among the Iberian kingdoms as an expansive European power. The death of Martin I in 1410 without direct heirs seemed to compromise its solidarity, for there were several claimants for the succession, of whom his great-nephew Louis III of Anjou, and his nephew Ferdinand, son of John I of Castile, were foreigners, while the nearest heir in the male line, James, Count of Urgel, was also his brother-in-law. The Catalans, who favoured the native Count of Urgel, were, however, irresolute, and the skilful diplomacy of Pope Benedict XIII, backed by the influence of the Valencian St Vincent Ferrer, produced the election of Ferdinand I (1412–16) by a commission drawn from Aragon, Catalonia, and Valencia in the 'Compromise of Caspe'. The new king had already proved his capacity as regent of Castile. He speedily quelled the insurrection of the Count of Urgel and secured the allegiance of the sub-sidiary kingdoms of Majorca, Sicily and Sardinia. He helped to extinguish the Great Schism by abandoning his patron Benedict XIII shortly before his own death. If he was always suspect to the Catalans, his son Alfonso V the Magnanimous remedied this defect by pursuing the ancient Medi-terranean ambitions of Catalonia and making Catalan the language of his court. He fixed his eyes eastward. He recalled his brother John from Sicily, which might have revolted, but compensated him by the hand of Blanche, the heiress of Navarre. He proceeded with the never-ending conquest of Sardinia. Hence he was called in by Queen Joanna II of Naples to support her tottering throne and to succeed her (1420). She soon changed her mind, and there arose a fresh war between Alfonso and the rival candidate, Louis III of Anjou. When in 1435 Joanna died, and left her kingdom to the dead Louis' brother René, Alfonso renewed his claims. His defeat at sea and capture by the Genoese proved to be the occasion of his victory, for he won over in captivity the Duke of Milan to his cause, and then warred down King René in Naples. After a transient support of the dying Schism, he had finally acknowledged Martin V (1429), but not till 1443, when he had captured Naples, did he induce the hitherto hostile Pope Eugenius IV to invest him as king and become his ally.

[1] See Genealogical Table 24 above, pp. 902–3.

1069

Henceforward till his death in 1458 Alfonso lived at Naples as the Maecenas of a learned and artistic court of the Italian Renaissance. He had fulfilled the dream of his predecessors, but at the cost of the heavy taxation and discontent of his Spanish kingdoms, which he left to the regency of his Queen, Mary of Castile. When he died, he left his conquest of Naples to his bastard son Ferrante, while his brother John II, the King of Navarre, succeeded to his hereditary kingdoms.

John had continued to reign in Navarre after the death (1441) of Queen Blanche, by whom he had Charles, Prince of Viana, and Eleanor, Countess of Foix. He was, however, more concerned in the discords of Castile,

Fig. 249. Alfonso V of Aragon and his Queen Mary of Castile attending Mass

whence he took his second wife, Joanna Henriquez (1447). Whereas Charles was desirous of peace with the Castilian faction of Don Alvaro de Luna, his father was bound to the opposite side. Opportunity was thus given to the lawless Navarrese nobles to engage in civil war, in which Charles's partisans had so much the worse that he fled to Italy. John's accession to Aragon made him heir apparent there also, and he returned, only to be imprisoned by his treacherous father. But he had become the emblem of Catalan autonomy, a revolt broke out, and he was released with an acknowledgement of his rights (1461). The same year he died, leaving the Catalans enraged with John and Joanna. War was waged between the *Generalitat* and the monarchs for years. The Catalans sought another prince, first Henry IV of Castile, then the Constable of Portugal, and lastly King René, in the latter case the attraction being his warlike heir, John 'of Calabria', anew evicted from Naples. John II ceded Roussillon to France.

1070

The years were filled with fighting, negotiations, and treaties with foreign powers. But in 1470 John of Calabria died, and King John II, who was already blind, and had obtained (1469) the much schemed-for marriage of his son and heir Ferdinand to Isabella of Castile, agreed in 1472 to favourable terms of pacification. His war to recover Roussillon failed, yet he had the satisfaction of knowing before he died in 1479 that Ferdinand V had become King-consort of Castile. John 'the Faithless', who vied with Louis XI in talents and diplomacy, had been the contriver of the union of Castile and Aragon. The little kingdom of Navarre passed to his daughter Eleanor of Foix (*ob.* 1479) and her French grandchildren.

During this period the history of Castile is a record of the anarchy of the lawless nobles and the ineffective efforts of the weak and incapable kings to control them. While Ferdinand was regent for his nephew, John II (1406–54), there was good government, but his accession in Aragon in 1412 left the monarchy adrift. The king grew up literary and showy. His minister, Don Alvaro de Luna, the Constable, was indeed fit to rule and quell disorder, but he lacked the steady confidence of the weak-willed John II, and would be banished and then recalled. At last the king's second wife, Isabella of Portugal, turned against him, and induced her feeble husband to arrest and execute the best friend of the monarchy (1452). Under his son Henry IV (1454–74), a miserable, abnormal cipher, nobles and court factions had free play for a scandalous twenty years. The king's only daughter Joanna was famed to be a bastard and was nicknamed La Beltraneja from her putative father. Henry's brother Alfonso and his sister Isabella were rival claimants of the succession. In 1465 an assembly of rebels at Avila declared Alfonso king. A reaction, aided by Alfonso's death (1468), restored Henry, who proceeded to recognize Isabella, not Joanna, as his heiress. But when Isabella married Ferdinand of Aragon (1469), the king veered round in favour of Joanna. His death in 1474 opened a civil war and foreign intervention.

The nobles were divided. Joanna was championed by her maternal uncle, Afonso V 'the African' of Portugal, who proposed to marry her. But his invasion of Castile was repelled, Louis XI of France was an ineffective ally, his Castilian partisans withered away, and he abandoned the struggle by treaties (September 1479, March 1480), which left Castile to Isabella, while safeguarding Portuguese interests in Africa. Joanna withdrew to a convent.

The Catholic Kings of the Spains, as Isabella and Ferdinand styled themselves, ruled conjointly in Castile, while Ferdinand was sole monarch of his hereditary kingdoms. Isabella (1474–1504), devout and high minded, and anything but negligible, was by far the most attractive of the pair; Ferdinand was endowed with the cold and ruthless craft and gift to rule of his faithless father. The two were bent on subjugating the nobles to the royal sway, and on completing the unity of Spain. The first task was, perhaps, easier than it seemed, for as elsewhere the unchecked baronial turbulence had burnt itself out in its own excess, and gentry and townsmen found employment and protection under the Crown and in the internal peace it enforced. The chief obstacle to unity was the Moorish kingdom of Granada, and this the Catholic Kings were resolved to subdue.

The war with Granada began in 1481, and the vitality of the Moorish kingdom was shown by the desperate resistance, at times victorious, which it opposed to the indefatigable Christians. The Moors, too, were hampered by internal divisions. Their kings, Abu'l-Hasan, his son Boabdil, and his brother 'Az-Zaghal', were at enmity with each other in a triangular duel. Abu'l-Hasan died (1485), and the weak-kneed Boabdil became a submissive vassal of Castile, but 'Az-Zaghal' held out heroically, though town after town was taken, until he was at last forced to surrender (1489). When Boabdil then refused to give up Granada itself as he had promised, he was besieged in 1491. The city capitulated in January 1492 on generous conditions, and the reconquest of Spain was completed. The terms, however, which included religious toleration, were not kept owing to the propagandist zeal of the Archbishop of Toledo, the eminent Cardinal Cisneros (Ximenes). A long and bloody insurrection of the Moslems ended in the decree (1502) giving them the choice of conversion or banishment from Castile and León. Thus was originated the class of Moriscos, whose Christianity remained very dubious. The Cortes of the Aragonese kingdoms, indeed, refused to allow their Moslem serfs, the Mudéjares, to be compelled to change their faith.

The same bitter intolerance was displayed by the Catholic kings in their treatment of the Jews. The unity of Spain seemed to them incomplete without religious unity, and in their persecution they were supported by the hatred of the Jews, fermenting since the disgraceful outbreaks a century earlier in spite of the intermixture of blood which existed. In disregard of the evil economic consequences of an attack on the trading and industrial Jews, by a decree of 1492 they were given the choice of conversion or expulsion. The results were the migration of Sephardim (Spanish Jews) elsewhere to the harm of Spain, and the multiplication of the suspect class of 'new Christians', who were often still Jews in secret. To root out Jewish practices and hold them in subjection, Ferdinand and Isabella founded (1477–90), in spite of opposition, the Supreme Council of the Inquisition, dependent on themselves, which held all Spaniards in terror. At the same time 'purity of blood' was made essential for office and dignity, clerical and lay.

All these measures were intended to strengthen the revived authority of the monarchy. A direct attack had already been made on the overmighty magnates. Resistance was sternly subdued, extravagant grants were annulled, the king neutralized the great Military Orders by taking their grand-masterships himself, castles were forbidden and dismantled, and justice was reorganized in the hands of middle-class men trained in the universities. Meanwhile the great nobles were tamed by honours and court posts, where they vegetated in decadent ostentation, an appeal to the vain pride which was their congenital weakness. At the same time the towns were strictly supervised under royal officials. After 1480 the Cortes of Castile were rarely summoned. An orderly despotism, fortified by the terrible Inquisition, took the place of outworn anarchy. In Castile the condition of the peasants was little changed; in Aragon proper, oppression by the nobles was still rife in spite of Ferdinand's efforts and their own revolts. Only in Catalonia, after a rising, did he succeed by the Decree of Guadalupe in lightening their burdens and enabling them to buy escape from serfdom.

The greatest event of the century took place under the aegis of the Catholic Kings. The Genoese shipman Columbus by perseverance obtained the support of Isabella for his project of sailing to China across the Atlantic. (The Azores were already known to the Portuguese, but the Iceland voyages of the eleventh century were in oblivion.) In 1492, with three ships and mainly Spanish sailors, he accomplished his momentous expedition and reached the Bahamas and West Indies. Without knowing it he had found the new and unsuspected world. His and others' achievements belong to Modern History. Here it must suffice to say that by an award of Pope Alexander VI (1493), modified by the Treaty of Tordesillas in 1494, a boundary was agreed upon between Spanish and Portuguese exploitation, a boundary which left the greater part of America for Spain. The Spanish Empire had been founded, and the Catholic Kings endeavoured (1500) to give an equitable organization to their growing possessions.

Ferdinand was more concerned with Spain and Europe. In 1494 he recovered Roussillon by treaty, and in 1512, in the course of the Italian wars, he conquered Navarre south of the Pyrenees. In those wars he also conquered the kingdom of Naples. His adroit and perfidious diplomacy, backed by the fighting qualities of the Spanish troops, served him well. Diplomatic marriages altered the balance of power in Europe. His eldest daughter Joanna was married to the Archduke Philip, Maximilian's son and ruler of the Netherlands. By her brother's death, she inherited Castile on the decease of Queen Isabella, but as she became insane and Philip I also died, her father Ferdinand took over once more the government of Castile until his own death (1516). His grandson Charles of Habsburg, the future Emperor Charles V, then succeeded, and the Spanish Empire entered upon a new phase.

The history of Portugal during the century showed a steadier progress towards absolute monarchy. The definite peace with Castile in 1411 left

John I's throne secure, but impoverished by his prodigal grants. The Portuguese, at peace by land, turned to expansion overseas. In 1415 the king achieved the conquest of Ceuta in Morocco, and his son, Prince Henry the Navigator, fixed his residence in Algarve, whence he organized the continuous maritime exploration of the west coast of Africa with a view to establishing a route to the east behind the belt of Moslem states. John's eldest son, King Edward (1433–8), besides continuing measures to remedy the poverty of the Crown by the resumption of estates, was the preparer of a new code of law (published under his successor) and the centre of a

Fig. 250. Portuguese ship, fifteenth century

literary movement. But his army met with disaster in Morocco. After his death his brother Peter obtained election as regent (1440) until his son Afonso V (1438–81) took the reins. Peter rebelled and was overthrown (1449). The king, besides encouraging the voyages of discovery, won the name of 'the African' by his conquest of Tangier in Morocco, but his war for the Castilian succession was, as we have seen, a failure. He died in debt, and the bastard line of the Dukes of Braganza, descended from John I, was almost equal to the Crown. His son John II (1481–95), however, was endowed with the resolute and ruthless character as well as the shrewdness which could build up an absolute monarchy. He relied on the townsmen against the overweening nobles. The Duke of Braganza, discovered in treason, was executed and his lands were seized. The Duke of Viseu, the king's cousin and brother-in-law, was stabbed by John himself, who then established a royal bodyguard. With the nobles subdued, John II was bent on making the Crown wealthy and independent of grants from the Cortes. His treatment of the banished Spanish Jews displayed a mean desire of gain. For a poll-tax they were permitted to stay eight months, and were then packed off to Morocco, as were their Portuguese co-religionists. The same keen business-instinct governed his treaty (1494) with Spain over the voyages of discovery. John II yielded the main part of the western continent then coming to light, while securing the Brazilian coastland, but for his share he kept the immediately profitable sea-route round Africa, which was soon to be the chief route to the Indies and to make Lisbon a rich emporium and the King of Portugal a wealthy potentate.

The circumnavigation of Africa and the discovery of the sea-route to the Indies and the spice islands were indeed the main achievement of fifteenth-century Portugal. It was no accident, but a well-thought out design. Prince Henry 'the Navigator' (although he barely crossed the sea) was its inspirer. He studied the meagre cosmography of his day; he selected and instructed pilots; he sent out his exploring ships year after year. In 1434 they mastered the difficult currents round Cape Bojador, and in 1436, passing the desolate Sahara coast, reached the fertile Rio

Fig. 251. Prince Henry the Navigator

de Ouro. Then the profits of trade in gold and negro slaves attracted adventurers. Senegal and the Cape Verde Islands were discovered. By 1460, when Henry died, the Indies seemed delusively within reach. In 1469 Afonso V leased the Guinea coast trade to Fernão Gomes on condition of discovering yearly 100 miles of coastline. By 1471 the Equator had been crossed. It was now clear that Africa extended far to the south. King John II, with his commercial intuition, took up the mantle of Prince Henry in organizing expeditions and knowledge. In 1488, when Bartholomew Diaz rounded the 'Cape of Storms', he renamed it 'Cape of Good Hope', and planned the voyage of Vasco da Gama to cross the Indian Ocean. Since he died in 1495, the crowning triumph of 1498, when da Gama arrived at Calicut, fell to his nephew and successor, Manuel I the Fortunate. Thus the sea-route to India was achieved, and it was not many years before the centres of European commerce shifted to the shores of the Atlantic from the Mediterranean. With the discovery of America and the circumnavigation of the globe, a new era began. In lasting significance these epoch-making voyages transcended that growth of absolute monarchy which was the political characteristic of the age.

(2) ITALY AND THE PAPACY

It was inevitable that Italy should be a storm-centre of the Great Schism, when the rival Popes fought and schemed for recognition. The struggle was complicated by the ambitions of the chief Italian states, eager for expansion, and by the internal throes of surviving republics and the petty tyrannies which pullulated more especially in the disintegrated papal lands. A new factor was the transformation of the Free Companies into native Italian bands under leaders, the *condottieri*, who besides their trade of war nourished territorial aims of their own. The crucial event in this change fell in 1378 when the Romagnol baron, Alberico da Barbiano, recruited his Company of San Giorgio. Next year he won the victory of Marino in the service of Pope Urban VI over the Breton mercenaries of Clement VII. Superior skill and discipline established the reputation of his troopers and made his company a school of professional warfare. After his death two of his lieutenants, Braccio and Muzio 'Sforza', were rivals in generalship as independent *condottieri*, but there were many others of eminence. The system of professional Free Companies produced a much more scientific strategy among the Italians, but their growing isolation in their peninsular warfare ended by leaving them far behind the transalpines in effective fighting. From the beginning of the century it was more profitable both for the condottiere and his employers to rely chiefly on horse-troopers in full armour, to the neglect of infantry, whether archers or pikemen. They were more highly trained and fewer to maintain. This led to a singular economy in these valuable troops and their horses. On occasions, which became rarer after the turn of the century, a condottiere would fight a pitched battle with heavy slaughter, but normally he preferred to win by skilful manoeuvre. Little enmity was felt by the opposing mercenaries. They preferred to put their dismounted prisoners, perhaps old or future comrades, to ransom. Further, their livelihood was war, and they had no zeal to end it. A disease of prolonged and indecisive campaigns afflicted Italy, in which the generals might earn the merited distrust of their employers for their collusive tactics. Often a petty tyrant from central Italy to start with, the condottiere aimed at raising himself in rank, territory, and power with little regard to the interest of the state which paid for his services. A decline in morale, if not in generalship, was the natural result. The infantry were hastily collected and inferior in this curious specialization; the advance in artillery beyond the Alps was overlooked; fortified cities were rarely taken; and spun-out wars on not too hard conditions burdened the greater states with taxation and with inconclusive results.

Map 26

It has already been told how in the course of the strife between the rival Popes the possession of the miserable kingdom of Naples was fought over by the successive Dukes of Anjou, Louis I (*ob.* 1384) and Louis II, and the

1077

Fig. 252. Venice, c. 1400

line of Durazzo until in 1399 King Ladislas of Durazzo was firmly established. At the time North Italy was being kept in agitation by the insatiable ambition of Gian Galeazzo Visconti, the Count of Virtù (Vertus). This master of dissimulation and diplomacy and most accomplished ruler in peace and war, who kept his ministers, cities, and condottieri well in hand from his seclusion at Pavia, succeeded his father Galeazzo II as tyrant of Pavia in 1376. He so hoodwinked his ferocious uncle Bernabò that he was able to capture him and acquire the whole Visconti state (1385), which he meant to enlarge into a kingdom of Lombardy at least. By adroit and treacherous mediation followed by force, he seized on the dominions of the two enemies, the Scaligeri of Verona and the da Carrara of Padua (1386–8). Thence he aimed at Bologna and Tuscany, where the absorption of Arezzo by Florence gained him allies in her alarmed neighbours. Florence, however, showed fight, and although Gian Galeazzo's armies were strong and well led, he was baffled by the skill of her general, Sir John Hawkwood, and her unsparing use of her wealth. He lost Padua to the da Carrara (1390), and was reduced to accept a peace (1392). If he gained a new status as a legitimate prince by the purchase of the title of Duke of Milan from King Wenceslas of the Romans (1395), he was obliged to see the anarchic city of Genoa accept the suzerainty of France (1396). Yet he was preparing for fresh aggression. He bought the signory of Pisa and received the willing submission of Perugia and Siena (1399–1400). Florence was all but encircled in the new war. Her ally, King Rupert of the Romans, failed ignominiously in invading the Milanese from the north, and Gian Galeazzo's generals conquered Bologna (1402). The duke's sudden death was hailed as a deliverance, yet he had so exhausted his duchy by taxation in the contest that it is doubtful if he could have exploited his victories. As it was, the ill-cemented state broke temporarily into fragments under his young sons.

His rivals, avowed or secret, took immediate advantage of his death. The last da Carrara of Padua seized on Verona, only to be overwhelmed by his quondam protector, Venice, who now extended her frontier to the river Adige (1405). Venice, however, being completely revived after the war of Chioggia, was soon involved in that war with King Sigismund which not only gave her back Dalmatia but added to her conquests Friuli, taken from the Patriarch of Aquileia. Her admirable and lenient rule won the hearts of her new subjects. In this way she definitely became a mainland state with command of her food-supply and the trade-outlets to Germany, while she still had on her hands the defence of the sea-routes to the Levant against the ever more formidable Ottomans. Florence, too, took the opportunity to starve out and annex derelict Pisa (1406), and thus acquire a coastline and a sea-port at Leghorn, but, in contrast to Venice, her oligarchs were not united, and, though anarchic Genoa threw off the French suzerainty (1409), she was exposed to the aggressions of an Italian power.

The aggressor this time was from the south. King Ladislas of Naples grew up warlike, astute, and ambitious, and giving up his Hungarian claims, devoted himself to the conquest of Central Italy, where the Schism and the disintegration of the Papal States furnished him with the opportunity. *Aut Caesar aut nullus* was his motto. Opposed by Florence and defeated by the pretender, Louis II of Anjou, he seemed baffled, but Pope John XXIII's mishaps and isolation changed his fortunes. He seemed on the eve of success when he died of his debauchery in August 1414 to the joy of his neighbours. He had unintentionally ensured the Council of Constance.

Meantime the reconstitution of the duchy of Milan had begun. It had broken up into city tyrannies wielded by Gian Galeazzo's condottieri or by local faction chiefs. His elder son, the insanely cruel Giovanni Maria, was quite incapable of controlling them, but the second duke's murder in 1412 fortunately coincided with the death of the most powerful general, Facino Cane, and enabled his younger brother Filippo Maria to take the reins. Although a neurotic recluse, he inherited his father's gifts of choosing and dominating men and of diplomatic deception, but the condottieri had become more dangerous and more set on tyrannies of their own. By craft and supple determination Filippo Maria outplayed his many opponents one by one, beginning by marrying Cane's widow and thus obtaining his troops and treasure. The subjugation of Genoa (1421) crowned his achievement: there was once more a solid Visconti duchy in central Lombardy. The duke governed his subjects well. Wily and treacherous in gaining and keeping power, he was an excellent financier and paymaster, who kept a watch on his officials, protected the peasantry, and encouraged industry. He was an example of the well-organized, despotic government of the century, which was superseding the particularistic, factious, and traditionally complicated regime of the outworn communes.

His mere success and known duplicity, along with his obvious wish to recover all the Visconti dominions, were enough to rouse his neighbours, who in their turn were bent on forming regional states in place of the shivered fragments of earlier times. Florence first took alarm. In 1423 she went to war, and in 1425 was joined by Venice, who now, guided by her doge, Foscari, leader of the war-party, proposed to protect her mainland, the Veneto, by enlarging it at Visconti's expense. The old reluctance to be involved in land politics disappeared in favour of aggression. Until 1454 fighting was all but continuous. It was the Golden Age of the condottieri. They were skilful generals, and if need be, hard fighters, but they warred for their own hand. To change their employer was their right, frequently exercised, but they might deal untruly with him to prolong operations or even commit sheer treason. For the last offence the celebrated condottiere, Carmagnola, was condemned to death by Venice (1432). The wars of Naples and the lure of forming petty states in the papal lands would draw off Braccio and Sforza to the south, and thus they lent a kaleidoscopic appearance to the intertangled political contests of the day. When they both died in 1424, their heirs, Niccolò Piccinino (ob. 1444) and Francesco Sforza, continued their rivalry and divagations.

Early in the war Filippo Maria lost Brescia and Bergamo to Venice, and in 1435 Genoa, enraged by his release of her foe, Alfonso of Aragon, revolted from him. He never recovered them. Francesco Sforza, cheated of the hand of the duke's only child, his natural daughter Bianca Maria, turned to Venice, and fought Piccinino with alternate vigour and lukewarmness. At last, Filippo Maria gave him Bianca and Cremona as her dowry (1441). Yet they soon quarrelled, until the duke, under pressure of a Venetian attack, recalled his son-in-law shortly before his own death (1447). That death and the extinction of the male line of the Visconti gave the signal for a general scramble for the duchy of Milan. Charles VII of France, now able to revive French ambitions in Italy, seized on Asti for his cousin, the poet-Duke of Orleans, who was the son of Gian Galeazzo's daughter Valentina, and had, perhaps, the best hereditary claim. Alfonso the Magnanimous of Aragon and Naples, the dead duke's ally, produced a questionable will nominating himself the heir. Venice proceeded with her conquest of the duchy. But a last flame of free government flared up in the city of Milan itself. The citizens proclaimed 'the Ambrosian Republic', and hired the philosophically practical Sforza for their general. Trust in this pretender they could not have; his successes in war made him the more dangerous. After the usual rapid changes of side the republic and Venice were combining against him (1449). Sforza played his game with skill; the money and influence of Cosimo de' Medici, the real ruler of Florence, were behind him; and he knew that the Ambrosian Republic, distracted by dissensions and misrule and starving from his blockade, was tottering to its fall. In February 1450 a revolution admitted his troops and acclaimed him duke.

The war was not over, for Venice and Alfonso banded against Sforza, but he had the alliance of Cosimo and Florence, which brought him both funds and diplomatic support leading to a passing intervention in the person of René of Anjou. Venice, hampered by her Turkish war, ended by giving way in the peace of Lodi (April 1454), by which she received Crema, and formed a league with Florence and Milan. Next year Alfonso entered into an alliance with the last two and with the Pope accepted a general league to prevent both Italian wars and French intervention. It was ineffectual, for Alfonso insisted on attacking his old enemy Genoa and thereby forced her to accept French suzerainty once more. Yet it showed at least the conception of Italy at peace and unmolested by foreign powers.

The straits of Filippo Maria and the success of Francesco Sforza had been largely due to Florence, then perhaps at the zenith of her banking, commercial, and industrial wealth, although her old staple, trade in cloth, had for a number of years been steadily declining in volume if not in vogue. Yet internally the foundations of republican government were undermined. The constitution, complicated and cumbrous in its attempt fairly to apportion office and power among the full citizens, the *beneficiati*, who belonged to the gilds, was a façade, behind which stood the narrow oligarchy of wealthy *ottimati*. Factious rivalry, linked with trading rivalry, was, as ever, the rock on which their unity was splitting. The family of the Albizzi under the very capable Maso held the lead for years, but when in 1417 he died, their power began to weaken, even when they manipulated the nomination to magistracies drawn by lot. Rinaldo d'Albizzi, the head of his house, had neither the perspicacity nor the moderation to guide a divided faction. The organization into gilds was losing real meaning, and the real division in Florence was between the rich and the poorer. Among the latter the chief influence was wielded by the very wealthy Giovanni de' Medici, who carefully eschewed politics, giving no handle to the oligarchs to crush him. When he died (1429), his son Cosimo, the ablest financier of the century, succeeded to his popularity. Meantime the oligarchs had discredited themselves by pressing on and then failing in the desirable conquest of the free republic of Lucca (1429–33). The death (1432) of their wisest man, Niccolò d'Uzzano, left Rinaldo free to force conclusions in his anxiety to prop up his tottering supremacy, using the old method of summoning a Parlamento, the fictitious general assembly of the citizens, to elect a packed Balía or committee with full powers, with the object of removing the now dangerous Cosimo by ruin, death or banishment (1433). Even the Balía was divided in opinion, however, public opinion was hostile, and Cosimo, who had influential friends abroad, got off with banishment to Venetian territory for ten years. His wealth was unimpaired. Rinaldo did not even venture to secure his partisans in office by a new selection of names to be drawn by lot for office. When his Balía expired next year, a Signory of Medicean partisans was drawn, a desperate appeal to force was a flash in the pan, and a new Parlamento and Balía recalled Cosimo and banished Rinaldo, and inaugurated the rule of the Medici.

Cosimo de' Medici was not, strictly speaking, a dictator but a private citizen, but his authority was overwhelming. Though he was an adept at intrigue and the various forms of buying support from offices and loans to direct bribery, he had behind him general opinion. He was the chief of a caucus, more numerous, even including some *ottimati*, more dependent on their chief, and more widely based than that of the Albizzi. Florence was accustomed to see real power exercised by cliques and personalities rather than by the fleeting magistrates as such, and the long predominance of the discreet Cosimo, which covertly substituted one-man rule for the free republic, was only resented by a minority. With them he dealt by exile, confiscation, and political disability in the time-honoured fashion, while unfair assessment for taxation was meanly used to weaken the independent remnant. This was facilitated by the system of property valuation, the Catasto, enacted in 1427 by the declining oligarchy and rendered far more onerous in its effects to the wealthier taxpayers under Cosimo's regime. Yet it was not only the money of the greatest banker and trader of Europe, it was the practical sagacity of his advice, which carried with him his critical and emulous citizens. It was exemplified when he turned Florence from her bickering alliance with his benefactor, Venice, to that with Sforza of Milan in the interest of stability and the balance of power in Italy. Even so, the renewal of the Balía to nominate the successive Signories was refused by the normal Councils, and it needed a Parlamento under military pressure to elect a fresh Balía of the usual kind and to establish a new trustworthy Council for Finance (1458). But Cosimo astutely let his ambitious henchman, Luca Pitti, be the leading actor in this unpopular proceeding of the faction, while he himself, save in foreign affairs, kept behind the scenes until his death (1464). He was mourned as the Father of his country, a peculiarly Florentine instance of the all-but despot, a cultured, generous, marvellously shrewd business man, no less genuinely pious than on occasion pitilessly hard. The contrasting strands of his character stand out unveiled, devoid of introspection.

The age was full of startling vicissitudes in the lesser states of Italy, of the juxtaposition of art, learning, and intellect with raging ambition and craft and hedonism, seldom checked by scruples, but their fascinating, if lurid, story cannot be followed in a brief outline confined to the greater powers. Of these the Papacy, with its European function, was the chief. Martin V (1417–31) was a Colonna, a Roman of the Romans. Moderate, practical, and thrifty, he had an iron will. As ruler of the Church, elected by the reforming Council, he, who had no wish for reform or for Councils to restrict his absolutism or to mitigate abuses, cannot be praised; as temporal ruler of the anarchic Papal States he was most skilful and fortunate. To recover secular independence and income for the Papacy by restoring some sort of order in Rome, by the use of his temporal suzerainty of Naples, by dexterous alliances and diplomacy, and by the exploitation of his ecclesiastical prerogatives, were the aims of his pontificate. He deftly

Fig. 253. Cosimo de' Medici

took the chances offered him. Naples was suffering from the changeable loves of Ladislas's sister, Queen Joanna II, and rapid revolutions. The Papal States were a prey to the warfare between the great condottieri, Braccio and Sforza, who held Rome itself. With the help of Florence Martin reconciled the two rivals for the moment, making Braccio his vicar in Perugia (1420). In 1421 the Pope was able to return to Rome. He had the cardinals, his kindred Colonna, and even the Orsini, their enemies, on his side, for all were weary of the mercenary troops. Once there, he brought order and prosperity. In Naples, meanwhile, Joanna and her reigning paramours, Braccio and Sforza, and her two rival heirs, Louis III of Anjou and Alfonso V of Aragon, were embroiling the kingdom in fickle and faithless combinations. When the two condottieri both died, their places were taken by Francesco Sforza and Piccinino (1424), until the Lombard wars drew them off. Martin changed sides as swiftly as any. When he died

1083

he was the ally of Louis III and Joanna, and was partially lord of his own legal dominions.

The unwisdom of Martin V's successor, the Venetian Eugenius IV (1431–47), was shown not only in his quarrel with the Council of Basle,

*Fig. 254. Triumphal arch commemorating the entry
into Naples of Alfonso I in 1442*

but in his mismanagement of Rome, the Papal States, and the knotty politics and wars of Italy in general. The 'great inopportunist' fled in 1434 to Florence, where he remained nine years protected by Cosimo de' Medici, while his ferocious legate and condottiere, Cardinal Vitelleschi, put down two Roman 'republican' revolts, and ruled as despot until his

ITALY AND THE PAPACY

usefulness was exhausted, and he was murdered by a like character, the Cardinal Chamberlain, Luigi of Aquileia (1441). Eugenius, with the prestige of the Union with the Greeks, returned to his see (1443). By deputy he had acted the tyrant as a secular ruler.

The unceasing troubles of Naples were not alleviated by the death of Louis III (1434) and of the worthless Joanna II (1435), for his brother King René and Alfonso V fought for the crown. Since Alfonso won the support of Visconti after his defeat and capture in the sea-battle of Ponza, Eugenius took the part of René, sending the fierce Vitelleschi to his aid for a time. The series of betrayals need not be recounted. René himself, brave and extravagant, did small good to his own cause. In 1442 he abandoned the country. Next year Alfonso entered Naples and was invested by Eugenius. The price was the expulsion of Francesco Sforza, who since 1434 had been consolidating a state in the March of Ancona, where he was papal vicar. He was hard pressed, when with Alfonso's encouragement he left the March for Lombardy to join Filippo Maria Visconti, then near ruin in the Venetian war. At this moment (1447) Pope Eugenius died at the height of his fortunes, secular and ecclesiastical. He can hardly be said to have deserved his triumphs.

By an odd coincidence two highly cultivated humanists were now the lords of South Italy. Yet it was natural, for humanism and art had become the intellectual passion of their day. Alfonso's court vied with those of upper Italy in its addiction to learning and splendour. The Papacy, already falling under the spell of classic antiquity, was filled in an election of compromise by a genuine scholar of humble origin, the Tuscan Nicholas V (1447–55), bred in intellectual Florence and possessed by an ardour of building and book-collecting. He was in character the best Pope of the century. With too little reverence or attachment for the medieval past or classic ruins, he was resolved to make Rome once more the imperial capital of art and letters in the new Renaissance fashion, and with unknowing vandalism planned to rebuild the Leonine (or Vatican) City as a temple, a palace, and a fortress, while he gathered round him the best artists and most eminent humanists of the time without regard to their lives or opinions. It was no unworthy, if not complete, ideal for the ecumenic Papacy.

In politics Nicholas V was a not unsuccessful man of peace. It was his fortune finally to close the schism with the Council of Basle; he saw peace established in Lombardy, and joined the league for the balance of power (1454); he maintained a tolerable *modus vivendi* with the petty local tyrants of the Papal States. Yet his pontificate was marred by two events. Humanism in Rome mingled with the traditions of the commune in the feeble conspiracy of Porcaro, which soured and alarmed him. The European disaster of the Fall of Constantinople in the same year (1453) broke in on his classic dreams, and unveiled his European impotence. The conclave on his death swung back to a foreign, political Pope, the aged Catalan, Calixtus III (1455–8). Energetic, but too old for his task, the new Pope did his best to fight the Turk amid general apathy, while he quarrelled with his patron King Alfonso, then adding to Italy's unrest by his unwise attack on Genoa. To the Papacy and Italy Calixtus did unexpected harm by his nepotism, for one nephew, the ill-famed Rodrigo Borgia (Borja), was made a Cardinal.

His successor, the Sienese Pius II (1458–64), had had a long experience as a slippery diplomat, indeed, a turncoat, in the Council of Basle and in Germany. As Aeneas Sylvius Piccolomini, he was remarkable for his versatile talent as a humanist author, modern in his aestheticism, his love of the countryside, his vivacious style, and his piquant personality. Now he appeared as an ardent Crusader and unbending Pope. Amid the turmoil of Naples, the turbulence of Rome, and the indifference of Europe, he pushed on the sorely needed Crusade in the Congress of Mantua. The scheme miscarried, and when, after the Neapolitan war was over, he desperately attempted to lead the crusade himself, he died at Ancona in the midst of a tragic fiasco. The pontificate of the attractive adventurer, turned idealist, had ended in failure. His successor, the Venetian Paul II (1464–71), was a man of business who had no love for heathenish men of letters. Them he did not tolerate, nor did he the desire of the College of Cardinals to fetter the autocracy of the Pope in favour of its own oligarchy. Since Martin V's death it had striven to impose capitulations on each new-elected Pope. Paul II, once elected, compelled their retractation. Secular magnificence in Rome was one note of his reign; the other was the workmanlike centralization of the Curia.

When Alfonso the Magnanimous died, Naples became the battle-ground of Italy. He had left his conquest to his bastard son Ferrante (Ferdinand) I (1458–94), whose early reign was full of violent vicissitudes. Calixtus III was against him, Pius II for him. So were Sforza and Cosimo de' Medici. But the Neapolitan nobles were as changeable and untrustworthy as ever, and John 'of Calabria', the spirited son of King René, invaded the kingdom, meeting with large, if dubious, support (1459), while Jacopo Piccinino the condottiere joined in. In 1460 Ferrante, routed by the river Sarno, was on the brink of ruin. Then there was a revulsion. Genoa revolted from the French, barons changed sides, and Ferrante won the decisive battle of Troia (1462). John soon sailed back to Provence, leaving his rival in possession. Broils further north continued. With his accustomed treachery Ferrante executed Piccinino, and Paul II was more often hostile than not, but the alliance of Naples with Florence and Milan held firm.

The other two allies enjoyed none too great stability. Francesco Sforza's last triumph was in 1464, when he annexed feud-torn Genoa, taking the city as a fief of France from Louis XI, who relinquished his father's policy of more active intervention. He never obtained the legal sanction of imperial investiture. In 1466 he died and was succeeded by his eldest son, Galeazzo Maria, a villainous but not incapable young man. He was obliged with the aid of Florence to foil the unfriendliness of Venice and the overt attack, prompted by her, of the great condottiere, Colleone (1467). Heavy taxation, faction, and nobles ousted from power rendered the duchy unquiet. When Galeazzo was deservedly murdered in the name of liberty by three conspirators in 1476, there followed no antiquated liberty but intrigues against the weak regency of his widow and her minister Simonetta, ended by its seizure in 1479 by the boy Duke Gian Galeazzo's uncle, Ludovico il Moro. Thenceforward Ludovico, a wily, gifted, vain connoisseur of art and government, ruled the duchy, but not Genoa, which had rebelled in the contest.

The tribulations of freer Florence were less ignoble with a better outcome. Cosimo's surviving son, the elderly invalid Piero, weathered a constitutional storm let loose by emulous members of the faction. He weathered, too, allied with Milan and Naples, the dangerous war with Colleone. In fact, the Medici owned the affection of most Florentines, who were not envious of their greatness or regretful of republican government— their wealth and their influence abroad seemed needful for the city's

Fig. 255. Ludovico il Moro

prosperity. On Piero's death (1469), his two sons, the genius Lorenzo and Giuliano the popular, took over the reins of unofficial, yet acknowledged, power with general assent. Lorenzo, the real ruler, had already shown his marvellous talents, but as yet he had not acquired the shrewd circumspection of his father, and he never did attain the skill in finance and trade on which his ancestors had founded their fortunes. He proceeded to extremities with the subject-city of Volterra on its revolt, and was unable to allay, indeed he somewhat increased, the friction between the greater states, to which Louis XI's diplomacy was no stranger.

The most stirring ruler in Italy was Pope Sixtus IV (1471–84), who, although not neglecting the perennial Turkish war, set his heart on making the Papacy a strong territorial power. A plebeian Genoese and a Franciscan

Fig. 256. The murderer of Giuliano de' Medici

friar, he bent papal nepotism to this methodical end. With nephews and other Genoese satellites he packed the College of Cardinals. Lay nephews he endowed by marriages. The acquisition of the tyranny of Imola in Romagna for one, Riario, was a blow to Lorenzo de' Medici, who saw Florence's trade-outlets by land endangered. The Pazzi, his banking rivals, who had financed the purchase of Imola, were mulcted of an inheritance, and Sixtus was flouted by him. Italy fell into two alliances, Florence, Milan and Venice, and Naples and the Papacy. The explosion came in the plot of Riario and the Pazzi to murder the two Medici. It failed, for only Giuliano was slaughtered, and the Florentines rallied round Lorenzo (Easter, 1478). An accomplice, Archbishop Salviati of Pisa, was hanged with the Pazzi, and the Pope, who had approved the plot while forbidding the inevitable murder, used this sacrilege as the reason for excommunicating Lorenzo, interdicting Florence, and war. The fighting went against Florence. It was only by throwing himself on Ferrante's mercy that Lorenzo obtained a generous peace from him and the unwilling Pope (1480). Henceforward the alliance of Naples, Florence, and Milan was restored.

Lorenzo now endeavoured to maintain a peaceful *status quo*, but Sixtus and Venice were not peacefully minded, if overawed by the capture of Otranto by the Turks (1480). When, however, an inefficient sultan, Beyazit II, succeeded Mahomet the Conqueror and the city was recovered, Venice and the Pope allied to partition the lands of the Duke of Ferrara, and were opposed by the Triple Alliance. In the course of this Ferrarese War and its varied chances (1482–4), Sixtus the loser deserted Venice the winner for the other side. Venice was outmatched, toyed with calling in the French, and finally bargained. The peace advanced her frontier against Ferrara to the river Po and killed the enraged Pope, whose territorial hopes were frustrated. Venice and the Papacy were now clearly marked out as the aggressive, adventurous powers, and the Triple Alliance as inspired by the dread of foreign intervention in these heedless conflicts.

The election of a kindly cipher, the Genoese Innocent VIII (1480–92), proved no antidote to war. The Papacy, negligent of its spiritual mission, had descended to tyrannic politics. The cardinals were factious, secular in life, and out of hand owing to continuous political and bad appointments. Their strong men, like Giuliano della Rovere and Rodrigo Borgia, were the partisans of foreign powers. Rome and the Curia were bywords for corruption and violence. Cardinal Giuliano was the firebrand who encouraged the Pope to relight a war with Naples. Ferrante, and his still more odious heir, Alfonso, were oppressive, needy, and extortionate, and provoked a revolt of their barons, who in any case hated a strict monarchical control. Faithless peace and feeble warfare took their turns. Ferrante treacherously put his pacified magnates to death, thus giving a momentary victory and long hatred to his dynasty and power (1487). From the Pope he received at last confirmation and alliance. Some months later (July 1492) Innocent VIII died, to be succeeded by Rodrigo Borgia as Alexander VI. He left the Papal States the prey to petty tyrants, more disintegrated than ever. In 1494, under the menace of the French invasion, Ferrante died, leaving his crown to the caitiff Alfonso.

Meantime Lorenzo de' Medici had toiled at his Sisyphean task of working for peace amid the blind bickering of all his neighbours. His lack of commercial and financial talent, combined with the new, untoward conditions of banking and trade as France and the Netherlands grew consolidated, was dissolving the money power of the Medici abroad, as distinct from his personal influence. In Florence the rule of this tireless diplomat and inspired patron of the arts and of culture was ever more popular. The disguised tyrant, still a great citizen in life and bearing, was assuring the domination of his faction by law. New Councils of Seventy (1480) and Seventeen (1490) were set up to select for office and watch over administration. It was expected that he would become the open head of the republic as Gonfalonier of Justice for life, when on 8 April 1492 he died, and his foolish son Piero succeeded him. His death closed a Golden Age.

The rational organization of the centralizing state, obvious in Naples and Florence and in lesser principalities and as yet vainly attempted by the localized, degraded Papacy, exhibited in Italy as elsewhere the temper of the century, which was turning to monarchy from the jumble of inherited, decadent, conflicting powers and institutions. Venice, 'the most

Fig. 257. Villa Medici Careggi

triumphant city' that the French statesman-historian Commynes had seen, was in the van of the movement. But there the sagely constructed state was republican and oligarchic. In powers, though not as yet in personal influence, the doge was a mere figurehead. Venice was held together by a clearer bond of common interests and a saner patriotism than existed elsewhere; yet, overmatched by the Turks, and incurably acquisitive in Italy, she was preparing for her future disasters, and the discoveries of da Gama and Columbus were to deprive her of her sea-born wealth. Ludovico il Moro, whose diplomacy was based on deceit and hand-to-mouth expedients, appears in another light as despotic master of the duchy. No prince was wiser in his economic policy, encouraging industry, agriculture, and commerce with systematic forethought. Yet Milan, burdened with taxation, had never really recovered from a century of costly wars, and was to be blasted by those to come, when Ludovico's fears and vanity precipitated the French invasion. In a century of comparative immunity from foreign conquest the multiplicity of emulous cities and courts had favoured the efflorescence of intellectual energy. When beset on all sides by greater states, the same characteristic rendered Italy divided and incapable of defence.

CHAPTER 38

THE RENAISSANCE: ITS GROWTH AND TRIUMPH

(I) EDUCATION IN THE LATER MIDDLE AGES

A cardinal feature of the later Middle Ages from the thirteenth century onwards was the spread of literacy, and that in two senses: the ability to read and write Latin, and to read and write in the vernacular, living tongues of Europe, both naturally accompanied with the wider diffusion and the intrinsic increase of the knowledge of the age. The large numbers of the clergy and of bureaucrats, lawyers, officials of all degrees, and of traders, who all required some sort of literate education for their various employments, for records, for laws, for communications, for thought, and for every kind of transaction, were the imperative stimulus to this diffusion. The growth of urban life enlarged the facilities for acquiring literacy. The part played by the universities has been already briefly indicated: they taught and exercised the learning and the reason of their *alumni*. But the earlier stages of elementary education were bound to be gone through elsewhere. The monastic Orders made small contribution save in the literacy of their own numbers, often perfunctory. Monks were· outdone by the friars in learning, and more and more after 1300 chronicles and the like ceased to issue from the monasteries. Similarly, the mere copying of books new and old became the work of professional scribes and illuminators.

In the same period there appeared north of the Alps beside the amphibious class of clerks in lower Orders, who might be married, that of literate laymen, who might frequently know Latin, as well as read and write in their vernacular. The means of education, however, remained under the control of the Church, as did the universities. After 1300 Western Europe was adequately provided with schools. Besides sporadic instruction by individuals, the song-schools of cathedrals taught the elements of reading and writing and of the Faith, as well as the beginning of Latin, to many other children besides their choristers. The grammar schools of cathedrals gave a real training in Latin, and were paralleled in other towns and supplemented in their own cities by like institutions of various origins. Chantry priests might combine a school with their duty of masses for the dead; benefactors, from kings and wealthy magnates and bishops, like William of Wykeham, the founder of Winchester School, down to humble citizens, endowed grammar schools; gilds and towns, all over the West, but most markedly in the Netherlands, did the same. The Brethren of the Common Life towards the close of the fourteenth century entered with zeal into the task of education, in which they wrought a revolution.

The grammar schools formed the gateway to knowledge. The Latin they taught was grammatical, much influenced by the Vulgate Bible, however unclassical and crabbed in philosophy and law. It was used by scholars and traders everywhere and was essential to intercourse in the world. It gave an impress of unity to the learning of the West; the student could be understood wherever he went. It was the language of the Church. The commonest grammars were the *Ars Minor* of Donatus and the *Doctrinale* (in verse, easy to learn by heart) of Alexander of Villa Dei (1199). Among popular texts for study Æsop's *Fables*, 'Cato's' *Distichs* (moral maxims), Christian authors such as Lactantius, and some Latin poets, such as Virgil, were the chief. The other subjects of the Trivium, Rhetoric (which included much general information as well as speaking and style) and Dialectic (logical argument), occupied a more modest place, along with the daily useful simple Arithmetic. Learning by heart, oral work, and, typically medieval, frequent disputations were the method.

In Italy, where the educated layman had always been common, the reading of classic authors was more widely practised, and the learned layman earliest appeared. But it is noticeable that in the thirteenth century and still more in the fourteenth, the use of the vernacular for chronicles, legal works, and serious treatises written by laymen, like King James of Aragon, Beaumanoir the lawyer, the poet Dante, the chroniclers Villani and Froissart, was showing the wider diffusion of literacy beyond the bounds of school instruction and the existence of what may be called a cultured public. Poetry of all sorts and romances of chivalry or fable naturally kept the lead in this growth, but it is significant that translations of classical works were being made for Charles V of France and his kinsmen. None the less the standard of general education was not high, especially in Latin literacy. The long time required to take university degrees and their specialized, scholastic nature made it impossible for the majority of aspirants to stay the course, and the subjects of instruction for those who did became somewhat petrified in a narrow, formalized range. The rural clergy were mostly ill equipped, and as a whole the secular clergy no longer maintained the superiority in literacy which they had earlier possessed.

In the north, the Brethren of the Common Life began late in the fourteenth century to bring about a change. Hitherto, the schoolmaster, whose status in society was not high, had merely attempted to force a modicum of literacy on his pupils. The Brethren aimed at educating the moral character of the boys as well as their learning; they relied for discipline on moral influence, reducing the universal practice of the rod. The books they taught covered a wider field. Imitative schools of high quality appeared in the towns of the Netherlands and Upper Germany. Yet this advance did not in general strongly affect the chivalric class or the women. Trained as a page and squire in the martial and athletic duties, the behaviour, and the mainly vernacular literacy of his rank, the average noble stood outside the learned education of the time. Girls received at home or sometimes in a nunnery a corresponding practical training, and acquired literacy in the vernacular if their rank allowed it.

Save among the Brethren of the Common Life, little attention was paid to the physique of the pupils of the grammar schools. It was in Italy that a more comprehensive conception of school education was set up in the fifteenth century. The process may be said to have begun when in the fourteenth century the poet Petrarch denounced the exclusive devotion of contemporary scholars to logic and dialectic and the supremacy of Aristotle in their reasoned thought. As humanism, the adoration of classic antiquity, advanced, and with it the cult of the development of the individual in all his faculties, the *Institutio Oratoria* of Quintilian, supplemented soon by Petrarch's *Paedagogia*, became the guide of the schoolmaster. The ideal combined the training of mind and body so as to bring out the best qualities of the pupil according to his capacity. The study of classic authors was the chief means, but an all-round instruction in other arts from moral philosophy to astronomy and music was included in the curriculum. The famous school, which approached nearest to the ideal among many far less successful, was the Casa Giocosa of the born educator, the high-minded Vittorino da Feltre (*ob*. 1446), near Mantua. He was a Christian humanist, at heart a monk and an aristrocrat, who united the worship of the ancient classics with the moulding of the pupil's character and the salvation of his soul. He insisted on games and physical training in the playing fields of his school, winning personal affection, maintaining excellent discipline, and removing bad companions. The body was no longer treated as a worthless enemy. Indifferent to personal profit and well supported by the Gonzaga, the local rulers of Mantua, he used the large fees of his wealthy pupils to give a free and identical education to promising poor boys. So, too, he gave to certain girls, who by exception showed both inclination and gifts for humanism, the same teaching. It was in Italy that the learned lady reappeared. His curriculum was thoroughly classic in the study of the now more widely known Latin authors and the newly known Greek authors, which were bringing a source of inspiration to Italy and thence to the north. It is to be observed that he and his like throughout the West despised the vernacular tongues as media of serious instruction and literature. While this prepossession impeded the development of national literatures, it gave an intellectual unity to Western Europe, in which for long new ideas and culture could easily spread, and movements be infectious, and the evolution towards a modern mentality be advanced.

Meantime the new spirit in literate education was making marked progress under the influence of the Brethren of the Common Life north of

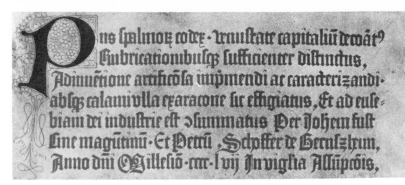

Fig. 258. Psalter printed by Fust and Schoeffer, 1457

the Alps. Scholars and teachers, such as Agricola (*ob.* 1485) and Hegius (*ob.* 1498), were teaching ardent pupils classic Latin and Greek, laying more stress on the Bible and early Christian Fathers than did the Italians. Their work culminated in the great Erasmus (1467–1536), the most learned and talented humanist of his day.

But it was a mechanical invention which multiplied enormously the effect of schools, universities, teachers, scholars, books, whether of the older or the new fashion, and of ideas. Printing by movable type, following, it seems, some obscure preludes in the Netherlands, was used at Mainz for reproducing books round about 1450 by John Gutenberg. Within a decade he and his allies, Fust and Schoeffer, had proved the new art capable of rivalling manuscripts in beauty and accuracy and of far surpassing them in productivity and cheapness. Pupils carried it rapidly over the West—it entered England (1476) with Caxton—and by 1500 many thousands of editions of books both ancient and medieval had been published. The extension of literacy and education was immensely furthered, and with it wide and rapid participation in learning, literature, and thought. Grammars, works of devotion, theology, and law, philosophy, and *belles lettres*, whether Latin or vernacular, became truly accessible to the literate at the close of the Middle Ages.

(2) PRIMITIVE SCIENCE AND SUPERSTITIOUS ABERRATIONS

With the growth of education there was an indubitable growth in the knowledge of the physical world, which formed the matrix of infant science, but it was clogged and hampered and almost concealed by the luxuriant accompaniment of irrational superstitions. These were largely, if not wholly, primeval, descended from heathen, not to say savage, beliefs. Elements from primitive German, Celtic, Mediterranean, and sophisticated oriental practices survived to meet and mingle in the medieval West. They were reinforced by the imperfect learning and contaminated knowledge which percolated among the scholars from Arabic versions of ancient Hellenic science, from imperial Roman sources, such as Pliny, none too enlightened, and from the deductive prepossessions of scholastic philosophy in the Twelfth-century Renaissance. Thus sheer magic, incantation and divination, witchcraft, unfounded convictions on the marvellous properties of stones and plants, alchemy and astrology all flourished to the detriment of the advance of sound knowledge of nature, which nevertheless did take place.

If we leave aside the belief of country folk in the spirits connected with fertility—in England the fairies, whose characteristics survive in Shakespeare's *Midsummer Night's Dream*—the most interesting superstitions, alloyed with knowledge, are those linked with medicine, alchemy, and astrology. Something like scientific knowledge was derived from the Arabs through translations, which brought some rational Greek medicine to the West, but it was deformed by ignorance and superstition, such as the vivid credulity in the occult properties of precious stones and in magical compounds and incantations. Folk-lore remedies, themselves mingled with magic, were often better than the too-learned physician's. Alchemy, likewise of Arabic origin, wasted itself in fruitless efforts to discover the philosopher's stone (for the transmutation of base metals into gold) and the elixir of life, based on false theory and tainted with magic. Yet the alchemists gave birth to the science of chemistry, if only by the habit of experiment and the observation of natural objects and their properties. It was, however, by transmission from the East, not by independent discovery, that the magnetic compass became known with its practical results for navigation, though the science of electricity and magnetism was yet unborn. Astronomy was mainly derived from classic sources, through Arabic translations. The Ptolemaic system of the central, motionless earth, enveloped by the successive spheres of planets and stars and the Primum Mobile, harmonized aptly with scholastic theology and reasoning. It encouraged accurate observation, but it was all but synonymous with the pseudo-science of astrology, which enthralled the belief of most. That men's characters were formed, events induced, and fate decided by the influence of the planets and their movements was a delusion which captivated learned opinion and led kings to maintain their astrologers. In this direction, as in alchemy, the very genuine desire to discover a stable natural law in the world and man, and to mitigate the capricious conception of phenomena, strayed into a blind alley.

Crude, irrational superstition, on the other hand, was resurgent in the witchcraft delusion, which stained the latest Middle Ages and the earlier modern centuries. Handed down among the masses, 'the common man' of present-day phraseology, prehistoric animism, with all its accompaniment of magic, charms, and spells, had received a pseudo-Christian embodiment in the belief in the perverted traffic and alliance of witches with the swarms of demons peopling the world and in the control of nature by means of magic mummery. Perhaps the more searching action of the Church on the population since the thirteenth century, perhaps the exhaustion of the scholastic attempt to construct an ordered, intelligible universe under Divine Providence took a share in giving a pronounced official recognition to these dark beliefs of inborn heathenism, and let loose, especially after the ignorant panic of the Black Death, savage horrors of repression. The real witchcraft practices, whether 'white' sorcery (which did not seek to inflict injury or commit sin) or 'black' magic (which designed both), were fantastically magnified by a depraved imagination. Cruelty and credulity joined hands.

To pass from these deplorable aberrations, there was a genuine growth of the scientific spirit, however halting and contaminated, visible from the thirteenth century. Some mathematical knowledge had come from Arabic writers. Robert Grosseteste (*ob.* 1253), the learned teacher and Bishop of Lincoln, had applied it to optics and urged the necessity of it for the understanding of nature. His pupil, the prophetic Roger Bacon (*ob.* 1292), had spent his life in insisting not only on the same theme but, as we have seen, on the need for extending the knowledge of facts to test the results of deductive reasoning by experience and experiment, in which he had been influenced by the Frenchman, Pierre de Maricourt. The influence of this inductive attitude, unluckily denuded of experimental research, but skilfully using mathematical reasoning, was to be seen in certain Masters of Arts at Paris in the fourteenth century. The most brilliant was Nicolas Oresme (*ob.* 1382), Bishop of Lisieux, who theorized on the laws of movement, and gave reasons for thinking that the earth revolved on its axis. It is in keeping that he attacked much of the astrology of his time and maintained that natural causes accounted for what seemed magical or due to starry influence. If this mathematical rationalism found but a small public, it remained alive to prepare for a less purely theoretic advance as the Middle Ages by our conventional division of history were ending.

(3) THE EVOLUTION OF PAINTING AND SCULPTURE

The term Gothic in relation to Art is merely a conventional label to denote the marvellous creative period after the fusion of Germanic and Romance peoples had crystallized in the resurgence of civilization in the Twelfth-century Renaissance. While it borrowed from Roman survivals and from Eastern infiltrations, its radiating centre was in the north, and more particularly in northern France. We have seen how this was the case in architecture, the dominating Art. Men 'had fallen in love with building'; sculpture and painting and the minor Arts grew up under its shade as subsidiaries to it and its purposes. They were pre-eminently decorative in spirit, and subserved the religious preoccupation of the Church for which they were evolved. Their gradual transformation is the index of their growing independence of their setting as the skill of the craftsman increased, and his interests were diverted from the architectural whole to his own art and the rendering of the visible human world. Not indeed until the fifteenth century did this constant progress towards naturalism win the day—the fetters of doctrinal symbolism and subject were too strong to be easily relaxed—but the tendency was always there, blending with the decorative and religious appeal.

Gothic art was thus intimately allied with the social atmosphere of its age, with whose changes it changed—from scholastic intellectualism to the drama of actual life. Realism first crept in through details and attitudes. In sculpture, the process may be watched in the focus of the Gothic style, in the great portals of the cathedrals of Chartres, Rheims, and Amiens (c. 1145–1288). The figures pass from hieratic rigidity to expressive, even vivacious, elegance, as time goes on. A similar development was to be seen sooner or later in other countries as the Gothic style of architecture radiated from northern France. It was modified as it spread, not by political frontiers, but by racial temperament, local traditions, and geo-graphical situation, and thus gave birth to provincial, not to say, national, styles. In England, the sculptors exhibit an almost lyrical quality, which in the fourteenth century is superseded by the general tendency towards dramatic emphasis and decorative mannerism, and in the prosaic fifteenth by a taste for realistic genre. In Germany the lingering Romanesque formalism gives way in the thirteenth century to an energy of characterization, which ends in violent realism and emotion, overloaded, anecdotal detail, and a certain obscuring of unity of design. In all, the liberation of the sculpture from its surroundings and the slow approach to naturalism were to be found in tombs and separate statues. In the thirteenth century there is little or no attempt at portraiture or natural recumbency on tombs, but round about 1300 individuality appears in some degree in the faces, while in Germany there were carved notable equestrian statues.

Colour was an essential part of Gothic art. The work of architect and sculptor was completed by the painter. Mouldings, vaults, tracery, and walls were decorated in vivid colours and gold. Religious and doctrinal scenes were painted on the spaces of church walls, and chivalric incidents had a place both there and in secular buildings. Most effective of all was the use of stained glass for the ever-enlarging windows of northern Gothic. Its peculiar beauty lay in the fact that the colour was fused in the glass as it was made, not applied later, and thus gave the jewel-like brilliancy of the medieval window. The pieces of glass, cut in shapes, were fixed in a leaden framework to make up designs and scenes. The typical thirteenth-century fashion was that of a series of medallions depicting scenes and figures, islands in a floral or geometrical pattern, but single figures, somewhat Byzantinesque, might fill a clerestory window. Towards 1300 the employment of grisaille glass for the field aided in developing new types of window-glass design, while the general progress of naturalism in floral and human representation drew towards the Renaissance of the fifteenth century.

For long the progress of painting and of stained glass was closely connected with the illumination of manuscripts. Manuscript designs were transferred to windows and an architectural setting appears in illuminations. England disputed with France for leadership in the north. The charming Winchester Anglo-Saxon style was replaced in England in the twelfth century by a heavier, richer, more emphatic style, very adaptable for wall-paintings, which nevertheless retained its agitated, somewhat grotesque tendency. A fresh wave of Byzantine influence in the West after 1200 produced a simpler, more naturalistic treatment with expressive outline and a closer study of nature. With the growth of the University of Paris and the rise it encouraged of the professional lay workshop a style of more advanced art was evolved with varied, supple drawing of figures and more realistic detail. An international Gothic style appeared, which strove for decorative effect along with vivid narration and attained its zenith towards 1400. In England, in London and the eastern counties, a great school of painting flourished. Psalter margins, richly decorated, provide a commentary, serious or satiric and burlesque, of contemporary life in the earlier fourteenth century; they inspired others abroad, but after the Black Death the main radiating centre was again France, where identifiable painters make their appearance.

These painters were much influenced by the Italians by way of Avignon, where the Tuscan schools were in favour. But realism was showing itself in genuine portraiture, and Flemish characteristics reinforced the instinct to study nature. In the *Très Riches Heures* (*c.* 1415) illuminated for the Duke of Berry, scenes for the Calendar exhibit both intense observation of animals and trees and skilful mastery in recording it. Yet the accurate detail does not build up a visual whole. Meantime Bohemia under the Luxemburg dynasty was displaying a derivative art, which from eclectic became exaggerated and affected in sentiment in spite of its luxuriant variety. The middle Rhineland and England each manifested a local variety of the reigning international Gothic, of which the portraits of Richard II furnish instances.

There was, however, a new spirit abroad, that curiosity as to man and the visible world, which was the central element in Renaissance thought. Painter and sculptor, although still decorating and expounding doctrine,

Fig. 259. Philip the Bold, Duke of Burgundy

were giving scope to their own personality and their perception of nature as a whole. Both the personality of the artist, a product of his native land, and the formation of large unitary states in the fifteenth century gave rise to nationalism in art. It was the southern Netherlands under the Dukes of Burgundy, where a numerous commercial aristocracy offered the artist a secure livelihood, which achieved the breach with late conventional

1099

Gothic. Claus Sluter (*ob*. 1406) sculptured individual figures of intense realism, hardly related to the architecture or to religious doctrine. With the brothers Hubert (*ob*. 1426) and Jan (*ob*. 1440) van Eyck the new ideals triumphed in painting. They made the picture a window into a real world. The scene was painted in scale, surrounded by atmosphere, and its forms were expressed not by mere line but by light and shade. In the *Adoration of the Lamb* (1432) detail and texture and landscape are of amazing accuracy: each figure is a distinct personality moving to the common goal. Yet only in his portrait-picture of Arnolfini and his wife did Jan succeed in making each perfect detail a part of an indissoluble whole (1434). At the same time, by improvements in the technique of oil painting, the van Eycks placed greater resources in the hands of their fellow-craftsmen. Realism and technical skill of the best were the common possession of their successors (who were not their pupils). Rogier van der Weyden (*ob*. 1464) expressed his own temperament. Dierick Bouts (*ob*. 1475) excelled in landscape, colouring, atmosphere, and characterization without uniting his personages in any common sentiment. The Rhinelander Hans Memling (*ob*. 1494) was a master of craftsmanship suffused by idyllic sentiment and outstanding in portraiture. He summarized the advance attained.

The revival of art in Italy, comparable with the Gothic movement, was somewhat later than in the north. There was no isolation. Northern influences repeatedly entered Italy; as often Italian influences travelled north. But assimilation was checked by national temperament and the strength of congenial classic traditions: the influence of ancient Rome persisted. Further, Italy was in closer touch with Byzantium, and harboured in Ravenna and the South Byzantine monuments of abiding inspiration. Byzantine influence, exquisite in building and colour, also maintained supreme its hieratic, symbolic art, intent on expressing abstract, dogmatic conceptions. Not till the thirteenth century did the human and realistic side of the life of Christ and the Virgin emerge, while the Franciscan impulse added the life of St Francis and quickened the interest in man and his surroundings. In Tuscan crucifixions the human agony of death is emphasized, and realism in detail appears at Siena.

But when the artist broke away from Byzantine models, he found freedom in classical tradition: form and balanced, harmonious treatment kept a dominant share in Italian art. Cavallini—individual names early occur— at Rome (1293) combined his religious theme, *The Last Judgement*, with individualization from life and a classical, Olympian conception of it. Even earlier, under the patronage of the Emperor Frederick II, there were revived in the South Roman types and technique in sculpture. From Apulia, it seems, Niccola Pisano brought this classic influence in sculpture to Tuscany, where it met a Gothic element coming from the north. He, and still more his followers, gave inspiration to artists to break the bonds of Byzantine tradition, introducing movement, character, and dramatic emotion: the classic nude begun by Niccola blended with the energetic rhythms of Gothic design. Sienese and allied Florentine painters were following a similar path. Into the still dominant Byzantine tradition Duccio of Siena and his compeers were introducing grace, variety, and expressiveness linked by their natural instinct for unity of design. In an atmosphere thus created the Florentine Giotto (1266–1336) was born. He was the first mural painter 'to knock a hole in the wall', creating the illusion of solid figures in three-dimensional space. His figures are full of vitality in gesture and action. In the Arena Chapel at Padua psychological insight and emotional intensity made a unity of each scene he painted, in which the use of light had its share.

After the imaginative genius of Giotto the leading influence in Italian painting passed to Sienese artists. Duccio's pre-eminence was succeeded by that of Simone Martini (*ob.* 1344). Here again Northern Gothic influence was manifest in vertical design and tracery and in the flowing lines of drapery as well as in a spirit of courtly elegance. With his subtle linear rhythms and his delicious harmonies and contrasts in colour Simone was a master of decorative effect. He imparts the mystical, contemplative bent of his own mind. Nothing could be more acceptable to the Church, and from Avignon, where he was employed, Sienese influence spread northwards to form a part of that international Gothic of the fourteenth century. Meanwhile in Siena itself the marked personalities of the two Lorenzetti (*ob.* 1349) were achieving a more native, less Gothic expression. Profundity of feeling and grandeur of design make Piero comparable with Giotto; both possessed the Sienese instinct for decorative effect.

Giotto's example was felt in northern Italy, but more potent was the Gothic influence of the northern illuminators seeping in over the Alps with its realistic detail and decorative charm. Yet the influence of the humanistic Renaissance was growing, and appears decisively in the medals of the Veronese Pisanello (*ob.* 1455). Commemorating human personality and achievement, the medal was a fit vehicle for humanism. The vigour of his portraiture is unsurpassed. His designs for the reverses exactly fit the space, exquisite in detail, but monumental in effect. The fundamental change, however, from medieval to renaissance art radiated from Florence. Primarily the Renaissance was a change in men's attitude towards life, which found a touchstone in classical literature and art. In art it affected both spirit and form. Man took God's place as the centre of the cosmos for the humanists. Religious themes were still in a vast majority, but the human element in them became more significant, and the divine more human. Classical themes and historical themes increased in number, while portraiture came into its own. In form we find the zeal for scientific inquiry, not merely realistic detail. Men investigated human anatomy and human

Fig. 260. Lorenzo Ghiberti's and Filippo Brunelleschi's specimen panels submitted in competition for the bronze doors of the Baptistery, 1401

movement and expression. Classic art was both an incentive and a restraint. Unlike the Flemings, the Italians sought for harmony, balance, and proportion. They studied perspective and light and shade. Unity of time and space was secured by reference to one source of light in a picture. In essentials they were anticipated by Giotto.

The sculptors took the lead. Lorenzo Ghiberti (*ob.* 1455), the winner of the competition in 1401 for the bronze north doors of the Baptistery of Florence, who also executed the east doors—'worthy of the gate of Paradise', said Michelangelo—showed unrivalled skill in modelling and in producing depth in bas-relief with a narrative and pictorial effect. Filippo Brunelleschi (*ob.* 1446), whom he defeated in 1401, became an original master of architecture, whose work at the cathedral of Sta Maria del Fiore and other churches and cloisters broke away from Italian Gothic to form arches, columns, and design of classic simplicity sometimes with a grace and harmony of extraordinary charm. Yet another defeated competitor, Jacopo della Quercia of Siena (*ob.* 1438), surpassed Ghiberti as a sculptor. The scenes in his masterpiece, the portal of Bologna cathedral, have all the grandeur and restraint of early Greek work, yet with no imitation of the antique. Greater than all was Donatello (*ob.* 1466). He widened the range of sculpture—his bronze statue of David in the nude was an innovation—and to established forms he gave new life. In him the Renaissance spirit of scientific observation was incarnate, driving him to a penetrating realism, saved from the sordid and commonplace by his sense of human dignity and his lyric instinct. He changed the whole current of art in northern Italy and laid the foundations for the following century.

In painting, the progress of the transition took much the same course. Fra Angelico (*ob*. 1455) remained faithful to Gothic ideals, but he used the new technique to express his mystical vision. In Paolo Uccello (*ob*. 1475) the decorative spirit of Gothic art was evident, but he showed a scientific passion for the problems of foreshortening and perspective. To reach the full Renaissance was the work of Masaccio. In his brief life (1401–*c*. 1428) he gave expression to every aspect of Renaissance thought and set Florentine painting on the road it was to travel until its decay. His frescos in Sta Maria del Carmine in 1426 reveal the fulness of his genius. Each figure seems a complete being, conscious of itself, of its own weaknesses and strengths. Yet they are not isolated: in the noble rhythm of his design, and in his power not only to render human emotion but to give it a point of dramatic concentration, Masaccio becomes a great artist. His art is founded on intense observation of men and nature, inspired by a vivid imagination and guided by a profound feeling for pictorial and dramatic construction. He picked up the torch lighted by Giotto and handed it on to Leonardo da Vinci, Raphael, and Michelangelo.

(4) HUMANISM IN THE RENAISSANCE

Like the growth of the arts the growth of humanism, so closely allied to them in spirit, was the product of the advance, intellectual and social, which was manifest in Western Europe as the fourteenth century began. Comparative increase of security and opportunity, exemplified in the universities, had given men more personal freedom and wider experience. Justinian, Gratian, and Aristotle had aroused and trained the critical and observing faculties, scholasticism had refined the reasoning powers, vernacular literature and architecture had strengthened the creative imagination and applied it to the real world of mind and matter men saw before them. The widest classification we can assign to the forerunners of humanism is that of individuality—not yet individualism—in themselves and in what they perceived. It was not Dante's world-scheme, so typically medieval, but his unsubmergable personality, making him 'his own party' in politics, his power of observing separate human characters and events, his eye for the particularities of nature, each object being seen as it exactly was at some special moment, that gave him his originality and made him the founder of modern literature.

But Dante's attitude to the cosmos was that of long-reigning scholasticism. Petrarch (1304–74) took the first steps towards humanism and modernity. His *Canzoniere* is the work of a master of style and a great poet. He was self-centred, and its poems are the introspective record of the changing moods of his own heart. This was conscious individualism. Nearly as remarkable was the confessed pleasure he took in natural scenery—he appreciated a landscape. This ecclesiastic, a Florentine born and living in exile, was possessed by a restless spirit, which sent him travelling over Italy and France and even to Bohemia. Something of the same curiosity impelled him to study the ancient Latin literature which satisfied his instincts for knowledge and style. He detested the awkward, barbarized Latin of the theological and legal thinkers of his day as well as their roundabout, abstract logic. In the classics he found the revelation of great personalities and the plain, direct reasoning he sought couched in the self-expressive style he admired. They were 'humane literature'. Though pagan, they belonged to a higher, past civilization, and they gave a consecration to human aspirations and human endeavour. Characteristically, he revered the still classic Father of the Church, St Augustine, but the objects of his devotion were Cicero and Virgil, Horace and Seneca. Many Latin authors in whole, or more frequently in part, had long been known, and some few were familiar to the learned. To increase his store Petrarch joined fervently the small band of Italians who searched for manuscripts of new works and forgotten authors. His chief quarry in his journeys was Cicero. He visited old libraries and copied, or procured copies of, new finds of him and other classics. He had the gift of rousing admiration and enthusiasm. It was his own Latin poems, rather than his inspired Italian, which procured him his coronation as poet at Rome (1341). He had struck the imagination of his contemporaries.

Fig. 261. Petrarch's handwriting and drawing of the chapel of Vaucluse

The atmosphere of the time, in fact, was growing, if slowly, favourable to the mental attitude he exemplified. Men would not be so shocked as they had been when Pope Boniface VIII erected his own portrait-statues, and Dino Compagni's Florentine character-sketches would be less of an isolated phenomenon. The most famous adherent Petrarch gained for humanism, the Florentine Boccaccio (1313–75), had already after several less mature works in verse and prose produced his masterpiece, the *Decameron* (1353), that collection of tales in choice Italian, instinct with life and movement and the ironic chances of existence, grave or gay or grossly sensual. He was a born story-teller and the tales he told were mundane to the core. In 1361 the now serious Boccaccio on Petrarch's advice turned his literary energies into a new channel. With amazing zeal, industry, and patience he devoted himself to the study and spread of ancient literature. His Latin works on eminent lives and on ancient mythology stimulated the interest both in humanity and the classics. Petrarch had realized from his Latin reading that behind and inspiring Latin authors were the Greeks, and Boccaccio underwent the penance of housing a repulsive Calabrian, whose tongue was Greek, and who translated Homer very badly into Latin.

The flame of classical humanism was now alight. Salutati (*ob.* 1406) and Marsigli (*ob.* 1394) were leaders at Florence, Barsizza (*ob.* 1431) occupied the chair of Rhetoric in Padua University. The one thing lacking was Greek, and this was supplied by the peril of Constantinople from the Ottoman Beyazit, which stirred the Byzantines to woo the West and more especially the Italians, already vainly eager to acquire the language and reach the fountain-head of classical civilization and its humane literature. The learned Manuel Chrysoloras (*ob.* 1415), an envoy of the Palaeologi, was invited to Florence in 1397 as Professor of Greek. It was a momentous event, for it marks the advent of Hellenic letters and thought in European humanism. At Florence and elsewhere Chrysoloras taught a band of pupils, among them the future schoolmaster, Guarino of Verona (*ob.* 1460). The search for and importation of Greek manuscripts now ran parallel with the fervid hunt for stray copies of ancient Latin works. Guarino, the Sicilian Aurispa (*ob.* 1450), and Filelfo of the March of Ancona (*ob.* 1481) brought back rich cargoes of Greek manuscripts from Constantinople. A stimulus to Greek studies was given in 1438 by the arrival of the large Byzantine deputation to the Council of Ferrara-Florence. Among its members were the learned Gemistos Plethon, the future cardinal Bessarion (*ob.* 1472), who remained in Italy, and Theodore Gaza (*ob.* 1475), the writer of the Greek grammar. After the fall of Constantinople Argyropoulos (*ob.* 1486) settled in Italy and was the ablest teacher. In this period Greek studies flourished, and attempts were made to assimilate Platonic, or rather Neo-Platonic philosophy. Pope Nicholas V was the planner of translations of Greek authors into Latin by humanists, whom he generously paid.

Meanwhile the search for Latin manuscripts went far afield. The Florentine Poggio Bracciolini (*ob.* 1459) ferreted out lost works in France and Germany, and other seekers had some success. By 1429 most of the now extant Latin books had been found. But the task of the humanist was not only to find them but to multiply copies and store them. Great libraries were collected by rulers and private booklovers. The later Ambrosian Library was formed by the Visconti and Sforza. The later Laurentian Library was amalgamated from those brought together by Niccolò Niccoli and Cosimo and Lorenzo de' Medici. Cardinal Bessarion's books were bequeathed to the Venetian Republic. Pope Nicholas V

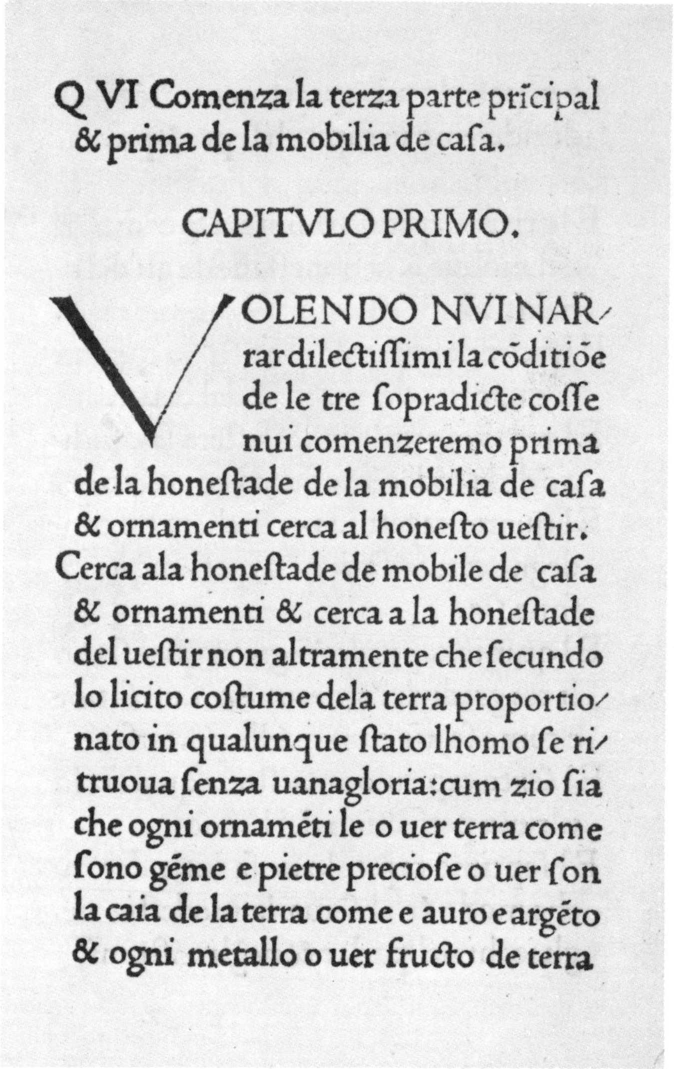

Q VI Comenza la terza parte prīcipal
& prima de la mobilia de caſa.

CAPITVLO PRIMO.

VOLENDO NVI NAR⁄
rar dilectiſſimi la cōditiōe
de le tre ſopradicte coſſe
nui comenzeremo prima
de la honeſtade de la mobilia de caſa
& ornamenti cerca al honeſto ueſtir.
Cerca ala honeſtade de mobile de caſa
& ornamenti & cerca a la honeſtade
del ueſtir non altramente che ſecundo
lo licito coſtume dela terra proportio⁄
nato in qualunque ſtato lhomo ſe ri⁄
truoua ſenza uanagloria:cum zio ſia
che ogni ornaméti le o uer terra come
ſono géme e pietre precioſe o uer ſon
la caia de la terra come e auro e argéto
& ogni metallo o uer fructo de terra

Fig. 262. Palma Virtutum, *printed by Nicolas Jenson*

collected the Library of the Vatican. Following the example of Petrarch
and Boccaccio, many humanists, like Niccoli and Poggio, were indefatigable
copyists themselves. Of them Niccoli, an artist in all things to his finger-
tips, introduced a revolution in book-script. By a slow change the elegant
and clear Carolingian minuscule of *c.* 800 had been transformed into the

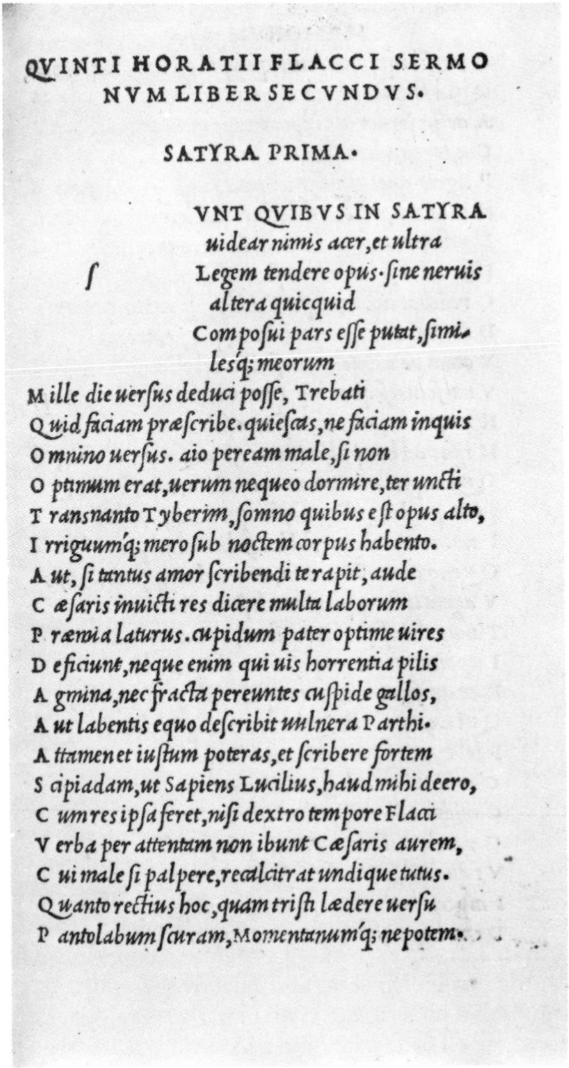

QVINTI HORATII FLACCI SERMO
NVM LIBER SECVNDVS.

SATYRA PRIMA.

VNT QVIBVS IN SATYRA
uidear nimis acer, et ultra
∫ *Legem tendere opus · sine neruis*
altera quicquid
Compofui pars effe putat, fimi-
lesq; meorum
M *ille die uerfus deduci poffe,* Trebati
Q *uid faciam præfcribe. quiefcas, ne faciam inquis*
O *mnino uerfus. aio peream male, fi non*
O *ptimum erat, uerum nequeo dormire, ter uncti*
T *ransnanto Tyberim, fomno quibus eft opus alto,*
I *rriguumq; mero fub noctem corpus habento.*
A *ut, fi tantus amor fcribendi te rapit, aude*
C *æfaris inuicti res dicere multa laborum*
P *ræmia laturus. cupidum pater optime uires*
D *eficiunt, neque enim qui uis horrentia pilis*
A *gmina, nec fracta pereuntes cufpide gallos,*
A *ut labentis equo defcribit uulnera Parthi.*
A *ttamen et iuftum poteras, et fcribere fortem*
S *cipiadam, ut Sapiens Lucilius, haud mihi deero,*
C *um res ipfa feret, nifi dextro tempore Flacci*
V *erba per attentam non ibunt Cæfaris aurem,*
C *ui male fi palpere, recalcitrat undique tutus.*
Q *uanto rectius hoc, quam trifti lædere uerfu*
P *antolabum fcurram, Momentanumq; nepotem.*

Fig. 263. The first Aldine Horace

pointed and less easily legible Gothic of the fourteenth century. Niccoli
in his transcriptions reverted to a beautifully formed version of the
Carolingian hand of his oldest manuscripts. The fashion spread not only to
Poggio and other humanists but to the professional scribes, who came
nearest to large-scale production. When about 1465 printing was brought

1107   73-2 into Italy from Germany the type was cut on the new 'roman' model, and is the parent of present-day roman types, while the more cursive hand, also devised by Niccoli, and used in the papal chancery, stands in the same relation to 'italic' type. The latest Gothic hand survived until *c.* 1600 for certain purposes in France and in English 'black letter', but only in Germany did it defy competition.

It cannot be said that the productions of these earlier humanists were as a whole worthy of the high claims they made for themselves. They were exploring an unhackneyed field of research with treasures of thought and knowledge to be rifled, a new and sovereign clue to the study of life. With the mundane view of life and man, daily gathering strength, and the long-descended fame of the ancient authors and their themes before them, fame among men seemed to them the best reward and the desire for it no excusable infirmity but the most laudable of motives. They thought it could only be enshrined in imperishable Latin, and despised the transient vehicle of the pithy and pungent vernacular—leaving a needless gap in their native literature. But with a vanity now absurd they overrated their own performances, which they fondly believed would give immortality to themselves and their patrons. The delusion favoured the vogue of humanism among ambitious despots, but tedious pedantry and imitative description enfeebled their narratives and praises. In their rivalries and quarrels they aped the scurrilous invectives to be found in the classics, while they even won approbation by celebrating the more pagan vices.

Not all their work, however, was vapid or scandalous. Their familiarity with manuscripts and copying gave them skill in textual editing, and they really advanced the science of criticism. Lorenzo Valla (*ob.* 1457) made a scientific study of the Latin language. A famous treatise proved the spuriousness of the Donation of Constantine (1440); he also showed that of the writings of Dionysius the Areopagite, so long influential in medieval thought. Biondo (*ob.* 1463) may be said to have commenced the treatment of Roman archaeology in a critical spirit. Besides, the attainment of a classic style in Latin was making progress. Pope Eugenius IV placed humanists in the papal chancery, and Nicholas V added to their number. Pius II was himself a man of letters and an observant lover of the country-side. His works, on all sorts of subjects, have worn better than those of most of his fellows. It was not long after that Politian (*ob.* 1494) at Florence and Pontano (*ob.* 1503) at Naples were writing Latin verse and prose with ease and freedom, while Politian lectured with a criticism, taste, and insight unknown for centuries.

Not less remarkable was the renewal of Italian poetry and prose under classic influences. Politian supremely and Lorenzo de' Medici himself with undeniable charm shaped old popular or rustic themes into Tuscan of a polish which owed its glamour to ancient literature, and something of the

Fig. 265. Cardinal Nicholas of Cusa

names includes Wessel (*ob.* 1489), Agricola (*ob.* 1485), Wimpheling (*ob.* 1528), Celtes (*ob.* 1508), the Abbot Trithemius (*ob.* 1516), Johannes a Lapide (*ob.* 1496), and Regiomontanus (*ob.* 1476), to mention no others, who propagated humanism at Zwolle, Heidelberg, Basle, Strasbourg, Nuremberg, Erfurt, and Vienna. Taken as a whole, they showed a preference for theology and the Fathers of the Church, along with their study of heathen authors, which stamped a special character on German humanism, and was among the causes of the sixteenth-century Reformation.

The bent towards Christian patristic learning in Germany led to the study of the Hebrew of the Old Testament. Not that it had been absent in fifteenth-century Italy. The Florentine Manetti (*ob.* 1459) had learnt Hebrew with a view to Christian apologetics. Pico della Mirandola (*ob.* 1494) read Hebrew and Arabic in the construction of his eclectic philosophy. Hebrew manuscripts were stored in the great libraries, and the Old Testament in Hebrew was printed in 1488. In Germany, Wessel and Trithemius were both Hebrew scholars, while Reuchlin (*ob.* 1522), a real Hebraist, provided the linguistic apparatus for future students. Here, too, the expansion of the field of knowledge and the recourse to antiquity and the understanding of its works were congenial products of the Renaissance.

RETROSPECT

Although the last decade of the fifteenth century is an arbitrary date at which to close the history of the period of European history which by a like arbitrary but convenient usage is named the Middle Ages, it yet forms an epoch-making landmark, not a frontier, in political events and in the growth of knowledge, just as the dissolution of the Western Roman Empire and the sinking of the level of civilization within its whilom boundaries did in the fifth century, a date almost as arbitrary. The emergence of the new, the decadence of the old, began long before either and continued long after. But the discovery of the New World and of the ocean route to the East, the French invasion of Italy, the erection of absolute monarchies ruling wide territories, mainly based on conscious nations, preceded by the fall at long last of the Eastern Roman Empire and the advance of the Turks in the Balkans and the Mediterranean, did together give a new set to European politics and economics. The oceanic stage was about to succeed the Mediterranean in commerce. The horizon receded in world politics. No less were humanism in literature and thought and naturalism in art marching to their victory. The spirit of ancient Hellenic rationality had begun to leaven the West, whose own mental evolution was making it receptive and equipped for a more inward appreciation of what the classics had to offer. Deductive scholastic philosophy, so marvellous in its speculative ingenuity, was slowly quitting its tenacious hold on the mind in favour of that ardent exploration of the sensible world, that exaltation of its beauty and wonder, and of man who could perceive and use it, which were akin to and embedded the early tentatives of infant science. By a happy coincidence the new device of printing was extending the boundaries of the educated classes and the range of the knowledge that they could acquire and impart.

At this halt, artificial as it may be, there is some advantage in attempting a backward view over some main lines of change which may be seen in the multitudinous events and unresting fluctuations of the millennium which has been traversed, in spite of the hazards of selection and the pitfalls thickly strewn in the path of the expounder. The Middle Ages began with the steady deterioration both of the fabric of civilized, centralized state government left by the ancient Empire and of the barbaric tribal cohesion, based on kingship and kinship, of the incoming Germanic invaders. Without literacy, without bureaucracy, without the orderly separation of functions, and, more than all, without the civilized tradition ingrained by centuries-old habits of order and organization, without the mentality of long-descended culture in the rulers or the reverence for it in the ruled, the West as a whole was crumbling into discordant fragments dominated by a local landed aristocracy and loosely held together by the tribal kingships. Yet in this degeneration were to be seen at least two factors of prime importance for the future, the amalgamation of barbarian and 'Roman', with its accompaniment of tenacious custom in the life of the countryside, and, more potent and fruitful still, the survival of the Christian Church, enshrining and propagating a higher ethos in thought and behaviour and a fertilizing remnant of the ancient culture, however subdued to its environment both it and they might be. Here was the significance of the conversion of England by the Roman mission sent by Gregory the Great and by the Irish monks. Quasi-civilized organization and an inspiring stock of learning and culture took root from them and reacted on the Continent. Monasticism in general, too, in its flight from the secular world and for all its facility in decay was yet a preservative of this inheritance and an exemplar of self-controlled life by an un-barbaric law.

On the heels of the Dark Ages came the Carolingian Empire. It did not endure, but its effects were enduring. For one thing the Carolingians restored over their wide lands the old, and more than the old, organization of the Western Church under the episcopate. The claims of the Papacy as its head were reinvigorated in alliance with the dynasty, and their exercise in some degree was made feasible by the transitory unification of the West. St Boniface, the Englishman, a champion of papal authority, achieved the lingering conversion of inner Germany, all but Saxony, beyond the Rhine. Under his guidance King Pepin and his brother Carloman reformed the incoherent Frankish Church. His theocratic son, Charlemagne, with his all-pervading energy controlled, vivified, and spurred it on in its secular task of civilization, while he strove to raise the level of his lay officials. St Augustine's City of God on earth was to be embodied in his theocratic realm. The sacring of the king, introduced by Pepin, implied a new conception of sovereignty in Francia to replace the barbaric, irresponsible right of possession of Merovingian times. The king was now God's Vicar

1113

with the duty of giving peace and justice to his subjects. The implications, whether for king or people, were never to be forgotten by the leaders of opinion. The idea culminated in the fancied revival, really the foundation, of the Roman Empire in the West, the not ineptly, though vainly, named Holy Roman Empire of later days. But the conception involved the seeds of a conflict. Christendom, the Empire, was guided by the two hierarchies of Pope Gelasius, the ecclesiastical and the lay, each under its chief, the Pope and the Emperor. Which, if either, of them was superior was to be a perennial debate, in which even compromise was uneasy and full of friction and the balance uncertain, and which led under the force of practical, urgent facts to open war between the spiritual and secular powers.

Not the least of the Carolingian achievements, bound up indeed with religion and the new imperialism, was the Carolingian Renaissance in thought and letters. Under Charlemagne it effected the salvage of the remains of Latin literature, theological and pagan, and thereby preserved it to form both the food and the mould of thought for future generations. Gathered from the fringes of his Empire, from England, from Italy, and from Spain, copies, zealously stored in monasteries and cathedrals, written in the beautiful Carolingian minuscule, itself a mark of the new ecumenic, not disaggregated, culture, were henceforth too widespread to vanish in the miserable devastations of the ninth century.

Even in the purely political sphere the Carolingian era left ineffaceable results for the future. The conquest and conversion of heathen Saxony by Charlemagne united at last all the inner German tribes under one sway and faith, thus creating the possibility of the German kingdom and nation, which at first dominated, and always was an essential factor in, medieval Christendom. In like manner Charlemagne's conquest of North Italy and the Spanish March set in motion forces which never ceased to work on both sides of the Alps and Pyrenees. It was also his continual wars, dependent in the last resort on the array of armoured, mounted vassals, brought by the great landed nobles, which made, in fact if not in law, for the speedy predominance of feudalism when once his strong grasp ceased to counteract the natural disintegration of a barbarized collection of lands and peoples.

In its very nature the Carolingian Empire was almost bound to collapse as its undisciplined constituents started asunder. The blind greed of the Carolingians themselves and the shattering impact of fresh invaders, Magyars, Moslems, and above all the Northmen, hastened and intensified this dismal progress to anarchy. The repulse or the settlement of the invading bands, completed, save in England, by the mid-tenth century, left Western Europe as a whole under the rule and as a prey of the local landed lords. Feudalism in this early, unregulated stage seemed rather the expression of anarchy than, what it became, its alleviation and subduer.

Private war was endemic and perpetual. Yet even the unruly petty feudal lords were obliged by their ideas of life and by their necessities to cherish the mutual duties of the feudal bond of lord and vassal, although passion, combativeness, and pride broke them on all sides. In fact, the feudal complex was an early example of that recourse to mutual association of like with like which was the refuge of a disintegrated society, and proved to be the typical creator of institutions in the creative Middle Ages.

Disintegration, however, did not rage unchecked throughout. The conservative German tribes retained their cohesion and gave strength to the kingship of the Saxon line. Otto the Great made alliance with the order-loving Church, mastered his nobles, and revived the Empire by his conquest of Italy. Thenceforward the power of the Emperors rested largely on the Church which they richly endowed, and which alone could provide the competent servants of their choice needed for administration in a rude, illiterate age. But the fabric was endangered by the very fact of Church reform. A spontaneous reaction against anarchy, a desire for the reestablishment of law and order in the Church at least, grew rapidly. It was favoured even by violent rulers. It gained men's reverence and enthusiasm. Reiterated reform of decadent or lethargic monasteries, the foundation of new, typified by the widespread congregation of Cluny, manifested the reawakened religious zeal, in which the episcopate took an increasingly notable share. The half-forgotten Canon Law began to be revived. Lastly, in the mid-eleventh century, reform captured the Papacy, just emerging from the miry slough of the anarchy, with none of its claims to rule the Church forgotten, but rather enhanced by Pope Nicholas I when the Carolingian Empire was dissolving. The German Pope Leo IX, strong in imperial support, asserted his authority over the daunted bishops, and began a new era. If the secular unity of Christendom under the Emperor was hardly more than a theory, its ecclesiastical unity under the Pope was in the way to become a living fact.

The first conflict between Pope and Emperor, merging into the Investiture Contest, was a natural consequence, for the Emperor was more dependent on his control of the Church than his fellow monarchs were, and owing to his Italian kingdom was most directly involved in the effects of the papalized reforms. The lame compromise of 1122 left the bishops with two masters and two possibly clashing allegiances. But the reform and the struggle, not confined to the imperial lands, had brought about more fundamental changes. The freedom of Church and churchmen from lay domination was an acknowledged doctrine and a partial practice. Still more important was the centralized organization of the Western Church under the papal monarchy, growing day by day. Finally, an extension of vast import had been given by Pope Gregory VII to the doctrine of papal supremacy. The Successor of St Peter, the Vicar of Christ, was supreme

1115

over all earthly potentates and persons, whose pastor he was, with power to set up and cast down. There was thus but one theocrat, the chief priest, in the earthly City of God. It was a doctrine upheld by later Popes. The Emperors and kings henceforward were on the defensive, confined to the claim that their office, the secular sword, was independent, derived from God alone.

These were Western developments. The Byzantine Empire, the continuation as it was of the ancient Roman Empire and civilization, remained a conservative, bureaucratic autocracy, where the Emperor was head of Church and State. Largely isolated by temperament, culture, and traditions from the West, it had been the bulwark of Europe against Asia, beating back Moslem and barbarian. But its strength was slowly waning, and it nearly collapsed before the Seljūk Turks. Then it was that the West, under the aegis of the Papacy, came to the rescue of Christendom in the Crusades. For some centuries the Moslems had been nearly masters of the Mediterranean Sea. But a reaction of Christendom had already begun, of which the Crusades were the completion and the fullest expression. It has been told how far they succeeded, and how they were perverted by the shameful attack on Constantinople in 1204.

The movement for Church reform and papal theocracy had not been merely a fervour to cleanse the religious life of the time. As the career of Gregory VII testifies, it had been an attempt to check rampant anarchy and the brutal rule of the strong. But a like, if rougher and less exalted, more contaminated intent was inspiring the lay potentates of the crumbled provinces of the West. Most spectacular was the history of the Germanic Emperors, but their Empire was too wide for their means and the structure of their institutions too obsolescent in their tribalism for them to achieve success in quelling local turbulence, when the Investiture contest lamed their power. A tardy growth of feudalism in Germany, reinvigorating ancient particularism and chieftainship, baffled their endeavours. Their Italian kingdom broke up into city-states. Elsewhere, however, for instance in France, the kings, endowed with resources not so disproportionate to their narrower sphere, found feudal law and feudal rights a valuable asset in re-establishing monarchic power. Their great vassals, engaged in enforcing feudal obligations on the unruly petty lords, unwittingly prepared the way. Thus arose the age of feudal monarchies. The kings made real their never-forgotten right and duty as the source of justice and protector of their subjects. They began to form bureaucracies; their administration became a blend of genuine officialdom and feudal delegation. Great statesmen, the first two Henries of England, Roger the Great of Sicily, Philip Augustus of France, mark the process.

The twelfth century was indeed the age of the resurgence of civilization. Growing security, growing trade and industry fostered the towns and the almost new class of townsmen, and produced new types of association, the commune, the gild, and the university. The Church, knit closely under the Papacy, gave a model of wide organization and reasoned law. The new federate monastic Orders fired for a while the religious imagination. In this new atmosphere the twelfth-century Renaissance played a decisive role. There appeared a thirst for knowledge. Zealots for learning studied the ancient Roman Law, or recovered through the Arabic translations, or sometimes through versions direct from the Greek, some parts of Hellenistic science. The schoolmen were busied in the adventure of the rational explanation of the universe and the construction of a Christian philosophy. In a spirit both aesthetic and practical, builders with carvers in their wake were devising in early Gothic architecture churches that were the fit home and expression of Christian worship. Poets and story-tellers were bringing to life in the vernacular tongues the unmuffled voice of a society astir.

The next century saw the sequel of this renaissance in achievement, in progress and decline, and in disaster. There was destruction, for the Byzantine Empire suffered an irremediable blow from the Fourth Crusade, and the Holy Roman Empire never recovered from its defeat in the third conflict with the Papacy and the fall of the Hohenstaufen, while its temporary annex, the Norman kingdom of Sicily, lost its brief, precocious eminence. There was also construction. Innocent III and his successors raised Papacy and Church to unexampled heights of centralized organization and methodical law, and the friars infused a vivid, penetrating Christianity into torpid beliefs or rebellious questionings. This advance was matched in lay creations. The kingdoms of England and France were acquiring internal solidarity permeated more and more by their central governments. The Italian communes amid their revolutions were inventing self-governing, would-be balanced institutions. The universities developed their constitutions and curricula. Craft-gilds multiplied. How wide a range the impulse for association among classes of the same social function was taking was shown in the prevalent conception of estates of the realm by which the clergy, the feudal nobles, and the trading townsmen formed separate groups in the new national assemblies. Men were classified less by the minutiae of rank and dependence than by the tasks they performed for the needs of human existence, and Christian moralists laid down their characteristic duties and rights.

Western civilization, surveying its gains, was possessed by the instinct to formulate and define. Not only institutions but theories of law and government assumed a clearer expression, a precision in application. The bull *Unam Sanctam* of Pope Boniface VIII was but one instance, if the most famous, of this tendency. It was seen in the coherent shape attained by the English Parliament and the French States General, to name no other assemblies, and in the functional elaboration of governments. The same endeavour was visible in scholastic philosophy, to which the recovery in translation of the works of Aristotle provided new and ample material for thought and a new starting-point. St Thomas Aquinas made his great attempt to formulate a complete scheme of man and the universe, combining reason and revelation. Dante's poem blended this cosmology with the daily lessons of human experience for all to see and feel in his vision of eternity. The mundane Marsilius of Padua set himself to disclose the immutable laws governing the best possible conditions of human society and the historic hindrances to their attainment, just when Dante had marked off the reciprocal limits of the traditional lay and spiritual rulers of Christendom.

After finality came the transition. For one thing, the raging wars between the greater states, like that between France and England, from which the lesser were not exempt, put a strain on hard-won order and organization which they could not bear. For another, the Black Death and its regular recurrence set a long-lasting check on the reduced population, afflicted its moral temper, and disturbed the balance of its economic habits. More fundamental, perhaps, was men's impatience of the new governmental structure, whether of the Church or the State, stringent, oppressive, and often corrupt, impatience, too, in economic life of the new-born capitalistic regime, which in certain centres of Europe-wide export bore remorselessly on its workmen and led to revolutions. The most formidable of all the restive elements was the greater nobility, strengthened by the wars, with ample lands and numerous troops, who even when their old legal feudal rights were decayed, retained their local predominance and by turns controlled or paralysed the royal government. How they wore themselves out, how their essential anarchy produced the remedy of the absolute monarch, is the story of the fifteenth century. Already, the like unbearable strife of class and faction had given birth to the Italian despot. In an analogous fashion the vexatious autocracy of the Popes of Avignon, lamed by the Great Schism, was faced by the Conciliar Movement. But Church reformers and Church rebels were at odds. The Papacy, like monarchy, held its ground, yet only by sharing effective power with the secular rulers. They were all to face the new European situation created by the Turkish conquest, religious revolution, and the rivalry of nation-states and their dynasties.

A slow break-away from earlier ideas, now on this side, now on that, was manifest in scholastic philosophy. Duns Scotus and Ockam called in question the rational basis of its reasoning; Wyclif impugned the traditional fabric of Church authority; Nicholas of Cusa spun a new web of metaphysics around accepted beliefs. The Italian Neo-Platonists endeavoured to construct an eclectic reconciliation of imaginative pagan thought with Christian doctrine. These were thinkers. In practical life the individual, the early capitalist, the soldier of fortune, and the despot, the artist and the humanist, was freeing himself from group-control. In spite of their enduring vitality, which long outlasted the fifteenth century, the innumerable lesser microcosms of vassalage or gild or corporation were yielding to the domination of the unitary state. It is in creative art that the new ethos, the new outlook on the world, becomes visible, transpiring through and transforming the formal garb of tradition and belief. From exact portrayal men moved to an engrossing curiosity and admiration of mankind and the world it inhabited. Coupled naturally with the individual enterprise of the humanists and their reaction to the impact of the ancient Greek and Roman world that they explored, this was the Renaissance and the propagation of modernity.

Beneath these movements displayed by the upper, directive layers of society, it may be asked what was the effect of them on the mass of the population, predominantly peasants, living a customary life, whose voice reaches us with a ghost-like faintness till near the close of the Middle Ages —the stiller deeps beneath the tumultuous waves. To judge from the sparse Carolingian records, the Merovingian storms passed with little formal change in the condition of the serfs and tenant freemen, bound to the soil they cultivated. But the subsequent invasions and anarchy not only debased crowds of freemen to serfdom but produced a thick crop of fresh customary exactions, the so-called abuses new and old. Yet the twelfth century witnessed a recovery from this abyss of gloom, a recovery which was accentuated in the thirteenth. The common interests of men, whether lord or serf, worked in the same direction. Many peasants absconded to the rising towns, others emigrated to new lands in the east, easier tenure was a lure to the assarting of the village waste which reacted favourably on the old original tenures, manumission from corporal serfdom at least was frequent. The growth of population implies the food to feed it. Round about the year 1300 seems to have been the peak-date for peasant welfare over much of Europe. Then came, with of course wide exceptions and variations, a decline. Famine, plague, and incessant wars and feuds told hardly on the villager. Devastation and pillage produced a starving peasantry in France. In Germany armed and needy lords revived the grievous incidents of serfdom. In East Central Europe the once happier cultivator was pressed down to a life of servitude. In North Italy the bourgeois landowner proved a more astute landlord than the vanquished noble. As was natural, the mentality of the countryman lagged behind that of the more mobile classes both in growth and in decay. In a less degree the same may be said of the less prosperous ranks of townsmen. Yet change, slow to come, was at work, less shown in conspicuous, temporary fashions, but in the end enduring and profound.

Taken as a whole, the history of the Middle Ages after the ruin in the West of the ancient civilization is one of progress, progress in society, government, order and organization, laws, the development of human faculties, of rational thought, of knowledge and experience, of art and culture. Men throughout had been restlessly creative and aspiring. But that progress to a better life had been perpetually thwarted and delayed, not merely by external disasters but by the passions and wilful ambitions of men themselves. They generated countless ills. Rough and ready, even skilful and inspired remedies brought with their benefits fresh misfortunes on mankind. Innate barbarism broke from its fetters time and time again. Potent delusions summoned their appropriate nemesis. In our distant retrospect we can perceive how crooked and perilous was the upward road.

APPENDICES

APPENDICES

(1) ROMAN EMPERORS (284–476)

The dates given are those of effective rule, not of nominal association as Augustus. The names of usurpers, and of emperors whose rule was recognized in Italy but not in the East, are in italics.

Diocletian	284–305
Maximian	286–305, 306–308
Constantius I	305–306
Galerius	305–311
Severus	306–307
Maxentius	306–312
Constantine I	306–337
Licinius	307–324
Maximin Daza	308–313
Constantine II	337–340
Constantius II	337–361
Constans	337–350
Magnentius	350–353
Julian the Apostate	360–363
Jovian	363–364
Valentinian I	364–375 (in the West)
Valens	364–378 (in the East)
Gratian	375–383 (in the West)
Valentinian II	375–392 (in the West)
Theodosius I the Great	378–395 (in the East; in the West from 392)
Maximus	383–388
Eugenius	392–394

IN THE EAST		IN THE WEST	
Arcadius	395–408	Honorius	395–423
Theodosius II	408–450	*Constantine III*	407–411
Marcian	450–457	Constantius III	421
Leo I	457–474	John	423–425
Leo II	474	Valentinian III	425–455
Zeno	474–491	*Petronius Maximus*	455
Basiliscus	475–476	Avitus	455–456
		Majorian	457–461
		Severus III	461–465
		Anthemius	467–472
		Olybrius	472
		Glycerius	473
		Julius Nepos	473–480
		Romulus Augustulus	475–476

(2) BYZANTINE EMPERORS (FROM 491)

The dates are those of effective reign, as distinct from honorary association on the throne.

Anastasius I	491–518	Constantine IX Monomachus	1042–1054
Justin I	518–527	Theodora	1054–1056
Justinian	527–565	Michael VI Stratioticus	1056–1057
Justin II	565–578	Isaac I Comnenus	1057–1059
Tiberius	578–582	Constantine X Ducas	1059–1067
Maurice	582–602	Romanus IV Diogenes	1067–1071
Phocas	602–610	Michael VII Parapinaces	1071–1078
Heraclius I	610–641	Nicephorus III Botaniates	1078–1081
Constantine III	641	Alexius I Comnenus	1081–1118
Heracleonas	641	John II	1118–1143
Constans II	641–668	Manuel I	1143–1180
Constantine IV Pogonatus	668–685	Alexius II	1180–1183
Justinian II	685–695	Andronicus I	1183–1185
Leontius	695–698	Isaac II Angelus	1185–1195
Tiberius III Apsimar	698–705	Alexius III	1195–1203
Justinian II (restored)	705–711	Isaac II (restored)	1203–1204
Philippicus	711–713	Alexius IV	1203–1204
Anastasius II	713–715	Alexius V Ducas	1204
Theodosius III	715–717		
Leo III the Isaurian	717–741	**LATIN EMPERORS**	
Constantine V Copronymus	741–775	Baldwin I	1204–1205
Leo IV the Chazar	775–780	Henry	1206–1216
Constantine VI	780–797	Peter of Courtenay	1217
Irene	797–802	Yolande	1217–1219
Nicephorus I	802–811	Robert of Courtenay	1221–1228
Michael I Rangabé	811–813	Baldwin II	1228–1261
Leo V the Armenian	813–820	John of Brienne (Co-Emperor)	1231–1237
Michael II the Stammerer	820–829		
Theophilus	829–842	**EMPERORS AT NICAEA**	
Michael III the Drunkard	842–867	Theodore I Lascaris	1206–1222
Basil I the Macedonian	867–886	John III Vatatzes	1222–1254
Leo VI the Wise	886–912	Theodore II Lascaris	1254–1258
Alexander	912–913	John IV	1258–1261
Constantine VII Porphyrogenitus	913–959	**EMPERORS AT CONSTANTINOPLE**	
Romanus I Lecapenus	919–944	Michael VIII Palaeologus	1261–1282
Romanus II	959–963	Andronicus II	1282–1328
Nicephorus II Phocas	963–969	Michael IX	1295–1320
John I Zimiskes	969–976	Andronicus III	1328–1341
Basil II Bulgaroctonos	976–1025	John V	1341–1391
Constantine VIII	1025–1028	John VI Cantacuzene	1347–1354
Zoë	1028–1050	Andronicus IV	1376–1379
Romanus III Argyrus	1028–1034	Manuel II	1391–1423
Michael IV the Paphlagonian	1034–1041	John VII (Co-Emperor)	1399–1402
Michael V Calaphates	1041–1042	John VIII	1423–1448
Zoë and Theodora	1042	Constantine XI	1448–1453

(3) GERMAN KINGS AND HOLY ROMAN EMPERORS

The dates are those of effective rule. Some monarchs were associated in the imperial office before their father's death, others were only crowned several years after their accession to the German throne.

Charles the Great	800–814	King of the Franks from 768.
Lewis the Pious	814–840	
Lothar I	840–855	
Louis II	855–875	In Italy.
Charles (II) the Bald	875–877	
Charles (III) the Fat	881–887	
Guy of Spoleto	891–894	In Italy.
Lambert of Spoleto	894–898	In Italy.
Arnulf of Carinthia	896–899	

Arnulf's successors in Germany (Lewis the Child, 899–911; Conrad of Franconia, 911–918; Henry the Fowler, 919–936) laid no claim to the Imperial dignity, which during the next half-century was disputed between various Italian dynasties and invaders from Burgundy. The true medieval Empire began with the imperial coronation of Otto the Great in 962.

Otto I the Great	962–973	German king from 936.
Otto II	973–983	
Otto III	983–1002	
Henry II	1002–1024	
Conrad II	1024–1039	
Henry III	1039–1056	
Henry IV	1056–1106	
Rudolf of Swabia	1077–1080	
Herman of Salm	1081–1093	Rivals to Henry IV.
Conrad of Franconia	1093–1101	
Henry V	1106–1125	
Lothar III	1125–1137	
Conrad III	1138–1152	Never crowned.
Frederick I Barbarossa	1152–1190	
Henry VI	1190–1197	
Philip of Swabia	1198–1208	Rivals. Philip was never crowned.
Otto IV	1198–1218	
Frederick II	1212–1250	
Henry Raspe	1246–1247	Anti-king. Never crowned.
William of Holland	1247–1256	Anti-king. Never crowned.
Conrad IV	1250–1254	Never crowned.
Richard of Cornwall	1257–1272	Rivals. Neither was ever crowned.
Alfonso X of Castile	1257–1273	
Rudolf I of Habsburg	1273–1291	Never crowned.
Adolf of Nassau	1292–1298	Never crowned.
Albert I of Habsburg	1298–1308	Never crowned.
Henry VII of Luxemburg	1308–1313	

Lewis IV of Bavaria	1314–1347	
Frederick of Habsburg	1314–1322	Anti-king. Never crowned.
Charles IV of Luxemburg	1347–1378	
Günther of Schwarzburg	1347–1349	Anti-king. Never crowned.
Wenceslas of Luxemburg	1378–1400	Deposed. Never crowned.
Rupert of the Palatinate	1400–1410	Never crowned.
Sigismund of Luxemburg	1410–1437	
Jobst of Moravia	1410–1411	Anti-king. Never crowned.
Albert II of Habsburg	1438–1439	Never crowned.
Frederick III of Habsburg	1440–1493	Last Emperor to be crowned at Rome.

(4) POPES (FROM 314)

The names of anti-Popes (including the Avignon Popes during the Great Schism) are printed in italics.

Sylvester I	314–335	Benedict I	575–579
Mark	336	Pelagius II	579–590
Julius I	337–352	Gregory I, the Great	590–604
Liberius	352–366	Sabinian	604–606
Felix II	355–356	Boniface III	607
Damasus I	366–384	Boniface IV	608–615
Ursicinus	366–367	Deusdedit I	615–618
Siricius	384–399	Boniface V	619–625
Anastasius I	399–401	Honorius I	625–638
Innocent I	402–417	Severinus	640
Zosimus	417–418	John IV	640–642
Boniface I	418–422	Theodore I	642–649
Eulalius	418–419	Martin I	649–655
Celestine I	422–432	Eugenius I	655–657
Sixtus III	432–440	Vitalian	657–672
Leo I, the Great	440–461	Deusdedit II	672–676
Hilary	461–468	Donus	676–678
Simplicius	468–483	Agatho	678–681
Felix III (II)	483–492	Leo II	682–683
Gelasius I	492–496	Benedict II	684–685
Anastasius II	496–498	John V	685–686
Symmachus	498–514	Conon	686–687
Laurentius	498–505	*Theodore*	686–687
Hormisdas	514–523	Sergius I	687–701
John I	523–526	*Paschal*	687–688
Felix IV (III)	526–530	John VI	701–705
Boniface II	530–532	John VII	705–707
Dioscurus	530	Sisinius	708
John II	532–535	Constantine	708–715
Agapitus I	535–536	Gregory II	715–731
Silverius	536–538	Gregory III	731–741
Vigilius	538–555	Zacharias	741–752
Pelagius I	555–561	Stephen II	752
John III	561–574	Stephen III (II)	752–757

Paul I	757–767	John XVII	1003
Constantine II	767–768	John XVIII	1004–1009
Stephen IV (III)	768–772	Sergius IV	1009–1012
Adrian I	772–795	Benedict VIII	1012–1024
Leo III	795–816	*Gregory*	1012
Stephen V (IV)	816–817	John XIX	1024–1032
Paschal I	817–824	Benedict IX	1032–1044
Eugenius II	824–827	Sylvester III	1045
Valentine	827	Benedict IX	1045
Gregory IV	828–844	Gregory VI	1045–1046
Sergius II	844–847	Clement II	1046–1047
Leo IV	847–855	Benedict IX	1047–1048
Benedict III	855–858	Damasus II	1048
Anastasius	855	Leo IX	1049–1054
Nicholas I	858–867	Victor II	1055–1057
Adrian II	867–872	Stephen X	1057–1058
John VIII	872–882	*Benedict X*	1058–1059
Marinus I	882–884	Nicholas II	1059–1061
Adrian III	884–885	Alexander II	1061–1073
Stephen VI (V)	885–891	*Honorius II*	1061–1072
Formosus	891–896	Gregory VII	1073–1085
Boniface VI	896	*Clement III*	1080–1100
Stephen VII (VI)	896–897	Victor III	1087
Romanus	897	Urban II	1088–1099
Theodore II	897	Paschal II	1099–1118
John IX	898–900	*Theodoric*	1100
Benedict IV	900–903	*Albert*	1102
Leo V	903	*Sylvester IV*	1105–1111
Christopher	903	Gelasius II	1118–1119
Sergius III	904–911	*Gregory VIII*	1118–1121
Anastasius III	911–913	Calixtus II	1119–1124
Lando	913–914	Honorius II	1124–1130
John X	914–928	*Celestine II*	1124
Leo VI	928	Innocent II	1130–1143
Stephen VIII (VII)	929–931	*Anacletus II*	1130–1138
John XI	931–935	*Victor IV*	1138
Leo VII	936–939	Celestine II	1143–1144
Stephen IX (VIII)	939–942	Lucius II	1144–1145
Marinus II	942–946	Eugenius III	1145–1153
Agapitus II	946–955	Anastasius IV	1153–1154
John XII	955–964	Adrian IV	1154–1159
Leo VIII	963–965	Alexander III	1159–1181
Benedict V	964–966	*Victor IV*	1159–1164
John XIII	965–972	*Paschal III*	1164–1168
Benedict VI	973–974	*Calixtus III*	1168–1178
Boniface VII	974, 984–985	*Innocent III*	1179–1180
Benedict VII	974–983	Lucius III	1181–1185
John XIV	983–984	Urban III	1185–1187
John XV	985–996	Gregory VIII	1187
Gregory V	996–999	Clement III	1187–1191
John XVI	997–998	Celestine III	1191–1198
Sylvester II	999–1003	Innocent III	1198–1216

Honorius III	1216–1227	Innocent VI	1352–1362
Gregory IX	1227–1241	Urban V	1362–1370
Celestine IV	1241	Gregory XI	1370–1378
Innocent IV	1243–1254	Urban VI	1378–1389
Alexander IV	1254–1261	*Clement VII* (Avignon)	1378–1394
Urban IV	1261–1264	Boniface IX	1389–1404
Clement IV	1265–1268	*Benedict XIII* (Avignon)	1394–1423
Gregory X	1271–1276	Innocent VII	1404–1406
Innocent V	1276	Gregory XII	1406–1415
Adrian V	1276	Alexander V	1409–1410
John XXI	1276–1277	John XXIII	1410–1415
Nicholas III	1277–1280	Martin V	1417–1431
Martin IV	1281–1285	*Clement VIII*	1423–1429
Honorius IV	1285–1287	Eugenius IV	1431–1447
Nicholas IV	1288–1292	*Felix V*	1439–1449
Celestine V	1294	Nicholas V	1447–1455
Boniface VIII	1294–1303	Calixtus III	1455–1458
Benedict XI	1303–1304	Pius II	1458–1464
Clement V	1305–1314	Paul II	1464–1471
John XXII	1316–1334	Sixtus IV	1471–1484
Nicholas V	1328–1330	Innocent VIII	1484–1492
Benedict XII	1334–1342	Alexander VI	1492–1503
Clement VI	1342–1352		

(5) CHRONOLOGICAL TABLE OF LEADING EVENTS

A.D.
- 284–305 Diocletian Emperor.
- c. 305–320 St Anthony and St Pachomius inaugurate monasticism.
- 306–337 Constantine the Great Emperor.
- 325 Council of Nicaea.
- 328–373 St Athanasius Bishop of Alexandria.
- 335 Death of Arius.
- 338 Death of Eusebius of Caesarea.
- 343 Council of Sardica.
- 346–420 St Jerome.
- c. 350 Wulfila, the Arian evangelist of the Goths, translates the Bible into Gothic.
- 354–430 St Augustine of Hippo.
- c. 360 St Basil establishes cenobitic monasticism in Asia Minor.
- 361–363 Julian Emperor.
- 366–384 Damasus I Pope.
- 374–397 St Ambrose Bishop of Milan.
- 378 Victory of the Goths at Adrianople.
- 379–395 Theodosius the Great Emperor.
- 381 Council of Constantinople (Second Œcumenical).
- 395 The Empire divided into East and West between Arcadius and Honorius.
- 402–417 Innocent I Pope.
- 406 German tribes break the Rhine frontier.
- 408 Execution of Stilicho.
- 410 Sack of Rome by Alaric.

418	Establishment of the Visigoths in Aquitaine.
426	St Augustine finishes *De Civitate Dei*.
429	Vandals enter Africa.
431	Council of Ephesus. Condemnation of Nestorius.
432	St Patrick begins his mission to Ireland.
438	*Codex Theodosianus*. Legal separation of East and West.
440–461	Leo the Great Pope.
c. 450	Anglo-Saxon settlement in Britain begins.
451	Council of Chalcedon.
	Defeat of Attila on the Mauriac Plain near Troyes.
454	Murder of Aëtius.
455	Sack of Rome by Gaiseric.
476	Deposition of Romulus Augustulus. Odovacar king in Italy.
482	The *Henoticon* of the Emperor Zeno. Schism in the Church.
486	Clovis the Frank defeats Syagrius and conquers North Gaul.
493	Theodoric the Ostrogoth conquers Italy.
494	Pope Gelasius I enunciates the doctrine of the two ruling powers (*sacerdotium* and *regnum*).
496	Baptism of Clovis.
c. 500	Theodoric issues his *Edictum*.
c. 500	British defeat the Saxons at Mons Badonicus.
c. 500	Dionysius Exiguus compiles his Latin collection of canons and papal decretals.
506	Alaric II issues the *Breviarium Alaricianum*.
507	Clovis defeats Alaric II at Vouglé and conquers Aquitaine.
c. 510	Clovis issues the *Lex Salica*.
518	The Emperor Justin I ends the schism.
c. 520	St Benedict composes his *Rule*.
523	Boethius writes his *Consolation of Philosophy*.
529–534	Justinian I publishes the *Code*.
532	Building of St Sophia begun.
533	Belisarius reconquers Africa from the Vandals.
535–553	The Gothic War of Justinian.
c. 540	Cassiodorus forms the monastic library of Vivarium (Squillace).
543–550	Formation of the Monophysite Churches.
546	Capture of Rome by Totila.
553	Fifth Œcumenical Council of Constantinople.
563	St Columba goes to convert the Picts. Foundation of monastery of Iona
568	The Lombards under Alboin invade Italy.
589	The Visigoths accept Catholic Christianity.
590–603	St Gregory the Great Pope.
594	Death of the chronicler Gregory of Tours.
595	St Columban leaves Ireland for Francia.
597	St Augustine begins the conversion of Kent.
602	Murder of the Emperor Maurice. Phocas Emperor.
603–628	The Persian War against the Empire.
610–641	Heraclius Emperor.
c. 617	Slavs settling in the Balkans.
622	Flight of Mahomet from Mecca to Medina. Era of the Hegira
622–623	Isidore of Seville's *Etymologiae*.
626	Siege of Constantinople by Persians and Avars.
627	Heraclius defeats the Persians at Nineveh.

632	Death of Mahomet.
634–644	Omar Caliph.
635	St Aidan begins to reconvert Northumbria.
636	Byzantines defeated by Arabs at the River Yarmuk.
637	Persians defeated by Arabs at Qadisiya.
638	Heraclius sanctions the *Ekthesis* (Monothelete).
641	Persians defeated by Arabs at Nihavand.
647	Arabs finally capture Alexandria.
648	The Emperor Constans issues the *Type*.
655–661	Ali Caliph. Civil War among Moslems.
660	Muāwiya, first Omayyad Caliph of Damascus.
663	Synod of Whitby.
669–690	Theodore Archbishop of Canterbury.
670	Foundation of Qairawan.
673	Synod of Hertford.
c. 679	Bulgarians settle in the Balkans.
680	Synod of Heathfield.
680–681	Sixth Œcumenical Council of Constantinople.
685	Battle of Nechtansmere.
687	Battle of Tertry. Pepin of Austrasia mayor of the palace of all Francia.
692	The Trullan (Quinisext) Council.
698	Moslems finally capture Carthage.
711	Moslems invade Spain and win battle of Lake Janda.
713	First election of the Venetian doge.
717–741	Leo III the Isaurian Emperor.
717–718	Constantinople repels the Moslems under Maslama.
718	Pelayo of Asturias defeats the Moslems at Covadonga.
719–741	Charles Martel mayor of the palace of Francia.
723	St Boniface consecrated bishop at Rome for his German missions.
725	The iconoclastic controversy begun by Leo III.
727	Revolt of Byzantine Italy.
732	Charles Martel defeats the Moslems at Old Poitiers (Tours).
735	Death of the Venerable Bede.
740	Leo III publishes the *Ecloga*.
741	Pepin and Carloman mayors of the palace of Francia.
742–745	Councils for the reform of the Frankish Church.
c. 750	Forgery of the *Donation of Constantine*.
750	Fall of the Omayyad dynasty. The Abbasid Caliphate begins.
751	Aistulf King of the Lombards conquers the Exarchate of Ravenna. Pepin 'the Short' elected and anointed King of the Franks.
754	Meeting of Pope Stephen II and King Pepin at Quierzy. Donation of Pepin to the Papacy.
754–756	King Pepin's intervention in Italy.
754	Death of St Boniface.
c. 754	Rule of St Chrodegang of Metz for cathedral canons.
756	Abd-ar-Rahman I founds the Omayyad emirate of Cordova.
757–796	Offa King of Mercia.
762	Baghdad founded by Caliph Mansur.
768–814	Charlemagne King of the Franks.
772–804	Charlemagne conquers Saxony.
774	Charlemagne conquers the Lombard kingdom, and confirms the Donation of Pepin.

778	Battle at Roncesvalles.
c. 780	St Benedict founds the monastery of Aniane.
781	Pope Adrian I ceases to date documents by the regnal years of the Eastern Emperors.
782	Alcuin of York attached to court of Charlemagne.
785	Charlemagne establishes the Spanish March.
787	Empress Irene holds Œcumenical Council of Nicaea which condemns iconoclasm.
788	Charlemagne annexes Bavaria.
	Establishment of the Idrisid dynasty in Morocco.
795–796	Charlemagne destroys the Avar kingdom.
797–802	Irene 'Emperor' of the Eastern Empire.
799	Outrage at Rome on Pope Leo III.
c. 800	The invasions of the Northmen (Vikings) begin.
800	Establishment of the Aghlabid dynasty in Tunis.
	Coronation of Charlemagne as Emperor by Pope Leo III.
802–825	The Northmen settle in Ireland.
802–839	Egbert King of Wessex.
804	Death of Alcuin.
809	Death of Caliph Hārūn-ar-Rashīd. Civil war begins in the Abbasid Caliphate.
809–810	King Pepin of Italy attacks Venice. The Venetians concentrate in Rialto.
812	Emperor Michael I recognizes Charlemagne as Emperor of the West. Venice acknowledged to be a Byzantine dependency.
813–840	Lewis I the Pious Emperor of the West.
813	Mamūn becomes sole Caliph.
815	Renewal of iconoclasm by Leo V and Council of St Sophia.
817	Lewis the Pious's scheme for dividing the Western Empire.
	Lewis the Pious and St Benedict of Aniane enforce the Rule of St Benedict of Nursia for Frankish monasteries and that of St Chrodegang for canons.
822	Death of St Benedict of Aniane.
824	Lewis the Pious and Lothar I issue the *Constitutio Romana*.
826	Exiled Spanish Moslems conquer Crete.
827–866	African Moslems conquer Sicily.
831–844	Paschasius Radbert writes and revises his treatise on the Eucharist.
833	Lewis the Pious deserted at the Field of Lies and temporarily deposed.
834	Continual attacks by Northmen on the Frankish Empire henceforth.
835	Resumption of Viking raids on England.
839	Treaty between the Russians and the Byzantine Empire.
840–871	Moslem pirates hold Bari in Apulia and ravage Italy.
840	Death of Einhard.
841–891	Viking invasions at their height.
841	Battle of Fontenoy between the Emperor Lothar I and his brothers, Lewis the German and Charles the Bald.
842	The Abbasid Caliphate of Baghdad begins to disintegrate.
	Lewis the German and Charles the Bald take the oaths of Strasbourg in French and German.
843	Division of the Frankish Empire by the Treaty of Verdun, between Lothar I, Lewis the German, and Charles the Bald. Beginning of modern France and Germany.

1131

843	Council of Constantinople under the Empress Theodora restores image-worship and ends iconoclasm.
c. 844	Kenneth MacAlpin unites Scots and Picts in Scotland.
845–882	Hincmar Archbishop of Rheims.
846	Moslem pirates sack St Peter's at Rome.
847	Pope Leo IV walls the Leonine (Vatican) City.
849	Death of Walafrid Strabo, compiler of the *Glossa Ordinaria*.
c. 850	Forgery of the *Pseudo-Isidorian Decretals*.
c. 850	The legendary Rurik, the Scandinavian, prince in Russia.
851	John the Scot (Eriugena) writes *De Praedestinatione*.
855	The Emperor Lothar I dies. His realm divided among his sons (Lewis II Italy, Lothar II Lotharingia, Charles Provence).
856	Death of Hrabanus Maurus, Archbishop of Mainz.
858–867	Photius Patriarch of Constantinople, first pontificate.
858–867	Nicholas I Pope.
860	The Russians appear before Constantinople.
863(?)	Mission of St Cyril and St Methodius to the Moravians.
864	Bulgarians under Boris I accept Orthodox Christianity.
867–869	Photian schism of East and West.
867	John the Scot writes *De Divisione Naturae*.
868	Death of Ratramnus.
869	Death of Lothar II of Lotharingia.
870–877	Danes colonize the Danelaw.
871–899	Alfred the Great, King of Wessex.
872–882	John VIII Pope.
872	Harald Fairhair, first King of Norway, wins battle of Hafrsfjord.
874	Norse exiles begin to colonize Iceland.
877–886	Photius Patriarch of Constantinople, second pontificate.
878	Alfred defeats Danes at Edington. Peace of Wedmore (Chippenham).
878(?)	The Emperor Basil I promulgates the *Prochiron*.
879–887	Boso, King of Provence.
c. 880	Death of John the Scot (Eriugena).
880	Duke Bruno and the Saxons defeated by Northmen on Lüneburg Heath.
882	Murder of Pope John VIII. Triumph of Roman nobles.
884	Charles the Fat reunites the Frankish Empire.
885	Recapture of London by the West Saxons. Alfred and Guthrum's Peace.
885–887	The Northmen besiege Paris.
887	Final disruption of the Frankish Empire.
c. 888	The Emperor Leo VI the Wise promulgates the *Basilics*.
c. 890	Moslem pirates seize Fraxinetum in Provence.
891	King Arnulf of Germany defeats the Northmen near Louvain.
895	The Magyars migrate to Hungary.
900	The Magyar raids on Western Europe begin.
907	Russian attack on Constantinople.
909	Fatimite Caliphate established in Africa (Qairawan).
910	Foundation of the Abbey of Cluny.
911	Treaty of St Clair-sur-Epte. Rollo becomes first Duke of Normandy.
915	The Moslem raiders defeated on River Garigliano.
919–936	Henry I (the Fowler) of Saxony German King.
925	Lotharingia finally united to Germany.
927–941	Odo, Abbot of Cluny.

928–936	St Wenceslas (Vaclav) Duke of Bohemia.
929	Abd-ar-Rahman III the Omayyad of Cordova declares himself Caliph.
932–954	Alberic prince of the Romans.
933	Henry the Fowler defeats the Magyars at Riade.
935	Death of Gorm the Old, King of Denmark.
935–970	Fernan Gonzalez, Count of Castile.
936	Otto I the Great crowned King at Aachen.
937	King Athelstan of England defeats Northmen and Scots at Brunanburh.
941	Russian expedition against Constantinople.
943	Dunstan made Abbot of Glastonbury.
951–952	Otto the Great's first expedition to Italy.
954	England under one king, Eadred of Wessex.
954–994	Maiolus (Mayeul) Abbot of Cluny.
954	Princess Olga of Russia becomes a Christian.
955	Otto the Great overthrows the Magyars on the Lechfeld and ends their raids.
955–964	John XII (Octavian) Pope and Prince of Rome.
959–975	Edgar the Peaceable King of England.
960–988	Dunstan Archbishop of Canterbury.
961–964	Otto the Great's second expedition to Italy.
961	Nicephorus Phocas reconquers Crete. Byzantine advance in Asia Minor begins.
962	Otto the Great crowned Emperor of the West. Commencement of the 'Holy Roman Empire'.
963	Deposition of Pope John XII. Election of Pope Leo VIII, the Emperor's nominee.
	Nicephorus II Phocas Emperor of the East.
968	Adalbert, first Archbishop of Magdeburg, appointed.
969	The Fatimite Caliphs annex Egypt, which becomes the centre of their power.
	John I Zimiskes Emperor of the East.
970–1035	Sancho the Great King of Navarre.
971	John Zimiskes annexes Eastern Bulgaria.
972	Capture of Fraxinetum, and end of Moslem brigandage in the Alps. Marriage of the Emperor Otto II and Theophano.
976	Basil II Bulgaroctonus takes over the government of the Eastern Empire.
978–1002	Almanzor, prime minister of the Caliphate of Cordova.
978–1016	Aethelred the Unready, King of England.
980	Renewal of Scandinavian invasions of England.
c. 980–1040	*Peace of God* movement in France and Burgundy.
982	Otto II defeated by the Moslems in Calabria. Revolt of the Wends from German rule.
983	Otto II nominates a Lombard Pope, John XIV, the first to take a papal name.
986–1018	The great Bulgarian War, in which Basil II conquers Bulgaria.
987	Hugh Capet, Duke of the French, crowned King of France.
989	Vladimir, Great Prince of Kiev, becomes a Christian.
992–1025	Boleslav I the Great, Duke of Poland.
994–1049	Odilo, Abbot of Cluny.
996	Basil II legislates against 'the Powerful'.
	Otto III nominates a German Pope, Gregory V.
999	Otto III nominates a French Pope, Sylvester II (Gerbert).

1133

c. 1000	The Christianization of Scandinavia.
1000	Foundation of archbishopric of Gniezno for Poland.
1000–1025	Burchard, Bishop of Worms, canonist.
1001	St Stephen crowned King of Hungary.
	Foundation of archbishopric of Gran for Hungary.
1002	Death of the Emperor Otto III.
	Massacre of Danes in England on St Brice's day.
	The Venetians defeat Moslem fleet at Bari.
1003	Death of Pope Sylvester II.
1004–1046	Richard, Abbot of St Vannes.
1007	Establishment of the see of Bamberg by the Emperor Henry II.
1007–1029	Fulbert, Bishop of Chartres.
1009	Profanation of the Church of the Holy Sepulchre by the Fatimite Caliph Hakim.
1012–1044	Popes of the Tusculan faction rule Rome.
c. 1012	Foundation of the Order of Camaldoli by St Romuald.
1013	Triumph of Swein of Denmark in England.
1014	Henry II crowned Emperor at Rome.
	Brian Bórumha of Munster defeats the Scandinavian Vikings at Clontarf.
1016	Arrival of Norman adventurers in South Italy.
1017–1035	Canute the Great of Denmark, King of England.
1018–1186	Bulgaria a Byzantine province.
1018(?)	Lothian added to the kingdom of Scotland.
1025	Death of the Emperor Basil II. Decline of the Eastern Empire begins.
1030	The Norman Ranulf becomes Count of Aversa.
1031	Break-up of the Caliphate of Cordova.
1032	Ferdinand I, first King of Castile.
1033–1034	The Emperor Conrad II becomes King of Burgundy.
1034–1037	The sons of Tancred of Hauteville arrive in South Italy.
1034	Foundation of the Abbey of Bec by Herluín.
1035	Ramiro I Sanchez founds kingdom of Aragon.
1035–1076	Raymond-Berengar I Count of Barcelona.
1035	William the Conqueror becomes Duke of Normandy.
1036	Death of Avicenna.
1037	The Emperor Conrad II issues the *Constitutio de feudis* for Italy.
1038–1063	Reign of Tughril Beg the Seljūk.
c. 1038	Conrad II declares Roman Law the territorial law of Rome.
1038(?)	Order of Vallombrosa founded by St John Gualbert.
1039	The *Truce of God* begins to be added to the *Peace of God.*
c. 1040–1100	Beginning of the transition from Romanesque to Gothic architecture.
1042–1066	Edward the Confessor King of England.
1042–1068	Wazo Bishop of Liége.
1043	Henry III of Germany holds the 'Day of Indulgence'.
	William of Hauteville Count of Apulia.
1043–1058	Michael Cerularius Patriarch of Constantinople.
1045	Foundation of the Law School at Constantinople.
1046	Henry III reforms the Papacy, and is crowned Emperor.
	Armenia annexed to the Eastern Empire.
1047	William the Conqueror defeats the Norman rebels at Val-ès-dunes.
1048	The Seljūks reach the frontier of the Eastern Empire.
1049–1054	Leo IX Pope.
1049–1109	Hugh Abbot of Cluny.

1049–1061 Humbert Cardinal-Bishop of Silva Candida.
1049   Leo IX holds the Synod of Rheims and begins the papal reform of the Church.
1050–1100 The earliest *Chansons de Geste* composed.
1053   Leo IX defeated by the Normans at Civitate.
1054   Schism of the Eastern and Western Churches.
1055   Tughril Beg master of Baghdad and the Caliph.
1056   Outbreak of the Pataria in Milan begins.
1057–1072 Peter Damian Cardinal-Bishop of Ostia.
1059   The Papal Election Decree.
           Pope Nicholas II concludes Treaty of Melfi with Robert Guiscard, Duke of Apulia.
           Cardinal Hildebrand becomes Archdeacon of the Roman Church.
1061–1091 Norman conquest of Sicily.
1063–1072 Reign of the Seljūk Alp Arslan.
c. 1063   First appearance of the Rule of St Augustine for canons.
1064–1069 Raymond-Berengar I promulgates the *Usatges* of Catalonia, the earliest known feudal code.
1065   End of the minority of Henry IV of Germany.
1066   William the Conqueror wins Battle of Hastings and becomes King of England.
           Death of Geoffrey de Preuilly, reputed inventor of tournaments.
1070–1089 Lanfranc Archbishop of Canterbury.
1071   Alp Arslan defeats the Eastern Emperor Romanus Diogenes at Manzikert.
           Downfall of Byzantine power in Asia Minor. The Seljūks occupy Jerusalem.
           Robert Guiscard takes Bari, and expels the Byzantines from Italy.
1072–1092 Reign of the Seljūk Malik Shah.
1073–1085 Gregory VII (Hildebrand) Pope.
1074   Henry IV grants a charter to the citizens of Worms.
1075   Gregory VII enunciates papal powers in the *Dictatus Papae*.
           First Investiture Decree.
1076   Council of Worms deposes Gregory VII.
           Gregory VII excommunicates Henry IV.
           The Order of Grandmont founded by St Stephen.
1077   Henry IV goes to Canossa.
           Accession of Sulaiman I, Sultan of Rūm.
1077–1080 Duke Rudolf of Swabia anti-king in Germany.
1080   Henry IV finally excommunicated and deposed by Gregory VII.
           Council of Brixen deposes Gregory VII and elects Guibert of Ravenna anti-Pope.
c. 1080–1130 General establishment of communes in North Italian cities.
1080   Robert Guiscard begins attack on the Eastern Empire.
1081–1118 Alexius I Comnenus Emperor of the East.
1084   Sack of Rome by the Normans under Robert Guiscard.
           Foundation of the Carthusian Order of Bruno of Cologne.
1085   Death of Pope Gregory VII.
           Death of Robert Guiscard.
1086   Compilation of Domesday Book.
           Death of Berengar of Tours.
1087   Genoa and Pisa capture Mahdiya in Barbary.
1088–1099 Urban II Pope.
1093–1109 St Anselm Archbishop of Canterbury.

1095	Pope Urban II received Emperor Alexius's request for aid at Council of Piacenza.
	Pope Urban II proclaims the First Crusade at the Council of Clermont.
1096	Massacres of Jews in France and Germany.
1097	The Crusaders defeat the Seljūks of Rūm at Dorylaeum.
	Alexius I begins reconquest of Asia Minor.
1098	Foundation of the Cistercian Order by Robert of Molesme.
1099	The Crusaders establish the kingdom of Jerusalem.
1100	Coronation charter of Henry I King of England.
c. 1100	Irnerius, the founder of the Glossators, teaches Roman Law at Bologna.
1104	Revolt of Henry V against his father the Emperor Henry IV.
1107	English compromise on Investitures.
1108–1137	Louis VI, King of France.
c. 1108	Lapse of practice of lay investiture by the King of France.
1111	Pope Paschal II captured and concedes lay investiture to Henry V, who is crowned Emperor.
1115–1153	St Bernard, first Abbot of Clairvaux.
1115	Death of Countess Matilda of Tuscany.
1119	Pope Calixtus II confirms the Cistercian *Carta Caritatis.*
c. 1120	Foundation of the Military Orders of the Templars and Hospitallers.
1120	Foundation of the Praemonstratensian Order.
1121	Condemnation of Abelard at Soissons.
1122	Concordat of Worms between Empire and Papacy on Investitures.
1130	Schism in the Papacy between Innocent II and Anacletus II.
	Roger II crowned King of Sicily at Palermo.
c. 1135	Geoffrey of Monmouth's *Historia Regum Britanniae.*
1137	Aragon and Catalonia united under Raymond-Berengar IV.
1138	Death of the anti-Pope Anacletus II.
1139	Afonso I Henriques first King of Portugal.
	Outbreak of civil war in England between King Stephen and the Empress Matilda.
	Pope Innocent II captured by Roger II at the battle of the Garigliano.
1140	Condemnation of Abelard at Sens at the instance of St Bernard.
1141	Death of Hugh of St Victor.
c. 1141	Compilation of Gratian's *Decretum.*
1143	Communal rising at Rome.
	Foundation of the town of Lübeck.
	German colonists begin moving east of the Elbe *en masse.*
1144	The Moslems capture Edessa.
1145–1170	The (Gothic) west portal of Chartres cathedral built.
1147–1148	The Second Crusade.
1147	Afonso I of Portugal takes Lisbon from the Moors.
c. 1148	St Bernard writes *De Consideratione* for Pope Eugenius III.
1148	Gilbert de la Porrée acquitted of heresy before the Pope.
1152	Marriage of Henry of Anjou to Eleanor of Aquitaine.
1152–1190	Reign of Frederick Barbarossa.
1153	Treaty of Wallingford between King Stephen and Henry of Anjou. End of English civil war.
1154	Death of Roger II of Sicily.
1154–1159	Adrian IV (Nicholas Breakspear) Pope.
1154–1189	Henry II King of England.
1155	Execution of Arnold of Brescia.

1156	Duchy of Austria created by Frederick Barbarossa.
1157	Diet of Besançon.
1158	Diet of Roncaglia. Imperial rights in Italy defined.
1159	Schism in the Papacy between Alexander III and Victor IV.
1160–1163	Henry the Lion of Saxony and Bavaria masters the Wends.
1162	Destruction of Milan by Frederick Barbarossa.
	Becket Archbishop of Canterbury.
1164	Constitutions of Clarendon.
c. 1164	Death of Peter Lombard.
1166	Assize of Clarendon.
1167	Beginnings of the Lombard League. Rebuilding of Milan.
	Frederick Barbarossa loses his army by pestilence before Rome.
1169	Egypt conquered for Nur-ad-din of Damascus.
1170	Peter Waldo begins to preach at Lyons.
	Strongbow begins Anglo-Norman invasion of Ireland.
	Murder of Becket.
c. 1170	Rise of the Universities.
c. 1170	Chrétien de Troyes *fl.*
c. 1172	Writing of the *Roman de Rou.*
1174–1193	Reign of Saladin.
1176	Emperor Manuel I defeated by the Seljūks at Myriocephalum.
	Frederick Barbarossa defeated by the Lombards at Legnano.
1177	Treaty of Venice between Alexander III and Barbarossa.
1179	Third Lateran Council. Majority rule for papal elections.
1180	Partition of the duchy of Saxony. Bavaria given to the Wittelsbachs.
	Death of John of Salisbury.
	Death of the Emperor Manuel I Comnenus.
	Foundation of the Serbian monarchy by Stephen Nemanya.
1183	Frederick Barbarossa makes Peace of Constance with the Lombard cities.
1186	Henry VI marries Constance of Sicily.
	Second Bulgarian empire founded.
1187	Saladin defeats the Christians at Hittin and takes Jerusalem.
1188	The Saladin Tithe.
	The Cortes of Léon contain representatives of the towns.
1189–1192	The Third Crusade.
1190	Foundation of the Teutonic Order.
c. 1190	Original composition of the *Nibelungenlied.*
1190	Massacre of the Jews at York.
1194	Henry VI conquers the kingdom of Sicily.
1197	Death of Henry VI.
1198–1216	Innocent III Pope.
1198	Death of Averroes.
	Civil war in Germany begins.
c. 1200	Italian cities are instituting *podestàs.*
1200	Philip Augustus grants charter to Paris University.
1201–1204	The Fourth Crusade.
1202	Death of Joachim of Fiore.
1202–1204	Philip Augustus conquers Normandy, Anjou, etc. from John.
1203–1227	Conquests of Jenghiz Khan.
1204	Sack of Constantinople and foundation of the Latin Empire.
1208	His vocation revealed to St Francis of Assisi.
1209	The first Albigensian Crusade begins.

c. 1210	Latin translations of Aristotle's *Metaphysics* in the West.
1212	Christian victory over the Almohades at Las Navas de Tolosa.
1213	King John of England becomes vassal of the Papacy.
	Frederick II grants the Golden Bull of Eger.
1214	Philip Augustus wins battle of Bouvines.
1215	Fourth Lateran Council.
	King John seals Magna Carta.
1219–1221	Fifth Crusade.
1220	Frederick II grants the *Privilegium in favorem principum ecclesiasticorum.*
c. 1220	Death of Wolfram von Eschenbach.
1221	Death of St Dominic.
1223	Final form of the Franciscan Rule confirmed by Pope Honorius III.
1221–1224	Composition of the *Sachsenspiegel.*
1226	Formation of the Second Lombard League.
	Death of St Francis.
1228–1229	Frederick II recovers Jerusalem.
1230	The Teutonic Order settles in Prussia.
	Final union of Castile and Léon under Ferdinand III.
1231	Frederick II grants *Constitutio in favorem principum.*
	Robert Grosseteste begins lecturing at Oxford.
	The bull *Parens scientiarum* establishes the independence of Paris University.
1232	Town representatives summoned to a Sicilian general assembly.
1233	Inauguration of the Inquisition by Pope Gregory IX.
1234	Gregory IX publishes his *Decretals* in five books.
1237–1241	Mongol invasion of Europe.
1239	Contest between Empire and Papacy begun by Gregory IX and Frederick II.
1242	Alexander Nevsky defeats the Teutonic Order on Lake Peipus.
1244	The Latins finally lose Jerusalem.
1245	First Council of Lyons deposes Frederick II.
	Death of Alexander of Hales.
1246–1248	St Louis builds the Sainte Chapelle at Paris.
1250–1258	Bracton writes *De Legibus et Consuetudinibus Angliae.*
1252	Florence coins the gold florin.
1253	Death of Robert Grosseteste.
1254	Knights of the shire summoned to English Parliament.
	Publication of the *Everlasting Gospel.*
	Mamlūk sultans begin in Egypt.
1254–1273	The Great Interregnum in Germany.
1256–1265	Compilation of the *Siete Partidas* for Castile.
1257	First clear appearance of the Seven Electors in Germany.
1258	Mongols capture Baghdad and end Abbasid Caliphate.
	St Louis surrenders suzerainty of Barcelona by treaty of Corbeil.
1258–1259	Provisions of Oxford and Westminster.
1259	Henry III surrenders claim to Normandy and Anjou.
	Death of the chronicler Matthew Paris.
1259–1282	Michael Palaeologus, Byzantine Emperor.
1259–1284	Reign of Kublai Khan.
1260–1278	Niccola Pisano *fl.*
c. 1260	Death of Accursius the Glossator.
1260	The Mamlūks defeat the Mongols at Ain Jalut.

1261	Recapture of Constantinople by Greeks of Nicaea. End of Latin Empire.
1264	Victory of the barons over Henry III at Lewes.
1265	Town representatives summoned to English Parliament.
	Defeat and death of Simon de Montfort at Evesham.
1266	Charles of Anjou conquers the kingdom of Sicily at Benevento.
1266–1336	Giotto.
1273	Rudolf of Habsburg elected King of the Romans.
1274	Death of St Thomas Aquinas.
	Second Council of Lyons and Union with Greek Church.
1277	Siger of Brabant condemned for Averroism.
1279	King Rudolf surrenders all imperial claims on Papal States and Sicily.
1280	Death of Albert of Cologne (Albertus Magnus).
1281	Pope Martin IV excommunicates the Greeks.
1282	The Sicilian Vespers. Peter of Aragon becomes King of Sicily.
	King Rudolf creates his sons Dukes of Austria and Styria.
1282–1283	King Edward I conquers the principality of Wales.
1283	The Teutonic Order completes the conquest of Prussia.
1284	Genoese victory of Meloria. Fall of Pisa.
1285	Death of Charles I of Anjou, King of Naples.
1286	Death of William of Moerbeke, translator of Aristotle direct from the Greek.
1290	Expulsion of the Jews from England.
1291	Mamlūks capture Acre and end the kingdom of Jerusalem.
	Edward I acknowledged as suzerain of Scotland.
	The Confederation of the three Forest Cantons founds Switzerland.
1293	Ordinances of Justice at Florence.
1294	Death of Roger Bacon.
1296	Edward I annexes Scotland to England.
1297	Edward I confirms the Charters with additions.
	Closing of the Great Council at Venice.
1297–1305	William Wallace leads the Scottish war of independence.
1298	Boniface VIII issues his *Decretals* (the *Sext*).
1299–1326	Osman Emir of the Ottoman Turks.
1300	The first Papal Jubilee.
	Pierre Dubois writes *De Recuperatione Terrae Sanctae*.
1302	The Flemings defeat the French at Courtrai.
	Philip the Fair holds 'States General' at Paris.
	Peace of Caltabellotta between Naples and Sicily.
	Pope Boniface VIII issues the bull *Unam Sanctam*.
1303	Capture of Boniface VIII at Anagni.
1305–1314	Clement V Pope. Papacy transferred to Avignon.
1306	King Robert I Bruce continues War of Scottish independence.
	Expulsion of the Jews from France.
1307–1312	Destruction of the Order of Knights Templar.
1308	Death of Duns Scotus.
1310–1313	Henry VII's expedition to Italy.
1314	Robert Bruce defeats the English at Bannockburn.
1315	Swiss defeat Leopold of Austria at Morgarten.
	Death of Raymond Lull.
1315–1319	Invasion of Ireland by Edward Bruce.
1321	Death of Dante.
1322	Statute of York. Commons recognized as an essential part of Parliament.

1324	Publication of *Defensor Pacis* of Marsilius of Padua.
1327	Death of Master Eckhart the mystic.
1328	Scottish independence recognized by treaty of Northampton.
	Ivan I of Moscow becomes Great Prince.
1329	The Ottomans capture Nicaea.
1335–1339	Pope Benedict XII issues reforms of the monastic Orders.
1337	Outbreak of the Hundred Years' War.
1337–1345	James van Artevelde rules Ghent.
1338	The Electors' Declaration at Rense. The German Diet by *Licet iuris* declares independence of Empire from Papacy.
1340	Edward III defeats French at sea by Sluys.
	English statute forbids taxation without consent of Parliament.
1342	Petrarch crowned at Rome.
1343	Peace of Kalisz between Poland and Teutonic Order.
1346	Edward III defeats Philip VI at Crécy.
	Stephen Dushan crowned Emperor of the Serbs and Greeks.
1347	Cola di Rienzo tribune of Rome.
1348	Emperor Charles IV founds University of Prague.
1348–1350	The Black Death.
1348–1349	Massacres of the Jews in Germany, and their flight to Poland.
1348(?)	Death of William of Ockham.
1353–1363	Cardinal Albornoz restores the Papal State.
1353	Boccaccio finishes the *Decameron*.
	Statute of Praemunire in England.
1354	The Ottomans take Gallipoli.
1354–1378	St Alexis Metropolitan of Moscow.
1356	Charles IV promulgates the Golden Bull.
1356	The Black Prince wins battle of Poitiers (Maupertuis).
1356–1358	French States General led by Etienne Marcel attempt reforms.
1357	The Ottomans capture Adrianople.
1358	The Jacquerie in France.
1360	The Ottomans recruit the Janissaries from tribute-children.
	Treaties of Brétigny and Calais.
1361	Death of Tauler.
1362	First version of *Piers the Plowman* being written.
1363	Philip the Bold becomes Duke of Burgundy.
1363–1439	Jean Gerson.
1365	Sultan Murat I makes Adrianople his capital.
1369	Renewal of the Hundred Years' War.
1370	Treaty of Stralsund between the Hansa and Denmark.
1374	Death of Petrarch.
1375	Death of Boccaccio.
1377	Wyclif's teaching in *De civili dominio* condemned by Pope Gregory XI.
1378	Revolt of the Ciompi in Florence.
	Dimitri Donskoy defeats Tartars on the Don.
	The Great Schism begins.
c. 1379	Wyclif teaches his doctrine of the Eucharist.
1380	Death of St Catherine of Siena.
	Genoese forces surrender to Venice at Chioggia.
c. 1380	Lollard translation of the Bible into English in progress.
1381	The Peasants' Revolt in England.
1382	Charles VI defeats the Flemings at Roosebeke.

1384	Philip the Bold becomes Count of Flanders.
	Death of Wyclif.
	Death of Gerard Groote.
1385–1402	Gian Galeazzo Visconti despot of Milan.
1386	The Swiss defeat the Austrians at Sempach.
	Conversion of Jagiello (Vladyslav II) of Lithuania and Poland.
1389	First Battle of Kossovo. Fall of the Serbian empire.
1391	Massacres of Jews cause the existence of crypto-Judaism in Spain.
1392	Treaty of the Hansa with Novgorod.
1393	Beyazit I annexes Bulgaria to the Ottoman Empire.
1394	Peace between Habsburgs and Switzerland.
1395	Beyazit I defeats the Crusaders at Nicopolis.
1396–1403	Chrysoloras teaches Greek in Italy.
1397	Union of Calmar.
1399	Deposition of Richard II and accession of Henry IV in England.
1400	Death of Chaucer.
1400–1464	Nicholas of Cusa.
1401	Statute *De Haeretico comburendo*.
1401–1429(?)	Masaccio.
1402	Timur overthrows Beyazit I at Ankara.
1402	John Hus begins preaching at the Bethlehem Chapel, Prague.
1409	General Council of Pisa. The Great Schism becomes threefold.
1410	Defeat of the Teutonic Order by the Poles at Tannenberg (Grunwald).
1414–1418	General Council of Constance.
1414–1460	Guarino of Verona teaches classics in North Italy.
1415	Henry V defeats the French at Agincourt.
	Hus burnt at Constance.
1415–1429	Frequent discoveries of MSS. of lost Latin works.
1417	Council of Constance elects Pope Martin V.
1420	Treaty of Troyes between Henry V and Charles VI.
1420–1446	Vittorino da Feltre conducts school of La Giocosa.
1420–1431	The Hussite wars.
1429	St Joan of Arc raises the siege of Orleans.
1431	St Joan of Arc burned at Rouen.
1431–1449	The General Council of Basle.
1432	*The Adoration of the Lamb* by the Van Eycks completed.
1434	Defeat of the Taborites at Lipany.
	Portuguese sailors round Cape Bojador.
	Cosimo de' Medici becomes ruler of Florence.
	Treaty of Arras between France and Burgundy.
1436	The *Compacts of Prague* between the Hussites and the Council of Basle.
1438	Charles VII issues the *Pragmatic Sanction* of Bourges.
1439	Council of Basle deposes Pope Eugenius IV.
	Union of the Greek and Latin Churches in Council of Ferrara-Florence.
1440	Lorenzo Valla proves the *Donation of Constantine* a forgery.
1443–1468	Skanderbeg's war in Albania against the Ottomans.
1444	Murat II defeats the Crusaders at Varna.
1446	Death of Brunelleschi.
1448	Murat II defeats the Christians at the third battle of Kossovo.
1448–1494	William Tilley of Selling *fl.*
1449	End of the Conciliar Movement.
1451	Mahomet II Sultan of the Ottoman Turks.

1452–1519 Leonardo da Vinci.
1453   Fall of Constantinople and end of East Roman Empire.
           Charles VII finally recovers Bordeaux. End of the Hundred Years' War.
1454–1485 The Wars of the Roses.
1454–1494 Angelo Poliziano (Politian).
1456   Mahomet II vainly besieges Belgrade.
           Gutenberg prints the Mazarin Bible at Mainz.
1461   Mahomet II annexes Trebizond.
1462   Ivan III of Muscovy becomes Grand Prince of all Russia.
1463   Philip the Good summons the Estates General of the Netherlands.
1465   Printing introduced into Italy.
1466   Peace of Thorn (Torun) between Poland and the Teutonic Order.
           Death of Donatello.
1467   The Unity of the Brotherhood institutes a separate Church in Bohemia.
1467–1494 Hans Memling *fl.*
1469–1492 Lorenzo de' Medici ruler of Florence.
1470   Printing introduced into France.
1474–1490 Botticelli *fl.*
1477   Overthrow of Duke Charles the Bold of Burgundy by the Swiss.
           Caxton begins printing in England.
1485   Battle of Bosworth. Accession of the Tudor dynasty in England.
1488   Bartholomew Diaz rounds the Cape of Good Hope.
1489   Venice aquires Cyprus.
1492   Conquest of Granada by the Catholic Kings of Spain.
           Expulsion of the Jews from the Spanish dominions.
           Columbus discovers America.

INDEX

Abdallah, Caliph, 235, 236
Abdallah, emir of Spain, 373, 374
Abd-al-Malik, Caliph, 213, 236
Abd-ar-Rahman I, Omayyad ruler of Andalusia, 240, 309, 372
Abd-ar-Rahman II, 373
Abd-ar-Rahman III, 374, 375
Abd-ar-Rahman (Sanchuelo), 376
Abelard, Peter, 561, 624, 628–9
Sic et Non, 629
Absalon, archbishop of Lund, 758–9
Abu Bakr, Caliph, 230–1
Abu'l-Hasan, Moorish king of Granada, 1072
Abu'l-Qasim, emir of Sicily, 371, 443
Abu Muslim, Abbasid general, 240
Acciaiuoli, Niccolò, grand seneschal of Naples, 865–6
Accursius, glossator, 619, 620
Achaia, Latin principality of, 734, 735, 931
Acquasparta, Cardinal, 773
Adalbero, archbishop of Rheims, 461, 465
Adalbero, archbishop of Trier, 559
Adalbert, archbishop of Hamburg-Bremen, 415, 457, 483, 485
Adalbert, archbishop of Mainz, 498, 554
Adalbert, joint king of Italy, 437
Adalbert, St, of Prague, 447–8
Adelaide of Turin, wife of Herman IV of Swabia, 456, 459, 486, 491
Adelaide, daughter of Hugh of Arles, second wife of Otto the Great, 430, 436, 437, 444
Adelaide, wife of Roger I of Sicily, 513
Adelard of Bath, translator, 620
Ademar, bishop of Puy, papal legate, 520
Administration, Byzantine
in fifth century, 103, 105–6, 114
under Justinian, 196–200
from Justinian to Basil II, 268–73
Administration, English
on eve of the Norman conquest, 401–3
after the Norman conquest, 586–7, 589
of Henry I, 595–6
reforms of Henry II, 603–5; of Hubert Walter, 718–21; of Henry III, 727–8; of Edward I, 804–6; of Edward II, 887–90; of Edward III, 891–2

Justices of the Peace established, 894
see also Parliament, English
Administration, French
Carolingian, 319–25
under Louis VI, 578
under Philip Augustus, 710–11
under Louis IX, 715–16, 717
Parlement of Paris, 715, 791
States General, 791–4, 872, 881–2, 977, 984
Administration, papal, 617–18
reorganized by Innocent III, 665–7
of Papacy at Avignon, 837–9
Administration, Roman, in the time of Constantine the Great, 15–20
Administration, Venetian, 779–80
Adolf, king of the Romans, count of Nassau, 789, 800–1, 858
Adolf, archbishop of Cologne, 648
Adolf III, count of Holstein, 559, 574, 610
Adoptionist heresy, 313, 328
Adrian I, Pope, 304–5, 312–14
Adrian II, Pope, 255
Adrian IV (Nicholas Breakspear of England), Pope, 416, 515, 564–5, 811, 943
organizes Church in Norway, 564, 655
and diet of Besançon, 566
conflict with Frederick Barbarossa, and death, 567
Aedh, son of Cathal Redhand, 812
Aegidius, lieutenant of Majorian, 98
Aegidius Romanus, *De ecclesiastica potestate*, 943, 944, 949
Aelfgar, earl of East Anglia, 400
Aelfgifu, wife of Canute, 397, 413
Aelfheah (St Alphege), archbishop of Canterbury, 392, 396, 398
Aelfhere, alderman of Mercia, 394
Aelfric, abbot of Eynsham, 329, 393–4
Aelle, 'ruler of Britain', 169
Aesc, king of the Jutes, 168–9
Aethelbald, king of Mercia, 180
Aethelbald, king of Wessex, 381
Aethelberht, king of Kent, 174, 175, 179
Aethelburg, wife of Edwin of Northumbria, 176
Aetheldreda, abbess of Ely, 177
Aethelfleda, daughter of Alfred the Great, 385; as 'Lady of the Mercians', 387–9

1143

plunder of Gaul and defeat by Julian, 50–2
capture of Alsace, 82
defeated by Clovis, 151–2
Alençon, John II, duke of, 1030
Alexander II, Pope (Anselm of Lucca), 480, 482–4
Alexander III, Pope (Cardinal Roland), 516, 540, 618
dispute with Frederick Barbarossa, 568–9, 571–2
supported by Louis VII, 582
and the murder of Becket, 600–2
decretals of, 616–17
Alexander IV, Pope, 675, 679, 697, 699, 700
Alexander V, Pope, 956, 964
Alexander VI, Pope (Rodrigo Borgia), 1073, 1086, 1089
Alexander, bishop of Lincoln, 598
Alexander, co-Emperor of the East, 257, 258
Alexander of Hales, 631, 675
Alexander Nevsky, St, prince of Novgorod, 746, 753, 760
Alexander I, king of Scots, 408, 409
Alexander II, king of Scots, 814, 815
Alexander III, king of Scots, 814
Alexander, Lord of the Isles, 1064
Alexander of Villa Dei, *Doctrinale*, 1092
Alexandria
church of, 31
riots instigated by Patriarch Cyril, 104–5
rivalry with Antioch, 116, 117, 118–19
captured by Arabs (642), 233
Alexiad of Anna Comnena, 538
Alexis, St, metropolitan of Moscow, 1018
Alexius I Comnenus, Emperor of the East, 281, 494, 519, 532–3, 540, 662
and the First Crusade, 521–2
hostility to Bohemond of Antioch, 522, 523, 524–5, 533–4
financial oppression by, 534–5
succession conspiracies and death, 535, 538
Alexius II Comnenus, Emperor of the East, 541, 730
Alexius III Angelus, Emperor of the East, 542, 612, 658
Alexius IV Angelus, Emperor of the East, 657–8
Alexius V Ducas (Mourtzouphlos), Emperor of the East, 658
Alexius Comnenus, nephew-in-law of Empress Mary, 541

Alexius Strategopoulos, Nicaean general, 735
Alfonso I the Warrior, king of Aragon and Navarre, 823, 826
Alfonso II, king of Aragon, 829
Alfonso III, king of Aragon, 769, 904
Alfonso IV, king of Aragon, 909
Alfonso V the Magnanimous, king of Aragon and Sicily, 1069–70, 1080–1, 1083, 1085, 1086
Alfonso I, king of the Asturias, 372
Alfonso VII, king of Castile, 826, 827
Alfonso VIII the Noble, king of Castile, 709, 711, 827–8, 829
Alfonso, king of Galicia, 823, 826
Alfonso V, king of León, 376
Alfonso VI, king of León, 822, 823
Alfonso IX, king of León, 655, 827, 828, 829, 832
Alfonso X the Learned, king of León and Castile, 764, 794, 798, 830, 832, 833
Alfonso XI, king of León and Castile, 906
Alfonso II, king of Naples, 1089
Alfred the Great, king of Wessex, 329, 366, 392
pilgrimage to Rome, 381
pays Danegeld, 381
defeats Danes at Edington, 384
'Alfred and Guthrum's Peace', 385
military and civil reforms, 385–7
scholarship of, 387
Ali, Berber chief, successor of Yūsuf ibn Tāshfīn, 823
Ali, cousin and son-in-law of Mahomet, later Caliph, 228, 230, 234–5
Alice, sister of Philip Augustus, 706
Almanzor (Mahomet ibn-Abi-Amir),vizier of Spain, 375–6
Alp Arslan, Seljūk sultan, 279, 281
Alphonse of Poitiers, count of Poitou and Auvergne, 712
Alphonse VII, count of Toulouse, 680
Alvaro de Luna, Don, constable of Castile, 1070, 1071
Amadeus IV, count of Savoy (the 'Green Count'), 866, 867, 934, 939
Amalafrida, sister of Theodoric the Great, 139
Amalaric, king of the Visigoths, 144
Amalasuntha, daughter of Theodoric the Great, 139, 140, 190
Amaury I, king of Jerusalem, 528
Amaury II, king of Jerusalem and Cyprus, 532
Amaury, son of Simon de Montfort, 665

Gerontius, general of Constantine the usurper, 86
Gerson, Jean, chancellor of Paris University, 958
Géza II, king of Hungary, 739
Ghazali, Persian philosopher, 279
Ghiberti, Lorenzo, 1102
Giacomo, archbishop of Capua, 686
Giano della Bella, 772
Gibraltar, origin of name, 148
Gilbert, earl of Gloucester, 728
Gilbert, duke of Lotharingia, 428, 430
Gilbert de la Porrée, bishop of Poitiers, 630
Gildas, British monk, 169
Gildo, prince of the Moors, 80
Gilds
  in Italian cities, 549, 698, 765, 772–3, 867–8, 1081
  in France, 553, 977
  in Germany, 553–4
  of merchants, in England, 596
  in Swiss Confederation, 858
  in Spain, 910
  in the Netherlands, 1035, 1037–40
  conflict among, weakens Hanseatic League, 1051
Giles, Brother, Franciscan friar, 670
Giotto, 1101–3
Gisela of Swabia, wife of Conrad II, 453
Giustiniani, Genoese defender of Constantinople, 1010
Glagolitic (Slavonic) alphabet, 254
Glass, stained, in medieval windows, 1097–8
Glossators, 619–20
Gloucester, Humphrey, duke of, 998–9, 1041, 1109
Gloucester, Thomas, duke of, 989–90
Glycerius, Emperor of the West, 100
Glyn Dŵr (Glendower), Owain, 994, 995
Godefrid (Guthrödr) the Dane, Scandinavian king, 312
Godefrid, Viking chief, 312, 367
Godegisel, king of the Vandals, 81, 82
Godfrey, duke of Lower Lotharingia, 436
Godfrey of Bouillon, duke of Lower Lotharingia, king of Jerusalem, 520, 522, 526
Godfrey II the Bearded, duke of Upper Lotharingia, 457, 480–1, 482–3, 485
Godfrey, archbishop of Milan, 483, 490
Godigisel, king of the Burgundians, 141
Godwin, earl of Wessex, 398, 399–400
Gorm the Old, king of Denmark, 429

Goths
  origins, 39
  as nomads in the Ukraine, 42
  defeat Romans at Adrianople, 58
  invasions of Italy, 80–1, 84–5; sack of Rome, 85
  revolt in Asia Minor, 81
  forced into Spain by Constantius, 87
  hostilities against Leo I, 109–10
  for Ostrogoths and Visigoths see s.vv.
Gottfried of Strasbourg, 637
Gottschalk, monk, 627
Gozelo I, duke of Lower and Upper Lotharingia, 457
Gozelo II, duke of Lower Lotharingia, 457
Gradenigo, Pietro, doge of Venice, 779, 780
Graham, Sir Robert, 1065
Gratian, canon-lawyer, 616
Gratian, Emperor, 53–4, 58
  measures against paganism, 74
Great Charter. See Magna Carta
Great Schism, 673, 674, 840, 927, 1003, 1069
  beginning of the schism, 953–4
  attempts to remedy, 955–6
  effects of Council of Pisa on, 956–7
  conciliar discussion on, 958–9
  proceedings of the Council of Constance, 959–62
  close of schism, 962, 1085
Greece, 9–10
  Latin Empire in, 658–60, 730–5, 931
  overrun by Ottoman Turks, 1011
  see also Achaia; Athens; Balkans
Greek fire, 211, 214, 243, 265, 271, 777
Greenland, Norwegian colony, 760, 1022
Gregory I the Great, Pope, 146, 156, 204, 218
  sends monastic mission to Britain, 174–5, 292–3
  truce with Lombard dukes, 224, 290–1
  early career, 289
  as an administrator, 290
  claims primacy of Church of Rome, 291–2
  as a theologian, 293
  character, 293
Gregory II, Pope, 222, 224, 248, 294–5
Gregory III, Pope, 160, 295, 298
  excommunicates iconoclasts, 248
Gregory IV, Pope, 341
Gregory V, Pope (Bruno of Carinthia), 445
Gregory VI, Pope, 459–60, 477

Henry III, king of England (*cont.*)
minority of, 724
character, 726
failure of foreign policy, 726–7
challenges administrative reforms, 727–8
civil war, 728
death, 729
Henry IV, king of England, 877, 880, 900, 924, 976
deposes Richard II, 993
suppresses rebellions in Scotland and Wales, 994–5
Hotspur's rebellion against, 994
expenditure restricted by Parliament, 995
death, 997
Henry V, king of England, 959, 962, 994
campaigns in France, 977–9
character, 997
command of the sea, 998
death, 998
Henry VI, king of England, 979, 982, 1030, 1042, 1059
minority of, 998
character, 999
and the dynastic conflict of York and Lancaster, 1054
captured at battle of St Albans, 1055
retreat to Scotland, 1056
reinvested with the crown, 1057
murdered, 1058
Henry VII, king of England, 1061
Henry, King, son of Henry II of England, 582–3, 601, 706
Henry I, brother of Otto the Great, duke of Bavaria, 430, 431, 437
Henry II the Wrangler, duke of Bavaria, 441, 444
Henry X the Proud, duke of Saxony and Bavaria, 554–5, 558, 559
Henry XI Jasomirgott, duke of Bavaria, 559, 562
Henry XII the Lion, duke of Saxony and Bavaria, 554, 559, 560, 561, 562, 571, 760–1
encourages expansion and colonization to the East, 573–4
deprived of his duchies, 574–5
opposes Henry VI, 610
death, 612
Henry II of Wittelsbach, duke of Lower Bavaria, 845
Henry of Carinthia, king of Bohemia, 801, 802, 842, 845, 915

Henry the Younger, duke of Carinthia, 441, 444
Henry I, king of France, 466, 469, 478
Henry of Champagne, king of Jerusalem, 531
Henry I of Trastamara, king of León and Castile, 828, 906
Henry II of Trastamara, king of León and Castile, 884, 906–7
Henry III the Invalid, king of León and Castile, 908–9, 1069
Henry IV, king of Castile, 1070, 1071
Henry, duke of Luxemburg, 449
Henry II, count of Champagne, king of Navarre, 782
Henry the Navigator, prince of Portugal, 1074, 1075
Henry II the Pious, duke of Silesia, grand prince of Poland, 745, 752
Henry of Lipa, marshal of Bohemia, 917
Henry Aristippus of Catania, translator, 620
Henry, earl of Lancaster and Leicester, 890–1
Henry of Langenstein, *Concilium Pacis*, 955
Henry, Don, of Castile, senator of Rome, 702
Henry Raspe, landgrave of Thuringia, anti-king, 692–3
Henry of Susa, cardinal of Ostia, 617
Henry of Blois, bishop of Winchester, brother of King Stephen, 597, 605
Heracleonas, co-Emperor of the East, 210
Heraclian, Count, 86–7
Heraclius, Emperor of the East, 231
overthrows Phocas, 205
escapes treachery of Avars, 205, and swears not to abandon the capital, 206
campaigns in Asia Minor, 206, 207–8
initiates government by themes, 208
fails to end Monophysite schism, 209
death, 209–10, 233
Heraclius, exarch, father of Emperor Heraclius, 204–5
Heraclius, generalissimo, brother of Leontius, 213
Heraclius, adviser of Valentinian III, 96, 99
Heraldry, 'science' of, 939
Herbert, Count of Vermandois, 358–9, 461
Heresies
Adoptionist, 313, 328

and the Swiss invasion of Franche
Comté, 1043–4, 1053
of Italian mercenaries, 1076
Military service
in Roman Empire, 17–18
under the Merovingians, 163
under Charlemagne, 322
as a feature of feudalism, 419, 806–7
of land-owning ecclesiastics under Otto
the Great, 434
in England: under Richard I, 719; under
Edward I, 809–10
in Scandinavia, 760
in the Free Companies in Italy, 861, 865
Mirandola, Pico della, 1112
Mircea the Great, prince of Wallachia,
1006, 1007
Miron, king of the Suevi, 144
Missi discurrentes (travelling envoys), 323,
340
Missionaries
sent by Pepin II to Frisians, 159; by
Gregory the Great to Britain, 174–5,
292
from Iona, 174, 177, 178
from Britain to the Germans, 294–5
missionary sees set up by Otto the Great,
435
sent by Germans to the Wends, 574
friars as, 670, 678, 755, 840
among the Magyars, 736
exterminated by Tamerlane, 1006
Mithraism, 25
Moechian controversy, 251
Moleyns, Adam, bishop of Chichester,
keeper of the Privy Seal, 999
Monasticism, Monasteries
development of monastic movement,
72–4, 123, 283
encouraged by Merovingians, 164
development of, in England, 178
overgrowth of, in Eastern Empire, 247
attacked by Constantine V, 249; by
Theophilus, 252
Rule of St Benedict, 283–8, 289; of St
Columbanus, 288
refuge for classical learning, 325–6, 1113
reform of, by Lewis the Pious, 338–9
sacked by Vikings in Britain, 364;
restored by Edgar, 392–3; encouraged
by Canute, 398
in Ireland, 410
degeneration in 10th century, 472–3
reforms by Cluniac monks, 473–5
Carthusian Order founded, 502

foundation and growth of the Cistercians, 502–4
evolution of Augustinian Canons, 504–5
Premonstratensian Order founded, 505
Military Orders, 505–6, 524, 526–7, 529,
530, 532
reforms of Innocent III, 666–7
relaxation of Rules under Avignon
Popes, 839–40
spread of, in Russia, 1017
Mongols (Tartars)
described, 42–3
as plunderers and invaders, 43–4
culture of, 44
invade Bulgaria and Hungary, 735, 738,
740, 752
conquests of Jenghiz Khan, 751–2
'Tartar Yoke' on Russia, 752–4
invasion of Persia, Syria and Asia Minor,
754
conquests of Tamerlane, 755–6, 840,
1006–7
defeated at Ain Jalut, 757
Monophysites, 110, 112, 114, 195–6, 204,
210
controversy of, 119–22
and the doctrines of Sergius, 209
persecution of Monophysite Copts in
Egypt, 233
Monotheletism, 209, 212
Montenegro, 1009
Montpellier, school of medicine at, 622
Morabit, leader of Saracen revolt in Sicily,
684
Morcar, earl of Northumbria, 400, 584–5
Morgarten, pass of, 858
Moriale, Fra, Hospitaller, 865
Mortimer, Sir Edmund, 994, 995
Mortimer, Edmund, earl of March, 895,
900
Mortimer, Roger I, earl of March, 887,
890, 899
Mortimer, Roger II, earl of March, 900
Moscow, 1017–20
Mozarabs, 373–4
Mstislav, great prince of Kiev, 750
Muāwiya, Omayyad governor of Syria,
211, 232, 234–5, 263
becomes caliph, 235
attempts to establish dynasty, 235, 236
Muhammad I al-Ahmar, Moslem king of
Granada, 830
Muhammad II, king of Granada, 904
Muizz, Fatimite caliph of Africa, 263
Mujahid, king of Denia, 371

Otto II, Emperor, king of Germany, 371, 461
marriage to Theophano, 439, 441
quells internal revolt, 441-2
defeated by Saracens in Calabria, 443
death, 444
Otto III, Emperor, king of Germany, 444, 743
regency of Adelaide and Theophano, 444
conception of Roman Empire of the West, 445
as 'servant of Jesus Christ', 446-7, with genuine religious enthusiasm, 447-8
death, 449
Otto IV, Emperor, son of Henry the Lion, 649
civil war with King Philip, 649-51
war with Frederick II and deposition, 651-3, 709
Otto of Nordheim, duke of Bavaria, 484, 486
Otto I of Wittelsbach, duke of Bavaria, 575, 651
Otto II, duke of Bavaria, 693
Otto of Wittelsbach, elector of Brandenburg, 850
Otto, duke of Brunswick, marries Joanna I of Naples, 866
Otto, Cardinal, papal legate, 726
Otto, son of Conrad the Red, 441
Ottobono, Cardinal, papal legate, 726, 728
Ottoman Turks
attack Byzantine Empire, 927-31, 934-5
military organization of, 931, 935-6
enter Europe, 933
crusades against, 934, 1006, 1008-9
attacked by Tamerlane, 1006-7
conquest of the Balkans, 1008-11
capture Constantinople, 1010-11
Owain Gwynedd, prince of north Wales, 599
Owen the Bald, Welsh king of Strathclyde, 407
Oxford
university of, 625; admission of friars to, 675; Wyclifite party at, 997
Franciscan school at, 676

Pachomius, St, 72-3
Paeda, king of the Middle Angles, 177, 179
Paganism
philosophic forms of, 26, 32
primitive, of nomads, 44
revival of, under Julian, 64-7
decays with rise of Christianity, 74-5
in early Britain, 172, 173
pagan university at Athens abolished (529), 194
Pallig, Viking chief, 395
Pandolf Ironhead, Lombard prince, 439, 442
Pandulf III, prince of Capua, 507
Pandulf, papal legate, 724
Papacy, the
power of, in Rome, 223-4
claims effective dominion over the East, 254, 275
break away from, by the East, 276
and Gregory the Great, 291-3
and Pepin the Short, 298, 300-1
under protection of Charlemagne, 304-5, 312-14
relations with Lewis the Pious, 339-40, 341
and the *Forged Decretals*, 346-7
degeneration after death of John VIII, 351
discredited by Sergius III, 437; by John XII, 438
relations with Otto the Great, 438; with Otto III, 445-7; with Henry III, 459-60, 476-7
reforms by Leo IX, 477-9; by Nicholas II, 481-2; by Alexander II, 483-4
election to, regulated by Lateran Council, 481-2
supreme authority of, claimed by Gregory VII, 487, 489-95
Investiture decrees, 490, 492, 495-6, 497-8
Concordat of Worms (1122), 499-501
policy towards Norman kingdom in Italy, 513-14
and the Crusades, 519-20, 758
schism of anti-Pope Anacletus II, 555, 558
hostility of Roman commune towards, 560-1
and Frederick Barbarossa, 565-6, 568, 572
majority rule in papal elections, 572
relations with William I of England, 590
hostility of, to Emperor Henry VI, 610, 612, 615
power of papal decretals, 616-17, 947
administrative machinery of, 617-18; reorganized by Innocent III, 665-7
financial basis of, 618, 667
and the Franciscans, 670-3, 676, 678
and Michael Palaeologus, 735

Rodolph II, king of Jurane Burgundy, 436
Rodolph III, king of Jurane Burgundy, 436, 451, 453, 455
Rodrigo Diaz de Vivar (the Cid), Castilian noble, 823
Roffredo of Benevento, 684
Roger, count of Andria, claimant of Sicilian throne, 610
Roger Borsa, duke of Apulia, 511
Roger, bishop of Salisbury, justiciar of England, 595, 597-8
Roger de Flor, German mercenary, 930
Roger, earl of Hereford, revolt of, 590
Roger Loria, Calabrian admiral, 768, 769, 771
Roger I, count of Sicily, 509, 511-13
Roger II the Great, king of Sicily, 538, 539
  character, 513
  proclaims the Regno of Sicily, 513
  enmity of the Papacy, 513-15, 558, 560
  sea power of, 515, 527
  Assize of Ariano (1140), 517-18
Roger III, king of Sicily, 612
Rokycana, Jan, archbishop-elect of Prague, 968, 969, 1048
Roland, Cardinal, papal legate. See Alexander III, Pope
Roland, warden of the Breton march, 309, 312
Rolle, Richard, English mystic, 841
Rollo, Northman, duke of Normandy, 358, 367
Roman, prince of Volhynia, 750
Roman Empire. See Empire, Roman
Romanus I Lecapenus, Emperor of the East, 258, 262, 267, 272
Romanus II, Emperor of the East, 258-9, 263
Romanus III Argyrus, Emperor of the East, 273
Romanus IV Diogenes, Emperor of the East, 278, 279
Romanus, Count, 52, 58
Rome (the city), 6, 22
  office of Prefect of the City, 17
  fortified by Aurelian, 18
  claims apostolic foundation for its church, 31
  pagan altars removed from, 74-5
  blockaded by Alaric, 84
  sacked by the Goths, 85; by the Vandals, 97
  emptied by Totila, 191
  attacked by Lombards, 223, 290-1
  power of the Papacy in, 223-4

Vatican walled after Moslem raid (846), 349, 370
  restiveness under degenerate Popes, 438, 439
  revolt against Otto III, 448-9
  sacked by Robert Guiscard, 494, 511
  commune of, 560
  and interdict of Adrian IV, 564-5
  captured by Frederick Barbarossa, 569
  Lewis the Bavarian's expedition to, 844
  Charles IV crowned in, 848
  Cola di Rienzo, Tribune, 863-4
  captured by Ladislas of Naples, 956, 957
  Martin V restores papal authority in, 1083
Rome, see of
  primacy proclaimed, 68-9, 116, 291-2
  rivalry with Constantinople, 212, 254, 275
  schism of East and West, 275-6
  seat of Papacy transferred to Avignon, 775, 786, 835-6; return to Rome, 953
Romuald, St, 448, 475
Romulus Augustulus, Emperor of the West, 100-1
Rory O'Conor, high-king of Connaught, 412-13, 810, 811, 812
Rosamund, wife of Alboin the Lombard, 218
Roscelin, scholastic dispute with Anselm, 628
Rostislav, great prince of Kiev, 750
Rostislav, Slav prince, 253
Rothari, king of the Lombards ('King Rother'), 220
Rotrude, daughter of Charlemagne, 305
Roussel de Bailleul, revolt of, 281
Rovere, Giuliano della, duke of Sora, 1089
Rua, king of the Huns, 93
Ruben, Armenian chief, 280
Rudolf I of Habsburg, king of the Romans, 738, 742, 764, 797, 798-800, 857
Rudolf II of Habsburg, duke of Austria, 799
Rudolf III of Habsburg, king of Bohemia, 801, 915
Rudolf IV of Habsburg, duke of Austria, 850
Rudolf of Rheinfelden, duke of Swabia, anti-king, 484, 487, 491, 492-3
Ruffo, Peter, vicar of Sicily and Calabria, 697
Rufinus of Aquitaine, praetorian prefect, 79, 80
Rūm. See Asia Minor
Rupert of Wittelsbach, elector-palatine, king of the Romans, 957, 1002, 1079

Scone, Stone of Destiny carried from, by Edward I, 816
Scot, Michael, translator, 620
Scotland, 760
  before Norman conquest, 406–8
  anglicization of (1057–1157), 408–10
  resists Norman conquest, 597
  submits to Henry II, 599, 603
  Gaelic pretenders, 814
  Norwegian sovereignty in western isles terminated, 814
  succession problems after death of Margaret of Norway, 815–16
  relations with Edward I of England, 816–17
  battle of Bannockburn, 818, 886, 898
  English claim to suzerainty surrendered at Peace of Northampton (1328), 818, 890–1
  Edward III's campaign in, 891, 897
  rise of Parliament, 898
  invasion of Ireland, 898–9
  insurrection against Henry IV, 994
  Orkney and Shetland ceded to, 1022, 1067
  Berwick ceded to, 1059
  insurrection against Edward IV, 1059–60
  strengthening of the monarchy under James I, 1064–5
  intervention in Wars of the Roses, 1066
  under James III, 1066–8
  see also Picts; Scots
Scots
  oppose the Romans, 41–2, 53
  Christianity of, 174, 177–8
  union with Picts (844), 406
  for further entries see Scotland
Scrope, Henry, Lord Scrope of Masham, treasurer, 997
Scrope, Richard, archbishop of York, 995
Sculpture, 1097, 1102–3
Sea power
  of the Vandals, 91
  of the Eastern Empire: against the Arabs, 211, 214, 371; against Charlemagne, 317; in the First Crusade, 533
  Moslem naval base at Alexandria, 234; defeat of Patrician John (698), 238
  decline of, in Eastern Empire (9th century), 262; recovery under Nicephorus Phocas, 263
  of Alfred the Great, 387
  of Roger II of Sicily, 515
  of Italian states in 11th century, 518–19, 523

of Venice, 538, 549, 656–7, 734–5, 756, 758, 779
of Sicily, under Roger Loria, 768–9
of Genoa, 769
of England, under Edward III, 877; under Henry V, 998
and Statute of Truces (1414), 998; repealed (1440), 999
  see also Vikings
Segarelli, heretic, 680
Seljūk Turks, 507, 538, 730
  migration to Persia, 278–9
  overrun Armenia, 279–80, and Asia Minor, 281, 532
  civil war and decline, 281
  capture Jerusalem and Antioch, 519
  relations with Manuel I, 540–1
  attacked and crushed by Mongols, 754, 927
  see further under Ottoman Turks
Sempringham, Order of, 505
Senuti, monk, murderer of Nestorius, 119
Serbia, 736
  conquest of territory from Byzantine Empire, 931–2
  under Stephen Dushan, 932–3
  conquest of, by Ottoman Turks, 1006, 1007, 1009
Serena, wife of Stilicho, 79
  executed, 84
Sergius I, Pope, 294
Sergius III, Pope, 359, 437
Sergius IV, Pope, 519
Sergius, patriarch of Constantinople, 205–6
  doctrine of the Two Natures, 209
Sergius, duke of Naples, 507
Sergius, St, patriarch of Radonezh, 1019
Severinus, abbot, 98, 136
Severinus, Pope, 209
Severus, patriarch of Antioch, 121–2, 195
Sforza, Francesco, duke of Milan, 1029, 1080–1, 1083, 1085, 1068–7
Sforza, Galeazzo Maria, duke of Milan, 1087
Sforza, Ludovico, Il Moro, duke of Milan, 1087, 1090
Sforza, Muzio, grand constable of Naples, 1076, 1083
Shahrbaraz, Persian general, 205, 206, 208
Shapur II, king of Persia, 36, 47, 49–50
Shapur III, king of Persia, 50
Shawar, vizier of Egypt, 528